DATE DUE

100
GREAT
KINGS, QUEENS
AND
RULERS
OF THE
WORLD

100
GREAT
KINGS, QUEENS
AND
RULERS
OF THE
WORLD

Edited by John Canning

BONANZA BOOKS
New York

This 1985 edition is published by Bonanza Books, distributed
by Crown Publishers, Inc., by arrangement with Taplinger
Publishing Company, Inc.

Manufactured in the United States of America

Library of Congress Cataloging in Publication Data

Main entry under title:

100 great kings, queens, and rulers of the world.

   Reprint. Originally published: New York: Taplinger Pub.
Co., 1968, c1967.
   Includes index.
   1. Kings and rulers—Biography—Addresses, essays,
lectures. 2. Queens—Biography—Addresses, essays,
lectures. I. Canning, John, 1920–   . II. Title: One hundred
great kings, queens, and rulers of the world.
D107.A15   1985   909 [B]   84-24386

ISBN: 0-517-458438

h g f e d c b a

Contents

CONTENTS

CONTENTS

7

CONTENTS

100 GREAT KINGS, QUEENS AND RULERS OF THE WORLD

Editor's Note

"THE BENEFITS of a good monarch are almost invaluable, but the evils of a bad monarch are almost irreparable," wrote Walter Bagehot in his classic study of the English Constitution. He was, of course, referring to the constitutional monarchy, but what applies to the constitutional monarch applies even more to the despot.

In this volume I have presented a personal selection of great kings and queens, the word "great" implying no moral judgement but used as a simple descriptive label for those whose significance for good or bad has been considerable. Most of them exercised absolute or near-absolute power, for the emergence of the constitutional monarch is a comparatively recent phenomenon. Bagehot, referring to the latter, says he has three rights: the right to be consulted, the right to encourage, the right to warn. And he adds that a king of sense and sagacity would want no others. For the rest he represents in his person all the dignified trappings of the state and is invested by his subjects with an almost mystical aura. He is the head of society. Even George III was a "consecrated obstruction".

However, by a unique combination of circumstance and national character the only major country with this type of effective yet controlled system was Britain, and it is significant that it is the only great nation in which royalty has survived to the present day (and even strengthened its position). Since Bagehot's time the great dynasties of Hohenzollern, Habsburg and Romanov have crumbled and vanished.

I have also included rulers who seemed to partake wholly or to a large extent in the royal mystique. Thus there is a certain resemblance between, say, Pericles, on the one hand, and Franklin D. Roosevelt and John F. Kennedy on the other. Pericles was almost the physical and spiritual embodiment of fifth-century Athens; Roosevelt and Kennedy, though their executive powers were not as great, nevertheless embodied to a quite extraordinary degree (as can any great American President) the sense of unity and purpose of their nation. All were performing a quasi-royal function.

The position of General de Gaulle is another case in point. Few Frenchmen throughout France's long history can so self-consciously have associated themselves with *la Gloire*, and his majestic and lofty utterances might well have been envied by *Le Roi Soleil*.

Conversely where this quasi-royal function is not involved, as in

11

societies where the executive and the dignified aspects of the state are separated—modern Britain for instance—I have not included statesmen who were undoubtedly great rulers: Gladstone, Disraeli, Lloyd George and Winston Churchill, for example. I have deliberately excluded also Hitler, Mussolini and Stalin. These have all been treated in earlier volumes of this series, and I felt that the space available should go to other interesting modern figures who have had a crucial influence on our age.

A word on method. For the sake of consistency, I have used anglicizations of names throughout. Also, where confusion might arise owing to the fact that a selected king has the same designation as another I have sought to clarify the matter by qualifying in the chapter heading the one being presented. Thus William I (the Conqueror); Philip II(King of Spain, Naples and Sicily); and Peter I (the Great).

JOHN CANNING

CHEOPS
(Reigned *c*. 2900–*c*. 2875 B.C.)

YES, HE certainly left his mark on the world, that Egyptian king or Pharaoh whose name was Khufu—or, as the Greeks transliterated it, Cheops. So far as we know (and in fact we do not know very much about him) he was not a great warrior, he made no far-spreading conquests, he showed no particular concern for the welfare of his people, he framed no code of laws for their guidance nor did he enlarge the bounds of knowledge or inspire the practice of new arts. And yet he made sure that he would be remembered when most of the dynasties have long since slipped into oblivion. He built himself a tomb. . . .

And what a tomb! There it stands today, some five miles from the west bank of the Nile, near the Arab village of Al-Gizah on the edge of the narrow trench that is the Land of Egypt: there it stands, the most stupendous mass of masonry that has ever been put together by human hands, the nearest approach to a man-made mountain that the world affords. We know it as the Great Pyramid; but Khufu, the man who gave the orders for its construction and saw to its completion, called it *Ikhet*, which in the tongue of the ancient Egyptians means "the Glorious". He chose the name well for something that is still "glorious" after the lapse of not far short of fifty centuries.

Nearly five thousand years have passed into history since Khufu reigned as Pharaoh at Memphis, if we may accept the dates commonly assigned to his reign of 2900 to 2875 or thereabouts before Christ. This means that the Pyramid was already very old when Joseph rode past it, as he must often have done when pursuing his official business as the Pharaoh's vizier; indeed, it would have appeared as ancient to Joseph as Westminster Abbey appears to us. No doubt he often stopped to view it, as it glowed in the burning sun or at night thrust its cone into the star-spattered sky. He must have pondered on its history, and thought of the mighty monarch who had built it; and perhaps he inquired of the priests who in the adjacent temple maintained a daily ritual of prayer and praise in honour of their royal founder.

When Joseph saw it, the Pyramid was bigger and higher than it

13

appears today, since in the course of centuries some twenty or thirty feet of the outer casing have been stripped away to be used in the building of the forts and gimcrack palaces of Cairo. Nothing remains of the inscribed slabs of smooth limestone or polished granite which originally enclosed it as in a skin. But even so, the statistics are impressive. The Pyramid is about 450 feet high, and it stands on a base of 755 feet each way, covering an area of 12½ acres. It has been calculated that more than two million three hundred thousand blocks of stone are incorporated in its huge frame, each weighing two and a half tons, and that in all there are over eighty-five million cubic feet of masonry still remaining after the depredations of time and the even more destructive man. And this monstrous construction was—not a temple to match the majesty of the gods, not a palace to exhibit the magnificence of a king, not a centre of imperial government, or an arsenal, or even the strongpoint of a system of national defence—not any of these things, but, as already stated, a tomb.

How Khufu's heart must have rejoiced as from his palace windows he watched it growing day by day, rising ever higher above the plain! It was not the joy of construction that drove him to it. He was not impelled by any urge to build the most magnificent, the greatest, of all the works of man. But it made him feel *safe*. Against what? Not the common run of enemies: he had nothing to fear from them, whether they attacked from Nubia in the south or from Syria or Arabia across the Red Sea—his armies were quite capable of taking care of *them*. But there was one foe that no armour was proof against, that no legions of soldiers could put to flight—the sting and stab of death. He knew, and needed no reminder from the priests, that even Pharaohs were mortal just as other men, and that the day must come when all his pomp and panoply of power would drop away and he would become a corpse.

This need not be the end of him, however: there was a way of dodging the finality of death, of keeping the dread spectre at bay, if not for all time at least for a time beyond measuring! There were sacred texts that showed how this might be done, formulae known to the priests and the initiated few, procedures that were powerful to preserve the spirit when it had quitted the body. The theology of ancient Egypt is a most strange and wonderful thing, and we shall never be able to understand it in all its profundities and complexity, but it would seem that it was believed that so long as something of the body was preserved, so long would the spirit be allowed by the gods to continue to share their life in the world beyond the setting sun. Hence the tremendous pains taken by the Pharaohs and other

great ones to secure their corpses from decay, by the weird process
of mummification, after which they were hidden away in places
which even the most determined and venturesome of tomb-robbers
would find it impossible to violate.

In the great age of the Pyramid-builders, the age of the Fourth
Dynasty of the Egyptian kings, it was the practice to bury the
Pharaoh in a chamber carved out of the solid rock beneath the
pyramid's centre. The construction of this pyramid-tomb became
the chief object and interest of each new ruler when he ascended the
throne, and to it he caused to be devoted the treasure and the
labour-power of all his dominions. He began it when he became
king, he continued the work through his reign, and he hoped for
nothing so much as that it might be finished before death overtook
him. For if it were completed in time, it would provide him with a
last resting-place in which *something* of his personality might
continue in being.

When the Pharaoh died, his corpse was given over to the corps
of official embalmers, who carried out the gruesome process according to the sacred, time-honoured formulae. On the day of burial
the body became the centre of a series of elaborate ceremonies
embodying occurrences in the life of the god-king Osiris who had
been killed but through magical processes had been brought to
some sort of life again, and was enabled to bestow a similar measure
of immortality on those who worshipped him and were mummified
as he had been. The royal mummy was conveyed to the pyramid,
to where in its side a shaft had been left open, leading down to the
tomb-chamber in the underlying rock. Down this the mummy was
lowered, and laid on its left side in a fine coffin of cedar-wood, which
again was deposited in a massive sarcophagus of granite or limestone.
Food and drink were left beside it, as well as a selection of toilet
articles, a magic wand, and a number of amulets for protection
against the horrid serpents and other enemies of the dead. Then the
deep shaft leading to the burial chamber from the outer air was filled
to the top with sand and gravel, and carefully sealed up so that not a
sign remained of its existence.

This, or something like this, was what Khufu—or Cheops, to use
the name by which he is generally known—had in mind when early
on in his reign he gave orders for the construction of the Great
Pyramid. As he sat on his throne he must often have thought of the
end of all this mighty work—this vast expenditure of materials and
labour, this direction of a nation's economy to a single object. And
what was the end he envisaged? Nothing other than a small chamber,

deep in the ground beneath the mightiest building ever made by human hands, in which his mummified body might lie on and on, snug and warm, while his spirit roamed among the palm-trees and rivulets of the Land of the Blessed!

More than two thousand years after Cheops's death and mummification, that inquisitive old Greek Herodotus visited Egypt, and of course he was shown, as tourists have always been shown, the Pyramid that covered the great king's tomb. He asked the priests of his acquaintance to tell him what they knew of him, and they hastened to oblige. What they had to tell was not complimentary, and it would seem that they bore Cheops a grudge. He had plunged into every kind of wickedness . . . he had given orders, as soon as he came to the throne, that no more sacrifices should be made to the gods and that all the temples should be closed. . . . Not content with these sacrilegious acts he (and here Herodotus must have pricked up his ears and got his wax-tablets ready) had conscripted all the people to work on a particular project of his own. This was the construction of a monster pyramid that he intended for his tomb. Herodotus took careful note of all that was told him, and in due course he included it in the history that he was writing.

A hundred thousand labourers were employed on the job, working in gangs of ten thousand, each gang working for three months at a time. Ten years were consumed in quarrying the stone. The principal quarries were on the farther side of the Nile, and the massive blocks were dragged along a specially constructed roadway to the river; and at high water, when the flats were flooded, they were floated across the valley to the base of the pyramid hill. Here an enormous stone ramp or causeway had been constructed—a labour that had taken ten years, resulting in something that was hardly less remarkable than the pyramid itself. Up this incline the blocks were dragged to the plateau on which the pyramid was to stand, and where more workmen had been engaged for years in excavating the subterranean tomb-chamber. Twenty years were occupied in building the pyramid itself. "It is composed of polished stones, none less than thirty feet long, and jointed with the greatest exactness"—so exact that the joints are in some cases of one ten-thousandth of an inch.

Of exceptional interest is Herodotus's explanation of the way in which the pyramid was raised stage by stage. After the first rows of blocks had been laid, a bank or platform of earth was raised against the wall, and up this the blocks for the next layers were dragged or hoisted with the aid of machines made of heavy timbers.

When this part of the work had been completed, another ramp or platform was built, and more machines were brought into action—or, as Herodotus is careful to state, they may have lifted the first set of machines and used them over again. "I should relate it in both ways," he says, "just as it was related to me." Then he goes on to tell us that he had been shown an inscription on the pyramid, written in the Egyptian characters (i.e. hieroglyphics), stating "how much was expended in radishes, onions, and garlic, for the workmen; which the interpreter, as well I remember, reading the inscription, told me amounted to one thousand six hundred talents of silver. And if this really be the case, how much more was probably expended in iron tools, in bread, and in clothes for the workmen!"

Ever on the alert for an interesting story, however fanciful, Herodotus adds that he had been told that Cheops ran out of money before the work was completed, and "descended to such a degree of infamy that he prostituted his own daughter in a brothel, and ordered her to exact—they did not say how much; but she exacted a certain sum of money, as much as her father had ordered her, and at the same time asked every man who came in to her to give her a stone towards an edifice which she had designed as a monument to herself . . . and of these stones they said the pyramid was built that stands in the middle of the three, in front of the great pyramid. . . ."

As already indicated, very little is known of Cheops apart from his Great Pyramid. He was not, it seems, of royal birth, but came of a noble family in Middle Egypt. Very likely he was a protégé of Seneferu, the first king of the IVth Dynasty, whom he followed upon the throne, and it is recorded that among the ladies of his harem was one who had been a favourite of Seneferu. He may have had his successes as a warrior and a statesman, but it is significant that the inscriptions that have come to light bearing his name are mostly in districts where his quarrying operations were carried on. He was not the inventor of the pyramid, but he set the model that his successors copied, and his own pyramid is the greatest and noblest of this very special form of construction. And our admiration for the monument, so writes the great American Egyptologist Professor Breasted, "should not obscure its real and final significance; for the Great Pyramid is the earliest and most impressive witness surviving from the ancient world to the final emergence of organized society from prehistoric chaos and local conflict, thus coming for the first time completely under the power of a far-reaching and comprehensive centralization effected by one controlling mind".

This was Cheops's achievement in the light of History, but when we remember what he himself had in mind we must arrive at the saddest of conclusions. The day came at length when the Khalif Mamoun, a medieval ruler of Egypt, inflamed by tales of immense wealth buried in the great Pharaoh's tomb, after spending an enormous fortune in breaking into the solid structure at length succeeded in forcing an entrance and penetrating the complex of passages to the underground chamber in which the royal mummy should have been deposited. Within it stood a splendid sarcophagus of red granite. It was without a lid—and it was empty.

HAMMURABI

(Reigned *c.* 1790-*c.* 1750 B.C.)

JUST LOOK at his letter, lying here in this case in the British Museum. You didn't know it was a letter? It looks like a piece of brick? Well, so it does, and in fact it is made of a lump of baked clay. But those marks on it that look like scratches—they are letters in the cuneiform (wedge-shaped) script of the ancient Babylonians, and it is a letter written getting on for four thousand years ago, by a king of Babylonia to one of his trusted servants.

Hammurabi was the king's name, and he was the sixth king in what is called the first dynasty of Babylon—the dynasty which was founded by a certain Samuabum and was continued by Sumulailum, Zabum, Apil-Sin, Sin-muballit (he was Hammurabi's father) and so in a quaint-sounding succession until the last of that particular line, whose name is given as Samsuditana. About most of them we know very little, but they belonged to the Semites, the race to which Jews and Arabs also belong, and seem to have established their rule in the middle portion of the Mesopotamian plain some time before 2000 B.C. There were already people in the land when they arrived, but they seem to have got on with them fairly well to begin with and were allowed to build cities, of which Babylon was the chief. To the south of them were the Sumerians, who were in a much more advanced state of civilization, dwelling in city-states of which the most important were Larsa, Erech, Isin, Eridu, and, most famous of all, Ur of the Chaldees as the Bible calls it. In course of time rivalries developed between the land of Akkad, as the region round Babylon was called, and the land of Sumer, and when Hammurabi came to the throne he inherited a war with Rim-Sin, king of Larsa. After a long and hard struggle, he won it; he took Rim-Sin captive, and put an end to Larsa as an independent state.

When this was we cannot be sure. Until recently it used to be generally stated that Hammurabi reigned about 2000 B.C., although some authorities put it some hundreds of years earlier, and some perhaps two or three hundred years later. It now seems most likely that he reigned at Babylon from about 1790 to 1750 B.C. Whenever it was, it was a very long time ago, and yet his reign is exceedingly well documented, what with the large number of tablets and inscriptions that have been preserved. Not least among these is the collection of letters in the British Museum, addressed by King Hammurabi to a certain Sin-idinnam, who seems to have been a trusted official of some kind. They are on a great variety of subjects, short and sometimes sharp in their wording, and absolutely clear. Most of them convey the king's instructions in matters of official business. Each letter—written on a small clay tablet—was enclosed in a clay envelope, inscribed with the address of the official for whom it was intended; the envelopes were thrown away when the recipient broke them open, but in a few instances small portions of the envelope still adhere to the letters. Both letter and envelope were baked in an oven before dispatch, and the envelope was dusted with dry powder to prevent it sticking to the letter that was put into it.

In the collection are some scores addressed by Hammurabi to Sin-idinnam, and in nearly all the latter is told to do something or the other. He is to order the dwellers on the Damanum canal to clean and clear it out within the current month, he is to arrest eight officials who have refused to do what they were told and to send them to Hammurabi in Babylon, he is to investigate a charge of theft of corn that has been brought against a man named Awel-ili by a man with the even stranger-sounding name of Awelu-tummumu, he is to send forty-seven shepherds to Babylon to give an account to the king of the flocks under their charge, he is to take steps to prevent certain fishermen from fishing in prohibited waters, he is to look into a dispute between a landlord and a tenant about the payment of rent for a plot of land, he is to make arrangements for a certain number of slaves to be provided on a particular day, he is to take on more sheep-shearers to get the job done in time, he is to appoint this man and is to give that other man the sack . . .

"Why haven't you sent Enubi-Marduk to me at Babylon as I ordered," demands Hammurabi; "as soon as you get this, tell him to start at once, and to travel day and night, and let him make sure that he arrives speedily." Time and again Sin-idinnam is enjoined to pay particular attention to the state of the banks of the Euphrates and of the canals dependent on it—a matter of the utmost importance in a land relying so largely on irrigation for its subsistence. Then there are letters dealing with the matter of the Goddesses—or rather, the images of the Goddesses—of Emutbalum, a district in the Elamite country to the east which had been recently raided by the Babylonian forces.

From what can be made out, it would appear that the "goddesses" had been captured and carried away in triumph to Babylon. But then the Babylonians had met with reverses, and the pious Hammurabi and his priestly advisers would very naturally assume that the goddesses themselves were angry at the insult that had been offered to them in being detained in a foreign land against their will. So Hammurabi took steps to have them returned to their own country. "Thus saith Hammurabi unto Sin-idinnam," runs the first letter; "behold, I am dispatching unto thee the officers Zikir-ilisu and Hammurabi-bani, that they may bring hither the goddesses of the country of Emutbalum. Thou shalt cause the goddesses to travel in the processional boat as in a shrine, that they may come to Babylon. And the temple women (their female attendants or priestesses) shall follow after them. For the food of the goddesses thou shalt provide . . . sheep, and thou shalt take on board provisions for the maintenance of the temple-women on the journey until they reach Babylon. And thou shalt appoint men to draw the tow-ropes, and chosen soldiers, so that they may bring the goddesses to Babylon in safety. Let them not delay, but make haste to reach Babylon." Sin-idinnam did as he was ordered, and then in a further letter he is told to arrange for the "goddesses" to be entrusted to troops under the command of one Inuhsamar, who would "bring them in safety", by which presumably is meant they would be returned to their shrines in Emutbalum, after which he might rest assured that he would be able to overcome the enemy with "the troops that are in thy hand".

Not only are there numerous letters from Hammurabi in the collection but many other documents, concerned in the main with legal and commercial transactions, and including deeds recording the buying and selling of houses and lands, leases of house-property, the hiring of slaves and labourers, the loan of money, the dissolution of business partnerships, the adoption of children, marriage contracts, bills of divorce, and so on. These in themselves are indications that the people over whom King Hammurabi ruled had attained a quite high state of civilization, an order of things to which many generations must have contributed. This conclusion is amply confirmed by the Code of Laws with which Hammurabi's name is indissolubly connected.

"Hammurabi's Code" is inscribed in ancient Babylonian characters on a pillar of black basalt that was discovered by French archaeologists in 1902, when they were excavating the remains of the ancient Persian city of Susa. The pillar was in several pieces when unearthed, but they were joined together and the restored monument has been for many years one of the most valued treasures of the Louvre Museum, in Paris; a very fine copy is in the British Museum in London. Originally the pillar may have been erected in the temple at Sippara (not far from the modern city of Baghdad), where it stood for perhaps a thousand years, until a king of Elam sacked Sippara and carried it away to Susa as a trophy. Then at some later date Susa in turn fell to a conqueror and was laid in ruins; Hammurabi's column was buried beneath piles of rubble until at length it was disinterred by the French archaeologists at the beginning of this century.

The pillar (or *stele*, to use the technical term for such a monument) is 7 feet 4 inches in height and 2 feet in diameter. On the upper part is carved in relief a picture of Hammurabi standing before the god Shamash, the Sun-god who in the Babylonian pantheon was also the god of justice in heaven and on earth. Shamash is seated on his throne; he is wearing a horned head-dress, symbolical of divine power, and from his shoulders rise flames of fire. Hammurabi is dressed in a long robe and is standing in the traditional attitude of worship with his right arm bared and raised; it is generally stated that he is receiving his "laws" from the god, but this is unlikely, since in the text the claim is made that they were originated by the king himself. (This claim is not strictly true, however; Hammurabi was a codifier rather than an originator, and the Code was based upon laws and customs that had acquired the sanctity of long tradition.)

The "laws" are engraved on the lower part of the pillar. There are 282 of them, and there were perhaps another thirty-five, but these were in the lower part of the column and have been erased, it is assumed, by the Elamite conqueror who wanted the room for an inscription of his own (which, however, was never added). They are preceded by an introduction, in which we are told that "Anu the King of the Gods, and Bel the Lord of Heaven and Earth had delighted the flesh of mankind by calling me, the renowned prince, the god-fearing Hammurabi, to establish justice in the earth, to destroy the base and wicked, and to hold back the strong from oppressing the weak . . ." Then follow more lines of eulogy, in which Hammurabi is styled among many other things the hero king, the wise and prudent ruler, the guardian of the city, the renowned potentate who has filled his people when there was dearth in the land, the far-seeing one who has provided them with pasture and drinking-water, the impetuous bull who overthrows his enemies, the grave of his foes, the promulgator of justice, the exalted one who humbles himself before the great gods. . . . "When Merodach (the god of Babylon) had instituted me governor of men, to conduct and to direct them, then it was that I established Law and Justice in the land, for the good of all the people. . . ."

Then follow the "laws", and it is noticeable that they do not seem to be arranged in any sort of order, and it would also seem that they cannot compose the whole Code since there are some very obvious gaps in the enactments. Thus punishment is prescribed for a man who steals from a temple or a "great house", but nothing is said about thefts from ordinary citizens. It may be that the laws given on the pillar are those about which there was most doubt, or perhaps they were those in most frequent demand, and there were many other rules of behaviour which were so generally accepted that there was no need to have them inscribed in this most public and permanent fashion. However this may be, the Code is the most complete and valuable collection of ancient laws to come down to us.

The Code opens with the enactment that "if a man has laid a curse upon another man, and it is not justified, then the layer of the curse shall be slain". This may strike us as decidedly harsh, but it is to be noted that capital punishment rather than fines or imprisonment is most frequently prescribed. Thus a man who has given false evidence in a lawsuit shall be slain, and likewise the thief above mentioned, a man who has broken into a house ("he shall be slain before the breach he has made, and there buried"), a receiver of stolen goods, a man who has harboured a runaway slave instead of restoring him to his owner, and a man who goes to help in putting out a fire and seizes the opportunity of making off with some of the householder's goods ("That man shall be thrown into the same fire"). A woman who kills her husband because she has become enamoured of another man shall be impaled on a stake. If disaffected persons happen to meet in a wineseller's, and she does not seize and take them to the "great house", she shall be slain.

Trial by some form of ordeal is provided for in certain cases. "If a married woman is found lying with another male, they shall both be bound and thrown into the river," runs one clause; but "if the finger is pointed against a man's wife because of another male, and she has not been found lying with him, then she shall plunge for her husband into the holy river"—in which case if she floated she was found innocent, but if she sank—well, she was obviously guilty and fully deserved her fate. Similarly, when a man has had "a spell thrown over him" he shall plunge into the holy river; if the holy river seize him, the layer of the spell shall take his house, but if he emerges safe and sound, the layer of the spell shall be slain, and he who plunged into the holy river shall take *his* house.

Coming now to domestic relations, a man may divorce his wife if she should prove barren, but he must return her dowry before sending her back to her father's house. If a wife mismanages her home and neglects her husband, all he has to do is to say "thou art divorced", and she must return to her father without her dowry; but a man is not permitted to divorce his wife just because he has got tired of her, but must maintain her as long as she lives. Several laws show a real concern for the woman. Thus a wife who has developed a deep aversion for her husband and says, "Thou shalt not possess me", may take her dowry and go back to her father, always provided she has given her husband no other cause for complaint. It is also recognized that a woman whose husband has been taken prisoner in the wars, and she is left destitute, may take up with another man, although if the first man should be released and return home she must go back to him.

Another group of enactments illustrates the old rule about "an eye for an eye". Thus, "if a man has destroyed the eye of a freeman, his own eye shall be put out". "If a man has knocked out the teeth of a man of the same rank, his own teeth shall be knocked out." But here class distinctions enter into the picture, for if the victim is a man of inferior rank or a slave, he or his master is to receive financial compensation only. That the practice of surgery was a dangerous occupation is illustrated by such a "law" as this: "If a doctor has treated a severe wound with a metal knife, and has caused the man to die, or has opened a man's tumour with a metal knife and destroyed the man's eye, his hands shall be cut off." Not long before the end of the Code is this pithy pronouncement: "If a mad bull meet a man in the highway and gore him, and kill him, that case has no remedy." So we come to the last one of all: "If a slave shall say to his master, 'Thou art not my master,' his master shall cut off his ear."

Then comes the epilogue, in which Hammurabi writes, "These are the judgments of justice which Hammurabi, the mighty king, has established, conferring upon the kingdom a sure guidance and a gracious rule. If a man heed not my words that I have written on this pillar, if he has scorned my malediction, nor feared the curse of God; if he has annulled the law that I have given, or altered my words ... may Anu, the Father of the Gods, extinguish his glory, shatter his sceptre, may he curse his end!"

THOTHMES III
(Reigned 1501-1447 B.C.)

THE OBELISK on the Thames Embankment in London which is called "Cleopatra's Needle" has nothing to do with Cleopatra, but was set up with another obelisk in the temple of Ra in Heliopolis by Thothmes III about one thousand and four hundred years before Cleopatra reigned. Mr. R. Engelbach, in his book *Problem of the Obelisks*, wondered what Thothmes III's feelings would have been "had he known that one (obelisk) would be taken to a land of whose existence he never dreamed (the U.S.A.) and that the other would fall into the hands of what was then a savage people; and, after undergoing such vicissitudes as ship-wreck and injuries from a German air-bomb, would still be standing, though thousands of miles away, after a lapse of nearly 3,500 years?" Not very far away from the obelisk, in the British Museum, is the giant head of Thothmes III, dignified and inscrutable.

Thothmes III, XVIIIth Dynasty, is considered to have been the greatest Pharaoh of the New Empire period and by some to have been the greatest in Egyptian history. He reigned for fifty-four years from 1501 to 1447 B.C. or, as recent authorities argue, from 1504 to 1450 B.C. He fought seventeen campaigns in Syria and maintained Egypt as the greatest military state of the time; his grandfather, Thothmes I, had been the first to militarize Egypt and send expeditions into Western Asia to make sure that there should be no repetition of the invasion of the Hyksos, who set up their own kings in Egypt. That invasion had left terrible and humiliating memories for the Egyptians so that Thothmes I and his grandson, Thothmes III, were regarded as heroes; the latter left annals of many of his campaigns inscribed on the walls of the great temple to the God Ammon at Karnak and on the walls of his tomb.

Thothmes III was an energetic and forceful man, becoming Egypt's great warrior Pharaoh, but for the first twenty-two years of his reign he was kept in the background by his co-regent, Queen Hatshepsut, who was probably both his step-mother and his aunt. She was, as far as is known, the first woman to rule as Pharaoh claiming divine origin; this was done by other Pharaohs, including

25

Thothmes III when he ruled alone. There was almost certainly a
party which supported Queen Hatshepsut and one which supported
Thothmes III, but there does not seem to have been any serious
trouble in the kingdom, even though it was very unorthodox to
have a woman as ruler, and they got round this by pretending that
she was a man. In nearly all the representations of her as Pharaoh,
wearing the double crown of Upper and Lower Egypt, she is
shown as a man, sometimes with a beard, though there is one relief
in which she is dressed as a woman; male pronouns are used in
describing her, but sometimes there is confusion between the
masculine and the feminine.

Ineni, the architect who built the first tomb in the valley, which
came to be known as the Valley of the Tombs of the Kings, states
in an inscription that Thothmes III followed his father Thothmes II
"as King of the Two Lands, having become ruler upon the throne
of the one who begat him . . . the Divine Consort, Hatshepsut,
carried on the affairs of the Two Lands according to her own ideas.
Egypt was made to work in submission to her, who was the excellent
off-spring of the God and who came forth from him". Some
authorities think that Hatshepsut and Thothmes III were married,
but this seems unlikely since he married her daughter Merytra
Hatshepsut, who became his Great Royal Wife and mother of his
successor Amenophis II.

There is little information about Thothmes III during the reign
of Hatshepsut and he is hardly mentioned in the inscriptions on
obelisks and monuments which she had erected during her lifetime.
He must have deeply resented his position, for when he ruled as sole
Pharaoh, not only was her name erased from her monuments but
those of her architect, Senmut, and of other officials were removed
from their monuments. Thothmes III "hated her with a deadly
hatred", wrote Wallis Budge, and is surprised that more of Queen
Hatshepsut's monuments were not destroyed, though other
authorities have expressed surprise that so great a man as Thothmes
should have shown his resentment in this way.

It is no discredit to Thothmes III that he remained in the background during the reign of Hatshepsut, for she was a most able
woman and he may, indeed, have held her in some admiration.
She was already in a powerful position when he became co-regent
as a young prince following his father's death. She was probably
co-regent with her father, Thothmes I, towards the end of his life
after his royal wife had died. His son, Thothmes II, who succeeded,
is believed to have been a rather effeminate character and was the

son of a secondary wife, so that to give him the royal power, which was considered so essential to a ruler by the Ancient Egyptians, he was married to his half-sister, Hatshepsut; purity of descent was reckoned through the female, rather than the male, line. Queen Hatshepsut's titles were "King's daughter, King's Sister, God's Wife and King's Great Wife" and she was certainly the ruler. By Thothmes II she had two daughters, Neferura, who died young, and Merytra; Thothmes III was the son of a secondary wife, Aset or Isis, so that when his father, Thothmes II, died, Queen Hatshepsut was officially made co-regent because she was of royal blood.

Queen Hatshepsut had, therefore, been in control of the government during her husband's reign of about thirteen years and by her talents and gifts she had won over to her able civil servants. Thothmes III, therefore, could do little except fret in the background; she was much too powerful and popular as a ruler to be overthrown by a palace revolution.

During her reign Egypt had peace and prosperity and the people of Syria and Palestine, conquered by her father, Thothmes I, continued to pay their tributes. She sent an expedition to the Land of Punt, which is now Somaliland, to do barter with the people of the country and bring back gold, skins and animals, but principally to bring back myrrh, which was used as incense at the ceremonies in the temples. The story is told in detail in delightful bas-reliefs on the walls of the beautiful funerary temple, dedicated to the Gods Amen-Ra and Hathor at Der el-Bahri in the Valley of the Tomb of the Kings. She died in middle age, worn out perhaps by the task of ruling a great kingdom. Her body has not been found in spite of all the elaborate arrangements she made at her funerary temple of Der el-Bahri.

The story of Queen Hatshepsut is important to the story of Thothmes III, since twenty-two years of his reign had passed by without his being able to display his talents to the full. It is a tribute to his character that he kept himself ready to rule the kingdom on the departure of the queen and that he did not become an embittered and angry young man. How well prepared he was is shown by the rapidity with which he led the Egyptian army on his first campaign in Palestine and Syria in the first or second year that he had assumed full power as Pharaoh.

On the death of the great queen the peoples of Syria and Palestine had revolted and refused to pay the tributes which they had done since the conquests of Thothmes I. It was a formidable revolt by well-armed and powerful peoples formed into a league under the

King of Kadesh whose territory lay by the Orontes river. "Behold,"
it is stated in the Annals, "from Yeraza (northern Judea) to the
marshes of the earth (the Euphrates) they had begun to revolt
against His Majesty." These Annals of Thothmes III's seventeen
campaigns are inscribed on the walls and obelisks in the temple of
the God Ammon at Karnak and in the Pharaoh's tomb. The King of
Kadesh, who was a redoubtable warrior, and was backed by many
peoples, including the powerful King of Mitanni to the east of the
Euphrates, had heard little of Thothmes III and probably thought
that he was a nonentity.

In April, 1479 B.C., or about that year, Thothmes III left with
his army from a fortress (later known as el Kantara) on the borders
of Sinai, and took the army in nine days the one hundred and sixty
miles to Gaza, and then on to Yehem on the southern slopes of
Mount Carmel. The King of Kadesh had advanced south from the
Orontes river in Syria, collecting troops of his allies on the way, and
they waited for the Egyptians near Megiddo with a well-equipped
army. Their soldiers were well trained and they had developed
chariot warfare, probably before the Egyptians had, and, indeed, the
peoples of Syria were in some respects more advanced than the
Egyptians. It was clearly going to be an important battle and the
result would be watched closely in Asia and elsewhere to see if
Egypt was to remain the dominant power or whether there would
be great changes.

Thothmes III, who was new to warfare, summoned a Council of
his generals. Among the official annals of the campaigns there is an
excellent account of this Council and of subsequent events, "the
earliest full description of any decisive battle" states Sir Alan
Gardiner in *Egypt of the Pharaohs*. It is also of great interest as giving
for the first time an insight into the character of the Pharaoh, who
shows himself, even before his first battle, to have been a born
commander. There were three roads the army could take to reach
the enemy drawn up before Megiddo; two of them were easy routes
and the most likely ones to be followed by a large army with
chariots, tents and baggage, while the other was a difficult track
over Mount Carmel. The generals advised strongly against the
difficult track: "How should we go by this road which is narrow
and risky . . . will not horse have to come behind horse and man
behind man? Shall our vanguard be fighting, while our rear-guard
is still halted over yonder in Aaruna and cannot get into action?"
Pharaoh did not take their advice; he must have realized that the
enemy would be expecting the Egyptian army to advance by the

easier road and have disposed their troops accordingly. It should be stated, however, that the official reports often show the Pharaoh to have been right and his generals wrong.

The Egyptian army led by Thothmes came through the pass without incident and the first stage of the battle was already won, for the Syrians were taken by surprise and had to reassemble their army to deal with the Egyptians who were in a strong position. Thothmes's boldness and the leisurely way he camped before the battle impressed the Egyptian army and caused consternation among the Syrians, who were defeated. The townsmen of Megiddo shut their gates in panic so that the army could not escape into the city though some of the leaders got in—"the people of the city . . . lowered clothing to pull them up within the walls".

Thothmes wanted to attack immediately while there was still confusion, but the Egyptian army was busy looting. "Then we captured their horses, their chariots of gold and silver were made spoil; their champions lay stretched out like fishes on the ground. The victorious army of His Majesty went round counting their shares. . . . Now if only the army of His Majesty had not given their heart to plundering the things of the enemy, they would have captured Megiddo at this moment."

The result was that the Egyptian army had to settle down to a siege of Megiddo and the King of Kadesh escaped from the city to stir up further trouble for the Egyptians in the future; but the opportunity to throw off the Egyptian yoke was lost by this first big defeat, for there was never again the same unity; on his subsequent campaigns Thothmes was able to deal with his opponents piece-meal. When Megiddo surrendered Thothmes showed magnanimity by granting terms and forbidding any killing. At the same time the city was despoiled and a long list is given of the plunder which showed how rich was this part of Western Asia. Thothmes returned to Egypt in triumph after a successful campaign lasting six months; there were ceremonies at the Temple of Amon at Karnak which was enriched with enemy spoils; hostages were brought from Syria and some were trained with the object that they should go back to their country as willing vassals.

While Thothmes was away on his many campaigns in Western Asia, Egypt was ably ruled by his Prime Minister, Rekhmara, who has left an account on his tomb of what he considered were the duties of a just Prime Minister, and he seems to have followed these precepts. It is probable that Thothmes enjoyed the military life which was very much freer for him than the life at Thebes with its ceremonies and rigid etiquette. He made sure that he lived comfortably on his expeditions; there is a stele in the Louvre on which Antef, the King's herald, describes how he used to go ahead with the advance guard and prepare a suitable palace or building for the Pharaoh's reception, so that when Thothmes arrived he found it "equipped with everything that is desired in a foreign country, I had made it better than the palaces of Egypt, purified, cleansed, set apart . . ."

The soldiers, too, seemed to have liked this rich country where there was plenty of plunder; in Phoenicia the annals state that "the army of His Majesty was drunk and anointed with oil every day as at a feast in Egypt". Thothmes had a collection made of the plants and animals, which were brought as an offering to the temple at Karnak and are recorded in bas-reliefs in a chamber which came to be called the "Botanic Gardens".

He made good use of his sea-power and formed bases in the coastal towns from which he could strike inland to capture cities such as Kadesh. The King of Kadesh continued to fight back and had shown his resourcefulness during the siege of his city by sending out a mare from Kadesh to cause confusion among the Egyptian chariots drawn by stallions, as they stood in battle array, but one of Thothmes's trusted captains, Amenemhab, dashed out and killed the mare before she reached the stallions.

On his eighth campaign in the thirty-third year of his reign Thothmes crossed the Euphrates at the "great bend" near Carchemish (fifty miles north-west of Aleppo) and attacked the King of Mitanni in Naharin—the Land of the Two Rivers (Euphrates and Tigris)—thus "extending the boundaries of Egypt". He then marched south to Niy, which he captured, and went elephant hunting; the story of how the Pharaoh's life was saved is recounted by Captain Amenemhab on his tomb at Thebes: "He hunted 120 elephants for the sake of their tusks. I engaged the largest which was among them, which fought against His Majesty; I cut off his hand (trunk) while he was alive before His Majesty, while I stood in the water between two rocks."

No country of the Near East had attained so large an empire or so much power as Egypt under Thothmes III. Rich tributes came yearly from Western Asia; Nubia paid tribute and there was a campaign there in the fiftieth year of his reign; the trade, which had been restarted by Queen Hatshepsut with the Land of Punt was maintained by Thothmes, and there were exchanges with the peoples of Crete and Cyprus. It was a period in history when war was profitable and Egypt's treasury was filled to overflowing, much of which enriched Thebes, the city of his beloved God Ammon. Thothmes added a colonnade of forty granite columns and almost as many pillars; on the walls of the temple were cut the names of the peoples he had conquered; repairs and additions were made to temples at Heliopolis, Memphis, Abydos, Denderah and Coptos. Thotmes died in the fifty-fourth year of his reign, loved and respected; his body was found in Queen Hatshepsut's temple of Der el Bahri in 1881 and lies in the Cairo Museum.

AKHNATON

(Reigned *c.* 1380–*c.* 1360 B.C.)

NOTHING MORE delightful has come out of Ancient Egypt than the
wall paintings and sculptures showing the young King Akhnaton
with his consort, the beautiful Queen Nefertiti, with the little
princesses who were their daughters. There is a simplicity about them,
a charming realism, a domestic intimacy that is altogether lacking
in the art that went before and most of what followed. Thus in
one we may see the king and queen in a fond embrace, the queen
sitting on her husband's knee; and in another the king is sitting on a
chair with the queen on a cushion opposite him, and the daughters,
according to their age, climbing on to his lap or standing or sitting
beside the royal pair. Then here is one showing them in their chariot,
and Nefertiti is reaching up as though to kiss the king, while their
little daughter, the Princess Mertaton, who is just tall enough to
see over the chariot's side, shows an eager interest in the pair of
prancing horses. And here in a vivacious fresco are two of the
princesses, naked save for their bead necklaces, fondling one another
as they sit on cushions at the feet of their parents.

Appealing as they are, it must be acknowledged that they are not
the pretty-pretty pictures that royal portrait painters have been
generally commissioned to produce. They are not in the least stylized
but bear all the signs of being true to life. But this is understandable
enough when we are told that the king who commissioned the
portraits assumed as one of his royal titles, as soon as he came to the
throne, "He who lives in Truth".

When he became king it was in succession to his father Amenhotep
III, and to begin with he himself bore the name of Amenhotep.
This was in 1380, or it may have been 1375 B.C., and he is supposed
to have reigned about twenty years. How old he was at the time of
his accession is a matter in dispute; some authorities hold that he was
a boy not yet in his teens, while others are of the opinion that he
was already a young man.

The XVIIIth Dynasty to which he belonged furnished Egypt with
some of her greatest and most successful sovereigns. Amenhotep III
had had a long reign of thirty-six years, and he bequeathed to his son

a realm that was prosperous and well-governed, and so extensive that it is more deserving of the name of empire than of kingdom. But the fourth Amenhotep was a very different man from his father, who had well earned his title of Amenhotep the Magnificent.

From the beginning of his reign he was much under feminine influence, at first that of his mother Queen Tiy and then on his marriage that of his wife, Queen Nefertiti, in addition, and of course the royal ladies had their own circle of courtiers and chosen counsellors. This is understandable enough when we remember his extreme youth, but as he grew older he showed a marked preference for the peaceful joys of his palace over the risks and ardours of military campaigning. Very clearly he was not cut out for the rougher tasks of kingmanship; which was a pity, since a period of instability had set in on the Egyptian frontiers in Africa and Asia. The governors in the outlying provinces were exposed to such pressures that they had great difficulty in holding their own, and to their imploring messages for assistance the young Pharaoh seems to have turned an almost deaf ear. He was not really interested in such things. Not politics but religion was what concerned him most. As Professor Breasted explains the situation, the philosophizing theology of the priests was of more importance to him than all the provinces of Asia; and so, instead of gathering the army so sadly needed in Syria, where the Hittites were overrunning the Egyptian defences, he immersed himself heart and soul in the thought of the time and gradually developed ideals and purposes which make him the most remarkable of all the Pharaohs—indeed (so Breasted claims) the first *individual* in human history.

A remarkable claim, and doubtless a well-grounded one; and yet it might be urged by one not so favourably disposed towards the young king that it was just this striking originality of his, in one special sphere, that contributed most to his failure as a monarch.

On the face of it, the signs for a revolution in religion were propitious. The old gods—the names of more than two thousand are known to us, and a queer lot they are!—were still worshipped in their temples up and down the land, but it was becoming increasingly recognized that they were too limited and too obviously local to answer the religious needs of what was now become an empire. "Our gods are too small," the more thoughtful of Egyptians must have concluded; "they have their worships, each in his own city, but they cannot adjust themselves to this new state of affairs, when the bounds of Egypt are no longer within sight of the waters of the Nile but lie far beyond the desert and reach unto the most distant

mountains". A super-state had come into existence: it was not
unreasonable to suppose that it should be matched with a super-
deity. "It can be no accident", Breasted has written, "that the notion
of a practically universal god arose in Egypt at the moment when the
king was receiving universal tribute from the world of that day".

Such thoughts as these had been passing through Amenhotep's
mind since he first began to think for himself, and it would seem
that as soon as he had the power in his own hands he resolved on
giving them tangible expression. If there was one god decidedly
superior to all his fellows it was Amen, or Amon, the state-god of
Thebes, the Egyptian capital; and very often his name was combined
with that of Ra, the sun-god whose chief centre of worship was at
On (Heliopolis) in the Delta. "Amenhotep" means "Amen is
content", but however it might be with the god, the king who was
named after him was *not* content. He decided to abandon the style
under which he had been known since he became king, and assumed
instead the name of Akhnaton (or Ikhnaton, or Akhenaten). This
word means "the Spirit of Aton", and Aton (or Aten) was the name
given to the god whose visible symbol was the solar disc. There is
not the least reason to suppose that the king thought of the sun itself
as a god, but it may well be that he was deifying, as it were, the
vital heat which he found accompanying all life on this earth. This
view is supported by the sculptured representations of the royal
family that the king caused to be placed in his palace and other
buildings. In these we see Akhnaton and Nefertiti and their daughters
basking in the light of rays proceeding from the solar disc—rays
which terminate in hands, each one of which is grasping the symbol
of life.

This outward symbol was a complete break with tradition. Up to
this time the gods had been represented in human shapes or animal
shapes or shapes that were half-human and half-animal. The simple-
minded Egyptians never doubted for a moment that these strange
creatures actually existed on earth and in heaven; and although the
educated classes may have had less crude conceptions of the divine,
there were few among them who were prepared for the substitution
of a symbol for the gods they and their ancestors had worshipped
from time immemorial. Akhnaton, however, had no patience with
their scruples, and he resolved to push ahead with his religious
revolution regardless of time-honoured beliefs and practices. What
his heart was set upon was a complete break with the past, associated
as it was with what he had come to believe was false and derogatory
of the Divine Unity.

If he had been an older man he might have been a wiser, and certainly he would have had more experience in that art of governing in which compromise has so large a part. As Pharaoh his powers were unlimited, however, at least in theory, and he soon demonstrated his intention to use them to the full. He hastened to establish Aton-worship as the religion of the State. He re-named Thebes as the "City of the Brightness of Aton", and in the middle of the precincts of the Temple of Amon, the god who was to be displaced, he caused to be erected a splendid sanctuary of the new worship. The priest-hood of Amon was a large and influential body, and they were supported by their colleagues throughout the land, but they seemed powerless to protect their possessions and privileges. One and all of the priesthoods were dispossessed, the official worship of the old gods ceased, and orders were given that their names should be erased from the monuments wherever they might be found. The name of Amon in particular was reprobated; and great must have been the consternation of the people when they saw workmen busily cutting away the god's name from the statues of the king's ancestors that lined the walls of the great temples at Karnak. Even the statue of the king's father was not spared, but the hated name was ruthlessly hacked out or otherwise made illegible. The word "gods" was also banned, for now the king had decreed that there were no longer gods but there was One God and only One.

When sullen resentment was intensified into bitter hate, Akhnaton determined to leave Thebes and build a new capital city on a site uncontaminated by old associations. The place chosen was midway between the Delta and Thebes, on a plain bounded on three sides by cliffs and on the other by the Nile. To this spot, in the sixth year of his reign, on the thirteenth day of the eighth month, the young Pharaoh drove in state in a two-horsed chariot; and in the presence of a crowd of officials and other notables he dedicated a large area (eight miles long from north to south and from eight to seventeen miles wide from cliff to cliff) as the site of the future holy city of Aton. The area was enclosed by fourteen boundary-marks hewn in the face of the surrounding cliffs, three on the west side of the Nile and eleven on the eastern side.

These monuments still exist, and are among the most remarkable relics of the civilization of ancient Egypt. The largest is twenty-six feet high. Each bears an inscription, sometimes as long as eighty lines, and above is a representation of Akhnaton and Nefertiti with one or more of their daughters, grouped beneath the rays emanating from the sun's disc. The site had been indicated by Aton himself, declared the king; and the name he gave to it was Akhetaton, meaning "Horizon of Aton". The modern name is Tell el-Amarna, and all about are the remains of the temples and palaces, government buildings and private residences, that were erected under the supervision of the royal architect, a man named Bek, who, we are told, was "instructed by his Majesty himself".

Akhnaton watched the city grow—that city which one of his nobles described (the description is still extant) as "Akhetaton, great in loveliness. . . . At the sight of her beauty there is rejoicing. She is lovely and beautiful, and when one sees her it is like having a glimpse of heaven". On the day when the temple was finished Akhnaton proceeded thither in his chariot, together with Nefertiti and their four daughters and a gorgeous retinue, and was received with loud shouts of "Welcome". The altar was piled with rich oblations, and we are told that in the evening ritual of "Sending the Aton to rest", Nefertiti joined with her "sweet voice" and her "beautiful hands" shook the sistrum, the jangling wire rattle used by the ancient Egyptians in their temple music.

Surely it is not unreasonable to suppose that included in the ceremonial was the recitation of one of those two Hymns to Aton that Akhnaton himself composed, and which are among the most remarkable specimens of the religious literature of the ancient world. "When thou settest in the western horizon of heaven," runs one of these noble pieces of poetry, "the earth becomes dark with the darkness of the dead. Men fall asleep in their dwellings, their heads are covered up, their nostrils are stopped and no man sees his neighbour. Everything that is theirs could be stolen from under their heads without them knowing anything about it. When it is dark all the lions come out of their dens, all creeping serpents likewise. The whole earth is silent, because He that made it and everything in it has gone to his rest. . . . But when day breaks, and Thou rejoicest and goest up on the horizon and givest light to the day . . . then the people of the Two Lands of Egypt arise, they stand up on their feet and rejoice. They wash themselves and put on their clothes, and they stretch out their hands to Thee in thanksgiving for Thy dawning."

"How manifold are Thy works!" runs another verse; "the works of the One and Only God, beside whom there is no other. It is Thou that makest the seasons, the cool of winter and the heat of summer. It is Thou who createst the man-child in woman, who makest the seed in man, who giveth life to the son in the body of his mother. To the chick within the egg-shell Thou givest breath, and when

Thou hast perfected him he breaks the shell and comes forth chirping with all his might and runs about on his two feet. . . . It was Thou who set the Nile in the Underworld, and another Nile in the sky to water the earth with rain. The lands of Syria and Nubia, the land of Egypt—Thou madest them all; Thou hast appointed each man to his own place, and provided him with everything that he needs . . ."

There's no denying that here there is evidence of something radically new. A new note has been struck, a new spirit of universalism has come into the world, and out of the dry and dusty bones of old Egypt has sprung vigorous young life. For it is no mere state-god that Akhnaton is hymning, no national deity, but One who has made the world and everyone and everything in it. "Aton, the father and the mother of all that He hath made." Seven or eight hundred years later very much the same note was struck by some of the Hebrew prophets, but there are good grounds for hailing this brilliant young Pharaoh Akhnaton as the first monotheist.

But it was after all a false dawn. The world was not ready for that sublimest of all religious conceptions, the One-ness of the Godhead. Akhnaton died, his empire on the verge of dissolution, when still little more than a youth, and his revolution died with him —or very soon after. Since he had no son he was followed on the throne by one of his sons-in-law, and he again, after a brief reign, by the husband of another of Akhnaton's daughters. His name to begin with was Tutankh*aton*, but after a time he quitted Akhetaton for Thebes and, even more significant, changed his name to Tutankh*amen*. His reign was short, but long enough to effect a complete restoration of the old worship of Amen and his fellow gods. He died, and was laid in a tomb whose magnificent treasures have been revealed in our own time. While as for Akhnaton, he was by now the "heretic Pharaoh", he was the "Criminal of Akhetaton".

MOSES

(13th Century B.C.)

MUCH OF the Old Testament—though not, perhaps, as much as it was once fashionable to think—is myth and fable, with the slenderest framework of fact.

But one of its tales, and perhaps the one best known to most of us, has been investigated so exhaustively and for so long that it is now established historical fact. Some of its details may err, but compared with much of more recent "history" it is factual indeed. Moses, as we shall see, was far from popular most of the time: no one had cause or incentive to go back, as has been done in our present century with "great leaders" in China, Russia, Germany and Italy —and elsewhere—to gloss over his faults, build up his achievement.

The words of Exodus are so familiar; the scene itself, painted on canvas, wood and stone by artists of every degree of skill for thousands of years, is so familiar, too, that the story needs little re-telling or amplification: "Moses stretched out his hand over the sea, and the Lord caused the sea to go back by a strong east wind all that night, and made the sea dry land, and the waters were divided. And the children of Israel went into the midst of the sea upon the dry ground; and the waters were a wall unto them on their right hand and on their left."

This must be Moses's most dramatic achievement. For as we know, the Egyptians galloped and thundered their way in pursuit—and were drowned to a man. The "children of Israel", the Israelites, got safely to the far side in their hundreds of thousands: years later, they reached their Promised Land, and founded their community, the state of Israel, in much the spot that it stands today.

And although we accept the fact—which, indeed, the Bible points out—that the waters were persuaded back by a freak wind and perhaps a monster tide, we cannot deny, as we follow the extraordinary adventures of these Israelite people in their search for freedom, that their ruler must have been one of the greatest in history. If we believe the Bible, he was divinely appointed: if we do not, he was humanly-, perhaps self-chosen. But until he came, the Israelites, the Jews, were in a sorry and desperate situation.

38

And the flight on which Moses led them was not just a dash across the border. This was the mass movement of a nation spanning no less than forty years; and while Moses was in command—as its ruler, in fact—two new generations were born, and one came to maturity. In the same extraordinary period of history the Jewish people were shaped into a pattern which has profoundly altered the shape of history since.

Before we go on to consider this man—condemned to death before his birth and on numerous occasions after it—we must take a brief, panoramic, look at the whole of Jewish history before him.

From the Persian Gulf, back "in the mists of antiquity"—or so, until fairly recently, men thought—the patriarch Abraham decided to move with his family to a more fertile, more attractive, land. His God said to him, "Get thee out of thy country, and from thy kindred, and from thy father's house, unto a land that I will show thee: and I will make of thee a great nation, and I will bless thee and make thy name great; and thou shalt be a blessing; and I will bless them that bless thee, and curse him that curseth thee; and in thee shall all families of the earth be blessed."

Abraham acted immediately on this advice: and now we know the date to have been somewhere between 2,000 and 1,700 years before Christ. He led his descendants to the coastline of Palestine, the "Canaan" or "Low Land" at the end of the Mediterranean Sea. Here they found land which was wonderfully fertile, a gentle but regular and adequate rainfall; and here the descendants of Abraham flourished and grew in numbers.

Many years later, the name "Children of Israel" was adopted by these migrants. "Israel" meant "God Fighteth", and God Himself told them, through Abraham's descendant Jacob, that he was, in effect, on their side, would always remain so: they should accordingly style themselves "Israel", or "Children of Israel". And scarcely had they done so than disaster struck: there was drought and famine in Canaan.

More advice came from above: Jacob was told to lead them to Egypt. Here, with the waters of the Nile irrigating farmland, there was little danger of drought affecting crops. The Children of Israel already knew that the finest corn crops of the known world came from Egypt; they had sent messengers and traders to obtain it. Now, once again, they girded their loins and set off.

At first the Egyptians and their ruler, their Pharaoh, welcomed them. There was room and to spare in Egypt: hard-working immigrants were just what the country needed. Joseph, Jacob's son, he of the many-coloured coat, had already found his way to Egypt, first as slave, then as a powerful man. To him Pharaoh now said: "Thy father and thy brethren are come unto thee: the land of Egypt is before thee; in the best of the land make thy father and brethren to dwell."

But soon, very soon, things changed. The Israelites settled eagerly, happily, into this new land—only to find that within a few years the Egyptians had panicked about their rate of increase. "The children of Israel", says the Old Testament, "were fruitful, and increased abundantly, and multiplied and waxed exceeding mighty; and the land was filled with them." And Pharaoh, alarmed, cried to his courtiers, "Behold, the people of the children of Israel are more and mightier than we: Come on, let us deal wisely with them; lest they multiply, and it come to pass, that when there falleth out any war, they join also unto our enemies and fight against us."

So orders were given that the Israelites be forthwith deprived of their flocks and their holdings of land: they would become prisoners of the Egyptian government, servants of the Egyptian people, building new towns, new cities. And if they faltered in the work they would be whipped to death by overseers. As afterthought, when Pharaoh realized these measures would have little effect on his real problem, orders were given that midwives would kill every male child born to an Israelite mother.

Moses entered upon the scene in the wake of this vicious edict. An Israelite woman called Jochebed gave birth to him, and bravely clung to him till he had reached the age of three months. Then, convinced that he must soon be discovered and put to death, she smuggled him to the bank of the Nile, made a little boat for him out of bulrushes and clay, and gently pushed him out into the stream. With luck—very great luck—someone might find him, perhaps not realizing that the little boy was Jewish, and save his life.

Jochebed's prayer was answered. A little further downstream, the child's tiny boat was discovered by almost the only person able to do something to save him: no less a person than Pharaoh's daughter, washing at the river bank. She lifted the child out, saw instantly that he was of Jewish birth, but gathered him gently into her arms and took him away. Before she handed him over to a wet nurse, to feed him at her breast, Pharaoh's kind-hearted daughter christened the little boy "Moses".

Somehow, though his appearance grew unmistakably Jewish and there could be no possible doubt of his origins, the young Moses was allowed to grow into manhood unmolested, even respected. Thanks to the royal favour which had been shown him, he was not made to perform manual labour like the rest of his people.

But he sorrowed greatly, watching them as they struggled to make bricks under the lash of the overseer. Day after day he was tempted to leap upon some brutish foreman and thrash him—but common-sense told him this could do no good at all to the suffering Israelites. The sight of one of their own men, mightier than themselves (for Moses had never lived on a starvation diet); mightier by far than the Egyptians (for they were a small race and Moses was by any criteria a well-built, strong-faced, man): this sight might cheer them for a moment. It might also spell their doom.

And then suddenly Moses, from the corner of an eye, saw an Egyptian foreman beating a small and helpless Jew with his cudgel. Without thinking, he flung himself upon the Egyptian, struck him a terrible blow, and killed him outright.

There was no hope of escaping detection: men had seen him perform the deed, and those who had not seen were only too anxious to incriminate this Jew, so unfairly honoured when most of the rest of his generation had been slaughtered at birth. The chase was on; and Moses fled the country.

He travelled many miles, to the land of Midian, north of the Gulf of Akaba, where he settled down to do whatever work might come his way. He became a shepherd, and being a fine-looking man, with obvious intelligence and powers of leadership, was chosen as her husband by Zipporah, daughter of a Midian chief. And it was while he tended their sheep that he had his first vision.

He was looking at a bush when suddenly it burst into flame. The fire spread till its gold had enveloped the whole plant—and yet somehow the bush was not consumed, the flame burnt on. As he watched in wonder, Moses heard a voice, then saw the figure of an angel, standing among the flames.

The angel spoke, with a message from God: "I have seen the affliction of my people which are in Egypt, and have heard their cry by reason of their taskmasters. I am come down to deliver them out of that land unto a good land, unto a land flowing with milk and honey; unto the place of the Canaanites, and the Hittites, and the Amorites, and the Perizzites, and the Hivites, and the Jebusites——"

And the angel ended with the words, "I will send thee unto Pharaoh, that thou mayest bring forth my people, the Children of Israel, out of Egypt."

Moses obeyed. He took leave of his wife, his old father-in-law, and headed for Egypt.

When he got there, things were even more difficult and unpleasant than he had imagined. Pharaoh, who had deplored the increase in Israelite numbers, now perversely objected to their removal: they were good workers, and he needed them to build his empire. Nor would he even allow Moses to take the elders out into the wilderness to perform a sacrifice. To show his anger at the suggestion, he decreed that henceforth the Children of Israel would make their daily quota of bricks, but without straw. They would have to scratch around in the stubble fields for something to bind the clay. And if they dropped by as much as one brick from their daily quota, they would be whipped to the point of death.

Moses had established himself, instantly, as the leader of his people; and a day or two later become the most unpopular member of the community. And yet, though the Israelites cursed and reviled him among themselves for being a meddlesome fool who had made their lives a million times worse, he was still their acknowledged leader.

Moses demanded explanation from his Lord—and much of what followed, seen over the gulf of years, has the ingredients of bad, "sick", comedy. Some of it, like the episode of the cudgels, is extremely funny. God told his servant Moses that he must impress Pharaoh by sorcery: he showed him how to change a stout stick, such as the Egyptian overseers carried, into a writhing serpent—and back again.

It seems that this trick was already well known in Egypt, was in fact a variant of the ancient snake-charmer's act, in which serpents are made to stand rigid, like sticks. Moses turned his "stick" into a serpent—and a moment later Pharaoh's sorcerers did the same with theirs. To make matters worse, Moses earned their undying enmity, and Pharaoh's, by being unable to stop his serpent gobbling up all the others. More restrictions, more sanctions, were piled on the protesting backs of the Children of Israel. And they made their feelings quite clear to Moses. It must have been with a feeling close to despair that he approached his God again and asked for guidance.

The Lord instructed him to threaten Pharaoh with a series of plagues if he maintained his refusal to let the Israelites leave, and Moses did so. Each threat brought a firm refusal and in its wake a sickening plague—which yet failed to move the Egyptian ruler. The waters of Egypt—after due warning—"turned to blood" and killed all the fish. Seven days of this was followed by a plague of frogs which oozed out of the blood-coloured rivers and spread, in slimy millions, over the whole of the land. Still Pharaoh refused to allow his Israelite slaves to leave. The frogs were followed by lice and flies, painful boils, hail, locusts and a total eclipse of the sun.

Pharaoh must have been the most iron-willed ruler in history. Only now, in the blackness of total eclipse, did he agree that the Israelites might leave: but not, decidedly not, with their sheep and cattle; these they must leave behind.

Moses insisted; Pharaoh was adamant.

Now came the last, most dreadful, plague of all. The Lord told Moses that "I will pass through the land of Egypt this night, and will smite all the first-born in the land of Egypt, both man and beast; and against all the gods of Egypt, I will execute judgement". If the Children of Israel wished to avoid this fate, they would have to take a certain, highly complicated, action—and from this action has descended one of the most hallowed observances of the Jewish people, the Passover. They must sacrifice lambs, mark their doors with the blood, then eat the flesh with elaborate ceremony: "It is the Lord's Passover."

And they were spared. "It came to pass that at midnight the Lord smote all the first-born in the land of Egypt, from the first-born of Pharaoh that sat on his throne unto the first-born of the captive that was in the dungeon; and all the first-born of cattle. And Pharaoh rose up in the night, he and all his servants, and all the Egyptians; and there was a great cry in Egypt——"

Moses—aided by his God—had won the day. That day was in about the year 1280 B.C.; and on it the Israelites left Egypt, the hateful land of their captivity, and headed for the land which none of them— none of those now living—had ever seen, but which was the Canaan from which their ancestors had departed, many years before, to seek better conditions in Egypt. And now there were more than half a million of them.

No sooner had they left than Pharaoh—can there have been another more impossible man to deal with, in all history, than this Rameses II?—decided to pursue them, bring back his slaves. Moses had led them via the marshy land at the north of the Red Sea and it was as they were camped here, waiting to move further north and cross on dry land, that they saw the dust of Pharaoh's chariots, as the Egyptians strove to catch them up.

The rest is history. The whole of Pharaoh's army perished with the returning waves, leaving Moses and his 600,000-or-so Israelites safe —if gasping a little for breath—on the far, eastern, side.

But there were forty years of privation and danger ahead. It was during these forty years, in which Moses became a very old man and two generations of his people died, that the Jewish people came to maturity. Time after time they raged at him, as ill luck dogged them, food and water grew short, and the wilderness hostile. But all the while God was instructing Moses in a code of thought and behaviour—a code culminating in the Ten Commandments, which were revealed to him at the summit of Mount Sinai.

There is a delightful, human, moment near the start of the forty years. Moses's old father-in-law heard that the pilgrims were coming through his land on the Gulf of Akaba, and he excitedly told his daughter, Zipporah, to make ready to meet her husband. They went out and met Moses at the head of his civilian army, and he was overjoyed at seeing them.

And this marked a turning point in the fortunes of Israel, for it took the wise old father-in-law, Jethro, no time at all to see that there was something very wrong in his son-in-law's organization of all these people. Why—the young chap was trying to do the lot himself, not *delegating*. Look, Jethro said, "the thing is too heavy for thee; thou art not able to perform it thyself alone".

And Moses, after listening carefully, took his advice, choosing able men out of the Israelite army and making them "heads over the people, rulers of thousands, rulers of hundreds, rulers of fifties, and rulers of tens——"

The years went by: the Israelites found that the present occupiers of their Promised Land were unwilling to let them enter it, and battles raged over the years. Many of the pilgrims were destined never to see it, to die in the wilderness. Children were born in that wilderness, told by their elders of the great future lying in wait.

And Moses himself was taken to the top of a mountain by the Lord, and at last given a glimpse. "This", said the Lord, "is the land."

Moses stared in wonder. This, then, was the Promised Land. After all these years, these trials——

But, the Lord went on, "Thou shalt not go over thither."

Moses died, was buried in a valley in the land of Moab. "And Moses was an hundred and twenty years old when he died; his eye was not dim, nor his natural force abated. And the children of Israel wept for Moses in the plain of Moab thirty days."

A little later, having worked a way round to the east of the land, to attack it from that quarter and cross into it over the River Jordan, they had reached their Promised Land. They were a nation, to be ruled henceforth—and literally—by the word of God. And, in God's words, they were his Chosen People.

Moses's work was done.

DAVID

(c. 1012–c. 972 B.C.)

DAVID: FEW names in history are more famous, more evocative, more fascinating. Western religion, myth, art and social history are full of its echoes. Yet the actual details of our knowledge of David are restricted to four Books of the Old Testament: I and II Samuel, I Chronicles, and the first two chapters of I Kings. The narratives contained in these are, however, most suggestive.

David's date was roughly 1000 B.C. He stands out as the first successful King of Judah and Israel, for his predecessor and strange enemy-friend, Saul, was tragically unstable. Indeed, his curious psychological relationship with David provides one of the most fascinating aspects of the younger man's character and career. All through his life David, at once warrior and musician, had an intense personality to which others reacted intensely.

This human trait has attracted all ages, and helps to compensate for certain acts of undoubted savagery. If we are apt to over-blame him for these, it is because the very name of David has become raised to a sublime level: though no plaster-saint, was he not the ancestor of Jesus Christ, his seed the vessel of Hebraeo-Christian salvation, his birthplace the equally humble birthplace of Christ? Even his un-questioned gifts as poet, musician and dancer (the three arts being then largely united) have made posterity attribute to him many of the Psalms which recent research has shown not to be his.

Surely David attracts because of his elusiveness and versatility. Which aspect is more significant, the comely shepherd lad anointed to be the future king, or that king himself in military and social splendour?; the stripling whose stone destroyed the giant Goliath, or the sweet singer and teacher of musical ecstasy?; the lover of many women, or the bosom friend of Jonathan and despairing father of Absalom?; the massacring general, the murderer of Uriah, or the gentle sparer of his foe Saul?; the historic monarch or the gipsy-like refugee from camp to camp and valley to valley? For David was all these things, in a mixture which most of posterity have found lovable.

David was born at a crucial moment in Hebrew history. The

45

youngest son of Jesse, a shepherd by the village of Bethlehem, his origins were humble. Yet so relatively flexible were social distinctions that this Jesse was the descendant of the well-to-do Boaz and of ancestors more impressive still. Even as a child David must have had some premonition of future greatness. When the prophet Samuel, directed by the Lord, came to Jesse's home to anoint *one* of his sons as the future chosen of the Lord, the father produced all but one of his sons in turn, and only at the prophet's insistence did he call the boy David in from his work in the fields.

Yet David seems to have had no doubt; his character already had a strange decisiveness. With typical versatility he had already slain both a lion and a bear that were attacking his sheep, and attained skill in singing and playing the harp. In fact it is in these last capacities that we next hear of him. The neurotic figure of King Saul, tragic rather than evil, now begins its extraordinary love-hate relationship with the youthful musician. The king, tormented by fears and visions, calls for a harpist to soothe his spirit. David is recommended, presents himself, and wins all hearts by his charm: Saul is delighted with him, congratulates Jesse on his son, and makes him his armour-bearer, for he had heard that the handsome lad was warrior as well as artist.

Now came a really crucial point in his career. The enormous giant Goliath, champion of the Philistines, was challenging any Hebrew to single combat. David, sent by his father with provisions for his soldiering brothers, was rebuked by them for his curiosity; but the lad amazed Saul with the proposal to fight Goliath himself, "that all the earth may know there is a God in Israel". Had he not slain a lion and a bear? Saul must indeed have been impressed, for he granted David's request. Refusing any cumbersome armour, the boy chose five smooth stones out of the brook: the first of these, thrown from his simple sling, hit Goliath on the forehead so that the giant fell. David ran up and beheaded Goliath with the victim's own sword. In panic the Philistines fled.

The delighted king took David to live with him, but his love froze into jealousy as he listened to the women dancing and singing: "Saul hath slain his thousands, and David his ten thousands." We read how "Saul was very wroth" and that he "eyed David from that day and forward". Neurotic jealousy of David's popularity, of his youth, handsomeness and skill, and an intuition that somehow this ex-shepherd boy would overpower the life and fame of Saul—all these factors led the king twice to throw a javelin at David while he was singing and playing to him. Yet David's own conduct was exemplary;

he was always to show for Saul the greatest respect. In him he found a father figure, while Saul may have found some kind of unreality and frustration in the relationship. It may well be that David's home life meant little to him; we hear little or nothing of any attempt to include his family in his good fortune, or later in his regal riches. Hence, perhaps, his eager, deep love for Saul, who at least showed some "temperament", if an unfortunate one. Throughout his life the artist in David felt bored with the ordinary. Gratitude and vanity also played their part.

For the moment he played safe, and his forbearance troubled Saul, who sent him away as a "captain over a thousand". Perhaps the upstart lad would blunder, become unpopular, or even get himself killed. He even promised him his daughter Merab in marriage, then gave her to another man, and offered David his other daughter Michal, who was already in love with him. Saul declared: "I will give him her, that she may be a snare to him, and that the hand of the Philistines may be against him." But still David observed all courtesies and was admired by all.

His greatest solace—and the most intense relationship of his life, other than his strange relationship with Saul and his love for his own son Absalom—was his close friendship with Saul's son, Jonathan. This unique bond has become a byword—more famous even than that of Achilles and Patroclus, or of Orestes and Pylades. The loyal, dashing, honest Jonathan and the genius David, prince who was once shepherd, were united on equal terms. Jonathan loved David "as his own soul", and they made a covenant of utter loyalty to each other and each other's descendants. Hence only Jonathan could act as intermediary and warn David of the king's mania to kill him. This involved much intrigue on the part of the two friends, as of the ingenious Michal also, who assisted her husband in escaping from a window, while she filled his bed with an image and a goat's-hair pillow.

When David absented himself from the royal table, Jonathan pleaded he had gone to Bethlehem on family matters and so incensed Saul that the latter threatened both his son and David with death. The final meeting between the two friends took place in a garden at night; speed was imperative; they swore eternal fidelity so emotionally that they "wept one with another".

David now embarked on some extraordinary adventures. At Nob, the priest Ahimelech gave him and his famished followers the sacred showbread to eat, as none other was available—a point raised later by the irony of Christ Himself. Fleeing to Achish, king of Gath, an hereditary enemy, he feigned madness and was successful in escaping. Next, in the cave of Adullam, he gathered a following of his own family, and of "every one that was in distress"—some four hundred men in all. Meanwhile Saul destroyed all living creatures in Nob, including Ahimelech himself. Now began a three-handed conflict between David's men, Saul's men and the Philistines. First David slaughtered the latter; then Saul pursued him. David, catching the king and his bodyguard asleep, merely cut off the skirt of Saul's robe. Such generosity moved the king and there was a brief reconciliation.

But David's cruel side soon showed itself. Because the landowner Nabal would not provision David's troops, he marched with the slaughter of Nabal's people in his mind, and was stopped only by Nabal's resourceful wife Abigail, who appeared with the required food and drink. The Lord slew Nabal and David added Abigail to his list of wives. Once more Saul harassed him; but the situation repeated itself, and David took from his sleeping enemy merely the spear and a cruse of water. Saul offered complete reconciliation, but David not unnaturally went his own way—but why to become the ally of Israel's perpetual foes, the Philistines? Here his lust for fighting and his sense of self-preservation triumphed over his patriotism and his religious feeling. As Achish's ally, his base at Ziklag, he massacred the Geshurites, the Gezrites and the Amalekites—he who had earlier slain two hundred Philistines and brought their foreskins as a marriage-gift to Michal!

The final test took place between Saul and the Philistines at Gilboa. Despite the pleas of Achish, the Philistines refused David as a treacherous ally, so he returned to Ziklag only to find it entirely destroyed by the Amalekites. Narrowly escaping stoning by his distraught people, he led them in vengeance and wiped out almost all the Amalekites. Meanwhile Saul's army was routed; he and Jonathan died. David received the news in a typical way: the news-bearer was put to death, but this was followed by one of the most exquisite and famous laments in literature. He praised and bewailed his enemy Saul and his beloved Jonathan: "Thy love to me was wonderful, passing the love of women."

David was now acclaimed King of Judah at Hebron. After long war with the house of Saul, led by Abner, David won the day, and was hailed king of a united Judah and Israel. In the event the union did not long survive his son Solomon's death; yet its spiritual impetus was enduring. The next obvious step was the conquest of Jerusalem from the Jebusites; from David's day the Holy City may date its splendour. Thither he brought the sacred Ark, and was commanded by God to build a Temple to house it. The arrival of the Ark produced wild, ecstatic dancing, in which David played a whole-hearted and graceful part—disgraceful, according to his prim queen, Michal, whose reunion with him had been a condition of his peace treaty with Saul's forces.

He now embarked on a series of aggressive wars: Philistines, Syrians and others were conquered and looted, their gold going to adorn Jerusalem's Temple, while Moab and Edom were at last annexed to the Kingdom. An account of every campaign would be wearisome; it is more heartening to think of recorded acts of royal kindness—his befriending of Jonathan's son, the lame Mephibosheth; his pardoning the shifty Shimei; and his gratitude to his aged benefactor Barzillai.

Troubles enough, however, afflicted David's reign. Some were due to his sensual temperament: by now he had collected several wives (whence nineteen sons and some daughters) and more concubines. Even so, he could not resist the sight of Bathsheba, wife of a gallant soldier, Uriah the Hittite. He made her pregnant, and then ordered Joab, his commander, to see that Uriah was killed in battle. He then married Bathsheba, but their first child died soon after birth. The prophet Nathan had sternly intervened and rebuked the king for his sin, thus creating a pattern of vital importance for the future, pointing the way towards Christian social ethics. The emotional David showed "true repentance". To compensate for the baby's death, the Lord decreed that David and Bathsheba's next son should be the wisest of all kings: Solomon.

Other offspring caused trouble. His son Amnon forced incest on his half-sister Tamar; this led to mounting feuds, in which Amnon was killed by Absalom, Tamar's full brother and David's favourite son. Absalom, an extremely handsome man, fled and soon led a revolt against his father, which won considerable support. Few pictures are richer in pathos than that of David suffering from divided emotions and the risk of a civil war. His favourite son, entangled in a tree by his long hair, was killed by Joab. Though peace was restored, the king wept and said aloud: "O my son Absalom, my son, my son Absalom! would God I had died for thee, O Absalom, my son, my son!"

There followed an unsuccessful revolt headed by the Benjamite named Sheba, and a three years' famine, appeased only by the slaughter of seven descendants of Saul, in reprisal for Saul's massacre of the Gibeonites. A subsequent victory over the Philistines (his former allies and protectors) inspired David with a magnificent hymn:

The Lord is my rock, and my fortress, and my deliverer . . .
He bowed the heavens also, and came down; and darkness was under his feet.
And he rode upon a cherub, and did fly; and he was seen upon the wings of the wind.
And he made darkness pavilions round about him, dark waters, and thick clouds of the skies.

These verses are typical of David's ecstatic style; the Psalms offer countless examples of it, as well as of softer imagery:

As the hart panteth after the water brooks, so panteth my soul after thee, O God.

Other Psalms (for instance, No. 150) call on man to celebrate God with every joy of music: "Praise him with the sound of the trumpet: praise him with the psaltery and harp." The brief lament over Saul and Jonathan is remarkably free from any mention of religion.

This humanity and artistry in David help us to sympathize with him in many seemingly monstrous misfortunes. The last chapter of II Samuel portrays an amazing "Divine Vengeance", and issues a dreadful warning. David had ordered the people to be numbered, and for the sin of taking a census he was faced by the prophet Gad with three calamities from which to choose one: seven years of famine, three months of fleeing from his enemies in hot pursuit, or three days of pestilence. Choice fell on the latter, after which David sacrificed and the Lord stayed the plague.

After forty years of reigning, David was old and physically weak. In his illness his advisers sought out a young virgin: "let her lie in thy bosom, that my lord the king may get heat." But the experiment failed, despite the beauty of Abishag the Shunammite. David's son Adonijah proposed to follow Absalom's example and usurp the kingdom. To ensure Solomon's succession, Nathan persuaded Bathsheba to plead with the ailing king for her son. David solemnly promised this, and gave Solomon a blessing and advice: "I go the way of all the earth: be thou strong therefore, and show thyself a man." His plans for the Temple and the safety of his kingdom in Solomon's keeping, David died.

The vast range of David's career, his human magnetism and versatile temperament, even some—though not all—of his faults, have endeared him across the centuries. "Son of David" was even a high title applied to Christ. Artists have found continuous inspiration in David's life and mind, two outstanding examples being Rembrandt's sombre picture of "David Playing Before Saul", in the Mauritshuis at the Hague, and Michelangelo's colossal nude statue of the shepherd-boy. Above all, David is the poetical genius of the Psalms. In one of them he enjoins us to "Praise God in the beauty of holiness". No Biblical figure has shone like David in the holiness of beauty.

SOLOMON

(Reigned *c.* 970–*c.* 932 B.C.)

SELDOM IN the history of any nation do its two most famous monarchs succeed one another as father and son; the most memorable exception is the case of David and Solomon. These two soar in importance above all other kings of Israel, of Judah or of Israel-Judah. To find a satisfying reason for this concentration of genius (though the two types of genius were widely different) is hardly possible. Why David himself chose Solomon as his successor out of his nineteen sons we cannot discover. The Bible simply tells us that the prophet Nathan foretold the birth of the future king as a divine ordinance.

Solomon's mother was Bathsheba, who had sexual relations with David while still the wife of the soldier Uriah. David arranged for this inconvenient husband to be killed in battle, and then married the widow. Their first child, however, died within a week, as a divine punishment. By compensation, the next child, Solomon, was destined to become king and excel all mankind both in wisdom and wealth. But not—so it turned out—in the purity either of his religious or sexual habits.

The career of Solomon is described in I Kings, 1-11; I Chronicles, 23 and 28-9; II Chronicles, 1-9—twenty-three chapters in all. Moreover, the account in Chronicles largely repeats that in Kings. Hence our relatively sparse information about Solomon. Even so, he stands out in his main qualities and in the chief events of his reign —the consolidation of the kingdom, the policy of peaceful neigh-bourliness with surrounding states, the numerous wives and concubines, most of them from these states, with the consequent influx of foreign customs and even creeds; the unprecedented luxury of his court, wisdom of his counsel, and—above all—prosperity of his people; the admiring visit of the Queen of Sheba; and the two contrasted aspects of the king's attitude to religion—his building of the splendid Temple at Jerusalem, and his later lapse into idolatry, largely under the influence of his foreign wives.

At once certain contrasts are apparent between Solomon and David. When first we read of Solomon he is the Crown Prince to whom God will grant the fulfilment of the Temple-building (denied to David as "a man of war"), whereas David appears first as a shepherd-lad. The ups and downs of David's reign may be contrasted with the security and peacefulness of Solomon's. David remains the revered ancestor of Christ and a symbol—heroic, artistic, human—for future ages. Solomon's fame is only a little less: wisdom, universal prosperity, and a luxury that did not at first deny the Lord—such are his hallmarks. This reign marked a point of rest in the long story of the tortured but imperishable Jewish people.

This "ideal" epoch was preceded by brief violence. Solomon's half-brother Adonijah had planned to seize the throne during David's last illness, gathering together a force which included Joab and the priest Abiathar; but David, informed by Bathsheba, had Solomon anointed king, and then summoned him to receive his last blessing and commands. Solomon pardoned his half-brother, but after their father's death Adonijah's tactlessness grew, and he begged Solomon (through Bathsheba) for the hand of Abishag the Shunammite. Solomon's ironic retort: "Why not ask for him the kingdom also?" showed his distrust of Adonijah; and he had him killed. Joab and Abiathar were next executed, according to David's last command; while Shimei was pardoned so long as he lived in Jerusalem. He stupidly left it in pursuit of runaway domestics, so he too perished.

The way was thus cleared for an epoch of unparalleled serenity. Splendour began with a sacrifice in the "high place" of worship at Gibeon, on whose altar the king presented a thousand burnt offerings. Then "the Lord appeared to Solomon in a dream by night: and God said, Ask what I shall give thee." Solomon, humble before the task of ruling an immense people, begged for "an understanding heart to judge thy people, that I may discern between good and bad."

Pleased that he had not requested riches, honour or long life, but wisdom, God gave him "a wise and an understanding heart; so that there was none like thee before thee, neither after thee shall any arise like unto thee", while He also awarded him what he had not asked for, "both riches and honour". In addition—"if thou wilt walk in my ways . . . then I will lengthen thy days". This is a remarkable event in the recorded story of kingship, when rulers, even when orthodox in religion, preferred the glories of battlefield and throne. Solomon awoke from his dream and came to Jerusalem; and "stood before the ark of the Lord, and offered up burnt offerings, and offered peace offerings, and made a feast to all his servants".

His wisdom was soon put to a practical test, which has become

53

proverbial. Now the husband of the daughter of the Egyptian Pharaoh, he was appealed to by two harlots, each of whom had just given birth to a child; one of the babies had died. One of the women accused the other of substituting her own dead child and taking the living one falsely as her own. Solomon had a sword brought and proposed cutting the child in half and giving each woman one of the halves. The real mother cried out against the murder of the child, preferring that the other woman should have the living baby. Solomon decided that her concern proved her maternity, so he awarded her the child. Thus we have an early triumph of psychology over mathematics. The nation was impressed by this and similar judgments, "excelling the wisdom of Egypt". We are told—"And there came of all people to hear the wisdom of Solomon, from all kings of the earth, which had heard of his wisdom."

Three thousand proverbs and a thousand and five songs were attributed to him, though we must be wary of such figures in an age without real historians. He is also said to have "spoken" about trees, beasts and fishes; and in all this attribution there is no doubt a core of truth. He must have made a deep and forcible intellectual impression. To wisdom was added joy: "Judah and Israel were many, as the sand which is by the sea in multitude, eating and drinking and making merry." With joy went security, for we learn that "Judah and Israel dwelt safely, every man under his vine and under his fig-tree". Peace attended Solomon also in his foreign relations, while his dominions reached from the Euphrates to the Egyptian frontier.

A special friend was Hiram, king of Tyre, a great admirer of David, who congratulated the new king and readily agreed to supply him with firs and cedars for the great Temple, receiving wheat and oil in exchange. An unbroken alliance was cemented. Then, in the 480th year after the Exodus, in the fourth year of his reign, Solomon began to build the Temple. Its magnificence, described in both Kings and Chronicles, has remained legendary and even symbolic; the actual edifice was razed to the ground in A.D. 70, apparently as an example of the "Roman peace".

Built of prefabricated stone, so that no sound was heard of hammer or iron tool, the building was overlaid within with pure gold. "Cherubim, palm-trees, and open flowers" formed a main feature of gold decoration. Tyre was famous for its brass and metal-work, so Hiram again willingly used his skill in fashioning pillars, large ornaments (including "a molten sea, ten cubits, from the one brim to the other"), and sacred utensils. After seven years the Temple was complete; and thither the Ark was brought, and a solemn consecration took place. So great was "the glory of God" in the form of a cloud, that "the priests could not stand to minister". Solomon's address to the people was deep and moving, likewise his humble prayers to the Lord: "When thou hearest, forgive."

Meanwhile he was building a splendid palace for himself. After twenty years, he gave Hiram twenty cities in Galilee, though these did not please the recipient. Immense levies, largely of the subject peoples, were raised to construct cities in the outlying parts of his domain, including "cities for his chariots, cities for his horsemen". In Ezion-geber, on the shore of the Red Sea, he prepared a fleet with Hiram's help; then once in three years came his ships from Tarshish with gold, ivory, apes and peacocks. Gold was everywhere; he drank only from gold vessels, while he "made silver to be in Jerusalem as stones".

Such luxury, and more, excited the feminine and regal curiosity of the Queen of Sheba in Arabia. Loaded with precious gifts, she arrived in Jerusalem to see whether Solomon's wisdom and splendour had not been exaggerated—but no, "the half was not told me". In mutual admiration the two rulers exchanged presents (the gorgeous spices of Sheba are mentioned), and legend has added a not improbable romance—considering Solomon's liking for women— which, however, is not referred to in the Bible.

Indeed Solomon "loved many strange women"; in flat defiance of the Lord's racial and religious intolerance he chose from the surrounding pagan peoples "700 wives, princesses, and 300 concubines; and his wives turned away his heart". Gradually he began to worship his wives' gods, building "high places" for them, and practising "abominations". His father's sensuality had in Solomon blossomed into full-blooded serene enjoyment. The fury of God descended on his triple unfaithfulness: religious, racial and sexual.

For David's sake Solomon would be enabled to keep his kingdom, but after his death vengeance was promised in the shape of civil and external war. Already in Solomon's lifetime, the Lord stirred up the Edomite Hadad, ruler of Syria, whose people had been slaughtered by David, and then Solomon's own protégé Jeroboam, who planned to usurp the throne: had not the prophet Ahijah promised him the ten tribes (other than Judah and Benjamin) from the Lord? Solomon pursued Jeroboam, who fled into Egypt. After a reign of forty years, Solomon died, and war followed, with the separation of Judah and Israel, and foreign conflicts.

To Solomon were attributed certain Biblical writings—

"Proverbs", "Song of Solomon", and "Ecclesiastes". Authenticity is doubtful, as it was a habit in Biblical times to attribute works to famous names (not all the so-called "Psalms of David" are by David). Yet some connexion may well have existed.

The book of "Proverbs" has been divided by scholars into four unequal sections: (1) chapters 1-9; (2) chapters 10-22, verse 16; here are 375 proverbs, many of Solomon's own authorship. This is the oldest part of the book, and it is significant and typical of the period that the name "Solomon" has in Hebrew the numerical value of 375; (3) chapter 22, verses 17-24; these "Words of the Wise" are not by Solomon; (4) chapters 25-29.

Though to some extent these sayings are repetitive, it is difficult, in the present space, to give a full impression of their variety. Worldly wisdom, spiritual maturity, crude pseudo-realism (e.g. "Spare the rod, and spoil the child", a recurrent motive), even poetic imagery—all are in evidence. The following examples may hint at their texture and admirable epigrammatic qualities:

"Hatred stirreth up strife: but love covereth all sins."
"There is a friend that sticketh closer than a brother."
"The beginning of strife is as when one letteth out water: therefore leave off contention, before it be meddled with."
"Pride goeth before destruction, and a haughty spirit before a fall."
"Reprove not a scorner, lest he hate thee: rebuke a wise man, and he will love thee."
"In the multitude of counsellors there is safety."
"Better is a neighbour that is near than a brother far off."
"He that oppresseth the poor reproacheth his Maker: but he that honoureth him hath mercy on the poor."
"He that hath no rule over his own spirit is like a city that is broken down, and without walls."
"Where no wood is, there the fire goeth out: so where there is no talebearer, the strife ceaseth."
"Where there is no vision, the people perish: but he that keepeth the law, happy is he."

"Proverbs" is full of contradictions, and a greater contrast still is found between that book and the next work attributed to Solomon, "The Song of Solomon" (or "Song of Songs"). Nothing less than a passionate love poem, exquisite in imagery, confronts us here. Unique in the whole Bible, it is interpreted by Jewish commentators as the union of Israel and the Sabbath, or Israel and the Torah (the "Law"), and by Christians as the union between Christ and His Church. Yet the poetry, to many modern readers, speaks for itself.

Both feminine and masculine beauty speak and hymn each other:

"Behold, thou art fair, my love . . . thou hast doves' eyes within thy locks: thy hair is as a flock of goats, that appear from mount Gilead. Thy teeth are like a flock of sheep that are even shorn. Thy two breasts are like two young roes that are twins, which feed among the lilies."

Thus is pictured the maiden who calls herself "the rose of Sharon, and the lily of the valleys". Alternately ecstatic and despairing, she seeks her beloved through the night-streets; she calls on the "daughters of Jerusalem" to tell him "that I am sick of love. . . . My beloved is white and ruddy, the chiefest among ten thousand. . . . His eyes are as the eyes of doves by the rivers of waters, washed with milk. . . . His cheeks are as a bed of spices, as sweet flowers: his lips like lilies, dropping sweet smelling myrrh. . . . His legs are as pillars of marble, set upon sockets of fine gold." And she in turn has "thighs like jewels" . . . "thy navel is like a round goblet: which wanteth not liquor. . . . Make haste, my beloved, and be thou like to a roe or to a young hart upon the mountains of spices." This is a truly lyrical portrait of the Sabbath, the Torah and the Church.

The third work attributed to Solomon, "Ecclesiastes", is nearer in spirit to "Proverbs", but more solemn and continuous. Who has not heard some of these phrases?

"Vanity of vanity . . . all is vanity. What profit hath a man of all his labour which he taketh under the sun? One generation passeth away, and another generation cometh: but the earth abideth for ever. . . ."
"All the rivers run into the sea; yet the sea is not full."
"To every thing there is a season, and a time to every purpose under the heaven: a time to be born, and a time to die . . . a time to weep, and a time to laugh; a time to mourn, and a time to dance. . . ."
"Cast thy bread upon the waters: for thou shalt find it after many days."

As to "The Wisdom of Solomon" in the Apocrypha, impressive though it is, "Wisdom" at times becoming personified, it is a Hellenistic work, centuries later than its alleged author; and it blends Hebraic and Hellenic qualities in several moods—lyrical, historical and mystical. Also attributed to the great monarch are the later "Psalms of Solomon", a mediocre work, and the resplendent "Odes of Solomon", an early and poetic Christian composition. None the less, the very association across the ages of Solomon's name with "wisdom" cannot have been without foundation.

The name of Solomon inspired countless legends in later, particularly medieval, Jewish literature, not to mention the reverence felt for him in Islam: the Koran, for instance, states how God gave him understanding of the speech of the winds and the birds. Despite certain exaggerations, the account of Solomon's splendour and wisdom must have some basis. We can admire in him also his balance and generosity, and his freedom from racial and religious intolerance, even though he did not reach the spiritual heights of another emperor of antiquity, the Buddhist Asoka.

The theme of Solomon has continuously inspired the arts. In music, for instance, there is Handel's genially regal oratorio, "Solomon", and a work for 'cello and orchestra, "Schelomo" (the Hebrew name for Solomon), by the Jewish composer, Ernest Bloch.

ASHURBANIPAL

(Reigned 668-626 B.C.)

AMONG THE nations of the ancient world the Assyrians have a
shocking reputation. For hundreds of years from their homeland
somewhere in the north of Mesopotamia they dominated the Middle
East, and they extended their conquests to Armenia in the north and
to Egypt in the south. Throughout, their record is one of almost
constant war, of battles and sieges, of cities burnt and sacked and
whole peoples carried away into captivity. Page after page in the
historical books of the Old Testament bear witness to their ferocious
ways of making war, while the Hebrew Prophets pointed to the
Assyrian monarchs as the most terrible workers of woe on those
whom the Lord found it necessary to punish. In a famous line Byron
wrote of the Assyrian who "came down like a wolf on the fold",
and that is what he seems to have been doing most of the time.

But the bitterest critic of the Assyrians must allow that from time
to time they produced kings of outstanding character, who were not
only great generals but displayed very considerable gifts of statesmanship and an active interest in the arts of peace. Of these the most
worthy to be remembered after the passage of more than two
thousand five hundred years is Ashurbanipal, who reigned as king
in his capital city of Nineveh from 668 to 626 B.C. And this for
several reasons.

In the first place, he was a great conqueror, although not so great
and successful as some others of his line. Secondly, he commissioned
sculptors to produce pictures in stone of his achievements on the
field of battle and in the chase, and in the British Museum we may
see whole series of these gigantic productions, that are among the
most splendid survivals of the art of the ancient world. Still this is
not all. Strange as it must appear, this vainglorious conqueror, this
furious hunter of men and of big game, was also a patron of science,
a lover of learning, and (so it would seem) more than a bit of a
bookworm!

That is indeed a strange thing to be able to say of one of the
Assyrian sovereigns, and we may suspect that Ashurbanipal would
have thought it hardly worth mentioning compared with what there

is to say about his career in arms. Of this there is abundance: Ashurbanipal saw to that; and pretty terrible most of it is, full of vulgar boastings, gloatings over defeated enemies, and the ferociously cruel treatment that he handed out to them. Take, for instance, the series of sculptures relating his warfare with Teumann, king of Elam, a country to the south-east of Assyria in what is now Persia, or Iran. Accompanying each picture is an explanatory text inscribed on the hard stone in the cuneiform or wedge-shaped characters of the Assyrian people.

In the month of Ab (the narrative begins), which was our July, during the festival of the "Great Queen", by whom is meant the goddess Ishtar, "I was staying in Arbela, the city that is the delight of her heart, to be present at her high worship. There they brought to me news of the invasion by the Elamite, who was coming against the wish of the gods". Teumann (the report goes on) had made a solemn vow that "he would not put out another drink-offering to the gods until he should have gone and fought with Ashurbanipal and overcome him".

Continuing with his story, Ashurbanipal says that "Concerning this threat which Teumann had spoken, I prayed to the great Ishtar. I approached to her presence, I bowed myself down at her feet, I besought her divinity to save me. Thus I spoke: 'O goddess of Arbela, I am Ashurbanipal, king of Asshur, the creature of thy hands. I have sought to do thee honour, and I have gone far to worship thee, O thou Queen of Queens, Goddess of War, Lady of Battles, Queen of the Gods. . . . Behold now, Teumann, king of Elam, who has sinned against the gods, while I, Ashurbanipal, have been doing everything in my power to please them and make their hearts rejoice—he has collected his soldiers, amassed his army, and has drawn his sword with a view to invading Assyria. So now, O thou Archer of the Gods, come like a bolt from heaven and crush him in the midst of the battle!' And Ishtar heard my prayer. 'Fear not,' she replied, and she caused my heart to rejoice. 'At the lifting up of thy hands, thine eyes shall be satisfied with the judgment, I will show thee favour. . . . Thy heart's desire shall be accomplished. Thy face shall not grow pale with fear. Thy feet shall not be arrested in their march; thou shalt not even scratch thy skin in the battle. Ishtar in her benevolence—she defends thee, and before her is blown a fire which will destroy thy enemies'."

Ishtar was as good as her word, Ashurbanipal hastens to inform posterity; and in the magnificent collection of sculptures in the British Museum we have a pictorial record of the ensuing battle.

On these great slabs, the engraver's chisel has preserved each episode in realistic detail, and above each is inscribed a few lines of commentary or explanation. "Urtarku, the son-in-law of Teumann, was wounded by an arrow, but not killed. He commanded an Assyrian soldier to kill him, saying, 'Come, cut off my head and carry it into the presence of the king thy lord, in order that he may take it for a good omen and show thee mercy' "—from which it would appear that he himself had small hopes of mercy if he should fall alive into Ashurbanipal's power. Then close by we see Teumann wounded by an arrow and kneeling on the ground, while his son Tamritu tries to keep off the attackers with his bow. In the next scene, father and son have fled and taken refuge in a wood. But not for long. "With the help of Ashur"—the great god of the Assyrians —"and of Ishtar, I, Ashurbanipal, seized them, and I cut off their heads in the presence of each other." This is followed by a scene of Teumann's head "being carried quickly to Assyria as glad tidings of my victory", and in yet another slab we have the end of the story. In the garden of his palace at Nineveh the great king is shown reclining at his ease, with his queen seated before him, quaffing a cup of wine; and there on the left, behind an array of musicians and with a girl playing a harp just below, hangs from one of the trees in the garden the gory trophy of Teumann's head.

Another set of sculptures illustrates a revolt against Ashurbanipal that was instigated and led by his brother, Shamash-shum-ukin, whom he had installed as viceroy of Babylon. The prince was defeated and was burnt to death when his palace was stormed by the king's troops and set on fire. "I am Ashurbanipal, king of hosts, king of Assyria," reads the inscription, "who achieved his heart's desire by the command of the great gods. The clothing, the treasure, the royal insignia that had belonged to Shamash-shum-ukin, the brother who was a traitor, his concubines, his officers, his soldiers, his chariot and carriage of state, his pair of horses, everything of his that was desirable, men and women, both great and small—all were brought before me. . . ."

Following upon this revolt, Ashurbanipal turned his arms against Elam, which had supported his brother, and made it an object-lesson of Assyrian "frightfulness". He vaunts of the way in which he "tore off the lips which had spoken defiance, cut off the hands of those who had held the bow to fight against Assyria", and winds up his narrative with the frightful statement, "The wells of drinking water I dried up. For a journey of a month and twenty-five days the districts of Elam I laid waste; destruction, servitude, and drought I poured upon them. I burnt the trees off the fields. Wild asses, serpents, beasts of the field I caused to lie down in them in safety. . . ."

A horrible picture, and yet Ashurbanipal the big-game hunter is a not much less repulsive figure than Ashurbanipal the conqueror. The king seems to have been a patron of almost every variety of the sport. He hunted wild asses and deer, stalked them across the plains and in the foothills, netted them and lassoed them, captured them in traps and had them driven before him in a battue. But the game which he particularly affected was the king of beasts, the royal lion, and he delighted to have himself represented riding in his chariot and discharging his bow at the pursuing beasts or, more dangerously, on horseback and wielding his spear. Sometimes he even followed the chase on foot, and in one of the scenes we see him pouring out a libation over four dead lions, of which the inscription reads: "I am Ashurbanipal, king of kings, king of Assyria. In my abounding might and princely strength I seized a lion of the desert by his tail, and at the command of the gods Enurta and Nergal, who are my helpers, I smashed in his skull with the axe I held in my hands." In another relief the hunt servants are shown laying out the "bag" at the end of the day's sport, and eleven dead lions are represented and seven more that are terribly wounded. Hounds were used in the sport, and powerful brutes they were, of a mastiff-like breed; Ashurbanipal must have thought appreciatively of them, for several statuettes of dogs have been found, modelled in terra-cotta, and each bearing on its back or collar its name—"Tear-the-foe", for instance.

In the representation of these hunting scenes the Assyrian artists reached the highest level of excellence, and there is nothing in ancient art to compare with them. Two in particular have been highly praised, though the animal-lover must have other feelings—that of a lion, mortally wounded by an arrow that still sticks in his body, coughing out his life-blood on the sand, and that other, no less pathetic, of a lioness, wounded unto death, with broken back and paralysed hindquarters, rising on her front paws to hurl a last roar of defiance at her pursuers.

What a relief it is to turn from these scenes of blood and savagery to what has invested Ashurbanipal's name with the most honourable distinction! We may watch the great king now, when perhaps he has returned from an exciting day in the hunting-field—he has bathed and put on a clean robe, he has dined and perhaps called on his favourite queen in her apartments, and now he has repaired to that quarter of his palace where he keeps his books. A lamp is burning on the table, the wine-jar is conveniently placed, a cushioned

seat awaits him. And going to one of the shelves that line the apartment he takes down a book—not such a book as we know, but a
clay tablet, closely covered with the marks of the cuneiform script.
He opens it—no, that is not the right word: how can you open a
brick?—takes it to the light, seats himself, and begins to read. . . .

For the discovery of Ashurbanipal's library at Nineveh we have
to thank the celebrated English archaeologist Austen Layard. He
came upon it by a most fortunate accident. In 1850 he was excavating
in the great mound or dust-heap at Kuyunjik, not far from Mosul,
in present-day Iraq. He had already retrieved some of the splendid
sculptures which we may see in the Assyrian galleries in the British
Museum, and had proved beyond a doubt that the site was that of
the ancient metropolis of Nineveh. But he kept on digging, and one
day he penetrated into two small rooms in what must have been
the palace of the Assyrian kings. They seemed to be empty, but he
noticed that the floor was covered to a depth of a foot or more with
what some years earlier he would have thrust aside in disdain as
"strange pottery", but since then had come to realize were inscribed
tablets of baked clay. They were of different sizes; the largest were
flat and measured about nine inches by six and a half inches, while
the smaller were slightly convex and not more than an inch or so in
length. They were all covered with cuneiform writing, although
on some it was so tiny that Layard had to use a magnifying-glass
to see it. He gave orders that the tablets were to be collected and
sent off to the British Museum, and in the course of the next few
years many more tablets were unearthed by Layard's assistant
Hormuzd Rassam, who was in charge of the diggings at Kuyunjik
after Layard had gone back to England. Altogether some twenty-
five thousand tablets reached the British Museum, but it was not for
some years that the work of translating them was put in hand. Then
that remarkable, largely self-taught scholar George Smith revealed
to an astonished world that what Layard had discovered by a lucky
fluke was nothing less than the royal library of King Ashurbanipal!

There was no doubt about it, for most of the tablets that had been
recovered from the rooms at Nineveh bore the inscription, "Property
of Ashurbanipal, king of hosts, king of Assyria," and many had in
addition a colophon or tailpiece in some such words as these:
"Palace of Ashurbanipal, king of the universe, king of Assyria,
who puts his trust in the gods Ashur and Belit, to whom Nabu
(the god of Wisdom) has given an open ear (clear understanding),
who has acquired a bright eye, with the exquisite skill of the tablet-
writer, which none of the kings my forefathers have learned—the

wisdom of Nabu so far as is written therein with the stroke of the stilus, this have I written on tablets that I may read it and learn it, and have laid it up in my palace. Whoever shall take them away or deface them, or write his name in the place of my name, may the gods curse him and root out his seed from the earth."

The "books" cover a great variety of subjects. A letter of Ashurbanipal's to the mayor of the city of Sippar has been preserved, ordering him to take with him certain named officials and seek out all the tablets that were in private houses or stored in the local temple, in particular those bearing astronomical data, magical formulas, incantations and prayers, battle stories, etc., and send them all to the king at Nineveh. Warrants were dispatched to government officials throughout the empire to the same purpose: they were to be most diligent and not overlook anything. Most of the material is of interest only to the chronicler, but among the books are the great masterpieces of Babylonian and Assyrian literature, including the Epic of Gilgamesh and the story of the Creation by Tiamat the female dragon and Marduk the hero-god.

Only fourteen years after Ashurbanipal's death, Nineveh was sacked and destroyed, and the great king's library was buried in the ruins. For two thousand years and more it lay forgotten, but then it was found and restored to the knowledge of men. And how astonished would the great king be if he were to learn that his fame as a book-collector has far eclipsed all that he won with his sword!

CYRUS THE GREAT

(d. 529 B.C.)

IN ALL the Bible's many hundred pages it would be hard to find a more dramatic episode than that of the mysterious writing on the wall that presaged the imminent fall of Babylon. We may read the story in one of the earlier chapters of the book of Daniel, told with an economy of words but in such vivid phraseology that we should have no difficulty in visualizing the scene.

In the banqueting-hall of his palace Belshazzar the king is making a great feast to a thousand of his lords, and a messenger has been sent to fetch "the golden vessels that were taken out of the temple of the house of God which was in Jerusalem", in order that the king and his princes, his wives and his concubines, may drink therein. And as they are drinking their wine, and praising the gods of gold and of silver, of brass and of iron and the rest—suddenly there come forth fingers of a man's hand, writing on the wall over against the candlestick. Then the king's countenance is changed, his thoughts trouble him, and his knees smite one against the other, and he cries aloud to bring in someone who may translate what is being written. And Daniel is fetched, and the words he speaks are words of doom. . . .

"In that night was Belshazzar the king of the Chaldeans slain. And Darius the Median took the kingdom." Here the chronicler is at fault: Belshazzar was not the king, and he does not appear to have been slain, and it was not Darius who took his kingdom but Cyrus the Persian, for whom the taking of Babylon was the crowning achievement of his career of stupendous conquests.

Who Cyrus was, what was his descent and origin and place in the world before the floodlights of History caught up with him— these are questions that are likely to remain without satisfactory answer. At least four different accounts were given of his early years by writers of antiquity, and it has not proved possible to reconcile them. The most picturesquely detailed is that given by the Greek historian Herodotus, who visited Persia about seventy years after Cyrus's time. According to him, Cyrus was the son of a Persian nobleman named Cambyses and Princess Mandane, only

65

child of King Astyages of Media, the country that lay between Persia (which was then a small territory bordering the Persian Gulf) and the Caspian Sea. Astyages had heard a rumour that his daughter's child would supplant him on the throne, and so he gave orders that the child should be killed. The savage order was not carried out, however; the boy was saved by a trick, and when he became a man he headed a revolt against his grandfather and dispossessed him and became king in his stead.

A pretty story, but probably too pretty to be true. The more sober historians of a later day have discounted practically the whole of it, with the exception that they are willing to allow that Cyrus may have been connected in some way with King Astyages. According to them, Cyrus belonged to the royal house of Anshan, a small kingdom bordering on Mesopotamia with Susa as its capital, and he succeeded his father as king of Anshan about 558 B.C. Then from a clay tablet preserved in the British Museum we learn that war broke out between Anshan and Media, and Astyages king of Media "collected his troops, and marched against Cyrus king of Anshan. His troops revolted against him, and he was seized and delivered up to Cyrus. Cyrus marched to Ecbatana, the royal city of Media. The silver, gold, goods, and substance of Ecbatana he spoiled, and to the land of Anshan he took away the goods and substance that were gotten."

In some such fashion as this, Cyrus became king of the Medes as well as of the Persians; Susa was the capital of the joint realm but Ecbatana shared its glory, and it is clear that the Medes were not at all loth to exchange Astyages for a sovereign who had already given abundant proof that he was a born leader of men. As for Astyages, Cyrus took him as a prisoner to Anshan, but (so Herodotus asserts) spared his life.

After a year or two as king of "Persia and Media and the other lands" Cyrus was moved to undertake further conquests. He invaded northern Mesopotamia, and then in 547 B.C. found his further advance checked by Lydia, the greatest power in the Western Asia of that day, and also the richest, as may be gathered from the fact that the name of its king has become proverbial for wealth.

On the face of it, King Croesus had all he could wish for. Immense treasures, a large and well-trained army, a realm which embraced the whole of Asia Minor, including the string of Greek cities along its Ionian shores. Yet he was nervous. Only the river Halys separated his dominion from that of Cyrus, and from all that he heard Cyrus was intensely ambitious and determined on a career of aggrandizement. For many years there had been good relations between Lydia and Media, and these had been cemented by family alliances, but Croesus was not at all sure that these good relations could be maintained with the new ruler of Media.

In the circumstances he thought it advisable to secure alliances with Egypt, Babylonia, and the Spartan Greeks, and he also dispatched emissaries to consult the oracles at Delphi and elsewhere, as to whether if he were to go to war with Cyrus he would be victorious? The answers returned by the oracles were ambiguous, but Croesus did not think them so. "If Croesus were to make war on the Persians," they ran, "he would destroy a mighty empire." Croesus at once jumped to the conclusion that the empire to be destroyed was that of Cyrus. But he was not quite convinced, and to make doubly sure he sent to Delphi again, putting to the oracle the question, "Shall I long enjoy my kingdom?" This time the answer was a strange one indeed. "When a mule shall become king of the Medes," it ran, "then do not waste a moment, nor blush to seem a coward, but *flee*." When his servants returned to their master with that answer it was in considerable trepidation, but Croesus was not in the least put out; on the contrary, he thought its gross improbability was a most favourable sign.

In the spring of 548 B.C. he set his armies in motion and crossed the Halys into Media, where he won an easy success against the town of Pteria, which he took and destroyed, enslaving its population. Cyrus came hurrying up but could not arrive in time to save the town, and the resulting engagement was indecisive. Then as it was getting late in the year Croesus decided to return home and go into winter quarters, thinking that Cyrus would of course do the same. But Cyrus declined to be so accommodating. He followed up Croesus's retiring forces and caught up with them outside Sardis, the Lydian capital, and inflicted on them a severe defeat. If Herodotus is to be believed, his victory was largely owing to his clever stratagem of mounting a number of his men on camels from the baggage-train and employing them as cavalry. Now, Herodotus explains, "a horse is afraid of a camel, and cannot endure either to see its form or to scent its smell". When the battle was joined, the Lydian horses no sooner sensed the camels coming towards them than they pranced and wheeled round, and in a few moments all Croesus's hopes of victory were dissipated. The Lydians hurried back to Sardis, hoping to find a safe refuge behind its walls, but Cyrus closely followed and took the place by storm.

Still following Herodotus's account, Croesus was captured and condemned to be burnt alive, but when the flames were already taking hold of the funeral pyre Cyrus was smitten with pity and ordered that he should be rescued, and he henceforth treated him with a kindly consideration. Of course the fallen monarch inquired into the prophecies that had pointed the way to his ruin. He understood clearly enough that he had misinterpreted the one about an empire that should be destroyed, but was still puzzled to understand how a mule could ever become king of Persia. The oracle was consulted again, and now it was explained that Cyrus was the mule intended, since he had been born of parents of different nations— his father a Persian and his mother a Mede. . . .

With the overthrow of the kingdom of Lydia, the dominion of Cyrus was extended over nearly the whole of Asia Minor, and soon the Greek colonies on the Ionian coasts and the adjacent islands were incorporated. In a matter of three or four years this prince of an insignificant little state had defeated two great empires and made himself master of an immense territory stretching from the Persian Gulf to the Dardanelles and Black Sea.

Still he was not satisfied. He recalled that while Babylon, no more than Egypt or Sparta, had actually assisted Croesus in his war against him, she had entered into an alliance with that end in view. They all three deserved to be taught a lesson, but Babylon was the nearest and therefore the first to be made to feel his resentment. For some years he bided his time, and no doubt completed his preparations. By 540 B.C. he was ready, and with characteristic vigour crossed the frontier and at the head of a large army marched down the Tigris and then cross country to Babylon.

Babylonia was still a great power, although not so great as she had been some twenty years earlier. In 556 B.C. Nabonidus had come to the throne of Babylonia, and he was not at all the sort of man to weather such a storm as now threatened his country. He has been described as an "amiable archaeologist", a man who delighted in digging up the foundations of ancient temples to read the inscriptions he might find there, and then adding to them a few lines of his own. He was also a keen student of comparative religion, and had formed the idea of centralizing the Babylonian religion, collecting the images of all the gods and goddesses and displaying them all together in one place in the capital. The priests were not at all taken with this idea, and (if they were to be believed) the gods and goddesses did not like it either. Thus when Cyrus drew near to the city there was something in the nature of a fifth-column at work in the place, in which, there is reason to believe, the Jews, whose fathers had been deported from Jerusalem to Babylon by Nebuchadnezzar, took a leading part.

Herodotus has some typically colourful paragraphs about what happened next. According to him the city held out quite a time, and Cyrus was greatly wrath at the delay. At length he thought out a plan. He diverted the stream of the Euphrates from where it entered the city, and then had men waiting in readiness to enter as soon as the sewer-gates were disclosed. When this happened, they rushed in, and took the Babylonians completely by surprise. Long after the outer works had been stormed, the people in the central part were still engaged in dancing and revelling, since the night was the occasion of one of their great annual feasts. It will be seen that this account is not inconsistent with the Bible narrative, although (as mentioned earlier) it was not Darius who was the attacker but Cyrus, and the king's name was Nabonidus and not Belshazzar— although Belshazzar may have been the crown prince.

Decidedly different is the account that is found on an inscribed cylinder of baked clay that is in the British Museum. The most important part of this reads: "Marduk (the chief god of Babylon) sought out a righteous prince, a man after his own heart, whom he might take in hand. . . . He beheld his good deeds with joy. He commanded him to go to Babylon, and he caused him to set out on the road to that city, and like a friend and ally he marched by his side; and his troops, with their weapons girt about them, marched with him, in countless numbers like the waters of a flood. Without battle and without fighting Marduk enabled him to enter into his city of Babylon; thus he spared Babylon tribulation, and Nabonidus, the king who feared him not, he delivered into his hand. All the people of Babylon, princes and governors, bowed down, they kissed his feet, they rejoiced in his triumph, and their countenances were bright with joy."

After the occupation of the city by his troops, Cyrus pleased his friends and went a long way towards conciliating those still opposed to him, by adopting a policy of the most complete religious toleration. He ordered that the images of the gods and goddesses should be restored to their old homes, and allowed the Jews (as we are told in the first chapter of the book of Ezra) to rebuild their Temple in Jerusalem that Nebuchadnezzar had destroyed, and he returned to them the valuable furniture and fittings that had been brought back to Babylon as spoils of war.

So ended the empire of Babylon, which had endured for fifteen hundred years. The city became one of the capitals of Cyrus's now vast empire, and there he now received tribute from "all the kings dwelling in palaces of all the quarters of the earth, from the Upper to the Lower Sea (i.e. from the Mediterranean to the Persian Gulf), and all the kings of the West Land (Arabia) who dwell in tents".

As king of Babylon Cyrus was overlord of Phoenicia and Syria down to the borders of Egypt, and Egypt was next on the list of his intended conquests. But for the present he had enough to do in organizing his huge empire. Tolerant and comparatively humane, clear-sighted and vigorous, he showed to as marked advantage as an administrator as he had done in military campaigning, and on his foundations of good government his successors were able to build for generations to come. And yet he died fighting, in a war on his eastern frontier against (according to the most generally accepted report) a tribe of savages known as the Massagetae. This was in 529 B.C., when he had reigned nearly thirty years.

Almost exactly two hundred years later another and even more famous world-conqueror visited Cyrus's tomb at Pasargadae, in the region that had been the homeland of his family. After he had read the epitaph (so Plutarch tells us), Alexander the Great ordered it to be re-cut in Greek characters. It was as follows: "O man! Whosoever thou art and whensoever thou comest (for come I know thou wilt), I am Cyrus, the Founder of the Persian Empire. Envy me not the little earth that covers my remains." The young conqueror read it, and then turned away, deeply moved.

DARIUS I

(Reigned 521–486 B.C.)

On a rock face at Behistun, high above the caravan route that in ancient times led from Ecbatana (the modern Hamadan), where the Persian kings had their Summer Palace, down south-westwards into Babylonia, is carved a great picture in stone. For more than two thousand years it has aroused the admiration and the curiosty of passing travellers. It was so old that its origins had been lost in the mists of time. Diodorus, a contemporary of Julius Caesar, told a wonderful tale that Semiramis, Queen of Babylon, had ordered it to be carved, and that in order to reach it the sculptors had climbed the face of the mountain on a heap of pack saddles taken from her baggage train.

Others who visited Persia in later times advanced even more fanciful explanations. One towards the end of the eighteenth century was quite positive that it shows Jesus Christ and the Twelve Disciples, and in 1827 the Englishman Ker Porter was of the opinion that the figures represent the Assyrian king Shalmaneser and the Tribes of Israel whom he carried into captivity. The Persian women from the neighbouring sordid little village had their own theory. According to them it was the tombstone of a saintly man of ever so long ago, and they used to hang little strips of rag on the bushes below as some kind of offering to his spirit.

All these imaginative excursions were dispelled, however, when in 1835 a young English army officer named Henry Rawlinson succeeded in climbing up to the site and deciphering the inscriptions which surround the picture. It took him years of study, but eventually he was able to show that the sculptures represent the "Great King" Darius I of Persia, triumphing over a rival and his confederates. We know that this actually happened, since Darius himself tells us so.

To understand the happening, we must go back a few years in Persian history. When Cyrus the Great (his story is given in the previous chapter), the founder of the Persian Empire, was killed fighting the barbarian tribes in a border skirmish in 529 B.C., he was succeeded on the throne by his son Cambyses. Not content with

71

the great realm that he had inherited from his father, the young king embarked on the conquest of Egypt. He won a surprisingly easy victory, but when he sent his armies to invade Ethiopia they suffered severe reverses, and Cambyses (so the story runs, as told by the ancient historian Herodotus—but Herodotus was a Greek, and not at all favourably disposed towards the Persians) went mad with the shock.

Then came news of a revolt back home in Persia, headed by a man who asserted that he was the king's brother Smerdis. Cambyses knew full well that this was rubbish, since he had himself given orders for his brother to be killed, and the orders had been carried out, but with the minimum of publicity. Cambyses forthwith started for the north with a portion of his army and some leading nobles, among whom was one Darius, whose father was Hystaspes, sub-king of a distant province, and who seems to have been a relative, perhaps a cousin, but certainly belonged to the royal family of the Achaemenids. On the way, somewhere in Syria, Cambyses suddenly died. The army went on, taking his body with them, and when they had returned at length to Persia they found that the pretender was in full possession of the power and glory, the treasures and the harem, of the previous monarch.

For the time being, Darius and the rest kept their own counsel and acquiesced in the new regime. Then suspicions began to be aroused among the other courtiers. The king never quitted his palace, not even to go hunting. He never gave audience to a Persian dignitary. Could it be that he was afraid of being recognized as being some other person than the real Prince Smerdis? Before long the doubts became certainty, and Darius became the centre of a small band of conspirators who were resolved to unmask the pretender and do him to death. Then came the day when Darius and six other young nobles, Persians all, made their way to where the "king" was staying, managed to obtain entrance to the palace, cut down the guards who showed resistance, and at last reached the royal sanctum and slew the pretender.

Herodotus has some particularly lively pages describing these happenings, and some of his stories are almost too good to be true. What shall we say, then, of his account of what happened next? The throne was vacant, Cambyses had left no children, and there was no heir apparent. Darius and his six associates argued the matter over and over, and at length it was agreed that one of them should offer himself as the new monarch. But which? Why, he whose horse should be the first to neigh next morning after sunrise. . . .

Now Darius had a very clever groom, and he told the man what had been decided and asked him if he could think of any way by which *his* horse should have the deciding voice. . . . The man told him not to worry: he would fix it. And this is how he did it—according to Herodotus . . . Darius's steed had a favourite mare, and after dark the groom took this mare and tied her up to a post somewhere in the suburbs. Then he brought Darius's horse to the place and walked him round and round before at last allowing them to meet. Then back to the stable. . . . Next morning the friends rode out together as they had agreed, and the wily groom saw to it that they should go very near to where the mare had been tethered the night before. Of course Darius's mount remembered—and neighed. Just at that moment, as though to clinch the election, there was a great flash of lightning, followed by a loud clap of thunder. This was taken as an indication of heavenly approval, and Darius's companions jumped down from their horses and bowed themselves in homage before the man whom they hailed as their new sovereign.

"Thus was Darius son of Hystaspes appointed king." Well, perhaps . . . But there is no doubt of the fact that he *was* appointed king, and the main outlines of the story receive striking confirmation from no less a person than Darius himself, as told in the sculptures and inscriptions on the Rock of Behistun mentioned above. We now know that the picture represents "the Great King, the King of Kings, the King of Persia, the King of the Provinces, whose name is Darius", receiving the submission of ten rebel kings or princes. Nine of the rebels are bound together by a rope passed round their necks, and their hands are tied behind their backs. The tenth is even more abjectly submissive: he is stretched on the ground before Darius, whose left foot is placed on his neck. Then in the panels surrounding the sculpture we are given the story of the revolt, told in three forms of the cuneiform, or wedge-shaped, scripts of Old Persian, Susian or Elamite, and Babylonian. Beyond the fact that the names are given differently—thus the true Smerdis is called Bardiya and the "false" Smerdis, Gaumata—the account is very much the same as what Herodotus tells us.

"When Cambyses slew Bardiya, it was not known to the people that Bardiya was slain. Afterwards Cambyses went to Egypt, and when Cambyses had departed, the people became hostile. Afterwards there was a certain man, Gaumata by name . . . he lied to the people, saying, 'I am Bardiya, the son of Cyrus and brother of Cambyses.' Then all the people rose in revolt, and from Cambyses they went over to him, both Persia and Media, and the other provinces. He seized on the kingdom. . . . There was no man, Persian or Median or of our own family, who could deprive Gaumata of the kingdom. The people feared him for his tyranny, but no one dared to say anything against Gaumata, until I came." Then, the inscription goes on, "I, with a few men, slew Gaumata. . . . I smote Gaumata. I took his kingdom from him. By the grace of Ahuramazda (the Good God of the Persian religion) I became king. Ahuramazda gave me the kingdom. The kingdom which had been taken away from my family, this I restored to its proper place."

Finally, in conclusion the king added a solemn warning to those who might come after. "Saith Darius the King: Thou who shalt read this inscription in days to come, thou who seest I have caused it to be engraved together with these figures of men—take heed that ye destroy it not nor deface it, see that thou keepest it whole. If otherwise, then may Ahuramazda slay thee, and bring thy race to naught."

For some years after his accession Darius had his hands full with revolts and dissensions of one kind or another, but as soon as he was able he devoted all his energies to the consolidation and good government of the vast empire that had fallen to his sway. His realm was indeed vast; in fact, nothing to equal it had been seen in history before, and there have been few empires to surpass it since. With its heartland in Persia, on the eastern side of the Persian Gulf, it reached to Macedonia in Europe on the one hand, and to the Indus valley in north-western India on the other. Included in the many millions of its population were peoples of very different standards of culture and civilization, ranging from Greeks in the Ionian colonies in Asia Minor to the barbarian Scythians who roamed the great plains in what is now southern Russia. Scores of different languages were spoken within its bounds, all the gods of all the religions had their worshippers in its great cities and innumerable towns and villages and the encampments of the nomad tribes. And this at a time when communications could be effected only by men on foot or on horseback.

Clearly, some form of decentralized government was imperative, and this is what Darius established. The task before him was tremendous; neither Cyrus nor Cambyses had had the time, or perhaps the capacity, to organize a system of government which would work, but Darius succeeded where they had fallen short. With the exception of Persia proper, which was considered to be deserving of special treatment as the home of the ruling race, the empire was divided into a number of provinces, or satrapies, to use the Persian term. Over the most important of these the governor or satrap was drawn from one of the great families connected with the Achaemenid dynasty, but in the case of the rest the satraps were drawn from a very wide field, the men chosen being from among the comparatively poor as well as the wealthy and high born, from the subject races as well as from the Persian stock. The satraps held office at the will of the king, and their tenure might be for life.

But however high-sounding their title, the satraps were not masters in their own house. They were almost entirely concerned with the civil administration, chiefly financial and judicial; the provincial military forces were under a commander, whose responsibility was direct to the central government. There was also in each satrapy a secretary of state, who again had direct relations with the king, and kept him informed of what was going on.

For the most part, the languages, laws, customs, and religious usages of the subject peoples were carefully respected; indeed, the Persian government showed a liberality that was in marked contrast with the attitudes adopted by other empires, contemporary and later. Darius himself, like the Persian ruling class as a whole, was a Zoroastrian in religion, holding the doctrines preached by the Prophet Zoroaster (Zarathustra) centuries before, and which are still held by the small body of religionists known as Parsees. But other religions were completely tolerated, just as the utmost liberty was granted to the Greek thinkers in the cities of Ionia to carry their speculations to the limit.

So far as the common people were concerned, it is certain that their condition was very much better under the Persians than it had been in centuries previously, or has been for most of the centuries that have elapsed since. There is no reason to believe that the rule of the satraps was oppressive. War was abolished over a very large area. The highways on land and sea were cleared of pirates and marauders, and men might move freely and safely from one end of the empire to the other. Greek travellers wandered here and there in search of knowledge or adventure or to spread the culture that was theirs. Trade was facilitated by the introduction of a coinage system that was noteworthy for its purity, and the gold "daric", named after King Darius, became the "sovereign" of the near and middle east. Of course people grumbled at the burden of taxation, but this was certain and regular, and once it had been paid they were left very much to themselves. Probably the obligation of military service was the most unpopular burden, but this affected only a small proportion of the young men, since the imperial standing army was remarkably small.

When his administration had been put on a stable footing Darius turned his attention to more magnificent if less useful projects. At Susa, the winter capital, he caused to be erected a splendid palace, but this was far eclipsed by the summer residence of the Persian kings that was built at Persepolis, "the city of the Persians", as the Greeks named it. Even in ruin this is still wondrously beautiful—ruin which was begun by Alexander the Great's mad act of arson in 330 B.C. What, then, must it have been like when the sculptures were fresh from the chisel, the coloured enamels glowed, the rich stuffs and embroidered hangings formed a fit and proper setting for the display of brave men and lovely women who were assembled at Darius's court!

For many years now the great complex has been in course of excavation, and extraordinary marvels have been restored to the light of day. Among the buildings that have been explored is that which housed the ladies of the court, but outstanding is the series of sculptured friezes—if placed end to end they would constitute a panel five or six feet high and nearly a thousand feet long—that adorn the staircase of the royal palace. Among the figures represented are men bringing tribute to the Great King, and what a magnificently varied crowd they make! Here stalk tall Sardians from Lydia, leading humped cattle and bearing shields and lances; and there are Susians from Bhuzistan, one of whom has a lioness in tow while others are carrying her cubs. These solemn-looking fellows in peaked caps are Scythians from Turkestan, these with the curled beards are Syrians, and those men in tight tunics and full trousers who are leading a camel come from what is now Afghanistan. Thus we have a most vivid picture of some of the peoples who were amongst the Great King's subjects. But even better is this splendid sculpture of Darius himself, seated on his throne, holding in one hand a sceptre and in the other a lotus, symbols of royal dominion.

Something more remains to be added, if we are to form a reasonably complete picture of the magniloquently styled monarch. Unchallengeably superior as he was as an administrator, Darius was a far from successful man of war. When he had been not long on the throne he led an expedition into Scythia, probably with the idea of securing his northern frontiers. He crossed the Dardanelles on a bridge of boats at the head of a great host of (so it is said) some 700,000 men, and reached the Volga. But then he had to turn back, and he got back home with the loss of 80,000 of his troops. Then in 498 B.C. his Greek subjects in Ionia revolted, with the aid of Athens and other Greek cities on the European mainland. The Ionians were crushed, but the Persian army which invaded Greece was defeated by the Athenians and their allies in 490 B.C. at Marathon, one of the really decisive battles of the world. Darius was preparing another and greater expeditionary force to teach the Greeks a lesson when he died, in 486 B.C. He was buried in a tomb cut in the rocks overlooking Persepolis, and still the inscription may be read: "I am Darius the Great King, King of Kings, King of countries inhabited by all kinds of people, King of this great earth, far and wide . . ."

LEONIDAS

(d. 480 B.C.)

ONE OF the most romantic figures in history is the Spartan King
Leonidas. We know little of his qualities as a ruler, for these have
been overshadowed by his abilities as a general, but it is reasonable
to assume that a personality and example which could make men
fight to the end for a lost cause would make them serve faithfully
and well as subjects.

It is in fact the quality of leadership for which we remember
Leonidas of Sparta. We cannot even be sure that he was a good
general, for generals need more than leadership to win their battles.
And Leonidas lost his.

But it is as leader and hero that he has earned a place in every
history of his period ever likely to be written.

That period is the fifth century before Christ, and the setting is
ancient Greece. One of the city-states in that confederation was
Sparta, set in a broad plain on the right bank of the River Eurotas,
twenty miles from the sea. It was a small and warlike state, dominated by a warrior caste of less than thirty thousand men calling
themselves "Spartiates" and controlling both "Helots" who had
been the original Achaean inhabitants and were now slaves, and a
provincial population of "Perioechi" who dealt with mundane
matters of trade and industry.

Leonidas succeeded to the throne of Sparta after the deaths of
his two elder brothers, in about 488 B.C., and married the sister,
Gorgo, of his half-brother Cleomenes. It was a difficult time for
the whole Greek peninsula, for the Persian Emperor Xerxes was bent
on a war of subjection which would make them all, much as the
Spartiates had made of their predecessors, slaves and bringers of
tribute. There had been skirmishes and worse, but six years after
Leonidas had mounted the throne of Sparta the Persian army was
on the move.

Ten years before, the Greeks had thrashed these same Persians
under their emperor Darius at the battle of Marathon. In the
meantime, Darius, harried by rebellious elements all over his empire,
had died, leaving the mounting of a huge attack which would

avenge Marathon to his young son Xerxes. Xerxes lost no time in doing so. His vast empire was divided into twenty "satrapies", and each of these was now called on to provide a contingent. As Herodotus put it: "There was no nation in all Asia which Xerxes did not bring against Greece."

News of Persian plans and Persian moves travelled ahead of Persian army and navy, and the Greek city-states had already called together a Pan-Hellenic Congress to consider the threat. Xerxes had sent messengers to all of them—all but the two he planned to crush forever, Athens and Sparta—demanding a symbolic gift, by return, of earth and water, twin symbols of submission. From Athens and Sparta the gifts would not be acceptable: bloody and total defeat was Xerxes's plan for these two.

And although a few states sent tokens, the great majority resolved to fight at the side of Athens and Sparta. The question was: where to make a stand against an army and navy so vast? There were thousand upon thousand of Persians crossing the Hellespont over the mile-long bridge they had slung across at the narrowest point, using three hundred ships, and laying a wooden roadway across their decks. Another bridge would soon be completed. But this was only a part of the force Xerxes was starting to deploy. In addition to this uncounted, uncountable, army marching into Greece, there was a fleet of three thousand naval transports preparing to sail across the Aegean in a massive Combined Ops expedition which would destroy for ever the ability of all Greeks—Athenians, Spartans and the rest of them—to wage war, or resist the spread of Persia.

The Pan-Hellenic Congress decided, in some haste, to defend Greece along the line of the Isthmus of Corinth, the narrow channel that divides the large southern part of Greece, the Peloponnese, from the northern and central parts. But when the plan was considered with more care, the Greeks realized that if the Isthmus were chosen as line of defence, the Persians could mount such an attack, using the whole of north and central Greece as base, that the Peloponnese must soon fall into their hands.

This was unthinkable.

If, therefore, Greece were to be saved, she must be defended, inch by precious inch, from the north down. But as both Greek army and navy (or the contingents, aggregated, from the city-states) were inferior in numbers to those of the Persians, this could only be done in the narrow seas and the narrow passes.

They decided to precipitate, if they could, a naval battle in the cramped and narrow Euboean Channel between their east coast and the large island of Euboea—a hundred miles long—and couple this naval tactic with the defence of the narrow pass of Thermopylae. This, they felt, was the only place the Persian army, marching south from its bridge crossing, could get between the impassable mountains and the sea. A picked band of men, it was argued, could hold the pass forever—or at least long enough to goad the Persians into trying to outflank them from the sea. Once Xerxes attempted the narrow channel with his fleet, the Greeks were confident of being able to defeat it. To this end they mounted a naval force out of all proportion to the mere 5,000 men they allotted King Leonidas of Sparta, with which he was expected to hold back the might of the Persian army. Three hundred men of Leonidas's force were his own Spartans.

Soon the Persian army, as had been prophesied, arrived at the Pass of Thermopylae. Like Leonidas's men, they camped and took stock of the situation. Xerxes had agile spies on horseback, able to describe the defenders to him: according to these there were a mere three hundred men in position.

This in fact was the Spartan contingent, the remainder of the five thousand being concealed from sight, and even when he learnt that these were Spartans, the most warlike people in Greece, the Persian emperor assured himself that no body of men, however brave, however well-armed, would take on any army several thousand times its own size. He waited four days: then, in some exasperation, he sent his first cohorts to crush them.

But as Herodotus was to report of that day, "The Greeks made it plain enough to anyone, not least to the Emperor Xerxes himself, that he had many men, but few soldiers." No soldiers, that is, which could be compared to the well-armed Greek ones, under the inspiring leadership of a Spartan king. The Persians had travelled many hundreds of miles and they always travelled and fought light. But their few, simple, weapons were of little use against the well-armed, well-armoured, Greeks. And though it was soon apparent to Xerxes's generals that they had five thousand men to deal with, rather than a mere three hundred, the Persian army was still enormously, absurdly, the larger force.

At the end of the first day the Persian vanguard had made no impression on the defenders of Thermopylae, whose bravery, arms, and discipline under Leonidas were assisted by the fact that the Pass was a mere fourteen yards across: no attacking army could deploy more than a few men at a time along so small a front. Xerxes replaced his vanguard by crack troops, "The Emperor's Immortals" under the general Hydarnes, but these fared little better. Leonidas, too, could replace his front line, using the various city-state contingents, the Thebans, Thespians, Corinthians and the rest of them, in strict succession, keeping only the Phocians, the largest single group, numbering a thousand, to guard a path to their rear. Were the Persians to discover this path, which ran from near their own encampment, right round behind the Greek position, they could easily outflank and threaten the defenders. In the unlikely event of this happening, Leonidas had posted the thousand Phocians around the southern end of the path, where it entered the valley behind him.

But Leonidas was betrayed. A Greek, Ephialtes, greedy for gold, approached Xerxes along this very path, and agreed to show it him, for a reward.

The deal satisfactorily completed, Ephialtes led Hydarnes and his Persians back along the path, and this large force surprised the Phocian defenders, cut off from the direct command of Leonidas, so that they fled in confusion, then regrouped themselves on a hilltop. Hydarnes ignored them, pressed on into the valley and up against Leonidas's rear.

And now there was consternation in the ranks of the Spartan king. For had not their seer, Megistas, prophesied defeat? And had not an Oracle stated that Sparta would fall to a foreigner unless one of her kings was killed in battle?

Part of the five thousand defected immediately: there was no point, if one believed in the prophecy of Megistas, no point at all in being present at assured defeat; and there was no point fighting—if one subscribed to the Oracle's point of view—for a king whose death alone would assure victory. And Leonidas, anxious to fulfil the Oracle's prophecy with his own life, sent others away, retaining only his own Spartans, with the Thespians and the Thebans. The Thespians, we are told, would not have left him, even if ordered, and he kept the Thebans to test their allegiance to the Greek cause,

Meanwhile the might of the Persian army was assembling behind this little force, assembling at the top of the slope which ran down to the valley, the slope down which thousands of barbarians would rush, when the order was given, to destroy Greece for ever. For this was what the young Xerxes, pouring a libation to the rising sun, had promised his generals, and this is what he firmly believed would be the outcome.

At last, as the sun rose the height of distant trees, the Persians flooded down. And now the character of the fighting changed: here were a few hundred men only, facing certain death, and determined to die well; taking ten, fifty, a hundred, each of the enemy with them before they could fight no longer. And they did. Led by the three hundred Spartans and their king, the Greeks fought with amazing gallantry and—though the outcome was foredoomed —amazing success. They fought first with spears; and when these broke, with swords, then with teeth and with hands. They inflicted such shocking casualties on the Persian hordes that, in order to get these into battle, the Persian commanders were forced to drive them on with whips.

But Leonidas, as the Oracle had foretold, died, at the head of his men, and all three hundred of his Spartans fell with him. Most of the other Greeks defected to the enemy, and of those who were not killed by them the majority were branded with hot irons as everlasting proof of their defeat.

One little band of men fought to the last to save the body of Leonidas, but, when they were heaped in piles around it, the Persians were able to seize it. Xerxes, enraged and horrified by the casualties which had been inflicted on his own army, ordered that it be decapitated, then crucified. The bodies of the others were buried where they had fallen, and later three memorial columns were erected at the spot in their memory.

These three columns might well commemorate Thermopylae, the Spartans, and, above all, Leonidas; for whenever heroism is mentioned the three spring to mind. In fact, that gallant defence of a lost cause against overwhelming odds had little bearing on the rest of the war. It inspired the Greeks—though its outcome distressed them—yet at the same time it inspired Xerxes and his Persians to an all-out effort to destroy them.

But Greece went on, from losing this battle so heroically, to winning the war, and we cannot leave this description of Leonidas and his battle without taking notice of the probable outcome. For if that war had been lost, the whole of Greek civilization would have been lost with it. We might now, in Britain, as all over the continent of Europe, share an Asian culture and speak in Asian tongues.

But this was not to be. (At least, not then: though there are ominous similarities in this history of the fifth century before Christ and that of the twentieth after Him.) The Greek fleet, outflanked from the land, sailed hurriedly south.

And now Themistocles of Athens came into his own. He had always maintained, against the advice, even the frank hostility, of others, that the saving of Greece would, in the long run, depend on its fleet. To this end he had built up a large one for his own Athens, and now, summoning to him the naval contingents, small and even smaller, of the other city-states, he was able to muster a powerful sea force. He rushed this towards the Island of Salamis in the Saronic Gulf, west of Athens, the last defence of the Isthmus of Corinth. By a trick, he was able to persuade Xerxes to try and "bottle up" the Greek fleet in the narrowest part of the Gulf, and here, with their heavier, more armoured—and far fewer—ships the Greeks were able to sail into the tightly packed mass of Persian shipping and rip it to bits. Persian oars were torn off, the hulls were rammed and sunk, and those that refused to sink were boarded and destroyed.

Xerxes and the Persian empire had received a blow from which they never recovered, but it was left to the following year, 479 B.C., for the final land battle of Plataea, and the final defeat of the Persians—by Spartans avenging their king.

PERICLES

(490–429 B.C.)

THE HISTORIAN Herodotus alleges that a few days before the
Athenian statesman Pericles was born his mother, Agariste, had a
prophetic dream: she dreamed that she would "bear a lion", a
son who would be a remarkable leader of men. In fact when this
son matured he was for three decades the outstanding personality
not only in Athens but in the whole Greek world.

Pericles's parents both belonged to the governing class of the
City. His mother was a great-niece of Cleisthenes, the law-giver,
and she had been given the name of an ancestor, the daughter of a
Synconian tyrant whose wooing—after a year of fierce athletic
competition—at the Olympic games had become legendary.
Pericles's father, Xanthippus, had held high command in an
Athenian naval unit which had defeated what remained of Xerxes's,
the Persian king's, fleet.

Xanthippus took a keen interest in political affairs. Athens was
then still governed by the Council of the Areopagus, a body which
originated in the seventh century B.C. The members of the Areopagus, called archons, all came from the two wealthiest classes of
the City. Few authenticated facts about the Areopagus have survived, but at the time of Pericles's birth many far-sighted Athenians,
including his father, already believed that the Areopagus system of
government was not as democratic as it should be. The reformers
were led by an activist, Ephialtes, who, in public utterances, discussed the corruption and fraudulent practices of which the archons
were frequently accused. Unfortunately little is known about
Ephialtes's life, but historians seem to agree that he himself was an
honest man.

There is no question that in Xanthippus's household Ephialtes's
activities were frequently discussed in the presence of young
Pericles. Though his parents were enthusiastic about reform, it is
doubtful whether, despite their intelligence, they understood the
dangers inherent in a sudden change of the system of government.
For in common with many liberals throughout the ages they did not
foresee that without an educated middle class the democracy they

contemplated was not workable in the long run. During the fifth century no effort was made to establish any kind of popular education. Intellectual life and learning was confined to a few wealthy families who could give hospitality and a position to resident tutors for their sons. This lack of a more general education was a tragedy for Athens after Pericles's death, because when, under his rule, Athens had become a world power, there were not enough trained men to carry on his work and maintain his achievements.

Pericles himself enjoyed the type of education his parents' wealth and position made possible. The boy had many tutors. From his earliest youth, as was usual for the sons of upper-class Athenians, his military training was never neglected, but he was also taught to develop and use his mind, to think logically, and, above all, objectively and dispassionately. Damon, a prominent scholar of the age, who had propounded various theories of music, was one of his teachers. Another was Zeno, the Eleatic philosopher from Cyprus, who explained to Pericles that he must distrust knowledge acquired purely through the senses; that he must instead rely only on logic and reason.

Young Pericles's most influential teacher was the philosopher-scientist Anaxagoras of Clazomenae, who, in modern terms, was really the earliest atomic scientist. For he believed in the existence of what he called "tiny seeds" from which the entire universe is made up. In other words, he impressed upon Pericles that all matter consisted of some kind of atoms.

Anaxagoras was convinced that all physical phenomena are based on natural causes. By imbuing his pupil with his attitude towards nature, he helped to liberate Pericles from the religious superstitions then widely accepted in Athens. Anaxagoras's influence on Pericles was permanent and far-reaching: for in his maturity Pericles helped to emancipate Athenian culture from the domination of the priestly class and it was he who gave his City the foundations of a secular civilization.

Pericles's character and temperament responded naturally to the discipline of his education. It was his nature to react to the problems of life in a cool, rational manner. His reserve seemed impenetrable and he was always a hard man to know well. He disliked and avoided convivial drinking parties, so popular amongst his contemporaries, and he chose his friends and associates with discrimination. His sculptured head by Cresilas, a copy of which is in the British Museum, shows us the calm face of a withdrawn and determined man who seems to be gazing into space above the troublesome conflicts of the moment. When one looks at the portrait it is difficult to remember that this apparently aloof and detached statesman was one of the most eloquent orators of ancient Greece.

Pericles presented a striking contrast to Cimon, the genial and very convivial hero of the Persian War, who was the leader of the conservatives in the Areopagus during Pericles's youth. Cimon wanted to bring about an alliance between Athens and Sparta— that is to say between the governing classes of the two City States— and when the serfs, the so-called helots, rebelled in Sparta, Cimon went with an armed force to help quell this rebellion. This intervention by an Athenian force in the affairs of Sparta was not generally popular in Athens. Even some of Cimon's drinking companions disapproved of what they considered his pro-Sparta attitude which they thought unpatriotic. Ephialtes and his followers in the democratic party welcomed this opportunity to discredit Cimon further, and he was finally ostracized and forced into temporary exile.

Cimon's disappearance from the political scene left the progressive party in the ascendancy. Pericles, by this time, was acknowledged as Ephialtes's second in the command of the party. Pericles, with Ephialtes and their followers, were now determined totally to reform the government and judicial system of Athens. Their opportunity was at hand, because, without Cimon's leadership, the conservatives on the Council of the Areopagus were disorganized and indecisive.

Ephialtes, for months past, had been preparing public opinion for the revolutionary changes he was contemplating. He had cleverly instituted proceedings against various Areopagites for fraud and corruption. Finally, a year after Cimon's departure, Ephialtes and Pericles officially deprived the Areopagus of all its power with one exception: the Areopagites were allowed to continue as judges in cases of murder.

A Council of Five Hundred—an assembly—and popular law courts took over the functions heretofore carried out by the Areopagus. The members of the Council of the Five Hundred as well as the men who served as judges and magistrates were now chosen by lot from all eligible citizens of Athens. Thus the government of the City was no longer conducted only by the wealthy and prominent; by the luck of the draw every citizen had a chance to take part in public and judicial affairs. It must, however, be mentioned in this connexion that, despite Ephialtes's and Pericles's reforms, the Athenians accepted as citizens eligible for government responsibility only a small minority of the population as a whole.

Ephialtes did not live to see the fruition of his ideas. The conservatives hated him too much, and he was assassinated. Pericles escaped the wrath of his opponents and succeeded the murdered man as the leader of the progressives. During the decade following Ephialtes's death Pericles firmly established the remarkable reforms they had planned together.

Pericles soon demonstrated that he was an imaginative as well as a practical statesman. He understood, for example, that many of the citizens chosen by lot could not really afford public service—which meant giving up gainful occupations—unless they were paid. He therefore introduced a system of payment from the public treasury for services to the state, a system unheard of in ancient Greece before this time. Judges and lesser magistrates, too, were paid a salary and jurymen were given a fee. Pericles also supported measures to give financial aid to the men (and thus to their families) called up for naval and military duties.

Patriotic or ambitious Athenians, now financially free to play a part in the government or the judiciary, were eager to have the luck of the draw. It was natural that they wanted to increase their chances, and the smaller the number of eligible citizens the greater were these chances. Before the age of Pericles the legitimate son of an Athenian father—regardless of his mother's origins—became an Athenian citizen when he was eighteen years old. Now there was great pressure to alter these rules. In 451 B.C. Pericles gave way to these pressures and a law was passed confining citizenship to men who were of Athenian descent on both sides. Not all Athenians welcomed this law, for they remembered many distinguished citizens—for example Cleisthenes, the law-giver, or Themistocles, the naval commander—who were not of purely Athenian origin.

Domestic reforms were not Pericles's only preoccupation. He was equally concerned with foreign affairs and he was radically changing the course of the City's foreign policy. His predecessors, though loyal Athenians, had been more willing to consider Greece as a whole. Pericles, on the other hand, was determined to create an Athenian empire, and to expand the geographical, political and commercial domination of the City. In about 461 B.C. he began to realize his expansionist vision.

He built up a large army and a superb fleet with which to fight for the expansion of Athenian power. To protect Athens itself against attack, fortifications were erected along the route to the port of Piraeus. He secured Athens's Aegean possessions and thus, after the defeat of Corinth and Aegina, made her the greatest trading nation in Greece. Athenian merchants now did business freely with Egypt and Carthage; their goods were sold in ports all over the Mediterranean. Politically, too, under Pericles's leadership, Athens became the dominant power in the Delian League. He also increased the influence of the City by settling groups of Athenians in the various territories conquered by his armies.

For thirty years—until 431 B.C.—Pericles was able to hold his empire together and to maintain the peace. He and his contemporaries could not have understood that the power structure he had created, the battles he had won, the cities he had conquered, would be forgotten by posterity except among scholars, or schoolboys struggling to remember dates and names for an examination paper. What posterity has never forgotten, and will never forget, is that Pericles by his encouragement of the arts and sciences created a lasting empire of the mind.

The Parthenon, largely the work of Phidias, the sculptor; the work of the great dramatists—Aeschylus's *Agamemnon*; Sophocles's *Antigone*, *Electra*, or *Oedipus*; Euripides's *Medea* or *Orestes*—none of these and other marvellous works of art would have been produced without Pericles's support and encouragement of the artists. One of the reasons why, under Pericles's guidance, the cultural life of Athens showed such a consistently high standard was his concern not only with men of genius, but with more ordinary artists and performers as well. Craftsmen as well as sculptors were encouraged; a concert hall, the Odeion, was built for popular concerts by flute and zither players, or singers who never became well known.

In his cultural and political life Pericles obviously had a remarkable ability to bring out the best in people. In his private life he was apparently less successful. He had no gift for the marriage relationship. His wife, a relative, remains a shadowy figure. Not even her name is known. He divorced her in 445 B.C. and his two sons by her were undistinguished and died young. To his mistress, Aspasia of Miletus, on the other hand, he was bound by ties of lasting affection and of mutual interests. It was said by one of Sophocles's disciples that Aspasia was accepted by Pericles and his circle of friends as an intellectual equal.

Aspasia remained faithful to Pericles when, in 431 B.C., the long peace ended, the Peloponnesian War began, and the Athenian Empire was finally destroyed. For the other Greek states had begun bitterly to resent the paramount authority of Athens and, led by Sparta, they had decided to make an effort to cause the downfall of "the tyrant Athens".

At home in Athens, too, Pericles now had many enemies. He had been in power for so many years that many Athenians simply wanted a change. The conservatives, of course, had always opposed him, but by this time some progressives as well were jealous of his dominating position. His adversaries began by attacking his friends: Aspasia, accused of impiety, was successfully defended by Pericles himself, and went free. Anaxagoras, arrested for atheism, was allowed to go into exile; Phidias, unjustly accused of stealing funds from the goddess Athene's treasure, died in prison.

These were bad days for Pericles, especially as the plague was raging in Athens. In 430 B.C. he was accused of fraud and deposed. But this gross injustice appalled so many Athenians that he was reinstated shortly before his death in 429 B.C. The history of Athens after his death showed that his passing was disastrous for the City: there was no man with his vision, authority and integrity to continue his achievements.

Shortly before his death, in a famous speech honouring the dead in the Peloponnesian War—a speech recorded by Thucydides— Pericles formulated for the last time his faith in his kind of democracy; he reminded Athenians never to neglect their political duties; he insisted that, despite their obligations as citizens or soldiers, they should cultivate their minds and their taste for what was beautiful in art and literature. "We shall assuredly," he wrote prophetically, "not be without witnesses . . . there are mighty monuments of our power which will make us the wonder of this and of succeeding ages."

ALEXANDER THE GREAT

(356–323 B.C.)

To few men of action, or other human beings, is the title "Great" given without hesitation: Alexander, son of King Philip of Macedon, and conqueror of Greece and the Near East, has always been one of these. His youth, his personal magnetism, the sweep of his conquests and the mere thirteen years they involved, his cosmopolitan vision and union of Western and Asian cultures, and his founding of international cities like Alexandria in Egypt—such are the reasons for his acclaim.

A fame which soon became literally legendary must in addition have enjoyed some rare personal origin of which we now possess mere hints. It is clear that he arrived at a psychological turning-point in the history both of Hellas and of the Near East. Alexander can be praised most for his vision, by which he accelerated—but did not create—a union and free flow of diverse cultures. His own marriages to Asian princesses formed a part of this policy.

But our admiration for his vision must not blind us to his many faults, let alone those of his un-visionary father, Philip. Centuries later Christianity achieved an equal cosmopolitanism without the necessity of war, as did Buddhism in India and the Far East. Alexander remains a "happy warrior", impulsive in battle and even endangering his life through his ardour.

The situation into which Alexander was born illustrates this. The year was 356 B.C. The many city-states of Greece were re-arranging the chessboard of their alliances and conflicts. To some—though not to Aristotle, himself teaching in Athens, though born at Stagira— the creative age of the city-state, the *polis* (hence our "politics", etc.), was past, and Greece needed to unite, both for her own political salvation and to propagate her culture. Further, only when united could the Greeks conquer Persia, their old foe in the "eternal war" between Asia and Europe—a fact that had never prevented one city-state from intriguing with Persia against another.

Now an apparent leader of the Greeks had arisen: curiously enough, from Macedon, a land to the north of Greece proper, inhabited by a somewhat primitive people ruled by kings of largely

Greek culture and race. Perhaps this marginal role of Macedon gave her king, Philip, a freshness of outlook and a "social-climbing" urge to conquer Hellas with her enormous prestige. Also, the relative primitiveness of his people implied strength and resolution.

Philip himself, in a stormy palace quarrel, had become king at the age of twenty-four; his son Alexander also incarnated the magic vigour of youth. By 338 B.C. Philip had subdued Thessaly, Illyria and Thrace, and had finally secured the mastery of Greece proper by his victory at Chaeronea over Thebes, Athens and their allies.

At the first pan-Hellenic congress held in Corinth, Philip proclaimed his intention to invade Persia. Yet the Greeks were not truly united behind him; their democratic traditions were against kingship, and Macedon was felt to be a semi-Greek outsider. The opposition to Philip, led by the Athenian orator Demosthenes, can thus be understood, however "inopportune historically".

His father's rash personal life provided a stormy background for the seething young Alexander. Philip dismissed the lad's mother, the fiery Epirot princess Olympias, to marry Cleopatra, niece of his general Attalus. At the wedding feast Alexander threw his drinking-cup at Attalus who had hinted that the prince was illegitimate; the sozzled Philip, sword in hand, reeled and fell. At which Alexander jeered: "Behold the man who would pass from Europe to Asia, and trips in passing from couch to couch!" Alexander fled; later Philip recalled him, but Olympias wove intrigues which culminated in Philip's murder in 336 B.C. Meanwhile Cleopatra had borne Philip a son.

Now king, Alexander was threatened on all sides: Greeks, Illyrians, his Thracian tributaries, all were restive, while Attalus in Asia supported the claim of Cleopatra's infant. Unlike his father, the impetuous Alexander acted swiftly; he had Attalus murdered (Olympias dealt with Cleopatra and the baby), subdued Thessaly, conquered the Thracian Triballi tribe on the Danube, received the alliance of some Celts, and rushed to save Macedon itself from attack by the Illyrians.

In the hour of victory he now learned that Thebes had rebelled, and that other Greek states were in ferment, intriguing with Persia. Thebes he smashed, and razed it to the ground; its people were sold into slavery. However, he left one house standing: that of the poet Pindar. This love of culture, which at Thebes stood in contrast to his general savagery, made him conciliatory to Athens. All Greece now stood under his command.

Young, magnetic, swift, beloved of the gods, Alexander was ready for the revenge *against* Asia. This must be emphasized, in view of the change his attitude underwent when once *in* Asia. It is only then that his cosmopolitanism awoke, and—in the words of the historian Eratosthenes: "As in a cup of friendship he mixed the nations." Only then could Plutarch's eulogy apply: "Virtue was by his side, and in him she engendered daring."

Philip was a bare conqueror; his son was to perceive the spiritual union and mission of Greece, and later still to extend this concept of friendship (*philia*) and "one-mindedness" (the Stoic *homonoia*) from family to city-state to Hellas up to Mankind itself. Yet can we blame the opponents of Philip and the early Alexander for not foreseeing this? Aristotle had been Alexander's tutor: from him the prince learnt Platonic philosophy ("kings shall be philosophers"); but to Aristotle's advice to be a political leader to the Greeks and treat them as friends, and to the "Barbarians" a mere enlightened despot, Alexander replies boldly.

In choosing advisers and assistants, "he did not mind whether one of them came to him with a Greek cloak and a spear or a Persian buttoned coat and a scimitar". Their "virtue or lack of virtue" was all that mattered. Yet Aristotle's instruction in the nature of the Greek city inspired Alexander to found Greek cities as far as Afghanistan (Bactria).

His career is now a blazing series of almost symbolic events. With 30,000 infantry and 5,000 cavalry he crossed to Asia Minor, vividly aware of his descent from the hero Achilles, sacrificing at places sacred in Greek tradition, commanding desolate Troy to rise again. Persians and their vassals of Asia Minor were defeated at the River Granichus, at Miletus, at Halicarnassus, all in 334 B.C. Halicarnassus suffered the same barbarous destruction as Thebes. The cities of the Ilyrian League submitted without resistance, so Alexander—like the Persians—left their constitution intact. The next year at Gordion, he cut with his sword the "Gordian knot", the cunningly tied cord of bark of a cornel tree, and so fulfilled the prophecy that he would rule Asia.

Meanwhile King Darius of Persia (who had ascended his throne in the same year as Alexander) resolved to join battle in Cilicia. A beloved monarch, he was no genius like the Macedonian. His empire was ill-organized, but he was employing 15,000 Greek mercenaries. On the plain of Issus Alexander gained a decisive victory; Darius fled in haste, leaving even his mother and wife behind. Alexander's extremely courteous treatment of these captives surprised the world and witnesses to a certain generosity in his nature.

Darius wrote a letter pleading for an alliance, but the victor's reply was haughty. Here Alexander founded the first of his cities, Alexandretta, the name clearly revealing his self-exaltation. The road being now open to Syria, he proceeded to attack the disunited Phoenician cities; Tyre capitulated after an eight-month siege (January-August, 332 B.C.), and suffered savage slaughter, while the remnants (some 30,000) were sold into slavery. The essentially compromising Darius sent Alexander an offer to the effect that he could have all the lands west of the Euphrates, and his daughter's hand. Alexander turned down the offer. Tyre was followed by Gaza, the Philistine capital, which endured slaughter on an even greater scale.

Egypt, always a restless part of the empire, was now cut off from Persia. No resistance was offered and, in the Pharaoh's capital, Alexander first showed his cosmopolitan vision by making sacrifices to Apis and other Egyptian gods, and so gaining goodwill. To deepen his rank as King of Egypt, he proceeded to the oracular sanctuary of Amen, where the priests arranged for the god to declare Alexander his son (a necessary title for all Pharaohs). Alexander never divulged his dialogue with the god. Here there may have been a genuine, if self-centred, "mystical" impulse blended with political opportunism. Cyrene submitted, and his domain adjoined that of Carthage.

Of vast historic importance was his founding of the city of Alexandria; its site was a stroke of genius. He filled it with Greeks, Asiatics, and the Jews to whom he always showed favour. Greek manners entered Africa, Greek trade prospered, and the native Egyptians to some extent suffered. None the less, Alexandria—city with the world's first lighthouse—became a beacon of multi-national culture whose effect on the future can hardly be overrated.

Returning to Asia, Alexander refused (though prudently) to "steal victory" by night, and in broad daylight put the Persians to utter rout at Gaugamela, 331 B.C. Darius fled into the mountains, his Persians with him, carrying along with them the troops already placed at the rear. Alexander hastened on to Babylon, a city as proud as Tyre, which yet received him with open arms. The satrap, Mazaeus, surrendered city and citadel, and the conqueror typically retained him in his post. As in Egypt, Alexander now appeared as the protector of the native faiths; those had been scorned and persecuted by the Zoroastrian "fire-worshippers" (though strictly they revered fire merely as a symbol of the Divine). Alexander restored the temples, notably the grandiose temple of Bel, which Xerxes had destroyed.

After resting in Susa, the luxurious summer capital, Alexander pressed on, forcing the tribes of the Uxian Pass to pay him tribute, towards the Persian Gates, a narrow defile leading to Persis. This pass seemed impregnable, and winter snow increased Alexander's dilemma, for this, the only route to Persia's royal cities, had to be crossed. Based on the clever device of dividing his forces, his nocturnal attack led to a sweeping victory. Then in ancient Persepolis he stayed four months, receiving the submission of local peoples, and—in a frenzy of Greek (and perhaps pro-Babylonian) vengeance—burning down the temple of Xerxes.

Meanwhile Bessus, satrap of Bactria, had conspired against his master Darius, who perished; but Alexander dispatched the royal corpse with all honour to the Queen-Mother and later hunted Bessus down and had him mutilated and crucified. In this, perhaps, he acted as an "Asiatic" monarch, punishing the killer of a fellow-king, like himself "divine". Alexander did not hesitate to adopt the arbitrary splendour of Eastern monarchism, despite the restiveness this caused among his democratic Greeks. He adopted Asian dress and customs, even encouraging prostration in his presence, in accordance with his general, and indeed enlightened, principle of putting Western and Eastern manners and men on an equality.

The foundation of mixed cities (usually called Alexandria in his typical mixture of vision and egotism) was part of this policy; he transplanted willing Asians to Europe and vice versa. Religions, too, were reconciled, though this was of course more natural in antiquity: at his great banquet at Opis on the Tigris, the loving-cups were shared by men of many races, and the libations chanted, by Greek seers and Persian Magi alike, to "God", not to Zeus or any Asian deity as such. He further encouraged his European associates to marry Persians, and he himself—though often judged indifferent to women—married Roxana, daughter of the Sogdian prince Oxyartes, and later added two other Asian princesses (this was not repugnant to custom, and was useful politically). In his assumption of Oriental pomp and "divinity" he naturally offended his Macedonians; yet his tremendous, cordial personality won them back— after a few executions!

The urge to conquest increased. Successfully he had manoeuvred his troops and his policies in regions scarcely known to the Greek mind. Now, emboldened, he subdued Hyrcania and Gedrosia in Afghanistan. Thus was opened the path to India across the Hindu Kush range. Bactria, Sogdia (with Samarkand) were vanquished after strenuous efforts in a rigorous climate, whose hardships

Alexander was willing to share with his humblest follower. Then, three years after the death of Darius, Alexander prepared to conquer India, thus anticipating by 2,000 years the next European conquest of those regions! The foresight, the organizational power, and the geographical intuition displayed by Alexander were enormous. He was accompanied, too, by merchants (often Phoenician), literary men, historians, craftsmen, engineers and other specialists.

India—which, to the Greeks, existed on the world's edge—lay before him. Skilfully playing one quarrelling state against another, he crossed the Indus and received the homage of the Prince of Taxila (a prized vassal) and other states. Taxila's rival, Prince Porus, defied Alexander but was routed with his elephants at the Battle of the Hydaspes (326 B.C.). Alexander then treated him with a generosity both genuine and opportunist. Next the Punjab was conquered; but at the River Hyphasis his weary troops, faced with a desert march of eleven days, struck, and Alexander yielded, thus depriving himself for ever of reaching what he *thought* to be the world's end, bounded by the ocean. Retracing their steps, his men subdued the warlike Malli. Alexander was wounded; his troops, believing him dead, indulged in a vengeful massacre. Sind was overcome with difficulty, and at last Alexander, full now of naval plans, sailed in the Indian Ocean. His friend Nearchus was detailed to discover a seaway for commerce between the West and the Far East.

Alexander himself marched through Gedrosia in the most terrible conditions of all his campaigns; then he reached Susa, Ecbatana, and proceeded to Babylon, on the way defeating the Cossaean brigands and receiving embassies from countries in three continents. At Ecbatana he suffered overwhelming grief at the death of his bosom-friend Hephaestion, and crucified the physician who had failed to save him. (Such contrasts are in character; here we can only touch on the murder of his foster-brother Clitus in a drunken brawl.)

But his next scheme was not to be fulfilled. Preparing to circumnavigate and conquer Arabia, he died of a fever at Babylon in 323 B.C., aged thirty-three. Since thirteen years produced such amazing results, who can tell what another two decades of life would have yielded? His mind, at once visionary and practical, would surely have explored new regions, discovering the true geography of India and at least making contact with China. His realm might well have extended from Libya to the Ganges, or beyond. It is this charting of ever new domains—of trade, geography, culture, as well as war, this raising of the Greek curiosity to a new dimension—which attracts us in Alexander still.

CHANDRAGUPTA MAURYA

(c. 321–c. 298 B.C.)

THERE HAVE been emperors of India right into the twentieth century, and many of them were foreigners. The "Mogul" emperors from central Asia were as little akin to their Hindu subjects in race, language or religion as was Queen Victoria.

And men may debate till the end of time whether it was Victoria or the Moguls who did the greater good—or the greater harm—to that subcontinent. There can be no real answer: yardsticks vary.

But though the achievement of the last Indian emperors may be in dispute, there is no argument about those of the first.

His name was Chandragupta Maurya.

He reigned for the quarter century between 321 and 296 B.C., founding his own family dynasty. From the rise of this Maurya dynasty, Indian history becomes suddenly clear: chronology, despair of the historian, begins to make sense. An empire has sprung into being, joining the fragments of what, till now, has been only a vast southern bulge on the map.

We know quite a lot about this period in Indian history, and for that we are indebted to three sources. The Greeks came to India with Alexander the Great and wrote of their impressions; there are lengthy stone inscriptions made by Chandragupta's grandson, Asoka; and there is a remarkable treatise written by Chandragupta's chief minister, Kautilya, which shows us clearly how the Empire was run.

Chandragupta, we learn, seized the throne of the kingdom of Magadha, in eastern India (and now part of Bihar), from the last of its kings. There is a theory that he was in fact the illegal son of that king by a low-caste woman, but in any case the seizure was effected by organizing a revolt within the kingdom. At the same time, the ambitious young Chandragupta launched an attack on the garrisons left behind by Alexander in the Indus basin. We know that Alexander died in Babylon in June, 323 B.C., and that the attack was launched against the forces of his successor. It was successful; the Macedonian garrisons were overrun; and Chandragupta now ascended the throne of an empire. He gave himself the title of emperor, and he is the first strictly historical person to hold it.

He had captured Alexander's Indian domains, but the successors to Alexander lost no time in trying to regain them. One of these, Seleukos, crossed the Indus again, but was roundly beaten. Chandragupta's terms for his surrender involved the handing over of a number of provinces: in return the new emperor magnanimously presented five hundred elephants and agreed to take a daughter of Seleukos as wife.

A treaty so concluded might well last, and we can be grateful that it did; for now Seleukos sent, as his ambassador to Chandragupta's court, a remarkable man called Magasthenes. The ambassador kept an account of what befell him in this eastern land, with a minute description of its institutions and geography. Sadly, we no longer possess that account, but so much of it was borrowed by other authors that we still retain a clear idea of the India of Chandragupta's day. We know that the emperor was a stern, even cruel, ruler, and that the Maurya dynasty he founded ruled with even greater efficiency than did the Moguls two thousand years later. The Moguls, despite their militarism (even cooks in the palace had a military rank), had difficulty in resisting European encroachment when it came, but Chandragupta had no difficulty in flinging back the might of Macedon and exacting large tribute. He had, as well as a fine army, a highly developed civil service capable, in theory at least, of controlling an empire of any size.

The capital was Pataliputra, near the site of present-day Patna, and built on a tongue of land jutting out into the River Ganges where the smaller Son River joined it. It was thus a natural defensive position, triangular in shape, with water along two of its three sides. Its ruins are almost hidden by the towns of Patna and Bankipore, and the river confluence itself has shifted, but we can still trace the old river beds, see the remains of jetties, as well as fragments of the wooden palisade which surrounded the city. There were 570 watchtowers looking over this wall, and 64 well-guarded entrances in it.

There was a magnificent wooden-and-stone palace in which Chandragupta resided and from which he conducted the affairs of his empire. The exterior columns were picked out in gold and silver, and the splendid park which surrounded it was dotted with fish-ponds, trees and ornamental shrubs. We know from Megasthenes and others that Chandragupta never appeared in public without being carried in a golden palanquin or on a gold-draped elephant. His clothes were of the finest cotton, richly embroidered, and the royal food was served from golden vessels, six feet across. He had what we today call a harem, though that word was to come later, with the arrival of the Muslims; and, rather surprisingly perhaps, his palace was guarded by a regiment of armed women, his Amazons.

The Hindu religion looks askance at hunting, but Chandragupta and his two great successors had large deer parks and game reserves set aside for their personal use, right up until the time that Asoka embraced Buddhism and gave it up.

In addition to the harem and the Amazons, there were the familiar "dancing girls" of Eastern legend, to provide almost every service a monarch could require, from actual dancing, via garland-strewing and housework, to diplomacy. Some, in the Mata Hari tradition, were active and dangerous members of the Secret Service.

Alexander's influence on India was comparatively slight and short-lived, but the fact that Chandragupta's empire in the west, in the Punjab, had lain close to the eastern limit of the Persian empire meant that many Persian customs were adopted; even, in certain situations, the worship of fire.

The emperor was absolute ruler of his domain, but in his minister's treatise on State craft, the "Arthasastra", we learn that "Sovereignty is only possible with assistance. A single wheel can never move. Hence the king shall employ ministers and hear their opinion." And this same work, by the hand of his old and trusted adviser, Kautilya, urges that the sovereign never take the advice of less than four ministers on any subject.

Sometimes Chandragupta did; often he did not. Certainly he had his way in most things, though well aware, as rulers must be, that if one antagonizes too many, one is likely to be deposed or even assassinated. So great was Chandragupta's fear of the latter fate that, according to Megasthenes, he refused to sleep in the same bed two nights running, or to rest at all in the hours of daylight.

His powerful army had four arms: infantry, cavalry, chariots and elephants. The Commander-in-Chief rode on a war elephant covered in armour, with sharp barbs on each tusk, and two soldiers to control it. Lesser officers travelled in chariots drawn by two or four horses, with infantry guarding them. Chandragupta's army at one stage numbered 600,000 infantry, 30,000 cavalry, 8,000 chariots and 9,000 elephants. It was superbly disciplined and it was paid, not feudally, but directly by the state. It had no difficulty in conquering all its enemies, from Seleukos to the rulers of bordering states. (Kautilya's treatise states flatly that "any ruler at the circumference of the empire is an enemy".)

The administration of this formidable force seems to have been on thoroughly modern lines, with a War Office divided into departments controlling Admiralty, Transport and Supplies, Infantry, Cavalry, Chariots and Elephants. The men were divided into squads of ten, companies of a hundred and battalions of a thousand.

The armament was as formidable as the organization. Each elephant carried three archers plus driver, each chariot a minimum of two fighting men plus driver, all armed with lances. The infantry carried broadsword, javelin, bow and shield; and every man and every beast was armoured.

There was an ambulance service with surgeons and female nurses.

But even with this immensely powerful apparatus at his disposal, Chandragupta preferred, whenever possible, to take the advice of Kautilya: "Intrigue, spies, winning over the enemy's people, siege and assault, are the five means to capture a fort."

The type of government is shown, perhaps, in Chandragupta's word for it. "Dandaniti" means, simply, "Punishment", and indeed any crime, however petty, was punished with great severity. Unless a suitable and rapid confession were obtained, torture was carried out to extort it.

But this cruelty was normal for the period, and India's first emperor can be counted one of her greatest. Even his death was noble. He had listened to the prophecy of a saint, Bhadrabahu, that his lands would suffer a famine for twelve years, and many men would perish: the only escape would be a wholesale migration to more fertile land in the south. But no one else would listen to the prophecy. When it seemed about to be fulfilled, Chandragupta, to point the urgency of the matter, abdicated, to the consternation of his subjects, and began to lead a party of emigrants south, exhorting others to join him. Amazed, uncomprehending, many did, and were saved, while a dreadful famine ravaged the lands they had left.

When Bhadrabahu died Chandragupta was grief-stricken. He starved himself to death.

The empire went on. The twelve lean years gave way to plenty and Chandragupta's son Bindusara took over what was, in every way, a going concern. He extended still further the bounds of his domain, so that soon it extended, literally, from coast to coast. He in turn handed it over to his own son, Asoka, who without materially increasing the size of the empire strengthened its organization. He became, late in life, the most devout of Buddhists (at which point he gave up using his game reserves) and dispatched missionaries to as many lands as he had heard of, or could reach. He was a great builder, largely of temples, and many of these stand today as his monument and that of the Maurya dynasty.

But, as Chandragupta had feared throughout his own, the life of an emperor, even of an empire, is at the mercy of the assassin's sword. The Emperor Brihadratha was killed by his own Commander-in-Chief in 185 B.C., and the Maurya dynasty ended. By this time the empire itself had begun to fall to pieces, lacking the firm hand of Chandragupta and his immediate successors. The subsequent history of India, for several hundreds of years, is confused and muddled. Then, at the start of the fourth century A.D., came a new, powerful, dynasty, that of the Guptas. This, by a confusing accident of nomenclature, was founded by another Chandragupta.

The Gupta dynasty brought a Golden Age of Hindu Culture, but it too fell, and was followed by a confusion of rulers until the tenth century A.D. Then the Muslim hordes swept down over the northern hills, bringing with them an alien religion, Islam, which owed allegiance to a "Caliph" outside India's borders. Previous to this, every invader from the north (and none, until the arrival of Europeans in the fourteenth century, came any other way) had been assimilated, his religion and his customs blending into the previous pattern. But with the coming of Islam that process ceased. Islam, to its adherents, was the one and only True Faith: any unbeliever must either be forcibly converted or put to the sword. The new invaders embarked on campaigns of punishment, but punishment unlike Chandragupta's "Dandaniti" which was designed to govern: punishment for its own sake, to show the infidel his worthlessness and grind him underfoot.

These early Muslim invaders gave place to a finer breed who shared the same faith. Believing them to be Mongols, which they were not, the inhabitants of India now styled them "Moguls" and under this alien Mogul empire the country again prospered.

India has had her share of great emperors. But perhaps the greatest was the first.

ASOKA

(Reigned *c.* 273–232 B.C.)

WAR HAVING been decided upon, the Indian army rapidly crossed the border into Kalinga and were soon carrying all before them. The troops they encountered were dispersed. Towns and villages were occupied, and those that put up any sort of resistance were stormed and burnt, and their populations put to the sword or driven into the jungle to die of hunger and exposure. The streets were piled with corpses. Tens of thousands were enslaved, and the cries of outraged women and children rendered fatherless were heard from one end of the land to the other. At length the war was won, and the victors returned home. The generals went to the palace to report to their royal master that the tasks entrusted to them had been successfully accomplished. They thought he would be pleased, as indeed almost any other monarch would have been pleased. But the man in the case was Asoka, and that made a difference.

At this time—the year was about 261 B.C.—Asoka had been king of most of northern India for some dozen years, or eight years if we date his reign's commencement from his coronation. He belonged to the Maurya dynasty that had been founded by Chandragupta Maurya in about 322 B.C., the year after the death of Alexander the Great, with whom he had had some friendly contacts when the Greek conqueror had penetrated as far as the Indus. Asoka followed his father Bindusara on the throne in 273 B.C.; he was not the eldest son, but he seems to have acted for some years as heir apparent, and no doubt he had shown signs of capacity to rule. Since his coronation or consecration was delayed for some years it has been surmised that there was some opposition to his accession, but the story that he killed ninety-eight or ninety-nine brothers in order to clear the way to the throne is a silly fable put out by the monkish chroniclers of Ceylon, who wanted to make out that he was a very wicked fellow before he became converted to their faith.

From what may be learnt from the inscriptions that he caused to be made (and there is not the slightest reason to doubt their essential truth) the young Asoka was not very different from the ordinary run of kings met with in Indian history. He lived as his predecessors had lived, surrounded by every luxury and tempted by every pleasure. He enjoyed his days in the hunting-field. He joined in the feasts and dancing and theatrical displays that helped to pass the time for his courtiers. We are told that he liked his wine and good food, being specially fond of peacock's flesh, and he spent much of his time with the ladies of his numerous harem. As a ruler he was not at all inclined to temper justice with any exceptional measure of mercy.

But the Kalinga war worked a great change in him. The Kalingas occupied the territory to the south-east of his kingdom in the coastal region of the Bay of Bengal. No doubt they had been making themselves a bit of a nuisance, and it would not be difficult to find a pretext for teaching them a lesson. So he gave the necessary orders, and his soldiers carried out their instructions. But the reports of victory gave him no pleasure; on the contrary, they filled him with anguish. He suffered a great revulsion of feeling, which found expression in an inscription for which it would be hard to find a parallel. It is one of the "Rock Edicts" that he had engraved on great slabs or faces of rock so that they might be read by all who knew how, and this is what it says:

"When the king had been consecrated eight years, Kalinga was conquered by His Sacred and Gracious Majesty. A hundred and fifty thousand persons were carried away from thence captive, a hundred thousand were there slain, and many times that number died. No sooner had the land of the Kalingas been annexed than His Sacred Majesty felt remorse for having conquered the Kalingas, because the conquest of a country that had not been conquered before involves the slaughter, death, and carrying away captive of the people. And that is a matter of the most profound sorrow and regret to His Sacred Majesty. . . ."

Thereupon (the inscription goes on) His Sacred Majesty had begun to take under his protection the Law of Piety, to show his love of that law, and to inculcate it. With the result that, "if a hundredth part, or the thousandth part, of all the people who were then slain, done to death, or carried away captive, were to suffer the same fate, it would be a matter of regret to His Sacred Majesty. Moreover, should any one in future do him wrong, that too must be borne with, as far as it possibly can be . . . For His Sacred Majesty desires that all living beings should have security, self-control, peace of mind, and joyousness."

Yes, indeed, it would be hard to find a parallel to this extraordinary document. A king whose dominions extended from what is now Afghanistan to as far down in the peninsula as Madras, had said—

what?—that he was sorry! Sorry for something that is a commonplace in the records of imperial power but which he had come to consider a crime against humanity.

Two further inscriptions, known as the Kalinga Edicts, emphasize the lesson that he had learnt and which he now wished to impress on all those who governed in his name. They are addressed to high officers in the provincial administration, and in them he asserts that "all men are my children" and warns them against displaying envy and impatience in their rule, lack of perseverance, harshness, want of application and indolence. Let them watch their behaviour in future, for they could rest assured that the king's eye was upon them and any failure in their duty would be visited with his extreme displeasure.

Up to this time Asoka had been, it would seem, an adherent of the Brahmanical form of Hinduism, but now he became a convert to the great rival faith of Buddhism, which had been first preached by Gautama the Buddha perhaps three centuries before. His instructor in his new religion, and perhaps the man responsible for his conversion, was one Upagupta, the fourth in succession from Buddha as the "patriarch" of the Buddhist Church. Together they toured the principal holy places of the Buddhist world, and at each Asoka caused to be erected a monument commemorating his visit. Perhaps it was Upagupta who persuaded him to give up hunting and the practice of eating meat, and to prohibit the slaughter of animals for the royal kitchen.

One tradition has it that the king became a Buddhist monk, and it may very well be that he did so for a time, after the fashion of Buddhists in Burma and elsewhere. What is quite certain is that he became a powerful supporter of Buddhist missions. From his inscriptions we learn that he dispatched missionaries to many parts of the Indian peninsula, to Burma, and even to the succession-states of Alexander's empire in Asia and North Africa. It is not impossible that some knowledge of the Buddhist faith may have been carried to Europe by one of the missionaries he sent out.

But the most successful of these missions was the one he sent to Ceylon, or Lanka as it was styled in those days. This was in about 250 B.C., in response to an invitation from Tissa, king of the island, who was Asoka's almost lifelong friend. A young man named Mahendra, who was Asoka's younger brother or perhaps his son, was the principal missionary, and to this day his name and fame is perpetuated by monuments and relics in various parts of the island. He was accompanied by his sister Sanghamitra, who, we are assured, was as successful in winning women to Buddhism as Mahendra was among the men. The mission was a complete success, as is evidenced by the fact that from that day to this Ceylon has been a predominantly Buddhist country.

Mention has been made of Asoka's inscriptions. There are many of these, made on rocks and pillars and on the walls of caves, and together they constitute what has been called the most remarkable set of inscriptions in the world. They are to be found scattered over the length and breadth of India, from the north-west corner of the Punjab to Mysore, on the coasts of the Arabian Sea and the Bay of Bengal. Some of them are historical, some are political, but nearly all are moral. Never before had a great sovereign taken such pains to instruct his people in the ways of good behaviour, and there have been few to follow his example. If we seek to know what Asoka's own personal code of morals was we may discover it most concisely formulated in one of the "Minor Rock Edicts", as follows:

"Thus saith His Majesty. Father and mother must be obeyed. In the same way respect for all living creatures must be enforced. Truth must be spoken. These are the duties of the Law of Duty which must be practised. The teacher must be reverenced by the pupil, and a proper courtesy must be shown to all relations. This is the ancient standard of duty, which if it is followed leads to length of days. And according to it men must act."

Time and again Asoka refers to the "Law of Duty". In what does this consist, he inquires in one of the Pillar Edicts; and goes on to answer, "many good deeds, compassion, liberality, truthfulness, and purity of life". In the Rock Edicts he states that it includes the proper treatment of slaves and servants, hearkening to what one's parents have to say, showing liberality to friends and acquaintances, relations, Brahmans, and ascetics, and refraining from killing living creatures. In another he bids men to beware of lauding their own faith too highly and of belittling the faith of others; the religions of other people are all deserving of reverence (he says), for one reason or another.

As was (and is) the custom in Oriental lands, Asoka's rule was an intensely personal matter. Deeply interesting is one of the Rock Edicts that shows him at work. "For a long time past," he says, "it has been the rule to do business only at certain times. But now I have made arrangements that at all hours and in all places—whether I am at dinner, or in the ladies' apartments, or in my private room, or in the royal mews, or in my carriage, or walking in the palace gardens—wherever I may happen to be, the officers bearing official reports should have immediate access to me on the people's business. I have given instructions that immediate report is to be made to me at any hour and in any place, because I am never altogether satisfied with the way business is despatched. All my exertions are directed to one end, that I may discharge my debt to every creature, and that while I may make some people happy in this world, they may all in the next attain to heaven."

In addition to the rock inscriptions, ten of the surviving pillars that Asoka caused to be erected on Buddhist sites are inscribed. One of these is in the Lumbini Gardens, just over the border in Nepal, marking Buddha's birthplace. Another, and the most famous, is at Sarnath, four miles north of the holy city of Benares, on the site of the Deer Park where Buddha preached his first sermon. Here there is a great stupa (domed mound) of solid brickwork, enclosing the much smaller stupa that Asoka built. Close by is the stump, still 17 feet high, of the Asokan Pillar; originally over 50 feet in height, it was cut from a solid block of stone, quarried more than twenty miles away, and dragged to this spot.

When Sir John Marshall, the pioneer of Indian archaeology, excavated the site he found lying near by the broken portions of the upper part of the shaft and a magnificent bell-shaped capital with four lions above, supporting in their midst a stone wheel, the symbol of the Buddhist Law or Dharma that Buddha first "turned" at Sarnath all those many centuries ago. Marshall was astonished by the excellent state of preservation of the sculptures. He acclaimed the bell and lions as "the finest carvings that India has yet produced, and unsurpassed, I venture to think, by anything of their kind in the ancient world". Another stupa with the remains of an Asokan pillar were located at Sanchi in Bhopal, and Sir John Marshall carefully restored the ancient monument to its original form.

After more than forty years on the throne, King Asoka died in 232 B.C. According to one version, he began to lose grip on affairs towards the end of his reign, and at length retired to a Buddhist monastery tired and disillusioned; but according to another, and, it is good to learn, better authenticated account, he continued to the end the same masterful striver after his people's welfare that he had been in his prime. His great name and example have never been forgotten, and to the founders of the Indian Republic in 1947 it seemed the most natural thing in the world that they should adopt the Sarnath capital as the device for the national seal, while in the middle of the national flag an "Asoka wheel" stands out in navy blue against the central band of white.

HANNIBAL

(247–182? B.C.)

HANNIBAL IS one of the very few great men of antiquity known to the wide public, who was neither Greek nor Roman nor Hebrew, though he was related by race to the latter. Moreover, he was an enemy of Rome: yet our tradition, in many ways Rome's successor, often admires him. His name itself, derived as it is from Baal, brings to mind the god who was Jehovah's rival in the Old Testament and whose priests were butchered by Elijah. It is interesting that a fellow-Semite, Sigmund Freud, tells—in his autobiography and elsewhere—how from boyhood he studied and admired the great anti-Roman hero.

We may further regard Hannibal as one of the line of significant North Africans, later to include great Christian thinkers like St. Augustine and Tertullian, as well as many of the creators of Moorish Spain with her tolerant international culture. Indeed such an exceptional figure as Hannibal may serve to make our historical judgments more subtle, create an awareness of the values that can exist on both sides of a conflict, and show us that our own culture and its ancestry are not unique.

Who was Hannibal? He was a Carthaginian, and Carthage was a long-standing, prosperous colony of Phoenicia. By Hannibal's time, Carthage was already mistress of a small empire, including territories in Sicily, long a source of dispute with the Greeks. Thus both a Phoenician and an African tradition were involved.

The Phoenicians, an unusual people, deserve considerable study. To them much of the pre-Hellenic culture of the Mediterranean Basin was due. Known in the Old Testament as Canaanites, they were principally a trading and maritime community; already in the middle of the second millennium B.C., their caravan routes reached, through Damascus, to the Euphrates, while in the West their commerce stretched, through Sicily, North Africa and Spain, as far as Cornwall. Pre-eminently they developed and traded in metals, fabrics and other products of a technical skill which, according to tradition, they handed on to Crete and thus Greece, and therefore the modern Western world.

To the Greeks they gave the principles of the alphabet, and the intermingling of Phoenician and Greek religious symbols (as with Aphrodite and Adonis) continued for many centuries. Trading with Babylon, they conveyed elements of its civilization to the West. Their subsequent conquests by Assyria, Babylon, Egypt, Persia and Greece (Alexander the Great) hardly concern us here; what is significant is that the Phoenicians were great colonizers, founding cities as far west as Cadiz (about 1100 B.C.), and also in Cyprus, Sicily, Malta and North Africa, and that as a result they were in perpetual contact and frequent conflict with the Greeks and their colonies.

One of the most powerful Phoenician colonies was Carthage, a few miles from modern Tunis, founded around 800 B.C. A natural site for international commerce, Carthage soon founded colonies of her own. After ousting the Greeks from the Spanish coast and most of Sicily, Carthage, the largest and richest city in the Western Mediterranean, had an empire comprising a number of coastlands— North African, Southern Spanish, Sicilian, Sardinian and Corsican. It was in Sicily that she first confronted Roman power. Carthage, like Venice later, preferred diplomacy to war, and she and Rome had made three treaties respecting "spheres of influence", before the tragic oversight of not defining such spheres in Sicily led to a conflict. This was over a third party, the Mamertines, discharged auxiliaries from Campania in Southern Italy, whose town, Messana, had been conquered by Hiero of Syracuse. A Carthaginian flotilla came to their aid, but the Mamertines then called in the Romans, as "fellow-Italians", to help oust the Carthaginians in their turn.

Through folly and obstinacy Rome and Carthage drifted into an undesired war—the First Punic (that is, Carthaginian) War, which lasted from 264 to 241 B.C. Rome built up her naval power, then invaded Africa, throwing away her victory at Ecnomus by demanding impossible terms of surrender, and goaded Carthage into an eleventh-hour rally which culminated in victory over Rome in the valley of the Bagradas, near Carthage (255 B.C.). Rome had to evacuate Africa. But the next years saw massive Roman attacks on Sicily, ending in another victory for Carthage: the exhausted Romans, who could have accepted a compromise which divided Sicily between Carthaginians, Romans and Greeks, wrecked their chances through listening to their diehard Regulus.

The tepid armistice gave time to Carthage to stage a decisive counter-blow under the young commander Hamilcar Barca, father of his country's most famous citizen, Hannibal. But eventually he had to accept peace on Rome's terms in 241 B.C. The very next year, taking advantage of Carthaginian dissensions, Rome sided with mutinous mercenaries in Sardinia and declared war on the legitimate government of Carthage, refusing arbitration. Carthage had no choice but to accept Rome's grabbing of both Sardinia and Corsica, and to pay a further 1,200 talents as indemnity. Whatever the Romans' fears of Hamilcar, through such high-handed sharp practice, they tarnished their reputation for fairness and increased their own insecurity by inciting Carthage to implacable revenge.

Hamilcar nursed his nine-year-old son, Hannibal, on hate, making him daily swear revenge on Rome by the family altar. If Rome by her greed and folly increased her own insecurity, it is equally tragic that Hamilcar, his son-in-law Hasdrubal, and Hannibal himself procured the far worse downfall of their country. At Carthage there was almost always a peace party, desiring merely the free passage of trade between Syria and the Atlantic; but the Barcas scorned this tradition. The First Punic War had been one of exhaustion: a course based on mercantile caution and the need to rely on mercenaries from the African interior. Hamilcar's dynamism and frequent imperialism changed this. Personality becomes important: Hamilcar and Hannibal possessed the genius of binding mercenaries in devotion to their own person, an art by which Caesar later reached monarchical rank in Rome. Today we think not so much of the individual Roman generals, but of Rome, while the name of Hannibal eclipses that of Carthage.

Under Hamilcar, Carthage recovered her resources through a series of conquests (obtained often by diplomacy) in the interior of Spain, rich both in mines and in military material. Rome gradually awoke to the situation, and made a treaty, protecting the Greek colony of Saguntum near Valencia, while Hasdrubal promised not to cross the River Ebro. In 221 B.C. Hasdrubal was murdered, and his severed head dramatically thrown into Hannibal's camp. The new leader—married to the daughter of one of the chiefs of Castulo—picked a quarrel with Saguntum, perhaps to forestall a second Messana incident with its resultant Roman aggression. But Rome, for once irresolute, accepted two rebuffs to her protests, while the Carthaginian peace policy of Hanno was brushed aside by the ardent Hannibal.

Hannibal's eight-month siege of Saguntum ended in victory, with the vanquished committing suicide on a pyre in their market-place (a tragedy repeated two generations later by the Carthaginians themselves). The Roman Senate, jolted into action, demanded the surrender of Hannibal. This was refused and Rome declared war in 219 B.C.

At this point Hannibal produced his master-stroke of strategy. He resolved to cut off Roman man-power at its source and cross the Alps into Italy—one of the most daring feats in military history, and one which has become proverbial. Unlike Napoleon's comparable march into Russia, Hannibal's plan met with success. Not that crossing the Alps proved easy: snow, ice and inhospitable cold combined with hostile mountain tribes to reduce Hannibal's man-power to some 26,000.

Yet he conquered Northern Italy within two months; the Roman general Cornelius Scipio, hastily recalled from Gaul, was no match for him in the preliminary skirmish by the River Ticinus; farther south, near Placentia, an enlarged Roman force suffered further defeat at the River Trebia, their 400,000 men being reduced to 10,000. On this the Romans withdrew from Northern Italy, leaving the hitherto hesitant Gauls to join Hannibal. Then Central Italy witnessed his great victory at Lake Trasimene, where he employed his usual tactics of decoying an attack on his relatively weak centre, followed by a surprise-rout of the attackers from all sides.

After Trasimene, Rome waited, adopting "Fabian" tactics, so called from the commander-dictator Fabius Maximus: the poet Ennius praised him as "the man who singly saved the state by patience". For, though theoretically Hannibal now had a clear road to Rome, no town of Central Italy threw open its gates to him, and he had no base for supplies. Preferring to ferment rebellion in Southern Italy, he received no welcome there, and was shadowed by Fabius, whose brush with him in Campania proved a failure, due to a really ingenious ruse of Hannibal: 2,000 oxen were driven by night to the Roman camp, their horns tied with lighted faggots, so frightening the Romans away. Yet Fabius's mere presence kept the allies of Rome in the south from joining Hannibal.

In 216 B.C. Roman impatience erupted and courted the disaster of Cannae: in this open Apuleian plain their 50,000 men were annihilated by Hannibal's 40,000, thanks to his usual tactics and the co-operation, in Greek style, between a containing and a striking force. Yet once again Hannibal's luck proved almost his undoing. Cannae turned out to be a lever for Roman revival; unheard-of patriotic sacrifices issued in a new effort; in the words of the Greek historian Polybius, the Romans were never as intractable as in defeat. Practically the whole of Southern Italy was won over by Hannibal (and his promise not to impose forced levies on them), while Capua, the chief industrial centre, was delighted to house and supply his army. Yet the ease and languor of that sensuous region undisciplined Hannibal's men, and the name of Capua in this sense became proverbial.

In addition, he had to face the growing increase of Roman man-power, while Central Italy's loyalty to Rome cut him off from his Gallic allies. He tried with little success to snare his enemies into fresh traps; in 212 B.C. he gained Tarentum (through treason), but the starvation of Capua into surrender in the next year out-balanced this. Rome meted out savage "peace-terms" to the Capuans. Three years later, by another act of treason, Tarentum was recovered by Rome; and Hannibal could only look for reinforcements from an external source—in fact, from Hasdrubal, who was allowed by his government to quit Spain, thus leaving it exposed to the Romans. This move helped to ensure the final Carthaginian defeat: for Hasdrubal was beaten by the Romans on the banks of the Metaurus, and he himself perished. Hannibal was allowed to retire for four years in the remote hills of Bruttium, in the Italian south. These periods of brooding seem typical, if ominous, throughout Hannibal's career.

Other factors, however, were already entering the situation. There were the kaleidoscopic relations of Rome and the varied powers of Greece, Sicily, and Asia Minor; but this was a war on many intermittent fronts. In 215 B.C. Philip V of Macedon allied himself with Hannibal, no doubt with the intention of winning an eventual foothold in Southern Italy. He was no match for the Romans, and the First Macedonian War (on Philip's territory) ended in his defeat. In Spain, after both brothers Scipio had perished with most of their forces, the younger Scipio (their son and nephew) achieved final victory there (206 B.C.).

Meanwhile Sicily was the scene of blood-letting operations; Hieronymus of Syracuse promised aid to Carthage, but was mur-dered before this could take effect; but his republican opponents and the pro-Carthage party united to oppose the Roman general Marcellus, who had landed on the island and massacred the inhabit-ants of Leontini. Marcellus defeated Syracuse through treachery, having broken his word to the Syracusans. The other Sicilian cities, terrorized by Roman atrocities, soon submitted. But Carthage was to be pierced still more vitally, on her own soil. A reluctant Senate was overruled by popular clamour, and permitted Scipio to retaliate upon Carthage the devastation of Italy.

Intrigues among African rulers increased the opportunities of both sides: the Numidian Syphax (Hasdrubal's son-in-law) fought for the Punic cause, while Scipio won over Massinissa of eastern Numidia; a to-and-fro conflict ended in the Roman victory of Cirta. The Carthaginians recalled Hannibal and Mago from Italy; Mago died on the journey; and Hannibal, deserted by his Italian allies, finally met Scipio in a fruitless personal interview. For Scipio's terms had been accepted by both sides; but their enormity (cession of Spain, reduction of the navy to twenty warships, and a huge indemnity) incited a group at Carthage to break off the armistice. The renewed conflict ended in the utter defeat of Carthage at Zama in 202 B.C. Hannibal himself, one of the few survivors, insisted sensibly on an immediate peace. Scipio doubled the previous punishment, while his further clause—that Carthage must not wage war without Rome's consent—led at length to the Third Punic War.

Carthage, by improving the cultivation of her hinterland, began to recover, and Hannibal showed himself a statesman, seeking to democratize his city's government, in both financial and other matters. But this decade of calm with Rome came to a harsh end when Hannibal's opponents accused him before the Roman Senate of collusion with Rome's enemies in the eastern Mediterranean, and even requested a Roman embassy to lay complaints against him before the council of Carthage—a sure sign of amicable relations with Rome. Hannibal fled to Tyre, and thence to Ephesus, the capital of Antiochus III.

He was coldly received and—against his advice—Antiochus, involving himself in the complex chessboard of Greco-Roman politics, answered the appeal of the Aetolians of Asia Minor and declared war against Rome. Hannibal led Antiochus's fleet and was defeated in 190 B.C. The king's military forces were destroyed in the same year at the battle of Magnesia. Rome took a deeper foothold in the Near East, and demanded Hannibal's extradition. He fled once more, this time to the court of Prusias, king of Bithynia, in North-west Asia Minor. Sensing that Prusias, who had enlisted him as a naval commander, would soon yield to Roman pressure, Hannibal took his life by poison.

His memory, and Roman dread of him, remained. Rome was so blinded by past memories that she did nothing when Carthage was invaded by Massinissa, the Numidian king, and Carthage had appealed for "permission to resist". Rome forced on a weakened Carthage the Third Punic War (149-146 B.C.), which ended in the Punic capital being razed to the ground, the survivors sold as slaves, and its site cursed solemnly into eternal desolation. Thus was fulfilled the refrain of the proverbially "honest" Cato who had concluded every speech with the words, "Carthage must be destroyed" (*delenda est Carthago*). The same year, 146 B.C., witnessed the Roman power "settle" the Greek question by razing Corinth to the ground, and selling the Corinthians as slaves. So the excuse—given by G. K. Chesterton and similar apologists—that Carthage had to be destroyed because of its primitive religion which at times included human sacrifice, is seen to be hollow.

Nor could the Rome of crucifixions and, soon, of gladiatorial massacres boast of humaneness. In any case Hannibal stands above such disputes. The calumnies of later Roman historians have been mostly disproved, and there is nothing to show—for instance—that Hannibal transgressed the usages of antique war. Still, the strength of the anti-Hannibal tradition indicates his magnetism. His long career, with its strange interludes of waiting and even of peace, his single-minded patriotism and ultimate series of defeats, mark him as a doomed, lonely figure. Of Hannibal's intensity, significance and tragic influence there can be no doubt.

JULIUS CAESAR

(102–44 B.C.)

THE GREATEST man in the Roman world—yes, there's no doubt that Julius Caesar was *that*. Some historians, and among them those of international authority, have made much greater claims for him. He was the greatest man not only of the Roman world but of antiquity; nay more, looking through the long lists of rulers, kings and emperors and the rest, they have failed to find an equal of this man who refused the style of king but whose name—Caesar—has become the synonym for commanding majesty and power. Great as a general, great as a politician, great as a far-seeing statesman, great as an orator, great as an historian and man of letters—Julius Caesar does indeed, as Shakespeare makes Cassius so grudgingly avow, "bestride the narrow world like a colossus. . . ."

Born in 102 B.C., or it may have been two or three years later, Gaius Julius Caesar, to give him his full name, was of the most ancient and aristocratic lineage. Although he himself, rationalist as he was, must have smiled sometimes at the conceit, there were some who said that he was not only of royal but divine descent, since Venus, the goddess of Love, had married a Trojan prince and so become the mother of the legendary founder of the Julian house. All the same, circumstances and perhaps personal inclinations attached him to the comparatively democratic "Popular" party. His aunt had married Marius, the leader of the *Populares*, and he himself was married as a youth of seventeen to the daughter of Cinna, another leader of the faction that was opposed to the aristocratic party under Sulla, Marius's great rival. A year or two later, when Sulla had become supreme in the state, the young man was ordered to put away his wife. He refused, and his life was saved only through the intercession of powerful friends in Rome. "You fools," Sulla is reported to have told those who pleaded for Caesar, "you little know what you are asking. That young fellow will prove much more dangerous than any number of Mariuses."

But though he had been reprieved, Caesar was far from safe, and for a time he skulked in the mountains until he managed to get across the sea to Asia Minor, where he served in the Roman army that was campaigning against Mithridates, the king of Pontus. At the siege of Mitylene in 80 B.C. he first distinguished himself as a soldier when he saved the life of a hard-pressed comrade. On the death of Sulla two years later, he hurried back to Rome, but for the while he kept himself aloof from the dangerous game of politics and made a career for himself at the bar. His political leanings were shown clearly enough, however, when he ventured to act as prosecutor of one of Sulla's principal lieutenants, who was charged with gross extortion and cruelty when he was governor of the Macedonian province.

To improve himself in rhetoric, Caesar went to Rhodes to take a course of lessons under a celebrated master of that art, and it was probably at about this time that he had his famous encounter with Mediterranean pirates. These ruffians captured the ship in which he was a passenger, and put him to ransom. While his messenger was away collecting the money, Caesar made himself quite at home with his captors. He told them amusing stories, joked with them, joined in their exercises, and, always in the highest good humour, told them what he would do with them when he got the chance. They laughed and joined in the fun. But Caesar was as good as his word. As soon as his ransom had been paid over and he had regained his liberty, he went to Miletus, hired some warships, and made straight back to the pirates' stronghold. He took the place by storm, captured the pirates, and ordered them to be crucified as he had assured them that he would. He also got back the money that had been paid as his ransom. . . .

Still on the fringe of the political arena, Caesar spent the next few years as a gay young man-about-town. His family were not rich, but there were plenty of moneylenders who were glad to accommodate him. He spent money like water, on expensive pleasures—women particularly, since he was as fascinating to them as they were to him—and on building up a body of popular support for the time when he might need it. Then in 68 B.C. he got his first official appointment under the Government, as a *quaestor*, which secured him a seat in the Senate, and in 63 B.C. he was appointed *Pontifex maximus*, a position of great dignity and importance in the religious establishment of the Roman state.

He was on the way up, and his rise was furthered by his successful administration of a province in Spain. So capable did he prove that in 60 B.C. he was chosen by Pompey, the famous general who was then the virtual head of Rome, to form with him and Crassus what is called the 1st Triumvirate. To strengthen the union between himself and Pompey, Caesar gave Pompey his daughter Julia in marriage. Then after a year as Consul, Caesar applied for, and was granted, the proconsulship of Gaul and Illyricum, the Roman dominion that extended from what is now the south of France to the Adriatic. His enemies—and he had plenty—were glad to see him leave Rome, and they no doubt thought that Gaul would prove the grave of his reputation. After all, he had up to now shown no special military gifts. But Caesar knew what he was doing. He realized that the path to power in the Roman State lay through military victory, and he believed, as firmly as he believed in anything, in his "star".

Nor was he wrong. In a series of campaigns he extended the Roman dominion to the Atlantic and what a thousand years later was to be known as the English Channel. Year after year his dispatches to the Government in Rome told of ever larger conquests, of ever greater victories. Sometimes he suffered a reverse, but not often; and when he did, he was relentless in his determination to win the last and decisive battle. His soldiers idolized him, even while they feared him. He demanded great things from them, and saw that he got what he demanded; but he showed them how to do it. He was no behind-the-lines general, ordering his men into the breach while he looked on from a distance. He was always up there, in the front line or very near it. He would march beside his legionaries on foot, and out-tire the best of them. He set the pace for his cavalry. He would seize a spade and give a hand in digging in. He ate the same food as his men did, he drank the same sour wine, he refused to sleep in a tent when his men were out in the cold and wet. He was never a specially strong man, physically: he seems to have been subject to epileptic seizures—but when campaigning he seemed as hard as nails. And of course he was brave. Many and many a time when his men were hard-pressed by the hosts of Gauls they were vastly cheered by the sight of their general hurrying up to their assistance, brandishing his weapons and shouting words of encouragement. "Cowards die many times before their deaths," are among the words that Shakespeare puts into his mouth; "the valiant taste of death but once".

If we would read the history of those years of almost constant campaigning, from 58 to 49 B.C., where better than in those *Commentaries* ("memoirs") of Caesar's own writing, that are among the masterpieces of Latin literature? Of particular interest to us are the chapters describing his two invasions of Britain. The first was in 55 B.C., when the Roman expeditionary force sailed from Boulogne and the men got ashore on the coast at Deal. This first "invasion" was nothing more than a reconnaissance, and after three weeks Caesar went back across the Channel. But in the summer of the next year he returned, and this time he penetrated as far as the valley of the Thames in Middlesex. After considerable fighting, the Britons under Cassivellaunus sued for terms, gave hostages and agreed to pay tribute. Whereupon Caesar sailed back to Gaul, where there was always a risk that the recently subdued natives might make a fresh bid for their independence.

In fact, they did rebel, and for several years Caesar found a worthy match in the young Vercingetorix. Once he was defeated, and the Roman position in Gaul was threatened as it had never been before. But Caesar managed to unite his forces, and at Alesia in 52 B.C. crushed the Gaulish armies and obtained Vercingetorix's surrender. This was the end of resistance to Roman rule: henceforth Gaul was a great and increasingly prosperous province of the Roman realm.

Caesar's victory was opportune, for affairs at Rome demanded his attention. The Triumvirate was on the verge of dissolution. Pompey was estranged, and Crassus had gone off to the east, where he met disaster and death in battle with the Parthians. Caesar's term of office in Gaul was nearing its end, and already his enemies in Rome were talking of what they would do to him when he had returned to civil life. They complained of his having overstepped his authority, of having embarked on grandiose schemes of conquest, of cruelties inflicted on poor inoffensive barbarians. . . .

All these things were reported to Caesar in his camp, and, being the man he was, it is not surprising that he resolved to get in the first blow. Although he had only one legion under his immediate command, and Pompey had been boasting that *he* had only to stamp on the ground and legions would rise up to do his bidding, he resolved to march on Rome. Early in January, 49 B.C., he took the decisive step of crossing the Rubicon, the little river that was the boundary of his command. As he watched his men plunging into the stream he walked up and down the bank, and some who were near said that he muttered the words *"Jacta alea est"*, "the die is cast".

Whether he spoke the words or not, the die *was* cast; and in open defiance of Pompey's government, Caesar marched with all speed on the capital. Pompey's support disintegrated, and he was forced to flee overseas. Ceasar entered Rome in triumph.

Almost without a blow Caesar had become master of Rome, and he was forthwith granted dictatorial powers. But Pompey and his friends rallied, and for the next five years Caesar was chiefly engaged in defeating, first, Pompey at Pharsalia in Greece, soon after which

Pompey was murdered in Egypt; next, Pompey's sons in Spain; and then the army of those Roman leaders who constituted what was known as the "senatorial party", i.e., those who clung to the old, time-honoured system of republican rule through the Senate.

A strange interlude in this torrent of campaigning is the time spent by Caesar in Egypt, when he had an affair with the beautiful young Queen Cleopatra, who bore him a son. After this he proceeded to Asia Minor, where Pharnaces, the son and murderer of King Mithridates, was causing trouble. Caesar made short work of *him*. In his message to the Senate he reported: *"Veni, vidi, vici"*: "I came, I saw, I conquered".

At length he returned to Rome, and was accorded yet another "triumph"—he had had four already. Vast crowds acclaimed him as he passed in his chariot through the streets on his way to the Capitol. Great hopes were centred upon him, great things were expected of him. The old system of government had broken down: a new system must soon come to birth—but what? We shall never know what vast schemes were fermenting in the brain of the man who was now hailed as *Imperator*, the first of the "emperors" to walk the stage of history, but we may perhaps get some idea of them from what he managed to accomplish in the all too short period that was left to him.

He reformed the calendar, in a way which has endured in its essentials to our own time. He planned the codification of the Roman law. He urged the establishment of public libraries. He reduced the rate of interest charged by money-lenders, and strove to lessen the burdens of taxation on the mass of ordinary citizens. He set up *municipia* in the towns, the forerunners of our local authorities. He dissolved the "clubs" by means of which the political gangsters in Rome had made a mockery of democratic forms. He cut down the issue of free corn to the lazy proletarians of the capital. He planted colonies of his veteran ex-servicemen throughout the land. He had plans drawn up for enriching Rome and the other great cities with splendid buildings, and he ordered a complete geographical survey of the immense region that had been brought within the realm of Rome. He proposed to drain the Pontine marshes, to give Ostia a bigger and better harbour, to dig a canal through the isthmus of Corinth.

These are only some of the schemes that were hatched within his teeming brain, and some of what he not only proposed but actually accomplished. But there was so much more that he wanted to do—if he had time! He was at the top of his form as an administrator,

as a captain, as a statesman of outstanding grasp and capacity. And
he enjoyed his position, no doubt about it. There was a marked
streak of vanity in his make-up. He sanctioned the re-naming of one
of the Roman months after him—the month that ever since has been
July, and approved the issue of coins bearing his engraved portrait,
a distinction granted to none before him. He was glad when they
authorized him to wear the splendidly embroidered robe and laurel
wreath that were the insignia of great and successful generals—
especially perhaps the laurel wreath, since this would serve to
disguise the baldness of which he was so painfully conscious. And
then there was the occasion when his chief lieutenant Mark Antony
offered him the crown—was he altogether sincere when he turned
it down, or would he have liked to have been pressed a little harder
to accept it? The greatest of men have their little infirmities of
mind. . . .

But now the last act of the tremendous drama was about to be
played. The "old order" had still plenty of supporters, and though
some of these were politicians on the make, others were high-minded
patriots who dreamed of a restoration of the ancient ways of
government. There were men like Cassius who resented their
"petty" condition. Now they joined together in an attempt to bring
him down, and foremost among the conspirators was a young man
named Brutus who had fought against Caesar and had been pardoned by him and admitted to high office. More than fifty persons
were in the plot, and news of it leaked out. Many people warned
Caesar of what was afoot, but he took no notice: he believed still
in his "star". The day appointed for the murder was the Ides of
March (15 March, 44 B.C.), and the night before Caesar's wife had a
fearful dream and on waking she urged him not to attend the meeting
of the Senate called for that day. Caesar hesitated, but there was
important business on the agenda, and he set out for the council-
chamber. On his way through the crowded streets several tried to
attract his attention with warning messages; a Greek philosopher
thrust into his hand a paper giving the names of the conspirators—
Caesar took it, glanced at it, and he was still holding it in his hand
when he took his seat in the chamber.

Then Brutus and his confederates drew near, and one of them
presented a petition for the great man's consideration. Others did
the same. Caesar put them on one side, whereupon one of the men
gave a pull at his robe. This was the pre-arranged signal, and they all
made a rush at him with their daggers.

For the most part they were young men and vigorous, and he was middle-aged and grown heavy and less active than in the days when he had soldiered with his men in Gaul. But he put up a good fight. He struggled, unarmed though he was, tried to push them away, and then struck at them with his metal stilus or pen. Then he saw Brutus was among his assailants. "What, you too, Brutus?" he said, and covering his body with his robe so that he should fall decently, suffered himself to be overborne. He fell, with twenty-three wounds in his body, at the foot of the statue of his great rival Pompey, which, with characteristic magnanimity, he had allowed to be re-erected in the Capitol.

Such was their mad fury, some of the murderers had wounded one another in their bloody work. Now they rushed from the scene, exultingly shouting that the Tyrant was no more! They called upon the people who were there to rejoice with them; but the people hung their heads, or muttered a prayer, or fled.

So Caesar died: "the noblest man", to quote from Shakespeare's immortal lines again, "that ever lived in the tide of times".

CLEOPATRA

(69–30 B.C.)

*"Age cannot wither her, nor custom stale
Her infinite variety."*

SUCH IS the tribute of Shakespeare in his *Antony and Cleopatra*, and it echoes the fame of centuries. More cynically precise, Pascal remarked that, had Cleopatra's nose been a little different, the history of the world would have been changed. To posterity the last queen of Egypt has indeed stood as a type of glamorous feminine beauty, luxurious in exotic cunning and colourful decadence.

Yet such a judgment does Cleopatra a real injustice. History, sparse in female rulers, has seen few to match her in political astuteness; for some thirty years she played—from her own standpoint—a wise game on the chessboard of Mediterranean politics, competing, amongst others, with the greatest statesmen and generals of Rome. That she should have made two of these—Julius Caesar and Mark Antony—her lovers shows in itself a firm political grasp, though naturally the personal element was not lacking. This is true particularly of her relationship with Antony.

Other queens and empresses have ruled, but few have surpassed Cleopatra; her end, which marked the end also of centuries of Egyptian tradition, and was due both to the childish quarrels among Roman leaders and to her meddling in their strife, was tragic. And we should think of her in tragic, or at least serious, terms, rather than frivolous.

Of course this is not to deny her personal attractiveness, of which she made conscious use as a diplomatic and political weapon. On one point the traditional attitude seems in error: Cleopatra was not specially "beautiful", as we can judge from the coins that have survived. She was rather the bewitching type, an enchantress in voice, movement, manners, mood and conversation; and it is certain that she was well educated, not only in the Egyptian tradition but still more in the Hellenistic art and thought around her. She befriended and subsidized the astronomers of her country, and lent one of them to Julius Caesar to assist in forming the new

Julian Calendar (which remained in use for many a century). Some intellectual quality must have added to her attraction for men; indeed, if she was inferior in this respect to Caesar, she was surely the cultural superior of Mark Antony.

Who, then, was Cleopatra, and how did she emerge on the turbulent international scene? One of the few queens in Egypt's history, and the only one in her own Ptolemaic dynasty, she was without Egyptian blood. A Macedonian Greek, she was descended from the first Ptolemy (Soter, "Saviour"), one of Alexander the Great's generals, who, on Alexander's death in 323 B.C. took charge of the province of Egypt. Themselves Greek in race and custom, the Ptolemies (especially the first two kings) took care to understand and respect Egypt and her traditions. They upheld the native religion and patronized the priesthood; they adopted many Egyptian customs, such as marriage between royal brother and sister; they sought the welfare of their land and brought it peace. While Egypt as a whole remained Egyptian, Alexandria and some other cities nourished a truly cosmopolitan life and culture, to which Greeks, Egyptians, Jews, Phoenicians, and many more, contributed. Alexandria's lighthouse was one of the Seven Wonders of the World, and its library unique.

To such a land, probably the most prosperous of its time, the growing might of Rome looked enviously; while Egypt in turn felt both the value of Roman friendship and an envy of Roman conquests in the Near East. Cleopatra symbolized both these tendencies: to the Romans, the magic and wealth of age-old Egypt, and, in herself, an ambivalent admiration and fear of Rome. She was born in 69 B.C.; curiously enough, the name of her mother is unknown. Cleopatra itself was a fairly common name (an instance is Cleopatra of Jerusalem, one of Herod the Great's wives). Her father was Ptolemy Auletes ("the flute-blower"); in 59 B.C., when Cleopatra was ten years old, he had been expelled by his own subjects, and had come to Rome to seek aid in his conflicts with relatives who had denied him the throne.

The triumvirate then governing Rome (Caesar, Crassus and Pompey) had long coveted Egyptian resources, and Caesar and Crassus proposed open annexation; Ptolemy's request played into Roman hands, with every influential senator intriguing for favour. Ptolemy found himself forced to pay over vast sums (to Caesar alone, 6,000 talents), underwriting huge loans from Roman bankers, who came in effect to control Egypt. Egypt accepted the suzerainty of Rome, to mark which, and to protect both Ptolemy and the usurious interest on the loan, a Roman garrison was stationed on her soil. Ptolemy also had to hand over Cyprus to the Romans.

The restored Ptolemy soon died, leaving his kingdom to his sixteen-year-old daughter Cleopatra and her ten-year-old brother Ptolemy (officially also her husband). But a faction favouring Ptolemy drove her out, and Egypt was governed by his guardian, the eunuch Pothinus, the rhetorician Theodotus, and the military leader Achillas. When Pompey and Caesar quarrelled and Pompey lost the battle of Pharsalia (48 B.C.), he fled to Egypt where Achillas feared that the Roman garrison might go over to him, their old commander. Caesar pursued him with 4,000 men and acted as conqueror.

Cleopatra now manoeuvred herself into the palace, by the ruse of being concealed in a mattress, and the notoriously sensual Caesar yielded to her bewitchment. But Caesar's bland assumption of power affronted both the Ptolemy party and the mass of the people, who, together with Achillas's army (which could be called both Egyptian and Roman), blockaded the palace, cutting off Caesar's communications with the island of Pharos and the sea. Five months of war ensued, with changes of luck on both sides. Caesar at one point had to swim for his life from a sinking ship, holding his notebook above water in his left hand. He also had the Egyptian fleet set alight; the famous library caught fire; and Caesar's men captured the lighthouse while the Egyptians were busy putting out the flames. Eventually, with the help of Mithridates of Pergamus, Caesar was victorious; the boy Ptolemy, trying to escape, was drowned, and Caesar set up Cleopatra and a still younger brother (also a Ptolemy) on the throne. At the same time Caesar married Cleopatra, affecting the religious beliefs which in Egypt linked kingship with divinity. Cleopatra bore him a son, Caesarion, her only child.

Meanwhile there was trouble elsewhere in the empire; and Caesar had just been named Dictator for the second time, and had appointed as Master of the Horse the young, ardent, magnetic Mark Antony. Clearly Caesar's presence at Rome was essential. Why did he delay another four months in Egypt? To consolidate his victory over Egypt, or over its queen? Mainly the latter, for Caesar was an enormously complex character, a fact which in itself must have charmed Cleopatra. His magnetism, his intellect both theoretical and practical, his strange "clemency" and lack of malice (well demonstrated in Bernard Shaw's *Caesar and Cleopatra*), his experience in many fields—all these surely made him a fascinating companion and influenced Cleopatra. We do him an injustice if we think of Caesar purely as an austere statesman and general: on the contrary, he was also incorrigibly sensual, and was notorious in youth for his amours.

With Cleopatra he journeyed down the Nile to Egypt's southernmost frontiers. Then he returned to his "business" elsewhere. But within two years he had invited her, with Caesarion, to Rome, seeking to make her his Roman consort. This, the pride of the Romans, still European and insular in some respects, could hardly stomach. On the model of the Pharaohs, he erected a shrine in the name of Jupiter Julius, with his own statues, and dedicated to Cleopatra, "Queen and Goddess", a temple of Venus Genetrix, the Goddess-Mother. It seemed that, in Egyptian style, he would become a God-King. Such activities increased Roman distrust and Cleopatra went home. Then, in 44 B.C., despite his many excellent reforms, Caesar was assassinated on the Ides of March. This caused an upheaval. For the moment, Rome had avoided a monarchy which would have made her interests subordinate to those of the ever-growing empire. Caesar's death led to civil war and indeed to the triumph of the monarchical principle in the person of Octavian, Caesar's great-nephew and adoptive heir. Mark Antony and Lepidus moved that Caesar's acts be recognized as law and a general amnesty granted.

Antony's arrogance and irresponsibility later provoked much hostility and he narrowly prevented some of his legions deserting to Octavian. Eventually these two forces came to blows and Antony was defeated near Mutina (43 B.C.). He escaped into Gaul, and in this venture showed his best qualities, sharing hardships with the ordinary soldiers. It was not for two more years that Cleopatra was to meet Antony in state and then in love. True, as a girl she had met him fourteen years earlier in Alexandria, and even then Antony's soul had taken fire.

Octavian sought reconciliation with Antony and Lepidus, and near Bologna the three agreed on a five years' triple authority—the "Second Triumvirate"—Antony's sphere of government being the two Gauls (France and Northern Italy), with the exception of the district round Narbonne. The three now embarked on a horrifying series of proscriptions and executions. Meanwhile Caesar's assassins, Brutus and Cassius, had manoeuvred and held the whole of the Eastern Empire. The Triumvirs made war against them, and in the two battles of Philippi were completely victorious (42 B.C.). The spoils were now re-divided: to Antony was allotted the Eastern world, to Octavian the Western, while Lepidus was given Africa.

Antony sped into Greece, there to extract cash from the miserable people of Western Asia. Establishing himself at Tarsus (later St. Paul's birthplace) in midsummer 41 B.C., he received the most momentous visit of his life. The next eleven years were his last, as they were to be Cleopatra's also, and their two lives became mingled as fire with fire. Now began one of the most famous love affairs in history. But our judgment of Cleopatra is partial if we ignore her political astuteness even in such a context.

She dreamt of expansion to the East—Syria, for instance—and she had somehow either to oppose, or to blend with, Roman expansionism. To achieve this, she needed to break the autarchy menacing her in Egypt itself: monopolies of the Royal Bank, of salt and oil, perpetual leases on state lands and so forth. All these she abolished, restoring freedom of trade and the money market. To create the necessary sound currency she reformed the finances of the Temples to the benefit of the state. This reform implied an increased military strength: surely her charms could win this from Antony!

This hard-headed voluptuary sailed up the River Cydnus to be greeted by Antony: attired as Venus, encircled by Cupids and Graces, and resplendent in a barge whose poop was burnished with gold, whose sails were purple and whose silver oars moved to the sound of music. Antony followed her to Alexandria, thus fulfilling both the erotic impulse and his yearning for the gorgeous East. Cleopatra could answer every trait in her lover's nature with superior cunning and finesse. Only his directness, his blend of nobility and coarseness which gained him the devotion of his soldiers, lay outside her competition. It was her sport to deceive Antony: her final ruse, the report of her suicide, led Antony to kill himself.

For two years they enjoyed every luxury life could afford. But Fulvia Antony's fourth wife, herself twice a widow and implacably ambitious, incited Antony's brother to make war on Octavian, furious as she was at being deserted for Cleopatra. At last Antony broke through his lethargy and left for Athens. Fulvia's death soon facilitated a reconciliation between Antony and Octavian, who gave Antony his sister Octavia in marriage. But quarrels reappeared, and after three years Antony returned to Cleopatra.

Cleopatra's influence was now complete. Antony handed her slabs of Roman territory, unfortunately including Jericho, the property of King Herod of Judaea, Antony's friend. Taking advantage of Antony's absence in Parthia, Cleopatra visited Herod, sold him back Jericho with its rich balsam-groves, and sought to seduce him. The brilliant, if cruel, Herod replied with mere courtesy. This insult she never forgave. With Mariamne, Herod's discontented wife, she kept up a correspondence of intrigue and sympathy. At one point she offered Mariamne and her mother refuge in Alexandria, but Herod foiled their plans.

Thus neither Cleopatra nor Antony shone in fidelity. Yet they complemented each other in their diversities and similarities. The latter included sudden rage, a streak of unbalance, "kingliness" and a taste for extreme luxury. If this trifling disgusted Octavian and other Romans, their anger grew into alarm when Antony celebrated a Roman-style triumph in Alexandria, when he aped the god Dionysus and adopted Greek habits, and when he posed as the god Osiris with Cleopatra as Isis, and her head appeared with his on coins. Antony's will leaked out; in it he had directed that he be buried in Cleopatra's mausoleum and that their children succeed to the Egyptian throne.

The climax came in 32 B.C., when Octavian declared war against Cleopatra—really against Antony. Antony then divorced Octavia and married Cleopatra, his sixth wife. Now Cleopatra made a fatal move: though as a woman unused to the reality of war, she still insisted on accompanying her fleet to Actium near Corinth, where Antony and Octavian faced a crucial battle. Before the decisive moment, she escaped with her fleet; and Antony followed suit, fleeing from Octavian into his wife's arms. Enraged at his desertion, his forces went over to Octavian, who soon, as Caesar Augustus, became emperor.

Shakespeare describes how Cleopatra's arts still overcame Antony's fury. For eleven months Octavian left them in nervous peace, which Cleopatra filled with abortive schemes like a flight east of Suez, where Rome's name was unknown. She then started secret negotiations with Octavian, trusting in her charms; Octavian's replies seemed encouraging and Antony locked himself up.

Eventually Octavian landed in Egypt; Antony marched against him, but retired when his fleet deserted him. Dreading his wrath, Cleopatra shut herself up in her mausoleum, and caused Antony to be told the news of her "suicide". He stabbed himself, and when almost dead learned of her last deceit; carried to her place of retreat, he begged to give her "of many thousand kisses the poor last". Heaved up by cords through the window, he was united with her shortly before his death.

Then Cleopatra consented to see Octavian; her intuition (and the words of the Roman envoy) told her that she had nothing to hope for from the emperor, whose courtesy was merely a scheme to bring her to Rome to grace his triumph. She had long been experimenting with poisons and means of death, and the bites of aspic-snakes soon soothed her, as well as her attendants, Charmian and Iras, into oblivion. There:

> ... she looks like sleep,
> As she would catch another Antony
> In her strong toil of grace.

Egypt's last queen has fascinated the ages. Of the numerous dramatic works based on her story may be mentioned Shakespeare's magnificent *Antony and Cleopatra*, Dryden's *All for Love* and, nearer our own time, the witty *Caesar and Cleopatra* of Bernard Shaw.

AUGUSTUS CAESAR

(63 B.C.–A.D. 14)

SOME MEN are born great, some achieve greatness and some have greatness thrust upon them. Gaius Octavius, generally known by the title bestowed on him by the Roman Senate in 27 B.C. of Augustus, is undoubtedly one of the men who achieved greatness. He was the founder of the Roman Empire. This empire was to last, at its fullest extent and with what is called the Roman Peace virtually unchallenged throughout the known world, for well over two hundred years.

During the reigns of Hadrian which began in A.D. 117 and of the two Antonine emperors who followed Hadrian, the empire was to know its most humanly civilized period. Even before the death of Marcus Aurelius in A.D. 180 the barbarians were beginning to cause alarm on the frontiers, and the third century was to be a time of decline and disorder; but at the beginning of the fourth century a new lease of life was brought temporarily by Diocletian and Constantine, the latter of whom founded the Eastern or Greek Empire. Rome as the Imperial City of the West was to disappear in the fifth century but was to leave behind a memory and an institution, the Holy Roman Empire, which was to haunt the minds of Europeans from Charlemagne to Napoleon.

The genius of Augustus moulded the Roman Empire. It was he who fixed its limits, who forebade, for instance, the Roman commanders of the legions to penetrate into the great oak forests and marshes of Germany. It was he who created its constitution— giving the emperor (Augustus never used the title himself) all ultimate power but preserving the old forms and some of the old powers of the Roman Republic. It was Augustus who made the system of administration which worked so well in Asia Minor, North Africa, Iberia, Gaul and Britain. Augustus Caesar was a patron of the arts on a grand and discerning scale and what is called the Augustan Age saw the genius flower of Vergil and Horace and of the great historians such as Livy. When, during the first two centuries of our era, men realized that they were living in peace and in a world unified by a single civilization which built roads and collected taxes from Asia Minor to the Atlantic, they recognized the work of Augustus.

The man of these great achievements lacked the lustre of many other great men. He was neither bold nor generous; he was not a great warrior and in his fight for power he won by duplicity and trickery and by making the right decisions cautiously. He was to a supreme degree a politic man, never unnecessarily making enemies, but ruthless when it paid to be. He was a cold fish in fact and as such he appears in Shakespeare's two great dramas *Julius Caesar* and *Antony and Cleopatra*. But in addition to his political gifts which are, in human terms, not altogether admirable, he had the ability to make friends, choosing them wisely and sticking to them. A slightly unfavourable view that one could have of him during his period of struggle is redeemed, in his later age, by his devotion to and ability for public affairs.

Physically he was not an imposing man, being about five-foot-seven in height and always negligent of his personal appearance. He did not enjoy good health, suffered from bladder trouble, and could not bear the cold; in winter he wore no less than four tunics with a heavy woollen gown, and beneath them a woollen chest-protector, underpants and woollen garters. He was inclined to doze a great deal in the day and not only when he was old. Sensual but not exaggeratedly so, he was frugal in eating and drinking. He entertained often but carefully and, when necessary, magnificently. Suetonius, the Roman historian who lived in the age of Hadrian but had many contacts with people who had known Augustus, described him, in spite of his physical deficiencies, as "remarkably handsome and of a very graceful gait even as an old man". His picture of Augustus in his old age is as follows:

"He always wore so serene an expression whether talking or in repose that a Gallic chief once confessed to his compatriots: 'When granted an audience with the Emperor during his passage across the Alps, I would have carried out my plan of hurling him over a cliff had not the sight of that tranquil face softened my heart; so I desisted.' Augustus's eyes were clear and bright and he liked to believe that they shone with a sort of divine radiance: it gave him profound pleasure if anyone at whom he glanced keenly dropped his head as though dazzled by looking into the sun. In old age however his left eye had only partial vision. His teeth were small, few and decayed; his hair yellowish and rather curly; his eyebrows met above his nose; he had ears of a normal size, a Roman nose and a complexion intermediate between dark and fair."

Gaius Octavius was born in 63 B.C. when the Roman Republic was the Great State of the civilized world, though torn with dissensions between rival generals and strife between the Patricians and the Plebs. When Alexander the Great's empire had broken up, the Romans had conquered all Italy rather slowly, from Naples to the north of the peninsula, and built a chain of forts guarding against the warlike Gauls who, in 390 B.C., had beseiged Rome itself. By 146 B.C., Rome, after three savage wars, had destroyed Carthage, the seat of the powerful Semitic commercial empire, selling the inhabitants into slavery and ploughing the blackened ruins of the great city into the soil. Rome had also conquered the Greek cities in the south of the Italian peninsula, Sicily, Iberia and most of Asia Minor. In 65 B.C. the Romans took Jerusalem. In 89 B.C. all free-born Italians were automatically Roman citizens, for, unlike the Greek City states, Rome knew how to assimilate, and this was indeed the essential part of her genius.

The Roman Republic during this period of immense expansion which followed the victory over Carthage was very different from the unified and disciplined aristocratic State which had waged its early wars against the Etruscans and Gauls. Strife between the Senate and the rest of the Roman Plebs, led often by discontented aristocrats, was continuous. It was made inevitable perhaps by the constitution of the Roman Republic which, out of fear of the ancient monarchy which was abolished in the sixth century B.C., split the powers of government between two Consuls, elected annually, and a number of other elected officers.

The aristocratic Republic could not keep peace in its own city at times, though its armies held down the conquered provinces most efficiently. In Augustus's childhood, spent in the country at Velitri where his family came from, two very great military commanders, Pompey the leader of the conservative party, and Julius Caesar, were fighting for supreme power. Julius Caesar had conquered Rome's last and greatest prize, Gaul, defeated Pompey, stamped out all resistance to his power in Africa and Spain and in 45 B.C. had returned to Rome, bringing to the task of re-organizing the government a mind at once supple, imaginative and experienced. He was inclined towards social reform, towards admitting greater representation of the people, a programme which inspired the Gracchi in the old days. With his popularity and his military reputation Caesar could have done anything. But he could not preserve his life and, on the Ides of March in 44 B.C., he was assassinated, falling under the daggers of Brutus and Cassius and a circle of determined defenders of the old order.

Augustus's father's family did not belong to the Patrician Order, although his father, Gaius Octavianus, had been admitted to Senatorial dignity. But, through his mother, the young Octavius was a nephew of Julius Caesar. The great man liked his nephew, used him in the wars and in his will made him his heir, adopting him into the Julian family. Thus after the Roman usage Gaius Octavius became Gaius Julius Caesar Octavius. Augustus was then nineteen. He was immensely rich and he was on the threshold, with some rivals, of supreme power; young as he was, he was determined to stake his chance. Brutus and the party which had opposed Julius Caesar retired from Rome. The young Augustus made himself the leader of the conservatives who hated Mark Antony, the brilliant lieutenant of Julius Caesar who was out and out for the people. There was a period of uneasy peace and then of war between the two avengers of Julius Caesar. However, when many military commanders, including Lepidus, declared themselves for Mark Antony against the conservatives, Augustus decided to desert the conservative faction and join his two rivals. As a member of the Triumvirate Augustus led an army into Asia Minor and defeated Brutus and Cassius at the Battle of Philippi. The empire was then divided between Mark Antony and Augustus, with Lepidus, already shown up as a man of no account, being given Africa until such time as his partners were able to oust him. Augustus chose as his share, Italy, and the poorer provinces of Gaul and Iberia, leaving to Mark Antony the rich lands of the East. Augustus had a lot of fighting to do in mastering his share of the world and he suppressed a revolt in northern Italy led by a brother of Mark Antony with a severity uncommon even in those days. He had to fight intermittently in Italy for eight years.

Mark Antony fell under the sway of Cleopatra, the Queen of Egypt, who had been once a mistress of Julius Caesar. For her he abandoned if not ambition at least the hard work which ambition needs. He still did not take his young partner Octavius very seriously and he repudiated Octavius's sister whom he had married as part of the pact between them. To a letter of reproof from Augustus Mark Antony wrote:

"What has come over you? Do you object to my sleeping with Cleopatra? But we are married; it is not even as though this is anything new—the affair started nine years ago. And what about you? Are you faithful to Livia Drusilla? My congratulations if, when this letter arrives, you have not been in bed with Tertullia or Terentilla or Rufilla or Salvia Titisenia—or all of them. Does it really matter so much where or with whom you perform the sexual act?"

War broke out finally between Rome and Egypt and at Actium in 31 B.C. Augustus's fleet defeated that of Antony and Cleopatra. After this battle Antony sued for peace, but Augustus ordered him to commit suicide and satisfied himself that he had obeyed by inspecting the corpse. Augustus was anxious to save Cleopatra as an ornament for his triumph and he actually summoned snake charmers to suck the poison from her self-inflicted wound, supposedly the bite of an asp. Though he allowed the lovers an honourable burial in the same tomb, Augustus put to death Caesarion, the son of Cleopatra and Julius Caesar, as well as Mark Antony's son by his own sister Fulvia. But for some reason or other he spared Mark Antony's children by Cleopatra and brought them up as his own.

The age of Augustus begins after the great battle of Actium. The empire was founded in 27 B.C. when the Senate with the agreement of the Roman people conferred on Augustus the title of Princeps (Prince of the Senate) and Father of his country. Augustus never used the title of Emperor and only, towards the end of his life, allowed altars to be erected to him as a God because he thought it helped to maintain order. He could not, as it were, escape the divine honours which were thrust on him. Retaining under his command the Legions—which were, of course, the source of real power—Augustus carefully preserved the established form of Republican government. From time to time he stood for, and was of course elected, Consul; he attended the Senate's proceedings and like anyone else asked permission to speak or give evidence in a law case; he voted in elections like an ordinary man of the people. The gratitude of the Senate towards a military leader who might have abolished their privileges was founded on obligation. The Equestrian order representing the upper-middle-class, members of which represented the people, felt, in their turn, that Augustus was entirely their man. Huge sums of money were collected for Augustus on his birthdays by popular subscription. Already rich, Augustus often used this money for the beautification of Rome. He rebuilt the temples of the gods. Together with control of the army, he kept under his direct rule all the Roman provinces outside of Italy. He modernized the administration both of Italy and of the empire, introducing accounting systems and bureaucratic methods used long ago in Egypt. He chose all the governors and minor officials, excluding ignorant amateurs of noble houses or adventurers. Two of his friends were of great use to him: one was Maecenas, the rich man who was the patron of Horace and who found Augustus many servants and officials; the other, Marcus Agrippa, his companion in arms and

131

adviser on military and political matters who married Augustus's daughter Julia.

Augustus married three times. The first marriage was of short duration. From his second wife, Scribonia, whom he divorced because she nagged him, he had a daughter Julia. His third wife, Livia, the one woman he truly loved until his death, bore him no children. He adopted the two sons of Agrippa and Julia and had them constantly with him. But both died young and Augustus had to adopt his stepson, Tiberius, as his heir. Tiberius had a dark and vicious character and he lowered the tone of Roman high society when he was emperor. But he was to prove, nevertheless, an able successor so far as the administration of the empire was concerned.

Augustus fell ill during a journey in southern Italy and on the way back to Rome stayed at his father's house at Nola where he died, some say in the very room in which he was born, on 19 August, A.D. 14. His will contained the following clause: "my estate is not large, indeed my heirs will not receive more than one million five hundred thousand gold pieces; for although my friends have bequeathed me some fourteen million in the last twenty years, nearly the whole of this sum, besides what came to me from my father, from my adopted father and others has been used to buttress the national economy." On the day before he died he frequently inquired whether the news of his illness was disturbing people. Suetonius writes: "Augustus called for a mirror, and had his hair combed and his lower jaw, which had fallen from sickness, propped up. Presently he summoned a group of friends and asked—have I played my part in the farce of life creditably enough?—adding a verse used by actors at the end of a play:

If I have pleased you, kindly signify
Appreciation with a warm goodbye."

The work of this great man was not only successful in materially re-organizing Rome and its dominions. He undoubtedly aroused a new spirit in the Italians and in other Roman citizens of the past empire. This spirit was a religious devotion to the greatness of Rome. It was not imperial glory or military chauvinism that Vergil expresses in his many verses about the destiny of Rome; it is rather the sense that this city, its people and citizens carry out a mission of ensuring peace and order throughout the world. In some ways this was not very different perhaps from the imperialist feeling in Britain at the end of the reign of Queen Victoria. The Romans felt that they were assuming "the White Man's Burden". Historical comparisons, however, are usually misleading. The Roman Empire was fundamentally different from that of Britain in the nineteenth and early twentieth centuries. Rome's power was based on the assimilation of *élites* and of subject peoples. Rome succeeded in imposing a unified civilization on the world, something Britain never tried to do. Augustus's great achievement, and the one which ensured that his system of government would last in spite of unworthy successors, was that the vast mass of Roman citizens from Mesopotamia to the north of Britain felt that the central power of Rome had become, in the words of H. A. L. Fisher, "consistently helpful, benign and even paternal".

HEROD THE GREAT

(Reigned 40–4 B.C.)

TWENTY CENTURIES of Judaeo-Christian tradition have not unnaturally found in Herod the Great something of an enigma. If he is "great", what then is greatness? One may answer: personality, will-power, historical, political or military importance; the moral element in greatness would seem to be lacking. And indeed Herod was all too often guilty of crime and atrocity, taking advantage of his position to commit or command brutal acts. Yet even here it is possible to exaggerate, or rather to set the whole picture in an unbalanced light; and modern research has certainly revised some of the harsher episodes: for instance, the Massacre of the Innocents, as described by Matthew (Chapter 2) and by no other evangelist, is now regarded as probably false.

As for the other qualities of greatness, there is no doubt but that the founder of the Herodian dynasty (though it lasted for only 140 years) possessed them. At one of the turning-points of the history of the West and the Near East he stands as a leading figure, in close contact with other protagonists—among others, the Roman emperors, the soldier-statesman Antony, the gifted and intriguing Cleopatra, Egypt's queen—and with all the main currents of belief and culture, Jewish, Greek, Roman, Egyptian.

Nor were these contacts, though full of manoeuvres, mere intrigues for power; he genuinely fought, for example, to protect the Jews from Roman oppression, reviving their glories while moderating their dangerous nationalism. It is a measure of his personal astuteness that Jews, in his lifetime and later, regarded him in this light, though this Semitic king was no Jew but an Edomite and an Arab. Again, by his passion for Greek culture and institutions he incarnated the generous, tolerant spirit of that cosmopolitan age; similarly, as the moving spirit behind many splendid buildings and new towns, and as a promoter of trade, he deserved well of his contemporaries. Famous, too, were his personal handsomeness and glamour, derived possibly from his Arab mother; these he bequeathed to his children and grandchildren. Yet, for political reasons, he could withstand the wiles of the almost naked Cleopatra!

134

In all he did one finds great independence and sense of effect; still more closely can he be compared to an Italian prince of the Renaissance, with the same force of personality, greed for power, sensitive culture and patronage of art, as well as a baffling blend of splendour, refinement, crudity and brutality. Surely such a personality deserves close study.

The origins of Herod, and thus of his whole dynasty, were indeed peculiar. It would seem almost incredible that they should lead to the jealously-guarded throne of David. Many details are obscure, but we know that Herod on his father's side was an Idumaean or Edomite from the country between Egypt and Palestine, containing the coastal town of Askalon, once of Philistine fame, in which Herod's grandfather is said to have been a servant in the temple of Apollo-Melkarth. This blend of Greek and Phoenician religions is certainly a strange background for a future Jewish king. A further tradition asserts that Herod's father was kidnapped by Edomites.

In any case his father, Antipas or Antipater (a name that recurs with some confusion among his many descendants, notably King Herod Antipas), was an outstanding man. Born a temple-cleaning slave, he quickly rose to military and diplomatic activity. With a skill his son was later to show, he manoeuvred his own advancement when Pompey captured Jerusalem in 63 B.C. Pompey made short work of the internecine conflict between the last of the Maccabaeans, and appointed Hyrcanus II ruler, though in fact Antipas wielded the power. Judaea—whose variable territory usually extended from Acre in the north to Idumaea and Egypt in the south—was made a tributary state of Rome. Antipas seized his chance in 48 B.C. to combine loyalty with ambition by aiding Caesar in his conflict with Pompey in Egypt. After Caesar's victory at Pharsalus, he made Antipas Procurator of Palestine, a post comparable to that of a modern Viceroy.

Antipas gave his son Herod the governorship of Galilee. The assassination of Antipas two years later led to Caesar appointing Herod Tetrarch (regional governor) of Judaea. Already he had begun his career of building by founding, or enlarging and adorning, towns like his Galilean capital of Sepphoris, and by erecting fortresses like those at Jotapata in the north, and Masada.

Sepphoris, where Herod lived for so much of his life, merits a short description. Its Hebrew name is Tsipori, from *tsipor* (bird), as the town stands "perched like a bird on the top of a mountain". Herod filled it with beauty: villas, gardens, palaces, a Greek amphitheatre and hippodrome. He followed this Hellenizing style also in Jericho, Samaria (rebuilt), in Caesarea (which he founded), and even in Jerusalem itself. Needless to say such building operations— Augustus mocked that Herod spent as much money on building as if he owned all Syria and Egypt!—pleased the mass of the people to whom they brought employment and prosperity, as well as the less bigoted among the educated; but the pious Jews abhorred the Greek influence which only emphasized the foreign origin, not of course Greek, of their daring *parvenu* ruler.

Herod seems to have been tortured by an ambivalent, love-hate relationship towards the Jewish religion. As a gesture he adopted the Jewish faith, but the inner and outer insecurity of his throne led him to stress his Hebraic sympathies (as in the superb rebuilding of the Temple in Jerusalem) and to defy the representatives of the tradition. Both the priestly hierarchy and the Sanhedrin, or High Council, soon were reduced to a smouldering obedience. Immediately on receiving the Tetrarchate, he daringly opposed the Sanhedrin, who protested against his illegal execution of Ezechias, a bandit leader, and gained his point.

All of which increased Jewish contempt for this descendant of the cursed Ishmael—from whom the Arabs, too, claim descent— the son of Abraham's concubine Hagar, the descendant also of the cunning and detested Esau. Many of Herod's acts of sudden cruelty may be partly explained by his guilty and terrified reaction to his origin and to his subjects' scorn on its account. For his mother Cypros—an Arab, a Nabataean, less Jewish still but less hated for her race—he felt a great devotion: he named his finest palace, at Jericho, after her. From her he probably inherited good looks, charm and generosity. Many critics would perhaps add, his arbitrary "Oriental" despotic cruelty, though of this the Arabs hardly possessed a monopoly.

From the day when, 40 B.C., Octavian (later known as the Emperor Augustus) and Antony together obtained for him the crown of Judaea, Herod's career may be divided into three periods. The first, 40-25 B.C., covers what may be called his years of development; the second, 25-13 B.C., saw the years of royal splendour; while the third, 13-4 B.C., consists largely of domestic troubles and tragedies. The characteristics of each period, however, reappear in the others. Thus in all epochs of his life he betrayed the qualities attributed to him by the Jewish historian, Josephus: "He was such a warrior as could not be withstood"; and ". . . a man of great barbarity towards all men equally and a slave to his passions."

Domestic tragedies indeed pervaded his entire career; his affection for his brothers Phasael (died in captivity 40 B.C.) and Pheroras (died 5 B.C.) stands out almost uniquely amid his tortuous personal relationships. As to wives, he had ten of them! The five most important were: Doris, daughter of a priest, whom he married in 42 B.C. (their son Antipater he caused to be killed thirty-eight years later, five days before his own death); then Mariamne, granddaughter of Hyrcanus II, from whom he had two sons (likewise murdered) and two daughters—Mariamne he also had slain; then he had another Mariamne, daughter of the high-priest Simon, by whom he had one son; Malthace, whose offspring included the future rulers Archelaus and Antipas; and Cleopatra of Jerusalem, mother of Herod Philippus, later Tetrarch of Ituraea, and the sole member of the line who was universally admired.

In 42 B.C. Parthian horsemen invaded Asia Minor, Syria and Palestine. Jerusalem was captured; Herod's brother Phasael committed suicide and in his memory Herod named the first of the three towers in his new palace at Jerusalem. At the same time the Maccabees, ever hostile to Rome, rose and allied themselves with the conquerors. The Maccabee Antigonus was proclaimed king and Herod fled. First he plunged into the wild rocky desert of Judah. Then he routed Antigonus's troops south-east of Bethlehem.

He now embarked on an exciting journey. His aim was Rome; but first he had to seek help in Alexandria from his friend Antony. Going by fast camel through Beersheba and the mountains, he passed through Raphim into Egypt. Here, unlike the easier-going Antony, he proved himself a match for the scheming Queen Cleopatra. He stood courteously firm against her wiles and proceeded to Rome. There, playing on his country's strategic position and Antigonus's hostility to Rome, he received the greatest prize of his life by being made king of Judaea. He was given Roman troops to suppress any rising of the "fanatical Jews".

He defeated Antigonus at the battle of Arbela. His enemies fled with their families, but Herod pursued them and killed them cruelly. Antigonus was executed at Antioch, and in the next year, 37 B.C., Herod won Jerusalem after stiff resistance. He executed all the members of the Sanhedrin except one whose eyes were put out. Then he married Mariamne, daughter of the widowed Maccabee Queen Alexandra. Beautiful and spirited, Mariamne fell for Herod's brilliance and charm, but politics and cruelty soon upset the marriage. Alexandra resented Herod and in addition had plans for her handsome fifteen-year-old son Aristobulus. Queen

Cleopatra also resented Herod's coolness towards her, and the two ladies conspired. Cleopatra, opposing Herod's expansionism with her own, aimed at possessing all Palestine. With Antony campaigning against the Parthians, she travelled to Jericho, where Herod received her with due splendour, but remained cool towards her sensual advances.

Meanwhile the stiffly pious Alexandra formed an anti-Herod league with Cleopatra. So in 35 B.C. she wrote for Cleopatra's aid in making young Aristobulus high priest. Cleopatra wrote to Antony, who sent his representative Dellius to survey the scene. Dellius schemed to bring Mariamne and Aristobulus to Alexandria, but Antony invited Aristobulus alone. Mariamne was turning against Herod by now because of his cruelty. Alexandra sought to escape with Aristobulus to Egypt, but her plot was foiled. Then Aristobulus was drowned in mysterious circumstances. Antony summoned Herod to explain the situation and Herod's charm won his old friend over. But Herod had begun to bring about his own destruction. The new high priest was a Hellenizing Sadducee, but Herod's passion for things Greek—theatres, sculpture, painting, baths, sports and hippodromes—thus offending the stricter Jews, proved dangerous.

In 31 B.C. Octavian defeated Antony off Actium, near Corinth, in one of the world's most fateful battles. Cleopatra made her escape, and the appalled Herod showed his nerve and skill by visiting Octavian at Rhodes and actually winning over the new victor, who admired his courage and confirmed him as king. But Herod's prudent fears as to his fate at Octavian's hands had made him place his family in safety. As usual, he went too far and handed Mariamne and her mother over to the "care" of two advisers, with orders for the two ladies to be killed if things went badly for Herod with Octavian. One of these advisers revealed the plot; on his triumphant return Herod had him executed.

Then, fearful for his safety, Herod bowed to suggestions that the two ladies were conspiring against his life and had them both murdered. These murders tortured Herod for the rest of his life. Never again was he to be himself. Remorse impelled him to name the finest tower in his new Jerusalem palace after Mariamne. His tormented conscience, added to a disease which provoked hallucinations, also led him to almost insane acts of criminal violence; yet with this there co-existed the keen-sighted, magnificent statesman.

He now began to build: not only fortresses to protect his own power, but he indulged in splendour and beauty for their own sake.

Thirty B.C. saw the beginning of the building of Fort Antonia in Jerusalem; 25 the creation of Caesarea both as a port and as royal residence; 23 his palace by the west gate in Jerusalem; and 20 his Jerusalem Temple, universally praised, and an object of both tourist interest and veneration. Further achievements were the building of Samaria and of Jericho (his Winter Palace, named after his mother Cypros, was excavated as late as 1951), the founding of Sepphoris, complete with Acropolis, hippodrome and Greco-Roman villas, and the building of a temple to Apollo at Rhodes and elsewhere to other pagan gods.

This building activity, perhaps his most inspired and permanent work, procured him popularity with a large number of his subjects, who saw him as the symbol of peace, order and achievement. Even so, by acts of folly he often played into the hands of the Maccabees, Pharisees and nationalists who detested him, even though they would claim him as a Jew when it suited their purposes. An instance is his nocturnal plundering of the treasures in the tombs of David and Solomon, to assist his building programme.

Sickening though it may be to record further murders (like those of two of his sons, or of Pharisees and others who had pro-phesied the end of his reign, or the possible Massacre of the Innocents), it can at least be noted that Herod bore with exemplary fortitude his appalling illness, a variety of the plague, beginning with a painful inflammation of the back of the head. Mental derange-ment and even hallucinations followed, aggravated by who knows how much remorse? Yet as a statesman he received and questioned the Three Magi on their way to Bethlehem, also convening a cowed Sanhedrin to answer learned problems.

In 4 B.C. Herod died at Jericho, having first ordered his son and daughter-in-law, Alexas and Salome, to gather all the priests and upper-class Jews to the Jericho race-course and have them massacred. Some 15,000 such persons were thus assembled after his death, but Alexas called off the massacre. Herod was buried with brilliant pomp in his own creation, the Herodian Palace nearby.

Despite his compulsive cruelties, Herod won the admiration of fellow-statesmen, who yet were not blind to his darker side. The Emperor Augustus, playing on the Greek words *hus* (pig), and *huios* (son), jested: "Better be a pig of Herod than a son". For Herod, the ambivalent persecutor of Jews and defender of their interests in the Diaspora, was still Jew enough not to eat pork. In the era of the psychiatrist Herod would have proved a fascinating and rewarding study.

BOUDICCA

(d. A.D. 62)

IN A.D. 59, King Prasutagus died.

He was a good man, proud of his East Anglian kingdom of the Iceni, and of his handsome wife, his two daughters. He admired the Romans who had entered his country, because they were wiser than he, and generous. Already they had made a large grant of money to the kingdom. On his deathbed, then, he had no doubts about making the Roman Emperor co-heir with his two daughters. This would be insurance against having Rome do harm to his kingdom or to his family—though in any case that was unthinkable —and it was a first step to having the kingdom of the Iceni incorporated peacefully within the great Roman province of Britain.

He died in peace—but his scheme failed entirely to achieve its object. No sooner was he dead than the Romans demanded back the "grant" they had made him: it had been nothing of the sort, it was a loan, and repayment had to be made immediately. Co-ownership of a kingdom which they regarded in any case as their own was not repayment. The Emperor Nero—if he ever learnt of this comic legacy—would laugh out loud.

And so, with a senseless brutality, the Romans decided to reclaim their loan in kind, by seizing the royal family, selling it into slavery. As for Prasutagus's widow, she was flogged almost to death, and her two daughters publicly raped.

But the widow, Queen of the Iceni, was no ordinary woman: she was Boudicca (or as it is sometimes spelt, with rather less accuracy, Boadicea) and in the words of the historian Dio: "She was huge of frame, terrifying of aspect and with a harsh voice. A great mass of bright red hair fell to her knees. She wore a great twisted golden necklace, and a tunic of many colours, over which was a thick mantle, fastened by a brooch."

A vivid picture of a Celtic heroine—the most vivid we have. If Boudicca was really like this, the Romans were indeed fools to molest her.

Generations of English schoolboys have waxed indignant over the indignities inflicted on Queen Boudicca. But it is reasonable to guess, knowing the way the Romans ruled their island province, that they were provoked to these atrocities. The Romans of the time were an inferior, subordinate lot in the east of England, led by the biggest Roman fool of all, Catus Decianus; but no doubt Boudicca refused to pay, and perhaps she even—considering her stature and her reputation—threatened.

At this moment in Britain's island history, the Roman governor, a fair-minded man by name Suetonius, was moving his legions westward to attack the Druids of North Wales, the mystic priesthood which had been inciting the Britons to resist. His absence with most of his army was put to good use. Inflamed by the red-haired Boudicca, the rulers of all the little British kingdoms—the Iceni, the Trinovantes, the Catuvellauni and nearly a score of others —got together under her banner. They had between them a number of grievances; and in the understanding phrase of another historian, Tacitus: "They compared grievances and inflamed each other by the constructions they put on them." The Iceni had the obvious one of an outraged royal family; the Trinovantes objected to the behaviour of Roman veterans billeted in Colchester. And so on. Each tribe had something of which it could complain. To cap it all, there was this news of a Roman advance against the cherished Druidic religion, in Anglesey.

And so, from all parts of Britain, a vast army assembled by stealth, small bands of men slipping through the forests to join the forces of vengeance massing in the land of the Iceni.

The legions under Suetonius reached the Menai Strait. Here they were held up briefly by an armed mass of bearded and dishevelled men and women, chanting, waving torches. Then the Romans crossed, by boat and horse, and methodically butchered the Druids, chopped down their sacred groves. And as they were consolidating this feeble victory, news came of revolt in their rear. The Roman town of Colchester had been sacked by Boudicca's forces.

The Roman garrison at Lincoln had sent a relief force of five thousand men taken from the IXth Legion and its auxiliaries—and this too had been ambushed and destroyed.

Suetonius, still in Wales, but preparing with all haste to return, digested the news. There was now no force in the east of England able to do battle with Boudicca, who must by now have an army of tens, perhaps hundreds, of thousands. Colchester had gone, in a sickening wave of atrocity which made the rape of Boudicca's daughters seem a triviality. And soon, for there was no time to save them, London and St. Albans must follow.

141

Suetonius, two hundred and fifty miles away, started his return with an advance guard of fast cavalry. By forced marches he reached the outskirts of London within a few days. The city had not yet been attacked but the situation was hopeless: the foolish, cowardly, Catus Decianus had fled overseas, taking soldiers with him, and the brash new city, still but twenty years of age, was indefensible. Suetonius had to take the painful decision of surrendering it to angry barbarians in the hope of saving the rest of Roman Britain. There was no hope of getting his main force in position: he had come ahead with cavalry alone, and the bulk of his army was still in Wales. Suetonius retraced footsteps and left the citizens of London to their fate.

Boudicca's army, much of it a rabble, was difficult to command, and even the forceful queen was delayed in her move south after the sacking of Colchester. Had she moved more swiftly, Suetonius himself would have been captured and his army made impotent. But he escaped to Wales, and the Britons, thirsting for plunder, took London. There was no resistance, and every kind of foul atrocity was perpetrated. The Roman women, and those British ones friendly to the Romans, or perhaps just unlucky enough to happen to be in Londinium, "had their breasts cut off and stuffed in their mouths, so they appeared to be eating them. Then their bodies were skewered lengthwise on sharp stakes."

Verulamium—St. Albans—followed a few days later. The three chief cities of Roman Britain had been destroyed with 70,000 of their inhabitants massacred. But none of these three was a military position, and this is where the red-haired queen made her big mistake. Vengeance was all very well, but unless she prevented a Roman counter-attack she was doomed. It was possible now for Suetonius to gather strength, get reinforcements, ponder the horrors which were being relayed to him.

But whatever force Suetonius mustered would be minute, in comparison with the vast number which had rallied, were still rallying, to the banner of Boudicca.

The queen, though, had her problems. Her forces were undisciplined and even the force of her personality failed to stop the looting, the wholesale murder that was going on in the three towns and in isolated communities between. She had little sympathy with the victims, but she desperately needed speed, to pursue the Roman general and destroy him before it was too late. Her rabble made that impossible.

At last she got it assembled and set off north-westward after

Suetonius. Wives of the British warriors travelled with the long column in ox-drawn waggons, and they trundled through the Chiltern Hills, on into the Midland forests.

We do not know where Suetonius chose to meet this army, but it seems the choice was his, for he had found a fine defensive position (perhaps near Towcester). It was early autumn. The site he chose—and wherever it was, it must now have been altered out of all recognition by centuries of deforestation and agriculture—had a forest in the rear, a level plain in front, and was set in a narrow defile. The Romans occupied this densely, for it was cramped, with infantry in the centre, cavalry on the wings. The British—the largest force ever to have been assembled in the island—filled up the open plain with waggon-loads of screaming women massed together at the back.

The Romans were nervous and probably very frightened, with this savage host in front, out-numbering them so enormously, but Suetonius held them together, much as Boudicca, in her way, was doing with her own force. "Don't think of booty," he ordered the legions. "Win the battle and you will have everything. Throw your javelins first, on the order, then move in with the short sword."

The British charged.

He waited to the last moment before ordering javelins. Then, in two big volleys, the slender spears sailed high into the air and down into the advancing horde. In the resulting confusion the infantry moved in with vicious short swords, far handier than the long British ones. The British had chariots, in one of which stood Boudicca, long red hair flowing behind her as she led the charge, but almost immediately these were disorganized by a disciplined enemy, and routed by Roman cavalry.

In the end it was waggons, hundred upon hundred of them which, in Celtic tradition, had been brought, loaded with women and supplies, to park behind the warriors, which brought ruin to Boudicca's army. The chariots, forced into unexpected retreat, tangled with the waggons, and the Roman archers, gleefully killing horses and oxen, watched while infantry moved in and finished the work.

It was soon over, with casualties, if we can believe them, of eighty thousand dead on the British side against four hundred on the Roman.

Boudicca escaped, hotly pursued, and knowing there could be no hope of clemency when she was caught. There was nothing for it but to take poison and this, with her two daughters, she did—much as Cleopatra, in a similar predicament, had done a hundred years before.

With the death of Boudicca—with the defeat of her force in battle—the confederacy of Britons ended, but the rebellion continued, tribe by tribe. It had been, for Rome, a major disaster, her three finest towns laid waste, her rule flouted, her citizens massacred. Viewed from Rome, there had been something sadly wrong with Suetonius's handling of the people, and of their revolt: he would have to go. But in the meantime rule would have to be re-established, by as brutal means as necessary. Thousands of mercenaries were rushed across the Channel and the North Sea to bring the provincial forces up to strength, and over. A terrible vengeance was extracted, particularly against the Iceni. Boudicca had taken her own life, but her people would suffer for her, and they did.

Our picture of the barbarian queen is a vivid one, but there are gaps in our knowledge, fancifully sketched, about which we may never know the truth. We know her forces were skilful with the tiny, manoeuvrable, chariots: we also know no British chariot ever had the scythed wheels of legend, which have been fitted to the impossible, bronze, vehicle, in which Boudicca rides along the Thames embankment. The Victorian sculptor Thomas Thornycroft had long dreamed of a colossal work depicting this early heroine. Slowly, lovingly, he planned his vast statue, and was given every encouragement by the Prince Consort. He had completed the plaster cast when he died, and the finished work in bronze was not ready to be mounted on its pedestal until 1902, fifty years after the sculptor's work had begun. In many ways it is a handsome work, but it bears little resemblance to the real Boudicca and practically none to her chariot. The queen's bronze vehicle has been, not inaccurately, likened to "an armoured milk float", and certainly no warrior would have been able to fight from it.

But the idea of Boudicca has long gripped man's imagination. These lines from the poet Cowper (they are on the statue's base) are only a few among many:

> "Regions Caesar never knew
> Thy posterity shall sway,
> Where his eagles never flew,
> None invincible as they."

Perhaps the words of Winston Churchill, who knew as much about the British people, present and past, as anyone, may serve to sum up the rebellion by which we remember the red-haired queen in her chariot. "This is probably the most horrible episode which our Island has ever known. We see the crude and corrupt beginning of a higher civilization blotted out by the ferocious uprising of the native tribes. Still, it is the primary right of men to fight and kill for the land they love, and to punish with exceptional severity all members of their own race who have warmed their hands at the invader's hearth."*

*History of the English-Speaking World.

TRAJAN

(A.D. 53–117)

"I NOW discharge my promise, and complete my design, of writing
the history of the Decline and Fall of the Roman Empire, both
in the West and the East. The whole period extends from the age
of Trajan and the Antonines to the taking of Constantinople by
Mohammed the Second——"

So wrote the historian Edward Gibbon in 1788, after the twelve
long years he had laboured over this history; the "years of health,
of leisure and of perseverance" for which he had prayed when he
began. His prayer was answered: he has left us perhaps the finest
historical work in the English language.

The Turk, Mohammed II, who, as Gibbon tells us, conquered
Constantinople and ended the Roman Empire, was a brilliant
general and a wise man, and we consider him in another article.
But what can be our excuse for including, in this compendium of
great rulers, a Roman Emperor who, according to the greatest
authority on the subject, started off a tragic "Decline and Fall"?

The reason is simply that one can fall only from a height: in
the reign of the Emperor Trajan the Roman Empire reached that
height. In Gibbon's words it reached with him "its full strength
and maturity".

It is Trajan's misfortune that as one of the greatest men of
antiquity his name is forever linked with the collapse of history's
greatest empire. It reached its greatest extent during his lifetime—
and from the moment he was taken ill in the year 117, a few months
before his death, it tottered to a slow, lingering and ignominious
collapse.

In fact, that collapse took rather more than thirteen hundred years:
Mohammed II's capture of Constantinople, the last-ditch, eastern,
capital of a dying empire, was not until 1453. But the process began
at the end of Trajan's life.

Marcus Ulpius Nerva Trajanus was—surprisingly perhaps—a
Spaniard, though there was Italian blood in his veins. He was born
near Seville in the year A.D. 53. His father was a general of some
distinction in the Roman army, an army in which promotion was

146

almost entirely based on merit, whose greatest generals might come from any Roman province between Gaul and Africa. The boy Trajan was keen to emulate him and he succeeded, working his way up from the bottom of the army pyramid to fight under his father's command in several theatres of war and get promotion as a brave and talented officer.

By A.D. 88 he was a man of thirty-five, commanding a legion in his native Spain, having already served as an officer in Germany and in Syria. His fame had spread back to Rome itself, not only to the senate and people, but to the emperor, who was keeping an eye on the career of this brilliant general. That emperor was Nerva, a mild and ineffectual little man, only too conscious that he cut a less imposing figure than his tyrannical predecessor, Domitian. Domitian had been unfortunate enough to get himself assassinated, but he was looked back upon in awe. Nerva was looked down upon —particularly by his own Praetorian Guard—and when this Guard mutinied in Rome at the end of the year 97, he hastily adopted as his successor a man who would be bound to appeal to it and to the Roman army. It was the custom, at this stage of Imperial history, for the emperor to choose his own successor, who need not—indeed, more often, should not—be a near relative: life within the family of an average Roman emperor was not likely to nurture qualities of greatness.

The obvious choice was Trajan, and the army accepted it with delight.

A few months later Nerva was dead. Trajan, good soldier that he was, did not rush to Rome to accept his honour. He had recently been appointed military governor of Upper Germany, he was on a tour of the Rhine and Danube frontier defences, and he completed it, ensuring that the empire would be able to look after itself in the troublesome areas before going to his capital to assume the purple.

His reign lasted twenty years. The empire, as we have seen, reached its greatest extent in those years, for he was above all a brilliant and ambitious general. But he was well aware of his responsibilities in other fields: the magnificent buildings, theatres, libraries, aqueducts and monuments which he ordered to be erected are as fine as any. He even ordered the digging out of the old canal between the Mediterranean and Red Seas. This had been originally made for very small craft in about 2000 B.C. and had fallen into disuse. The Persian Darius had it re-opened in the sixth century B.C., but it soon silted up, grew useless. Under Trajan it became a valuable waterway—though after his death, too, it was allowed to silt up.

Seventeen hundred years later it was reclaimed as "The Suez Canal".

But it is as a just and gallant conqueror that we remember him: his reign was the last major extension of the Roman Empire by conquest. As Gibbon puts it, "he received the education of a soldier and possessed the talents of a general. The peaceful system of his predecessors was interrupted by scenes of war and conquest; and the legions, after a long interval, beheld a military emperor at their head. The first exploits of Trajan were against the Dacians, the most warlike of men, who dwelt beyond the Danube and who, during the reign of Domitian, had insulted with impunity the majesty of Rome. To the strength and fierceness of barbarians they added a contempt for life, which was derived from a warm persuasion of the immortality and transmigration of the soul."

Dangerous indeed: such an enemy, with such a creed; and these inhabitants of what is now Rumania and part Hungary had for many years forced their more civilized neighbours to buy them off with large annual payments of gold. Trajan defeated them, made their land a Roman province. "Decebalus, the Dacian king, approved himself a rival not unworthy of Trajan: nor did he despair of his own and the public fortune till, by the confession of his enemies, he had exhausted every resource both of valour and of policy. This memorable war, with a very short suspension of hostilities, lasted five years; and as the emperor could exert, without control, the whole force of the state, it was terminated by the absolute submission of the barbarians."

Decebalus committed suicide and Trajan, annexing all his lands as a Roman Province, declared a public holiday in Rome: the celebration and feasting in honour of this great victory went on for one hundred and twenty-three days.

Almost immediately after this he moved south-east into what is now Jordan, took the capital, Petra, and the remaining country of the Nabataeans, incorporated them successfully into the Roman Empire.

Parthia is the ancient name for what is now a part of Persia, but in the time of Trajan it was the centre of the large Parthian Empire, sometimes an ally and sometimes a vassal of the Roman. There had been skirmishing on the border between the two empires and in 114 Trajan set off to annex the Parthian Empire. He wintered at Antioch and in the spring of 115 began a brilliant campaign which subjugated almost all of it. He then pressed south along the River Tigris, "in triumph", says Gibbon, "from the mountains of Armenia to the Persian Gulf. He enjoyed the honour of being the first, as he was the last, of the Roman generals who ever navigated that remote sea. His fleets ravaged the coasts of Arabia. Every day the astonished senate received the intelligence of new names and new nations that acknowledged his sway."

But while he was away on this southern conquest, a revolt broke out behind him, in Parthia. He returned to the Parthian capital, Ctesiphon, punished the ring-leaders and appointed a strong, wise man as King of Parthia.

But still: "Trajan was ambitious of fame; and as long as mankind shall continue to bestow more liberal applause on their destroyers than on their benefactors, the thirst of military glory will ever be the vice of the most exalted characters. The praises of Alexander, transmitted by a succession of poets and historians, had kindled a dangerous emulation in the mind of Trajan. Like him, the Roman Emperor undertook an expedition against the nations of the East, but he lamented with a sigh that his advanced age scarcely left him any hope of equalling that renown."

This was true: he had greatly extended the Roman Empire (extended it too far, his successor was to decide), but was in his sixty-fourth year. He fell ill in Parthia, headed back for Rome.

At Selinus in Cilicia, now part of Asiatic Turkey, he died. His body was cremated and the ashes taken to Rome where they were placed inside the tall column he had erected in the Forum Trajanum.

And so, like other great rulers, Trajan died miles from home, victim of one of his own campaigns. He left his empire far larger than it had been on his accession, and Rome a more beautiful city; left behind a well-deserved reputation for fairness, mercy and honesty in addition to that of a great soldier, so that two hundred and fifty years after his death the Roman Senate, greeting a new emperor, could hope that he would "equal the virtue of Trajan".

But by this time the empire over which Trajan had ruled was crumbling on all sides. Trajan perhaps may be blamed for some of this: he chose as his successor the young Publius Aelius Hadrianus. The Emperor Hadrian, as he thus became, on the eleventh of August, 117, was determined to make his empire more manageable, and in order to achieve this he began by abandoning Mesopotamia and Assyria to the Parthians. He adopted a policy—which would have made Trajan's ashes turn over inside his column—of appeasing dissident tribes, so that his empire dwindled further. Soon the River Euphrates was re-established as the eastern boundary.

Among the people Trajan conquered were many Christians, and Christianity has something for which to thank him. It was an age of great cruelty, great religious intolerance, particularly towards the infant religion of Christ. The Emperor Nero had set the tone of the era by massacring Christians in their thousands in the autumn of A.D. 64. There had been a great and grievous fire in Rome—for which some historians hold Nero responsible as incendiary—and the blame for this was laid on the Christians as reason for the massacre. Subsequent emperors dealt harshly with the survivors and with other Christians swallowed up in the empire, but Trajan, as one can see from his correspondence, bent over backwards to be lenient, while carrying out the laws of Rome. The younger Pliny, Roman Governor of Bithynia in Asia Minor, had written to Trajan in the year 112. Should he punish Christians, according to the law, even when no other offences were proved?

"Do like this," wrote Trajan. "Christians are on no account to be sought out. If, however, a man is actually accused and then, after careful process of law, proved to be a Christian, he must be punished. But if he *now* says that he is not a Christian any longer, he is to be pardoned, whatever he may have been in the past."

This—in such a period of history—was generosity indeed. Later emperors were less lenient and there were many mass matyrdoms, notably in the years 250 and 257 under Decius and Valerian. At last, in the fourth century, the Emperor Constantine became a Christian himself and stamped out religious persecution with his Edict of Milan.

HADRIAN

(A.D. 76–138)

FOR NINE people out of ten the vices and follies of the emperors who succeeded the great Augustus, who died in A.D. 14, remain the dominant impression about the early Roman Empire. This applies not only to those whose knowledge is largely drawn from the many popular novels written about Rome, but also to those who in their youth studied the classics and Roman history.

Tacitus, one of the most fascinating historians who have ever lived, contributes greatly to this impression. Tacitus was a stern Republican of the old school and his great and sombre history of the Roman Emperors is concerned with the misdeeds of the wielders of a power whose existence he hated. He is a powerful witness for the prosecution; but a wise judge would sum up the period rather differently. Tiberius, Caligula, Nero and Domitian were, in differing ways, sinister characters, criminally self-indulgent, and they debased Roman society. On Nero's death there was a short period of anarchy, and had this lasted the empire would have been shaken to its foundations. But the vices of the emperors did not alter the administrative machinery which governed the civilized world, nor had their extravagances affected the provinces. In the small market town of Chaeronea, Plutarch could correspond with intellectuals and politicians all over the world and compose his Lives of Greeks and Romans. Egypt knew peace and in Gaul and in far-away Britain cities were founded on the Roman model, complete with temples, baths, amphitheatres and bookshops. Great roads holding the empire together continued to be built.

In any case, the period when there was folly at the top was not a very long one. In A.D. 69 a rough practical soldier, Vespasian, became emperor and there began a period when capable, well-meaning men succeeded each other, each emperor collaborating with and adopting his successor. This period, the Golden Age of the Roman Empire, lasted for 111 years until the death of Marcus Aurelius in A.D. 180.

In the middle of this period, from A.D. 117, reigned the Emperor Hadrian, soldier, administrator, man-of-letters, intellectual; a ruler who more than any other worked to civilize his subjects and who seemed to embody Plato's ideal of the philosopher king. Hadrian indeed had a great love for the strong Greek element in Roman culture. Now like Trajan, his predecessor, the last of the conquering Roman Emperors and a great builder of cities, temples, triumphal arches and aqueducts, Hadrian was a Spaniard, a fact which shows how far the Roman Empire had ceased to be first of all Roman and then Italian and had become world-wide. Hadrian's ancestors, it is true, were Roman, but his family had lived in Spain for well over one hundred and fifty years—so that he would properly be called a Roman-Spaniard in the way that Algerians whose fathers had come from France between 1830 and 1870 were known as French-Algerians. Trajan, and even more Hadrian, felt themselves different from the Italian aristocracy in that they quite naturally thought in terms of the whole empire and considered themselves as citizens, and rulers of an empire, not as the chief men of Rome.

Publius Aelius Hadrianus was born in A.D. 76, lost his father in early youth, one of his guardians being Ulpius Trajanus, who became emperor in A.D. 98. Trajan employed his ward, who was a soldier, on various frontiers, and when Trajan died Hadrian was commanding the Roman army in Asia Minor. Though he was adopted by Trajan, Trajan's intentions never seem to have been absolutely clear as to whether Hadrian was to be his successor. It is said that he became emperor partly because Trajan's wife, Plotina, also a Spaniard, was determined that he should be. Trajan died, as he was leaving Asia Minor for Rome, in a small port of Cilicia. It is possible that Plotina forced the obstinate old man on his deathbed to declare Hadrian his successor, and there is a story that, in a darkened room, Trajan's physician counterfeited his then unconscious patient's voice and read out his last wishes.

Hadrian, in Antioch, was consumed with the anxiety of ambition which was about to be thwarted or realized. He consulted soothsayers and magicians and had brought up from one of the dungeons a prisoner awaiting crucifixion whose throat was slit in his presence by a sorcerer, in the hope that in some way or other the man's soul would reveal the future. Hadrian's army enthusiastically backed him for victory in the imperial stakes. When he was declared emperor, there was no opposition from the Senate or from the people in Rome.

Shortly after his accession, however, when he was away from the capital, four men of consular rank were put to death by the chief of Hadrian's Praetorian guard for conspiring against Hadrian's life. One of these, Lucius Questus, who had been governor of Mauritania, was an old rival of Hadrian and had tried to kill him in a contrived hunting accident. Hadrian on his return was extremely angry at this action, or pretended to be, because it was illegal to punish men of Senatorial rank without the agreement of the Senate. He promised the Senate that such a thing should never happen again. It was obviously part of his policy to build up the prestige of this body which had been severely damaged by its servility towards the unworthy emperors of the past. He strove to maintain what was by now partly a fiction—that the Roman Empire was ruled not only by the Emperor as Princeps or prince of the Senate, but also by its old Republican constitution. Hadrian may also have been alarmed by the conspiracy for, when he placated the Senate, he gave large sums of money to the people and cancelled arrears of taxation, having the evidence of such arrears publicly burnt in the great Forum built by Trajan. Thereafter, Hadrian had no fear of domestic enemies and he spent no less than twelve of the twenty years that he was to be emperor outside of Italy.

The empire over which Hadrian ruled had largely been created by the Roman Republic. On the north-west of the empire was the island of Britain which, though visited by the legions of Julius Caesar, had been largely conquered later by the Emperor Claudius. The frontier of the Roman Empire ran along the Rhine and the Danube to the Black Sea. It embraced Asia Minor west of a frontier with Armenia and along the Euphrates with Mesopotamia. The empire included Palestine and the Arabian Peninsula, Egypt, Libya and all that is now called North Africa; and then it included all the Iberian peninsula and Gaul. The Mediterranean was an entirely Roman sea. Trajan had crossed the Euphrates and had also conquered Armenia; one of Hadrian's first decisions was to give back Mesopotamia and Armenia to their former rulers and so to strengthen the Roman frontier. Trajan had also crossed the Danube and occupied what the Roman cartographers called Dacia which corresponds to modern Rumania and Transylvania. Hadrian thought of retiring from Dacia but for various reasons was unable to do so.

The first of the many journeys which took up the greater part of his reign was to Britain where he built a great rampart from the Tyne to Solway Firth, known as Hadrian's Wall. This was a part of the shrinking policy. During Trajan's reign, and particularly during his Eastern wars, Roman legions had had to be withdrawn from Britain and the IXth legion had been cut to pieces by the Picts and Scots during an uprising. In Eboracum (York) Hadrian, on a green knoll, watched the first levy of British auxiliaries march past him. This was a sign of the times for, before the end of the century, the Roman Empire was desperately enlisting native troops—kinsmen of the very Goths and German tribes who were threatening it. The Roman legions, the bodies of perfectly trained, long-service, heavily armed but quick-marching infantry with their own artillery and cavalry, were getting very thin on the ground. They were no longer able to recruit from the good country stock from which most of their soldiers had come at the beginning of the century.

Hadrian knew that the Roman Empire had not nearly enough men to defend it. He spent a whole winter in Londinium (London). The first Roman Emperor to visit the remote island for any length of time, he was also the first to give long and detailed attention to the British administration. One city had got into debt through building baths on too ambitious a scale; with problems such as this the emperor concerned himself as well as with strategy of the empire.

A great deal is known about Hadrian's character, not only through his public acts but through letters and chronicles and through the work of two near-contemporary historians, the Latin, Spartianus, and the Greek, Dio Cassius. Both of these writers had copies of an autobiography which Hadrian wrote in the latter part of his life and published under an assumed name. Unfortunately all copies of this autobiography disappeared shortly after his death. Hadrian was first of all a man of works, an administrator who, as Roman Emperor, was able to work directly on realizing his dream of unifying the empire. The administrator was concerned with re-organizing the systems of agriculture throughout the empire with increasing shipping and industrial enterprises, with increasing the numbers of professional men such as doctors, lawyers and engineers. Hadrian was a great builder of cities. He was also, and above all, an artist. An historical reconstruction of Hadrian by Marguerite Yourcenar, called *The Memoirs of Hadrian*, describes Hadrian's dominant impulse:

> *"My ideal was contained within the word 'beauty', so difficult to define despite all the evidence of our senses. I felt responsible for sustaining and increasing the beauty of the world. I wanted the new cities to be splendid, spacious and airy, their streets sprayed with clean water, their inhabitants all human beings whose bodies were neither degraded by marks of misery or servitude, nor bloated by vulgar riches; I desired that the schoolboy should recite correctly useful lessons; that the women presiding in their households should move with maternal dignity, expressing both vigour and calm; that*

gymnasiums should be used by youths not unversed in arts and sports; that the orchards should bear the finest fruits and the fields the richest harvests. I desired that the might and majesty of the Roman peace should extend to all; that the most humble traveller might wander from one country or one continent to another without vexatious formalities and without danger, assured everywhere of a minimum of legal protection and culture; that the sea should be furrowed by brave ships and the roads resounding to frequent carriages; that in a world well ordered, the philosophers should have their place and the dancers also. This ideal, modest on the whole, could easily be realized if men would devote to it one part of the energy which they spend on stupid or cruel activities; great good fortune has allowed me a partial fulfilment of my aims during the last quarter of a century."

In Athens, the city he loved most and felt most at home in, he built the temple of Olympian Zeus and restored many old buildings. As an intellectual he was passionately interested in the religions of Greece and Asia Minor and was initiated into the Eleusinian mysteries. It was in Athens that Hadrian received a long missive from the Christian bishop Quadratus. His views about Christians and Christianity are ably summed up in *The Memoirs of Hadrian.* They were those of a highly civilized, highly educated and tolerant man.

"I read Quadratus's work and was even interested enough to have information collected about the life of the young prophet named Jewus who had founded the Sect, but who died a victim of Jewish intolerance about a hundred years ago. This young sage seems to have left behind him some teachings not unlike those of Orpheus, to whom at times his disciples compare him. I can discern through this teaching the appealing charm of the virtues of simple folk, their kindness, their ingenuousness and their devotion to each other. Within a world which remains, despite all our efforts, hard and indifferent to men's hopes and trials, these small societies for mutual aid offer the unfortunate a source of comfort and support."

But Hadrian was aware of what he considered dangers. Glorification of the virtues befitting children and slaves was made, he thought, at the expense of more virile and more intellectual qualities. He felt too that with all the appealing qualities of Christians there was the fierce intransigence of the sectarian in presence of forms of life and of thought which are not his own, the insolent pride which makes him value himself above other men. Hadrian believed that the Christian injunction to men to love one another was too foreign to the nature of man to be followed with sincerity by the average person who, he thought, would never love anyone but himself.

Towards the Jews Hadrian displayed great practical tolerance. He constantly met their leaders and listened to their complaints which he judged understandable but insufficient to explain their refusal to live amicably with the Greeks and Romans in Palestine. Much of Jerusalem had been destroyed by Vespasian in the previous century. Hadrian began the rebuilding of Jerusalem under the name of Aelia Capitolina. Although he favoured treating Jewish susceptibilities with respect he did not succeed in preventing a Jewish revolt in A.D. 132, and at his death relations between the authorities and the Jewish people were in confusion.

As a young man Hadrian married Trajan's niece Sabina, largely as a stepping-stone in his career. She was apparently a cold and rather formal woman. As empress she was not surprisingly annoyed by Hadrian's long absences. She held a court of her own. Hadrian mildly disapproved of certain tendencies among the intellectuals at this court. His marriage was largely a matter of convention. He had affairs with high-born women in Roman society and frequently visited the many places of debauchery in Antioch, Alexandria, Capri and elsewhere. Like many Greeks and Romans, his love was for boys rather than women. His great favourite Antinous died on a journey with Hadrian in Egypt. He had Antinous embalmed and was for long inconsolable. Hadrian founded a city in South Arabia in honour of Antinous. The city was in ruins by the end of the eighteenth century and by the middle of the nineteenth century what remained of its triumphal arches and theatres had been carried off for use in a neighbouring Arab town.

Towards the end of his life, Hadrian named a young patrician of considerable gifts, with whom he had been in love in his youth, as his heir. But Lucius Ceionius died, and Hadrian's choice finally fell on a middle-aged respectable Roman land-owner of great honesty called Arrius Antoninus, the first Antonine emperor. Hadrian insisted that Antoninus should at the same time adopt his successor and that this should be a young man, Annius Varus, who ruled later under the name of Marcus Aurelius.

Hadrian's last years were spent in Rome, where he built his great mausoleum which forms part of the Castello St. Angelo, several temples and his huge villa at Tibur. He disliked the public games, circuses and gladiatorial combats which took place so frequently at Rome, but he learnt to preside over them with equanimity and dignity. A man of the empire, he never felt quite at home in his capital. Throughout his reign he paid immense attention to the betterment of Roman and all human societies. He forbade the sale of slaves for gladiatorial and immoral purposes, and he made the enfranchisement of slaves easier. He abolished the giving of gifts either by rich or poor to the emperor. The authority to collect taxes was no longer sold as an office of profit; taxes were collected throughout the empire by State officials. A postal service was instituted throughout the empire. This soldier who preferred peace as a policy, this aesthete who was also a practical man, was above all a great civilizer, a well-wisher for mankind as a whole. He wrote a number of poems—his best-known, *Animula Vagula Blandula*, translated by Alexander Pope, treats of the human soul as it is about to meet death, a subject always much in his mind.

In his private life, Hadrian showed some of the not-unexpected defects of a man-of-letters who is also an all-powerful ruler. He liked the society of learned men, but he was inclined to be jealous of them and he frequently turned them to ridicule. His character was at times contradictory. Spartianus has described him as "grave and gay, affable and over-dignified, cruel and gentle, mean and generous, only consistent in his inconsistency". Possibly this was written of Hadrian at the time when his personal character showed itself at its most capricious, during a long and painful illness—dropsy of the heart. By the people of Rome he was more feared than loved and, according to Gibbon, the Senate doubted, after he died, whether he should be pronounced a god or a tyrant. The final honours given to his memory were largely procured through the offices of the emperor who succeeded him. This was a somewhat unkind fate for the most capable and the most well-meaning of all the Roman Emperors and the man who worked most steadfastly for the public good. Perhaps, however, the reluctance of the Senate to pronounce him a god was all the same an indirect tribute to the liberal attitude of mind which the Emperor Hadrian had always encouraged.

MARCUS AURELIUS

(121-180)

INSPIRED AND perhaps misled by Gibbon, historians have placed too much emphasis on the alleged causes of the fall of the Roman Empire. More remarkable than its fall was the fact that the Roman Empire held together for so many centuries and bestowed upon its subjects generations of peace, prosperity and security such as they had never experienced before and did not experience again for more than a thousand years.

The empire lasted for five centuries—longer than any other empire in history. For all its faults and deficiencies, it was the most successful empire ever devised by man. It was more successful than the British Empire, because the Romans practised no colour or race bar. Its very existence sets the Romans apart as one of the truly great peoples of history. They were not brilliant intellectuals like the Greeks. They were a practical people: they did not innovate, they adapted. They had a sense of law and justice which has endured through the centuries. The Roman Peace they gave to Europe and North Africa was one of the blessings of history. The fall of their empire was inevitable, part of the process of history and of the evolution of the European races.

In a famous passage in his *Decline and Fall*, Gibbon says that the age of the Antonines was "the period in the history of the world during which the condition of the human race was most happy and prosperous".

Roman civilization was at its zenith. Large, well-built cities, with amphitheatres and great aqueducts whose stately remains astonish us to this day, were connected by means of splendid roads. Their prosperity can be seen in the lavish scale of the public entertainments which had to be paid for out of public funds. Under the wise rule of such emperors as Trajan and the Antonines, the empire grew more humane and more united. Cultural and political harmony was reached, with all the provinces in the empire attaining equal status, as Julius Caesar had originally planned. The age of the Antonines has been called "one of those rare interludes when humanity seems to be given a respite from its self-inflicted sufferings". It achieved

158

what the Middle Ages strove for in its conception of "Christendom", and what the modern world hoped for in the League of Nations and the United Nations.

Under the excellent rule of the Antonines, the empire enjoyed a standard of living not reached again in Europe for many centuries. It increased to its greatest extent under Trajan. After that it slowly declined. But what the Romans had built was so enduring that its disintegration took hundreds of years. It was not, for instance, until A.D. 410 that the Legions finally left Britain.

The beginnings of decline were seen under Marcus Aurelius, when the empire suffered its first serious invasions from the outside, and war and pestilence were brought to the heart of the Roman world.

Marcus Aurelius, the greatest of the Antonines, was born on 25 April, A.D. 121, during the reign of Hadrian, under whose enlightened autocracy the empire was vigorously strengthened. Marcus started life as Marcus Aurelius Annius Verus, after his father Annius Verus who was Prefect of Rome and three times Consul. They were a Spanish family who had received patrician rank under Vespasian. Marcus's father died when he was three months old and the child was brought up by his grandfather, Marcus Annius Verus, a distinguished Senator who was Consul three times, a singular honour.

Annius Verus senior had a splendid mansion in the fashionable Caelian district of Rome and here Marcus spent his tender years in the very best Roman society. Romans had their snobberies as other peoples, and one of them was the necessity of speaking Greek from an early age, Greece being the source of all culture. Roman parents employed Greek girls as wet nurses for their children, with the result that they grew up bi-lingual.

Marcus was a serious and solemn child from infancy, despite being brought up by his grandfather, a genial man with a taste for sports. Emperor Hadrian, who took a great interest in young Marcus, called him Verissimus on account of his academic accomplishments.

Hadrian had adopted as his successor Titus Antoninus Pius, the uncle of Marcus Aurelius, on condition that Antoninus in turn adopted both Marcus, who was then seventeen, and Lucius Verus, then seven, whose father, Aelius Caesar, had originally been intended by Hadrian to be his successor, but who had died before Hadrian.

Antoninus was an experienced administrator, a man of great personal quality and intelligence, and when he adopted Marcus he made the youth break his earlier betrothal to Ceionia Fabia in order to become betrothed to Faustina, who was the one surviving child of Antoninus.

Marcus had already come under the influence of the Stoic philosopher, Apollonius of Chalcedon. Stoicism was the most important school of philosophy at Rome just then, and Marcus was profoundly influenced by it, and was in fact its last great exponent.

The Stoic philosophy has been described as one of endurance rather than of hope, and the word stoic has passed into the English language with this meaning. Stoicism was of course a great deal more than that. For Marcus Aurelius it was a way of life, a pattern of behaviour of the highest ethical and moral kind. It was a philosophy which required an iron will and a spartan mind. It was the philosophy of the intellectual and the aristocrat and embodied all the best Roman attitudes.

A Stoic always died in the finest and most edifying manner. Seneca, forced to commit a Roman suicide, dictated eloquently to his secretary to his last breath, while the poet Lucan, dying a similar death, expired while reciting his own verses.

In the year A.D. 139 Marcus was designated Consul, in preparation for his future role, and took up residence in the House of Tiberias on the Palatine Hill. Here he pursued the simple philosophic life as well as his political duties as Consul and Quaestor to Emperor Antoninus. His consular duties required him to take a leading part in the proceedings of the Senate and the administration of affairs, and he was a member of the Imperial Council which conducted the business of the empire.

He and Faustina were married in A.D. 145. He was twenty-two and had become Consul for the second time. Coins were struck to celebrate the occasion. He also received the title Caesar.

Verus, whom Antoninus had also adopted at the behest of Hadrian, and who was destined to be co-emperor with Marcus, was a very different type of young man. He liked sports and pleasures of all kinds and revelled in the sanguinary gladiatorial spectacles of the circus, while the studious Marcus found the circus boring and always took a book to read.

Antoninus Pius died in A.D. 161 at the age of seventy-five, and his end was as tranquil as his life had been. He commended Marcus to the state as his successor, and said nothing about Verus, well knowing that that young man was not cut out for the imperial role.

However, Marcus had a genuine reluctance to assume supreme power in the empire. His *horror imperii* was partly due to a natural modesty, and he also wished to honour Hadrian's desire that he and Verus should rule jointly after Antoninus. Marcus insisted that

Verus should share the imperial power with him, despite the urging of the Senate that he should take the sole administration.

The Senate bowed to his wishes and decreed the joint imperatorship, and Marcus became Imperator Caesar Marcus Aurelius Antoninus Augustus, while Verus was designated Imperator Caesar Lucius Aurelius Verus Augustus. Marcus, at forty, was plainly the senior partner and was ten years older than his co-emperor.

Their first duty—as of all the Roman emperors—was to secure the support of the Army. They paid a large sum (20,000 sesterces) to the Praetorian Guard in return for their oath of allegiance.

Antoninus, who was deified at his death, left the bulk of his large fortune to his daughter Faustina, who in the year of her husband's accession gave birth to twins, one of whom was the ill-fated Commodus.

At the beginning of the new reign trouble broke out in the empire. The King of Parthia invaded the Roman-protected Kingdom of Armenia, and war was threatening in Britain and on the German frontiers. Neither Verus nor Marcus had any military experience, their training for the purple having been seriously neglected in this important respect.

Nevertheless, Verus, being the younger and more robust, went to take command of the Imperial Armies at the Parthian front, and with him went wise and experienced military advisers. Both the Senate and Marcus were anxious to get Verus away from Rome where his pleasures and immoralities were becoming something of a scandal. It was hoped that army life would reform him.

It did nothing of the kind, of course. Verus took his military duties lightly, and showed more interest in the fleshpots of the Eastern Mediterranean than in the dusty battlefields of distant Parthia. Command of the army was left to more competent and responsible men, which was as well. Verus naturally took the credit for the inevitable Roman victory. The troops hailed their absent commander as Imperator, and he was given the title Armeniacus. By A.D. 166 victory in the East was complete. Verus's contribution to it had been confined to riotous living at Antioch where he revelled in all the Levantine vices.

The victorious army returned home, bringing disaster with it, for it had become seriously infected with the plague in Mesopotamia. As the troops returned to their homes in the various parts of the empire, they spread the pestilence with them and the result was the most widespread plague in all antiquity which had serious economic consequences for Rome.

In A.D. 169 Verus died suddenly of a stroke. Rome was full of rumours of the wildest kind—that Verus had been murdered by Marcus, by his wife, by Marcus's wife—none of which were ever seriously believed.

Marcus Aurelius now ruled alone and was probably relieved to be no longer encumbered by Verus. Marcus, with more experience and confidence, now fully embraced his destiny in true Stoic spirit.

Although the *pax Romana* reigned over the majority of the empire, there was always fighting to be done on the frontiers. In the northern provinces the war against the barbarian intruders was going badly, and Marcus now spent several years fighting with his armies.

In A.D. 170 the Marcomanni, a German tribe, came across the Alps and invaded Italy itself—the first time an invader had been on Italian soil for hundreds of years. Barbarian armies also invaded the Balkans and overran Thrace and Macedonia with much pillage and slaughter. In A.D. 171 the Moors crossed the Straits of Gibraltar and invaded Spain. Marcus's legions took vigorous counter-measures and the invaders were no match for the Roman arms.

In all these wars, alarms and military operations, Marcus was always the fair and temperate ruler who never failed to listen to the advice and opinions of his subordinates. In addition to the mammoth task which occupied his day-to-day life, he found time not only to conduct judicial affairs, but also to write his book *Meditations*, upon which mainly rests his noble reputation as the epitome of the philosopher-king.

He was not a strong man and suffered greatly from the cold of the northern winters. He ate little and developed chest and stomach trouble—probably an ulcer—which gave him great pain. He took a drug called *theriac*, which contained opium, to alleviate the pain. He later found that he could not do without the drug, which suggests that Marcus Aurelius became an opium addict. But he used opium only to ease his constant pain and make him sleep.

His latter years were also troubled by rumours of the unfaithfulness of his wife. According to the stories, Faustina, with that wantonness which seemed not uncommon among the high-born ladies of ancient Rome, disported herself with many lovers. She was said to have had a great fancy for low-born ballet-dancers and gladiators. She had been accused of sexual intimacy with Emperor Verus and even of murdering him. But Rome had always been a hotbed of vicious slander and calumny, particularly about the Imperial family, and Marcus was satisfied that none of the charges was true.

In A.D. 175 Marcus received news that Avidius Cassius, Commander of the Roman Army in Asia, had revolted and proclaimed himself emperor. Faustina was again accused of being behind this. She was reported to be in despair about Marcus's health, and not unreasonably fearful about their son Commodus becoming emperor. But Cassius's revolt came to nothing as he was murdered within three months of his bid for power.

Marcus visited Egypt, Palestine and Syria on a successful journey of pacification, during which time Faustina died at the age of forty-six. She had borne him eleven children. He had always trusted her despite the malicious gossip about her, and he greatly mourned her death, which event was naturally enough surrounded by rumours of the most sensational nature in Rome.

The emperor had been absent from Rome for eight years, and he returned there in A.D. 176 with the object of preparing his son Commodus for the succession. Marcus was fifty-five, in ill health and knew he had not much longer to live. Establishing his son as his successor was perhaps Marcus Aurelius's only act of unwisdom. History has criticized him for sacrificing the well-being of millions to his fond partiality for his worthless son, and for choosing a successor in his own family rather than from among men who were infinitely better qualified to rule. Even if he had been ignorant of Commodus's true character, he must have been aware that the boy had not inherited his virtues and his talents.

The persecution of the Christians has also been held against him as a bitter paradox in such a pure and noble man. Marcus, however, under Roman law as it stood had little option but to take action against the Christians who ostentatiously refused to take part in emperor-worship which was part of the fabric of the Roman state. The emperor was the incarnation of government and his deification was more a political than a religious act. No one really supposes that the irreligious, free-thinking Romans regarded their deified emperors with the same emotional awe and reverence as the Christians regarded their God. The primitive Christians were fanatical and narrow and obsessed with martyrdom. The secrecy of their worship gave rise to scandalous rumours about their practices. They were dead to both the business and the pleasures of the world. Until the rise of the Papacy they contributed nothing to the practical conduct of affairs. To them the Roman Empire was an evil thing and they ardently prayed for its destruction. Persecution was inevitable.

In the last few years of his life Marcus Aurelius had no peace. In A.D. 179 he and Commodus were with the Army on the German frontier where a great victory was won. In March of the following year he was taken seriously ill at Vindobona (Vienna) and he knew his time had come.

The Army loved Marcus, and when they heard they were stricken with grief. He commended Commodus to their protection. On the evening he died a tribune came to him and asked him for the watchword.

Marcus Aurelius said: "Go to the rising son, for I am already setting."

CONSTANTINE THE GREAT
(288?-337)

IN THE summer of A.D. 306 the Roman legions in York, who had with them some troops drawn from Gaul, proclaimed Constantine, the son of their commander Constantius who had just died, as *Caesar et Imperator*. It is not clear whether the soldiers intended to make Constantine the Caesar of Britain and Gaul, or the ruler of the vast Roman Empire. Constantine himself, a prudent but determined young man then in his thirties, may not have made up his mind either. But, after nineteen years of civil war fought in Gaul and then in Italy which his troops invaded rapidly, Constantine became the Roman Emperor, with no one to dispute his absolute sway from Persia to Britain.

His reign is of immense importance for two reasons. He made Christianity the official religion of the Roman Empire and, twenty years after he had crossed from Britain, he decided to remove the seat of government from Rome to the East. He built a city on the Bosphorus on the site of two ancient cities, Chalcedon and Byzantium, which he called Constantinople. This city was to carry on, in a manner of speaking, the Roman Empire in a Greek guise after Italy, Gaul, Britain, Spain and Africa had been lost to the barbarians.

Along with the founding of Constantinople, the reign of Constantine begins a period when the empire becomes distinctly like an Asiatic empire; an all-powerful monarch was addressed as "Lord" and his subjects prostrated themselves on the ground before him. The great Augustus who founded the empire had ruled as *Princeps'* sharing power with the Senate. This principle of government was continued by Trajan and Hadrian, both of whom, and particularly the latter, respected the Republican form of government. But under Constantine this was no more the case and the Roman Empire became in form what it had long been in practice, a despotism.

The emergence of Christianity, the founding of an eastern empire and the transforming of the political institutions of the empire were all the consequences of the terrible events which fell on the Roman Empire after the Golden Age, the reigns of Nerva, Trajan,

Hadrian, Pius Antonius, and Marcus Aurelius. From then, until the arrival to power of Diocletian, a peasant soldier from Illyria who was the predecessor of Constantine, the empire had had twenty-three emperors of whom all but three were killed by their rivals. These emperors were many of them bad, but all were insecure. After the dark and gloomy Commodus, the son of the philosopher-king Marcus Aurelius, it was the legions, from their headquarters in Gaul or Dalmatia or the East, who were liable to choose the Caesar Augustus, either on account of his wealth and generosity or his popularity. One, the Emperor Phillip, in the middle of this troubled period, was alarmed by a revolt which broke out among the legionaries of Dacia shortly after his accession. A stern and courageous Senator named Decius rebuked him and said the revolt would easily collapse. The emperor sent Decius to quell the revolt. But when Decius arrived in Dacia the rebel legions proclaimed him their leader and forced him, or persuaded him, to comply with their wishes. In due course Decius defeated the Imperial Army, put Phillip and his family to death, and was compelled to accept the purple.

It was in this terrible third century that the invasions of the Goths, Visigoths, Vandals, Franks and Alemanni, which were later to overwhelm the Western Empire, began to become a major danger. Already in the reign of Marcus Aurelius the Marcomanni and the Quadri, tribes who lived in Bohemia and Moravia, had broken the Roman peace, invaded Italy and besieged some towns in the north of the peninsula. Throughout the century insecurity was as general as peace had been before; at the end of the century, one of the capable emperors, Aurelian, thought it necessary to fortify Rome itself. Writing of the middle years of this century, the historian Gibbon says:

> "During that calamitous period, every instant of time was marked, every province of the Roman world was afflicted by barbarous invaders and military tyrants, and the ruined Empire seemed to approach the last and fatal moment of its dissolution."

The Roman legions and regular auxiliaries amounted to a force of no more than 650,000 men, a small number to defend so large an empire. It was, however, adequate so long as Roman training and superior Roman weapons were in the hands of tough peasants drawn, at first, from Italy and the hardy regions of Greece and then from Gaul and Spain. But it became impossible to maintain the quality of the far-flung legions or their numbers. The peasant population of Italy had decreased. The birth-rate had fallen. A terrible plague had decimated the population of Italy during the reign of Marcus Aurelius and again at the end of the third century. The instability throughout the territories of the empire meant that able men no longer came forward to serve in the municipalities of the empire. Some of the great Roman roads, the foundation of the imperial military power, fell into disuse through disrepair. Yet, strangely enough, the third century did not witness the dissolution of the Roman Empire. In the East some territory was lost to oriental princes, but substantially the *Imperium* was maintained. Along the Danube and the Rhine, the old limits set by Augustus, Rome preserved her frontiers. In Britain, Hadrian's wall was re-fortified and improved by the Emperor Severus; Constantine's father, on the eve of his death, had just repulsed an invasion of Picts and Scots.

But if the empire was largely maintained, it was necessary to adopt a policy of allowing the barbarians to settle inside the empire and, in return for helping to defend it, to enjoy their own customs, which often remained warlike. The Roman peace and the Roman civilization were becoming threadbare. Unquestionably the great structure was on the verge of collapse when in A.D. 284 the legions stationed on the north-east of Italy made Diocletian, a peasant soldier from Illyria (what is now Yugoslavia), emperor.

Diocletian was the reincarnation of a type of soldier-administrator who had made Rome great from the days of the Republic. Men such as he had recurred sufficiently frequently throughout the life of the empire to save it. Diocletian tackled the two great dangers— the insubordination of the legions, which led to constant civil wars and the instability of the imperial power, and the ever-growing pressure of the barbarians, by one ingenious master-plan. The empire should henceforward be ruled by a college of four men— two imperial rulers, the Augusti, and under them two Caesars who should be their successors in due course. At the same time he de-centralized the military command and the civil administration. Rome became simply the nominal capital of the empire.

From Treves on the Rhine, Constantius, one of the two Caesars, governed Gaul, Britain and Spain; and from Milan another Caesar looked after the provinces of Illyria, Dalmatia and the north-east. The second Augustus was in charge of Africa and Italy, whilst Diocletian himself governed the East from Nicomedia in Asia Minor. From a military point of view, the system was at first remarkably successful. Gaul, which had been particularly disorderly, was pacified. A serious revolt in North Africa was ended and Egypt was reconquered. All the Asian provinces acknowledged the

Roman sway. At the age of fifty-nine, having only once visited Rome which he disliked, and that only for a Triumph, Diocletian and his fellow Augustus, Maximian, abdicated in order to enjoy the pleasures of private life.

The political remodelling of the empire collapsed at once under the effect of rival ambitions. There were at one time no less than six rival Caesars in the field. Constantine's conquest of power was repeating what had happened in the past, and when he emerged finally victorious there was no question of ruling the empire through a college. But there was no going back on Diocletian's obviously correct view that Rome was unsuitable as the centre for the defence of the huge empire against the many pressures, from many sides, of the barbarians.

Constantine had been a protector of the Christians long before he mounted the imperial throne. Like some of the Frankish and Gothic kings of the early Middle Ages, Constantine is said to have had a vision assuring him that it was the Christian god who would give him victory. Indeed Constantine is said by a contemporary historian, Eusebius, to have seen a Flaming Cross with on it the words "By This Conquer" as he was about to cross the Alps in a surprise invasion of Italy in A.D. 312. Constantine's character makes it unlikely that his conversion to Christianity was the result of a vision of this kind or of any genuine spiritual experience similar to that of St. Paul.

In *The Decline and Fall of the Roman Empire*, the great English historian Gibbon has pointed out the curiously discordant and almost irreconcilable elements in the character of Constantine. Of Constantine's admirable qualities he writes:

"The person, as well as the mind, of Constantine had been enriched by nature with her choicest endowments. His stature was lofty, his countenance majestic, his deportment graceful, his strength and activity were displayed in every manly exercise; from his earliest youth to a very advanced season of life, he preserved the vigour of his constitution by a strict adherence to the domestic virtues of chastity and temperance. He delighted in a social intercourse of familiar conversation, and though he might sometimes indulge his disposition to raillery with less reserve than was required by the severe dignity of his station, the courtesy and liberality of his manners gained the hearts of all who approached him."

But yet the man who accomplished the conquest of the empire and its re-organization, and for a while its re-vitalization, was certainly the murderer of his son Crispus, who had become too popular with the people and with the army, of at least one nephew, and of many respectable and intimate friends whom he had begun in his old age to suspect of treachery. He was also probably the murderer of his second wife, Fausta, the mother who bore the son who succeeded him. Seated securely on the throne, the great man of action became, late in life, the easy prey of rumour-mongers and the victim of sycophants. It was, no doubt, this side of Constantine's character which so ardently followed the example of Diocletian in breaking with the austere Roman political traditions and adopting its style of an oriental despot. Not only the inner nature of this great man seemed to have altered after his accession to the throne; he even changed his appearance, and this hardy soldier wore false hair of various colours and loaded himself with diadems, gems, bracelets and rings.

The idea of Constantine as a saintly Christian ruler, which was, not surprisingly, propagated by the Fathers of the Church, is somewhat damaged by the fact that Constantine did not himself become a Christian until he was on his deathbed, in A.D. 337. Constantine's policy towards Christianity must be seen rather as that of a far-sighted ruler than a believer.

So far as statistics are reliable, the Christians at the beginning of the fourth century A.D. did not comprise more than a fifth of the population of the empire and were most numerous in Asia Minor, North Africa and Gaul. The severity of the persecution of Christianity in the reigns of Nero and some emperors in the third century has been greatly exaggerated; the persecution in the reign of Diocletian was undoubtedly far more severe. But Christianity had emerged the stronger from being a persecuted and forbidden religion. The growing insecurity of the third century, the breakdown of values, had no doubt drawn many of the best and most ardent men and women towards a religion of love, which placed its chief accent on the after life. Intelligent men no longer, as in the time of Hadrian, were disposed to dismiss Christianity as a noble philosophy perhaps but one which had a debilitating affect on a virile character. Many of the Fathers of the Church appeared, even to non-Christians, as men of character and remarkable energy. It was Constantine's mind rather than his heart which made him the protector of Christianity. As H. A. L. Fisher writes:

"The Christians had given their proofs. They had survived persecutions, they were organized. Constantine made up his mind to enlist the support, to control the activities and to appease the dissensions of this influential society ... The barbarians, the legions, the vast proportion of the civilian population of the West were still pagan. But there was this difference between paganism and

Christianity, that while the pagans, with polytheistic hospitality, were willing to receive the Christian god, the Christians regarded the pagan divinities as malignant demons ... To a deserving prince a well-organized and convinced minority fortified by sacred books and a clear-cut creed, might well seem to be a better ally than a superior number of indulgent and various-minded sectaries."

Constantine's services to the Church were immense. He became a lucid mediator in the many disputes between rival Christian sects and, therefore, exerted a direct influence in the formation of Christian dogma. In A.D. 314 the sect of African puritans, known as the Donatists, were cast out of the Church. More important still was the Council of Nicaea held in A.D. 325, the first Ecumenical Council of all Christian churches, which witnessed the rejection of the Arian heresy and the drawing together of Church and State.

Constantine, like Diocletian, was an Illyrian by birth, coming from Nish. He therefore all the more readily saw that the empire could not be defended from Rome and he was determined to choose as the capital of the empire a city which would also be the best strategic defence centre. He decided on the shore of the Bosphorus as the point from which Europe and Asia Minor could best be ruled and defended, and therefore he began to build the great city of Constantinople. Constantine's idea in founding a new capital was not only defensive and military. The new Latin city (Roman senators and knights were encouraged to move to Constantinople) was also to be the first Christian capital of the world. Constantine himself, carrying a lance in his hand, led a great procession which fixed the boundaries of the new city. To those who remonstrated that he was taking in too much land, the emperor is said to have answered: "I shall still advance until He, the invisible Guide who marches before me, bids me to stop." Large as Constantine planned the city, it had to be enlarged not fifty years after his death, so great was the influx of citizens behind the fortified walls.

A description made around A.D. 430 of Constantinople stated that there were, when the city was founded, a Capitol, or school of learning, a circus, 2 theatres, 8 public and 153 private baths, 52 colonnades, 5 granaries, 8 aqueducts or reservoirs of water, 4 spacious halls for the meetings of the Senate or courts of justice, 14 churches, 14 palaces and 4,388 houses which, for their size and beauty, deserved to be distinguished from the multitude of plebeian habitations. It was undoubtedly a splendid city, but the greatest architectural glories such as the Church of Saint Sophia were to be built much later. Constantine's creation was decorated with copies of masterpieces brought from Greece and the great cities of Asia Minor. Its beauty was second-hand, for the decadent Roman Empire had none of the aesthetic vitality and dignity of Athens. It is noteworthy that skilled architects and masons were so hard to find when Constantinople was being built that apprentices had to be trained hastily in special schools set up by the emperor's orders.

Constantinople never became a Latin city and, indeed, shortly after its foundation, the Roman Empire of the West crumbled away before the renewed onslaughts of the barbarians, combined with continued civil wars between Romans. On the other hand, Constantine's child was to stand until the middle of the fifteenth century—for over a thousand years—as a bulwark of Christian and Greek civilization until in 1453 it was captured by the Turks. However much of the character of Constantine may have degenerated in his later years, there can be no doubt of the greatness of his achievements and the sureness of his vision of the future.

ATTILA

(d. 453)

MORE PERHAPS than any other nation, the Huns have a history which is that of their greatest son. We know remarkably little about them before the arrival of Attila and very soon after his death they vanish from the pages of history.

Who were they?

No one really knows. There is a pleasing and convenient theory that they were once the warlike Hsiung-Nu tribes of Asia, referred to in Chinese histories, but there are plenty of good arguments against it, and we can only submit it as a theory. At least one historian has debunked it in the grand manner: "It is a mortal step from the kingdom of the northern Zenghi to the steppes of Russia, and he who takes it is supported on the wings of fancy and not on the ground of fact."

So much for the problem of their coming. As for their going, they left their name behind them, to be applied by the Romans to every wave of savages which assailed them. And we ourselves have been known to use the word "Huns" when we wish to speak evil of our enemies.

Their greatest leader—if greatness be measured by power— was Attila, the "Scourge of God", who reigned less than twenty years and was remembered, in terror, for a thousand. A contemporary summed him up as: "Short, squat, with deep eyes, flat nose and thin beard. He is truculent and blustering, but of simple tastes. While his lieutenants dine off silver and eat luxuries, Attila eats only meat, and off a wooden plate."

Hardly an attractive fellow. But Attila, the Scourge of God, hacked out a place for himself in history, while many of the educated and the beautiful whom he slaughtered have been forgotten.

There is a legend which persists in many East European tongues that years after the Huns were (or were not) the Asian Hsiung-Nu, a large group of them settled in the Caucasus. For a brief period in history they were peaceful folk, tending their cattle and their little ponies. One day a heifer was stung by a gadfly and tore off

172

westward, splashing into the marshy waters of the Strait of Kerch. The herdsman followed it and was surprised to find that the marsh which spread out over the horizon, and had always seemed the western limit of the world, gave way to fertile, rolling plains. He retrieved his frightened heifer, got it back to the land of the Huns, and then told his friends of the paradise he had discovered. A little later the Huns waded over to this eastern Crimea and slaughtered the Goths who lived there.

From now on Hunnish legends, and what little history exists, deal entirely with conquest and slaughter.

We know that in A.D. 395 these new barbarians launched their first big invasion of the Roman Empire, pouring westward over the River Danube. At the same time, they launched a great attack on the Romans' Eastern Empire, based on Constantinople. "Behold, the wolves, not of Arabia, but of the North, were let loose upon us last year from the far-off rocks of Caucasus, and in a little while overran great provinces. How many monasteries were captured, how many streams reddened with human blood! Antioch was besieged, and the other cities washed by the Halys, Cydnus, Orontes and Euphrates. Flocks of captives were dragged away; Arabia, Phoenicia, Palestine and Egypt were taken captive by their terror. Suddenly messengers ran to and fro and the whole East trembled, for swarms of Huns had broken forth from the far distance. They filled the whole earth with slaughter and panic alike as they flitted hither and thither on their swift horses. The Roman Army was away at the time and was detained in Italy owing to the civil wars. May Jesus avert such beasts from the Roman world in the future! They were at hand everywhere before they were expected: by their speed they outstripped rumour, and they took pity neither upon religion nor rank nor age nor wailing childhood. Those who had just begun to live were compelled to die, and in ignorance of their plight would smile amid the drawn swords of the enemy——"

So it was written at the time.

Eventually the Huns were held in the East, though they retained many of the lands they had overrun. Then, at the start of the fifth century, they took another plunge westward. This time they drove other barbarians before them: Vandals and Alans poured westward over the Rhine, fleeing in terror into the Roman province of Gaul, while the Huns at their back laid waste to Germany.

The first Hun we know is Uldis, who in A.D. 408 led another expedition against the Eastern Empire and was narrowly stopped from seizing it all. But it was Uldis who finally made the Romans see that a crash programme of defence must be put in hand immediately: and if it had not been for Uldis and his depredations, the ravages of Attila might have been still greater: there might today be a nation of Hunland.

In about A.D. 432, one Rua enters the pages of history as the leader of the Huns. He sent emissaries to the East Romans demanding tribute, and when these played for time he prepared a massive campaign against them. The empire was saved—for the time being—by Rua's death and the accession of his two nephews, Bleda and Attila. The two young men decided they stood to gain more by repeating their demand for tribute than by waging war, and they summoned Roman emissaries to their city of Margus (now Pozarevac in Yugoslavia) where they parleyed with them, on horseback. The Huns were happiest on the backs of their fleet little horses, but for Romans this was an uncomfortable, indeed undignified, position. Yet it would have been even less dignified to stand on the ground and talk up to the little men, and they remained, like their hosts, unwillingly astride.

Perhaps this accounts for the crippling terms to which they agreed. Old Rua had fixed an annual tribute of three hundred and fifty pounds of gold: Bleda and Attila, with their threat of a devastating campaign, were able to force this up to seven hundred pounds a year, at the same time imposing a number of other conditions in this "Margus Peace" of A.D. 435.

The peace lasted some six years. Then—perhaps the Romans had been dilatory in their tribute—the brothers attacked again, in 441. The Huns razed a number of East Roman cities, including Singidunum, which is now Belgrade. There was a brief truce in 442, but the attack was continued in 443, and the barbarians got to the walls of Constantinople where at last they were held, though they had completely wiped out the large Roman force in the Peninsula of Gallipoli. The Romans sued for peace and now the brothers were able to demand arrears of tribute amounting to some 6,000 pounds of gold. No one dared to question the arithmetic; the huge tribute was handed over, and the annual stipend was now trebled, to 2,100 pounds.

In 445—and the incident is brushed aside in chronicles of the period as being of small account—Attila murdered his brother Bleda and took over the running of what had now become a Confederacy of tribes, by himself. From now on he was an absolute ruler, more absolute and autocratic, perhaps, than any other in

history. He planned his campaigns down to the last detail without
any advice from his followers; his negotiations, though he might
send others to conduct them for him, were planned in the same
way, and however long he might allow them to take, Attila knew
the outcome from the beginning.

Justice for all his people was in his hands and his alone. A case
would be brought to him, sometimes from the farthest part of
his shifting, horse-borne empire, and the parties would stand
meekly outside the little man's log hut and say their piece. The
leader's judgement was given instantly, without reference to
anyone else, and it was never questioned. Some of this unquestioning
obedience sprang from superstition, which the sharp-witted Attila
was quick to use to his own advantage. A few years previously
a herdsman had found a very old sword buried in the grass and
brought it to the leader. Attila promptly declared that this was the
long-lost sword of the War God: fate had decreed that he, Attila, was
to inherit it, and from now on none of his campaigns would fail, and
no nation—including his own—would be able to stand against him.

In 447 he launched another huge attack—far larger than that
of 441—against the Eastern Empire. He devastated the Balkans,
went on into Greece. Three years of negotiation then followed.
Attila attached great importance to these negotiations: not to
their outcome, which he had already planned, but to their duration.
He sent as emissaries, when he did not go himself, large parties
of his closest lieutenants, who would then be fêted and made much
of by the terrified opposition, to return months, sometimes years,
later, laden with gifts. This helped ensure the loyalty of the lieutenants, for there was little, apart from tribute gold, which the
king of the nomadic Huns could give them.

But slowly, as ideas of luxury and easy-living filtered in, the
character of the Hun nation was changing.

A treaty was signed after years of profitable negotiation with
the Emperor Theodosius. The Romans agreed to pay still more
tribute and evacuate a wide belt south of the Danube, which thus
became Hun territory.

A little later Attila turned his attention westward, to Gaul.
No doubt he could have overrun the country in a few weeks,
but the taste for negotiation had seized him, and he now declared—
much as Hitler was to do fifteen hundred years later—that he
wanted only the small Visigoth kingdom within Gaul, based on
Toulon. He had no more territorial demand than this: the Western
Emperor, Valentinian, need have no worries on that score.

We will never know what Attila's real intention had been, for now came the notorious affair of Justa Grata Honoria.

Honoria was the Emperor Valentinian's sister. She got herself involved with a royal steward; the liaison was discovered, and the man put to death. Honoria was then engaged, against her will, to an elderly Roman senator and in her despair wrote to Attila begging him, in return for a large gift of gold, to come and marry her himself.

In fact, her motives were completely political: she had planned to make her steward emperor and become his empress; the elderly senator was a non-starter for this sort of contest; Attila might well succeed. She sent a messenger to him, bearing her ring as proof of authenticity, and he duly delivered his message. What Attila's reaction was at first we do not know, but the messenger was captured on his return and made to pour out the whole dark secret to the Emperor Valentinian before he was executed. Honoria was hastily despatched to her mother, and we hear no more of her.

But now, of course, Attila demanded Honoria as his bride, and with her half of the Western Empire as dowry.

This time he had bitten off more than he could chew. The Romans resisted him and allied themselves with the Visigoths he had already decided to conquer. A war broke out, and at first it seemed the Huns were winning. They nearly captured Orleans before the tide of battle changed dramatically, and the barbarians were flung out of Gaul, in this Attila's first and only defeat.

He recovered sufficiently from this stunning blow to his pride to attack Italy in the following year, where he sacked a number of northern cities, including Milan and Verona. Plague, though, was raging in the peninsula and he decided not to pursue the campaign across the Apennines.

Meanwhile, in August, 450, a new Eastern Emperor had taken over, a strong man who refused flatly to hand over any further annual tribute. Negotiation took place and Attila failed in this as he had failed in battle: the Romans refused to budge, even refused to hand over the usual lavish gifts to the negotiators.

Furious, Attila prepared another attack on the East, an attack so devastating that there would be no doubt left in any Roman mind that his orders were to be obeyed, and promptly.

And now another woman was his undoing, and the undoing of his kingdom.

Just before the campaign was due to begin, in 453, Attila decided to take another wife. She seems to have been German and of great beauty, and we know her name was Ildico. As usual, Attila drank enormously before, during and after the wedding ceremony and retired to the marriage bed in a coma. When he drank his nose often bled, and it had done so more than once during the evening, round a roaring fire. When he was escorted to bed the bleeding had stopped.

But the next day, the sun was high in the sky and starting to descend when Attila's servants decided to enter his room. They forced their way in and found him dead, drenched in blood and with his weeping bride beside him. There was no trace of a wound and there is little doubt that he had suffocated in his sleep during another violent attack of bleeding from the nose.

His body was laid out in a silken tent, and while this was being done the most skilled horsemen in the kingdom galloped round him, chanting war cries. Others slashed their own faces with their swords, so that "the greatest of all warriors should be mourned with no feminine lamentations and no tears, but with the blood of men".

So ended the life of the greatest ruler of the Huns, and with it the strength of the nation. The kingdom was parcelled out among his sons who, unlike Attila and his brother Bleda, chose to rule their portions separately. This, coupled with the growing taste for new luxuries, and Roman inducements for Hun warriors to enter the Imperial armies, weakened the Hun nation so that within a hundred years it had ceased to exist.

But as a name symbolizing ruthlessness, rapacity and skill at arms, it remains, with that of its greatest leader.

JUSTINIAN I
(483–565)

To those for whom history is largely based on English history, Justinian, the Byzantine monarch of the sixth century, warrior and law-giver, who for a brief moment reconquered Italy and Spain from the Barbarians, is a dim and baffling figure, belonging neither to the Ancient world nor to the Middle Ages. He reigned during a period when English history also was dim and baffling, when dates and facts are uncertain.

Constantine, the Roman general who had started his conquest of power from Britain at the beginning of the fourth century, had, for a while, revived the great Roman Empire of which the British people felt themselves to be part. But by the end of that century, Goths, Visigoths, Vandals and then, behind, the Huns had poured into Western Europe, driving before them Franks and Alemanni and the Angles and Saxons. The Roman Empire was no more, and perhaps its final date was 453 when Rome, having been captured by a Gothic chieftain in the pay of the Eastern Emperor in 410, was sacked once again by the Vandals who had settled in North Africa. It was incidentally in Romanized Britain that the invading barbarians met the fiercest resistance and, as Gibbon states in his *Decline and Fall of the Roman Empire*:

The continent of Europe and Africa yielded, without resistance, to the barbarians; the British island, alone and unaided, maintained a long and vigorous, although an unsuccessful, struggle against the formidable pirates who, almost at the same instant, assaulted the northern, the eastern and the southern coasts.

Whilst the western part of the Roman Empire collapsed before the conquering hordes, no victorious Goths entered the eastern capital of Constantinople; and the Roman provinces of Greece and Asia Minor, though disturbed by invasions, still largely accepted the rule of the Eastern Emperors. For this much was due to the great land walls which protected the city on the west and to the supremacy which the Graeco-Romans, and later Greeks only, maintained on the sea. Constantinople was impregnable by land or by sea. Its Greek and oriental population, though lacking the stern civic virtues which had once been those of the Romans, were militarily far more disciplined and skilled than the invading barbarians. The policy of the Greek Empire was directed by civilized and cunning leaders who knew how to use both their military power and their wealth.

Christianity survived in the West, particularly in Italy and in Gaul, where the first Frankish king, Clovis, who united most of France, adopted the religion which had its centre in Rome. It survived because the barbarians accepted it. But Christianity played a major part in preserving the unity of the eastern part of the Roman Empire. It was the bond between Constantinople and the provinces of Asia Minor and Greece. Constantine had been supremely wise in making the second capital of the Roman Empire a new city which would, from its foundation, be a Christian city. Then, in the last half of the fifth century, when the ruin of the western part of the Roman Empire was consummated, and into the beginning of the sixth century, the Eastern Empire was ruled by three men of great ability, Leo I, Zeno and Anastasius I. They were cautious and prudent rulers, men of energy, but who never were led into rash enterprises or wars which would have drained away the resources of their city and the loyal provinces.

When the Emperor Anastasius died in A.D. 518, a violent quarrel over the succession broke out, and civil war seemed likely. But Justinus, the commander of the Imperial guard, was proclaimed Augustus by his soldiers and the Senate acquiesced. Justinus, who reigned as Justin I, was sixty-eight, a quiet unambitious man, virtually illiterate when he came to the throne. Like Diocletian and Constantine he came from Illyria (Yugoslavia today). He reigned for nine years: the only event of note during this period was that he put an end to a schism between the churches of Rome and Constantinople which had lasted for forty years—and was of course to come alive again. Justin I died in A.D. 528 and was succeeded by his nephew Justinian, who, during his uncle's reign, had been thoroughly prepared for taking over the throne.

Justinian had the virtues of a hard-working civil servant of great intellect with the peculiar stamp of what is today called Byzantinism —persistence in aim, refinement of thought and extreme deviousness and cunning. Neither he nor Zeno nor Anastasius were men who appealed to the imagination or the affection of their subjects. At the height of his power, Justinian was derided by rioters in his imperial city and perhaps only saved his throne because of the boldness of his wife, the Empress Theodora. Yet, but for a few internal crises of which these Nika riots were the most dangerous, Justinian exerted an unquestioned authority which was both that of a great military conqueror as well as a pernickety hide-bound official who poked his nose into everything. Under his rule, the economy of the empire prospered, Constantinople grew richer and more beautiful. One of Justinian's passions was building, and particularly the building of churches—the world-famous church of Saint Sophia was one of the fruits of this passion. His most indisputable achievement was the codification of Roman law, which Justinian put in hand and supervised, and which is known as the Corpus Juris Civilis.

The fundamental conception of Roman rule, whether in the time of the republic or of the empire, founded by Augustus, was the importance and indeed the sanctity of Law. The Byzantines respected the law as a written heritage from the past, regulating man's relations to other men and to society, with fervour and with even more intellectual and disputatious passion than the Roman world of Augustus or Hadrian. But by the time of Justinian the huge mass of law had become unwieldy and excessively complicated; it was additionally complicated when Christianity became the official religion of the empire in the fourth century during the reign of Constantine. Justinian's commissions of lawyers headed by the celebrated Tribonian laboured, and laboured successfully in the opinion of posterity, to simplify and co-ordinate this heritage.

About a fourth section of the great corpus of Law, the Novellae, the new laws issued by Justinian subsequent to the publication of the Code, opinions are more divided. The Novellae are far less widely known even by lawyers than the Code. Many historians consider that they show a too rigid conservatism, and amount to a somewhat depressing attempt to enforce religious orthodoxy on every department of life. Nevertheless, the Novellae constitute an attempt to unify Graeco-Roman and Christian traditions, and if they are somewhat over-didactic they are often subtle and sometimes rather curious, as witness the following extract dealing with gardens:

> He had been receiving many complaints about the misdoings of gardeners in this blessed city and its suburbs. They form a union which underestimates the value of gardens when the owner is letting them out and tremendously overestimates the value when the owner is taking them over again and paying compensation for improvements. The prefect of the city is to put an end to this abuse.

Justinian's imperial policy was a more spectacular achievement than his work as a legislator. Justinian deliberately set himself to restore the whole of the Roman Empire. In fact, he never attempted to recover Gaul or Britain. As for Britain, his map-makers and generals seemed to have been doubtful exactly where it was, some considering it an island off the coast of Spain and others confusing "Brittia" with Denmark.

However, Justinian's achievements were considerable. Having defeated Persia, the only menace in the East, in a three-years' war, Justinian sent his greatest general, the justly famed Belisarius, to the conquest of North Africa, which was in the hands of the Vandals. This was carried out successfully and the Vandals were virtually exterminated and, indeed, pass out of history. Italy was in the hands of a number of Gothic kings, many of them Christian and some of them professing respect and even paying homage to the empire. It might have been a wiser policy on the part of Justinian to have tried patiently to persuade or bribe them into a fuller obedience and then perhaps to have forced them to renounce their independence and become servants of the empire. But Justinian decided on conquest and, in A.D. 535, Belisarius landed in Sicily with a small army of some eight thousand soldiers. He captured Naples and Rome with great speed, defeating a number of Gothic armies. The Greek mailed cavalry and mounted archers and the clever use which they made of sea power was invincible at first. By A.D. 540 a Byzantine official, known as the Exarch, nominally ruled Italy from Ravenna on the north-east coast.

But the fortunes of war were to change. Fresh waves of barbarians under a new leader, Totila, poured into Italy, and for a time the Goths recovered all Italy except Ravenna and Ancona. The Byzantines enlisted Goths on their side: this may have made the fighting even more savage, giving it the character of a civil war. According to a Byzantine historian of the time, when the Goths and Burgundians recaptured Milan in A.D. 539 they slaughtered the whole male population of this city, some three hundred thousand. Belisarius, whom the emperor treated with harsh injustice and whom the empress hated, was recalled. Victory went to Justinian in the long run and the power of the Goths was broken for a long time by the generalship of a typically Byzantine figure, an aged eunuch, Narses, who united military ability with a most unscrupulous diplomacy. Italy was devastated by these wars which lasted twenty-eight years. Rome became an impoverished city of a few thousand people with its great entrepôts, granaries and aqueducts in ruins. But Justinian could write to the imperial proclamation which said:

> God has permitted me to bring the Persians to conclude peace, to subdue the Vandals, the Alemannis and the Moors, to recover all Italy and Sicily and we have good hope that the Lord will grant us the rest of the Empire which the Romans formerly extended to the limits of the two oceans and which they lost through indolence.

About Justinian's personal character and abilities there is a diversity of opinion among historians. Most agree that he was a man of extraordinary industry and quickness of mind and a man with bold ambitious views. Throughout his life he was accustomed to spend whole nights in study, particularly of his dominant interest which was theology. He was able to choose able servants, though many of them were extremely corrupt, and towards the end of Justinian's reign the economy of the empire suffered from legal plundering as well as from the fact that Justinian undertook too many things at once.

He was obviously very much influenced by his wife Theodora, who was not only empress but a co-sovereign. The subtle Justinian turned to profitable use the fact that he and his wife were known to have differing views on certain subjects. If he was ungrateful and suspicious, he disliked putting people to death and had, on the whole, a reputation for clemency. He was not a morally impressive character, but he was almost certainly not the highly unpleasant individual who emerges from the contemporary account of the historian Procopius. Procopius wrote the official history of Justinian's wars and then later, and perhaps moved by resentment from insufficient favour, the celebrated *Secret History* in which Justinian appears as a monster. Inspired as it is by hatred, pure hatred at moments, Procopius's view of Justinian has to be taken into account because it is that of a contemporary with a first-hand knowledge and that of a man of considerable intelligence. Of Justinian's character Procopius writes:

> He was neither particularly tall, nor stunted, but of moderate stature; not thin, however, but slightly plump. His face was round and not uncomely and even after two days fasting his complexion was ruddy. Of his character I could not possibly give a precise description; he was at the same time malevolent and gullible, the type people describe as being both fool and knave. He never spoke the truth himself, but was always crafty both in word and act, and yet always easily at the mercy of those who wish to succeed him. His character showed, indeed, an unusual blend of foolishness and maliciousness. He was full

of dissimulation, treachery and affectation; he secretly nurtured resentment, was double-faced, a past-master in the art of acting a part; his tears were always ready, not in response to suffering but because he could always turn them on to help the requirements of the occasion. He was always lying, not just casually but on paper and with the most solemn oaths and that too to his own subjects. As a friend he was faithless, as a foe implacable. He had a consuming passion for murders and money. Such being Justinian's character how could anyone portray it adequately? For these vices, and many others worse than these, he displayed in a superlative degree. It seemed as though nature had taken all the wickedness of all mankind and planted it in the soul of this one man.

If one puts on one side Procopius's attribution of evil motives as the root of Justinian's nature, maybe some of the characteristics described hit off the real man.

Procopius's portrait of the Empress Theodora has been adopted by some serious historians such as Gibbon and has been the basis for many popular novels which show her as one of the most wicked and debased women in the world. In her youth there is little doubt that she was an actress and a prostitute; the two professions in Byzantium were often combined. Justinian made her acquaintance when she had returned from a number of discreditable adventures in Libya and Alexandria. He married her not without having to overcome opposition from the wife of his uncle, the emperor. His love survived his marriage.

She may have been cruel to her enemies and delighted to witness their torture in the dungeons of her palace; she may have had her illegitimate son put out of the way; she was certainly a woman of character and spirit and a faithful wife as well as a useful one to Justinian. She was small in stature with beautiful features, large eyes with a piercing glance. The stiff saintly figure of the contemporary mosaic portrait of the empress in the Apse of San Vitale in Ravenna would appear the antithesis of the monster described by Procopius. The true character lies no doubt somewhere between. Her career shows that she was at the very least an extraordinary woman, born to shine in any situation or in any country.

If, in retrospect, Justinian's great wars may be considered errors, nevertheless they undoubtedly enhanced the renown of the Byzantine Empire, and Justinian's reign as a whole certainly contributed to the astonishing survival of this Greek heir of the Roman Empire. Thanks to Byzantium, the Slavs of the Balkans and of Russia made their first and unforgettable contact with Christian civilization and thought, whilst in Asia many states imitated the institutions of a city which had shown such a high survival value. Though often defeated by the Moslem armies in the early Middle Ages, Byzantium was never conquered by the Saracens and long helped to defend the West. It lasted as a Christian citadel until 1453, when it fell to the Turks.

The greatness of Justinian does not rest on his wars. It rests as much if not more on his great buildings and on his work as a lawgiver. His character is difficult to determine accurately, but he was certainly bigoted, despotic and without many humanly attractive features. In one of his many brilliant summings up of great figures in history, H. A. L. Fisher writes of Justinian:

A man so jealous, vain, and irresolute, a man of whom no design was too great, no detail too small, no superstition too absurd, and no subject irrelevant or remote, cannot excite admiration. With almost infinite resources of skill and industry, he appears to have lacked the higher gifts of statesmanship, the energetic will, the true sense of proportion, the capacity for taking unpleasant decisions. Few men whose personality is so uncertain fill a greater place in history. As for a moment we tread beside him through the corridors of the past, we seem to see the shades of night battling with the blood-red sunset of imperial Rome.

MOHAMMED
(570?–632)

ARABIA AT the close of the sixth century was a country of gross idolatry, superstition, ignorance and intemperance, a divided country where tribe warred with tribe, clan with clan. Miraculously, one man, Mohammed, by the force of his tremendous personality, completely transformed the life of this people; in the incredibly short space of twenty odd years he united them in the bonds of a lasting faith and laid the foundations of a mighty empire.

Mohammed was born in Mecca around A.D. 570. His clan was the powerful Koreish to which all the Meccan notables belonged. The Koreishites were the guardians of the Kaaba within whose walls were 360 crude stone effigies of deities. From all parts of Arabia an endless stream of pilgrims came to Mecca to worship in the holy shrine.

Mohammed, who had lost both parents (his father had died before his birth, his mother when he was six), was brought up by Abu Taleb, his uncle. Abu Taleb was a merchant, and in due course Mohammed became the leader of his caravans. It was during the long journeys across the desert that the contemplative side of his nature was formed.

Honest, truthful, reliable, Mohammed was well-liked in Mecca; although not much of a talker, he had a pleasant manner, a ready laugh and an attractive smile. He was considered an oddity, however, for his kindness to animals and his complete lack of interest in women.

At twenty-three, Mohammed entered the service of a wealthy widow, Khatija. Khatija, who was in her fortieth year but still comely, gradually lost her heart to her handsome young camel-leader, and at the end of two years offered him her hand. Surprisingly, she bore her husband six children, four daughters and two sons, both of whom died at an early age. The marriage was an extremely happy one, and during the twenty-one years that it lasted Mohammed never gave a thought to another woman.

Mohammed's tastes were simple, but while wealth meant nothing to him it gave him leisure for contemplation. Khatija's cousin, an old man named Waraka, had often accompanied him on the caravan journeys; a convert first to Judaism and then Christianity, he had taught Mohammed much about these two religions. Mohammed now had time to ponder over what he had learnt, and the more he pondered the more he doubted the ritual of the Kaaba; finally, he rejected it altogether, utterly convinced that there was only one God. There is nothing strange in the fact that he identified this Supreme Being with Allah, the Lord of the Kaaba, for Allah is a contraction of *al-ilah* which signifies *the* God. A prophet was needed to teach men that Allah alone, the source of everything in this life and the hereafter, should be worshipped, Mohammed told himself: surely, he thought, this prophet would soon appear. . . .

A great need for solitude filled Mohammed. Not far from Mecca was a towering boulder, Mount Hira, and in the small, dark cave in its rocky side he passed long hours in meditation. In A.D. 610 came the Call.

One day, when he was at home, he suddenly began to tremble violently, the sweat broke out all over his body, and he lost consciousness. When he had fully recovered from this mysterious attack, he went as usual to the cave, and at nightfall lay down, wrapped in his mantle, on the rocky floor. He had scarcely closed his eyes when a voice called: "Mohammed!" At first he dared not open his eyes, but it repeated his name so insistently that at last he looked up. There before him stood a shining Being. "Recite!" it commanded him, "Recite in the Name of the Lord who created all things, who created man from a clod; recite in the Name of the Most High who taught man the use of a pen, and taught him what he knew not." Awestruck, Mohammed obeyed, and when he was word-perfect the Being said: "Oh, Mohammed, truly thou art the messenger of Allah, and I am the angel Gabriel." With that, the angel vanished.

Overcome with this stupendous announcement, Mohammed stumbled out of the cave, hastened blindly home, woke Khatija and stammered out the revelation that had been made to him. Instantly, joyfully, she accepted him as Allah's chosen Prophet.

Mohammed had expected a second revelation almost immediately, but when none came he was assailed by doubts and fears. The story goes that in his despair he was about to fling himself from Mount Hira when Gabriel reappeared and said once more: "Truly thou art Mohammed, the Messenger of God." It was, however, through prayer and fasting that Mohammed became convinced that he had not dreamed the Call.

The most important members of Mohammed's first small band of converts were his close friend, Abu Bekr, a rich merchant (Abu Bekr was to become the first Caliph), and Ali, the young son of Abu Taleb, whom Mohammed had taken into his home.

The meetings of these early converts were held in secret, for Mohammed was fully aware of how bitterly the Koreishites would oppose him. "Recite," he would say to his listeners, and they would memorize the words Allah spoke through his mouth. These sayings were later written down, traditionally on palm-leaves, and after Mohammed's death were embodied in a single manuscript: the Koran.

The second revelation made to Mohammed was all-important. In four years he had made only forty converts; now he was commanded: "Rise and Warn."

Mohammed did not hesitate. He summoned the Koreishites to Mount Hira, and standing above them on a rock, an impressive figure in his mantle, with his flashing black eyes and flowing beard, he said solemnly: "I am commanded to warn you that you will know no profit now or hereafter if you do not acknowledge the One and Only God." The enraged Koreishites stopped to hear no more.

From now on Mohammed openly preached Allah's precepts which constituted, in effect, a whole programme of social reform. As more and more Meccans professed the Faith, Islam*, the Koreishites, thoroughly alarmed, took steps to suppress the movement. Led by Abu Sofian, commander of the Meccan army, and Abu Jahl, an important official, the persecution of Mohammed and his followers, the Moslems, began. Mohammed was beaten up and stoned, and many of his supporters were savagely tortured. Unafraid for himself, Mohammed persuaded a band of Moslems to seek safety in Abyssinia; convinced that the Prophet intended to establish an army there, Abu Sofian confined the Prophet and his adherents in a wretched quarter of the city where they remained for three years. Not long after they had been released, worn out by the hardships she had endured, Khatija died.

At fifty, Mohammed found himself a poor man once more, for Khatija's wealth had long vanished. This did not trouble him, for the sole use he had for money was to give it to the needy.

Within a few months of Khatija's death Mohammed married

*The name Islam is derived from *Salama*, meaning peace, submission to God. *Salama* is also the root of Moslem which signifies one who surrenders to Him.

again—married twice. Sawda was middle-aged and plain, the widow of a Moslem who had died for the cause—Mohammed married her to give her a home. Aisha was only seven; she was the daughter of Abu Bekr, and Mohammed probably married her to honour his friend. He did not consummate the marriage until Aisha was ten, an age at which many girls in the East are mature. Aisha was the only virgin he was to know. Mohammed subsequently took six more wives, only one of whom, Zeinab, can be said to have attracted him; he married the other five either to afford them his protection or to ally himself with an important clan. Aisha, spirited and gay, while she could not take Khatija's place in his heart, was his favourite wife. She was barren, and strangely none of the rest bore him a son.

In A.D. 620 an apparently trivial incident proved to be the turning-point in Mohammed's life. A small band of pilgrims from Medina heard him preach. Now the Medinese were vaguely monotheistic owing to the fact that one or two Jewish tribes lived close to their city; they also knew from these Jews that the Hebrew people lived in expectation of a prophet. The impression made by Mohammed on this band of pilgrims was so great that they were convinced he was the prophet in question. The following year, with a large number of their fellow-citizens, they returned to Mecca, embraced Islam, and begged Mohammed to come and dwell amongst them. Their invitation could not have come at a more opportune moment, for the persecution had grown so severe that the Moslems went in daily fear of their lives. Mohammed, therefore, made a pact with the Medinese: provided they would give refuge to his followers, he would do as they wished. The pilgrims gladly agreed.

A.D. 622 was the year of the Hegira, the Year of the Flight or Emigration. One by one, small parties of Moslems secretly left Mecca until finally only a handful remained in the city. Mohammed was making the necessary arrangements for these few to follow the rest when he himself was suddenly forced to flee.

One evening a Moslem burst into the Prophet's house with the dire news that Abu Sofian and Abu Jahl intended to kill him that very night. Ali, snatching off his uncle's cloak, told him and Abu Bekr to fly for their lives; as soon as they had gone, he bolted the door, barred the shutters, and, wrapping himself in the cloak, lay down on the bed. When the would-be assassins arrived they found that they could not get in without using force; peering through a crack in the shutters, they saw the well-known mantle and decided to wait till Mohammed came out in the morning. By the time they discovered they had been tricked, Mohammed and Abu Bekr were some miles away in the desert.

Mohammed had foreseen that if he and Abu Bekr started off for Medina by camel, the Koreishite horsemen sent to pursue them would follow their track and would swiftly overtake them. The fugitives, therefore, had set out on foot by a devious route, and when daylight came they hid in a cave. It so happened that a small band of Koreishites, finding no camel-tracks, made a detour which brought them to this cave; they dismounted, intending to search it, but when they noticed a spider's web across its mouth they decided it was a waste of time.

At last Mohammed and Abu Bekr reached an oasis near Medina where they rested and bathed and gave thanks to Allah. The news of their arrival soon reached the city, and a crowd of Moslems hastened to greet their Prophet. Mounted on an almost white camel, Mohammed rode into Medina where he was given a tumultuous welcome. The legend goes that he said he would build his mosque wherever the camel halted—that intelligent animal stopped at the perfect site! Mohammed had not been long in Medina before Ali, together with the few Moslems who had remained in Mecca, rejoined him in the city.

In spite of repeated demands by Abu Sofian and Abu Jahl, the Medinese obstinately refused to expel the Prophet. Seething with anger, Mohammed's two arch-enemies dispatched skirmishing parties to raid the outskirts of the city. These razzias were common amongst the Arabs, therefore Mohammed saw nothing wrong in ordering his followers to ambush Meccan caravans. When one Meccan was killed, Abu Sofian and Abu Jahl had the pretext they needed for taking up arms against the Moslems.

In A.D. 624, the Fourth Year of the Flight, news reached Mohammed that Abu Jahl with an army of a thousand men was marching towards Medina. Although he had denounced the shedding of blood in battle, the Prophet, as the defender of Islam, proclaimed the Jehad, the Holy War.

Mohammed could only muster some three hundred ill-trained, poorly armed men, but undaunted he led them out of the city and decided to make his stand at Jadr, a sandy plain crossed by a brook which had been dammed here and there to form reservoirs. With inspired strategy, he stationed his "army" round the reservoir nearest to the enemy, and blocked the others; he thus had command of the all-important water supply. Mohammed, watching the progress of the battle from a hill, saw that the Meccan troops, forced to fight in the blazing heat, unable to quench their thirst, were nevertheless gaining the upper hand. Scooping up a handful of sand, he flung it towards them, shouting, "Confusion on your faces!" As if by a miracle, a sudden sandstorm arose and blew straight towards them; stung by the burning grains, they began to fall back. "On, on!" yelled Abu Jahl, and galloping forward, engaged a Moslem leader who, after a furious combat, unseated him and cut off his head with a single sweep of his scimitar. With their leader dead, the Meccan forces withdrew ingloriously.

Abu Sofian swore revenge, and in the Fifth Year of the Flight he marched against the Moslems with a far larger army. This second battle took place at Mount Uhud. Mohammed, who had disposed his small force as brilliantly as at Jadr, had given his archers strict orders not to move from their position. Unfortunately, as the enemy reeled back beneath the onslaught of the Moslem swordsmen, the archers disobeyed him and rushed forward to attack, thus leaving a gap through which the Meccan soldiers poured. Mohammed, as he galloped into the thick of the mêlée to rally his men, crashed to the ground beneath a hail of spears and javelins; Abu Sofian saw him fall, and shouted aloud in triumph, but after the Moslems had been forced to retreat to Medina, he searched in vain for Mohammed's body amongst the slain. It was not until he was on his way back that he learned that, far from being killed, Mohammed had only been slightly wounded. Furious with rage, as soon as he had mustered a huge army he set out to take Medina by force.

A Persian convert, experienced in siege warfare, saved the city. He told the defenders to dig a trench too wide for a horse to leap across; thus when the Meccan troops galloped forward to attack, they found themselves separated from the walls by this moat, from behind which the Moslem archers shot their arrows with deadly accuracy. Day after day they vainly returned to the assault; night after night they shivered in their camp in the bitter winter weather. Then the rain came pelting down, and when a sudden tearing wind blew down their tents, causing their horses to stampede, they retreated in wild disorder.

After this humiliating failure to take Medina, Meccan prestige fell very low, while that of the Prophet soared. All the tribes in the vicinity of the city rallied to him and embraced Islam. He became so powerful that Abu Sofian was forced to conclude a treaty with him, which among other concessions gave him the right to lead Medinese pilgrimages to Mecca. An infringement of this treaty roused Mohammed's just anger, and in the Seventh Year of the Flight he marched on the Holy City.

As Mohammed advanced across the desert the Bedouins flocked to join him; it was with an army ten thousand strong that he reached the gates of Mecca. Abu Sofian surrendered abjectly, and the Prophet entered the city. There was no bloodshed—Mohammed even spared the life of his arch-enemy.

Once within the walls, Mohammed donned the pilgrim's white robe, and with a party of his followers similarly attired made his way to the Kaaba. One by one the stone idols were ground to powder; the moment that Mohammed had dreamed of so long had arrived at last.

Abu Sofian and all the Meccans professed Islam. From Medina, Mohammed, now virtually ruler of Arabia, dispatched ambassadors to Rome, Egypt, Persia, Abyssinia to spread the Faith.

The Tenth Year of the Flight saw what was to become known as the Farewell Pilgrimage. Forty thousand pilgrims followed Mohammed to Mount Arafat; from its summit as dawn broke, he led them in prayer and recited to them from the Koran. Then in a loud voice he cried: "Oh Lord, I have delivered my message and accomplished my work."

Not many months after his return to Medina from this pilgrimage his health began to fail. In A.D. 632, the Eleventh Year of the Flight, Mohammed died with his head in the lap of Aisha, his favourite wife.

Of all great leaders, none has been so much maligned as Mohammed. Many of his detractors have called him an arch-impostor, an accusation to which his tremendous achievement gives the lie. Only a man of burning sincerity, utter integrity, could have established a Faith which today draws more converts than any other religion.

ABD AL-RAHMAN

(d. 788)

WHEN THE Abbasides (descendants of Mohammed's uncle, Abbas) overthrew the Omayyad Caliphate in Syria in 750, two brothers fled to escape the ensuing massacre and sought refuge in a village near the Euphrates. Run to earth, they plunged desperately into the river. The elder, eighteen, managed to struggle to the far bank. Exhausted and dripping, he looked back for his thirteen-year-old brother to see that the youngster had been overtaken and hauled back; a moment later he was beheaded before the horrified watcher's eyes.

The surviving brother was Abd al-Rahman, and this grim tragedy was to mark his first step on a road that was destined from then on to be punctuated with violence and peril, but which, nevertheless, was to lead the young fugitive to great eminence and power as founder of the Moorish emirate (later caliphate) of Cordoba, in Spain.

Abd al-Rahman's belief in his destiny had been deep-rooted since a day when, as a child, a prophecy had been voiced in his hearing by his great-uncle, Maslama ben Abd el Malik, who had looked in to see his grandfather, the caliph Hisham.

The caliph had been on the point of sending his grandson away, but the great-uncle had restrained him, saying: "Let the child be, for I see in him the man of the Omayyads who will revive this dynasty after its fall."

From that moment, Abd al-Rahman observed that his distinguished grandfather seemed to display a special partiality towards him.

After his breathless escape from the Abbasides, Abd al-Rahman became a wanderer. In time he got to Palestine and then crossed Egypt into Ifrikia, following the established caravan route. He stayed for a while at Kaironan, in Tunisia, until suddenly arrested and brought before the Governor of Ifrikia, Ibn Habib. He was recognized by a former servant of his great uncle who promptly proclaimed him as "destined to conquer Spain, and no doubt Africa as well". He declared that it had been prophesied that the

192

conqueror would have two curls upon his brow. When the Governor saw that the wanderer did indeed have two such curls his first impulse was to have him put to death as a potential rival to his authority. But the old servant intervened and vowed that destiny would never permit that.

So Abd al-Rahman was spared, though his followers were killed and had their goods seized.

Whether legend, or superstition, based upon Eastern fatalism, tipped the scale in favour of the wandering Syrian from the territory of Damascus cannot be said; but it is a fact that he went on to fulfil the prophecy.

He knew that Ibn Habib was ambitious of creating an independent realm for himself in Africa, so deemed it prudent to resume his wanderings. He made his way through Morocco and settled for a time near Ceuta, among a Berber tribe, the Nafza, to which his mother, a former African slave, had belonged. These tribesmen befriended him, and plans began to take shape in his mind. Spain, in the grip of anarchy, lay near, and there were Omayyad partisans there whom he hoped to gather round him. He sent one of his followers, Badr, to take soundings among old soldiers from Damascus, now known to be in Elvira and Jaen.

At that time a dissolute and brutal tyrant called Somail had conquered the Yemenites, aided by the governor, Yousouf, so the Yemenites welcomed Abd al-Rahman's approach, which offered a chance of revenge. Eventually, Abd al-Rahman struck, and in a battle on the banks of the Guadalquivir, between Seville and Cordoba, Somail and Yousouf were defeated. Their conqueror was hailed as Emir of Spain in 756, and it is said that on landing at Almunecar he felt "wholly possessed by his great-uncle's prediction"* made so many years before.

What kind of man was this young conqueror of twenty-five? He had already demonstrated energy, generalship and vision. Some accounts refer to him as one-eyed, but all agree that he was an impressive figure of a man; very tall, with reddish-yellow hair. The two distinctive curls upon his forehead have been referred to already. He was exceptionally virile, utterly without fear; a persuasive and eloquent talker.

Of his iron resolution in persistently following what he firmly held to be his inflexible destiny there can be very little doubt. Once he had crossed into Spain he lost no time in making himself fully independent of the Caliph of Baghdad and pursued his dream of

* The History of Spain. Bertrand and Petrie.

setting up a completely new Syrian-Arab dynasty. Though he made every haste to consolidate his position, he was allowed barely one year's respite from strife. Somail was much too debauched in his habits to present any real challenge; but Yousouf was sufficiently determined to venture upon rebellion once he had managed to raise 20,000 supporters.

Aided by the Governor of Seville, Abd al-Rahman met this challenge to his authority and the revolt was suppressed. The emir decided to make an example of the rebel chief and had Yousouf beheaded together with his son who had been held as a hostage throughout the rebellion. By Abd al-Rahman's command both severed heads were placed on public display on the bridge at Cordoba. As a further lesson to would-be rivals he had Somail strangled.

Though he had thus succeeded in ridding himself of his two chief rivals, his troubles were far from being over. A Yemenite rebellion, followed by a revolt in Toledo, forced the emir to stand siege in Carmona for two months. When ultimately victorious in quelling these insurrections he decided that an even more forceful gesture was called for. He had the heads of the leading rebels cut off as before; but this time he had them stuffed with salt and myrrh, packed in boxes, and sent over the long caravan route to the Caliph of Baghdad who was suspected of having stirred up the revolt. What the caliph thought of this grisly gift does not appear to be on record.

It was the Berbers who next turned upon the ambitious young emir, and they were only subdued after a series of prolonged struggles.

Then came a completely new threat in an insurrection in the north, where another of Yousouf's sons and a son-in-law had joined forces with the Governor of Barcelona. This was a formidable challenge indeed, for the trio had also invoked the powerful aid of the mighty Emperor Charlemagne, who, accompanied by his doughty nephew, Roland, marched across the Pyrenees with every intention of laying siege to Saragossa. It looked as if a tremendous clash was inevitable, but, in the event, Charlemagne and Abd al-Rahman were never destined to meet, though some historians were later to compare the character of the emir with that of the emperor. For some reason battle was never joined and the invading forces withdrew. This was the historic occasion of the epic stand made against Basque mountaineers in the Pass of Roncesvalles—the rearguard action fought so desperately by the emperor's nephew and immortalized in "The Song of Roland".

What might have been a decidedly interesting historic clash of great leaders was avoided, Abd al-Rahman was kept feverishly engaged for most of his troubled administration in combating and crushing one conspiracy after another. He never shirked any challenge but fought tirelessly and courageously, dealing out the most savage punishments to the various enemies he brought to submission.

As the years went by, nearly everyone who could conspire against him must have done so. Even one of his brothers was among the rivals whom he had to subdue. It is small wonder, then, that his grim experiences turned him into a fearsome tyrant, obliged to rule by force. Indeed, the day was to come when the emir could move only under the staunch protection of an Imperial Guard of specially recruited Berbers; and it was always necessary for him to maintain a standing army of 40,000 European slaves (Slavonas) ever ready in the background.

The destiny he had chosen to follow so unswervingly thus turned out to be one that constantly necessitated the waging of remorseless warfare against threats of internal strife for upwards of thirty years. The wonder is that in spite of this ever-present handicap to settled rule he did succeed in establishing a centralized power and never for one moment abandoned the ideal of creating something worthwhile.

Surrounded and menaced, as he was, by every conceivable kind of barbarity, intrigue and revolt, it is probably fair to concede that a great many of the cruelties laid to his name were inevitably forced upon him by sheer weight of circumstance. Nevertheless, he was capable of showing forbearance and it has been recorded that he showed clemency towards the Christians. At least one commentator, Ibn el Athir, has described the better sides of his complex character and has credited the emir with being: "Benignant, well-informed, resolute; prompt to crush rebellion, he never remained long in repose or given over to idleness; he never entrusted the care of his affairs to anybody, and relied upon no judgment but his own."

The same commentator mentions that Abd al-Rahman was endowed with profound intelligence. And, speaking of his great courage, says that he united bravery "pushed to the point of daring" with great prudence. He also "showed himself broad-minded and generous".

When scattered scraps of information concerning Abd al-Rahman are pieced together there emerges a picture of a man of many parts. As an administrator he certainly sought vigorously to establish law and order. He organized a Council of State; reorganized the judiciary under a senior Cadi; and divided Spain into six military provinces.

His capital, probably of Carthaginian origin, and carefully colonized by the Romans, actually doubled its size under the dynasty he established.

He is credited with having started the Great Mosque at Cordoba on the site of a Roman temple and a Visigoth church, his dream being to establish a great religious centre in his chosen capital to rival those of the East. His mosque finally became the great cathedral world-famous for its beauty today.

Abd al-Rahman not only beautified his capital; he provided schools and hospitals; he also adapted and improved the old palace of Cordoba and built a country seat for himself, naming it Ruzafa to honour the memory of his grandfather, Caliph Hisham, who had built the Damascene Ruzafa.

That he was able to accomplish so much constructive work of this nature while fighting almost ceaselessly against successive threats to his realm is surely evidence enough of his boundless energy and strength of character. His capital became famous for its silversmiths, its silk embroideries and for a special kind of leather. Under his guidance it became progressive in every way.

It is obvious that the emir can have enjoyed scant leisure to devote to family life, yet he sired a family of twenty children—eleven sons and nine daughters.

One more interesting facet of his many-sided character must be mentioned. This doughty warrior, who usually dressed all in white, had great poetic yearnings, and though very little of his verse seems to have survived there are sufficient fragments to indicate the existence of a tender, deeply reflective side to his nature. Some historians have been moved to express astonishment that a ruthless man of action should have betrayed an ingrained love of beauty and refinement amounting almost to a sentimental streak. But is this so astonishing? Haven't a great many men of action revealed similar tendencies? It may even be an inevitable reaction—the assertion of a sincerely felt longing for peace and beauty to offset the turmoil and ugliness that has dogged their lives—a longing for serenity that can be captured only on paper.

The surviving verses of Abd al-Rahman undoubtedly betray a nostalgic yearning for his beloved Damascus. In one poem, inspired by the unexpected appearance of a lone palm tree in the grounds of his new Ruzafa retreat, he likens himself to this unique growth.

This palm tree, he says wistfully, "has strayed into the soil of the West, far from the land where dwell its peers. There, I say to myself, is my image. I, too, live in far-off exile".

The self-same theme is repeated with even greater feeling in another surviving fragment and suggests a veritable cry from the heart of the poet.

> Traveller, You who go to my country, take with you there the salutation of half of myself to my other half.
>
> My body, as you know, is in one place, but my heart and its affections are in another.
>
> Marked out as it was by Destiny, the separation has had to be accomplished, but it has chased sleep from my lids.
>
> The Divine will that ordained this divorce will perhaps decree, some day, our reunion.

That desired reunion was not to be. The self-made Emir of Spain, who had wandered so far in following what he devoutly believed to be his pre-ordained path of destiny, died in "exile" in his fifty-seventh year.

CHARLEMAGNE

(742–814)

CHARLEMAGNE REIGNED in France and over most of Western Europe from 764–814. His reign was a period of order and enlightenment at the end of what is called "the Dark Ages", but it was a brief period only and chaos came again before the civilization of the Middle Ages of the twelfth and thirteenth centuries.

Charlemagne was a contemporary of Offa, King of Mercia, the most powerful of the Anglo-Saxon kings at that time and the only monarch in Europe whom Charlemagne treated as an equal. Legends grew up about Charlemagne, and in the eleventh and twelfth centuries he was presented as a hero of chivalry. Indeed some of the troubadours and trouvères wrote about him and his knights as of another King Arthur and the Round Table. Charlemagne, however, exists as a very real and historical personage. He can be seen through the eyes of contemporaries and there is one full contemporary record, that of Einhard, a German monk, who wrote *Vita Caroli Magni*.

One must look at Charlemagne not as a knight in shining armour but rather as a recently civilized Frankish chieftain, dressed in a short tunic or linen shirt, wearing breeches cross-strapped with leather and, in the cold, a waistcoat of otter fur with a cloak. He had his legendary white beard, but certainly also the long thin moustaches of Frankish warriors. He used to carry a cane cut from an apple tree with symmetrical knots. He was probably not the gigantic figure of legend, but of moderate height (his father was called Peppin the Short), with a thick neck and a protruding stomach. He had a somewhat high voice. He was, however, a most imposing personality, choleric, tyrannical, watchful. He had much of the crude cunning of the barbarian chief, the ruler of savage men. His immense respect for learning and for wise men, which helped to make him a great ruler, had a naïvete but also a strength which a sophisticated emperor might not have had.

The atmosphere which surrounds this great monarch is not that of the Middle Ages, as we understand the term, but one much more similar to that of Anglo-Saxon England. As we shall see, in many ways England in the eighth century was more civilized than the continent. She had only so far had to face the onslaught of the Angles and Saxons and not the successive waves of barbarian conquerors which had broken over the continent as the Roman Empire had lapsed into nothingness.

In discussing the future of Europe today, the term "Charlemagne's Europe" is often used to denote a Europe based on the unity of Germany, France and Italy. Charlemagne did for a short while unite most of Western Europe, and he was crowned Holy Roman Emperor in 800 by Pope Leo III. Those of his contemporaries who could read and write, and these were mostly ecclesiastics or great nobles, saw Charlemagne literally as the restorer of the Roman Empire. The Roman Empire had officially ceased to exist in 475 when a Gothic chief, Odoacer, had deposed the last Roman Emperor and decided not to appoint another. But it had ceased to exist a long time before that when the empire had been over-run by Germanic tribes—of whom the largest were the Goths, Visigoths and Vandals. The Vandals had sacked Rome in 455 and the Goths, under Alaric, had sacked it 410. Yet the fiction of a Western Empire had been preserved.

The invaders, who kept on coming into the west all the time, settled in the empire, and Romans and Gallo-Romans (the Gauls of France who had long been Romanized) believed that the empire would completely absorb them. In 451, under a Roman general Aetius, Frankish and Alemmani tribes had defeated the Huns under Attila in a great battle near Paris in which 300,000 men had been engaged. But after the fifth century the idea that the empire would survive lived on, though as we can see today nothing really justified the belief.

A Frankish kingdom under Clovis, the first of the Merovingian kings, proved the most powerful of the kingdoms which the barbarians had hewn out of the empire: the Franks were the people who had settled in northern France and the Rhineland. After defeating a Roman general, Syragus, at Soissons, Clovis then turned on the Alemmani, a rival Germanic tribe, promising to become a Christian if he could defeat them. His wish was granted; his promise was fulfilled. Then in 507 Clovis defeated the Visigoths who possessed most of France south of the Loire and all of Spain. Clovis gave the name of France, land of the Francs, to the country which had hitherto been Gaul, the great Roman province and the land of the Celts.

The Merovingian Frankish dynasty lasted for three hundred years, longer than did the Valois or the Bourbon kings. Clovis's heirs, however, were savage despots who, as debauchery wore out their stock, lapsed into incompetent puppets. They lost many provinces which Clovis won and had little control over the rest of their kingdom. One of the last Merovingians to rule more or less effectively was Dagobert in the seventh century. But he died of old age at thirty-four, prematurely worn out, it is said, by his numerous concubines.

If Clovis's kingdom did not break up it was due to the Church, whose bishops, priests and monks supplied what existed of an administration. The Church indeed was what remained of the Roman Empire, its real heir. There were also Roman towns, in which Franks and Gauls lived like campers in a deserted palace, Roman roads, aqueducts, baths and arenas, but these were disused or ruined, except in parts of the south of France where something remained of the old civilization. The Roman Church alone worked, of all the institutions of the old empire.

At the beginning of the eighth century, the Arabs who had conquered Spain advanced into France. Officials of the Merovingian court, called the Mayors of the Palace, now took charge of the kingdom, and it was one of these, Charles Martel, who with a force of Frankish infantry defeated a Moorish army near Poitiers in 732, from which time the Arab invasion of France gradually ended and the invaders were pushed back into the Pyrenees. Charles Martel's son, Peppin the Short, was allowed by the Pope to depose the last of the Merovingian kings and, in 754, the Pope, Stephen II, came to France and crowned Peppin King of France, giving his two sons, Charles and Carloman, the title of Patricians of the Romans.

The Carolingian dynasty was now legitimate and was given a religious character or sanction which the French monarchy possessed henceforward. In return, Peppin subdued the Lombards, a Germanic tribe long settled in northern Italy (which, indeed, ruled over most of the peninsula), and handed over to the Pope territories which he took from the Lombards in central Italy. These territories had belonged to the Empire of the East, the Byzantine Empire; they became the Papal States and they were to last, as the property of the Pope, from the eighth century to 1870. The power of the Papacy increased at the same time as the power and prestige of the Frankish monarchy.

This perhaps helps to make it clear why the nobles and ecclesiastics who lived in France and Italy considered that Charlemagne, who succeeded his father Peppin the Short, had the mission to restore the secular Roman Empire, called Holy because of its indissoluble alliance with the Sovereign Pontiff. Charlemagne himself, a man of good sense, did not see himself as a Roman Emperor. He called himself "Emperor governing the Roman Empire", for he did not wish to supplant the legitimate emperor at Byzantium and, in any case, considered himself a Frankish king. But he was deeply impressed by Rome which he visited in 774; and then in 800 he had gone there to help Pope Leo III again. He was not perhaps altogether displeased when, on Christmas Day, as he was kneeling in prayer before the altar, the Pope placed the Imperial Crown on his head and a number of people present cried out: "Long life and victory to Charles Augustus the crowned of God, the great powerful Emperor of the Romans." But Charlemagne forbade his son to accept the Imperial crown.

Charlemagne was engaged in wars throughout his life. One of the first was against the Lombards, whom his father had fought; and like Peppin he fought at the behest of the Pope. But he had a personal quarrel with the King of the Lombards, Desiderius. Charlemagne had succeeded to only half the realm of his father, the northern half, his brother Carloman reigning over the rest. Carloman died three years after Peppin and Desiderius proclaimed Carloman's widow and children as rulers. Legally, this was the custom of the German tribes, who did not recognize primogeniture. Charlemagne disposed quickly of Desiderius, whom he deported to France, and crowned himself King of the Lombards.

When he went to Rome he was deeply impressed by the Christian relics, and dazzled by the splendid Church ceremonies and the beautiful Gregorian music. It was from then on that he called himself "King by the grace of God". In Rome, Charlemagne had no difficulty in legalizing his repudiation of his first wife, Desiderata, the daughter of the former Lombard king. He married a Princess Hildegarde of the Alemmani. He had already had a son from an illegal union with a Frankish noblewoman by name Himiltrude. He was to marry, later on, on Hildegarde's death, Fastrada, also a Frank, and on her death in 794 a German princess named Luitgarde. With four wives he had many mistresses, keeping them in his great palace at Aachen (Aix-la-Chapelle) which, with its baths and innumerable marble columns, was built like a Roman palace. Order reigned in the palace, which was never the scene of debauchery and drunkenness as in Merovingian times.

He brought up his family strictly and tried, unsuccessfully, to prevent his daughters marrying until he had found them the husbands he wanted. Among his pleasures in the Aachen Palace was that of swimming, and at that, even as an old man, the monarch excelled, beating young men in races.

Charlemagne fought no less than forty campaigns during his reign of forty-three years. These were, however, most of them, military expeditions which began in the late spring and ended in the summer before travelling became difficult. Some of his early wars, which were to subdue Aquitaine or Burgundy, were really more or less military promenades. So too were most of his expeditions to Italy, where he took Venice, though, later on, the Emperor of Byzantium recaptured it. The serious wars were against the Avars in Hungary and the tribes of North and East Germany, particularly the Saxons. The Saxons—the hard race which had in the past over-run Britain—wanted neither to be ruled over by Charlemagne nor to accept Christianity. They were defeated in a number of campaigns, after one of which Charlemagne had four thousand men beheaded in a single day. But this act of barbarism was exceptional. As a rule Charlemagne, when he had overcome a tribe or a group of tribes and had had homage paid to him and taken hostages for good behaviour, allowed the conquered to rule themselves according to their own laws, provided they accepted Christianity.

In some cases he brought back the population of a conquered region to Gaul and gave them land—sending Franks to colonize the conquered territory. His empire extended eastwards to the Elbe and across the Danube and to the borders of the Byzantine Empire. His success can no doubt partly be explained by the quietening of the onrush of the barbarians from the east which had already lasted four hundred years.

Charlemagne was a great man of war, but equally great as a man of peace. He organized his empire, or at least the parts of it which he could manage, such as France, the Rhineland, and Bavaria, with a new accent on justice. Like St. Louis in the thirteenth century, he employed monks and learned men as his representatives, sending them to visit all the provinces. A monk or bishop travelled with a count or military commander and they were known as the Missi Dominici—the master's envoys. One of these envoys was the Bishop of Orléans, a learned man called Theodulf, and he did not fear to over-rule local lords, to denounce bribery. In certain parts of France, Theodulf succeeded in ending certain old customs, such as trial by boiling water or red-hot irons, when there was no conclusive evidence. Instead, an accused man was made to stand upright and with his arms extended in the form of a cross: prayers were then recited by monks—and if the man made no movement at all he was judged innocent. Charlemagne himself periodically went to the less civilized centres of his realm such as Ratisbon or Paderborn to hold assemblies. He and his retinue lived in tents and so too did the chiefs and their tribesmen from distant parts who camped around the emperor waiting for their turn to consult with him.

Charlemagne summoned scholars from all over Europe to his court at Aachen. One of his aims was to set up new ecclesiastical schools in great cities such as Paris and Toulouse and to translate and restore manuscripts. One of his assistants was Alcuin, the scholar who had the celebrated monastic school at York, one of the best in Christendom. Alcuin and Theodulf busied themselves also with reforming Latin as a spoken language and re-ordering the way mass was to be said in churches and monasteries. At Aachen Alcuin presided over a sort of learned academy attended by Charlemagne, his wives and daughters and counsellors; at this school the emperor became a pupil and was known as David. Charlemagne, who could read a little but had never learnt to write, would in his old age sleep with writing tablets under his pillow so that if he was sleepless he could practise writing. Manuscripts were searched for by Charlemagne's emissaries in Italy, Greece and at the court of the great Caliph Harun-al-Rashid in Baghdad. The caliph sent Charlemagne a clock which was no less a wonder than an elephant, another gift of the caliph.

The Arab world at that time was a most civilized part of the globe and still remained skilled in war. It was against the Arabs of Spain that Charlemagne fought his only unsuccessful campaign. He invaded Spain in 778 and failed to take Saragossa, where the Moorish king defied him. Forced to retreat from Spain because of trouble in Saxony, a small rearguard of the Franks commanded by Hroudland, the Margrave of the Breton marchi, was ambushed and annihilated by the Basques in a valley of the Pyrenees called Roncesvalles. This comparatively unimportant military episode was to become a popular epic, and before the battle of Hastings in 1066 the minstrel Taillefer encouraged the Normans with a popular version of Charlemagne's deeds in Spain and the gallant Roland's great fight. Roland and Oliver and the rest of the Frankish knights were turned into typical heroes of medieval romances. The *Chanson de Roland*, one of the greatest epic poems of the world, was given its final form by monks in the twelfth century, some three hundred years after Charlemagne was dead.

No historical ruler has ever been more the subject of myth than

Charlemagne. It was said a hundred years after his death, and widely believed, that he had made a pilgrimage to Jerusalem. Charlemagne is also supposed to have had a sword called Joyeuse which contained the point of the lance with which the Roman soldier had pierced the side of Christ on the Cross. Many more extraordinary stories were told about him, which bear practically no relevance to history.

In German myths Charlemagne was said, like Frederick Barbarossa, to be awaiting a resurrection when he would win back his empire. In a Bavarian myth, Charlemagne was said to be upright in his tomb at Aachen with his white beard still growing: when his beard had three times encircled the stone table before which he was sitting the end of the world would come. His name was given in the Middle Ages to the constellation of the Great Bear which is sometimes called in English Charles's Wain (Karlswagen).

Myths apart, Charlemagne's empire was a great achievement. But the search for the unity of Christendom, which has never been successful, was more impossible in the ninth century even than in the thirteenth. Charlemagne's grandsons divided his empire into three parts. Most of Germany went to one son and France was divided into two: Lotharingia, east of the Rhône and the Saone; and Neustria, that part of France to the west of those rivers. The continent was once again in the melting pot, and in November, 885, seven hundred sailing ships full of Vikings or Norsemen were in the lower Seine, some miles from Paris. It was to be left to the Counts of Paris to create France.

HARUN-AL-RASHID

(763–809)

HARUN-AL-RASHID, caliph of the Abbasid Empire which stretched from India to North Africa, was born in 763 (though some consider it was two years later) and died in 809. His reign of twenty-three years and that of his son, the caliph Mamun, came to be regarded as a golden age for its luxury and for its renaissance in learning; it was celebrated as such by the poets, musicians and writers of the time and achieved world-wide fame through the stories of *The Arabian Nights*, in some of which the caliph Harun figured prominently.

Though the origin of many of the stories are Persian or Egyptian, they give a very good picture of the teeming life of Baghdad with its magnificent palaces and its wealthy merchant class, for the site of the city on the Tigris had been wisely chosen by Harun's grandfather, the caliph al Mansur, who had said "there is no obstacle between us and China; everything on the sea can come to us by the Tigris". Indeed, the round city of Baghdad spread in all directions and it became a centre of a world market with ships sailing up to its wharves with silks, spices and jewels from China, India, Ceylon and East Africa. Wars brought in slaves so that the market was full of Greek, Circassian and African boys and girls, the most beautiful being taken for the caliph and the nobility of Baghdad. Mr. H. St. John Philby, in his biography of Harun-al-Rashid, describes the slave market as constituting a monster chorus of beauty and talent beside which the splendours of Hollywood paled into insignificance; "sexual extravagance was the order of the day among the wealthy, while the common herd, who paid heavy taxes to support the estate and court, would seem to have been limited by economic pressure to a system of practical monogamy". The fantastic world of contrasts and uncertainties depicted in *The Arabian Nights* was not by any means all fiction; the slave in Baghdad could suddenly become powerful and the wealthy man be reduced to poverty.

The most interesting aspect of caliph Harun's reign, and the most widespread in its effect throughout the Arab world and Europe, was the renaissance in learning. The orthodox theologians

205

of Islam, who had had great influence, knew little of the philosophy and science of ancient Greece, and anyway the whole idea of a questioning philosophy based on logic was abhorrent, for to them there was no such thing as cause and effect, but every happening was brought about directly by God; and since the Koran contained the answers given by God to everything it was impious to start asking questions about the universe.

Although Harun-al-Rashid was religiously a very devout man and did the long pilgrimage to Mecca on foot almost every other year, he was intelligent and curious, so that orders were given that the works of ancient Greece and Indian works in Sanskrit should be sought out and translated into Arabic. This saved much of the ancient wisdom from oblivion and was even more enthusiastically carried on by the caliph Mamun. It helped towards the later flowering of Averroes and Avicenna, who brought the knowledge of Aristotle and other writers to the universities of Europe. Another great advance was the introduction from China of the art of making paper, instead of having to rely on parchment and papyrus. The caliph appreciated poetry and music and there were schools of musicians under the famous Ibrahim of Mosul and Ibn Jami.

A great impetus was also given to learning by the increase at court of foreigners, especially Persians, and Magians with the learning of India; they brought with them intellectual curiosity, artistic talent and a new kind of poetry. This predominance of foreigners, who were mostly Muslims, constituted one of the main differences between Abbasid rule and that of the earlier Ummayad dynasty centred on Damascus with an Arab empire which extended to Spain in the west and to India in the east. It had been an efficiently administered empire based on the Arab aristocracy; the Arabs were given precedence over the Persians, Magians, Byzantine Greeks and others who had become Muslims, but were second-class citizens and known as *Mawali*, or "adherents". In the end the *Mawali* revolted and helped the Abbasids, who were descendants of the Prophet Mohammed's uncle Abbas, to come to power in 750; no difference was made between Arab and non-Arab and, in fact, under the caliphs Harun and Mamun the Persians had precedence in the administration, while Turks from the Oxus formed the caliph's bodyguard.

But the unity of the Arab empire was broken up into rival caliphates in Spain, North Africa and Asia. Though cruel and treacherous, the caliph Harun was an energetic ruler, sending embassies to China and to Charlemagne, who had been crowned by the Pope Emperor of the West in 800. To Charlemagne the caliph sent an elephant, a water-clock and the keys of the Holy Sepulchre at Jerusalem, but their exchanges did not lead to any closer contact; "their public correspondence was founded on vanity", wrote Edward Gibbon, "and their remote situation left no room for a competition of interests". Against the Greeks of Constantinople and revolts in the Abbasid Empire the caliph on several occasions left his life of luxury in Baghdad, or at ar-Raqqa in Syria, to lead his armies.

Harun was born soon after the great circular city of Baghdad had been founded in 762 by the second Abbasid caliph Abu Jafar, known as al Mansur, who moved from al Kufa, south of Baghdad, when his new capital was completed. Al Mansur had sent his son Mahdi, who was nominated his successor, to crush a revolt of the Governor of Tabaristan in Persia; after defeating the Governor, Mahdi had taken two Persian maidens from the Governor's household as part of the loot; one of them was Khaizaran, who bore Mahdi two boys, Hadi and Harun, at Raiy near Teheran; by the other Persian, Mahdi had a girl called Abbasa, who was to suffer a tragic end at the hands of Harun. Also at Raiy, and at the same time, Fadl was born, son of the Persian Yahya ibn Barmak, whose father, Khalid, held high office under the caliph Mansur. Harun and Fadl became foster-brothers, for the two mothers were friends and used to exchange infants at the breast.

Nothing much is known about Harun until after the death of al Mansur in 775, when the new caliph, Mahdi, sent his eighteen-year-old son Harun in command of an expedition of one hundred thousand men against the Greek Empress Irene of Constantinople. With Harun as adviser was Yahya ibn Barmak, who came of a distinguished family of Persian landlords and whose grandfather had been the *Barmak*, or guardian, of the principal Zoroastrian temple in Persia; but both Khalid and his son Yahya had become Muslims. Harun's expedition pursued the Greek army to the Bosphorus and forced the empress to sue for peace and to pay a large annual ransom. The caliph Mahdi was so pleased with his son's achievement that he nominated Harun to be Governor of the western provinces from Syria to Azerbaijan. He was also given the title of al-Rashid—the Virtuous or Orthodox—and nominated second in succession to the caliphate after his brother Hadi.

Harun's mother, Khaizaran, had been made queen by marriage with the caliph over whom she exerted a considerable influence. Her favourite son was Harun and she persuaded Mahdi to make him the next caliph instead of the elder brother Hadi; but Hadi, who was fighting a campaign in Persia, refused to be set aside, and the caliph, accompanied by Harun-al-Rashid, set out with an army from Baghdad to enforce respect. On the way the caliph ate a poisoned fruit, intended by a jealous concubine for another woman, and died at the age of forty-three. Harun-al-Rashid then showed great statesmanship; he had the army with him and he could very easily have carried out his father's wishes and assumed the caliphate, but instead he sent a message to Hadi to come at once to Baghdad to be made caliph, an act which infuriated Khaizaran. Under the new caliph she was confined to the women's quarters and not allowed to have the influence that she had had before, but among her ladies-in-waiting she planned Hadi's downfall.

The caliph Hadi made the mistake of setting aside Harun's rightful claim to the succession and nominating his own son to succeed him; when Yahya did his best to dissuade the caliph from this action, he was thrown into prison. While Hadi was at Mosul he fell ill and was smothered by his concubines, a death which had almost certainly been planned by his mother, Khaizaran, who had everything prepared for the proclamation of Harun-al-Rashid as caliph. This was done without opposition in 786 when Harun was twenty-three years of age. Harun's son, al Mamun, was born to a Persian slave-girl on the day of the caliph's accession; later another son was born to his wife Zubeida, who was granddaughter of the former Caliph al Mansur, and therefore her son took precedence in succession over al Mamun. Later, after Harun's death, the conflict between the Persian-born son and the Arab-born son was to be fought out in a civil war, leading finally to the victory of the abler al Mamun and the Persian element.

The rivalry between Arab and non-Arab Muslims continued during the reign of the caliph Harun, but the Persian element was dominant, largely because of the great power wielded by the Barmakis, as Yahya and his two sons, Fadl and Jafar, came to be called. Yahya, then forty-eight, was vizier, a fit recompense after being imprisoned for defending Harun's right of accession; Fadl was his deputy in the administration of the empire and the younger son, Jafar, was made Secretary and Controller of the Imperial Household; both sons were known as "the Little Vizier". Jafar, because of his eloquence, intelligence and charm, became the boon companion of the caliph, who suffered from sleeplessness and liked someone intelligent to talk to, or there would be carousal with drink and women late into the night and perhaps a visit to different parts of Baghdad in the early hours of the morning. In some of *The Arabian Nights*' stories the caliph is accompanied by Jafar, as well as by Abu Nawas, the poet and licensed jester, and Mesrur, the Negro executioner. The caliph's relations with the Barmak family were very close, and as they administered the empire it was natural that Persian customs should predominate, which was welcomed by the caliph.

Whereas under the Ummayad dynasty there had been some semblance of the Arab democracy brought from the deserts of Arabia, at least for Arabs, and the ruler was kept under some check, under the caliph Harun the Persian doctrine was accepted that the ruler had divine right. Any opposition to the caliph was treason and it was regarded as natural that he should be despotic and have people imprisoned, tortured and killed at his will; Harun made at times tragic use of his despotic powers. While the court presented a gay, learned and civilized aspect, there were unfortunate ex-favourites lying in prison and perhaps being tortured to obtain information on others.

The caliph was a generous spender, but the empire was efficiently administered and it is estimated that the annual income from it (after Spain and most of North Africa had been lost) amounted to about sixteen million sterling a year. That was great wealth in those days, especially when the Government did not bother about general education or the social conditions of the masses; Harun thought of the poor to the extent of giving forty pounds daily in alms. As part of his religious devotion Harun-al-Rashid maintained rest-houses along the route of the pilgrimage to Mecca. Communications within the empire were well looked after; there were, for instance, the desert route from Baghdad to Damascus and thence through Palestine to Egypt and across North Africa, and the roads north-westwards to the Byzantine frontier, but the most important route was the Persian highway eastwards with fortified caravanserais throughout its length, which helped armies to be moved quickly; there was also a remarkable postal system with post-masters acting as spies for the caliph. Most of the trouble came from Syria and Persia, and about eight years after his accession Harun moved his capital from Baghdad to ar-Raqqah in northern Syria, so that he could the better control these areas and deal with the contumely Emperor Nicephorus, who had succeeded the Empress Irene.

There are various views of the caliph Harun-al-Rashid; some refer to his energy, ability and intelligence, while others emphasize his cruelty and treachery, but all have condemned his treatment of the Barmak family. Not only had Yahya and his two sons worked hard and efficiently for the Abbasid Empire, but the family had always been very close to the caliph; Yahya, his guardian as a boy, Fadl, the caliph's foster-brother, and Jafar, his boon companion— how intimate were the relations of the caliph and Jafar has been much discussed. There is a story that the caliph was found staring across the Tigris at Yahya's large palace and exclaiming: "Yahya seems to have taken all the business in hand without reference to me. It is he who is the caliph in reality, not I."

That may have been part of the reason that made him turn against the family, but it was probably another form of jealousy, for the first to die was Harun's boon companion Jafar, executed by Mesrur while he prayed; the head was brought to Harun, who addressed his charges to a Jafar who could not answer as he used to do. The most likely reason for this murder concerns Abbasa, Harun's half-sister, for whom he had a great admiration; the caliph wanted her to be present when he and Jafar had their carousals, but this would not have been correct Islamic etiquette. He got over the problem by arranging that Jafar and Abbasa should go through a marriage ceremony, but it was made clear that this was only nominal and it would anyway have been unfitting for a commoner to marry a close relation of the caliph. Abbasa, so the story goes, fell in love with Jafar and arranged that she should take the place of a slave girl who used to be sent on Friday nights to Jafar's room. Jafar was horrified, fearing what the consequences might be, but even so they continued to meet and two sons were born who were sent away in secret to be brought up in Mecca. One story says that the caliph had Abbasa and her two sons also killed.

Yahya, now an old man, and his son Fadl were cast into prison at ar-Raqqah and orders issued that all the property belonging to any member of the Barmak family was to be confiscated. Fadl became paralysed from the shock of his brother's death and he and his father died in prison a little time before Harun himself died in 809. The caliph died of cancer in Persia at the age of forty-seven while accompanying his army on an expedition to suppress a rebellion led by Rafi ibn Leith of Samarkand. The caliph had reached a place called Tus when he knew that he was dying and he had his grave dug close by. Just before he died the rebel leader's brother was brought as a prisoner and the caliph was asked what should be done. "If I had no more breath left," said Harun the Virtuous, "but to say a single word, it would be *slay him*."

ALFRED THE GREAT

(849–99)

IN THE annals of the English nation no man merits a higher place than Alfred the Great: stainless in character, brilliant as warrior, statesman, lawgiver, scholar and champion of Christianity. He delivered his country from brutal invasion and conquest by hordes of heathen Danes, and began the task, completed by his son and grandson, of welding the whole of England into one united realm.

It had not always been that. When the Anglo-Saxons emerged, at the end of the sixth century, from the Dark Ages, during which their hordes had flooded, wave after wave, into Christian Britain, plundering, massacring, obliterating all traces of its ordered Roman civilization, they were divided up into some seven petty kingdoms, which made ruthless war upon each other. Although in the eighth century the kings of Mercia, the midland state, claimed sovereignty over England, Northumbria, Wessex and Kent still had their own kings. In 828, Egbert, King of Wessex and grandfather of Alfred, defeated the Mercians at Ellandune, and became ruler of all southern England from Kent to the Devon border.

But now internal strife was stilled by a darker menace. Near the end of the eighth century the first Viking raiders had made their appearance. Three of their long ships attacked the Wessex coast. Then they ransacked the monasteries of Lindisfarne, Iona, Ireland and North Wales, collecting rich plunder and massacring the monks or taking them to sell as slaves. Amazed at such easy success, the Danes and Norsemen set out in ever-growing numbers on these marauding expeditions, which grew from raids to invasion, conquest and land settlement. Danes subjugated East Anglia, Yorkshire and Mercia, while Norsemen penetrated Cumberland and Lancashire, and joined hands with their Danish cousins across the north of England.

Finally the Danes set about the conquest of Wessex. Advancing up the Thames valley in 871, they met the West Saxon army at Ashdown, in the Berkshire downs. The Saxons were in two forces, under King Ethelred and his younger brother, Alfred. While Ethelred prayed for victory, Alfred plunged furiously into the fray.

211

Presently his brother joined him and in savage fighting they routed the Danes, who fled in confusion back to Reading. It was their first defeat in pitched battle in England since their invasions in force.

The war continued fiercely, and in the first half of 871 nine battles were fought. Then Ethelred died, and his brother Alfred, who had won the enthusiastic trust of the Saxons, was elected king by the Witan—the national council.

Alfred, born at Wantage in 849, was now a young man of about twenty-two; of poor health, a cultured scholar, with an unusually wide outlook for a man of that time. His father had twice taken him as a boy to Rome, where he was confirmed by the Pope and saw something of the world beyond Britain. In 868 he had married Ealhswith, who bore him two sons and three daughters.

Shortly after his accession he suffered a severe defeat at Wilton, and saw he must gain time to re-organize his defences. He made a peace treaty with the Danes, who were themselves not unwilling to disengage their forces from Wessex. Presumably he paid them a "Danegeld" to buy the treaty. But it gave him five years of relative peace to consolidate his realm. The Danes drew back into the Midlands, where they firmly established themselves and many of them settled down to farm life.

The more mobile warriors among the Danes, however, still were resolved to conquer Wessex, and under their new chieftain, Guthrum, they planned in 877 a system of combined attacks by land and sea. They drove overland to Wareham and by sea to Poole Harbour. Alfred tried to buy them off again. They swore a peace and forthwith broke it and captured Exeter. But their sea army was smashed by a storm near Swanage, which sank 120 ships and drowned over 5,000 warriors. The Danes swore a fresh peace.

Five months later, in January, 878, came Alfred's darkest hour. As he and his army were celebrating Twelfth Night at their headquarters in Chippenham, the Danes struck. The Wessex army scattered, its survivors creeping home or flying overseas. Alfred with a few faithful followers took refuge in the Isle of Athelney, among the marshes of Sedgemoor. He had no army, no money, no visible prospect of being able to resume the offensive against the victorious Danes, who now deemed themselves masters of Wessex.

Legends have gathered round his doings during this period in hiding. Men told how, disguised as a harper, he visited Danish camps and gained information about their strength and probable movements. They recounted, for the age-long delight of youngsters, how the housewife of the cottage where he was concealed left him to watch the baking of cakes. Intent on his plans, he did not heed them, and was roundly berated by the angry woman when she returned to find them burnt.

Somerset still kept pockets of Saxon resistance here and there. A Danish force, after plundering in Wales, attacked a stronghold in Exmoor. But the Saxons made a sudden sortie and killed the Danish chief and most of his troops. Alfred saw that the time had come to strike. He had established contact with the thanes of Wiltshire and Hampshire, who were groaning under the Danish yoke, and now he summoned them to join him and the men of Somerset at a point near Selwood.

There was magic in the name of Alfred; and a large army gathered and hailed him as one risen from the dead. He led them towards the Danish headquarters at Chippenham. The Danes issued forth to meet him at Ethandune (now Edington) and the greatest battle of his career was fought with desperate fury. It ended in victory, and he pursued the Danes and beleaguered Guthrum's camp. Guthrum begged for peace, offering to give hostages and withdraw from Wessex.

Alfred had a better plan. Dane and Saxon must learn to live together in England. A lasting peace must somehow be established between them, and it would not be achieved by slaughtering the defeated enemy. So he brought Guthrum and thirty of his chief earls into his camp and induced them to accept Christianity and be baptized. He himself was Guthrum's sponsor. Then he feasted them and settled with them the Treaty of Wedmore, by the terms of which the Danes were to remain to the east of Watling Street, the Roman road running from London to Chester. Thus the east and north of England—known as the Danelaw—were for the time being left in Danish hands; but the Midlands and the South were acknowledged as Alfred's realm. In 886 he gave his eldest daughter, Ethelflida, in marriage to Ethelred, the Mercian regent, thus binding the Midlands to Wessex. In 885 he had swept the Danes from London, which he fortified and re-established as the major port it had been in Roman times.

After the Treaty of Wedmore, Alfred enjoyed for fourteen years an uneasy peace, or something as near peace as those troubled times allowed. He busily employed this respite to bring his powers of statesmanship to bear on the organization of his country for defence. He divided the "Fyrd"—the mass rally of the country's manpower—into two parts, so that if one half of the men were summoned to battle, the other half would be guarding their families and tending their fields. He fortified the country by building defensive boroughs along the Thames valley, the south coast and the western borders. To each was assigned a district which would provide its manpower and maintain its fortifications. He saw the need for sea-power to resist the pirate raids of Danish long-ships, and to this end built a fleet of bigger vessels. Thus Alfred became the founder of the British Navy.

After his capture of London, Alfred made in 886 a further treaty with Guthrum. It defined the frontier of the Danelaw as running up the Lea Valley, east of London, thence to Bedford and by the Ouse to Watling Street. To check the constant fighting between Danes and English, a tariff of compensation payments was fixed for anyone killed of either race: 200 silver shillings for a Danish or English peasant, and 8½ marks in pure gold for men of higher rank. Such money settlements reduced the danger of blood feuds.

Alfred now set to work to codify the laws of England, which had been a chaos of local rules and customs. He sought to revise and combine these with regulations borrowed from Mosaic laws and Christian principles. His Book of Dooms (laws) formed the basis for administration of justice in Courts of the Shires and Hundreds, and with additions and modifications became the ancestor of our Common Law of today. He instilled throughout the nation so great a respect for law that it was commonly said that in his day one might leave precious jewels hanging on a roadside bush, and no one would venture to take them.

Alfred was not content to make his realm strong and law-abiding. He was determined it should become educated. Though forced by circumstances to fill the role of a warrior, he was at heart a scholar. In these more peaceful years he set himself to provide his people with literature in their own tongue. He translated from Latin into Anglo-Saxon Bede's *History of the English People* and various religious works. He translated or compiled handbooks of theology, history and geography and rendered parts of the Bible into the common tongue. He brought over scholars from the Continent and drew learned refugees from the Danelaw. He started the first "public schools" for the sons of the nobility, to teach them to read and be better fitted to undertake administrative responsibilities. He started the compilation of the Anglo-Saxon Chronicle, which from his time kept a continuous record of the nation's history.

Alfred specially concentrated upon reviving the life of the English Church. In those dark and troublous times it could become influential to educate and unify the nation, and to link it with the former heathen of the Danelaw, among whom Christianity was now rapidly making progress. The Church had been shattered by the Danish invasions, in which monasteries had been destroyed and churches robbed and burned. The quality of the priesthood had fallen so low that few of them could read, still less understand, the Latin of their missals. Alfred founded monasteries and built churches. He brought distinguished churchmen from the Continent, corresponded with leading scholars, and is even alleged to have sent a mission to India.

Alfred was that rare bird, a really all-round man, interested in all the many facets of the life of his time, and gifted more than most for dealing with them. He was a keen huntsman, who could teach verderers and falconers the skills of their callings. He fostered the manufacture of high-quality jewellery and goldsmiths' work. He was a builder, pressing on with the building or restoration of towns, and constructing fair dwellings for his own courts. His court indeed became famous abroad for its learning, piety and culture.

He was yet to face further trouble with the Danes. In 891 Guthrum died, and the rather wavering peace he had kept with Alfred was at an end. At the time a great Viking host was ravaging northern Europe, besieging Paris and devastating northern France. Meeting desperate if disorganized resistance, they grew famished in the desolate countryside; so they decided to invade England and settle there. In 892 this great heathen army disembarked on the south coast of Kent and set up camp at Appledore. Another party sailed up the Thames and landed near Sittingbourne.

Thanks to Alfred's re-organization of her defence system England could put up a far stronger resistance than fifteen years before. Alfred himself was in poor health, but he had capable deputies in his son Edward and his son-in-law, Ethelred of Mercia, to lead his armies. They set about mobilizing the Fyrd, while Alfred tried to make terms with the Viking leader, Haesten. A peace was signed, but quickly broken, not before Alfred had induced the heathen Dane to let his two sons be baptized.

Haesten made a fortified camp at Benfleet, but Edward and Ethelred brought an army from London and stormed it, killing or scattering the invaders, burning their boats and looting their stores. Haesten's wife and sons were captured. Alfred sent them back to him. People thought this generosity to a brutal foe incomprehensible. But the Christian deed had a happy sequel. Haesten never fought Alfred again.

Another Danish force, drawn from Danes of the Danelaw, came round by boat to attack Exeter and thrust inland. But Edward and Ethelred, riding to its relief, met a column of Danes near Aldershot, defeated and pursued them for twenty miles, till they swam the Thames to get away. Yet another force brought their boats up the Lea, but Alfred barred the stream below them, and they fled across country, leaving their ships behind. By 896 these fresh Danish thrusts weakened and the invaders withdrew to the Danelaw or Normandy.

Intermittent raiding and conflict went on, however, for another forty years, until the ultimate unity of the land under English rule was achieved by Edward, Alfred's son, and Athelstan, his grandson, when not only the Danelaw but Northumbria, Strathclyde and the Welsh princes accepted the supremacy of the English crown. There was one last struggle when in 937 the Scots, Danes and Northumbrians, with Vikings from Iceland and Ireland, met the English in the great battle of Brunanburgh. Alfred's grandson, Athelstan, won an overwhelming victory, and thereafter styled himself King of All Britain—*Rex totius Britanniae*.

Alfred had not lived to see this consummation of all his efforts to unite the English realm, of which he had by arms and statesmanship through thirty critical years laid so well the foundations. He died in 899 at the age of fifty-two, leaving an England which from warring tribes he had transformed into a nation, and delivered from being overrun and obliterated by hordes of heathen invaders; an England with an established system of national and local government; with good laws and just administration; with a rising standard of education, literacy and art; with a universal acceptance of the Christian faith and an increasingly powerful and active Church.

He was reverenced and loved by all his people. In the following age they told of his exploits, held by his laws, and established his fame in history as Alfred the Great.

KING WENCESLAS

(d. 929)

THE LITTLE central-European country of Czechoslovakia—considerably smaller than Britain—is one of the most ruggedly attractive in the world: its capital of Prague has often been called the most beautiful city in Europe. The city is set in the middle of the Bohemian plain, a hill-rimmed saucer, tilted so that it slopes gently from south to north. It seems peaceful and quiet—yet some of history's darkest, most bloody deeds have been perpetrated there, over the past one thousand years.

The country itself is a recent creation, hacked out of the old Austro-Hungarian Empire at the end of the first world war and embodying a number of one-time kingdoms: Bohemia, Moravia and Silesia which speak the Czech language, and others, farther east, which speak Slovak. Each of these areas has a long and vivid history: none more so than Bohemia.

Caesar and Livy both refer, with some respect, to a powerful Celtic tribe, the Boii, and it is from these first inhabitants that Bohemia derives its name. Shortly before the birth of Christ they were defeated by other invading tribes and vanished from the pages of history. Their conquerors vanished, too, in the fifth century A.D., when the warlike Czech tribe took over. A few hundred years later, Christianity was introduced into the country and adopted by the ruling dynasty of these Czechs—though not, as we shall see, by all of them.

The greatest member of this ruling (and to West European ears, unpronounceable) dynasty, the family Premyslide, has a name known to schoolboys over half the world: Good King Wenceslas. Not too many kings are remembered as "good", but every verse of that long and rollicking carol points out that Wenceslas deserved to be.

He was born in the last days of the ninth century A.D., elder son of Uratislas, the Duke of Bohemia. The Duke was a devout Christian, but his wife was a pagan. This sort of situation, with husbands or wives espousing the new religion and their wives or husbands the old, was fairly common in these early years of

European Christianity. The pagan wife Drahomira bore her husband two sons, Wenceslas and Boleslas, managing to retain a hold on the younger boy while Wenceslas, at the Duke's insistence, was sent to be brought up by his grandmother Ludmilla. The old lady was as devout a Christian as her son the Duke and she sent young Wenceslas to a Christian college a few miles outside of Prague. Here he was diligent in his studies, particularly the sciences, in which he made great progress, and in all the varied accomplishments necessary for a European nobleman of the ninth century. He was also fortified greatly in his faith and was singled out as a good and virtuous Christian. He was exceedingly kind to any man or woman in trouble or distress, and the Christmas-carol story, of his inviting the poor man into his palace to share a meal, is only one of a great many. We learn that Wenceslas from an early age had "all the virtues which compose the character of a Christian and a saint".

He was still a very young man when his father died, and his pagan mother Drahomira seized the reins of government. While her husband lived she seems to have kept her hatred of Christianity in some sort of check, but now she rapped out a whole series of laws, closed down all Bohemia's churches and prohibited the teaching of the new religion. Christians were forbidden to teach children, whether the subject be mathematics or music or Latin, and an infringement of this law was punished by death. Many Christians were massacred.

Young Wenceslas, horrified at this, managed to get most of the power out of his mother's hands and assert his new position as Duke of Bohemia. He was backed by the majority of his Czech people, who agreed when he divided the country into two spheres of influence in order to give his younger brother Boleslas a domain of his own.

Unfortunately for Wenceslas, his young brother, who had been brought up by the pagan Drahomira, was as rabidly anti-Christian as she, and the pair of them now began to plot ways of overthrowing him and his religion. No doubt it would be necessary to have him killed, and that would be messy and troublesome, but in these early days of the tenth century it would hardly be unusual.

First they would have to put the old grandmother to death.

Ludmilla soon learnt of the plot against her life, but she was calm and philosophical, making no effort to avert a fate which she believed to have been ordained for a purpose. If by her death the Christian religion could be furthered, then it would not have been in vain. She began to give away all her goods to the poor, to pray daily that she might meet her fate with dignity and without rancour.

The assassins sent by Boleslas found her kneeling at prayer in her own private chapel, and they strangled her there, with her own veil.

Wenceslas, viewed from our vantage point of a thousand years on in time, seems to have been rather too forgiving a Christian for his own good. Instead of having his brother and mother locked up or put to death for this hideous crime, he devoted himself to prayer that they might be converted from their wicked ways. They were left in freedom to continue their plotting against him. At one point it seemed to the young duke that his prayers were being answered, for Boleslas came into his chapel one day and knelt down at the altar.

(If it served to lower the Duke's defences, Boleslas cared not a whit how often he went into a church, how ostentatiously he knelt to pray.)

The Holy Roman Emperor Otto I ruled a large area of Europe which included Bohemia, and that year he called a meeting of his subordinate rulers at Worms on the Rhine. Wenceslas made haste to attend. He travelled on horseback as fast as he could, often riding by night, but still arrived late for this "Diet", having stopped to pray for a deliverance for his country. While many of the other small rulers resented this, the great Otto knew a good man when he saw him, and respected Wenceslas for it. He immediately gave him the title of King of Bohemia, with the privilege of bearing the imperial eagle on his standard.

(Wenceslas, incidentally, went on to the end of his short life styling himself simply as Duke—but over all Europe he was known as the King of Bohemia.)

Otto also handed over some precious relics of St. Vitus and St. Sigismund which the devout and grateful Wenceslas took back with him to Prague, planning to build a new church to house them.

But in his absence his mother and brother had again been imposing restrictions on Christians: their excuse was that Christians had been holding meetings, making themselves a menace to Bohemian law and order. Wenceslas duly investigated the charges, found them false and reversed the laws. He warned his mother that any further intrigue would be punished.

"My son—how could you, for one moment, think that your own mother, who carried you in her womb, would intrigue against you? How ungrateful you are!"

"Perhaps——"

"But come, let us forget these family quarrels and feast together. Your brother's wife has been safely delivered of a son, there will be music and feasting——"

And Wenceslas, who had sworn a vow of virginity, but was glad that his brother and his brother's wife were now parents of a son who would some day rule Bohemia, agreed to attend the celebrations.

It was 27 September, in the year nine hundred and twenty-nine.

A chill evening, for Bohemian winters are as icy cold as the summers are hot: there was much drinking of mulled wine. The King of Bohemia's brother and mother greeted him effusively, showed him the infant, which had been placed on a skin-padded wooden bench to be admired, and the child whooped with delight as Wenceslas picked it up.

The music began, the candles were lit as the sun dropped over the edge of the Bohemian plain, there was wild dancing and eating and drinking. The hours flew past, and almost before he knew it the time was a minute to midnight.

"Come, my brother, to this little chapel in the trees, for I know that at midnight you will pray, as you always do——"

"Yes," said Wenceslas. "I pray. And I will go to your chapel."

Boleslas left the festivities to lead him there and the king went into the chapel alone. He made his way to the altar and knelt.

But now Boleslas, exactly as he had planned, was leading six men up the street from their hiding place, leading them back to the chapel and, on tiptoe, through the door. So devout was the king that he heard not a sound as the seven men approached.

They were behind him now, an arm's length off, and they halted, listened for a moment to the muttered prayer. Then Boleslas gave the signal.

The first man's dagger plunged deep into the back of the kneeling king. He half turned, a look of horror tinged with sadness on his face, and the second man knifed him in the shoulder.

The king seemed to feel no pain as the third and fourth blows were administered; he rose slowly to his feet as Boleslas prepared for the *coup de grâce*.

"Why, my brother, oh *why*?" were the last words the king was heard to say, as the lance sank deep into his chest. Still he came on, and the assassins, shocked by what they had done, backed away.

Surely the man should be dead, with so many grievous wounds, the blood gushing over his kingly robes?

He came on, one more step. Then, hands clasped in a final silent prayer, he fell.

He lay there and the slowly widening pool of red reached the altar steps, spilt down them. It was a few minutes after midnight on 28 September.

King Wenceslas was soon avenged. The Emperor Otto heard of the crime and led a vast army, virtually a crusade, into Bohemia, laying waste in his anger a large part of it. The wicked Drahomira, evil power behind the throne, was put painfully to death, and Boleslas, though his life was spared, was at first imprisoned, then released to become a vassal king of a subject Bohemia. On the Emperor Otto's orders all banished priests were recalled, the Christian religion was restored, and Christians throughout Bohemia were given freedom to worship where and how they wished.

The martyred king was entombed in Prague and almost immediately miracles were reported. Blind men touched the tomb and their sight was restored, the sick were made whole, the dead brought back to life. No doubt much of this was fanciful but the legend of the martyred king and his miracles spread rapidly, and Boleslas, fearful that the people would now rise up against him in their anger and shame, ordered that the body be moved to another resting place, the Church of St. Vitus in Prague. He would dearly loved to have burnt it or thrown it into the Vltava, but he knew the people of Bohemia would never countenance it. Perhaps, though, a change of location might put an end to the miracles?

It did not. For many, many years people reported miraculous happenings in the Church of St. Vitus.

Boleslas died, a guilty, unloved king, tortured by his own conscience and the contempt of his people. He was succeeded by his son Boleslas II, who was a pious and good man, basing his life on that of his uncle, "Good King Wenceslas". He was in addition a good general and extended his rule into Moravia and parts of Silesia and Poland. Bohemian history at this time is noted for the alternation of good rulers with bad, and the next one, Boleslas III, was a disaster, losing all Bohemia's foreign possessions and his own throne, to be replaced by a Polish prince, Vladivoj.

There are many churches to the memory of St. Wenceslas: the first, surprisingly, being erected in Denmark, a few years after the martyr's death. He is remembered widely, even in present-day Communist Czechoslovakia, as a wise ruler and an early Christian martyr.

OTTO I (THE GREAT)
(912–973)

EMPEROR CHARLEMAGNE, King of the Franks, who had been crowned in Aix-la-Chapelle (Aachen) in 800, had consolidated his realm and had made a supreme effort to establish a permanent Western empire which included some lands beyond the River Elbe. Charlemagne's plans had, however, been frustrated after his death, for he had appointed his three sons as his heirs. Then Louis, called the Pious, who finally succeeded Charlemagne, divided the empire amongst *his* three sons, who were all weak and ineffectual men, and during their reign Charlemagne's great dominions fell apart.

It was not until one hundred and fifty years later that this empire was revived and expanded by Otto I, called the Great even while he lived. He not only strengthened the power and the prestige of the empire itself, but dramatically made Italy a part of his dominions. This inclusion of Italy brought about the creation of the Holy Roman Empire in the medieval world.

Otto was born on 23 November, 912. He was the eldest son of Henry I, called the Fowler, Duke of Saxony, who in 919 had been chosen as German king by the other German rulers. Otto, Henry's son by his second wife Matilda, had two younger brothers and three sisters. Henry, a simple straightforward man, cared more about his country than about his own aggrandizement. He went to war not to exercise and to show off his armies' prowess, but only when he thought armed conflicts inevitable.

Matilda, Otto's mother, on the other hand, relished her position of power and regal dignity. She was a domineering woman who acknowledged only God as her superior. She was pious in the extreme and finally ended her days in a convent.

Henry's and Matilda's marriage was not a peaceful relationship. Otto's childhood was disturbed by his parents' quarrels. For Matilda was quite determined that her second son—several years younger than Otto—was to succeed her husband. Henry was equally determined that Otto was to be the heir to the throne. These altercations continued until Henry's death in 936, when Otto, then twenty-four years old, did in fact succeed his father.

In his younger days Otto must have welcomed the weeks he spent away from his mother, and he gladly joined his father's troops when they were fighting recalcitrant tribes in Bavaria or Swabia. It was also a relief to Otto when, at the age of seventeen, he was married to Edith, a daughter of Edward the Elder of England, and established his own household away from his parents.

Otto's education bore no resemblance whatsoever to the modern meaning of the word. He was, of course, by his mother, given a thorough religious training. Throughout his life he was considered a deeply religious man. He rarely missed early mass. He founded a number of famous convents and appointed many new bishops. He revered the Church, but he never considered himself a servant of the Church. He was her master.

Otto had no book learning. In fact he was never taught to read or to write. As a mature man this lack of education and his dependence upon his literate courtiers irked him. His illiteracy is not, however, reflected in those of his letters which have been handed down to us, for they clearly show how well he formulated his ideas and intentions in the documents dictated to his secretaries.

Despite his own lack of learning Otto respected scholars and always welcomed them to his court. And when he was thirty-five years old he taught himself the letters of the alphabet and acquired a certain ability to read manuscripts. He learned a little French, but did not speak the language. He had no knowledge of Latin, at a time when a proficiency in Latin was the mark of a man's real culture. Otto's lack of education did not hinder the development of his keen native intelligence. He had a splendid memory and very good judgment of men.

He loved hunting and riding wild horses and was a man of great physical courage. His manner was reserved and he was usually calm and dignified. Even as a young man he was more respected than loved. For his calm demeanour could sometimes suddenly change: he had a violent temper, though he forgot his outbursts more quickly than they were forgotten by the men in his court.

Otto's physical presence encouraged the awe with which he was regarded by his followers. There are no pictorial relics of Otto—apart from blurred likenesses on great seals—but Widukind, the Saxon historian, left a vivid description of Otto's person. This historian recorded that Otto was a tall, powerfully built man who demanded and got implicit obedience. "His eyes sparkled," Widukind wrote, "and struck men at whom he was gazing like a stroke of lightning . . . the hair on his chest was so thick that it was like a lion's mane. . . ."

When Otto was crowned in Aix-la-Chapelle in 936 by Hildebert, Archbishop of Mayence, he made it quite clear that he intended to be an absolute ruler. To emphasize the subservience he demanded from all of the German nobles, Otto had the Dukes of Bavaria, Swabia, Franconia and Lorraine wait upon him at the banquet which followed the coronation ceremonies in the cathedral.

This personal service by the dukes was a most important symbolic act. Otto's father had treated the other dukes almost as his equals; during his reign Germany had been something like a confederation. Otto, on the other hand, when he was waited upon by them during the banquet, indicated that henceforth they would be his vassals and that power would be vested in his person alone.

The dukes naturally resented this decrease in their influence. Soon some of them gathered together bands of armed followers and revolted against Otto. One of his half-brothers, Thankmar, went so far as to rebel against Otto in Saxony itself. Eberhard, the Duke of Franconia, came to Thankmar's assistance, but Otto succeeded in quelling this rebellion with the help of the Duke of Swabia who—luckily for Otto—had quarrelled with Eberhard.

Soon another insurrection followed. This time the insurgents were led by Otto's brother Henry, who was still angry because—despite his mother's wishes—Otto and not he had been chosen to succeed their father. Henry was joined by Giselbert, Duke of Lorraine, and by the Duke of Franconia. Henry and his allies marched from Lorraine towards the Rhine. Otto hastened with his troops to meet the rebels, but he did not have enough boats to ferry his entire force across the river. When he met Henry's armies, therefore, he was greatly outnumbered. Nevertheless, Otto was victorious—he was a clever strategist—and his victory was attributed by his superstitious people to a "Holy Lance" he carried. With this "Holy Lance" in his hand he continued, in a number of battles, to defeat Henry and his friends. Henry finally fled and escaped to the court of King Louis IV of France.

After the routing of his enemies Otto was too clever to seek further revenge. His aim was peace and unity in Germany, and when enough time had elapsed for the revolting nobles to calm down, he tried to win their friendship. His brother Henry was forgiven, appointed Duke of Bavaria and became a loyal follower of his king and brother. Otto retained a personal overlordship of Franconia, but he pacified Hermann, Duke of Swabia, by marrying one of his sons to one of Hermann's daughters. One of Otto's loyal followers, Conrad, the Red, was created Duke of Lorraine.

When peace within Germany seemed established, Otto made known that he planned to "secure" his Eastern frontiers. In common with other German rulers and leaders since Otto's days, he wanted to conquer and hold the tribes and territories in the East. Otto's *Drang nach Osten*—which made him a popular figure during Hitler's regime—caused him, first of all, to conquer Bohemia.

Then he turned to the Slavonic tribes living beyond the rivers Elbe and Oder. This war against the Slavs was terrible, causing vast devastation, mass executions and cruelty on both sides. It could have been but little comfort to the inhabitants of these ravaged regions when, after their defeat, Otto founded several bishoprics in the district. Garo, Otto's uncompromising representative in the Slavonic territories, was named as the Bishop of Magdeburg.

While Otto's eastern lands were being "pacified", he was having trouble with France. Louis IV, who had harboured Henry after his flight, was hoping to gain sovereignty over Lorraine. Otto had strong family feelings and he was particularly displeased with Louis who had married Otto's sister. Otto was too angry to attempt negotiations with his brother-in-law. He marched his troops into France and successfully attacked Louis. Later Louis was again defeated, this time by his rival Hugh the Great, Duke of France. Hugh irritated Otto as much as Louis had done, for Hugh, too, was Otto's brother-in-law: the husband of another sister. Now Otto was tired of these family quarrels. He defeated Hugh's forces at Rheims and then insisted that Hugh and Louis settle their differences amicably. Otto appointed himself as an arbitrator and intervened whenever Hugh and Louis seemed on the verge of fresh dissent.

Otto's prestige in Europe as well as in Germany was soon very great and it was not surprising that he became involved in Italian affairs. In Italy, Berengar II, Margrave of Ivrea, a cruel and unscrupulous man, had succeeded King Lothar. Berengar was trying to seize the dowry of Adelaide, Lothar's widow. The Italian bishops, who themselves had suffered under Berengar's rule, were enraged when he imprisoned Adelaide. She was a clever and attractive woman and she had managed to escape. She was still, however, in danger and the bishops and her other friends appealed to Otto to come to their assistance. He responded to this appeal, came with an army to Lombardy, and forced Berengar to accept the subordinate position as his vassal in northern Italy. Otto then assumed the title of King of Italy. In the meantime he had fallen in love with Adelaide. Several years had now passed since the death of his first wife, Edith, and he and Adelaide were married in Pavia.

Already Otto hoped to include Italy in his empire, but before he could make plans to realize this ambition he was summoned back to Germany where his son Ludolf—fearing the rivalry of Adelaide's future sons—was conspiring with the disloyal Archbishop of Mayence and others to undermine Otto's authority. At the same time some of Otto's Magyar vassals were in revolt and had attacked Bavaria.

While Otto was quelling these insurrections in Germany the situation in Italy had become more unsettled than ever. The Duke of Lorraine—whom Otto had appointed as his representative in Lombardy—had joined Berengar in an effort to undermine Otto's position in Italy. In 961 Pope John XII—notorious for his debauched way of life—appealed to Otto to help him get rid of Berengar. Otto returned to Italy, and after Berengar's resistance had been broken Otto was generally acknowledged as King of Italy, and his sovereignty of southern as well as northern Italy was firmly established.

Otto's power was now supreme in Italy, and on 31 January, 962, in St. Peter's in Rome, he was crowned with all pomp by John XII as Holy Roman Emperor. Not only had Otto thus achieved supreme secular authority in Europe; beyond that—and this is historically of the greatest importance—he made himself the head of the Church. For he forced the Pope to swear an oath of allegiance to himself, and John XII thus became Otto's vassal. Later, when John showed signs of regretting this oath, Otto deposed him. Otto selected Pope Leo VIII as John's successor and decreed that henceforth no Pope should be elected without his consent.

The bitterness felt by most churchmen because of this decree was expressed by Benedict, a Roman monk, who wrote: "Woe to thee Rome that thou art crushed and trodden down by so many peoples; who hast been seized by a Saxon king . . . and thy strength reduced to nought."

When Otto had settled affairs in Rome he returned to Germany, but after the sudden death of Pope Leo in 965 the Roman clergy and nobles tried to elect the Pope of their choosing without Otto's consent. He hurried back to Rome and against the wishes of the Romans he appointed the Bishop of Narni as the new Pope. He was Pope John XIII. The Romans were dissatisfied, temporarily drove John XIII into exile, and Otto faced an awkward situation. However, by 966 he had imposed his will on the Romans and John XIII returned to Rome.

Then Otto left Italy for the last time and the closing years of his life were peaceful. He died on 6 May, 973, and was buried in the Cathedral of Magdeburg which he had built. He had accomplished what he set out to accomplish: he had revived Charlemagne's Holy Roman Empire, he had forcefully subdued the turbulent German tribes and instilled in the Germans the beginnings of a national pride. He had spread the teachings of Christianity—as he understood them—and at the same time had brought the Papacy under his control. He had increased Germany's *Lebensraum* in the East.

Whether or not, in the long run, Otto's expansionist policies benefited Germany and Europe as a whole only students of Germany's history after Otto's reign can judge.

BRIAN BORU

(926–1014)

"STOUT, ABLE, valiant, fierce, magnificent, hospitable, munificent, strong, lively and friendly. The most eminent of the west of Europe."

Quite a testimonial. It is for Brian, from a contemporary; and from what we are able to piece together about him, accurate, even discerning. He was all these things, and we can add to the list that he was a Christian and devout: he was slain—a very old man—as he knelt near the battlefield to pray. He had resisted all entreaty to take himself to a place of safety.

Like many great men of his period, Brian had a pedigree that was largely imaginary, an Arthurian fantasy of blood-drenched heroes stretching back through the dawn of history, through darkness and out into the magic world of mythology. But from the ninth century we can trace it with some accuracy, thanks largely to the vivid details we have been given of ceaseless, bloody war between Irishman and Dane.

The Danes came to Ireland early in the ninth century, stealing up the River Shannon in long, slender boats, leaping ashore to lay waste to the country, plunder what they could from it and move on: or, when the fancy took them, to settle.

A little later they met shattering, unexpected defeat at the hands of the tribal chief Corc and here history begins. We can follow Corc's line down through his successive descendants, Lachtna, Lorcan and Cenedid, the gallant Cenedid who died fighting the Danes, a hundred and twenty years after his great-grandfather had thought, with reason, that he had flung them into the sea forever. Cenedid—a name more memorable in its modern form of Kennedy —was killed in 951. He left two sons, Mahon and Brian, and these continued the fight: waging non-stop, guerrilla war against the Danes from the unbroken forests which, in those distant days, swept down to the edge of the Danish town of Limerick. They suffered impossible hardships, never able to stay in a spot long enough to organize supplies, always harried, pursued, by a larger, better-armed, well-fed force.

228

Eventually the young King Mahon, weak from wounds and starvation, seeing no end to the conflict, made peace with the Danes.

But his brother Brian refused to do so, went on attacking, his force getting gradually smaller. At last, with only fifteen able-bodied supporters left, he confronted his brother.

"Why, O King," he demanded, "have you chosen to make this wicked truce? Is not your country my country, the country of our father who was killed for it? Do we not both wish it to be free? Can you not fight for it, with me?"

"Your country," said Mahon, "is mine indeed. But look at those you have made fight for it. Where are they now? Dead, for the most part, homes and villages burnt to the ground."

"Better death than dishonour."

"A fine thought. And how many are there to share it with you? Fifteen men, it would seem, in all Ireland."

"There are more—and they will come."

"You are a brave man, my brother. And a fool. Why should the blood of Ireland be spilt in a hopeless cause? Look—my own supporters are at peace with the Danes. At peace, well-fed. And alive."

A strong argument, but Brian ignored it—and so strong was his personality, so right his cause, that he brought Mahon over to his side. The Kingdom of Munster, under its king and his younger brother, prepared for war. Inspired by the alliance, the people of Munster rallied to the flag.

When the attack, after careful preparation, was launched against Limerick, it was strikingly successful. The Danish stronghold was wrested from its commander, Ivor, thousands of Danes were killed. The capture was followed by wholesale, systematic looting, of jewellery, leather, satin, silk—and of boys and girls for slavery.

And then Mahon, King of Munster, most respected king in all Ireland, indulged in an odd form of sport. Having slaughtered almost all the male population of Limerick, he led out the women, young and old, hundred upon hundred of them, and made them get down on hands and knees in a large circle. The circle was some two furlongs round, on a stretch of open land outside the burning town. And here, within and around this circle, he and his men engaged in running races throughout the whole of one day, the border of their track marked out by the kneeling bodies of Danish women.

When night fell and the sports were over, the women still capable of getting to their feet were allowed to do so. Those not wanted by the victors trooped back to the charred remains of their city, to fossick in the ruins.

Months went by and the Danes returned with a fleet, but by now the spell of Danish power was broken and they were easily beaten off. Mahon was King of Munster in reality, with none—or so it seemed—to contest his claim. Nine good years passed.

But in 976 Mahon was butchered by a gang of conspirators, a bloody ruse of the sort that has punctuated Celtic history. Donnabhain, trusted friend of the king, paid him a visit, partook of his hospitality, overpowered him and called up the rest. One of these, Maelmuadh, butchered the king. Maelmuadh, when the news came out, was cursed by all the clergy of Munster.

A little later, he, too, was butchered on the battlefield. But by this time the Danes, invited back by the conspirators, were spreading over Munster.

Brian was now a reluctant king and he swore to avenge his brother. Gathering an army about him, he first killed Ivor the Dane; then, systematically, he cleared islands and forts of Ivor's men. Donnabhain, the Judas who had handed Mahon over to his death, now panicked and sent for Harold, the Dane who styled himself King of Munster. Harold assembled a large force and met Brian. In the battle that followed, the Danes were soundly beaten and Harold and Donnabhain killed.

By 984 Brian was truly King of Munster and supreme in the south of Ireland. He then easily subjected the titular "King of All Ireland", Maelsechlainn, who ruled in Meath. Gradually he overcame both Connaught and Ulster. And now to the man who was real King of Ireland, tribute and captives poured in. (His title of "Boru" comes from the old Irish "boroma", or "tribute".) He was all-powerful. At the same time, he was a good and wise ruler. He sent abroad for books that his people might learn wisdom, established professorships all over his kingdom and paid the incumbents lavishly. He built churches. There was lawlessness in the land and Brian of the Tribute set out to punish this with a severity which would be horrifying today, but was typical of the period: eleventh-century hands and feet were hacked off for venial offences, tongues and eyes torn out for what might merit a stiff reprimand in the twentieth. Slowly, law, order and the blessings of knowledge settled into Munster, began to spread over Ireland. There is a belief in Ireland that the first years of the eleventh century were good and peaceful, under the strong rule of Brian; but history fails to confirm this. Plots, insurrections, murders and assassination continued apace, with the ever-present Danes to complicate each issue, give each plotter and assassin hope of reward.

This idyll of peace and prosperity—and though it was largely illusory, Brian deserves great credit for his efforts to achieve it— was shattered by a new and vicious quarrel between Brian and the King of Leinster. Leinster's king, with Danish backing, had decided he, not Brian, should be acknowledged King of All Ireland. He challenged the army of Munster to dispute his claim.

And so, on 23 April, 1014, Brian crossed the Shannon to engage the armies of Leinster and the Danes. He was eighty-eight years old, still strong in mind and body, still in absolute command of his army and its strategy, and of the hearts of its men. He had no doubt that with God's guidance he would defeat the enemy, for he was fortified by the knowledge that he defended the religion of Christ against the heathen worship of Odin.

At Clontarf the two armies met. For Brian and his followers it was a Crusade, and banners with the Cross of Christ were whipping in the wind when the first steel met. The battle had begun with the premature charge of a part of Brian's force under his son, the headstrong Murchadh, which was repulsed. The two opposing forces settled down to bloody combat at close quarters.

A little apart from the fighting, but in his own small tent, pitched far in front of the Munster encampment, the aged King Brian prayed. He sang psalms, recited prayers, a Pater Noster. According to Irish sources, he did this accompanied only by one young page, completely unprotected, as the battle raged less than a mile away. Danish history agrees that the old king was in an exposed spot, but states that, apart from the young page who prayed with him, Brian was at the centre of a ring of armed men.

The boy, hearing ever-louder sounds of battle, the groans of the dying, the clash of metal, asked his king whether he would not move. The outcome of the battle was far from clear, but the danger to an old man was growing. "I pray you, Sire—move before it is too late!"

"Oh God, thou boy, retreat becomes us not. And I myself know that I shall not leave this place alive. And what would it profit me?"

"But, Sire——"

"Enough."

A moment later the boy looked out and cried, "Blue, naked, people are advancing on us". And this, to one who had not yet seen them at close quarters was exactly what the Danish soldiers looked like, in their close-fitting blue *byrnies*.

"It matters not, boy."

The tent flap was flung open, three men burst in. They ignored the page and seized the old man, still on his knees.

"The king," said one.

"It is not the king. It is one of their priests. He is praying."

The old man, ignoring them, went on praying.

"One does not slay a priest."

"But this is no priest. Look—that is a king's mantle. Kill him."

And the three Danes killed Brian of the Tribute, King of Munster and All Ireland, in his tent.

He had been, by the standards of his time, a good king, and, by any criteria, a wise and brave one. He had succeeded, not entirely for reasons of aggrandizement, in making himself ruler of an all-but-united Ireland. Had his line been spared, he and his descendants might have made that unity a real thing, made Ireland strong and great, for even in the moment of his death Brian's army was winning a resounding victory against the Danes and his Irish enemies.

But with Brian gone, and with him his son Murchadh, who had begun the Battle of Clontarf and was to survive it by only a short time, the line had ended. Ireland descended again into the pit of intrigue and petty warfare from which she took so many years to rise.

In his long life—but a moment against the span of Irish history —Brian Boru won for himself undying fame as a great and good ruler who proved his country could be united. He has been compared with King Robert Bruce of Scotland, and the Battle of Clontarf with that of Bannockburn, for both men were wise rulers and both battles inflicted shattering defeat on their enemies. But Bruce's Scotland was more stable than Brian's Ireland, and Bruce was fighting with his country behind him against a single, clear-cut enemy, not a fifth-column like that which was helping the Danes. And Bruce survived the battle, was able to consolidate his victory and bring to Scotland the peace and justice for which he had fought.

But though Brian's line was extinguished and therefore his victory not as conclusive as it might have been, he has gone deservedly into history as a wise and brave ruler, one of his country's greatest sons.

CANUTE
(995–1035)

ENGLAND'S POSITION as an island has always been considered her greatest protection against invasion. But England's immunity from invasion dates only from the Norman Conquest. Before that Saxon Britain endured centuries of invasion, and was pillaged and plundered, its inhabitants slaughtered by generations of sea-borne invaders who came mainly from Scandinavia. These bold and ruthless Vikings—the Northmen or the Danes, as the English called them—ravaged the coasts of all Europe, from the Orkneys to the Isles of Greece.

The word Viking simply means warrior. The fiercest and most successful of them came from Denmark, and they were not all uncivilized. They had settled in the valley of the Seine and formed the Dukedom of Normandy. William the Conqueror was one of their descendants.

Two Vikings who had a great effect upon English history were Sweyn Forkbeard, King of Denmark, and his son Canute.*

In 1013 Ethelred the Unready was on the throne of Wessex, the last Saxon kingdom in a Britain where the Danish influence had been spreading for a long time. Ethelred was a weak and cowardly man, quite unfit to rule. After a generation of peace from the ancient enemy in Denmark, the country was once more subjected to Viking raids. In vain the ineffectual Ethelred tried to buy the invaders off with the traditional Danegeld. He then attempted to strengthen his position by marrying Emma, sister of Duke Richard of Normandy. He gained a beautiful wife, but little more. Emma was called the Pearl of Normandy on account of her beauty.

Ethelred found that there was no way of buying off Sweyn. He was determined to add England to his dominions, and in 1013 he landed with a great army and claimed the crown. After some bitter, sporadic fighting, the country capitulated. The craven Ethelred fled to Normandy with his bride.

But Sweyn died within a few weeks of his success, and Canute, who had accompanied his father on the expedition, was proclaimed

*The true form is Cnut. Canute is the Latin name used by medieval historians.

king. He was nineteen, a brave and talented young man, to be numbered among England's greatest rulers.

However, with the death of the terrible Sweyn Forkbeard the English gained heart. The Witan, a more or less haphazard assembly of ecclesiastics, nobles, royal officials and other magnates which existed to advise Anglo-Saxon kings, then plucked up courage and invited Ethelred to return to the throne. This Ethelred eagerly did, taking full advantage of the revulsion of feeling in his favour. But his subjects found him unchanged, and as mean, cruel and faithless as ever. Fortunately for his unhappy realm he was a sick man and he died in 1016, to be succeeded by his son Edmund Ironside.

Edmund was a brave and worthy man, in direct contrast to his despicable father, but the Saxon sun was setting, and though London and other parts of the country accepted him as king, the north, which was mainly Danish, was for Canute, who was in the country with a great fleet and a strong army. During 1016 Canute and Edmund fought bitterly for the English crown. Canute tried several times to take London, without success. He eventually defeated Edmund at Assandune (now Ashington) in Essex, but there was nothing final about the victory and Canute had to agree to partition of the kingdom. The two monarchs, both men of worth, met at Olney, an island in the Severn, and decided that Canute should rule Mercia and Northumbria, while Edmund should have Wessex, London and East Anglia.

Edmund did not live long to enjoy the fruits of this patched-up peace, which on the face of it did not seem likely to last for long. Within a few months he was dead, poisoned it was said by one, Edric Streona, who during the late fighting had joined whichever side seemed to have the best chance of winning. The Witan, weary of the war, then elected Canute as king of the whole kingdom.

Canute more than justified the wisdom of their choice, even though no exercise of wisdom was involved in this particular instance. The Witan had no choice and only wished to have an end to this wretched squabble for the crown. Kings were not so important in Anglo-Saxon England as they were after the Conquest when they became hereditary. Before 1066 the monarchy was largely elective.

Canute was no Viking adventurer. The age of the Vikings was at an end, as Canute well knew. On his mother's side he had Slavonic blood in him and this tempered the fierce and reckless Viking blood. He was also something of a statesman and this showed immediately in his dealing with the two young sons of Edmund Ironside—mere children of course, but important children. Canute did not put them to death, which might have been excusable in that rough age. Instead he sent them to the court at Sweden. It might be thought that Canute set a good example—which was not followed—to the monarchs who sat upon the English throne after him, a number of whom were faced with the problem of disposing of persons dangerously near an insecure throne. The more probable explanation for Canute's apparent generosity lay in the fact that the English throne, being largely elective, the children were no threat to him.

One of the first things Canute did was to put away his Danish wife and propose marriage to Emma, widow of Ethelred. Despite the lady's legendary beauty, this was a political marriage above all else. He wished particularly to have friendly relations with Emma's brother, the powerful Duke of Normandy, who despite his own Viking ancestry could not have viewed the events in England with any great favour. Even then the Dukes of Normandy had their eyes on the desirable throne of England.

Emma, who well knew the unpleasant character of her late husband, was not averse to the match. On the contrary, she was prepared to leave the two sons she had borne Ethelred in her brother's care in Normandy, and once more ornament the English throne as consort to the young Canute. She was older than he, yet she had retained her beauty. She put but one condition to the union—one which Canute found not unflattering. It was that the succession to the English throne should go to the son which she would bear him, and that the sons by their other unions should be excluded. Canute agreed, and the beauteous Emma once more became Queen of England, and bore Canute a son who became Hardicanute, and king after his father.

One of the first of Canute's forthright measures was to put to death the perfidious Edric Streona, who was suspected of poisoning that valiant adversary Edmund Ironside. Canute had no use for men like that. Canute also sent back to Denmark the army which had enabled him to gain the throne, and he paid off the great Viking fleet which had brought the army to England and whose existence was a threat and a source of fear in the country. This wise but difficult act of demobilization was only brought about by paying £83,000 in Danegeld, an enormous sum in those days, which the country had to raise in the form of taxes. But it was a wise and statesmanlike move.

One of the most important things that Canute did for England was to reconcile the Danes and the English, and give them equal rights before the law. This had been one of the grievances of the English in Mercia and those parts dominated by the Danes.

Canute gained great favour among the monastic chroniclers by his attitude to Christianity. His father had been a pagan and Canute himself had been nurtured in the worship of Woden. Legends exist about the miraculous manner in which he was converted to the true faith. But in those days Christianity was the mark of civilization (such as it was), and Canute was anxious to shake off his Viking role and join the mainstream of history. All the Vikings who had settled in Europe became Christian, and Canute did so with great enthusiasm and gained high favour among his contemporaries by founding abbeys, making gifts to monasteries and churches, by promoting churchmen to high office and doing reverence to saints and holy places. He made laws for the rigorous payment of tithes and church dues, for the observance of the Sabbath and the suppression of heathenism. In 1026 he went on a pilgrimage to Rome and was present at the coronation of Emperor Conrad III.

Canute was one of the great law-givers of English history. He gave to free Englishmen the first charter of liberties, and his legal system survived and formed the basis of English law under the Norman monarchs. What was known as "Cnut's law" in the succeeding centuries was a system of government which recognized the ancient and approved customs.

He was the first English king to establish a strong central government in the country. He travelled around with his staff of secretaries, scribes and legal advisers, and was the first king to have this kind of permanent secretariat.

Canute was not the first foreigner to rule successfully over a people whose customs, language and manners were at first strange to him, and he was certainly not the last. But England was only part of his great kingdom. In 1018 he became King of Denmark, then much larger than it is now, and he also conquered Sweden and Norway during his busy and eventful life. No other English king before or since has ruled over so large a portion of Europe. His comparatively early death prevented the establishment of a powerful Nordic empire bridging the North Sea, the possible historical consequences of which make interesting speculation. Canute's successors looked across the English Channel rather than the North Sea, and thus paved the way for the Norman Conquest.

In 1031 Canute conquered Scotland and forced King Malcolm to recognize his overlordship. Malcolm's nephew Duncan also did homage to Canute, and also a certain Maelboethe, both of whom were immortalized by Shakespeare, the latter as Macbeth.

It is evident that Canute thought more highly of England than of any of his possessions. He sent English missionaries to convert his pagan subjects in Scandinavia to Christianity. He gave England an especial undertaking that the country would be free from Viking raids which it had suffered for so long. When he was in Rome he wrote to the English people a letter containing, besides many elevated moral sentiments, regrets for his past misdeeds and promises for the future. In it he ordered his royal officers to do justice to all men whatever their estate, and not to extort money wrongfully under the pretext of the royal necessities. "I have no need," he said magnanimously, "of money gathered by unrighteousness".

Like all monarchs, he suffered from fawning courtiers. There is the famous story of when he was at Southampton, and was addressed as "Lord and master of the sea as well as of the land". To establish the literal incorrectness of this sentiment, which is certainly not so fulsome as some which have been bestowed upon rulers, and as a lesson in Christian humility, he had a chair placed at the water's edge before the incoming tide, and he challenged the sea to wet the feet of him whose ships sailed upon it and against whose land it dashed. The tide accepted the challenge and wet Canute's feet and clothes and Canute said: "Behold how feeble is the power of kings of men, for the waves will not hear my voice. Honour the Lord only, and serve him, for to him all things give obedience."

The story may or may not be true and to many it merely illustrates Canute's rather ostentatious religious sentiments, which were natural and perhaps necessary in an age when men were being converted from the old paganism to the new religion which was to be the cornerstone of Europe in the centuries to come.

But Canute, Dane though he was, deserved well of his adopted land, to which he had given order, law, unity and good government.

Canute died in 1035 at the age of forty, which was not young in those days when men lived hard and the normal span of life was short, but it was not long enough for Canute's work to be enduring. All too quickly England slipped back into the old chaos and disorder. It had to wait for the coming of Canute's kinsfolk, the Normans, to be moulded finally into the kingdom and country we know today.

WILLIAM I (THE CONQUEROR)
(1027?–1087)

THE ONLY English ruler who is given the title "The Great" is the noble Alfred. He merits the title but he was not King of all England: it would be more fitly given to William I, Duke of Normandy, usually called "The Conqueror". Attila, Genghis Khan and Napoleon were conquerors. William was a great warrior but he was above all the man who founded England, and, being a great administrator, gave it some of those features which made England, in less than a hundred years' time, already the first modern nation.

The Norman Conquest brought the Anglo-Saxon realm out of the orbit of the Scandinavian Empire and into the evolving world of Latin Christianity and feudalism. The Norman Conquest was the final ingredient which made the England of today. The very English language was transformed as a result of the Conquest into the language of Chaucer and Shakespeare. The effect of the Norman Conquest was to drive the Anglo-Saxon language underground, to make it a tongue only spoken by the ruled, by the simple and poor. Anglo-Saxon in the mouths of such men lost its Germanic inflections and general heaviness, and when, as happened astonishingly quickly, Normans and Anglo-Saxons found they were one people, the language emerged as more simple, direct and flexible than it had been and also enriched by Norman French. So the very English language was the fruit of the Norman Conquest.

Not much more than one hundred and fifty years before 1066, Norsemen, sailing in their conquest of foreign lands, landed at the mouth of the Seine, and the first leader of these men, Rolf the Ganger, agreed to hold the lands he had won as vassal of the King of France. Very quickly these Norsemen conquered what is now all Normandy. They were a warlike and cunning people, more ferocious and ruthless than the inhabitants of the surrounding areas. But they took to Christianity and were great admirers of learning which was largely in the hands at that time of the Church. The Duchy became a very well organized unit, and the Duke had much more power over his subordinate nobles and chieftains than had the French king over his.

William was born in 1027. He was the fruit of a love affair between his father, Duke Robert of Normandy, and Arletta, the daughter of a tanner of Falaise. Duke Robert had no legitimate issue and so in 1042, when he went on a crusade from which he never returned, he left his bastard as Duke. Tall and strongly built, with an air of majesty even as a young man which inspired awe, William had first to suppress various revolts which broke out against him, leading his men himself with a huge battle-axe.

The inhabitants of Alençon rebelled against him and to mock his birth they hung hides on the walls of their city with "Work for the Tanner" written across them. William cut out the eyes and cut off the hands of the prisoners he had taken and threw them into the city. He was soon undisputed master of his Duchy and when the King of France twice invaded Normandy he twice defeated the French armies.

No knight under heaven, it was said at this time, was William's equal. And no man dared say him nay. He showed, however, another side of his nature to those men of the Church, by no means all, whom he respected. From Abbot Lanfranc, afterwards to be Archbishop of Canterbury, he took advice. Once in a fit of temper he ordered the great scholar Anselm, who was also to play an important part in the history of England, out of the country. Hearing Anselm was proceeding very slowly he rode after him to hurry him on. "I'll go faster if you'll give me a better mount than this poor palfrey," said Anselm. The Duke laughed and they became friends.

William looked across the water. From nearly the beginning of the century to 1042, England had been ruled by the great Danish King Canute and by his unworthy sons. The House of Alfred was restored in Edward the Confessor who had spent his youth in Normandy at the court of William's father. Edward lived as a monk, and though married was obviously going to have no children. He loved the Church above all things and preferred the civilized Normans to his own subjects. He gave land to Norman knights on the borders of Wales and he installed Normans as bishops.

The heir to Edward the Confessor's throne by blood was a young boy, Edgar the Atheling; but though blood counted, no one could be king without the consent of the great Anglo-Saxon nobles or thanes. The monarchy in fact was partly elective. Edward had almost certainly promised William of Normandy the crown after him. The saintly king was no ruler and there was no central power of law anywhere in the land, each thane doing what he liked in his own domains. The kingdom was in fact falling to pieces, and sooner or later seemed likely to lapse back into the hands of the Scandinavians. No wonder then, when Edward the Confessor died in 1065 the English thanes decided that in spite of rivalries they would elect the strongest of their nation, Harold Godwin the Earl of Wessex, as Edward's successor. Harold, who had very carefully placated Edwin and Morcar, the lords of the North, by siding with them in a quarrel with his own brother Tostig. And so, in the words of the Anglo-Saxon chronicle, on the very day that Edward died:

Earle Harold was now consecrated King and he met little quiet in it as long as he ruled the realm.

William fell into a fury when the news was brought to him, as he had expected to be summoned to the Witan in London at least to state his claims. If Edgar the Atheling were set aside he had a certain claim in blood which, apart from his bastardy, was a better one than Harold's. Edward the Confessor was the son of a daughter of William's grandfather.

Still more was he angered because of a curious incident. Harold Godwin had either been wrecked off the coast of Normandy or, according to the Normans, sent by Edward the Confessor on a mission to William of Normandy to assure him of the throne. In any case, however it happened, William received Harold with great friendship and took him on a military expedition in Brittany— thus in fact showing that Harold served under him as a warrior and was therefore his vassal. Before Harold was allowed to return to England he had to swear fealty to William as future King of England in the presence of a large concourse of knights and barons. He took the oath, he could not in fact do otherwise; and then according to some sources, having sworn on a simple altar table, the table was shown to conceal the bodies of various holy martyrs. Harold's perjury was considered so serious that even on the eve of the Battle of Hastings some of his advisers thought he should not fight against William in person.

By Christmas of that year he was crowned king in Westminster Abbey, the great Saxon church which it had been Edward the Confessor's life work to build. Though there was bitter fighting in the north and west of England, though the Danes were to help the English rebels, the success of William's achievement was never in much doubt after the events of 1066. England was substantially conquered by an army of some twelve thousand Norman and French knights, men-at-arms and archers at the Battle of Hastings, or as it is sometimes called Senlac, fought in October. Harold was killed in the battle and with him many of the famous nobles and warriors.

Harold had been obliged in the late summer to raise an army and march north to fight a Scandinavian invasion led by Harold Hardraada, with his brother Tostig. After the victory at Stamford, he learnt that the Normans had landed in Sussex. Instead of waiting for William near London and getting the largest possible forces together, he decided to dash to Hastings to give battle. William very wisely hoped he would do this and had on purpose remained near his ships. When William had landed he had slipped on the sand and his followers, aware that they were on a rash enterprise, were alarmed. "See," said the Duke, rising to his feet, "I have firmly grasped the soil of England in my hands."

The battle was a hard-fought one. The English, dismounted, fought in a close formation protected by their huge shields. One Norman attack, uphill, was decisively beaten back. William ordered his cavalry, later, to pretend to flee from the battle. The English ranks broke up in pursuit and the Normans turned on them. Even then the English were able to reform, and it was not until late in the evening—with the Norman archers shooting up into the air so that their arrows would strike downwards, and William himself leading the furious attacks of the Norman knights—that victory came. Harold died, an arrow through his eye, and William refused him burial; and so the last Anglo-Saxon king rotted on the ground.

After Hastings, William again delayed. Edwin and Morcar, the thanes of the North, did not proclaim Edgar the Atheling as king at once. This they were to do, too late, in 1068. After this rebellion William devastated practically the whole of Yorkshire and the northern thanedoms of Burnisia, on the borders of Scotland. The truth was that though the Anglo-Saxons under local leaders such as Hereward the Wake in the fen country would fight bravely, the kingdom itself was so anarchic that it was not possible to rally men against Normans for the defence of the country. In 1067, for instance, William was already able to use the English Fyrd, the armed militia of the Anglo-Saxons, against some forces under the command of Harold's sons at Exeter and in the west.

However, William had to use all his driving force and ruthlessness to make himself really master of all England and to secure the nominal vassalage of the King of Scotland. When Edwin and

Morcar rebelled with the help of the Danish king, and the Welsh poured across the border into Cheshire to fight the Normans, the king answered with terror, devastating most of Yorkshire and County Durham. After "the harrying of the north" the great Norman castles were quickly erected on huge earth mounds piled up by Saxon serfs. The citizens of London saw the huge dungeon of the Tower dominate the city. Though the peasants pursued their ancient systems of farming as before, and though the Norman king was inclined to help the townspeople and merchants and to grant them charters, large parts of England, particularly the marches of Wales and Scotland and the Danelaw in the east, were very much under a military occupation. And the majority of the Anglo-Saxon nobles lost their lands forever.

Good came from the very thoroughness of the Conquest. King William had no intention of allowing Saxon thanes or Norman barons to challenge the power of the Crown. He refused to allow any single lord to hold large estates grouped together but scattered their lands about the country. The king, therefore, was far more powerful than any of his subjects, and accordingly his sheriffs and governors were respected. England, like Normandy, became a more modern and centralized kingdom than anywhere else in Christendom. The king, as his subjects knew, was avaricious—not personally but for his kingship. The great Doomsday Book was an extraordinary innovation for the eleventh century. The Anglo-Saxon chronicler describes it with wonder and also with the sort of scornful surprise that a king should bother so much about such things.

> Then the king sent his men over all England into every shire and had them find out how many hundred hides there were in the shire, or what land or cattle the king himself had in the country or what dues he ought to have in twelve months. Also he had a record made of how much land his Archbishops had, and his Bishops and his Abbotts and his Earls—and they are related at two great lengths—what or how much everybody had who was occupying land in England, in land or cattle, and how much money it was worth. So very narrowly did he have it investigated, that there was no single hide nor yard of land, nor indeed (it is a shame to relate but it seemed no shame for him to do) one ox nor one cow nor one pig wa. there left out and not put down in his record: and all these records were brought to him afterwards.

From his wife Matilda, a daughter of the Count of Flanders, he had four sons: Robert Duke of Normandy; Richard, killed as a youth whilst hunting; William II and Henry I, both of whom succeeded him; and five daughters. He was a faithful husband without personal vices. In old age he was somewhat corpulent, but still muscular and agile, with short moustaches on each side of his upper lip and close-cropped hair. A monk of Caen wrote:

The King excelled in wisdom all the princes of his generation, and among them all he was outstanding in the largeness of his soul.

He was great in body and strong, tall in stature but not ungainly. He was also temperate in eating and drinking. Especially was he moderate in drinking, for he abhorred drunkenness in all men and disdained it more particularly in himself and at his court. In speech he was fluent and persuasive, being skilled at all times in making clear his will. If his voice was harsh, what he said was always suited to the occasion. He followed the Christian discipline, and whenever his health permitted he regularly, and with great piety, attended Christian worship each morning and evening.

His death took place during an expedition in Normandy to punish the men of Mantes who had raided his territory. During this expedition the great king was struck with violent pains in his intestines. On Tuesday, 9 September, 1087, he woke from sleep and heard the great bell of Rouen Cathedral and saw the sun—but died soon after. As often happens when a great man died in those days, those around the bedside were filled with alarm. A monkish chronicler notes that the physicians and others who were present, who had watched the king all night, seeing him expire so suddenly and unexpectedly were much astonished and became as men who had lost their wits. The wealthiest of them mounted their horses and departed in haste to secure their property. But the inferior attendants, observing that their masters had disappeared, laid hands on the arms, the plate, the robes, the lining, and all the royal furniture and, leaving the corpse almost naked on the floor of the house, they hastened away. William was afterwards buried in great pomp in the Cathedral at Caen.

An Anglo-Saxon chronicler states:

This King William was a very wise man and very powerful and more worshipful and stronger than any predecessor of his had been. He was gentler to the good men who loved God, and stern beyond all measure to those people who resisted his will. Amongst the good things he did, the security he made in this country is not to be forgotten—so that any honest man could travel over his kingdom without injury with his bosom full of gold: and no one dared strike another however much wrong he had done him. And if a man had intercourse with a woman against her will, he was forthwith castrated. He ruled over England and by his cunning it was so investigated that there was not one hide of land he did not know. Wales was in his power, he built castles there and entirely controlled that race.

However, the Anglo-Saxon chronicler also goes on to speak of William's pride and ends:

Alas, woe, that any man so proud should go, and exalt himself and reckon himself above all men. Though Almighty God show mercy on his soul and grant unto him forgiveness for his sins.

The judgment of posterity is certainly with those who admire William's greatness of soul and mind, and rather less with those who bemoaned his pride. He can claim to be the begetter of the English realm.

FREDERICK BARBAROSSA

(1120–1190)

In a cavern in the Kyffhäuser mountain in Thuringia there has been sitting for nearly eight hundred years an old man in royal robes with a crown on his head. He is asleep so that his eyes cannot be seen, but they are large and blue. A slight smile plays round his broad humorous mouth. His hair is silver, but his beard has touches of red in it and has grown so long that it has pushed right through the table before him. Ravens fly round the mouth of the cave and some day, when they depart, the old man will wake up, take his shield and sword and save Germany from her enemies. So runs the legend of Frederick Barbarossa (1120-1190), and it is still alive in Germany today, for the red-bearded emperor has rightly been called the greatest figure in early German history after Charlemagne.

Elected king in 1152 in succession to his uncle, Conrad III, he faced a formidable task. Germany was like a melon sliced into segments, and in the centuries following Charlemagne's division of his empire amongst his sons these segments had tended to split off. In a vast country stretching from the North Sea to Italy and from Burgundy to the boundaries of Poland, the tribal groups of Burgundians, Swabians, Bavarians, Saxons and East Franks had developed an independent life under their own rulers, held together only by an elected king whom German princes looked on not as a superior, but as the first among equals.

This loose conglomeration faced a number of threats. Danes, Northmen, Poles and Magyars pressed in from the perimeter. Rival dukes, when they were not repelling invaders, fought for power among themselves, and for many years before Frederick's accession there had been an internecine struggle between the House of Hohenstaufen (called the Waiblings) from which Frederick came and the Saxon House of Welf, which since the eleventh century had supplied three German emperors.

There was also a complicated issue of spiritual versus temporal authority within Germany. Charlemagne had been declared by the Pope to be Emperor of the Roman Empire and this established a precedent for future Popes to appoint the man of their choice as temporal ruler over Christendom. In the early Middle Ages the theory was that Christianity had both a spiritual and a temporal head—Pope and Emperor—and this was symbolized in the picture of two swords which defended the Faith. But this segregation of powers never took place. The Popes had their political ambitions and within Germany they sought to influence the whole life of the country through their legates and bishops recognizing them as the supreme head, temporal as well as spiritual, of whom the emperor was merely a kind of liegeman. This German emperors could not accept, particularly as they needed the support of churchmen in maintaining their own authority.

So under Frederick's predecessors a continual struggle for supremacy had developed between emperors and popes, made more acute in the time of Otto the Great (see earlier chapter) by his invasion of northern Italy, its reduction to a satellite kingdom and his banishment, on grounds of treachery, of the Pope who had crowned him emperor in Rome. Otto then styled himself Holy Roman Emperor, a title which was not finally dropped until 1806.

Thus was born the Imperial Idea to which much of Frederick's life and energies were dedicated and the Idea was quite new, fitting the times. Frederick gave it form. Within Germany the long-standing contest of Welf and Waiblingen would be brought to an end, not by crushing the Welfs, to whom he was related on his mother's side, but by making them yet stronger and then enlisting their support to create a new Imperial splendour. This was based on the idea of power derived directly from God, confirmed, not conferred, by the Pope. A clear division must be made once more between spiritual and temporal authority, the Pope must be relegated to his proper sphere and be deprived of the capacity to make trouble. This meant that the cities of northern Italy must be thoroughly subjugated to the Imperial rule so that they could not intrigue with the Pope and he would have the Imperial power on his door-step. The wealth of the cities would also fill Frederick's coffers, providing him with the resources which his German kingship lacked.

To realize this Idea Frederick possessed outstanding qualities: political skill, courage, perseverance, piety, a love of adventure and the ability to conciliate which went with great personal charm. After his election he hastened to make peace with his proud and powerful Welf kinsman, Duke Henry the Lion, by restoring to him Bavaria, part of his dukedom which Conrad had seized. Two years later he toured the Rhineland and the Palatinate, ruthlessly suppressing feuds between rival lords until throughout the Reich, as it was said, "it seemed better to keep quiet, as the emperor was restlessly travelling around, hanging or beheading every peace-breaker he captured". He then turned to Poland, technically held by its Dukes in fief to the Reich, where Duke Boleslav, nicknamed Curly-Hair, was building the country into a threatening and independent power. Within a month Frederick had subdued him, imposed a crippling fine and restored Boleslav to his allegiance.

Meanwhile, Frederick with a thousand knights had journeyed to Italy for his coronation in Rome by the English Pope Hadrian IV, had freed Hadrian from a Roman mob stirred up against him by the religious fanatic Arnold of Brescia, but aroused the Pope's deepest suspicions by refusing to hold his stirrup for him when he dismounted from his palfrey. Soon Hadrian was claiming that he had "conferred" the crown as though it were a benefice and Frederick was retorting, in a circular published throughout the Reich, that he had received it from God alone "through the election of the Princes" and would rather die than accept such a doctrine.

The controversy between Pope and Emperor became more acute. Faced with the possibility of Italy united under Hadrian, Frederick tried to strengthen his grip on the northern cities. In June, 1158, he appeared in Verona with an army fifty thousand strong and on the pretext that Milan was oppressing her smaller neighbours besieged the city and compelled it to capitulate. At Roncaglia, with the help of Italian lawyers, he then issued a series of laws, regulating the dues to be paid to him by the cities and appointing royal officers to administer them and prevent strife between rival factions.

This was a success, but the Italians did not willingly submit and the death of Hadrian brought Alexander III to the Papacy, a man as intelligent and resolute as Frederick himself, who deeply mistrusted him and saw his Chancellor Reinald as the arch-enemy of Christendom. Frederick secured the election of an anti-Pope, Victor IV, held his stirrup and kissed his feet; but the puppet proved of no account. Alexander excommunicated the emperor and Milan promptly revolted. This time the population was starved out and the city razed to the ground.

It was war to the knife. The Lombards rose against the harsh German administration, actively encouraged by Alexander III, who had taken refuge in France. The walls of Milan were rebuilt. Frederick kept his grip on the Italian towns with difficulty and redoubled his efforts to destroy Alexander's influence. When Victor IV died in 1164 he had another anti-Pope elected, Paschal III, and three years later stormed into Italy with a large army to capture Rome itself. The city fell. Alexander, who had meanwhile returned, fled to Sicily and Frederick procured the enthronement of Paschal. But retribution, apparently divine, then descended. In the summer heat plague suddenly struck the army, the soldiers died like flies and Frederick was forced to make an ignominious retreat with the survivors through the northern territories flaming with revolt. He crossed the Alps without arms, disguised as a servant.

He was now faced with a Lombard League sworn to wrest independence from the Germans, and in 1176, descending for the last time to reassert his authority, he was heavily defeated at Legnano and obliged to make terms which left him with a vague imperial suzerainty over cities which from now on counted as allies rather than subjects. The time had come for reconciliation with the Pope. Both Frederick and the aged Alexander saw it as their task to give "eternal peace" to a war-weary world. In October, 1176, the Emperor's emissaries prostrated themselves before the Pope at Agnani and difficult negotiations began, resulting in an arrangement which left the Pope still dependent on the emperor's temporal power and placed the northern cities under their joint supervision. Well might Frederick be prepared, in a splendid ceremony at St. Mark's in Venice, to kneel to Alexander and receive the kiss of peace.

Nine years later Frederick bequeathed a promising strategic situation to his Hohenstaufen successors by marrying his eldest son Henry to Constance, heiress presumptive of the Norman King Roger of Sicily. By that time Frederick was undisputed master of Germany and the threat of a warlike nobility from the north, coupled with a well-trained Saracen army and a powerful fleet from the south, was well calculated to soften the Papacy. But in the long result neither Popes nor emperors were the victors. The Hohenstaufen dynasty was destroyed, but the Popes became subservient to France, lost heavily in prestige and the way was opened for the Protestant Reformation. Meanwhile, in his declining years, Frederick, once "Hammer of the Godless", became the "Most Christian Son of the Church".

Within Germany his success was unqualified. Here all his fine qualities combined to consolidate the Reich, foster trade, prosperity and learning. Henry the Lion, placated in earlier years, refused to accompany the emperor on his later Italian expeditions and built up a Saxon empire within the empire stretching from North and North-west Germany to Thuringia. His aggressiveness earned him many enemies among his princely neighbours, and when they complained and he refused to obey an Imperial summons to answer their accusations, Frederick in a lightning campaign occupied Saxony and banished his rival to France. Henry's Duchy was then sagaciously divided amongst the nobility, now put on its best behaviour by the dismal fate of the Lion.

By smashing the most powerful duke in Germany Frederick set the seal on his claim to be Holy Roman Emperor in fact as well as in title. Without the support of the nobility and of the Church, which he was able to dominate owing to the weakness of the Papacy, he could not have created the conditions needed for commercial and social prosperity. During his reign fine roads were built in Swabia, establishing new trade routes for transcontinental traffic. Between 1150 and 1175 the number of German towns, all of them in Staufian territory, almost doubled, their construction heavily subsidized by Frederick. On his initiative special trading centres were set up for the European market. A unified coinage was introduced in the area of the Lower Rhine. The middle class, comprising craftsmen and merchants, was strongly encouraged and a rigid caste system was softened by permitting members of the Imperial administration to rise into the aristocracy. Thus a basis was formed for the later glories of the Hohenstaufen period when trade, security and territorial expansion went hand in hand and the refinements of medieval chivalry flowered into splendid literature.

Frederick was regarded in his time as the perfect knight and it was as a Crusader that he died. Now, nearing seventy, as the ruler of an empire comprising more than half the Christian world, he answered the call of Pope Clement III to lead the princes of Europe to Palestine where the Holy Places were again in deadly peril. The Imperial glory was laid aside. Donning simple dress, thinking himself no more than a pilgrim and a follower of the Lord, he summoned the princes of the Reich to a "court-day of Jesus Christ", leaving the throne empty in symbolic fashion. They promised their help; a large army was collected and to the admiration of Christendom the old man led it in person overland towards the Bosphorus while the English crusaders under Richard Coeur de Lion and the French under King Philip chose the sea-route.

At first everything went well. From rulers along the route and the Emperor Isaac at Constantinople promises of provisions and an unmolested passage had been obtained. But trouble started as soon as the army reached Byzantine territory. The encampment was attacked at nights, food was scarce and the population had fled from the towns, taking everything with them. An army which Isaac sent to attack the Crusaders was defeated and, despite this extreme provocation, Frederick bargained with him afresh with tolerable good humour. Agreement reached, the army arrived at the Hellespont almost a year after it had left Germany.

The advance through Asia Minor began and Frederick addressed his troops: "Brothers, be strong and full of confidence, the whole land is ours!" Isaac helped him on his way and no more trouble was met till in May the army reached the kingdom of the Seljuk Turks. Here, too, the Sultan Kilidsh Arslan had promised his support, but it was soon clear that he had no intention of keeping his word. The men marched on through mountainous country bereft of cattle and all sign of life. It was extremely cold. Swarms of hostile horsemen descended. Frederick and his army seemed to be trapped.

They plodded on with their heavy horses and massive armour, aiming for a town beyond the mountains where they hoped to find food. But a hostile army thirty thousand strong blocked the only pass. Half starved, they struggled over by a different route and pressed on towards the town—to find it foodless, deserted. There they celebrated Whitsun and after mass there was a banquet consisting of boiled horse-skins.

Thirty miles away was the Sultan's capital, the wealthy Iconium. Still harried by savage, elusive horsemen, the crusading "army", now dwindled to six hundred knights, groped towards it, clinging to this last hope, another mirage perhaps. Their wits were beginning to turn: the Bishop of Würzburg had a vision of St. George in the sky and many said they had seen miraculous white birds circling the emperor's tent.

Iconium was garrisoned and a Seljuk army was waiting outside the town. No one knows the exact size, but perhaps the German chroniclers are right when they say that Frederick with his starving few scattered a force a hundred times as strong. At any rate, they reached the Sultan's gardens, then split into two parties, one to capture the town, the other to act as rearguard under Frederick's command. When assailed again by the reformed horsemen he spoke to his knights with tears streaming down his face and his words are on record: "Why do we hesitate? Why do we tremble? Christ conquers, Christ is King, Christ is Emperor. Our death is our reward. Into battle, warriors; win the Kingdom of Heaven with your blood!"

That night the Sultan was begging for peace, offering mules, horses and food, and within a week the band of brothers, refreshed and confident, having won one of the most brilliant victories in German history, was moving, the last obstacle gone, towards the Holy Land. Ahead went Frederick, the old man of whom his chronicler wrote: "In all the world there is not his equal to be found."

Did he remember the prophecy that he would die by drowning, or that other saying that he would win the Reich like a fox, preserve it like a lion, but die like a dog? Not at this moment, surely. The spiritual goal was beckoning and he felt strong for all his years. Near Seleucia, on the coast opposite the eastern end of Cyprus, mountains had to be crossed and Frederick chose a path bordering a fast-flowing river. It was June, the heat was intense and the going very difficult. Sometimes he and his friends had to crawl on all-fours, until a ford was found and he crossed with his horse to the far side. There, resting in the burning sun, he had some food, then said he would bathe again. The other men warned; he disregarded them and went down once more into the cold water. They saw his arm suddenly rise, then he disappeared. Much later, after a difficult search, they found his body. It was Sunday, 10 June, 1190.

The chronicler closed his book. On meeting in Seleucia many of the knights who had come so far turned their horses for home and within twenty years his bones, even, at first carefully preserved in Tyre, had been lost. But legend brought them home and today, when they see the clouds surging up above the Kyffhäuser, German peasants still say with mingled fear and hope: "Kaiser Friedrich is brewing!"

SALADIN

(1138–1193)

SIR WALTER SCOTT, in his introduction to *The Talisman*, explained that he was drawn to his subject by the "singular contrast" between Richard I, King of England, and his opponent in the Holy Land, Saladin the Sultan: "The Christian and English monarch showed all the cruelty and violence of an Eastern Sultan; and Saladin, on the other hand, displayed the deep policy and prudence of a European sovereign, whilst each contended which should excel the other in the knightly qualities of bravery and generosity."

This seemed a paradox to the novelist in 1830, for the countries of Europe had long been powerful, while Islam had lost much of its great civilization of the past; but at the time of Saladin, born in 1138 and died in 1193, the Saracens were heirs to a civilization four centuries old, and medieval Europe came to learn much from Arab literature, science, architecture and state-craft. To the Muslims the Christians were idolators, for they worshipped a Trinity of three Gods; to the Christians the Muslims were infidels to be destroyed.

Saladin stands out among Saracens as well as Christians as a great general, a just, religious and kind man, whose generosity was often so quixotic that the Crusaders were astounded and his own companions critical; he always kept his word even though the Crusaders repeatedly broke theirs, absolved by their priests on the argument that an oath to an infidel was invalid. His high qualities are described by Christian as well as Arab chroniclers at the time of the Third Crusade. In Europe Saladin is remembered for his qualities as a man, while in the Arab world he is honoured more for political reasons, because he succeeded in uniting Egypt, Syria and Mesopotamia in one empire and because he freed most of Palestine of the invaders. "Jerusalem," wrote Saladin to Richard, "is holy to us as well as to you . . . Think not that we shall go back therefrom . . . And as for the land, it was ours to begin with, and you invaded it; nor had you taken it but for the feebleness of the Muslims who then had it; and so long as this war lasts God will not permit you to set up a stone on it."

Forty years before Saladin's birth the First Crusade would

probably not have succeeded if the great Seljuk Sultan, Melik Shah, had not died in 1092, so that when the Crusaders arrived the empire was already broken up into petty kingdoms ruled often by former Mamluk slaves. One of these was Zengy, ruler of Mosul, and it was through him that Saladin's family received preferment.

When Zengy and his army suffered a defeat in Mesopotamia they wanted to avoid being massacred by retreating across the Tigris at a point controlled by the castle of Tekrit, commanded by Ayyub Nejm ed-Din, a Kurd of the Rawadiya clan, born near Dawin in Armenia. Ayyub agreed to let Zengy and his army be ferried across, although he knew that this would infuriate the Abbasid Caliph of Baghdad; indeed, he and his brother, Shirkuh, were later ordered to go. On the night they left in September, 1138, a son, Yusuf, was born to Ayyub; later he was to be given the title of Salah ed-Din, "Honour of the Faith". The family sought refuge with Zengy, and Ayyub, in recompense for saving the army, was made Governor of Baalbeck, and there Yusuf, or Joseph, spent his childhood; when he was nine years old Zengy was murdered in his tent and Ayyub had to move to Damascus, where he became commander of the army. His brother Shirkuh, known as "the mountain-lion", had taken service with Nur ed-Din, who had succeeded his father, Zengy. Nur ed-Din wished to occupy Damascus and sent Shirkuh in command of his army to negotiate with his brother, Ayyub, who treated the matter as a family affair, handed over the city and became governor.

Yusuf or Saladin seems to have led a retired life, interested in literature and discussing religion with the ulema, but at the age of twenty-six, much against his will, he was drawn into the battle for Egypt. Nur ed-Din was now King of Syria and a powerful rival to Amalric, the Crusader King of Jerusalem, so that neither wished to allow the other to increase his power by capturing Egypt; this was under the nominal rule of a young Shia caliph, el-Adid, the last of the Fatimid dynasty which had ruled for two hundred years. Amalric invaded Egypt in September, 1163, and Nur ed-Din ordered Shirkuh to take the army there with Saladin who distinguished himself as a soldier and was given his first command as governor of Alexandria; there he was besieged for seventy-five days, but peace terms were arranged on 4 August, 1167, under which it was decided to leave Egypt to the Egyptians, at any rate for a period. Saladin was a guest in Amalric's camp and made friends with a famous Crusader, Humphrey of Toron, showing great interest in the vows taken by Christian knights. It was related by the Christian chroniclers, but not by the Arab, that Saladin went through the ceremony of Christian knighthood; perhaps these stories were told to try to account for Saladin's knightly qualities which could not, they thought, be derived from Islam.

There was another expedition to Egypt, and Shirkuh, who was now Vizier, died from over-indulgence in March, 1169. The caliph chose his nephew Saladin as Vizier, largely because he seemed an unambitious and pliable young man, but the caliph was soon to regret his choice. Saladin's strong religious beliefs, which had made him a recluse, now became an inspiration to him to establish a Muslim empire which would be strong enough to drive the Crusaders out of the Holy Land. "When God gave me the land of Egypt," said Saladin later, "I was sure that he meant me to have Palestine as well." The older emirs were jealous that a man of thirty should have so coveted a post, but Saladin took up their challenge and showed great tact, wisdom and cunning in winning many to his allegiance. He overcame plots, army mutinies and Crusader invasions; when the caliph died at the age of twenty he made the chief eunuch at the palace, Kirkush, see to it that there were no more Fatimites capable of ruling Egypt. Saladin was Sultan of Egypt in all but name.

Nur ed-Din had himself become jealous of Saladin's rapid rise to power and planned to bring an army to Egypt to humble him, but he died suddenly in May, 1174, at the age of fifty-six. His loss was felt deeply, for he was a pious, just and able administrator who used the public revenues for the good of the people. The only person to benefit was Saladin. There was now bitter hostility between the house of Zengy and the house of Ayyub and it was not until April, 1175, that Saladin was in a position to declare himself King of Syria as well as King of Egypt. He could now plan his *jehad* or holy war.

King Amalric had died soon after Nur ed-Din and there was a regent for King Baldwin IV, a boy of thirteen and a leper. Saladin was back in Cairo for a year in 1176, supervising the building of colleges, the great dyke of Giza and planning his citadel. It was a life of great activity supervising the administration of two such different countries as Egypt and Syria, dispensing justice, receiving envoys, settling the jealousies of an elaborate court; most of all he enjoyed the company of poets, philosophers and religious men, putting all at ease, so that the noise of the conversation shocked those who had been accustomed to the staid levees of Sultan Nur ed-Din when each man sat rigid "as if a bird were perched on his head".

He lived piously and simply and was extraordinarily patient; he considered always that he held his high post for the good of the people. "Seek to win the hearts of your people and watch over their prosperity," said Saladin to his favourite son, ez-Zahir, when he was being sent to take over a provincial government; "for it is to secure their happiness that you are appointed by God and by me . . . I have become great as I am because I have won men's hearts by gentleness and kindness". This was true and it was a remarkable achievement, considering the size of the kingdom he controlled and the wild independence of some of the many races making up the Saracen world from Armenia and Kurdistan in the north to Tunisia in the west and the Sudan in the south. "He was," writes Sir Steven Runciman in *A History of the Crusades*, "a Kurd of no great family who commanded the obedience of the Muslim world by the force of his personality".

Saladin left Cairo for the last time on 11 May, 1182, and set up his headquarters in Damascus. There had been breaches in a truce with various emirs, but he made no move against them until the truce had expired and then he subjugated Mesopotamia and captured Aleppo. He was a great general, taking much care to reconnoitre the ground himself where he intended to give battle; he controlled his troops from his headquarters or would ride through the arrows between the battle lines accompanied only by a page with a spare horse; he would appear in all parts of the battlefield encouraging his men but he did not fight himself unless the enemy were gaining an advantage.

It was his good intelligence service and his careful choice of ground which won him the great battle of Hittin, a little west of Lake Tiberias, on 4 July, 1187, when the Crusaders had to fight after a long march in the summer heat without water. It was one of the most important battles in the history of the Middle East and the greatest reverse that the Crusaders had suffered; Jerusalem was taken in September and all Palestine was at the mercy of the Saracens. For nearly a hundred years Jerusalem had been the capital of the Latin kingdom, and when Saladin came in September to besiege it the thousands of Christians within must have been fearful lest the Muslims should take revenge for what had been done when it was first captured. Stanley Lane-Poole, in his biography *Saladin*, refers to "the savage conquest by the first crusaders in 1099 . . . when the blood of wanton massacre defiled the honour of Christendom and stained the scene where once the gospel of love and mercy had been preached", but, as he adds, "never did Saladin show himself greater than during this memorable surrender". There was no revenge or indiscriminate killing and all the people were ransomed. The Christian chronicler Ernoul, Squire to Balian of Ibelin, who had commanded the defence, wrote that the Muslim guards kept strict discipline so that there was no ill-usage of Christians, "such was the charity which Saladin did of poor people without number"; but when the refugees reached Tripoli on the coast, which was still held by the Crusaders, they were refused entrance.

The overwhelming defeat of the Crusaders at Hittin and the fall of Jerusalem had caused consternation in Europe. Archbishop William of Tyre had hurried to Sicily to get aid and then to France and England. The Pope issued an appeal to the knights of Christendom and thousands prepared themselves for the Third Crusade. Kings and princes contributed treasure, but the largest contribution came from what was known as "the Saladin tax", which was, in the words of Edward Gibbon, "the noblest monument of a conqueror's fame and the terror which he inspired"; he points out that, although it was raised for the service of the holy war, it was so lucrative that it was continued and became "the foundation of all the tithes and tenths on ecclesiastical benefices". Huge armies with their supplies, horses and siege-weapons gathered under the most powerful kings and knights of Europe—the ageing Emperor Frederick Barbarossa, King Richard I (who had succeeded Henry II to the throne of England), and King Philip of France. There were gathering of troops and plans drawn up between the kings at the hill-top Cathedral of Vezelay in Burgundy.

It took them a long time to reach the Holy Land and Saladin had plenty of time to complete the defeat of all the Crusaders in Palestine, so that the armies of the Third Crusade would have found no easy means of gaining a footing on the coast. But Saladin made the very great mistake of withdrawing from the siege of Tyre which became a rallying point for the Christians. Saladin was suffering from recurrent illness and he always had difficulty in keeping his troops together for a siege; nor did he follow up the defeat of the Crusaders in front of the great fortress of Acre in a bitter fight on 4 October, 1189. The situation changed radically with the arrival of strong forces from England, France and Germany with their huge siege-engines.

In July, 1191, the Saracen fortress of Acre was surrendered. Humiliating terms to save the lives of the garrison had to be accepted by Saladin although his large army was undefeated; but Richard, in cold-blood, ordered the beheading of two thousand seven hundred hostages. "After Saladin's almost quixotic acts of clemency and generosity, the King of England's cruelty will appear amazing," wrote Stanley Lane-Poole. Richard's extraordinary strength and courage put heart into the Crusaders and they won the battle of Arsuf, but they never reached Jerusalem. The Crusader army turned back to the coast in 1192, defeated by the cold of a Palestine winter and the fact that Saladin's army was still intact; a treaty was signed at Ramla in September; Richard left Palestine in October. Saladin held Jerusalem and all Palestine except for the coastline from Tyre to Jaffa.

Saladin agreed that Christian pilgrims should come to visit Jerusalem and he granted the request of Hubert Walter that four Latin priests might celebrate their service in the Church of the Holy Sepulchre; a similar request from the Byzantine Emperor for priests of the Orthodox Church was refused; this was the origin of that quarrel between the French and Russians over the custody of the Holy Places which nearly seven centuries later was one of the causes of the Crimean War. It was at this interview with the Bishop of Salisbury that Saladin said that he admired Richard's bravery but thought that he often incurred unnecessary danger. They had, indeed, a great respect for one another and exchanged many courtesies; when Saladin had seen Richard fighting on foot during one battle he had had a horse sent to him, but Saladin had always refused to meet him. Saladin told the bishop that he would himself rather be gifted with wealth, wisdom and moderation than "with boldness and immoderation". He thought that Richard got too involved with the fighting himself; Saladin, however, always seemed to be at the place he was most needed, either in defence or attack. When it was thought that the Crusaders under Richard would march on Jerusalem and there was considerable consternation among the Saracens, Abdel Latif, a well-known Baghdad physician, was surprised to see Saladin personally supervising the defence of the city, "even carrying stones on his own shoulders and everybody, rich and poor, followed his example".

By the age of fifty-five Saladin had worn himself out and he died leaving no personal possessions on 3 March, 1193, in Damascus where is his tomb. "Our Sultan," wrote Baha ed-Din, his secretary and biographer, "was very noble of heart, kindness shone in his face, he was very modest and exquisitely courteous".

HENRY II OF ENGLAND

(1154–1189)

THE STRONG administration of William the Conqueror served England well. William II, known as William Rufus, was a self-indulgent, reckless king, but he maintained the royal authority against the fierce ambitions of the barons. His younger brother, Henry I, the man who said, "An unlettered king is a crowned ass", married the daughter of the King of Scotland who, on her mother's side, was descended from Anglo-Saxon kings.

During Henry I's reign the towns of England were granted, many of them, charters, thus helping to deliver the merchant classes from the domination of the barons. Great prelates like Anselm and John of Salisbury encouraged learning and the Church produced a generation of clerks and lawyers who no longer thought of themselves as Norman or Anglo-Saxon but as English. The army with which Henry I firmly defeated his brother Robert Duke of Normandy and which, at the victory at Tenchebrai in Normandy, avenged the Battle of Hastings as it were, was an English army though its leaders bore Norman names. Under Henry I's strong rule England prospered.

But on Henry's death in 1135 a period of misrule began. Henry's only son, William the Atheling, had been drowned off the coast of France, and when the king learnt the news it was said he never smiled again. He had one daughter, Matilda, whom he had married first to the Holy Roman Emperor and then, when she was widowed, to Geoffrey Plantagenet, Count of Anjou. The nobles swore to accept Matilda as queen. But on Henry's death, Stephen, Count of Blois, the son of one of William the Conqueror's daughters, Adela, claimed the throne. It was indicative of the new forces of the times that though most of the nobles of the south of England held aloof from Stephen, the City of London's acceptance of Stephen was decisive. Matilda invaded England and a long period of civil war followed, a dark night for the people of England in which every baron and local chieftain did what he liked. However, and this again was significant of the new times, the influence of the Church and of the great Archbishop, Theobald of Canterbury, restored peace, though an uncertain one. It was agreed by the various factions that Stephen should reign until his death and be succeeded by Matilda's heir, Henry, Count of Anjou.

England was then to have one of the greatest of all her kings and one of the most extraordinary men called to the throne. Henry, the son of Geoffrey Plantagenet, was first of all very much a foreigner, having been born in Anjou and possessing, through his father and grandfather Henry I, other parts of northern and western France. Shortly before he became King of England he married Eleanor of Aquitaine, who owned most of south-western France and who had been the bride of Louis VII, King of France, whom she could not stomach. When she left the French king, she it was who proposed herself to Henry Plantagenet to whom she had long been attracted. Henry thus became the ruler of an empire which ran from the Cheviots to the Pyrenees, and included the highly civilized cities of the south-west of France with a small court where the troubadours flourished as well as the wild tribes of Wales and the grim fortresses of northern England.

Henry spent much of his time out of England, yet England was always his chief concern. He left his foreign fiefs to his lieutenants and then later, with unhappy results, to his sons. Although his empire rivalled that of the Holy Roman Emperor and in size eclipsed the land of the King of France, Henry was of all kings the man who loved grandeur and pomp the least. He had a contempt for the trappings of monarchy, dressed himself very carelessly in ordinary clothes and mingled as familiarly with peasants and merchants as with his courtiers. He was a scholar speaking many languages and, inspired by the civil and political ideas of the rising civilization of Italy, he was above all a man of business and progress. Nobody could have been better fitted for such a vast task as the Angevin Empire—as Henry's domains were called—for he had a passion for administration and was a man of ceaseless, restless energy. Gerald of Wales, a writer of mixed Norman and Welsh ancestry, a scholar of Paris and who, as royal chaplain, had known the king well, described him:

Henry II, King of England, was a man of reddish, freckled complexion with a large round head, grey eyes which glowed fiercely and grew bloodshot in anger, a fiery countenance and a harsh cracked voice. His neck was somewhat thrust forward from his shoulders, his chest was broad and square, his arms strong and powerful. His frame was stocky with a pronounced tendency to corpulence, due rather to nature than to indulgence which he tempered by exercise. For in eating and drinking he was moderate and sparing and in all things frugal in a degree permissible to a prince. He was addicted to the chase; at crack of dawn he was off on horse-back, traversing wastelands, penetrating forests and climbing the mountain-tops, and so he passed restless days. At evening on his return home he was rarely seen to sit down either before or after supper. He was a man of easy access, and condescending, pliant and witty, second to none in politeness, whatever thoughts he might conceal in himself.

It was no joke being attached to Henry's court, and this bow-legged, hot-tempered monarch had little concern for those who followed him as he went about England enquiring into the administration of justice, or the way taxes were collected, or why such and such a castle erected without permission during the war of Stephen's reign had not been pulled down. Professor Coulton's *Life in the Middle Ages* reproduces the complaints of a certain Peter de Blois, one of Henry's servants, who after complaining of the poor food and drink served out by the royal stewards, bemoans the king's restlessness:

If the king had promised to stay anywhere, then be sure that he will set out at daybreak, knocking all men's expectations by his sudden change of purpose. Whereby it cometh frequently to pass that such courtiers as have let themselves be bled, or have taken some purgative, must yet follow their prince forthwith without regard to their own bodies, and, setting their life on the hazard of a dice, hasten blindfold to ruin for dread of losing that which they had not nor never shall have. Or again if the prince had proclaimed his purpose for setting out for a certain place, then he will surely change his purpose; doubt not that he will allow it be until mid-day. Here wait the sumpters standing under their loads, the chariots idly silent, the out-riders asleep, the royal merchants in anxious expectation, and all men murmuring together; men flock around the court prostitutes and vintners to get tidings of the king's journey.

He speaks of the king's entourage wandering for three or four miles through unknown forests at night and fighting for huts more suitable for swine than men to sleep in. He ends by asking God to teach the king to know himself to be but a man.

Although Henry was never haughty and liked good conversation and laughter, he had a diabolical temper. His son, Richard Coeur de Lion, said that one of his father's maternal grandmothers was a demon who could not abide the secrets of the mass. Her husband, according to the story, had ordered four knights to take her to church. "When there she threw away her mantel that she was holding and left her two sons under her right side of her mantel, and with her other two sons that she had under the left side of the mantel she flew out at the window of the church in the sight of all men and was never seen after that time." Henry's hot temper led him to quarrel with his son Richard, and it was partly responsible for the act which earned him the greatest notoriety, the murder of Thomas à Becket, Archbishop of Canterbury, in 1171.

Henry was not directly responsible for this murder. At the height of his quarrel with the Archbishop Henry was in France and was reported to have said: "Will no one rid me of this turbulent priest?" Four knights took him at his word, crossed the sea and murdered Thomas à Becket in the cathedral. Henry made a public act of contrition and submitted to the Papal Legates, promising to carry out all their conditions for absolution—some of which he had not the slightest intention of performing, nor they, as a matter of fact, of enforcing. He admitted, however, before the Papal Legates that: "He had been the cause of the Archbishop's death, and that what had been done was for his sake."

Henry's relations with Thomas à Becket and the causes of their quarrel throw a great light on Henry's character and on his work. Thomas à Becket was the son of two Normans in a humble position who had settled in London. He was educated by the monks of Merton Priory, introduced as an able young man to Archbishop Theobald, was sent to Rome, came to Court, and within a month or two of Henry's accession to the throne was made Chancellor of England—an astonishingly rapid rise for a young man of no birth.

Henry found in Becket, sixteen years older than he, the qualities he most admired—conscientiousness, energy, intelligence and at the same time an agreeable manner, a love of singing and dancing and jesting which the Angevins brought into England with them. Thomas à Becket, six feet high, with a strong jaw and a slight stutter in his speech which only made more attractive his ready wit, loved luxury and dressed in scarlet furs with gold-work on his cloak. Though the king himself had no fancy for luxury, the two men were the closest of friends and Henry treated Becket as his equal.

When Henry made Becket Archbishop of Canterbury, the latter told the king that there might be trouble between them. He knew Henry's plans for the Church. Henry was determined, in the interests of good order in his kingdom, that the Church Courts, which had the right of trying and sentencing any monk or cleric, or any servant of the Church, should no longer interfere in the course of justice. It was said that in Henry's reign no less than a hundred murders had been committed by a "clerk" who had escaped with light punishment. After Thomas à Becket's appointment various test cases took place and the Archbishop clearly felt himself obliged to fight in favour of the Church. Becket was not supported by all the bishops and was forced to a half-retreat, answering the question did the bishops obey the king with the phrase: "Aye, my Lord, saving our Order." The king grew enraged with the man who had once been his closest friend. They made an attempt at a personal reconciliation, meeting on horseback in a field near Northampton; but here too after some friendly words they began to quarrel.

At the Council of Clarendon in 1164 the king summoned the bishops to sign and seal an agreement which was much wider in scope than merely the question of the Church Courts. Becket tried and failed to leave the country. The quarrel dragged on. Becket went into exile for six years, and there was a reconciliation when the two met in 1170.

Becket went back to Canterbury. Local magnates who had been given his land, and who had now to pay homage for them, were hostile, but the common people who considered that Becket was a saint waded out into the sea to meet him. The Church was still the friend of the people, a help against local tyranny and a giver of education. Becket preached a sermon on Christmas Day, 1170, in which he excommunicated some knights who had been offensive to him and spoke of his own likely martyrdom. It was after this that the four knights who were with the king in France took ship to Canterbury and committed the murder, in the Cathedral itself.

Although the people venerated Becket, Henry's work for order in the realm was securing their attachment. The greatest of King Henry's work lay in the reform of the law. He introduced trial by jury. What Henry did above all was to make the Crown, through its courts, the source of all justice, one which completely took the place of the private courts and tribunals of the barons. The whole of England was governed by the king's servants—sheriffs, judges and coroners; much of France, the King of France's domains, remained a number of separate states, each duke or count being the source of power and justice in his territory, only acknowledging the King of France as overlord.

Above all, the system of law Henry adopted was the ancient common law, enriched by Norman-French legal concepts, and not a new code of law drawn up by the king which could be changed by another king. Henry completed the work which William the Conqueror had begun, using as his instruments the new science of politics, developed in the Italian cities, and the new educated men, who came out of the middle classes, as his agents. In the Assize of Arms in 1181, Henry II encouraged his subjects to keep their own arms and armour. The yeoman archers who were to do such good service at Crécy and Poitiers were the first fruits of this policy. The king trusted his subjects, and regarded the local militias, which could take up arms at any moment, as his best assurance against any rebellion by the nobles.

This restless, energetic, unostentatious, highly intellectual monarch, who worked so well for England and for his vast domains in France, who was for a time the most powerful monarch of Europe, had to face, at the end of his life, trials which did not wreck his work but which brought him to a miserable end. He had, from the beginning, dominated his powerful wife, Eleanor of Aquitaine, and taken mistresses as he wished. Although strongly attached to his family, he behaved not only as an autocrat but with a certain meanness towards all his children, except to his youngest son, John.

He behaved as a tyrant towards his sons in that he gave them rank and lands but kept them short of money. His son Henry he had crowned King of England so that there could be no dispute about the succession. Yet this son rebelled against his father with the help of the King of France and of his fourth son, Geoffrey. The revolt was suppressed and later the young King Henry died of fever.

Eleanor encouraged Richard and Geoffrey against their father. Richard, known later as Richard Coeur de Lion, was a remarkable man endowed as was his father with restless energy and intellectual qualities, though not of such a practical disposition. The Angevins had in all of them something of the same demonic energy as Henry. They were liable to be suspicious and unforgiving. Richard, Duke of Aquitaine, made war on his father for a second time and had as his ally the new King of France, Phillipe Auguste, a powerful ruler. The youngest son John joined them, unknown to his father, Henry II was forced to retreat before his enemies at Le Mans, though vowing vengeance. He fell ill and was obliged to sue for a truce; when he met Richard and Phillipe Auguste to parley the shadow of death was on his face.

When he lay sick at his castle at Chinon, having been forced to accept the terms of his foes, he was told that John his favourite had joined his enemies. That night in high fever his bastard son, also called Geoffrey, held him in his arms and the king acknowledged that he alone had been a true son; he muttered the well-known phrase, "Shame, shame on a conquered king". He was buried at Fontevrault near Chinon and the last act of this great king was, like the first, played out in France. But his lifework had been for England. As the historian G. M. Trevelyan has written:

"*Of all the holders of the island crown, no one has done such great and lasting work as Henry Plantagenet, Count of Anjou. He found England exhausted by nearly twenty years of anarchy with every cog in the Norman machine of State either broken or rusty with disuse. He left England with a judicial and administrative system and a habit of obedience to government which prevented the recurrence of anarchy in spite of the long absences of King Richard and the malignant follies of King John. After the death of Henry I, the outcome of bad government was anarchy; after the death of Henry II, the outcome of bad government was constitutional reform. And the difference is a measure of the work of the great Angevin.*"

RICHARD, COEUR DE LION

(1157–1199)

THE MEMORY of Coeur de Lion, the lion-hearted Plantagenet king, was for centuries dear and glorious to his English subjects. He was extremely popular in his day, despite his extravagant and rapacious demands upon England's treasury, and his almost total neglect during his absentee reign of the country's administration. He was remembered in subsequent ages as one of the great knights of chivalry, unsurpassingly brave, a man who placed valour and honour above all other qualities.

The Turks and Saracens against whom he fought remembered him in a different way. For generations his was a terrible name in the Holy Land. Syrian mothers used it as a bogy-man to silence their infants, and if a horse turned unexpectedly from its path its rider would exclaim: "Dost thou think King Richard is in that bush?"

He was born in 1157, the second son of Henry II by Eleanor of Aquitaine. His mother was a lady of great significance in English medieval history. She was a woman of remarkable beauty, character and ability, whose immense dowry included the great duchy of Aquitaine, which comprised the whole of South-west France, then the homeland of chivalry. Eleanor's marriage to Henry II brought this large new area of France under the English crown, which already ruled over Normandy and the rest of North-western France.

Eleanor had been married to King Louis VII of France, but in 1152 the marriage was annulled. She then married Henry Plantagenet*, Count of Anjou, who was technically speaking a vassal of the King of France. But when Henry succeeded unexpectedly to the throne of England as Henry II in 1154, Louis realized what a mistake he had made in divorcing Eleanor. The acquisition of Aquitaine made Henry's territories in France larger than his English realm. His vast possessions made him more powerful than France, and even than the Holy Roman Empire. Louis was mortified and thus began the long series of wars between England and France which were waged intermittently for three hundred years.

* From the family badge *planta genesta*, a sprig of broom.

Eleanor had the reputation of being something of a virago, and Henry found her extremely difficult to live with. She had of course much to complain of, for he was constantly unfaithful to her. They quarrelled bitterly and frequently. She bore him five sons and three daughters, and she supported her sons in their great rebellion against their father in 1173.

Henry instituted a machinery of government which brought about the end of the personal rule of the Norman kings. After the miserable anarchy of Stephen's reign, England readily accepted Henry's bureaucratic monarchy, the benefit of which was plainly seen in the ensuing reign—or non-reign—of Richard I.

Richard spent his youth in his mother's homeland of Aquitaine and there he acquired a passionate love of music, poetry and chivalry. When he was eleven his father made him Duke of Aquitaine. With the title also went the power to rule Aquitaine independently, and this he did for a number of years. His iron rule caused much discontent. He became so powerful that his elder brother Henry, the heir-apparent, demanded that Richard should do homage to him. Richard's scornful refusal led to a fratricidal war in which Henry invaded Aquitaine and was killed during the fighting in 1183.

Henry II's struggles with his rebellious sons brought an outstandingly successful reign to an end in bitterness and confusion. Richard's relationship with his father was of the worst. Richard had many reasons to feel personally aggrieved. He had, for instance, been betrothed to Alice, sister of Philip II of France. Henry, who had the morals of a tom-cat, took a fancy to his son's affianced and seduced her with the result that she gave birth to a son.

When Richard became heir to the thrones of England and Normandy, Henry wanted him to renounce Aquitaine in favour of Prince John, his beloved younger son. Richard flatly refused. He loved Aquitaine. It was his home. England and Normandy were foreign countries to him. Another civil war ensued, Richard sought alliance with King Philip (Philip Augustus) of France, whom he recognized publicly as the overlord of his French possessions. Henry's attempt to crush Richard's rebellion failed ignominiously, and the old king's heart was broken when he found that his youngest and favourite son John had joined Richard against him.

On 6 July, 1189, Henry died. At this time Queen Eleanor was held in "honourable captivity" at Winchester. For fifteen years she had been more or less a prisoner owing to her ardent and active support of her sons' rebellion.

Richard was the undisputed heir, even though Henry had

obstinately refused to acknowledge him as such. The first thing Richard did when he heard of his father's death was to order his mother's freedom and he made her regent until he came to claim his kingdom.

On 20 July he was acclaimed Duke of Normandy, and on 13 August he landed at Plymouth and began a royal progress which culminated in his coronation on 3 September. Though he had been born in England, he had lived all his life in Aquitaine and had returned to England only for two short visits, at Easter, 1176, and Christmas, 1184. He was therefore not only as much a foreigner as Dutch William and George I, but he was also a complete stranger to his people, though of course they knew a great deal about him by reputation.

He was thirty-one, tall, strong-limbed, splendidly handsome, with reddish-gold hair and piercing blue eyes. He caught the imagination of his people right from the start. He was a Crusader, having taken the Cross in 1187, the first prince on the north of the Alps to do so, and this, combined with his legendary valour and chivalry, made him a romantic hero in the eyes of his people.

In the age of faith the Crusader was a hallowed figure, the Champion of Christ. When Richard ascended the throne of England, people were still inflamed with the magic and the wonder of the Crusades, a movement which had the double purpose of satisfying at the same time the dictates of piety and the craving for war and plunder. So great in fact was the prestige of the Crusader that Richard retained the love and loyalty of his English subjects, even though he squeezed their treasury dry to pay for his life of wasteful warfare, and though he regarded the English with barely-disguised contempt, and spent a mere six months of his ten years' reign in England.

Richard was well aware of his brother John's treacherous character. John was vain, capricious and grasping, lacking in the administrative ability which had distinguished his father. He was also totally lacking in principles, and Richard showed little disposition to trust him, though he provided for him well enough by giving him the south-western part of England as his principality in the vain hope that it would keep him quiet and out of mischief.

Richard's magnificent coronation is the first one in English history to be described in detail by contemporary chroniclers. The feast which followed was described as being "of the greatest profusion, richness, variety and plenty".

Richard had prohibited all Jews from his coronation feast,

and the people interpreted this as royal licence to indulge in a little anti-semitism on their own account—a very popular pastime in the days of the Crusades, as at other times. The mob added to the coronation festivities by beating up and killing all the Jews they could find, and plundering their property. Many Jews barricaded themselves in their houses, which the mob then set on fire. Soon there was a full-scale riot going, and half of London, then nearly all built of wood, was ablaze.

Richard was a man of no mean temper, and when he found his coronation feast disturbed in this manner his anger knew no bounds. He had been insulted on the day of his crowning. The plunder of the Jews who were under his royal protection was an especial loss to him, for the Jews paid him well—a kind of protection money. The Jews had been brought into England by William the Conqueror. As they were the historical enemies of Christ, anti-semitism was the logical consequence of the crusading zeal which was sweeping Europe.

Though Richard ordered condign punishment for the rioters, only three of them were found and hanged. None of the others could be identified. Richard gave strict orders for the protection of the Jews in future.

As soon as he was crowned, Richard busied himself planning for the Crusade which he was to make in the company of Philip of France and Leopold of Austria. He used reckless methods of raising the money. Offices and honours were put up for auction to the highest bidder. He raised 15,000 marks by remitting to William the Lion of Scotland the rights over Scotland which Henry II had secured by the Treaty of Falaise. Having sold all he could in the way of offices and privileges, Richard departed from England in the summer of 1190 with a force of about 4,000 men-at-arms and a fleet of about 100 ships.

He left the country in the corrupt hands of William Longchamps, a Frenchman who hated and despised the English. Longchamps's oppressive rule resulted in a great struggle between him on the one side and Prince John and the barons on the other. The barons, growing in power and responsibility, enforced the submission of Longchamps without bloodshed. In previous reigns these men would unhesitatingly have plunged the country into civil war. Henry II's life-work had not been in vain. In fact it saved England from anarchy during the non-reign of his son.

It was Richard who showed the greatest irresponsibility. He was unmarried and had no heir, and he had left for the Crusade, with all its attendant personal dangers, without making any provision for the succession.

On the journey to the Holy Land he wintered in Sicily where he occupied himself in quarrelling with Philip. In the spring he interrupted the voyage to Palestine in order to conquer Cyprus, and did not join the Crusaders besieging Acre until June, but he immediately made his presence felt, Acre being finally conquered mainly owing to his energy and skill.

Though this Third Crusade has been described as the most "courtly, chivalrous and romantic" of all, the temper of its leaders could hardly be so described. They hated each other more fiercely than they did the common enemy. Richard's arrogance earned him an unpleasant reputation among the Orientals of the country in which they fought. They considered that his magnificence and military renown were depreciated by the lack of dignity he displayed in his unprincely quarrels with Leopold of Austria and Philip of France.

Philip, a better statesman than warrior, wisely decided he had sacrificed his health and interests long enough in this barren though glorious enterprise. He had likewise had enough of Richard's insults, so he sailed for home and made more effective retaliation by entering into negotiations with Prince John with the object of invading Richard's French possessions. He offered John the hand of his sister Alice into the bargain.

It cannot be imagined that John was tempted by the prospect of marrying this much-soiled royal maiden who had been the mistress of his own father, but he was unquestionably interested in filching his brother's French possessions. The fact that Philip was Richard's suzerain, or overlord, in France, gave some kind of legality to the offer. Doubtless Alice had been introduced into the bargain with the object of these Plantagenet realms being eventually reunited to the French throne.

However, Queen Eleanor got wind of what was afoot and that formidable lady had no difficulty in bringing her treasonable son to heel.

Meanwhile in the Holy Land Richard won a brilliant victory over the forces of Saladin and twice led the Crusader host within a few miles of Jerusalem. But dissensions among the warriors of the Cross made it impossible to continue, and so the Crusade ended ingloriously but not inexpediently on 2 September, 1192, with Richard making a truce with Saladin whom he seemed to like rather better than his fellow Christian warriors.

Alarmed by reports of John's intrigues in England and France, he hastened home. But owing to the hostility of Philip he could not take the obvious route through Marseilles, and Toulouse was in the hands of his enemies. He decided to return via the Adriatic and Austria. But, passing through Vienna on 20 December, 1192, in disguise, he was recognized and captured. He was held in the Castle of Durenstein by Leopold of Austria whom he had grossly insulted at the time of the fall of Acre, and who now demanded an enormous ransom for his release. But early the following year Leopold was forced to surrender his valuable prisoner to Emperor Henry V. Despite the fact that Richard, as a Crusader, was under the Church's protection, the enormous sum of 150,000 marks had to be paid for his release.

This considerably taxed the resources of England. All the same they gladly paid and gave Richard a tumultuous welcome when he returned in March, 1194, and they also insisted upon giving him another coronation, this time without the anti-semitic embellishments.

A curious relationship now existed between Richard Coeur de Lion and his English subjects. It is difficult for us to imagine the awe and adoration in which they held him—the returned Crusader whose lion-like courage and daring deeds of valour for the cause of the Holy Cross were the talk of the known world. Like Churchill, he had become a legend in his lifetime. Richard of England was the hero of half of Christendom on that day and his people were overwhelmed with pride to be his subjects.

But Richard did not return this feeling. England had disappointed him. He had come back from the Holy Land a changed man, disillusioned with crusading, embittered by the indignity of his incarceration in Austria, angry at the plotting that had been going on behind his back while he was far away fighting for the True Cross. He was lean and tanned by the Levantine sun, his face lined with illness, his frame toughened by his privations. He had never spared himself and he never asked his soldiers to encounter dangers which he was not prepared to face himself. And when he looked upon his stay-at-home subjects, his fleshly barons, and the plump, prosperous citizens of London, he was displeased. Coldly he acknowledged their ecstatic plaudits, and just as coldly he demanded more money from them.

He stayed in England merely a few weeks and then returned to France and devoted the rest of his reign to Normandy and Aquitaine, determined to avenge himself upon Philip of France who had incurred his especial anger for deserting the Crusade in order to plot against him.

Richard did not return to England again. He left its government in the competent hands of Hubert Walter and devoted the rest of his life to his favourite occupation and that at which he most excelled—war. Although he got the best of Philip in the field, he was unable to sustain the economics of war with his inferior resources, despite the exactions he made upon England.

He met his death as he would have wished, on the field of battle, being wounded in the left side by a bolt-shot from a crossbow at the siege of Châlus Castle on 26 March, 1199. At first he concealed his injury and tried to pull out the bolt himself. It broke off, leaving the iron head in the wound. Mortification set in and he died on 6 April after naming his brother John heir to the realm of England and all his other lands.

GENGHIS KHAN
(1167?–1227)

THERE HAVE been conquerors galore, throughout history, who have sprung from nothing. Napoleon, the moody little Corsican from an undistinguished family, went on to hold half Europe to ransom. Mao Tse-tung, small-time teacher, became ruler of a vast population. Hitler had his day.

But one man stands alone.

There has never been another like him. There can never be another, since that first bomb dropped on Hiroshima. If ever half the world is laid waste, it will be done impersonally, almost without human intervention. There will be a barren waste, a desert—with no one left, to loot or rape or plunder.

But, in the thirteenth century, and within the walls of a single city, Herat, in what is now Afghanistan, the Emperor Genghis Khan supervised the massacre, in one blood-filled week of vengeance, of 1,600,000 people. And before those men, women and children were dead, many had suffered torture and mutilation of a kind which is almost impossible to imagine. Arms, legs, were hacked off, and the bleeding, screaming trunks were flung into the road, to roll helplessly away and die in agony. Children, a dozen or more at a time, were skewered like shish-kebab on lances, or burnt alive in great wailing heaps, while their mothers, hideously mutilated, were forced to stand by and await their turn.

A man is product of his time, and the time was cruel. But Genghis Khan—"perfect warrior", the name meant—was the most bloodthirsty man in history. Under his example and his orders, men performed prodigies of sadism, unrepresentative of any time, even their own.

This great ruler, as historians usually point out, was born in a tent. But this is the least remarkable fact about him. Everyone, for as far as eye could see or imagination reach, was born in a tent: there was no other form of habitation in that part of Asia. It was near the shores of Lake Baikal, and he was named Temuchin by his father Yesukai, leader of a group of small Mongolian tribes who warred constantly with each other. He had just killed a rival

272

chieftain of that name: on returning to his tent he found the new-born child with its mother, his wife, and prised open the infant's clenched fist. Inside was a red-brown clot of coagulated blood, like a stone. This, to the superstitious father, represented the body, the fortunes, of the Temuchin he had just slain, and he gave the name to his son.

Temuchin found himself on the throne at thirteen, when his father died: almost immediately a number of the small tribes which comprised the kingdom began to secede. Temuchin had no experience of dealing with such a situation, but his indomitable mother, a Mongolian Boadicea, rallied troops and brought the rebels back into the fold. The leaders were punished with great cruelty, while the young ruler watched.

Soon he was able to take over the rule of the kingdom from his mother—rule which consisted largely of subduing or trying to subdue every tribe on his borders, then ensuring that it remained well-disciplined. He soon showed qualities of generalship and an aptitude for large-scale treachery which even in those times must have evoked the admiration of his contemporaries. Before long he had made himself emperor of all the Mongol tribes, and in 1206 he summoned the most notable men within this empire and allowed them to name him Genghis (perfect warrior) Khan (king).

He was now strong enough to indulge in a private dream. He would invade distant China, the fabulous, almost mythical Cathay. There had been many Mongol attempts to penetrate her Great Wall, but all had failed. Now Genghis Khan was able to muster an enormous army of horsemen and by sheer brute numbers to burst through the Chinese defence. Burning, killing, raping, the Mongol hordes penetrated to the sea, destroying much of an ancient civilization, one of the oldest and finest in the world.

Having reduced Cathay to a smoking, stinking ruin, corpses piled high in every town and village, the Perfect Warrior retired to his capital. One of the reasons for his continued and increasing success may have been an insistence on keeping his capital at desolate Karakoram, that bleak Mongolian city, when he could have had any of the fine cities of China, or later, Persia, for the taking. His vast army was not allowed to get soft from easy living in conquered lands. It remained, between campaigns, camped outside the walls of Karakoram, mile upon mile of felt "yurts", or tents, full of warriors ready to be formed up, mounted, and sent to any part of the world.

It was not long after the Chinese campaign that Genghis,

learning of the riches to be had in the west, decided to cross the Hindu Kush, that huge mountain range which had always cut the Mongols and other plains-people off from the civilizations of western Asia.

In 1219 he set out—on one of his few peaceful missions. He had sent messengers to the large Muslim state of Khwarizm, stating that as he now had conquered China his country was "a mine of silver and a magazine of warriors", and he had little interest in fighting but much in trade. What could he get from Khwarizm in exchange for some of his own riches?

The Shah, Mohammed, was at first well-disposed to this, but the local Governor, in Otrar, was foolishly rude. Genghis had anticipated a reply by sending a small advance party of traders and these were pointlessly, callously, butchered by the Governor. Genghis, beside himself with rage, demanded the Governor be extradited and sent to him for justice.

Mohammed refused.

Thus began a campaign which, in its speed and ruthlessness, eclipsed the one into China. It began with two Mongol armies, under two of Genghis's sons, Juji and Jagatai, which swept all before them. One army, Juji's, was resisted at first by Mohammed's larger one, a force of 400,000 men, but the Mongols went through these like a knife through butter, and within hours 150,000 of the defending army were dead on the field.

Meanwhile the second army, under Jagatai, had penetrated to Otrar, the offending city, and laid siege to it. The siege lasted five months, but at the end it fell and every inhabitant was put to the sword, including the Governor, for whom a particularly public and revolting torture was provided first.

A third army leap-frogged Otrar, and a fourth, commanded by Genghis himself, headed for Bokhara. The cities of Tashkent and Nur surrendered to him as he approached—which helped them not at all, for they were both sacked—and Bokhara put up a short resistance before capitulating. As he entered it, Genghis shouted to his officers, "The hay is cut: give your horses fodder!"

This picturesque invitation to plunder was seized on by the entire army. Everything portable was taken, everything not small enough was smashed to convenient pieces. Every inhabitant was butchered, many after the most appalling tortures and mutilation; almost every building was burnt to the ground.

Within a day, one of the world's great centres of learning, the "Centre of Science", was a smoking ruin.

Genghis retired to his Court at Karakoram, leaving the "mopping up" to others, who successively laid waste to the cities of Ness, Merv and Nishapur. This last offered a determined resistance, street by street, but was at last overpowered. Apart from some four hundred skilled workers who were sent in chains to Mongolia, every soul was butchered. The city of Herat miraculously spared itself by surrender—unlike those less fortunate ones on the way—and the Mongols put a governor in charge. They continued their pursuit—first, of Mohammed, then, when they learned he had died suddenly of pleurisy, of his son Jelaleddin, whom they pursued deep into India. When he took sanctuary in Delhi, they gave up the chase, but by this time they had ravaged Lahore, Melikpur and Peshawar.

Suddenly news reached Genghis that the Governor of Herat, the one he himself had put in charge, had been deposed. He decided instantly to send a punitive expedition. When it reached there, the doomed city fought bravely and held out for six months, but at last Herat fell.

It was during the week that followed that 1,600,000 people were massacred.

From this hideous campaign of vengeance Genghis turned to the business of extending his Mongol empire. The most attractive direction now seemed due west, and his armies were ordered through Azerbaijan into Georgia. They took Astrakhan, near the Caspian Sea, pursued its fleeing defenders to the River Don.

The Russians now chose to defy him: Genghis sent them envoys whom they killed. A little later the Russian army had been destroyed and the Mongols, after ravaging Bulgaria, began their long, slow, progress home.

While all this had been going on, Genghis, from a distance, was controlling another campaign in China, and that whole land of Cathay and the regions about it had become a Mongol province. As soon as his western campaign had been cleared up, he made his way to China to take charge.

Like his father, and most Mongols, Genghis Khan was a superstitious man. Late one night during this expedition to China he saw five planets in a certain conjunction, and his courage died within him. This, to a simple man—and Genghis had never learnt to read or write—was the end. He would die, and soon.

He gave up his command of the campaign, headed home for Karakoram, and almost as soon as he began the long journey the "sickness" came over him.

The spirit had fled from the greatest conqueror of all time. He continued the homeward journey, but death grew ever nearer and he made no effort to hold back its approach.

He reached one of his "travel palaces", a large rest-house for his own use, on the banks of the River Sales in Mongolia, and there he died.

He had decreed that his son Ogotai should succeed him, but the death of the world's greatest ruler, miles from his capital, boded so evil for the empire, held such dire possibilities of treachery and *coups d'état*, that as the body was carried northward to its final resting place the guards killed everyone that passed. Only in this way could they maintain secrecy until Ogotai had been proclaimed ruler.

A few generations after Genghis Khan's death his empire had vanished. Under degenerate successors it had shrunk to nothing, leaving only the memory of a wholesale cruelty which has never been surpassed. To be fair to the man, we can remember him for one or two other things: he was, as well as a general, an imaginative ruler. There was complete religious freedom in his empire, for Genghis allowed all his varied subjects to worship in their own way, and Karakoram was full of different places of worship. He also had one of the world's best postal services, with a chain of relay stables stretching from China to the Dnieper, to let the great Khan keep in touch with every part of his domain.

In the main, we have much to remember about the great Genghis Khan—but little for which to thank him.

FREDERICK II

Roman Emperor and King of Sicily and Jerusalem
(1194-1250)

FREDERICK II, who was born in 1194 and died in 1250, was described as *Stupor Mundi*, "Wonder of the World". Between Charlemagne, who was crowned Roman Emperor by the Pope in 800, and Napoleon Bonaparte, there was no ruler to equal Frederick in genius. It was a brilliant and extraordinary life made tragic by his prolonged battle with the Papacy which prevented him from carrying out in full his great reforms for the creation of the first state in Europe.

"We, who read and ponder the annals of history, never found such an instance of intense and inexorable hatred as that which raged between the Pope and Frederick," wrote Brother Matthew Paris, monk of St. Albans, who was the fairest and most detailed chronicler of the time. He is referring especially to the battle between Frederick and Pope Gregory IX who had taken his name from that other Gregory, the VIIth, who had excommunicated the powerful Henry IV, Emperor-elect of Germany and Italy, and forbade anyone to serve him as king. It was a fearful enough sentence in those days to bring Henry to Canossa and beg on his knees that the Pope should lift the ban. Even the great Emperor Barbarossa, Frederick I of Hohenstaufen, paid homage to the Pope on his knees, after the defeat of his armies by the Lombard League, the Pope's allies.

When the Emperor Barbarossa was drowned leading a Crusade to the Holy Land he was succeeded by his son, Henry VI, in January, 1186. Henry married Constance, the daughter of Roger II of Sicily, and presumptive heir to that kingdom which consisted of the island and the south of Italy. The Pope, Celestine III, was opposed to the marriage, since the Emperor Henry intended to try to unite Germany and Sicily under one empire which would threaten the encirclement of the Papal States of central Italy, but the Pope was constrained in the spring of 1191 to crown Henry and Constance as emperor and empress. Henry then proceeded to the conquest of Sicily which had been divided up among a number of feudal barons, who had elected as their king Tancred, an illegitimate grandson of King Roger II; but three years passed before Henry won Sicily and this he did by massacring many of the Sicilian aristocracy in a terrible act of treachery. In December of that year, 1194, Constance gave birth to a son at Jesi, near Ancona, and he was christened at Assisi with the names of his two distinguished grandfathers, Frederick and Roger; Frederick, who was to become Emperor Frederick II, had already been made "King of the Romans", the title held by the emperor-elect.

The Emperor Henry VI fortunately died before he could carry out any further cruelties, which were shocking even to an age which was accustomed to refinements of torture, but his early death left his wife to deal with a gang of German soldiers of fortune who expected to take over Sicily for themselves. Constance was regent and a capable woman, determined that her infant son should be king, and she turned for help to the Pope, now Innocent III; she and her son were crowned in Palermo in the summer of 1198. She died in the autumn and Frederick became a ward of the Pope in a kingdom of confusion with rival factions fighting for control.

Frederick was ignored and would have starved if the poorer citizens of Palermo had not taken pity and looked after him in their own houses. At the age of seven he was kidnapped by men sent by the Markward of Anweiler, who was intent on obtaining the kingdom for himself. Even at that age Frederick's precocity and his consciousness of his position is revealed in a letter written to the Pope by a man in Palermo: "Nor did he forget his royal estate and, like a mouse who fears the pursuit of a ferocious animal, he threw himself upon those who were about to seize him, trying with all his force to ward off the arm of him who dared to lay hands upon the sacred body of the Lord's anointed."

Fortunately the Markward died a few months later otherwise Frederick might have been blinded and castrated as Tancred's son had been by order of Frederick's father.

After that Frederick was left free to lead his own wild life with grooms and huntsmen; this did not improve his manners, but taught him how ordinary people lived, which was an advantage when he came later to draw up his famous laws for his kingdom. He studied languages, including Arabic, and read widely; he was encouraged by the Papal Legates and by Muslims at the court who carried on the learning which had helped to make Sicily under the Norman kings the most cultivated court in Europe.

"He is never idle," wrote a contemporary of Frederick, ". . . and so that his vigour may increase, he fortifies his agile body with every kind of exercise and practice of arms. . . . To this is added a regal majesty and majestic features and mien, to which are united a kindly and gracious air, a serene brow, brilliant eyes, and expressive face, a burning spirit and a ready wit. Nevertheless his actions are sometimes odd and vulgar, though this is not due to nature but to contact with rough company."

At fourteen Frederick came of age and the Pope chose as his wife Constance of Aragon, who was widow of the King of Hungary; she was ten years older than Frederick and taught him some manners. A son, Henry, was born, and Frederick was determined to try to ensure his son's succession to the empire although Frederick himself had only a precarious hold over his kingdom of Sicily. Frederick's right to succeed his father as emperor had been ignored and Otto had been elected by the Ghibelline, or pro-papacy princes of Germany; at the age of seventeen Frederick had to prepare against an invasion of the island of Sicily after Otto had occupied all the mainland part of the kingdom. But suddenly there was a reversal of fortune; the Guelf faction in Germany, who were in favour of the Hohenstaufen family, succeeded in overcoming the Ghibelline faction. The Guelf princes deposed Otto and elected Frederick as emperor, and at the beginning of 1212, when Frederick was eighteen, the German ambassadors came to Sicily to invite him to Germany as emperor-elect.

Frederick would have been a happier man if he had remained King of Sicily, but he was conscious of what he considered to be his destiny and he accepted. The Pope insisted that he should first come to Rome to pay homage and made him promise to give up Sicily to his son, who had been made King of Sicily. Innocent III believed that by having a regent under his control he would avoid the danger of the unification of the empire with Sicily, but Frederick had other ideas which he was wise enough to keep to himself.

There were many factions hostile to Frederick in Germany, but through his diplomacy he managed to overcome them. He was crowned with various titles but he still had to be crowned by the Pope to confirm him as emperor. Frederick did not care for Germany and was longing to return to Sicily. He took two steps which would clearly antagonize the Papacy, but Innocent III had been succeeded by the gentle Honorius and Frederick believed he could overcome opposition by promising to lead a Crusade to retrieve Jerusalem.

Frederick had his wife and infant son brought to Germany and had him elected in April, 1220, as the future King of Germany, without the consent of the Pope; by this means Frederick believed he had ensured his son's succession to both Germany and Sicily. He next wrote to the Pope to say that he wished to discuss with him and obtain "the favourable issue to our demand that we may keep to ourselves the Realm of Sicily for our life". In great state he came to Rome. Frederick's decision to equip and lead a Crusade did much to mollify the Pope, for Frederick was now the most powerful ruler in Europe and was the only leader likely to succeed in the capture of Jerusalem; Frederick also agreed that the administration of the kingdom of Germany and that of Sicily should be kept entirely separate. On 22 November, 1220, the great ceremony was held in Rome and Frederick received at the hands of the Pope the imperial crown of Charlemagne. He had achieved his ambition of being anointed emperor and retaining Sicily, so that his empire could be compared to that of the Roman Caesars with lands touching the English Channel, the Baltic and the Mediterranean. He had made concessions with regard to ecclesiastical privileges within his empire, but this did not affect his power as a temporal ruler.

Frederick hurried back to his beloved Sicily and at Capua issued a series of laws based on earlier Norman laws, which had made the kingdom of Sicily the most prosperous in Europe. By excluding the Genoese and Pisans he saw to it that the rich wheat and wool trade, and the fact that Sicily was a great entrepôt for commerce between Africa and Europe, should enrich the state and not other middlemen. He encouraged the growth of new crops and improved the breed of horses and mules; mares, according to the detailed Capuan laws, were to be covered by horses and asses in alternate years. Castles built since the reign of William II, the last of the legitimate Norman kings who had died five years before Frederick's birth, were to be destroyed or become state property; a fleet and an army were built up. The first modern state of Europe was being created by Frederick, "the greatest single force in the Middle Ages", wrote H. A. L. Fisher.

There was considerable resistance from those who lost castles and lands; Frederick had no intention of setting out on the promised Crusade until his kingdom was in order; besides he needed time for Sicily to become prosperous again so that he could finance the great undertaking. He had agreed to construct a fleet of fifty transports to carry two thousand knights and ten thousand soldiers;

the ships were very ingeniously built; part of a side could be let
down so that the knights disembarked mounted and ready to meet
the enemy; Frederick was ahead of his time with many of his ideas.
A further reason for delay was a war against the Muslim population
of western Sicily; after finally defeating them he settled several
hundred thousand Muslims as farmers on the plains of Apulia and
formed a Saracen army garrisoned at Lucera where an entire
Saracen town was created.

The gentle Honorius died in 1227 and was succeeded by Gregory
IX, who was to be Frederick's formidable opponent. Frederick,
after waiting seven years, was at last preparing to go on the Crusade.
The fleet sailed with its great army, but after three days at sea
Frederick developed an epidemic which had already killed many
hundreds of Crusaders and he turned back while the others went on;
he decided that he would recover in Sicily rather than die at sea.
Gregory IX was furious, considering that this was just another
excuse for avoiding the Crusade, and excommunicated him,
issuing a violent attack on Frederick for what were considered to be
his misdeeds against the Church: "We shall proceed against him as
if he were a heretic; we shall absolve his subjects of their oath of
allegiance, and we shall strip him of his kingdom which is our
fief." The Crusade could only achieve success if the emperor were
in the Holy Land, but it was more important to Gregory to discredit
him. No one believed that an excommunicated man would lead a
Crusade and most of the forty thousand knights and soldiers who
had set off with the emperor returned from the Holy Land when
they heard of the excommunication.

Historians, such as Mr. T. L. Kington, have criticized the Pope
for his hasty action; Miss Georgina Masson, in her *Frederick II of
Hohenstaufen*, argues that Pope Gregory was intransigent and
vindictive because he had the intelligence to realize that Frederick's
ability and his newly organized system of government would be a
dangerous threat to the Church of Rome and, indeed, the lay state
and the Reformation did ultimately reduce the powers of the
Roman Catholic Church.

Frederick hit back in a circular to all the rulers of Christendom
setting out his case: "The Roman Empire, the bulwark of the
Faith, is being assailed by its own fathers." The kings, clergy and
people of Europe watched to see whether the outcome would be
another Canossa and a victory for the Pope. Frederick tried in vain
to make his peace with Gregory. He had no intention, however, of
being stopped from going on his Crusade. When he had fully

recovered from the epidemic and set his kingdom in order, for the Pope's hostile acts had caused him many difficulties, he set out for the Holy Land, to the amazement of Europe and to the annoyance of the Pope.

It did not seem possible that the emperor could achieve anything, for the Pope was the dominant figure in all Crusades, and the knights in the Holy Land were divided in their allegiance. Jerusalem had been in the hands of the Saracens since its capture by Saladin forty years earlier, in 1187, and neither the Third Crusade with King Richard I of England and King Philip of France, nor the Fourth nor the Fifth Crusades, had succeeded in winning it back. But Frederick had for a long time had good relations with al-Kamil, Sultan of Egypt, and his ambassador Fakhr ad-Din; through diplomacy Frederick was able to gain what the armed might of Christendom had failed to achieve. In the Treaty of 1229 those parts of Jerusalem which were holy to Christians were returned to them, while the Muslims retained what was holy to them, the Dome of the Rock and the Mosque of al Aqsar. In the Church of the Holy Sepulchre Frederick crowned himself King of Jerusalem, for the Pope's Patriarch would have nothing to do with the ceremony.

Frederick returned to Sicily triumphant; the legend had begun to grow that he was *Stupor Mundi*. The Pope was chagrined and, after forcing Frederick to make many concessions, the ban of excommunication was lifted in August, 1230; but he continued to be very watchful. The Pope disliked many things in Frederick's remarkable Constitutions of Melfi, drawn up by a team of able jurists; there were, for instance, schools for training civil servants and doctors; men were taught law to dispense justice on the principle that all were equal before the law, so that prelates and nobles no longer had jurisdiction in criminal cases. Although an autocrat, Frederick was concerned about the freedom of the individual. "Nothing is more odious," he said, "than the oppression of the poor by the rich."

The Pope also hated and condemned Frederick's sophistication and curiosity, probably gained from his early association with cultivated Muslims. The emperor, said the Pope, only believed what was proved by reason or shown to exist in nature; for the Pope this was a most serious accusation. Frederick's court was full of learned men and elegant poets who wrote, as he did himself, in the Sicilian dialect; Dante was later to describe him as the father of Italian poetry, though he consigned him to hell for his unbelief. The emperor's book on the Art of Hunting with Birds (*De Arte Venandi cum avibus*) showed great observation and has remained a classic. He encouraged the well-known philosopher and astrologer, Michael Scott, to translate important works from the Arabic, such as Averroes's commentaries on Aristotle's works, and he was himself a student of Aristotle, whose works were condemned at that time by the Church. Frederick's court was an early flowering of the Renaissance, but such learning and sophistication did not show itself again in Europe for another two hundred years.

Frederick was, too, a great builder. He established castles in Apulia and the island of Sicily to maintain lines of communication for the administration of his empire, but they also expressed his love of beauty and of nature. The site and design, for instance, of the famous Castel del Monte, looking over the Apulian coastal plain, has an honoured place in the history of architecture. Some of these castles had luxuries borrowed from the East, such as bathrooms and lavatories with running water, probably unknown elsewhere in Europe at that time; indeed, the fact that the emperor believed in cleanliness and took a bath every day was regarded as a scandal. The imperial caravan when it travelled through Italy must have roused great wonder—the Saracen cavalry, an elephant, a giraffe (the first to be seen in Europe), hounds, falcons, hunting leopards and cheetahs, lions and lynxes; and on the camels, curtained in mystery, came the emperor's harem of lovely Saracen dancing girls about whom the prelates made sure that Europe should hear much. The emperor, auburn-haired and slim (he ate only one meal a day), rode in the caravan on his black charger, Dragon.

The struggle with the Papacy continued and it was inevitable since it was a dispute over temporal power. Frederick was not content to rule his kingdom of Sicily and leave Germany entirely to his son Henry, for both countries were part of the empire. In order to maintain his lines of communication between the two he needed to overcome the hostility of the states of the Lombard League which lay across his path—Milan, Brescia, Piacenza, Bologna, Faenza and Parma. The Pope, however, could not agree to see these powerful allies of his subdued, since without temporal power in those days the Pope would have had little influence. If Frederick had succeeded in vanquishing the Lombard League, Italy would have been united over six hundred years before it was achieved under the House of Savoy; whether it would have remained united is another matter.

Frederick considered that the Pope, by his support of the Lombard League, was encouraging insurrection against the empire, which was to him a sacred institution, based on the natural laws of society; people needed the empire, for they required order and it was for the empire to fulfil their need by having just laws. When Frederick found his ambitions to achieve orderly government continually opposed by Gregory he decided on a policy of trying to deprive the Papacy of all temporal power. It was a clash between two beliefs fervently held—a battle that had to come sooner or later, but it was tragically epitomized in the persons of two passionate individuals, Frederick and Gregory. It led to the destruction of Frederick and his whole family and to the shelving for several centuries of imaginative ideas and principles of government; later it led to the Pope's exile to Avignon and eventually to the stripping of all temporal power from the Papacy.

In the spring of 1239 Gregory excommunicated Frederick for the second time; it was the only way he could try to subdue the emperor who had become extremely powerful, supported as he was against the Pope by most of the kings of Christendom, who were apprehensive of the support given by the Pope to the insurgent Lombard League; the Pope, commented Matthew Paris, had tried to persuade the people "that obedience consisted in revolt, and duty in forgetting oaths". In a circular letter to the rulers of the west Frederick had written: "This matter touches you and all the kings of the earth; when your neighbour's wall is on fire, your own property is at stake."

The kings of England, France and Hungary sent forces to help the emperor against the Lombard League. In a famous encyclical Gregory IX, who was nearly a hundred years old, attacked Frederick violently for all manner of sins, many invented: "A furious beast has come out of the sea whose name all over is written *Blasphemy*; he has the feet of a bear, the jaws of a ravening lion, the mottled limbs of a panther . . ." Frederick replied by calling "this false Vicar of Christ", Anti-Christ. He decided to end the Pope's power by capturing him in Rome, for the people were calling for the emperor and many of the cardinals had deserted the ageing Gregory.

It seemed to Frederick, as he approached Rome, that he had achieved his final ambition and that he would reign in the imperial city of the Caesars with the Pope doing his bidding. Gregory himself believed that he had lost the battle; the indomitable old man led a procession through the Roman streets full of hostile crowds and flanked by a few faithful cardinals, who carried the most sacred relics of the Church, the heads of St. Peter and St. Paul. At a moment when he could make himself heard the Pope declaimed:

"These are the ancient relics of Rome for which your city is venerated. . . . It is your duty, Romans, to protect them." Taking the Papal tiara from his head he laid it on the relics exclaiming: "Do you Saints defend Rome if the men of Rome will not defend her?" In a sudden emotional fervour the Romans swung to the support of the Pope and the walls of the city were manned.

Frederick retired, for he did not intend to lay siege to Rome. Twice more Frederick advanced on Rome and retired; the first time Gregory died as Frederick's army was advancing to the city; the second time the new Pope, Cardinal Fieschi of Genoa, who became Innocent IV, escaped dressed as a soldier and helped by the Genoese; he set up his court at Lyons, where he held a Council at which he deposed Frederick in 1245. "For too long I have been the anvil," declared Frederick, "now I wish to be the hammer"; but he had only five more years to live and his position was gradually being undermined. In Germany he had had to depose his son for incompetence and for allying himself with Frederick's enemies, the Milanese; Frederick had lost much of his popularity because he had not come to the help of the Germans when they had to withstand the invasion of the Mongols who had overrun Hungary, although he sent circulars to rulers urging resistance.

He suffered a serious setback in February, 1249, when he failed to capture Parma and his main route across the Appenines was closed to him. There were various attempts on the emperor's life planned by the Pope, and Frederick became suspicious of all, including his closest companions. In 1250 he died still fighting for freedom from the Papacy, and was buried in a porphyry sarcophagus in Palermo. "Let those who shrink from my support," the Emperor had written in one of his letters to rulers, "have the shame, as well as the galling burden of slavery. Before this generation and before the generations to come, I will have the glory of resisting this tyranny."

LOUIS IX (SAINT LOUIS)

(1214-70)

THE FRENCH kings who are the subjects of essays in this book represent, each of them, the spirit of an Age and not only of a reign in French history. Louis XIV is the central figure of the solemn and magnificent seventeenth century; Henry IV, with his pointed beard, his wit, his gallantry, his commonsense, is a typical Elizabethan; and the at once ridiculous and terrible Louis XI, the Spider King whom Sir Walter Scott portrayed in *Quentin Durward*, is the king who, in the early Renaissance, laboured to make a nation against the old order—like Henry VII of England.

To those who only read history occasionally, Louis IX, St. Louis, is a much vaguer and less attractive figure. This is largely because the thirteenth century seems part of a very long, dreary period known as the Middle Ages, principally concerned with the endless battles of kings and nobles from, let us say, William the Conqueror until the Tudors. We may all have been attracted by the Crusades and by the story of Crécy and Agincourt; we may, some of us, realize that in Italy life was more varied and interesting in the Middle Ages than it was in northern Europe; nevertheless, one century seems much like another, and the important men wooden and unconvincing as human beings.

Yet the thirteenth century, in France and in England, was a time of enlightenment and achievement. France had one of her greatest ages from 1180, when St. Louis's grandfather, Philip Auguste, became king, until the death of St. Louis's grandson, Philip the Fair, and the beginning of the Hundred Years' War between France and England early in the fourteenth century. The kings of the House of Capet won back their lands from England and, with the aid of the people of France, had subdued the great nobles who were, some of them, richer and more powerful than the King of France.

In Paris great masters such as St. Thomas Aquinas and Albertus Magnus taught at the Sorbonne where Roger Bacon studied. Owing to the work of monks and friars during the past two hundred years there were plenty of educated men, even of humble rank, in the towns and, thanks to relative peace, there were people of every sort. Indeed, the population of France was probably greater in the reign of St. Louis than it was at the time of the French Revolution, whilst England at the beginning of the reign of Edward III had a larger population than one hundred and fifty years later.

The towns flourished. Many of them had paved streets and in Paris there were no less than twenty-six large bath-houses, for cleanliness of body had become a passion with the new city bourgeoisie. France had grown rich, in part because it lay on the great trading routes to northern Europe along which travelled the luxuries which Europe had discovered in the Middle East during the Crusades of the eleventh and twelfth centuries. Lowlands and marshes were drained, forests were cleared. Farm animals, particularly sheep and pigs, increased enormously in numbers during the thirteenth century. All sorts of plants were first introduced from the East, such as the apricot tree, rice, maize, spinach, artichokes, shallots and many kinds of herbs. The popular literature of folk tales and fables shows the independence of mind of the time. Among the major arts which were first created in the twelfth and thirteenth centuries in France and Flanders was that of stained glass.

This brings us to the greatest aesthetic achievement of the time, the building of the Gothic cathedrals. Some were built or largely built in the twelfth century: others were completed in the fourteenth century; but the great period of construction lies in the thirteenth. Now a point about these Gothic cathedrals is that they cannot be considered like the Pyramids as the work of a society which crushed the individual and used him as a mere servant. The cathedrals are the work of planners and architects about whom we know comparatively little in the first place; but every cathedral or church of this time cries out that it is the expression of hundreds of skilled artisans in wood and stone and in iron and bronze. Individual fantasies in gargoyles, carvings of bishops' thrones, screens or misericords shows that hundreds of ordinary men took part in creating these great works of art. Nor was enthusiasm restricted to artisans and craftsmen; writers of the time record that noblemen and their ladies, shopkeepers and peasants harnessed themselves to the carts bearing the heavy stones, wood, lime or oil needed for building. Minstrels and trumpeters headed great processions of people bearing materials, and when at night such a procession arrived on the site the carts were emptied by the light of torches, hymns were sung, and it was said that blind men recovered their sight and that the paralytic walked.

Throughout the land, particularly during the reign of St. Louis, there was a feeling of security. The king reigned and dispensed justice, not as a tyrant but as the representative of God and as the head of an ordered society. How different life was to be during the next hundred years, after Philip the Fair, when, as the result of the Hundred Years' War and the Black Death, France was delivered over once again to the robbers, barons and marauding soldiers, and when men were to live in caves and eat grass. The very secret of building the Gothic cathedrals was to be forgotten.

Louis's father reigned for only a few years after the death of Philip Auguste. Louis was only twelve at his father's death and his right of succession was disputed. Twice, factions of the nobility took up arms. Louis's mother, Blanche of Castile, one of those dominating female figures such as Catherine de Medici or Anne of Austria, fought with courage and cunning for her son. The support given to the Crown by the people of the towns and by the Church was so strong that the issue was never very much in doubt. St. Louis's reign really begins in 1236, after he had been married for two years to Marguerite of Provence, who brought her lands into the royal domain. Queen Blanche did not abandon power lightly to her son, and Louis appeared extravagantly respectful to his mother. The old queen, presumably out of jealousy, wanted to keep Louis from seeing too much of his wife and so, early in their marriage, Louis and Marguerite had to meet on a small private turning stair which linked their apartments in the Palace at Pontoise, near Paris, where they lived for much of the time. But, in the long run, Louis was a much stronger character than his mother and, although until her death he put up with her caprices, he had his way in all essential matters.

His wife Marguerite bore him nine children. She too had something of her mother-in-law's determination to play a part in politics, and Louis, but with greater sternness than he had shown to his mother, kept her at arm's length. He was anything but uxorious. However, he took her with him on his first Crusade: this was that she might also reap the spiritual reward which came to those who fought for the Cross.

Louis, both as an adolescent and grown man, was of striking beauty. He was firm and smooth of face and, as all his contemporaries noted, his look was mild and kind. Many people speak of his "dove's" eyes. He was extremely tall and elegantly built, and when he was in armour with a gold crown on his helmet, Joinville writes: "Never was so fine a man under arms, for he stood alone, above all his people from the shoulders upwards." From an early age Louis fulfilled his Christian duties as man and king with a sort of fanaticism. He would leave his palace early in the morning to distribute money as anonymously as possible to the poor. He would rise from bed at midnight to hear the Mass for the dead, and regularly attended all the offices of the Church throughout the day. When he rode abroad, his chaplains accompanied him to read the appropriate services. On Fridays he avoided any kind of gaiety and on that day he never wore a hat in memory of the Crown of Thorns. Often in church he would prostrate himself on the stone floor for so long that his attendants grew impatient. When he roused himself he would sometimes not know where he was. Of course, like Henry III and most medieval monarchs, he washed the feet of the poor.

As close companion Louis kept with him a monk who was a leper, and in Palestine during his Crusade he helped bury the putrefied remains of massacred Christians. He was avid of mortification and confessed that he took on repugnant tasks not because they were necessarily the most useful but because they were the most disagreeable to him. Only after his death did men discover the many practices and torments he imposed on himself.

With all these religious extravagances, the king was careful not to overdo his Christian acts so that they might in any way undermine his authority. He liked, for instance, dressing in a monkish habit, and there is the story that his wife once reproached him for his dislike of dress and for his simple robes trimmed with rabbit or squirrel. "Madame," he answered, "if it pleases you to see me richly dressed I will be so; but since conjugal love enjoins on each spouse to please the other, then you must do me the pleasure of leaving your rich dresses and conforming to my fashion as I do to yours." No more was heard on that subject from the queen.

On occasions he appeared in all the magnificence of a monarch with a vermilion surcoat, ermine and jewelled sword. "In such a fashion one must dress that wise men will say that one does not overdo it, nor young men of the time say that you do too little," said Louis. He was of such a totally integrated character that he was never at a loss for a reply to man or woman. Once, to a fishwife who shouted out as he passed that he was more like a monk than a king, he answered gravely: "You speak the truth I am sure. I am not worthy to be a king, and if it had pleased our Lord there would have been another in my place who would have known better how to govern the kingdom."

Louis had the inner gaiety and confidence of a saint and loved jests and songs with his companions. He was a man of action, totally unlike the saintly Henry III of England, and so strong was his will that all men feared him. The worldly cautious Joinville, who was to be his chronicler as well as his friend, not only appreciated Louis's greatness but loved him dearly. Louis once asked Joinville if he would rather wash the feet of lepers or commit a mortal sin. Joinville answered that he would much rather commit a mortal sin. "That is ill said," answered the king; but it did not impair their friendship.

It was inevitable that this most Christian king should take the Cross. He went, in 1248, on a Crusade which was directed at Egypt where the power of the Saracens was centred. With eighteen ships and accompanied by his two brothers, Alphonse of Poitiers and Charles of Anjou, as well as by his wife, Louis took Damietta on the mouth of the Nile in 1249 and ought then to have advanced at once on Cairo, which he would infallibly have taken. But instead the Crusaders dallied and enjoyed the fleshpots of the Near East, whilst the king prayed. The Sultan brought up reinforcements and fifty of his officers who had abandoned Damietta were strangled. When Louis's army finally marched towards Cairo it was delayed at a river crossing near Mansourah and could not succeed in building a bridge. Fourteen hundred French knights crossed by a ford and took Mansourah; unfortunately the infantry could not cross by the ford and the knights were unable to hold their own on the opposite bank. The Egyptian Mamelukes were strengthened, the French advance-guard and the rest of the army, was beseiged on all sides. The Saracens blocked the river from Damietta so that no food could reach the French. An attempt was made to retreat but Louis's army was decimated by dysentery from which he himself suffered, and he was finally forced to surrender. In Damietta the queen and a small force held out.

The captured king was made to embark in a war-galley on the Nile. He was escorted by a large number of Egyptian boats which led him in triumph to the sound of cymbals and drums, whilst, on the bank, the Egyptian army advanced beside the ships. The prisoners followed the army with their hands bound. The Egyptians were embarrassed by the too great number of prisoners and, one night, these prisoners were led in bands of three or four hundred to the banks of the Nile where, after having their heads cut off, they were thrown into the river. Louis and those of his nobles still alive were ransomed and returned to the queen at Damietta, which, of course, was surrendered to the Egyptians. Characteristically, King Louis refused to take advantage of an error of calculation made by the Egyptians in the amount of his ransom and he insisted on the proper sum being paid.

After this disaster, Louis spent two years in Palestine where he did his best to prop up the Christian principalities. But this, too, was on the whole unsuccessful. The crusading ardour of Europe was over and Louis received little help from other Christian countries.

If this Crusade can be blamed as a folly on the part of the king it nonetheless redounded to his credit in the Christian world. After his return he won two great victories at Taillebourg and Saintes over the English who had invaded South-western France in support of some rebels against the king. To the surprise of all his subjects Louis, after these victories and the retreat of the English, gave back three provinces of France to Henry III, stating that it was fitting that between Christians and cousins there should be peace and amity. Louis, however, stipulated that the English king should pay him homage for these provinces, and also should abandon all claims to the throne of France. Louis, in this, showed a touching faith in the continuance of the feudal system—for why should he not let the English king own land in France as his vassal? He failed to foresee that already national feeling was stronger by far than feudalism. But this spectacular policy of seeking Christian friendship was in keeping with the medieval tradition of Christendom, and, had there been more men as Christian and as powerful as St. Louis, Europe might have become, by the fifteenth century, a politically united continent. His political unwisdom, however, had at least one reward in his time. Henry III and his barons submitted their quarrels later to the arbitration of St. Louis, another unprecedented act.

Much of Louis's time was devoted to the administering of justice. Joinville had this picture of the king holding his informal court in the wood of Vincennes, just outside Paris:

> Many times it happened in the summer that the king went to sit in the wood of Vincennes after hearing Mass, and leant against an oak and made us sit round him, and all those who had affairs to attend to came to speak to him without disturbance of an usher or anyone else. And he would ask: "Is there no one who has a plea?" And those who had rose and then he said: "Keep quiet all of you and judgement will be dealt to you in turn." He then summoned lawyers to speak.

Joinville also describes him as administering justice in Paris in the same way. "I saw him several times in the summer going to judge cases for his people in the Palace garden, dressed in a coat of coarse stuff with an outer coat of tyretaine (a stuff half wool and half cotton) without sleeves, a mantle of thick black silk fastened round his neck, his head well combed out and without a hat but with a coronet of white peacock feathers around his head. And he had a carpet spread for us to sit round him; and all the people who had matters to bring before him stood round him and he gave judgment in the way I have described before in the wood of Vincennes."

All over his kingdom Louis sent seneschals, or *baillis* as they were called, to ensure justice, choosing very often poor friars or men who knew the conditions of the humble as his agents. In his instructions to his son, Louis describes the principles on which royal justice was to be carried out. "Dear son, if it should be that you come to reign, see that you have the mark of a king, that is to say that you are just and that you will never refuse justice on any consideration. If it happens that a dispute between rich and poor comes before you, support the poor rather than the rich, and when you've heard the truth, do justice to them. And if it happened that you have a dispute with another, support the claim of the other before your council and do not show your great interest in the dispute until the truth be shown."

In the summer of 1270 Louis embarked from Aigues Mortes on his second Crusade, which was against Tunis. He believed, quite wrongly, that the Bey of Tunis was intending to become a Christian and therefore his Crusade would turn into a visit of friendship. Other people say he was persuaded to sail to Tunis by his brother, Charles of Anjou, who had become King of Sicily and wanted someone to check the pirates who used the port. Joinville strongly advised the king against the Crusade. "Those," wrote Joinville, "who recommended the Crusade to him were guilty of mortal sin; for the whole kingdom was at peace and he with all his neighbours . . . a great sin did those commit in view of King Louis's great bodily weakness. He could not bear to be carried in a vehicle or to ride on horseback. His weakness was so great that it gave him pain when I carried him in my arms from the house of the Count of Auxerre to the Franciscan monastery where I took leave of him. And even though he was so feeble, if he had remained in France he could still have lived and done much good and many good works." Louis landed at Carthage in mid-summer. The pest was raging in Tunisia, and after a victorious fight before the walls of Tunis the

French army was immobilized by sickness. On 25 August the king himself died of the plague.

As a ruler Louis was perhaps less able and successful than his grandfather and his grandson. He made mistakes—the two Crusades, the giving away of land to the English. He stood for a cause, that of a united Christendom, which was a lost cause and perhaps always an impossible one. Yet, as a ruler, he reinforced the belief of the French people in monarchy: indeed, he made the idea of monarchy beloved among the people. As a chronicler says of him: "He shunned discords, he avoided scandals and he hated disagreements. For which reason the waves of bitterness were held back on all sides and disturbances were driven away." St. Louis embodied a unique moment in history when a saint successfully ruled a great kingdom. During his reign the manuscript painters with their vivid designs and bright colours flourished. Their illustrations of some of the Book of Hours leaves behind an impression of extreme devotion, vividness, and childlike power such as no other art has attained to. Joinville, writing of St. Louis, says: "And as the writer who has finished his book illuminates it with gold and blue, so the said king illuminated his kingdom."

KUBLAI KHAN

(1215?-1294)

In Xanadu did Kubla Khan
A stately pleasure-dome decree:
Where Alph, the sacred river, ran
Through caverns measureless to man
Down to a sunless sea.

KUBLAI KHAN has haunted the imagination of man for seven centuries. Coleridge's half-glimpsed vision in his magic lines has all the strangeness of a broken dream, and the remarkable story of the Mongols, of whom Kublai Khan was the last and the greatest, is an astonishing mixture of awful nightmare and glittering splendour such as the world has not known before or since.

The Mongol saga which astonished and dazzled the world lasted for a brief century. The fierce nomadic tribes of the Mongolian plains had always fought each other until the beginning of the thirteenth century, when they were miraculously welded together into a nation under Genghis Khan, a leader of great genius and ruthless ambition. They thundered into history, invading China, India, Turkestan, Persia and Russia. They were irresistible and their number seemed limitless. They were savage and ruthless and gave no quarter as they ravaged and butchered across the whole continent of Asia and into Europe.

These terrible horsemen from the distant plains aroused such dread and committed such wanton slaughter that they made an outstanding contribution to what was called "the Martyrdom of Man". The Mongols are said to have won as much by the terror they inspired as by actual fighting. Two and a half million corpses marked their passage across the central Asian state of Khorasan. At Balkh, a great and splendid city, every single man, woman and child was massacred, and when Marco Polo passed through the place fifty years later it was still just a pile of ruins. Genghis Khan erected immense pyramids of skulls to remind the inhabitants that he had passed that way and resistance was useless.

The strange thing was that after the slaughter of these terrible invasions the Mongols proved to be wise and enlightened rulers of the vast empire they conquered. It could be said that those who survived the sword of Genghis Khan were lucky in more than one sense. Previous to the invasions most of these people lived in squalor and servility. Those who survived enjoyed a period of peace and prosperity such as had not been known before. There was complete religious toleration—something unknown in those times—and all the trade routes of Asia were open to travellers and merchants from all lands.

The empire of Genghis Khan stretched from the Black Sea to the Pacific Ocean and as far south as the Himalayas. His sons had been trained as leaders and rulers to hold down his immense conquests, but Genghis had little faith in them. He died in 1227 at Ha-lao-tu, on the banks of the River Sale in Mongolia, his sons and grandsons standing around his bed, and it was said by the Mongol chronicler Sanang Setzen that the dying man pointed to his eleven-year-old grandson and said: "One day he will rule and his will be a greater age than mine."

The boy thus picked out for greatness was Kublai, the second son of Tule, who was the youngest of four sons of Genghis by his favourite wife. Kublai had to wait for more than thirty years before he could even begin to fulfil his grandfather's prophecy. In the meanwhile family quarrels threatened to break up Genghis's vast dominions.

Kublai's brother, Mangu, became Grand Khan before him, and under his rule more conquests were made. Baghdad was captured and the last of the Abbasid Caliphs was tortured to death and three-quarters of a million of his subjects massacred. All of China was conquered and subdued at the cost of the lives of eighteen million Chinese. Mangu died fighting at Ho-Chow in 1259, and Kublai succeeded him as Grand Khan after some dispute with other members of the family, which was settled in the usual sanguinary fashion.

Kublai had very different ideas to those of his bloodthirsty and barbaric family, who loved war for its own sake and seemed to revel in the slaughter and bloodshed which had made their name synonymous with the worst kind of barbarism.

When his brother had been Khan, Kublai's preference for negotiation rather than slaughter had brought him under the displeasure of the warlike Mangu, but when Kublai succeeded he soon proved the superiority of his more pacific policies. But he was no weakling. His rule was firm. He was the first to rise above the innate barbarism which had so far characterized the Mongol rulers.

He was forty-four, of medium height, dark-eyed and, according to Marco Polo, who knew him well, had a prominent and splendid profile, a fair complexion and an impressively regal air.

His long and busy reign transformed the huge Mongol Empire and brought a peace and prosperity to Asia which it had not known before and which it did not experience again for many centuries. The prosperity was centred on China, which was then the wonder of the world and enjoyed a wealth and luxury unknown in Europe. The splendour and magnificence of Kublai Khan's empire, as told by Marco Polo, haunted the imagination of the West for centuries and inspired the great voyages which later set out from Europe to discover the fabled riches of the Indies and Cathay.

China's two leading cities, Peking and Hangchow, were its main centres of trade. To their gold and silver markets came traders from all over Asia. The streets were full of rich bazaars, and magnificent warehouses lined the waterfronts. Rivers and canals, spanned with innumerable bridges, carried a constant stream of merchandise in gaily coloured junks. The people prospered on the highly skilled industries which made cloth of silver and gold, fine silks and taffetas. Merchants travelled many thousands of miles to buy these beautifully made luxury goods of China.

All the roads and trade-routes of Asia were open to travellers at this time. An Italian handbook for merchants published in 1340 said that the road to Cathay "is perfectly safe whether by day or by night, according to what the merchants say who have used it". This could not be said for travel in Europe at that time, but during the Mongol Dynasty the whole of Asia was open. Chinese silk was brought to Europe for the first time since the days of the Roman Empire, and it was highly prized.

It was the first time in history that an Emperor of China was known by name and deed in Europe. Kublai's seals on letters sent from Tabriz to France are still preserved in Paris. Adventurers and travellers from eastern Europe, as well as the Polos from Venice, served Kublai as ministers, generals and governors.

Kublai Khan encouraged Europeans to come to China in order to solve his administrative problems. His own Mongols were not civilized enough to govern an educated and sophisticated country like China, and he dared not put Chinese in high administrative positions in case they rebelled and undermined his authority. He sought men of talent and education from all over the known world.

At his court in Peking were received ambassadors from every country on earth.

Just as Europeans took every opportunity of this unprecedented chance to get to know more about the mysterious East, Kublai Khan on his part had an inexhaustible curiosity about what took place beyond the distant limits of his immense empire. He was a man of keen intelligence and an insatiable desire for knowledge. China had exercised its age-old spell upon its conquerors and the Mongols were eager to be educated by their highly civilized subjects. They abandoned their old capital of Karakoram, and Kublai built the splendid city of Cambaluk, or Peking, the glories of which so impressed Marco Polo.

Kublai seemed to possess a good deal of natural benevolence and magnanimity. He also had a great love of splendour. The magnificence of his court was the marvel of the world. His palace at Peking was large enough to accommodate a thousand knights and was surrounded by a wall sixteen miles in circumference. His banqueting hall seated six thousand guests. It was decorated with tapestries of green and gold and ornamented with chrysoprase, silver and gold. The walls of Kublai's private apartments were lined with skins of ermine, and the audience chamber was decorated with ermine and zibelline, delicately worked in intaglio.

The gardens of the mighty Khan were nature reconstructed, as befitted the greatest emperor upon the earth. There were gardens and fountains, rivers and brooks, lakes and forests and artificial hills.

> So twice five miles of fertile ground
> With walls and towers were girdled round:
> And there were gardens bright with sinuous rills
> Where blossomed many an incense-bearing tree;
> And here were forests ancient as the hills,
> Enfolding sunny spots of greenery.

Coleridge was doubtless inspired by Marco Polo's rhapsodies on the subject.

Kublai Khan was treated like a god. When he ate, his attendants stuffed silk napkins in their mouths so that their breath should not contaminate his food. Silence was always observed in his presence by all ranks of his subjects. Courts at Peking were traditionally held in almost complete silence, and no noise was permitted within half a mile of where the Khan was. Everyone attending court took slippers of white leather so that the beautiful carpets, which were curiously wrought in silk and gold in a variety of colours, should not be soiled. They also took small cuspidors with them, for obviously no one could spit upon such priceless floor-coverings.

Kublai had a number of wives—at the time of Marco Polo, towards the end of his reign, there were four "of the first rank who are esteemed legitimate"—and he also had a harem of concubines on the grand scale as befitted the greatest emperor upon earth.

These girls were selected according to a well-established custom of the Mongol princes. Every two years his agents went to the Tartar province of Ungut, whose women were noted for their beauty and fairness of complexion. Several hundred maidens were assembled and their beauty judged as though they were precious stones, in carats, each feature—hair, mouth, countenance, figure—being judged separately and receiving a certain number of carats. Those estimated at twenty or twenty-one carats were taken to the Khan's court for further elimination.

After personal inspection by their prospective lord and master, thirty or forty chosen maidens were entered for the final heat as it were. Following the most intimate physical inspection, each girl was placed in the care of the wife of a noble whose duty it was to see that they had no concealed imperfections. The matrons slept with the girls to ensure that they had sweet breath at all times, that they did not snore, toss and turn in their sleep, or suffer from body odour.

The presumably fortunate girls who came through this final scrutiny then had the honour of sharing the emperor's bed. The intimacy, however, was not à deux, for Kublai Khan always had five girls at a time. These girls waited on his every wish, and as Marco Polo delicately puts it, "he does with them as he likes". Each party of five girls remained with him for three days and three nights, when the next five girls on the rota came on duty. He had no personal male attendants, but throughout his reign was always waited upon by relays of beautiful young females. He thus became the father of forty-seven sons, and daughters who were not numbered. In battle his army was largely officered by his own sons.

Kublai Khan was extremely interested in religion. Such was his liberal mind that all religions interested him and he made a study of each one. He had earnestly considered the religions of the Jews, the Buddhists and the Moslems. But it was Christianity which fascinated him the most.

When Nicolo and Maffeo Polo arrived at his court about 1265 they were the first Western Europeans he had met, and Kublai was particularly interested in them as they were Italians who came from the very home of the Christian Church. The Polo brothers, wise and prudent travellers, had already taken the trouble to master the Tartar language, and found themselves immediately at home in the company of the Grand Khan. Traders to their fingertips, there was nothing in the way of material things which they could sell to the Khan, who possessed everything man could wish for upon earth, so they sold him their religion.

Kublai was fascinated, particularly in the story of Jesus Christ, though the subtlety of the Crucifixion escaped his oriental mind. He could not understand why such an exalted man should have made the sacrifice of permitting himself to perish miserably on the Cross. What really interested him about Christianity was the institution of the Papacy. The Pope, with his wealth and pomp and enormous but mysterious power, was someone after his own despotic heart. This he could readily understand and this perhaps was the thing about Christianity which really appealed to this great Eastern ruler.

He told the Polo brothers that he would like them to return to the Pope at Rome as his ambassadors with the request that a hundred men of learning should be sent to instruct the Tartar people in Christianity and the liberal arts. Years later the Polos returned with Nicolo's young son Marco. The Dominican friars the Pope had sent with them had lost heart early in the journey across Asia and turned back.

They did not succeed in converting Kublai Khan to Christianity. Although he recognized its intrinsic superiority, it did not have the spectacular powers, the miracles, the black magic and the general entertainment value which protagonists of the more barbaric religions then practised in China used as methods of conversion. It was probable that Christendom's failure to provide the teachers he asked for was the real reason why Kublai Khan turned to Tibetan Buddhism as the most effective means of civilizing his countrymen. Tibetan Buddhists were given positions of great power in his empire.

Kublai Khan made several attempts to extend his realms, but generally without success. Two bids to conquer Japan failed, as did an attempt to invade Cochin China (South Vietnam) and Java. He did, however, successfully subjugate Burma.

He died in 1294 at the age of eighty-two, greatly revered by his subjects, and renowned all over the then known world.

His death was marked by one of those dark Mongol customs

which has made their name a by-word for barbarism. It was said that all of his wives were buried alive with him, and that any of his subjects who dared to look upon his bier as it was borne to its last resting place were summarily slain by his Mongol mourners with the injunction: "Your master needs you in heaven. Go and serve him there."

But he was not a barbarian and would not have approved of servants thus acquired—supposing that he found his way to heaven.

Kublai Khan was a giant figure in the tumultuous centuries of the Middle Ages, standing astride the world like a colossus, ruling more territory, more subjects, than any other monarch on the face of the earth. He bridged the two worlds of East and West, then unknown to each other, and for a brief and magic period opened the way for them to know and understand each other. His reign was a bright gleam of light and reason in the dark centuries which went before and which followed.

After his death the Mongol Empire collapsed, the darkness once more descended upon the vast spaces of mysterious Asia, and the barriers of misunderstanding and suspicion came down between East and West.

EDWARD I

(1239–1307)

SOME MONARCHS are remembered by their personalities or their capacity to stir the imagination, others by the vigour and force of their actions. King Edward I stands apart in English history, for he is best remembered by his good works—the Model Parliament of 1295 and the improvement in the laws and the legal system which he carried out. Some of his laws are still in force today.

The eldest son of Henry III, he was born in 1239. In his early years he witnessed the disastrous rule of his father, who was influenced by favourites and the French followers of his queen, Eleanor of Provence, who swarmed into England in her train and were soon filling the chief positions in the land.

In 1258 the barons, led by Simon de Montfort, compelled Henry to hand over government to them. De Montfort, a Frenchman of far-reaching intelligence and ambition, whose family had made a great fortune out of the unspeakable Albigensian Crusade, had come to England to claim the earldom of Leicester, had become one of the leading barons in the land, and had married the king's sister.

Led by de Montfort, the barons took up arms against the king and defeated him, and de Montfort became virtual dictator. He summoned what has been regarded as the first real English Parliament in 1265. He formed the great conception of Law as something above the king, and held that the king's true strength lay in Parliament. In de Montfort's 1265 Parliament an important new class of members was present—the Commons, which was destined to give it its future greatness.

Edward had originally come to an understanding with de Montfort and for a time it looked as though the two men might make common cause. This naturally brought Edward into conflict with his father. But Edward's main concern was the preservation of the Plantagenet dynasty, and he strove to persuade his father's royalist party to adopt a more liberal and national spirit. During the fighting between the king and de Montfort, Edward fought on his father's side.

The two armies met at the decisive Battle of Lewes on 14 May, 1264, an encounter which does nothing for Edward's reputation as a soldier. De Montfort and the rebel barons, whose soldiers were said to have worn the white cross of the Crusader, were joined by a large body of Londoners. Henry had the advantage of numbers and quality, though his forces were tired from long marching.

This advantage, however, was thrown away by Edward, who at the head of his knights impetuously pursued the left wing of de Montfort's army, consisting mainly of Londoners, off the field. As de Montfort's standard was in this left wing, Edward ruthlessly chased the Londoners into the swampy ground near the River Ouse, killing large numbers of them and capturing the de Montfort standard.

When Edward returned to the main battle, flushed with what he imagined was victory, he found that de Montfort had not been where his standard had flown, and during Edward's absence had won the day.

After the Battle of Lewes both Edward and his father were virtual prisoners of de Montfort and the barons. But dissension broke out between de Montfort and his followers during which Edward escaped, gathered an army and met de Montfort's forces at Evesham on 4 August, 1265. Edward had learned the lesson of Lewes and himself employed a stratagem which led de Montfort into a trap and to his final defeat on Green Hill outside Evesham, where, after a heroic resistance, de Montfort was slain among his devoted friends and followers.

Edward now showed his true statesmanship and was soon in firm control of the policies of his discredited father. He sought no vengeance on de Montfort's followers. In fact he assimilated many of the de Montfort ideals, with the result that he was acclaimed by the Londoners as de Montfort's heir and successor.

Peace now settled upon England after the civil war which was terminated by the Battle of Evesham. The moderate spirit which seems to have come to the conflicting elements in the kingdom was due to several reasons. The people had faith in the heir to the throne, and knew he would give them the kind of government they wished. England, too, was conscious of emergent nationhood after centuries of being part of an Anglo-French kingdom. Her sovereigns had lost most of their French possessions, and although the battle to retain them was to last a hundred years and more, England was now the centre of the monarch's interests and activities, whereas during the reigns of Henry II and Richard I France occupied as much if not more of the king's time as England did. Thus England came more and more to realize her nationhood and independent power.

So peaceful were the final years of Henry III's reign that Edward went on a crusade in 1270, the funds for which were willingly provided by the country, which was in the mood to expiate for its civil strife by mounting an attack upon the enemy of Christendom. Edward and his followers arrived at Acre in May, 1271, despite the fact that a truce had been concluded with the infidel. Edward refused to be party to this treason to Christendom, but neither his energy nor his valour could do much to prop up the decaying Crusading movement. News of the declining health of his father was used as an excuse to come home.

He was in Sicily when he heard of the death of Henry III on 16 November, 1272. Four days later at Henry's funeral he was recognized as King Edward I of England by the English barons. Affairs in England were so peaceful that Edward came home leisurely, and made a royal and friendly progress through Italy, France and Gascony, his own hereditary duchy. He arrived in England in August, 1274, and was that month crowned at Westminster.

He was thirty-five years old and a magnificent figure of a man, towering above his contemporaries to the then rare height of six feet two inches. Like his knightly ancestor, Richard Coeur de Lion, Edward was a romantic, but he was a practical one. Though his mind was steeped in the legends of King Arthur, his boundless energies were devoted to the establishment of a really effective administration. A man of considerable intelligence, he had a complete mastery of the law, and was an eloquent and convincing orator. Though reasonable in the council chamber, his Plantagenet temper was uncertain and was greatly feared. He was no saint, and was guilty of vindictive cruelty, in the typical Plantagenet manner, to his enemies.

But his domestic life was above reproach, and his friends and subordinates could always rely upon his loyalty and his trust, which was unusual with a medieval king. He had married Eleanor of Castile in 1254 and she bore him four sons and nine daughters, though only one son (Edward II) and five daughters survived infancy.

Thus the man who succeeded Henry III was a very different person to the cavalry leader whose impetuosity had lost the Battle of Lewes eight years previously. Edward's character had developed and hardened in the rough school of duplicity and double-dealing which characterized the politics of his age.

Edward has been described as a revolutionary conservative. Although maintaining the *status quo*, he revolutionized the English administration, and brought to an end feudalism in the country's political life. Nothing that he did was either new or original, but it was necessary to the development of the nation. He limited the amount of money which was paid to Rome, and ended the Papal overlordship of England which his grandfather King John had been forced to grant as the price of patching up his damaging quarrel with Pope Innocent III.

Apart from occupying himself with administration and legislation, Edward set about the conquest of Wales in the early part of his reign. The Welsh of the mountains had never submitted to any of the conquerors of Britain. Neither Roman, Saxon, Dane or Norman had subdued them. Strong fortresses had been built by the Anglo-Norman nobles who had been granted Welsh lands and who were engaged in constant warfare with the native clans. Edward extended this method of conquest and built many castles in Wales, some of which, including Conway, Rhuddlan, Carnarvon, Caerphilly and Harlech, can be seen today.

Prince Llewelyn (the Last) of Wales had been recognized by Henry III as Prince of Wales—the first and also the last native prince to bear that name. Edward required Llewelyn to pay homage to him as his overlord. Llewelyn, over-estimating his power, refused to do this. So in 1277 Edward invaded North Wales where Llewelyn had his stronghold and after a skilful campaign forced him to surrender. The attempt to put Wales under an English administration failed and war broke out again. Llewelyn was finally killed in a skirmish in 1282. The resistance of the Welsh was crushed and Edward divided the country into shires and hundreds, introduced English laws and issued charters to encourage commerce.

In 1284 Queen Eleanor gave birth to a son at Carnarvon Castle, and there is a legend that Edward presented the babe to the Welsh as their own prince who could speak no English. Young Prince Edward was formally created Prince of Wales in 1301.

Between the years 1285 and 1289 Edward was on the Continent. Philip III of France had died and was succeeded by Philip the Fair, to whom Edward performed an act of public homage, the French king being his overlord for Edward's possessions in France, and Edward was very punctilious about these necessary medieval formalities. His business on the Continent included attempts to improve the administration of his duchy of Gascony and a successful mediation of a quarrel between the houses of Anjou and Aragon.

While Edward was abroad the administration at home deteriorated to such an extent that the country was thrown into confusion. When he returned he found he had to dismiss most of his judges and ministers for corruption.

Persecution of the Jews had grown worse. They had been introduced into England by William the Conqueror, their legal position being that of royal chattels. The kind of religious fervour which the Crusades had inflamed led to all sorts of atrocities being perpetrated upon the Jews, who could not leave the country to escape the terror unless they obtained royal permission. In 1290 Edward expelled all these unfortunate people from England. This was not an act of terror but a merciful release. It was three hundred and fifty years before the Jews returned in any numbers to England.

Having conquered Wales, Edward then turned to Scotland, which he found a much more difficult task and one which was to occupy him for the rest of his life.

After the death of Alexander III the Scottish throne had several claimants. Edward was asked to arbitrate and he chose an Anglo-Norman named John Balliol, whom he claimed as his vassal and from whom he demanded homage. At first the new king was prepared to agree, though his subjects were not. Balliol himself soon rebelled but was defeated by Edward at Dunbar.

As a sign of the intended incorporation of the Scottish kingdom with the English, Edward took the Coronation stone from Scone and carried it to Westminster, where it remains to this day, a matter over which some Scottish nationalists are still at issue with the English Crown.

Edward's great work was the Model Parliament. He was determined to govern with the support of his own subjects. "What touches all," he declared, "should be approved of all."

In 1295 he summoned the most representative Parliament that had met in England up to that time, comprising the three estates, lords, clergy and commons. It is called the Model Parliament because all subsequent Parliaments in England have followed the same pattern. At first it sat in a single chamber and was presided over by the king sitting on his throne. Before him was his Council, headed by the Chancellor and comprising judges and justices. The chamber was flanked on one side by the bishops and clergy and on the other by the lords and barons. At the far end of the chamber was a bar, on the other side of which stood the Commons whose leader was later known as the Speaker.

When the king had put his proposals to Parliament, the various estates retired to separate chambers and discussed and voted on the proposals, then returned to the Parliament chamber with their decisions. It was not until after the death of Edward I that Parliament split into the two Houses of Lords and Commons. But Edward established the Parliamentary constitution of England and instituted the government which we have today. That was his great work, and he brought to bear upon it an intelligence unrivalled in his day, a mastery of the law, and an idealism inspired by the best virtues and philosophies of his time.

Edward, however, did not form Parliament for it to govern. His intention was that it should be a consultative body. The idea of delegating any of his royal authority or dispersing any of his powers was as foreign to him as it would have been to any Plantagenet. The decisions were taken by him in consultation with his Council. He called Parliament for a discussion and an exchange of views in the national good. Parliament was to augment the royal power by approving the decisions he had already made. Democracy was not in anyone's mind, and was in fact quite foreign to the philosophy of thirteenth-century government. But it did give Lords, Commons and Clergy a sense of responsibility and implanted the seed of government by consultation, agreement and debate in which representatives of all sections of the country took part—the seed, in fact, of democracy.

The reign of this great king ended in turmoil and frustration. Again and again Scotland rose in revolt under their leaders, William Wallace and Robert Bruce. Again and again Edward marched north and defeated them. In 1298 William Wallace, betrayed into Edward's hands, was brought to London and executed.

The century ended in bloodshed, with Robert Bruce once more raising the standard of Scottish liberty. In 1307 Edward, now old and worn, raised his finest army against Bruce, but he was detained at Carlisle by illness. He sent an advance guard ahead under the Earl of Pembroke who routed Bruce at Perth. Edward followed, carried on a litter. On 7 July he died, and with his last breath asked that his body should be borne at the head of his army until Scotland should be completely subdued.

But it was not to be. His son, Edward II, who was destitute of any great purpose in life and thus the complete opposite of his father, did not seriously pursue the campaign after Bannockburn.

ROBERT BRUCE

(1274–1329)

Bannockburn betwixt the braes,
Of horse and men so chargit was
That upon drownit horse and men
Man might pass dry atour it then.

AND INDEED the narrow stream, the Bannockburn, as this
eye-witness report tells us, was stuffed—piled high—from bank
to bank with dead and dying English chivalry. Knights, chargers,
filled it: the water was stained dull crimson.

But the English, under Edward II, were brave and determined.
The forces had met just before dusk, contact was broken off for
a few hours during the semi-darkness of a northern night, and
fighting began as the sun rose on the second day. Much deployment
and re-deployment had taken place during the night, with the
Scots under Bruce digging pits about their several positions and
covering these with grass and straw, like traps for wild animals.
Outnumbered, they prepared to meet their enemy in tight circles
of armed infantry, and when dawn came these "schiltrons" proved
all but impervious to the horsed attacks launched on them. The
English knights, finding lances suddenly useless against a solid mass of
mutually supporting armour, a vast tank with a hundred legs, hurled
swords and maces in despair before turning to flee.

And then, with the appearance of what seemed a whole new
Scottish army—in fact they were camp followers, whooping with
delight, eager to join the soldiers—the English fled in shameful
defeat, many of them across the Bannock Burn, running blood-
stained to the Forth and the sea.

The Scots under their king Robert—Robert Bruce—had won
in these two June days and a night of 1314 a resounding victory,
against vast numerical odds. They had dealt England and her
foolish, effeminate king (the first Prince of Wales, he had been) a
blow which was to make Scotland free of English domination.
Had Bruce not then behaved with rather more magnanimity than
was wise, had he and his army been more prepared for their

thumping victory, relations between the two countries might have stabilized at once into a lasting peace, instead of drifting unhappily on for a number of years.

But Robert Bruce, even if victory took him unawares, had achieved a great one, the greatest in Scots history. He was able to concentrate the remaining fifteen years of his life on being a king—on the wise and just rule for which he is now remembered. When he died, in 1329, in his simple house on the west coast—not for Bruce a castle or a palace, but a modest dwelling where he could watch his young son grow up a Christian, away from the sound of war—he was, to all his subjects, and many who were not, "Good King Robert".

"Good" is an epithet sparingly distributed among Scottish sovereigns—and half an hour with any book of Scots history will make the reason abundantly clear—but Robert was a profoundly good one. Kingship seems to have made him so, for there is much with which we can find fault before his accession. But as king he established, as no ruler of Scotland had or has done, a complete understanding and sympathy with his subjects.

He was—once he reached the throne—utterly just, endlessly patient, and for a brilliant leader in time of war surprisingly wise in matters of peace. He died, aged fifty-five, mourned throughout his kingdom, not yet certain that he had achieved its freedom or not, and sad that he had never fulfilled his vow to embark on a crusade. His last request was that his heart be taken from his body, embalmed and carried by a goodly knight to Jerusalem. It never got there: Sir James Douglas was killed on the way. The relic, in its silver box, was eventually deposited in the monastery of Melrose, while Bruce's body was buried in the abbey church of Dunfermline. Six days later, the Pope issued a bull permitting Robert Bruce's coronation by the Bishop of St. Andrews.

History is the study of accidents, and the thrones of England and Scotland might well have been joined by this time, with Bruce remaining a law-abiding Earl of Carrick. But this was not to be. In one of the more romantic accidents of history, the last Scots king of the Canmore line died through a whim to be bedded with the young French wife he had left on the far side of the River Forth. It was 18 March, the year was 1286, and Alexander III had been dining in Edinburgh castle, drinking the good red wine of Bordeaux, when the urge seized him. Ignoring the warnings of his nobles, he got from the table, mounted a steed and rode furiously to the ferry at Dalmeny. Here the ferry-master implored him to return to his castle, but the king brushed aside the entreaty and was rowed across two miles of icy, churning water to Inverkeithing. Once again he was urged, this time by one of the bailies of the town, to go back, or at least spend the night in Inverkeithing. A storm had got up, the wind was howling in from the North Sea, there was no moon. It is interesting to compare the man-to-man relationship between Scottish monarch and his subjects with the respectful attitude of the English to their own. "What are you doing out in such weather?" said the bailie. "Get back, get back! How many times have I told you, midnight travelling will do you no good——"

But King Alexander III refused, as bluntly, to return. It was true the weather had got worse, but the urge to visit his young Queen Yolande, the fact that he had already survived a perilous trip across the Forth, made it impossible for a man of spirit to retrace footsteps or even postpone till the morrow reunion with his wife. He set off along the coast road to his manor of Kinghorn—and was never seen alive again. Somehow in the dark he got separated from his guides and was found the next morning at the foot of the cliff, his neck broken.

Yolande, only six months wed, had been his second wife: now she was his widow. The two sons of the first marriage were already dead, and now the heir to the throne of Scotland was a sickly little girl of three, across many miles of water. This "Maid of Norway", little Margaret, was the child of Alexander's daughter, also dead, once married to the King of Norway.

At first it seemed a desirable state of affairs. England, Scotland and Norway were all in favour of a marriage between the little Maid and the heir to the English throne. But in September, 1290, after all arrangements had been made, the Maid of Norway died on her way to England. She was to have been joined with a young man she had never seen, a man who would, twenty-four years later, be thrashed at Bannockburn by another who had taken the throne of Scotland.

On her death, the bridegroom's father, Edward I, took matters into his own hand and marched into Scotland to claim the country and its castles, on the shaky grounds that he must have them to pass on to the successful contender for the Scottish throne. He followed this up by selecting, with some show of legality, a king for Scotland, John Balliol. It was the reluctance of this vassal king's subjects to stump up money and men for the English monarch's adventures in France that brought about Balliol's downfall. He was forced to renounce his allegiance to the English throne, then to abandon his own.

Edward now appointed, as he had for Wales, a "Governor" for Scotland. It was done with more show of legality, and agreed to by a fair proportion of Scottish nobles, who no doubt regarded it as a temporary expedient which would let them retain lands they had acquired in England. But among the disaffected was William Wallace, who rose, with thousands of others, in an ill-starred revolt. After years of see-saw campaigning, he was captured by Edward in 1305 and brutally executed as a traitor, his head impaled on London Bridge.

At this time the young nobleman Robert Bruce had just passed his thirty-first birthday. Already he had lived a full, not to say dramatic, life. His grandfather had been claimant to the Scottish throne when little Margaret died—the throne awarded to John Balliol—and the younger Bruce, though angry that his family's claims had been overruled, decided at first to support Edward. Confused, ambitious, he then proceeded to change sides with some frequency, fighting both for and against the English king. It was the hideous death of Wallace which finally decided him to have no further truck with England. His father had died in the previous year; Robert Bruce was now owner of vast estates in Scotland, another in England, a house in London and a manor at Tottenham: so we can discount any theories that he was a disappointed man. But he had made up his mind by the end of 1305 to win the throne of Scotland for a Scotsman, and preferably himself. His family's claims had been only marginally less valid than Balliol's, and now that Balliol ("Toom Tabard," the Scots called him, the "Empty Coat") had proved himself incompetent, Robert Bruce's mind was made up.

Soon, though, he was involved in the least savoury episode of his life. Another claimant was John, "The Red," Comyn, and in a quarrel within the sacred precincts of Greyfriars Church in Dumfries, Bruce killed him. Historians disagree as to the reason behind the deed. Some maintain Comyn was about to betray to the English king a joint plan of revolt. Others maintain it was just rivalry for the throne of Scotland. Some say Bruce did not strike the fatal blow, that it was done by his companions. Others, on the contrary, say Bruce had the dying man brought to him at the altar steps and there dispatched him. Some say Bruce wounded Comyn and that his companions made sure of his death. It seems likely, though, that the killing was unpremeditated and the climax of a sudden quarrel.

Six weeks later, knowing he had set in motion half a dozen different chains of events—the Pope had excommunicated him, Edward thirsted for his blood, every man's hand was against him—and knowing it was too late to turn back, Bruce had himself crowned King of Scotland at the traditional site in Scone, even though the Stone of Destiny had been removed to Westminster, and the crown was still with Balliol. Only four bishops and four earls, from all Scotland, were present as the Countess of Buchan placed the golden coronet, specially made for the occasion, on the new king's head.

A little later the Countess was captured by the English. For her crime, she was locked in a cage and suspended *four years* from the wall of Berwick Castle, to be gaped at by the populace. A similar fate befell Bruce's sister. Both, miraculously, survived to be released.

The history of the next years is confused. King Robert captured a number of English-held castles and extracted oaths of allegiance from a large part of the population. But he was a hunted man, with most of his family in captivity or done to death, and the English in hot pursuit. For months he and a few loyal supporters were harried through the highlands of Perthshire. A little later he had to leave Scotland and hide on the island of Rathlin: by the spring of 1307 he was an exile on the Isle of Arran. Perhaps it was now that he observed the determination of the spider, trying again and again to spin its web, finally succeeding, which has come down to us through the years as part of the Bruce story. Edward I —"Hammer of the Scots" he liked to be styled—came within an ace of capturing him on several occasions, but at last that irascible monarch died, during a last northward advance, in Cumberland. Old and ailing, he had been carried for most of the way in a litter at the head of his army. His dying words were to hand over the task of conquering Scotland—and Bruce—to his son, that Prince of Wales whose child marriage with the Maid of Norway had been frustrated. Fortunately for Bruce and for Scotland, the new Edward II was not of the same calibre as his father. Slowly the tide began to turn in Bruce's favour, as he and his ever-increasing band of followers captured, one by one, every castle held by the English till only Stirling held out.

And so we come to Bannockburn, and the summer of 1314. The English Governor of Stirling Castle, surrounded by a force led by Robert's surviving brother, Edward Bruce, agreed to capitulate

311

if the English failed to relieve him by Midsummer Day. It was a gentlemanly sort of arrangement and Edward Bruce for his part agreed to wait.

Thus, thanks to a gesture unappreciated by the ruler of either country, the decisive battle drew near. Robert was averse to a pitched battle against the far greater numbers of an English army, and Edward II, comfortable in England, had little desire to lead one. But honour now compelled them both. It also determined the day, for 24 June would be Midsummer Day, and for Edward there was no time to lose. He rushed north with an army which may have numbered 100,000, and was in any case far larger than Bruce's.

As we have seen, the Scots won a resounding victory. Edward II reached the castle he had come to relieve, a tattered fugitive: the Governor, Sir Philip Mowbray, told him he was about to capitulate, and the unhappy English king fled to Dunbar. He was lucky. Many of his followers were struck down in their retreat—though Bruce had a kinder heart than was customary in those days—and those that were captured were used to ransom Scots prisoners, including Bruce's wife the queen and her daughter. The ransom extracted by the Scots for English prisoners brought sudden, undreamed-of wealth to the country.

Bruce's victory was not the end of the war, but it was decisive. The blood that flowed for nine more years served no purpose at all. The Scots captured Berwick in 1318 and were able to plunder northern England almost at will: the English came north again, looted the abbeys of Melrose and Holyrood and burned Dryburgh. But in 1323 Edward made a truce for thirteen years. It was broken by fighting between his young and warlike son, succeeding to the English throne in 1327, and small bands of Scottish raiders, but a year later a treaty was signed, in Northampton, which formally recognized Robert Bruce as King of Scotland. A year after that Bruce was dead.

Without doubt, he was a great king. We can largely discount his shifts of allegiance before he became one: patriotism in 1300 was a different thing to that of six hundred years later: a man had to fight for the side his family wanted, preferably the one most likely to win, or it would mean extinction. As king, he defeated his country's enemy, tried hard for and finally succeeded in a just peace, and made sure there would be no disputed succession after his death by tying up the details with strict fairness and legality. He made a lasting treaty with France at Corbeuil in 1326, re-organized the Scottish parliament to include representatives of the Burghs—a new and startling innovation in a feudal society—and left his country ordered, prosperous and proud.

Robert Bruce combines in a unique and fascinating way the qualities of brilliant general and skilful knight-at-arms—a knight who could rally an army, in the early stages of Bannockburn, by reining aside and smashing with an unbelievable blow the heavy helmet and the skull of Sir Henry de Bohun as the Englishman charged him. He was with it a schemer, probably a murderer, and the wisest, fairest ruler in Scots history.

EDWARD III

(1312-77)

THE FIFTY-YEAR reign of Edward III from 1327-77 stands as one of the most glorious in English history, in spite of miseries at its close. Edward, for a time, appeared the most powerful monarch in Europe and his court the most brilliant in Christendom.

Among the Norman and Angevin or Plantagenet kings who had ruled England since the Norman Conquest there had been weak and bad rulers such as John and Edward II, the father of Edward III, but the strong and able dominated. A powerful royal administration had been established throughout the country, and so the English, enjoying more internal peace and security than did their neighbours on the Continent, began to see themselves as one nation. The archers and men-at-arms who won the great victories of Crécy and Poitiers and the naval battle of Sluys felt themselves to be free men, subjects of the king and not of local barons.

Since the reign of Henry II they had been encouraged to use their own weapons and were organized in local militias, obedient to the Crown. England had grown rich too, not only in the export of the best wool in the world to Flanders, but also in the manufacture of woollen cloth. In one year, it is said, Edward III received the huge sum in those days of £80,000 from duties levied on wool. The towns flourished. In the reign of Edward III the total population of England, about three million, was greater than that a hundred years later. It was above all the fact that England had become a nation which gave, in the middle of the fourteenth century, a special lustre to the island kingdom, for all that its people had not the industrial ingenuity of the Flemings or the civilization of northern Italy and the south of France.

The English language was now that of nobles, yeomen, as well as of the peasants. Edward III was the first English king to speak English and not French as his natural tongue. "Let clerics indite in Latin," writes an author who translated French Romances into English at this time, "and let Frenchmen in their French also indite their quaint terms, for it is kindly to their mouths; but let us show our faculties in such words as we learnt in our mother tongue."

Geoffrey Chaucer, the first and one of the greatest of English poets, appeared in the reign of Edward III. Chaucer's verse, and above all the *Canterbury Tales*, is a monument to the English civilization of the time.

Edward III, like his great grandfather Edward I, had a troubled succession. His father, Edward II, had been a weak king. A man of fine stature, athletic, good at handicrafts, he showed himself unfit for the business of ruling. He had strong homosexual tendencies and it was his undue partiality for his favourites which caused his wife Isabel, the daughter of the King of France, to lead a rebellion against him. He was forced to abdicate in favour of his son and was imprisoned and cruelly treated until he died.

Edward III became king at the age of fifteen and was married a year later, in 1328, to Philippa of Hainault. The paramour of Queen Isabel, the Earl of Mortimer, was the real ruler of England for some time after Edward's accession. It was touch-and-go whether Edward would survive the increasing enmity of the ambitious Mortimer. But during a Council meeting at Nottingham, Edward and his supporters entered Nottingham Castle, where Isabel and Mortimer were living, by a subterranean passage at night, forced their way into Mortimer's apartments, trussed him up and sent him to the Tower of London. Mortimer was later drawn on an ox-hide to the gallows at Tyburn and hanged in public. The queen was gently treated by Edward, in spite of her complicity in his father's murder.

The handsome Edward, an accomplished knight, versed in lore of hunting and falconry, was a great performer at joust and tourney. It was inevitable that war should be his pastime. Very soon after he began to reign he resolved to avenge his father's defeat by the Scots at Bannockburn. He made war on his own brother-in-law, King David, and won a great victory at Halidon Hill over the Scots; but he wisely gave up the hopeless attempt of conquering Scotland. His eyes turned towards France for many reasons—France had helped the Scots, French interference with the cities of Flanders with whom England did so much trade, and Edward's great possessions in France—which still included most of Aquitaine in the south-west.

When Charles II, the father of Edward's mother Isabel, died, he left as direct successor to the French throne a fifteen-year-old daughter who, already a widow herself, gave birth to another daughter. The French nobles proclaimed Charles's cousin, Philip of Valois, King of France, and this was generally acknowledged by the nation. Isabel, however, claimed that her son Edward, who was a nephew of Charles VI, had a better right than Philip. However, in 1329, Edward III, in the Cathedral of Amiens, paid homage to Philip for his lands in France. This did not prevent him later from reviving his claim and proclaiming himself King of France, a title which thereafter every English sovereign bore until George III.

But the Hundred Years' War between England and France was not, in substance, a dynastic war. Some of its roots were undoubtedly in rivalry over the rich lands of Flanders that were the main causes of Anglo-French wars. But the war, never a continuous affair but rather a series of discontinuous campaigns waged by smallish invading English armies, had its origin largely in the martial ardour of the English. Like their master King Edward, the young knights and squires were burning to prove their strength and chivalry overseas. It was the parliaments composed of barons and representatives of the land-owning classes and even the rich burgesses of the towns who, at first, urged Edward to conquer France and supported him with men and money. Froissart, that great chronicler of Europe in the fourteenth century, wrote:

The English will never love nor honour their king unless he be victorious and a lover of arms and war against their neighbours and especially against such as are greater and richer than themselves. They take delight and solace in battles and slaughter; covetous and envious are they above measure of other men's wealth.

This was certainly true at the beginning of Edward's reign, though the Commoners were heartily sick of war by the end.

Edward III at first tried to invade France through Flanders, and he entered into league with the German princes whom, as Pitt did against Napoleon, he supplied with money to fight the French. But this came to little except a great waste of money. In 1340, however, 150 English ships with the king in command sailed from Suffolk and engaged "a great fleet of masts"—some 190 ships of the French king—in the harbour of Sluys. The ships were manned by Normans and the men of Picardy who were good sailors. The English sailed into the harbour and used grappling irons to attach themselves to the enemy's ships and, as at Crécy, the long-bow archers caused havoc among the enemy. English nobles and men-at-arms swarmed over the enemy ships and, by sunset, the French were beaten. Edward III was wounded in the leg. This first English sea victory made Edward famous. He was offered the title of Holy Roman Emperor, which he refused. But his wars and the subsidies to Flemings and Germans had nearly bankrupted him—indeed he defaulted on his debts to the great banking houses of Florence, two of which were forced to go into liquidation.

But six years afterwards, in July, 1346, Edward set out on the great direct invasion of France, capturing Caen, in Normandy, a city larger than any English city of the time except London. Edward took his army within a dozen or so miles of Paris. But he could not take Paris. The French king was approaching with a huge army whilst Edward's had suffered heavy losses from disease as well as fighting. He had to retreat northwards for home, and he crossed the Somme near its mouth. He halted in Ponthieu, near the village and the forest of Crécy, turning at bay on his enemies much as Henry V was to do at Agincourt.

On 25 August, in a great thunderstorm, the large French army, mainly of heavily armoured and beautifully caparisoned knights and mounted cavalry with Genoese crossbowmen, caught him up. There was great confusion, for King Philip first ordered the advance columns of his army to halt and then, groups of French knights in the rear protesting, decided to begin battle at once. His Genoese crossbow archers and infantry, tired by marching, blinded by a sudden storm after the rain, fell in hundreds before the English bowmen: they flung away their weapons and started to retreat. As they fled, they were ridden down by the French knights anxious to be at the English. Edward's army was drawn up in two forward arrays of dismounted men with archers, one commanded by the Black Prince, Edward's son, then aged seventeen. King Edward commanded a centre formation slightly behind the other two: the king himself, with a white staff in his hand, mounted on his war-horse, stood by a windmill overlooking the field.

The French made fifteen separate charges on the English during that day, each time suffering terribly from the arrows of the English. At one moment a messenger was sent to Edward to say that the Black Prince was sorely pressed. "Is my son dead or hurt?" the king asked the messenger. "No, sir," answered the messenger, "but he is hardly matched, therefore he has need of your aid." "Return to him," said the king, "and say that they can send no more to me as long as my son is alive: and say to them that they suffer him this day to win his spurs; for if God be pleased I wish this day to be his, the honour thereof, and for them that be about him."

After Crécy, Edward had nothing for a while to fear from the French king's army. According to English reports, eleven princes, one thousand two hundred knights and about thirty thousand common men lay dead on the field. Few prisoners had been taken,

an unusual thing for war at that time and due to the small number of
the victors and their fear of taking any risks. Edward continued his
march homewards, and settled down to the siege of Calais which his
fleet was blockading. The siege lasted a long time and this much
annoyed him. When the town at last surrendered, Edward at first
intended to sack it and to murder most of its inhabitants, but then
agreed not to do this provided that six of the most prominent
burghers of the town appear before him with halters round their
necks ready for hanging and the keys of Calais in their hands.
The king received them angrily and proposed to execute them at
once. He was only deterred, unwillingly, by the entreaties of his
queen.

It is interesting to compare the king's surly behaviour to these
commoners who had defied him and fought bravely with the way
he treated some noble prisoner who, later, had attempted to recapture Calais. To their leader Froissart makes the king say: "Sir
Eustace, you are the most valiant knight in Christendom. I never
have yet found anyone in battle whom, body to body, has given
me so much to do as you have this day. I adjudge you the prize
of valour. I present you with this chaplet as being the best commander of this day, and I beg of you to wear it all this year for love
of me. I know that you are a lover of damsels and noble ladies;
therefore tell it wherever you go that King Edward gave this to
you. You also have your liberty, free of ransom, and may go
tomorrow, if you please, wherever you like."

The king returned to England in 1347, and there was a period
of revelry and jousting and magnificent entertainments. The king
fought the Spaniards at sea, and accepted a personal challenge to
combat from a French knight. In 1356 his son, the Black Prince,
won a victory even more splendid than that at Crécy. This was
at Poitiers, and he won it again thanks to the valour and discipline
of the English and the out-dated tactics of French chivalry. King
John of France was captured. The Black Prince served his illustrious
captive bare-headed as a mark of respect, and himself brought him
to London. Other less successful forays into France were undertaken. Finally the Treaty of Calais gave the English the whole of
Aquitaine, that is most of South-west France, free of homage, and
Calais. In return Edward renounced his claim to the kingdom
of France.

Before Edward's death the war in France underwent a new
phase. In 1369 Charles V repudiated the Treaty of Calais and
Edward III re-assumed his claim as King of France. But the French,

under leaders such as Bertrand du Guesclin, fought very differently, avoiding large battles, ambushing the English forces and harrying them on their forced marches through hostile country. Most of Aquitaine was lost and the English people grew tired of the war. The Black Prince, sick of a fever which was shortly to carry him off, returned to England. When a truce was made in 1375 all that remained in English hands were the ports of Brest, Calais, Bordeaux and Bayonne. The whole Angevin empire was lost.

During the later years of the king's reign the Black Death hit England several times. It was a time of social unrest which broke out in great violence at the beginning of the reign of Richard II, the son of the Black Prince. Edward III, always much given to the lusts of the flesh, went into a sort of premature dotage in his infatuation for his last mistress Alice Perrers. The king's third son, John of Gaunt, was the real ruler of the kingdom, although his corrupt faction was opposed by the Black Prince. In 1376 the Black Prince, supported by the Commons and by many ecclesiastics, triumphed over John of Gaunt and called what was known as "the Good Parliament" in London. Alice Perrers was banished from the Court and John of Gaunt's exactions were ended. But the death of the Black Prince gave John of Gaunt the chance of returning to power and reversing the acts of Parliament. Edward's reign ended in general disappointment. He died suddenly at Sheen, near Richmond, apparently talking merrily with his courtiers a few minutes before he grew pale and his breath failed. As he expired, most of the courtiers having run away in fright, it is said that Alice Perrers pulled the rings off his fingers.

Edward III was not as strong and resolute a king as William I or Henry II, and inferior perhaps in strength of character to his grandfather Edward I. But he was a brave knight and an excellent commander of men, even if, as a general, his plans were too ambitious as a rule to be carried out. For all his warlike and amorous propensities he had an eye to the well-being of England and could claim to be the founder of the English fleet. All his life he protected the English and foreign weavers whom he had been persuaded to settle in East Anglia. If he died after his best period, it was clear there was something august and calm about this king who represented England at the time when national self-confidence was so strongly expressed. The tomb in Westminster Abbey, made from a wax portrait modelled from Edward's dead body, expresses the greatness of a king who, in the words of a chronicler of the time, was brave in war, affable and pleasant to all men.

TAMERLANE (TIMUR)

(1336–1405)

THE DEEPEST lake in the world—well over a mile, straight down, between its glassy surface and its pitch-dark, stony bottom—is in southern Siberia. It is four hundred miles from the north end to the south, and at its widest point a fisherman would have to row fifty miles to get from one bank to the other. It abounds in freshwater fish of strange and exotic variety: delicacies to the human community which lives around its shores, as well as to the colonies of seals that inhabit the rocky northern fringes.

It is called, in the language of the easy-going, peaceable Mongol people who live there, *Dalai-Nor*, or The Holy Sea. The Russians, who control this part of the world, call it Lake Baikal, the name by which it is most familiar to us, but it is as *Dalai-Nor* that it has been known for centuries. It was here that the far-from-peaceable Genghis Khan was born, in the middle of the twelfth century, here that he inherited a small Mongolian kingdom at the age of thirteen, and from here that he set out to conquer the world. His exploits are dealt with in another article, but we may stop for a moment to consider the people from which he sprang; the strange, wild land which gave them birth.

They were Mongols, short squat men with narrowed eyes, living a nomad life and sleeping in tents of matted hair and rancid butter. They lived by hunting: when they killed an animal they devoured the whole thing, raw. They were horsemen, probably the finest horsemen the world has ever known, and their staple drink was mare's milk. For festive occasions they drank it fermented, often from the skull of an enemy. (The term "Tatar", usually mis-spelt "Tartar", is variously used for all Mongols of this period, or for one tribe, or for a group, and has, for this reason, little meaning. It also has no traceable etymology; except that in medieval times the word "Tatary" was used in Europe to mean Central Asia.)

There were many of these Mongol tribes: *Kipchaks*, *Karaits*, *Naimans*, *Uighurs* and *Kirghiz* were but a few abounding in the time of Genghis Khan. Others, hundreds of years before, speaking

320

the same language, had fought a way westward off their wide Mongolian plain, left their mark on Europe. These were *Huns, Goths, Seljuks, Vandals*: like their successors they were happier in the saddle than out of it and able to go for days without food or water. When the time came, they were ready and anxious to make up for this privation by orgies of food and drink.

They were fighters: a man was seldom without his breastplate and his spear.

Genghis Khan built up a superbly successful military machine, a machine which laid waste to much of the known world, taking what it could carry in the way of riches and slaves, dragging it back to the Mongolian plain, destroying the rest. But after the death of Genghis, the quarrelling of his descendants started to break up his empire and his army. The rot was halted for a time by the great Kublai Khan, who ruled for thirty-five years in the latter half of the thirteenth century, and was a wise man who loved art and literature. He did much to hold the empire together in peace and to encourage the arts throughout it: while he lived, the Mongol empire remained great.

But after this golden age it separated into a squabbling confederation of tribes—much as it had been at the birth of Genghis. It was in one of these tribes, the *Barlas* clan, living in the hills south of Samarkand, that the chieftain's wife gave birth to a son and named him Timur. It was 1336.

Timur, not without plotting and intrigue, succeeded his father and was crowned king, or "Khan", of the tribe, in 1369, when he was thirty-three. By this time he had conquered a number of other small Mongol clans and was lord of a considerable territory. He had also been badly wounded in the foot by an arrow so that he became, in the Mongol language, *Timur-i-leng*, or "Timur-the-Lame".

In a very few years' time, when fame, notoriety, had spread westward, the European mispronunciations "Tamerlane" and "Tamburlane" would strike terror into the hearts of men.

His army, smaller than that of his predecessor—though it would soon be as large—was better armed, better trained. It could travel fantastic distances non-stop on its little ponies. It was heavily armed with spears, lances, maces, scimitars, both long bows and short; its soldiers wore finely meshed armour and pointed helmets.

It was supported by spies who went ahead and reported on the enemy before contact was made. It had gunpowder.

It was a formidable force. And yet the most powerful Mongol

group was not Timur's but the so-called "Golden Horde", an assortment of tribes which had banded together to ravage their neighbours. So great had been their success that they travelled from battle to battle bearing huge quantities of loot, earning for themselves a name which sowed envy and panic.

Timur resolved to defeat them, take away their power, their gold.

Fortune played into his hands. There was a quarrel in their ruling house and one of the princes, Toktamish, fled to the little court of Timur and demanded asylum. This Timur gave eagerly, and when the Khan of the Golden Horde demanded his return a highly convenient war broke out, with "underground" supporters of Toktamish supporting Timur's forces. Very soon Timur had overthrown the Golden Horde and placed Toktamish as his own puppet on the throne.

He now invaded Persia, where the proud city of Isfahan resisted him. When eventually it fell, he decided to use it to terrorize the rest of his enemies, present and future. He massacred the inhabitants, piling seventy thousand of their heads into one hideous pyramid beside the city wall. From here he pushed his army down to the Persian Gulf, on to Kabul and Kandahar, laying waste the country as he went. His armies also pushed westward into Europe, with Timur organizing and supporting as many as half a dozen different campaigns at the same time. One of these was soon directed against Toktamish, the puppet king of the Golden Horde, who had managed to raise a large force against him—men who resented this usurper from the once-humble tribe of *Barlas*. But Timur managed to defeat the Golden Horde this second time, to scatter it for ever. It was probably his greatest military feat—though it sounds small in comparison with the destruction of North India or of Persia—for the forces involved were the greatest in the world. At the end of the campaign the defeated tribes which had not been dispersed beyond recall, to end their days as bitter little groups moving aimlessly over the Asian plain, rallied to Timur and became part of his swelling Mongol Empire.

And so his progress, much of it mere senseless brutality, went on, rising to a bloody crescendo in the last half-dozen years of his life. He captured Baghdad: when it rose a little later in revolt against him, he ordered that each of the ninety thousand Mongol soldiers who had helped quash the rebellion bring him one enemy head. These, too, he piled in a pyramid, before turning towards India, going down through the Khyber Pass, sacking the cities of Meerut and Multan on the way. Once on the Indian plain, he was faced, as Alexander had been, with the new weapon of war—elephants: the master tactician and strategist lured the ruler of Delhi and his elephants out into the open where the little Mongol cavalrymen could manoeuvre. The Indians were easily overcome and Timur captured their elephants, taking them back in triumph to Samarkand, bearing the spoils of India, leaving behind him utter devastation. India had been ruled for several hundred years by Muslims—followers of the same, Islamic, faith as Timur—but he destroyed this ruling house, massacring its Hindu and Muslim subjects indiscriminately, and made no effort to replace it with anything else. All he had wanted from India was loot: as a territory it was too far away, too inaccessible, to add permanently to his dominions.

(It was over a hundred years before a new ruling house established itself in India. Then, at the start of the sixteenth century, another band of Central Asian Mongols, with the blood of Timur, and of Genghis, and of Kublai Khan, flowing in their veins, set up a great Indian empire, the Mongol, or "Mogul", Empire.)

This reluctance on the part of Timur to consolidate so many of his conquests saved many kingdoms and cultures in Europe and Asia. After his victorious sweep across North India, he turned west again to attack the Turks (who as descendants of another Mongol chief, Osman, or "Ottomans", had overrun Asia Minor) and also the Egyptians. He swept across their lands, capturing the Turkish capital of Brusa, sacking Damascus, inexplicably sparing Jerusalem. In the first year of the fifteenth century, Timur was standing with one foot in South-east Europe.

He turned back again, to Samarkand, the city he loved; and Europe and Christianity were spared. By now, well over sixty years of age, he had become obsessed with beautifying Samarkand, so that it might outshine the beautiful and opulent cities with which his travels had brought him in contact. He sent for craftsmen and artists from these lands and set them to work as masons, wood-carvers, sculptors, goldsmiths in Samarkand. He had definite ideas of his own, and impressed his own sombre taste on all their work. Soon Samarkand was one of the wonders of the world, with vast palaces, handsome dwellings, innumerable monuments, all of them covered with ornate and sometimes beautiful carved work in stone, wood and precious metals.

Still the urge to conquer was with him. He began, in 1402, planning the conquest of China. This strange Eastern land had already been subjugated by Mongols: Kublai Khan had set himself up as first emperor of the "Yuan" dynasty. He had been a wise and good emperor and during his reign China became more powerful than ever before or since, extending from the Dnieper River to the Pacific Ocean, from the Arctic Ocean to the Straits of Malacca. But after Kublai's death the Mongols had been thrown out and replaced by the native "Ming" dynasty. Now Timur resolved to regain China.

As we have seen, he was capable of conducting several campaigns at the same time, and while he was laying plans for the Chinese assault he attacked and defeated Turkey.

But at last, in 1405, Timur-the-Lame set off for China. And it was during the journey that he was overtaken suddenly by a violent illness and died—much as his ancestor Genghis Khan had done—and in the course of a similar expedition.

Indeed, there are many points of resemblance between the two great Mongol conquerors. Both were helped greatly, as youths, in the early establishment of their power, by the loyalty and bravery of womenfolk, mothers and sisters who planned and intrigued for their advancement. Both men loved fighting for fighting's sake, caring less for territorial expansion than for loot and the smell of battle. Both were followers of Islam, but whereas Timur was devout, almost bigoted, Genghis Khan had been easy-going in matters of religion and encouraged absolute freedom of worship throughout his vast empire. Both combined great personal bravery with an absolute ruthlessness: between the pair of them, the numbers massacred must have exceeded the total bag of any hundred other conquerors in history.

The conquests of Timur make those of Napoleon and Caesar insignificant, for he had every attribute to which a commander can aspire: he was brave, hardy and incredibly strong; he understood the minds not only of his own men but of his enemy; he was a master tactician and strategist. In the brief intervals between campaigns he would indulge himself in long hours of chess, sometimes against relays of opponents—and he always won. Chess is not a fast game, but Timur adapted his chess moves to the field of battle and played them at speed. One of his favourite maxims was: "It is better to be on time, at the right place, with ten men, than late with ten thousand." Another, still more characteristic, perhaps, was: "Might is right."

With the death of Timur, as with that of Genghis, the Mongol Empire relapsed into warring factions. Thanks to Kublai Khan, it had recovered after Genghis; after Timur it was finished.

SIGISMUND

(1368–1437)

THE DEATH of Charles IV, Emperor of the Holy Roman Empire, King of Bohemia, on 29 November, 1387, marked the end of an epoch. Wise, clever, ruthless, Charles had brought prosperity to Bohemia and had founded the University of Prague. He has been called the last splendid embodiment of the Middle Ages.

His garish funeral at Prague was lit with touches of half-barbaric medieval chivalry—the five hundred and sixty-four black knights with huge smoking candles pounding the January dawn to the wild and doleful music, the columns of slouching monastics, the ten sombre horsemen proudly bearing the banners of the ten lands ruled over by the dead emperor, who followed upon his bier, magnificently crowned, wrapped in purple and gold, splendid rings glittering upon his white-gloved hands, his great black beard gleaming in the smoky dawn—more regal in death than he was in life, when he had not been an impressive-looking man.

Behind the splendid corse and the sea of banners walked ten-year-old Sigismund, destined to be more famous than his formidable father, though now he was second to his 26-year-old brother, Wenceslas, upon whom the purple fell after the death of his father, and who had already been elected king of the confederation of German states, which carried with it the title of emperor, with a power which was only nominal. An emperor who wished to wield the powers implicit in this ancient Roman title had to seize them and force his will upon his widely scattered empire which bridged the Alps and stretched down to Italy and the Mediterranean.

Wenceslas was not made of this stern stuff and failed to reach the high standard of his father. He had a greater passion for hunting than for statecraft, and was so fond of his hounds that he took them to his bed, and there was a story that his first wife, Johanna of Bavaria, was bitten to death by one of them. He was a perverse man. He took to drink and would roam the streets at night and break into houses and violate the wives of respectable citizens. A cook whose roast did not meet with his approval was himself roasted upon the spit by Wenceslas.

Discontent at his incompetence, perfidy and continual absence from the seat of government, lost him the empire. One by one its cities and territories turned against him, and in 1400 the Rhenish electors declared him deposed and elected Rupert III, Count Palatine of the Rhine, in his place.

It was an age of cruelty, cunning and treachery. The only rulers who survived the jungle of those medieval monarchies were those who exercised the most cunning, the most ambition and the most ruthlessness, and in the exercise of these unlovely but necessary qualities Sigismund far excelled his elder brother.

Sigismund had grown up something of a dazzling figure. Tall, slim, he had a fine face—a splendid nose, deep-set eyes and a long, forked, well-cared-for beard. He was every inch the stop-at-nothing king of medieval legend—a great hunter, a great drinker, a great womanizer, without morals but possessing a fierce religion, cultivated and cruel, charming and ambitious, greedy and faithless. A great orator, he could speak fluently in seven languages. His domestic life was something of a scandal even in those dissolute times. He had mistresses even before he was in his teens. His beautiful second wife, Barbara, Countess of Cilly, exerted an extraordinary influence over him, and was just as licentious as he was, openly seeking lovers for herself while he was womanizing.

Sigismund had become the Margrave of Brandenburg on his father's death, and had been educated at the Hungarian court which he had scandalized with deeds of amour not usually associated with schoolboys. He was crowned King of Hungary in 1387, after a series of dynastic murders over the succession, sharing the crown with his first wife Mary, who was heir to the throne and who died in 1395.

While brother Wenceslas, with his mixture of perversity and stupidity, was gambling away the imperial family inheritance, Sigismund's time was occupied in trying to hold the unstable throne of Hungary, and also in holding in check the Turks who took advantage of the state of affairs in Hungary to invade the country.

This resulted in a crusade against the infidel being proclaimed by the Pope Boniface IX, and Sigismund presented something of a shining image by leading the combined armies of Christendom against the Turk. Nobles and knights, distinguished adventurers, war-loving princelings flocked in their thousands from every part of Europe to fight under the banner of the Cross which Sigismund held aloft in Hungary. Insubordination in this motley army of individualists and quarrels with the Pope, rather than lack of generalship on Sigismund's part, was responsible for the defeat of the forces of Christendom in 1398. Sigismund then fell back upon a defensive policy for Hungary, with more success.

Sigismund now turned his attention to the more attractive proposition of succeeding his childless brother, Wenceslas, as emperor. But Wenceslas had thrown away the great family heritage while Sigismund had been fighting the Turk, and had already been deposed. Sigismund never forgave his brother. He had to wait until Rupert III, who had succeeded Wenceslas, died in 1410.

During the intervening years Sigismund was busy with war and suppression. He returned to Hungary to put down popular uprisings due to the spread of the dangerous teaching of John Huss that all men were equal. To this wicked doctrine was added the heresy that man should worship God according to the dictates of his conscience—evils which had to be stamped out with every instrument of terror and oppression. Hungary was only cleansed of these satanic delusions after great slaughter, mainly the work of the Papal Inquisition which completely depopulated large areas of the country in the process.

Meanwhile Sigismund had been elected emperor in 1411 and he then addressed himself to putting right the great and terrible scandal which existed in the Church. During the fourteenth century the Popes had been residing at Avignon where they had reigned in opulent and magnificent state. In 1377 Urban VI was elected Pope and decided to return to the historic Papal seat at Rome. The College of Cardinals, who were mostly French, were so incensed that they elected another Pope and declared the election of Urban void. But Urban refused to be deposed, and so there were two Popes, each excommunicating the other, and each having his supporters in different countries.

This state of affairs so damaged the reputation of the Church and was creating such widespread anti-clericalism that the leaders of the Church met at the Council of Pisa in 1409. But they merely made matters worse by electing a third Pope. As neither of the other Popes recognized the authority of the Council, there were now three Popes each claiming the supreme power and authority of Christ's Vicar on earth.

The most dangerous result of this state of affairs was the heresy of Protestantism (though this name was not used until the time of Luther, a hundred years later). It was not a new discovery that many of the eternal truths taught by the Church were not to be found in the Bible. The thing which aroused so many people against the Church was the wealth, immorality and corruption of the clergy, which contrasted unfavourably with the life of Christ and His Apostles. Men like Wycliffe and Huss did more than ask questions to which the lax Church of their day had no effective answer. They did not so much want to reform the Church. They questioned the whole idea of Papal authority. The Great Schism merely underlined everything Wycliffe and Huss were saying. The Papacy indeed seemed to have the death-wish in the fifteenth century and did nothing to put its house in order until it was too late.

John Huss became one of the Protestants' great martyrs and none of those responsible for his martyrdom suffered more obloquy than Sigismund.

Huss became rector of the Bethlehem Chapel in Prague in 1402 and began violently attacking the immoralities of the clergy and challenging the authority of the Papacy itself. Weakened by the Schism, the Church found it difficult to deal with him, for whichever Pope tried to tackle him had enemies supporting one or other of his rivals, who were thus able to use Huss and his heresy as ammunition for the battle which was going on in the Church.

Wenceslas, though he had lost the empire, was still King of Bohemia, which was a more realistic and substantial sovereignty and which was inherited and could not be taken away from him by the German Electors.

Wenceslas, as did all rulers, supported one or other of the rival Popes, and he stood by Huss when the Prague clergy tried to bring him to book for heresy in the name of Gregory XII of Rome. Wenceslas did this merely because he was opposed to the Bohemian Church supporting this Rome Pope. Wenceslas used Huss as a pawn in his battle with his own clergy, supporting him in the teeth of their opposition. This kind of support, though it may have delayed his going to the stake, did Huss little real good.

Sigismund in the meanwhile was setting about the great task which was his most important historical act—the re-unification of Christendom by healing the Great Schism. For this purpose he persuaded John XXIII, who had succeeded the Pope elected by the Council of Pisa, to convoke the Great Council of Constance. In calling this Council Sigismund had to use all his powers of statesmanship and persuasion in order to get together the secular as well as the religious princes of Europe. Union of the Church must be brought about at any cost, he told them, and with this everyone agreed. The scandal of the triple Papacy could no longer be tolerated.

The Council of Constance met on 5 November, 1414, and lasted until 22 April, 1418. It was one of the most famous occasions in the history of Christendom. It was a vast and tumultuous assembly of prelates, monks, doctors of law, princes and ambassadors, and it was held in an atmosphere of incomparable splendour and uninhibited immorality which was remembered for centuries in the good city of Constance.

The most important act of the Council was the deposition of the three Popes and the election of a new one, Martin V, thus bringing to an end the Great Schism.

The Council had also been set up to deal with heresy in the Church, and Huss was summoned to appear before it. Huss agreed to go to Constance after Sigismund had promised him protection and a safe return to Prague. Sigismund was not foolish enough to imagine that once the Council had got Huss into their power that they would let him return free to Prague—if they found him guilty of heresy, which was a capital crime in the eyes of the Church. Sigismund has in fact been harshly criticized for an act of bad faith which cost Huss his life.

There are two points to be made in Sigismund's favour. Firstly, as an obedient son of the Church he would have committed a mortal sin himself if, the Council having found Huss a heretic, he had enforced his promise and returned Huss to Prague. Sigismund could, and did, argue that when he gave Huss his promise he did not know he was a heretic, and no good son of the Church could protect a heretic.

The second point is perhaps more important. Granted duplicity on Sigismund's part—there was evidence that Huss was a heretic before he promised him safe conduct—the life of Huss was of less importance than the reunion of Christendom. When Huss was first arrested at Constance, Sigismund threatened to release him by force, but the cardinals came to see him and gave him to understand that in their view the extirpation of heresy was even more important than healing the Schism in the Church. It may have been a bluff, but Sigismund was not prepared to risk a breach with the Church over Huss and have the work of the Council of Constance ruined. Huss was a pawn in the game, like so many others had been. But Huss was emotional dynamite in the centuries to come, and so Sigismund's reputation in history—at least so far as Protestant countries are concerned—was ruined.

Some reports say that Huss was sentenced to death in the presence of Sigismund, others that he was absent from Constance during the martyrdom. It makes no difference. Sigismund had made it plain that he was not prepared to lift a finger to save a heretic from the flames.

In fact after the death of Huss, Sigismund sent a manifesto to his brother Wenceslas demanding vigorous action to suppress the Hussite movement in Bohemia. Huss was supported by many knights and nobles in Bohemia, who sent a letter to the Council of Constance, condemning Huss's execution in the strongest terms. Sigismund was also violently denounced for his part in Huss's death. Disturbances broke out and in the middle of them Wenceslas had a fit of apoplexy and died.

This left Sigismund the titular King of Bohemia, but it was seventeen years before his estranged subjects would acknowledge him. Meanwhile violent fighting broke out in Bohemia and the long trail of bloodshed began as Queen Sophia, the widow of Wenceslas, whom Sigismund had deputed to rule, tried to put down the Hussites, but in vain. Sigismund, reviled as the betrayer of Huss, was unable to get the support of the German princes for his war against the Bohemian heretics, and a Papal crusade against them was without success.

An important element in Sigismund's utter failure in Germany was the attitude of the German princes, who wanted to strengthen their power at the expense of his, and who were moving away from the Papal orbit, whatever sympathy they might or might not have had with Huss's teaching. In the spread of Protestantism lay the key to their independence, as they discovered in the coming century.

Whatever his failures in Germany, Sigismund succeeded in Hungary where he established good government and introduced many prudent political reforms. After the abortive crusade against the Turk, he changed his tactics and organized such excellent defences against the invaders that Hungary was able to keep them at bay for decades to come.

He became King of Lombardy in 1431, was crowned emperor by the Pope in 1433, and recognized, though only nominally in Bohemia, where he was never forgiven, in 1436. He died at Znaim in Bohemia in 1437 in his sixty-ninth year, and has gone down in history as one of the few far-sighted rulers in a century of unenlightened princes.

HENRY V (OF ENGLAND)

(1387–1422)

ON SUNDAY, 11 August, 1415, a great armada of fifteen hundred ships put to sea from creeks and harbours facing the Isle of Wight and headed towards France. From a clear sky a hot sun poured down on brightly painted bulwarks, sails embroidered with heraldic beasts, pennons, helmets, shields and the glossy rumps of horses.

From the masthead of the king's flagship flew a banner representing the three persons of the Trinity and the arms of St. Edward, St. George and England. A crown of copper-gilt shone on the top-castle. On board the fleet were 2,000 men-at-arms and 8,000 archers, about 25,000 horses and a large number of specialists— miners, carpenters, armourers, smiths, gunners—as well as members of the king's retine which included fifteen minstrels. The baggage was enormous. Each man-at-arms had his suit of armour and personal weapons—sword, dagger and mace or hatchet—each archer had his long-bow and forty to fifty arrows of which a reserve stock was also carried. There were tents and all their equipment for the king and his senior nobles, the royal beds, the royal cutlery of silver, crowns and boxes of jewels. In the holds were stored massive siege equipment, gunpowder for the artillery and siege-guns, some of which measured two feet across the mouth.

As the fleet manoeuvred out of the Solent, three ships caught fire. This was considered a bad omen and timid advisers urged the king not to sail with his troops. But he ignored them. He had made his will, his clergy had given a unanimous blessing on the enterprise, he was convinced that he was about to fight in God's cause and had no doubt of its justice.

The cause was to take possession of Normandy in absolute right—territory held to be the domain of English kings since William the Conqueror—and also to lay claim to the throne of France, asserting a right of succession through Henry's great-great-grandmother Isabella, wife of Edward II and daughter of King Philip IV of France. The claim had first been raised by his grandfather, Edward III, and already the English nation looked

331

back on nearly eighty years of sporadic warfare in France which had left Edward III as sovereign over one-third of the country. But some of his gains had since been lost, lands still held in France were not conceded by the French as absolute possessions and the royal throne was as distant as ever. To Henry V, young, tested in battle against the Welsh, with his warrior's soul, his realistic, calculating mind, his ambition, his trust in heaven, this situation proved an irresistible lure. A glorious achievement, sealing his grandfather's labours, gleamed ahead. Behind, still within the memory of old men, shone the magnificent victories of Crécy and Poitiers. Afire with militant piety, the king even dreamed, once France was under his sway, of leading Western Europe in a crusade against the Infidel.

But he was not trusting only in God and his strong right arm. His hopes were based on practical realities. In France rival factions distracted the country. Since 1380, the feeble, vicious and demented Charles VI had been on the throne, but for many years the real power had been disputed between Louis of Orleans, the king's youngest brother, and John, Duke of Burgundy, his cousin. In 1407, Orleans had been murdered at the instigation of the Duke and the rivalry between their parties had flared into bitter hatred. The Orleanist cause was supported by royal dukes and their hopes centred on the Dauphin, a sickly boy whom they expected in due course to dominate as they dominated his father. Meanwhile, their power was threatened by the Duke of Burgundy who apart from the Duchy ruled wide tracts of land in northern France and, through marriage, most of what are now Belgium and Holland. With both parties Henry had negotiated, fruitlessly, as he expected and perhaps intended, with the Orleanists and more hopefully with the duke, whose hatred of the Orleanists was matched by a desire to maintain friendship with England because his Flemish weavers were dependent on English wool. Henry could count on his neutrality, if not on his active help.

Behind him Henry left a kingdom more secure than ever it had been in his father's time. Henry IV had been a usurper and spent most of his reign, until disease enfeebled him, quelling revolt at home, in Wales, in Ireland and invasion from Scotland. From the age of sixteen his son had helped him in his task, acting as the King's Lieutenant in Wales against Owen Glendower, leading the charge against Henry Hotspur at the battle of Shrewsbury and, after rebellion had been crushed, sharing in government as a member of the Royal Council, as Warden of the Cinque Ports,

Constable of Dover and Captain of Calais. He still found time, it was said, for riotous living, being "in his youth a diligent follower of idle practices, much given to instruments of music and fired with the torches of Venus herself". But responsibility brought out the iron in his temperament and his coronation banquet presented a symbolic picture: amid the revelry and feasting the twenty-five-year-old king sat remote with a serious expression, not touching the food. This set a note of intensity for the new reign. Henry felt sure of his heritage and sure of himself. His courteous but purposeful demeanour aroused admiration and loyalty. His appearance was impressive: smooth, oval face, a long, straight nose, full lips, a powerful jaw and hazel eyes, normally mild as a dove's, but blazing when in anger. Behind them men sensed an unconquerable spirit and they remembered his ancestors, Edward III and the Black Prince.

> *You are their heir; you sit upon their throne;*
> *The blood and courage that renowned them*
> *Runs in your veins; and my thrice puissant liege*
> *Is in the very May-morn of his youth,*
> *Ripe for exploits and mighty enterprises.*

At home, in the first months of his reign he felt strong enough to release from imprisonment the young Earl of March, rightful heir of Richard II. But on the Lollards, descended from the "poor preachers" of John Wycliffe, his hand fell heavily. These men, proclaiming the supremacy of the individual conscience, became allied to political revolt and were regarded with terror by contemporaries. We should call them Christian Communists. Their offence was heightened by their attitude to articles of faith dear to the pious and it was their declared policy to plunder the Church. They seemed to threaten the very fabric of the State. They had been persecuted under Henry IV and the process was intensified by his son. Armed demonstrations were crushed and their leader, Sir John Oldcastle, a former companion in arms of the king, was executed. For a Lollard the alternatives were clear: renunciation of his heresy or the stake. These severities enabled Henry to sail for France with a reasonable assurance that the country was secure behind him.

The crossing took three days and early on 14 August the troops began to disembark at the mouth of the Seine near Harfleur. It was a professional army, not a medieval levy, indentured for service and paid at regular rates. But it was not homogeneous. Besides English, there were many Welshmen, Irishmen, Gascons and other foreigners in the ranks and to control his force the king imposed strict discipline.

Harfleur, valuable as a base from which to advance into Normandy or towards Paris, was in a naturally strong position on the north side of the Seine estuary. The only possible approach was from the south-west, but a wide moat, an alert and enterprising garrison and heavily strengthened defences made attack difficult even from this quarter. For a month the siege went on in broiling heat, while dysentery scourged the army, killing or putting out of action more than two thousand of the troops. Henry's miners tunnelled and the French countermined. Their men-at-arms made damaging sorties. English siege-guns hurled huge stones at the walls—and as fast as they crumbled the French repaired them. All this time the king worked as hard as any of his men, planning, supervising, inspecting, encouraging.

Finally, short of food and ammunition and closely beset at the south-west gate, the garrison surrendered, and Henry, clothed in royal gold, enthroned in a silken tent on a hill-top, received the keys of the town from a delegation wearing shirts of penitence with ropes round their necks. He told them they had withheld his town of Harfleur from him in defiance of God and all justice. Nevertheless he would be merciful. An English garrison was installed. The inhabitants were allowed to remain provided they took an oath of allegiance; gentlemen of wealth were required to ransom themselves, and only the infirm, the aged and the very young were turned out of the town—useless mouths, a source of weakness to the garrison. This was considered just by the standards of the time.

The troops available for further operations were now reduced to 900 men-at-arms and 5,000 archers. A march on Paris was out of the question. There remained three possible courses: to go home, to enlarge the district around Harfleur, or to march inland, regardless of resistance offered, as a demonstration of the royal claims. The last was obviously a dangerous course. The whole force might be destroyed, the king killed or captured. Nevertheless, against the strong advice of his war council, he chose it. He had already challenged the Dauphin to single combat for the throne of France and received no answer. To go meekly home now, or to sit at Harfleur would be to abandon his cause, which he believed was also God's. "Even if our enemies", he said, "enlist the greatest armies, my trust is in God, and they shall not hurt my army or myself. I will not allow them, puffed up with pride, to rejoice in misdeeds, or unjustly, against God, to possess my goods. . . . I have a mind, my brave men, to encounter all dangers. . . ."

So, on 6 October, the king with his small army, mostly on foot, set out, heading near the coast towards Calais, 160 miles away. This was not to be a pillaging expedition. The inhabitants and their property were to be respected and the troops were not to take anything beyond essential food.

Days passed almost without incident. Cannon fire from the towers of Arques, south-east of Dieppe, was met by a warning from the king that he would burn the town if resistance was offered. Twenty miles farther on, at Eu, a sortie by French men-at-arms was driven back and the troops calmly encamped for the night beyond the town. Thirteen miles ahead lay the River Somme and the ford Blanche-Taque which Edward III had crossed and Henry now looked forward to finding guarded by English troops which he had ordered to be detached from Calais.

Then, six miles from the river, came disastrous news from a solitary French prisoner, quickly confirmed by Henry's scouts. The ford was guarded on the far bank not by Englishmen but by a force of six thousand French. . . .

Incredibly, this French force had come up from nearly a hundred miles away to the south and got to the ford before the English. There was nothing for it now but to turn back to Harfleur or march east up the left bank of the Somme to find another crossing-place. The army marched east, but faced with an uncertain route and a strong enemy ahead spirits began to falter.

More disappointments were in store. Upstream at Abbeville the bridge over the Somme was guarded and French troops were in force on the far side. The little army slogged on and every crossing proved impassable, either destroyed or strongly defended. Rations were running short. The men were living on walnuts and dried meat. And every step they took was leading them farther away from Calais and safety. Now, avoiding a northward bend in the river, the king took them still farther eastwards, to a point near the headwaters of the Somme. The archers were marching with the increased burden of stakes, sharpened at both ends, which the king had ordered to be cut down and used, planted in the ground, against cavalry attacks. At last, two unguarded fords were found and the army, with its horses and baggage, was able to cross entire. That night the men went to sleep in good spirits. No major obstacle, they believed, now lay between them and Calais.

But at that moment, six miles away to the north, a French army of 24,000 men was entering the town of Péronne. This huge force had come from two directions: a part from Blanche-Taque and another north-east from Rouen, where King Charles VI and his Dauphin had sped its departure. United, the royal dukes, the flower of French chivalry, had only one aim: to bring the English to battle and destroy them. Heralds were sent to King Henry to inform him of this and inquire his route. He replied without anger or fear: "Straight to Calais".

21 October. It was raining heavily as the English resumed their march, north-west, towards the coast. The French army was no longer in Péronne, but a mile outside a cross-roads churned by thousands of feet showed that it had moved east to advance parallel to the English. They gazed on these "strangely trodden" tracks with awe and the chaplains prayed earnestly that God would turn away the power of the French.

Three days later, fifty miles farther on, a scout descended at full gallop from a hill-top and reported: in the valley beyond, the French like "an innumerable host of locusts" were streaming inwards towards the Calais road to cut off the advance.

The king remained calm, committed himself and his army to God and deployed his men on a ridge facing the enemy. It was there that, in his hearing, a knight expressed longing for 10,000 more archers and the king rebuked him. He would not, if he could, increase his number by one. "For those whom I have are the people of God, whom He thinks me worthy to have at this time. Dost thou not believe that the Almighty, with these His humble few, is able to conquer the haughty opposition of the French?"

But there was no battle that day. The light would soon fade and fighting in the dark was no part of medieval tactics. The French had formed into line of battle, but now they moved off in columns again until, like an unwieldy centipede, they came to rest athwart the Calais road and encamped for the night near a place called Agincourt.

Half a mile away, Henry billeted his men in a village. But many had to sleep in the open, exhausted and hungry under almost continual rain. Next day, the Feast of St. Crispin and Crispinian, they expected to die. Earlier, the camp had been noisy, until under dire penalty the king enjoined silence. All the greater seemed the clamour of the French as it drifted across the fields. Their fires burned brightly. Knights sat dicing and drinking on bundles of straw. Servants bustled, shouting, to and fro. At the back of their camp it is said that there was a brightly painted cart in which they intended to parade the captured English king through Paris.

Henry certainly would not be captured alive, but, outnumbered by over four to one, he doubted despite his brave words that victory was possible. Negotiators were sent to the French seeking a free road to Calais in return for the surrender of Harfleur, but the bargain was rejected. So the night wore on, the only sounds in the English camp the clanging of armourers' hammers, the murmuring of priests as they gave the men absolution. The king, too, must surely have moved amongst them, as he had done earlier in the day, "animating them with his intrepid demeanour and consoling expressions".

25 October, 1415. With the daylight both armies slowly moved into position, one thousand yards apart. At the north end of a field sown with young corn and flanked by woods the French formed three lines of battle, each five or six men deep, the first two lines consisting of dismounted men-at-arms and the third line of horsemen. On each flank a body of six hundred cavalry was stationed. Crossbowmen and gunners completed the array. To the south, the English had troops only for a single line of men-at-arms, four men deep, divided into three divisions interspersed with wedge-shaped clumps of bowmen with more archers on the wings. The centre was commanded by the king, resplendent in a suit of shining armour and a surcoat embroidered with the arms of England and France.

Priests were brought to the fore and told to pray continually. Henry received the Sacrament, then put on his gold-plated helmet surmounted by a gold crown studded with jewels. He addressed his troops, reminding them of former victories, of the justice of his cause and that at home in England wives, children and parents awaited their return covered with glory. "Sir," they replied, "we pray God give you a good life, and the victory over your enemies."

For four hours the armies faced one another, the French well knowing that the English would have to attack that day or else perish from cold and hunger. So at eleven o'clock Henry gave the order to advance and the whole line moved forward to within bowshot range, which at extreme distance was three hundred yards. A hail of arrows descended on the French and stung their cavalry into a charge.

The English long-bow now came into its own. Not until the American Civil War were there weapons of equal range and accuracy. At two hundred and fifty yards a skilled archer could lodge his shaft in the eye-slit of a knight's helmet and he could fire an arrow every ten seconds. As the heavy cavalry rolled forward, riders and horses were shot down pell-mell. Many that reached the archers were impaled on the stakes which had been planted slant-wise in the ground and the whole attack broke up in confusion, riderless horses plunging back into the front line of French men-at-arms now lumbering slowly forward in full armour towards their English opponents.

A situation disastrous to the French now developed. A knight required space in which to wield his weapons, but the French started their advance too closely packed and to protect themselves, as they thought, against the archers they formed into columns yet more dense. The arrows took a murderous toll. Outside ranks pressed in towards the centre and when the French reached the English men-at-arms many found themselves barely able to lift an arm. Their impetus dented the front, but then those pressing from behind knocked them over and, unable to get up, they were clubbed to death where they lay. The English rallied and soon corpses in their hundreds were piling up before the line. Then the archers from the flanks, a shrilling, tattered throng, dropped their bows and picking up abandoned weapons started hacking nimbly in the unwieldy mass. The heaps of killed, suffocated and wounded grew higher and higher. The French second line came forward, suffered the same fate and an hour after the battle began the fighting had ceased and the English were sorting out the prisoners.

Some time later, while the English were still busy with their prisoners, a party of marauders broke into the baggage train at the rear and a dangerous situation arose. The French third line of cavalry had so far not moved and was watching the scene from afar. If it attacked now the English scattered over the field might be caught in front and rear and some of those French knights still lying on the ground might be helped to their feet and start slaughtering their captors. To avoid this possibility, which might turn victory into disaster, Henry ordered all prisoners to be killed. This has since been described as a "cruel butchery", but contemporary writers were not so severe.

But the French horsemen withdrew from the field and, after this alarm, the search for plunder filled the rest of the day. Evening saw King Henry at table in the nearby village, modestly ascribing the victory to God, and next day, having killed eight thousand of the enemy in battle to their own loss of a few hundreds, his troops marched forward, booty-laden and escorting fifteen hundred prisoners, all of them nobles, on the road to Calais.

338

The glittering victory of Agincourt marks the high-point of Henry's career. It made him, says Sir Winston Churchill, "the supreme figure in Europe". Thereafter, in further campaigns, he subdued all of Normandy and his position was consolidated by Charles VI who, in 1420, recognized him as heir to the Kingdom of France and regent during his life. To seal the compact, he married Charles's daughter, Catherine, and it seemed possible that all of Western Europe might become united under his sway in a Crusade against the Heathen.

But in 1422 Henry died in France, probably of dysentery, while his nominal regency was still far from established in fact and thereafter, until the Hundred Years' War came to an end in 1453, English military fortunes fluctuated in France until the intolerable scourge of war created a national spirit and the Maid of Orleans brought about a turning of the tide.

Harfleur was finally lost in 1449, Rouen in the same year, Normandy in 1450, and at last the English were driven off the Continent and left with only one possession—Calais. Two years later, England plunged into civil war yet more murderous, more destructive of life than the long and fruitless campaigns in France.

So perished the vision of Henry V. But there is left a picture of a true Englishman inspiring to all generations, a brilliant soldier, an able organizer, a sound diplomatist, in the words of the historian Stubbs: "Splendid, merciful, truthful and honourable; discreet in word, provident in counsel, prudent in judgement, modest in look, magnanimous in act." No king in English history has been so dearly loved.

LOUIS XI

(1423–83)

TRAVELLING IN the French kingdom became safe again around 1447, for the first time since over a hundred years, when the English invasions and other disorders had destroyed the king's peace. Charles the Bold, Duke of Burgundy, the last and greatest enemy of the French kings, died in that year, leaving no male heir. His Duchy reverted to the French crown.

Many travellers on the roads of that time were liable to meet a cortège consisting of a few mounted Swiss archers, a few men-at-arms bringing up the rear and, in the middle, riding on a mule, a little man with very thin legs and a long crooked nose. He would be dressed in a coarse cloth, with a large fur-lined hat from which was suspended a number of little medallions of saints. With him would be four or five companions also soberly dressed. The unknowing traveller would have stared curiously at what might have been a well-protected party of merchants. But if the traveller had known it was King Louis XI of France he would have trembled.

The king was not majestic but he was terrible. Everyone had heard of "the King's Orchard" at Plessis-les-Tours, near Amboise, where the bodies of the king's enemies swung to and fro from the branches of trees, of the château itself with its powerful fortifications and look-out points, its packs of dogs and its iron cages in which other enemies of the king were shut up to waste away slowly. Unless the king was in a great hurry, the traveller might well be summoned to speak with him and he would meet someone who was like a man of business, easy and jocular in discourse, who would ask a number of practical questions—if he thought the traveller had any useful knowledge about the state of farming, the kind of industries and crafts of the neighbourhood, the best kinds of wines and food.

For King Louis XI went about his country informing himself ceaselessly. No king cared less for ceremony or appearance: when he reached a town, he often entered it by a back street, to the confusion of the mayor and the notables of the district waiting for him. At Tours once when a great mystery play had been prepared for his entertainment, and the painter Nichols Fouquet had designed a

340

special backcloth, the king refused to attend and said he took no pleasure in such things.

His court was very boring no doubt for the nobility, and though on occasions the king gave a great fête, this was rare. The king himself was liable to be found on a Sunday after mass eating in a tavern. He took pleasure in drinking with some of his advisers and counsellors who were drawn from the middle classes, and with these, seated between their flattered wives, drinking and exchanging coarse jokes, the king seemed at his happiest. At his house in Paris—he never lived in the royal palace of the Louvre—and at Plessis-les-Tours men of all sorts were summoned to meet him. Many of these were paid agents or royal spies; and the king kept a huge number of dossiers concerning the lives and habits of his important subjects. He admitted to boundless curiosity. To a friend he wrote: "I have a woman's nature; when someone tells me something in obscure terms, then I must know, at once, what it means."

In the hundred years from the middle of the fourteenth century to the middle of the fifteenth, French civilization had all but been destroyed. The wars with England which began in 1340, with Edward III's naval victory at Sluys and his first invasion of France, war had indeed only been intermittent; but the armies had brought disorder and devastation and, when the armies were gone, the countryside and towns were terrorized by bandits, demobilized companies of men-at-arms, French and English, commanded by pirate captains. Anarchy affected a very large part of the kingdom—Normandy and Brittany, the whole south-west as far east as Rodez and Montpelier, all the north of France, the Paris region and the country around Orléans. In those parts of France which had been so prosperous and peaceful in the reign of St. Louis there were large regions where people lived in caverns, ate grass and roots and sometimes took to cannibalism. In the less affected parts, where agriculture continued in some fashion, bullocks, cows and even sheep learned by instinct to run for shelter behind the village walls when the church bell tolled the coming of marauders.

The first part of the war saw the great English victories of Crécy and Poitiers where the French nobility with out-of-date tactics were defeated by the smaller but more modern army with its long-bow archers. At Poitiers, the French king, John, was captured and spent the rest of his life in London. But by 1380, forty years after the war had begun, the English had been swept out of the country and lost all the rich provinces they had held before the war began. France in 1364 had had an able king in Charles V, who chose his advisers from men of ability. The French troops were led by Bertrand du Guesclin, who avoided pitched battles and used guerilla tactics against the English. The English ships were chased from the sea.

But thirty years later Henry V once more invaded France and once more the French nobility, who had learnt nothing, were completely defeated by the English at Agincourt. Ten thousand men fell in this battle, one of the bloodiest in the Middle Ages. When, two years later, Henry V invaded France from Normandy, the French king Charles VI was already mad and France was torn by a civil war between the king's brothers, the Dukes of Orléans and Burgundy. The latter, John the Fearless, sided with the English. When, in 1442, Charles VI and Henry V both died within three months of each other, the young child Henry VI, in Windsor, was proclaimed King of France. The Dauphin, "the King of Bourges", as he was called in mockery, gradually won back his crown, with the help of Joan of Arc. By 1450 the English were once more driven out of France, out of all but Calais, which Edward III had captured and peopled with Englishmen. They even lost the great port of Bordeaux.

Although a sense of patriotism had been born in these terrible wars and the Burgundians were now considered traitors, French unity based on the king in alliance with the Church and people, a king powerful enough to withstand the great nobles, was still to be restored. The great nobles indeed, and with them scores of lesser barons and knights, had been accustomed to doing as they wished during the hundred years of anarchy. Many of the great nobles claimed to be sovereign owners of their lands. Some such as the Duke of Brittany and the King of Provence were richer than the King of France. Above all the Duke of Burgundy, prince of the Blood Royal, was an independent sovereign of far greater power than his nominal overlord. His province of Burgundy had been relatively untouched by wars; and he owned also the more prosperous and civilized Low Countries to the north of France, with a capital at Brussels.

Nor was the King of France in the fifteenth century assured, as had been the old monarchs of France of the House of Capet, of the loyalty of the Church and the towns. After the first phase of the war with England, when King John had been captured, Paris and other cities had set up what had amounted to short-lived republics and there had been peasant risings in northern France. The Church, which in the twelfth and thirteenth centuries produced so many great philosophers and men of action, had lost her mission of scholarship and good works. There were two, and at one moment three, Popes in the fourteenth century. Religious feeling, though still ardent, had become superstitious in the extreme. It was the age of witch-hunting, when the civilized world listened to a German friar Sprenger with his violent admonitions against women and his capacity to arouse the crudest superstitious feelings.

The arts flourished in Italy and in Germany, but in France around 1450, when it was desired to repair the great bridge across the Loire at Orléans, not even a master mason could be found capable of such work. The art of building the great Gothic cathedrals was no longer found in the country which the Germans across the Rhine had, in the thirteenth century, thought of as God's country—"*Gott im Frankreich*".

1461 saw the English expelled from France and engaged in their own civil war—the Wars of the Roses. The Dauphin, whom Joan of Arc had succoured—the lazy, trifling, timorous Dauphin of whom it was said that when young he had the soul of an old man—reigned at last in peace. His spirit seemed to be reborn as a result of a liaison with a beautiful woman called Agnes Sorel. Charles VI, known as the Well Served, surrounded himself with wise and able counsellors, including the great merchant of Bourges, Jaques Coeur, and good soldiers such as Dunois and Richemont, who had fought side by side with Joan of Arc. He did much to restore the kingdom. Nevertheless, he was unable to tackle the major task of re-asserting the monarchy against the great nobles, and when the Duke of Burgundy refused to come to Paris to pay him homage he was obliged, out of prudence, to allow the duke to abstain from doing so. He had to fight a rebellion of other vassals and to see his own son, the Dauphin Louis, join the rebels. He had few illusions about Louis's loyalty, but he had some idea of his abilities. When Louis, after the rebellion, took refuge with the Duke of Burgundy, Charles said: "The Duke is harbouring a fox who one day will eat all his hens."

Charles suspected Louis of having poisoned Agnes Sorel. He also suspected that he himself in 1461 was the victim of his son when he died of a constriction of the throat and probably of a cerebral haemorrhage. He had never attempted to disinherit his son, a sign perhaps that the prescience of a king was stronger than the rancour of a man. King Charles's doctor was Louis's agent and had kept him informed about his father's health which, since 1457 when the king had suffered from a thrombosis of the leg, had been precarious. Louis had a mania for spying and plotting. He made no pretence about being anxious to succeed to the throne. But men everywhere in those days all too readily saw poisoning as parricide: Louis can almost certainly be acquitted.

Louis was thirty-eight on his father's demise. Still in exile, he dashed to Paris at once. His coronation was celebrated with great splendour, and his uncle, the Duke of Burgundy, attended it and even put the crown on the new king's head. The duke gave many sumptuous entertainments to citizens of Paris—where, since the beginning of the century, the Dukes of Burgundy had been popular. Yet, strangely enough, when the duke measured himself against his puny and undignified nephew he didn't succeed in getting his way. The men he proposed for important posts in the kingdom were politely set on one side. Someone asked Duke John, as he was leaving Paris, how he had enjoyed his stay. "I do not know," said the duke, "but it has pleased me so much that I am glad to be gone".

At the beginning of his reign King Louis XI threw down a challenge to all his powerful enemies. In the north he bribed the towns in Belgium which were claimed by Burgundy to declare for France. He deliberately offended the Duke of Normandy, the King of Provence and other powerful vassals by attempting to impose the royal authority. There was soon a League of the Public Good, as it was called, formed against him and, after a short, undecisive war, Louis was forced to promise his enemies all they asked. But he had, as it were, unmasked them. He learnt their secrets and weaknesses in the negotiations. The King of France suffered by being forced to make concessions; but the great nobles were exposed to the whole nation as self-seekers, enemies of unity. The king gained.

Louis never minded humbling himself for the moment. Fearing that the English, who were then at peace under Edward IV, might invade France in alliance with the Duke of Burgundy, Louis paid an annual tribute to the King of England and bribed some of his Ministers. He allowed Edward IV to call himself King of France without protest and even signed his letters to him as Prince Louis.

John the Fearless, Duke of Burgundy, died and was succeeded by Charles the Bold, a more bitter enemy of Louis than his father, proud, unbending, but, fortunately for Louis, devoid of a sense of the possible. Charles was grand and rash. In his long struggle with him, Louis made one mistake. Having bribed the duke to accept a temporary truce, he went to visit him at Peronne with a safe conduct. Alas for the king. Whilst he was the duke's guest the news came that Liège had revolted against Burgundy and that the revolt had been encouraged by Louis's agents. For a few days the king was caught in a trap. But he agreed he would go with Charles to suppress the rebels, and he had the humiliating experience of seeing the citizens of Liège crying "Vive le roi" just before they were butchered by Burgundian men-at-arms. Cardinal Balue, who had led the king into the trap at Peronne, was shut up in an iron cage at Plessis where he stayed for many years.

From all his misfortunes Louis learnt something which he put to account. Gradually, what with natural deaths, assassinations and seizures of lands, he broke the powers of the individual dukedoms and his rule bit by bit became unquestioned from the Pyrenees to the Low Countries, except for the great wound of Burgundy in the east. Charles the Bold was encouraged by Louis to go to war in Italy and with the Swiss. After two defeats at the hands of the Swiss, Charles the Bold met his death when he was trying to capture Nancy in eastern France, which he wished to make the capital of Lotharingia, a new kingdom embracing Burgundy and the Low Countries. By Salic law his only child, a daughter, could not inherit the royal duchy, though she kept Flanders, which was a private possession. Burgundy reverted to Louis. On the news of Charles's death it is said the king could not contain himself with joy. He took possession of Burgundy at once, bribing the duke's followers, executing those who made difficulties. Louis was called "the universal spider", and the largest and fattest fly had at last entangled himself in his web.

Louis devoted himself to the prosperity of his kingdom. To carry out his tasks he enlisted the more able administrators he could find abroad, including Englishmen and Scots, into his personal service. He invented the first postal system, carrying letters by fast post-chaises between the principal towns. He encouraged the nobility to enter trade. He started to reduce the customs barriers which existed between one province and another and often one town and another. He brought Italian artisans to settle in France and introduced the great silk industry to Lyons. He made it compulsory to develop minerals. He was no friend of the poor or needy and it was the rich merchants and bourgeoisie who profited from his reign. But what a tragedy it would have been for France if a more virtuous, but less able and unscrupulous, king had come to the throne in this bitter period when recovery was beginning and still unsure. The true value of his reign was not perceived until long after it had ensured for France a period of solidity and prosperity.

Louis did for France very much what Henry VII did for England.

Both were men of similar characteristics. But Louis's task was harder than that of the Tudor king, as it required a character which was so extreme as to be a sort of horror and a sort of wonder. Louis was extremely religious, but it was the religion of the base merchant not of the prince, and a matter of superstition rather than faith. He thought that God, the Holy Virgin and the saints could be bought to help him in his affairs as well as to guarantee him salvation. He even believed in bribing the saints of his enemies, and professed particular devotion to St. Claude, who was the patron saint of the Duke of Burgundy.

Like many great men Louis was an odd mixture of contrasts. With all his cunning he was extremely talkative and apparently indiscreet. Commines, a statesman and historian whom Louis seduced from the service of the Duke of Burgundy, records that Louis once said: "What harm my tongue has done me." He had few affections and treated his family badly. He had mistresses but none had any influence on him. He could never bear to be still, a characteristic reinforced by a skin disease he contracted in old age which he exacerbated by too much wine drinking. He was in appearance and manners anything but master of himself, yet master of his kingdom he certainly was. His energy was extraordinary—his skill at embroiling his adversaries remarkable as was his resolution. He was without conscience or pity.

For many years Louis had paid his doctor a large sum each month to look after his health, yet he also surrounded himself with quacks and astrologers. When he died at Plessis-les-Tours in 1483, probably of dropsy which was followed by two attacks of paralysis, he remained to the end master of himself—speaking, as Commines noted, "driely as though never ill and incessantly saying things which made good sense". Politics and prayer alternated. On his own orders he was buried, not in St. Denis, but very simply in a small church at Clery. Fifteen years after his death it was said of him that he was the most terrifying king France had ever had. He had certainly put all his diabolical qualities to good use.

MOHAMMED II (THE CONQUEROR)

(1429–1481)

THE TURKEY of today is a proud country—but it is in size a mere
fraction of the great empire of years gone by. At one stage this
"Ottoman Empire" embraced the whole Balkan peninsula, includ-
ing most of what are now Greece, Bulgaria, Rumania, Hungary,
Albania and Yugoslavia. Now only a small part of what remains
Turkish is in Europe: less than 10,000 square miles out of 296,000.

The rise of this Central Asian people is one of the most fascinating
tales in history. Unlike the Mongols who had come from the same
area, led by Genghis Khan and Tamerlane, men who entered
Europe and Asia Minor only to kill and plunder, the Turks stayed
behind to build. They were eager to learn from the more cultured
people they overran, and they consolidated their new empire,
made it strong. They were, on the whole, good to those they
conquered.

It was in the year A.D. 1000 that these nomads from the Asian
plain crossed the River Oxus under their leader Seljuk and swept
on down to the Anatolian peninsula between the Black Sea and
the Mediterranean. Their move had been forced upon them by
other tribes at their back; and soon, in their flight, they found
themselves up against the eastern boundary of the Byzantine
Empire. They were resisted and they fought the Emperor Romanus
and his forces, defeating him in 1071, advancing deep into Anatolia.

This, they decided, was where they would stay. They treated
the local Christians with respect, settled themselves around the
town of Konia, which became their capital.

They spent the remainder of the eleventh century consolidating
their position, dividing Anatolia into provinces, appointing a
ruler for each. While they were doing this they eagerly absorbed
what they could of the Greek and Persian cultures which had
preceded them. They began to build fine houses, adapting the
styles of these two civilizations to their own tastes and needs,
began to encourage all manner of art. They had arrived in Anatolia
as nature-worshippers, animists, but now they embraced Islam,
the religion of Allah and his Prophet Mohammed.

Like other empires, the Turkish one under Seljuk and his successors was destined to fade away: the Turks grew soft in their new environment and at the same time found themselves with too small a population to fill the administrative posts which were required to run an empire. The Seljuk empire withered.

But another branch of the same, Turkish, people, led by a man called Osman and variously called "Osmanlis" and "Ottomans", came to take their place. They, too, had been fleeing from Mongol tribes in Central Asia, and they settled with delight into the fertile Anatolian plain.

They remained, peaceably at first, under the control of the decayed Seljuk empire, but when one of its rulers, Ala-ed-Din, chose to select an Ottoman to be governor of the north-west of his territory, the newcomers began their process of assimilation. They grew rapidly in numbers and in strength, and by virtue of being hard-working and intelligent soon had numbers of the people around them working for them, as servants, artisans, farm managers. Like the Seljuks, the Ottomans had arrived in the area as pagans, and went on to embrace Islam, in the early fourteenth century. At the same time, they were prepared to tolerate Christianity as practised by the Greeks, and very soon they had absorbed many people from that older civilization. Ottoman mosques began to be built like Byzantine churches. The Greeks were allowed to worship in their own churches, but many of them, fed up with the controversies of medieval Christianity, embraced Islam.

The Greek city of Brusa was surrendered by its commander to the Ottoman Turks and this became their first capital. By now their eyes were turned firmly towards Europe and a policy began of conquest alternating with peaceful infiltration. Gradually the Turks spilt over into Europe, settling among the people, inter-marrying, following the example of their rulers who married European princesses.

Many of the people overrun in this way welcomed the Turks: the Bulgars greeted them with delight as a protection against their cruel Christian neighbours.

Within a few years the only part that remained outside the Turkish dominions—or, to be more accurate, inside it, but not subject to Turkish rule—was the city of Constantinople on the Bosphorus. There was no sign of its people, however feeble and decadent, handing over this capital of a once-great Roman Empire.

The Turks decided to take it.

But in 1402 their plans were rudely shaken. The Mongol Timur, or "Tamerlane", swept down into Anatolia: in July of that year a big battle was fought at Ankara, and the Turks were utterly defeated.

But—as we can see in the article on Tamerlane—the great Mongol's conquests were usually in the form of paralysing raids. He laid waste, took as much loot as his army could carry and made his way back to Samarkand. This is what he did in 1402, and the Turks were able to regroup and recover. It is interesting to note that the Greek and Slav prisoners who had been incorporated into the Turkish army made no attempt to desert or mutiny when that army was crushed by the Mongols. One of these contingents was the so-called "Corps of Janissaries", composed of conquered Christians. This had become one of the finest units in the Turkish army and would remain so for hundreds of years, until its disbandment.

There were other, smaller, Turkish communities in Asia Minor —for the Seljuks and the Ottomans had not been the only groups to flee from Asia. These little "Emirates" were peacefully absorbed, often by straightforward purchase, into the rapidly expanding Ottoman empire.

When the Sultan Mohammed II became ruler in 1451 he sat on the throne of a powerful empire extending to east and west of the city of Constantinople. Half a century before, his people had prepared to take it by force: Mohammed made plans to do so now. During the half-century the Turks had been content to leave this foreign outpost in their territory, much as the Chinese are prepared, for the moment, to tolerate Hong Kong, but with the accession of Mohammed II all that changed. He was a man of boundless ambition, soon to be known as "Al Fatih", or The Conqueror; he prepared to make this the first, the greatest, conquest of his reign.

He made sure of his flanks by diplomatically paying a visit to nearer Asia to sign a treaty with a rebellious Emir, and to Europe to do the same. Then he built a powerful fortress covering both sides of the Bosphorus. When the Emperor Constantine XI protested, Mohammed simply declared war.

Constantine was a brave man and with only eight thousand soldiers he refused to surrender against Mohammed's quarter of a million. The city was surrounded by water to north, east and south, projecting as it does from Europe into the Bosphorus. That on the north was a narrow inlet from the Bosphorus, the "Golden Horn". Landward defences were extremely strong, as were those covering the Bosphorus, and Mohammed, failing to breach any of these, tried to force his Turkish fleet into the Golden Horn. This was thwarted by a boom placed across the entrance by Constantinople's defenders.

Mohammed now performed the first of the military miracles for which he is famous. He decided to move his fleet *overland* from the Bosphorus into the Golden Horn.

His commanders assured him this was impossible. He brushed aside their objections.

A few days later a road was built, under his personal direction. It was rather more than a mile long and surfaced with wooden planks. It ran from a point on the Bosphorus north of the impregnable entrance to the Golden Horn and climbed a hill of almost three hundred feet to descend again to the narrows of the Golden Horn.

Regiments of men were put to work greasing it with animal fat.

A day later the defenders of Constantinople were appalled to see a Turkish fleet bear down on them from the north, overland. Each ship had sails spread and two men on board, at bow and stern, while other men drew it at the end of long ropes. Eighty large vessels had made their way overland in the course of a night, and now, as dawn broke, the last ones slipped silently into the narrow waters of the Golden Horn, a few hundred yards from the north wall of Constantinople.

The ships opened fire, and simultaneously the soldiers attacking overland, from the west, doubled the ferocity of their attack.

Despite this the defenders hung on gallantly, almost incredibly, for another seven weeks.

Mohammed's Christian Janissaries were his crack troops and these he kept in reserve until the very end. Then, at the head of them himself and shouting, "Advance, the city is ours!", he made his charge. Constantine, last of the Roman emperors, died gallantly commanding his defenders: Mohammed entered the town over his dead body.

It was 29 May, 1453.

The siege had been long with heavy casualties on both sides, and much of the city destroyed. But Mohammed, when the fighting had ended, did everything possible to ensure that what was worthwhile in the Byzantine Empire would be retained. A few institutions were altered and laws changed, but Greek names were kept and—by the standards of the day—respect was shown for the conquered. As against the plunder of Constantinople two centuries previously by the Christian Crusaders, hardly any looting took place—though, of course, Constantinople was by this time an impoverished city, with little to loot. Slaves were taken, but the Christian communities that remained were given full equality: the Greek patriarch was even crowned by Mohammed himself.

But despite this show of magnanimity, many of the learned men and scholars of Constantinople began to make their way westward, into Europe. It was Turkey's loss, but for Europe as a whole a tremendous gain, for these men re-lit the flame of scholarship which had been snuffed out by the coming of the barbarians, and carried it over a dark and decadent Europe.

Gradually everything worthwhile left Constantinople—the culture, the art, the learning—only the vice and corruption of an old and cynical city remaining.

Mohammed could see the process happening before his eyes, and he was saddened by it. He remembered the fate of the Seljuk Turks who had lacked capable administrators, and he implored the conquered Greeks and other nationalities to stay and help him run what he hoped would be the greatest, the wisest, empire in history.

As far as Constantinople was concerned, he had no success. But his consolidation of the rest of his empire was sound and he went on to make further conquests. The fleet which had so dramatically surprised Constantinople was doubled, trebled, in size and went on to become the "Scourge of South Europe". Greece was taken over in the five years between 1456 and 1460, and a few years later Mohammed The Conqueror entered Italy.

The Turkish, or Ottoman, Empire reached its greatest extent after the death of Mohammed, but he had shown the way. And to our present time there are men who talk of The Day the Ships Came Sailing Overland.

IVAN III (THE GREAT)
(1440-1505)

IT WAS once said that Russia occupies a greater place on the map than it does in history. This may not be true today, but it certainly was in the Middle Ages.

The peoples who originally settled in the vast lands of Russia were made up of many tribes—Slav, Norse, Hun, Balt, Turk and others. The Russian peoples adopted the Greek form of Christianity in the tenth century. They knew little of Europe to the west of them, but had frequent intercourse with Constantinople. This might have led to a rapid advance in civilization and culture—for Constantinople had guarded the learning which was then lost to Western Europe—but for a great historical catastrophe which set Russia back for centuries.

Lying squarely in the path of the Mongol hordes who swept in from the vast spaces of the east in the thirteenth century, Russia took the full force of this terrible human onslaught. Huge armies of savage horsemen under Batu Khan, one of the successors of Genghis Khan, invaded Russia about 1237, and ravaged the country with fearful slaughter and destruction.

Many of these Mongols settled in Russia and were known as Tartars (or Tatars). Among them was Batu himself. He pitched his magnificent, so-called golden, tent on the banks of the Volga and became the first Tartar Khan. His Tartars and their descendants were known as the Golden Horde.

The Russian princes were for a long time dependants of the Great Khan in China and had to make humiliating pilgrimages to his distant court, some three thousand miles away, and prostrate themselves before him. Both their crowns and their heads were frequently disposed of by this oriental despot and his successors.

The great Mongol Empire crumbled, but the Tartar occupation left its mark and the Tartars remained in Russia. The princes of Moscow imitated the khans rather than the western rulers of Europe, of whom they knew nothing. In their crude and barbarous court they adopted an Asiatic ceremonial and etiquette. Their manners, customs, dress and accoutrements of war were Chinese.

The name Czar, adopted by Ivan the Terrible in 1547, is Asiatic in origin, and is not, as many think, derived from Caesar. Russia did not become Europeanized until the time of Peter the Great.

Moscow emerged as the dominant Russian principality during the years 1240 to 1480 when Russia was under the yoke of the Golden Horde. Each prince of Moscow had to make a shameful journey to the Khan of the Golden Horde at the Tartar capital of Saray, near the mouth of the Volga, to receive investiture from the Tartar overlord. The khans regarded the Muscovite dukedom as the most important in Russia which led to the rise of Moscow. The Muscovite princes gradually extended their boundaries and became more and more powerful as the Tartars of the Golden Horde gradually declined, so that by the middle of the fifteenth century the Tartars were no longer capable of imposing their will on Moscow.

The Prince of Moscow who finally put an end to the Golden Horde and united all of Russia under his own rule was Ivan III, known as Ivan the Great. A hard-headed man of single purpose, he devoted his whole life to the goal of an all-Russia union to replace the existing confederation of princes which was both anarchic and inefficient.

The son of Vasily II, he was born in 1440, and was co-regent during the last few years of the reign of his father, who was blind. Vasily lost his sight in a manner typical of the times. In the early years of his reign he had to fight for his throne with his cousin Kosoy, who was seized and blinded at Vasily's orders. Ten years later Vasily fell into the hands of Kosoy's brother, who put his eyes out in revenge.

Ivan came to the throne on his father's death in 1462. He inherited a wild and backward state, whose progress had been stunted by the devastations of the Mongol invasions.

No country in Europe had suffered so much from these Asiatic hordes whose effect was to stultify every aspect of national growth. While the rest of Europe was progressing towards some kind of civilization and order, the principalities of Russia were under the yoke of an Asiatic oligarchy, which professed no religion at a time when religion was vital to man's progress,* whose past glory lay in senseless slaughter and destruction, and whose sole genius lay in war. Unlike other European intruders, they never assimilated with those they conquered, and were thus going against the stream of history.

*The Tartars later became Moslems.

Ivan went about the uniting of all Russia under his rule in a way which showed that he had a cool, strategic plan. His main military operation was to be against the Grand Principality of Lithuania, which in those days occupied roughly what is now the western part of the U.S.S.R.—Belo-Russia and the Ukraine.

Lithuania had largely escaped the Mongol invasions of the thirteenth century. The Lithuanians were a virile and powerful people who had peacefully infiltrated into the West Russian lands about the time of the terror of the thirteenth century, in a way which considerably benefited the inhabitants.

Before he undertook the task of annexing Lithuania, Ivan secured his other three fronts. The Golden Horde to the south was troublesome, though by now greatly enfeebled. To the east was the Khanate of Kazan, another Tartar horde, in the middle reaches of the Volga, independent of the Golden Horde in the south, more powerful and more dangerous to Moscow. To the north was the Republic of Novgorod, a large territory centring upon the prosperous trading city of Novgorod on Lake Ilmen. The city enjoyed a restricted kind of democracy, and its population was said to be in the region of 400,000 in the fourteenth century. It escaped the Mongol invasions, the hordes of cavalry being unable to cross the marshes which protected the city.

Ivan first turned his attention to Kazan. After preliminary incursions he began a full-scale invasion in 1469, but the campaign was only partially successful. After some indecisive fighting, Ivan's brother, Prince Yury, laid siege to the city of Kazan, which capitulated upon honourable terms when he cut the water supply. Ivan did not conquer Kazan, but at least neutralized it while he turned his attention to Novgorod and Lithuania.

Novgorod had many ties as well as differences with Moscow. Vasily II had died in the middle of one of these quarrels, and during the first eight years of Ivan III's reign relations worsened and tension mounted. Ivan's representatives were insulted at Novgorod. He had plenty of pretext for war.

Novgorod sought a military alliance with Casimir IV, King of Poland and Grand Prince of Lithuania, but Casimir did not respond, although Lithuania had always been on friendly terms with Novgorod. Casimir had no desire for war with Moscow, though he was willing enough to plot against Ivan.

Ivan invaded Novgorod in 1470 and obtained a speedy victory. He did not at first claim total sovereignty over the conquered Novgorodians but made them abandon their alliance with Poland

and Lithuania and cede to him a large part of their northern colonies.

With oriental patience Ivan then awaited a pretext to strip Novgorod completely of its independence. This occurred in 1477 over the apparently trivial matter of the Novgorodian ambassadors addressing him as "Sovereign" instead of "Sir". As there was a strong pro-Muscovite faction at Novgorod this was perhaps not significant. But when Novgorod repudiated its ambassadors' use of the title Sovereign, Ivan's troops once more set out for the obstinate city. Novgorod surrendered again and was forced to recognize Ivan as sovereign. Ivan then stripped it of every pretence of independence, and crushed a further show of resistance by removing one thousand of the most influential and wealthy families to Moscow and replacing them by powerful families from Moscow.

Thus Novgorod lost its proud independence, its wealth and its trade with Europe. It was forced to cut all its ties with the West and with the Hanseatic League. Several other minor principalities were also absorbed into Ivan's territories, either by conquest, annexation or marriage.

Ivan now turned his attention to his southern flank where he was faced with two Tartar khanates—that of the Golden Horde, or the Khanate of Astrakhan, whose ruler was named Ahmed; and the Khanate of Crimea, which included a large part of southern Russia as well as the peninsula of Crimea itself and which was ruled by Mengli Girey.

Fortunately for Ivan's plans, there was bitter rivalry between these two khanates. Ivan sought an alliance with Mengli, while King Casimir, no doubt divining Ivan's intentions upon his own territories in Lithuania, urged Ahmed to attack Moscow, promising that he would invade from the west.

The princes of Moscow had for centuries paid tribute to the khans of the Horde whose ancestors had conquered them. In 1476 Ivan flatly refused to do so, and curtly rejected Ahmed's claim of overlordship. In 1480 Ahmed's armies invaded the territories of his rebellious vassal, in the expectation that Casimir would support him by attacking Ivan's western flank. But Casimir had internal troubles of his own, and failed to fulfil his part of the bargain. His troubles were added to by the marauding attacks upon his provinces of Podolia (now South-west Ukraine) by the forces of Mengli Girey at the instigation of Ivan.

Ahmed lost his nerve. The two armed hosts glowered threateningly at each other across the River Ugra, and after a few skirmishes

Ahmed retired to the Volga where his practically undefended camp was attacked by the forces of an obscure Tartar chieftain from Siberia. Ahmed was killed and the whole operation against Moscow collapsed. The Golden Horde disintegrated. Ivan's hand was no doubt behind the raid on Ahmed's camp, and the act marked the end of Russia's two hundred and fifty years of subservience to the descendants of the conquering Mongols.

The year 1480 is a milestone in Russian history. It was the date when she emerged as a nation. Never again was a Prince of Moscow summoned before the once-dreaded ruler of the Golden Horde. Ivan III accomplished this historic victory mainly by diplomacy and with a minimum of military effort. He had plenty of trouble with the Tartars afterwards, but their yoke had been thrown off for ever.

For the next two decades Ivan occupied himself with the subjugation of Lithuania. King Casimir died in 1492, and his son, the Grand Prince Alexander, became the ruler of Lithuania.

Though fighting began in the 1490s in the form of border affrays instigated by the Muscovites, Ivan was busy in the diplomatic field before he sent his main armies in.

Alexander did not want war. He put out peace feelers, and suggested a marriage with Ivan's daughter Elena. He was left in no doubt that Ivan wanted back the Lithuanian territories which had originally been Russian. The marriage nevertheless took place at the Lithuanian capital of Vilna in February, 1485; after much haggling and argument between the contending parties, Elena, who had no say in the matter of course, obediently going to her fate to marry a man she had never seen. Her fate could have been worse, for Alexander was a dashing and handsome young man.

Ivan's hopes that the marriage would enable him to infiltrate into the Lithuanian court came to nothing. Alexander did not want Elena's crude and rough-mannered retinue in his more civilized Western court, and sent them back to Moscow, to Ivan's intense annoyance. Ivan intended his daughter to be a spy for him in the enemy's court, and instructed her to influence her husband politically in favour of Moscow's interests.

In this respect the marriage was a total failure. Though it was not a failure from the conventional point of view, Elena seems to have fallen in love with her good-looking and gifted young husband. He treated her well and her loyalties soon changed to his. It is likely, too, that she found the more civilized court of Alexander an agreeable contrast to the crudities of the Kremlin.

But she would not change her faith. Her husband was a Roman Catholic and she was Greek Orthodox, and despite great pressure she refused to join the Roman Church. In 1500 Ivan used this as a *casus belli* for starting the Lithuanian war. Alexander had pledged that he would not use pressure to make Elena change her faith. This undertaking apparently was not kept. Great pressure was put upon her by members of the Lithuanian Catholic Church, who were urged on by no less a person than the Pope himself (Alexander VI, the Borgia Pope). Members of the Greek Orthodox Church in Lithuania were also subject to persecution. Ivan, who always liked to have a pretext, then officially declared war on Lithuania.

The Russian and Lithuanian armies met at Vedrosha, where the Lithuanians were routed after a long and bloody battle. Alexander lost the greater part of his army and the Russian casualties were heavy, too. Vedrosha gave Ivan large territories of eastern Lithuania which he desired to add to his domains. But the war dragged on until 1503 when Alexander was forced to sue for peace. Elena also pleaded with her father to cease the war, denying she was persecuted for her faith and saying that in Alexander she had found the perfect husband, who was tolerant and generous and had shown her great kindness.

A truce, rather than a peace, was agreed by which Ivan kept all the Lithuanian territory he had conquered. Some idea of where Ivan's conquest had led him may be gained from the fact that the boundary still fell short of Smolensk and Kiev, which remained in Lithuania.

Thus at the end of his turbulent reign Ivan the Great realized his dream of ruling all Russia and shaking off the hated Mongol yoke. Russia became a single country, and systematic foreign relations were for the first time started.

We have very little knowledge about Ivan himself and his private life. He was an autocrat who rode rough-shod over all opposition and he dealt firmly with his often rebellious relations. His personal appearance, we are told, was remarkable. Tall, thin, slightly stooping, there was something about his face, it was said, which inspired such awe that women fainted at the sight of him. His only known vice was gluttony.

An interesting figure in his life was his second wife, the mother of Elena. This was Zoe, niece of the last Byzantine emperor, who is thought by some to have introduced Byzantine etiquette and ceremony into Ivan's somewhat crude court. After marrying Zoe— whom the Russians called Sofia—Ivan adopted the Byzantine

Imperial double-headed eagle in his emblem. Following the fall of Constantinople and the Eastern Empire in 1453, many people regarded the Grand Dukes of Moscow as the successors of the Byzantine emperors.

Nineteenth-century historians have portrayed Sofia as a haughty Byzantine princess who urged her husband to rid himself of the shameful Tartar yoke in 1480 and inspired him to the unification of all-Russia under his rule. Modern scholarship, however, does not bear out this romantic view of Sofia. Ivan needed no such inspiration for his life's work. His marriage with this last princess of Byzantium is certainly significant, and doubtless she brought some of her rich cultural background with her, but there is no evidence that she influenced his policies. She bore him seven children.

Ivan the Great died on 27 October, 1505, at the age of 66, after a reign of 43 years. He died apparently unmourned and unloved, yet Russia owed him much, for he made her into a nation. He deserved the appellation "the Great" as much as Peter I and Catherine II.

RICHARD III

(1452-1485)

THE BRIEF and sombre reign of Richard III, battle-filled, stained with treachery and murder, centres on a short, slight, tight-lipped figure whom historians, from Tudor times to the present day, have defended or attacked with equal zeal. Many contemporaries looked on him as the Devil Incarnate and twenty years after his death Sir Thomas More in his history started the legend that Richard was deformed in body as well as soul. Shakespeare sees him as the greatest monster in English history and puts into his mouth the line: "I am determined to prove a villain." That he was a villain, despite efforts to prove the contrary, seems clear.

He was born, sickly and undersized, in October, 1452, as the twelfth of the thirteen children of Richard, Duke of York, and Cecily, known as "Proud Cis", the daughter of the first Duke of Westmorland. On his father's side he was descended from Edmund, the fifth son of Edward III, and on his mother's from Lionel, Duke of Clarence, the second son. Thus the House of York had prior claim to the throne after the murder of the childless Richard II, himself the son of Edward III's heir, the Black Prince. But the House of Lancaster, descended from Edward III's third son, John of Gaunt, also had a claim, and though it was inferior it had forcibly been made good in 1399 by Henry Bolingbroke who had invaded England, seized Richard II and established himself on the throne as Henry IV.

The Wars of the Roses between York and Lancaster broke out in 1455, when Henry IV's grandson was on the throne, and as a toddler of three young Richard saw his father return from the victory of St. Albans, the first blood-letting in the thirty years' struggle, where the Duke had gained possession of Henry VI and soon after forced the feeble-minded monarch to grant him the succession to the throne.

The violent shifts of the dynastic struggle filled Richard's childhood. His father's pact with Henry VI disinherited the king's son, Edward, Prince of Wales, and Queen Margaret of Anjou, one of the most determined and resolute women in history, took up arms

359

in his defence. Gathering a Lancastrian army, she defeated a Yorkist force at Ludlow, the Duke of York fled to Ireland and at the age of seven his son Richard became a temporary prisoner of war. Released after a Yorkist victory, he moved with his mother to London, where, early in 1461, they received tidings of disaster. The Duke had been killed and now his head with a paper crown was rotting on Mickle Bar, the highest gate of York city. His grieving widow, in terror for her son, dispatched him to Holland.

Another change of fortune brought him back. His admired and handsome brother Edward, despite defeat by the Lancastrians, found the road to London open, entered it with his army, was greeted with enthusiasm by the citizens and declared himself king. As he grew up Richard became an ardent supporter and Edward soon needed his subtle brain. As a redoubtable soldier he could deal with Lancastrian revolt, whether centred on Henry VI who was carted round like a piece of luggage from battle to battle, or on the still indefatigable Margaret of Anjou who clung through amazing vicissitudes to her son, the Lancastrian heir. Edward triumphed over them all and in 1464 the unprotesting person of King Henry was seized in Lancashire, conveyed to London and after a mock procession through the streets with a straw hat on his head conveyed to the Tower. But then the Earl of Warwick, who claimed a large share in these successes, turned against his master, allied himself to the Lancastrian cause and succeeded in restoring Henry to the throne. Edward, with his brother Richard, fled to the Court of Burgundy.

At this point Richard emerges into the full light of history. In Burgundy he planned with Edward an armed descent upon England and, an essential prelude to its success, the weakening of Warwick's power by winning back to his Yorkist allegiance their brother George, Duke of Clarence. Clarence, aged twenty-one, had been won over by the king-maker in the hope of obtaining the succession and had contributed handsomely to his success. But now Clarence was beginning to wonder: would the throne ever be his so long as the son of Margaret of Anjou was alive, that handsome heir of Henry VI? Richard sent emissaries, played on his doubts, and Clarence, already once foresworn, prepared to play traitor again.

Under the management of his dynamic brother, Edward landed at Ravenspur in Yorkshire. York would not open its gates until, on Richard's advice, he pretended that he had only come to reclaim his personal estates. But then, refreshed, he marched southward, managed to slip past Warwick's forces coming to meet him and placed himself between his enemy and London. At Banbury, Clarence, marching from the west ostensibly to attack him, embraced him instead and their two armies joined forces. It was a triumph for Richard, made complete soon after at Barnet where Warwick was killed and his army routed. Richard's own company had dealt him the death-blow.

Edward was now king again. Henry VI, mild and unprotesting, was taken back to the Tower. But his wife Margaret, newly landed with a force from France, offered Edward a new threat. Again the diplomat Richard got to work and persuaded one of her captains to change sides. The battle was fought at Tewkesbury, the nineteen-year-old Richard, his slim, wiry form encased in white German armour, commanding the van of four thousand men. It was a disaster for the Lancastrians. Margaret was taken prisoner and her son, the Prince of Wales, slain.

With the last hope of the Lancastrians dead and the White Rose triumphant there remained only one possible rallying point for Edward's enemies, Henry VI, devout, uncomprehending, eking out his days in the Tower. After Tewkesbury, Richard hastened to London on his brother's orders and spent the night of 21 May, 1471, in the Tower. On that night Henry died, of "sheer melancholy", it was claimed.

For the next twelve years Edward reigned unchallenged, much occupied with sensual pleasures and bored by the task of government. Richard built up a solid reputation in the north as a zealous and fair-minded administrator. With his wife, Anne Neville, daughter of Warwick the king-maker and former wife of Edward Prince of Wales who was killed at Tewkesbury, he lived a quiet life, but his mind revolved an interesting question: when Edward died who would succeed him? He had two sons, born in 1470 and 1473, but Richard knew that before marrying their mother, Elizabeth Woodville, Edward had been "troth-plighted" to a Lady Eleanor Talbot. The union had been consummated, but no marriage had taken place. Could not this fact be used to illegitimize Edward's children? In that case, only one barrier stood between Richard and the throne: his elder brother Clarence, and in 1478 Clarence was convicted of high treason, sent to the Tower and seen no more— drowned, it was said, in a butt of Malmsey wine. So Richard watched and waited, grave, competent, impeccably loyal.

The king died suddenly from his excesses in 1483, having appointed Richard in his will to act as regent for his son. At York, very correct, he dressed himself and his gentlemen all in black, attended a Requiem Mass and took the oath to Edward the Fifth. But he did not forget the troth-plight and, when he came to think of it, he could remember rumours that his own deceased brother had not been sired by his father, but by some person unknown. Such rumours were damaging to Proud Cis, but they could be used. And there was another circumstance of the greatest importance. Secretly, much to the fury of the higher nobility, Edward IV had married a lady of low quality. Elizabeth Woodville was a daughter of Sir Richard Woodville, one-time steward to the Duke of Bedford. This was bad, but worse was the reckless way in which the king had showered favours on his wife's brothers and sisters, of which she had twelve. Rancour against him had simmered for years and now, after his death, Richard knew that he could rely on a large body of the nobility for their support.

Methodically Richard made a plan. The first step was to gain possession of the boy-king who was at Ludlow on the Welsh border. This was easily done. The king, with a heavy escort commanded by his maternal uncle Lord Rivers, was intercepted on his way to London by Richard in Northamptonshire. Rivers and other officers were arrested, the escort was embodied in Richard's forces and the proud regent, with deep obeisance, led the way to the capital—ostensibly for his sovereign's coronation. Rivers and his friends were executed within a month.

In London Richard also acted swiftly. On the feeble pretext that it would be safer and more dignified for him there, the twelve-year-old king was lodged in the Tower. Meanwhile the Council of Regency was empowered to issue writs in his name and ordered to prepare the Coronation. The moment had almost arrived for the *coup d'état*, the accusation which would give Richard the throne. One last rival had first to be disposed of—Richard, the king's nine-year-old brother—and incredibly his mother surrendered him to the smiling Protector from sanctuary at Westminster and he, too, vanished into the Tower. Now the stage was set.

The Coronation was fixed for 22 June. Three days before, the Bishop of Bath and Wells was prodded into publicly proclaiming Edward IV's troth-plight with Lady Eleanor Talbot, the consequent illegality of his marriage with Elizabeth Woodville and the bastardy of all his children. Richard professed to be much surprised. The Coronation could not, of course, take place, and on the day itself, instead of the boy-king enthroned in splendour, London saw one Doctor Shaw, a firebrand preacher, repeat the accusation at St. Paul's Cross on the text "Bastard slips shall not take root" and call on his audience to acclaim Richard, who conveniently happened to be present, as their rightful king and true son of his father. Even Edward IV's legitimacy was impugned. The appeal fell flat, likewise another public harangue delivered by Richard's friend, the Duke of Buckingham, in the following week.

But this did not prevent a dutiful and packed Parliament proclaiming the deposition of Edward the Fifth and, soon after, with much show of reluctance, Richard, besought by Buckingham, accepted the throne. He was crowned with impressive ceremonial on 6 July, 1483. Perhaps he felt joy and satisfaction on that day, but he was to feel little thereafter.

He went on a progress through the Midlands, righted wrongs, bestowed favours and courted popularity. But the people were suspicious and, in the south, where resentment at his usurpation was particularly strong, the demand was raised that the princes should be released from the Tower.

So we come to Richard's principal crime. In the same month of his coronation he resolved that the princes must die. Sir James Tyrell, devoted and ruthless, was sent to London with an order to the Constable of the Tower to deliver him the keys for one night. His groom, Dighton by name, and one of the gaolers did the deed, suffocating the boys while they slept and burying the bodies under a mass of rubble by a staircase leading to the chapel in the White Tower, where the bones were found during alterations in the reign of Charles II. From this time, as the story goes, Richard knew no peace, but saw enemies everywhere, was forever fingering his dagger and at night pacing, ghost-haunted, in his chamber.

Troubles soon descended. Buckingham, the former bosom friend, rose in rebellion, concerting his plans with Henry Tudor, Lancastrian heir to the throne. At the same time there were risings in the south, provoked by rumours that the princes had been murdered. Richard crushed all with ruthless hand. Henry returned to Brittany whence he had come; Buckingham was captured and immediately beheaded.

Richard was granted a strife-free interlude in which he showed himself an enlightened reformer, but his crime clung to him, and when, in April, 1484, his young heir, now Prince of Wales, died the question of succession was reopened and many Yorkists as well as Lancastrians flocked to the banner of Henry Tudor in Brittany. A marriage was projected between him and Elizabeth, daughter of Edward IV, and Englishmen saw in this prospect of uniting the Roses a means of ending the sickening bloodshed.

Early in 1485 news came that Henry meant to land in the spring. Richard acted with resolution, setting up his headquarters at Nottingham, arranging for relays of horses to bring early news of an invasion, collecting money and troops. In June he issued a proclamation. It was meant to be a rallying cry against "Henry Tydder, descended of bastard blood" and his band of "murderers, adulterers and extortioners", but it had little effect and troops were slow in coming in.

Two months passed. Richard went hunting in Sherwood Forest, in the summer-decked glades pondering the innocence of nature, the treachery of his enemies. Then, on 7 August, 1485, Henry Tudor's expedition landed at Milford Haven and, though with only two thousand men, he at once proclaimed Richard a usurper. With his force enlarged by three thousand Welshmen, delighted to welcome a descendent of Owen Tudor, he marched eastwards, gathering more recruits as he went. But when the rival armies finally met at Market Bosworth, the king had managed to muster twelve thousand men, while Henry had only half the number. All depended on the Stanleys of Cheshire. They marched with the king, but would they fight for him?

On the night before the battle it is reported that Richard had fearful dreams. But next morning he harangued his captains in splendid style. "Dismiss all fear... Everyone give but one sure stroke and the day is ours. What prevaileth a handful of men to a whole realm? As for me, I assure you this day I will triumph by glorious victory or suffer death for immortal fame."

No Mass was said. The king took no food. Fasting, he entered battle at eight o'clock in a suit of polished steel, wearing his crown. The country was undulating, with dales and hills. On one of these, Ambien Hill, Richard's forces were arrayed with the Stanleys on lesser hills to either side. Henry attacked from the south, facing a steep slope topped by cannon brought from the Tower of London. The fighting with axe, mace, lance and arrow was confused and bloody. Henry's men were halfway up the slope when Richard called on Lord Stanley to attack them in the flank. Instead, Stanley marched his soldiers to Henry's succour. Crying "Treason!" and seeing that all was lost, Richard galloped down with about a hundred knights into the thick of the fight—his aim to slaughter the Welshman. Sir William Stanley from the other flank could have helped him at this moment, but stood his ground. Hand-to-hand, Richard slew Henry's standard-bearer and Sir John Cheyney, his Cavalry Master, then Stanley with his horsemen surged into the struggle—for Henry, not for Richard. A mace crashed on his helmet. He was borne down, axed, stabbed and trampled. His crown was retrieved from a bush and placed on Henry's head and the mangled corpse of the last of the Plantagenets, with the long hair hanging down, was tied naked on a horse and carried into Leicester as a show for the people.

So Henry Tudor reigned and, marrying Elizabeth, daughter of Edward IV, brought the long and murderous Wars of the Roses to an end. In the thirty years' struggle it is calculated that 100,000 men had died, died for a reconciliation which now, at last, placed a new dynasty on the throne. All Englishmen believed that a new age had dawned.

FERDINAND V (THE CATHOLIC)
(1452–1516)
and
ISABELLA I
(1451–1504)

THE STORY of Ferdinand and Isabella is the story of the birth of
Spain as a nation. Their marriage enabled Spain to become a united
country after seven centuries of war and anarchy. They laid the
foundations for the vast Spanish Empire in the newly-discovered
Americas, and put Spain upon the road to greatness.

In this joint enterprise in kingship, Isabella was unquestionably
the senior partner. Not only was she more gifted than her husband,
she greatly excelled him in integrity and moral qualities. She had a
talent for statesmanship, while his talents were more for warfare.
They made a remarkably effective partnership.

Isabella was born on 22 April, 1451, daughter of John II, King of
Castile, and was a descendant of John of Gaunt, third son of
Edward III of England. Isabella's father was an amiable, indolent
intellectual who neglected his kingdom for his literary pursuits and
left the affairs of state to his favourites with disastrous results. This
accomplished but incompetent king had two wives and three
children—by his first wife a son who succeeded him as Henry IV,
and by his second wife a son and daughter, Alfonso and Isabella.

Ferdinand's father was King of Aragon, also called John II.
Ferdinand was born on 10 March, 1452, and at the age of ten became
heir to the throne upon the death of his brother. From that date
Ferdinand was taken away from his studies and spent his life on the
battlefield and in the saddle by the side of his father, whose long and
turbulent life was spent in conquest, violence and civil war, typical
of fifteenth-century kingship.

The two kingdoms of Castile and Aragon then made up the Spain
as we know it today. Aragon comprised the north-eastern part from
the Pyrenees to just below Alicante, and Castile the rest of the
country. Castile was much larger, more important and powerful.

Isabella was four when her father died and her brother Henry IV became King of Castile. He was known as Henry the Impotent, and impotent he was in every meaning of the word. Extravagant and debauched, he possessed none of the cultivated tastes which were his father's redeeming feature. In 1462 his beautiful and unvirtuous queen, Joanna of Portugal, gave birth to a female child, also called Joanna, which though accepted by the impotent Henry was widely believed to be illegitimate.

Upon her father's death Isabella was sent with her mother to live in seclusion in the little town of Aravalo. Here under her mother's guidance, and far from the corrupting atmosphere of her brother's immoral court, she was trained and brought up with care and wisdom, and well instructed in the practical pieties of the age. She was naturally of a pious disposition and her mother implanted in her serious mind such strong religious principles that nothing in after-life could shake them.

The disputed child of Queen Joanna brought the question of the succession into violent dispute, and Henry summoned Isabella and her brother Alfonso to his court to keep an eye on them, well knowing that his rebellious nobles would try to use them. He was right. In 1465 young Alfonso, then eleven, was set up as King of Castile in opposition to Henry, and the country was riven by strife.

Isabella was then sixteen—a tall, demure, attractive girl, with a clear, fresh complexion, light-blue eyes and auburn hair. Her portraits depict her as having well-nigh faultless features upon which sat an engaging expression which was a mixture of intelligence and feminine sweetness. It has been said that Isabella's Spanish admirers were so smitten by her moral perfections that they tended to exaggerate her physical beauty.

She was, of course, a very marriageable commodity. Not only was she exceedingly personable, but much more important was the fact that on the death of her brother Alfonso in 1468 she was declared heiress to the throne of Castile, the claims of Queen Joanna's child being set aside.

The princes of Europe contended with each other for her hand, but Isabella, who had reserved the right to pick her own husband, showed an unerring judgment and faith in her destiny by choosing her cousin Ferdinand of Aragon, with the conscious object of uniting Spain into one kingdom. Ferdinand was no stranger to her. They spoke the same language and enjoyed the same customs and institutions.

Ferdinand was eighteen, and a well-built, muscular young man, a great horseman, who excelled in all the field sports of his day and who was already experienced in battle. Even in his youth his receding hairline gave him an almost bald appearance. He had a sharp-voiced eloquence by which he had no difficulty in asserting his considerable authority. But his rather cold and suspicious nature alienated him from many of his future subjects.

The marriage articles signed on 7 January, 1469, firmly established Ferdinand as the junior partner in this historic dynastic union. In vain Henry IV opposed the marriage, which took place on 19 October, 1469, in his absence. Henry's profligate and unheroic reign continued in uninterrupted anarchy and corruption until his unlamented death in 1474, when Isabella ascended the throne of Castile amid general rejoicing.

Ferdinand immediately showed the less pleasant side of his character as well as demonstrating a typical essay in fifteenth-century kingsmanship. Rushing to Isabella's side, he claimed the crown of Castile for himself on the ground that a female was excluded from the succession and that the sovereignty devolved upon him as the nearest male in line. Spain's highest ecclesiastical court decided that a female could sit upon the throne of Castile, though not upon the throne of Aragon. Ferdinand would not at first accept their judgement, but Isabella smoothed his ruffled pride with true feminine tact and guile. He was forced to capitulate anyway, for his attempt to grab the throne for himself had no support in Castile, where it would not have been tolerated. The Castilians wanted Isabella, well aware of her great qualities which were not shared by Ferdinand. In 1479 Ferdinand's father died and Ferdinand ascended the throne of Aragon, and the two kingdoms were united.

Administratively Isabella made a splendid start, converting the dismal anarchy of the previous reign into a state of order such as Spain had not known before. She reformed justice, re-codified the laws, regulated trade, agriculture and the currency, and re-established the royal authority which had fallen into contempt during the lawless reign of her brother. She brought the rebellious nobles of Castile to heel. With the firm re-establishment of royal authority, the Spanish grandee acquired dignity and responsibility, as well as a splendour which was to dazzle and astonish the world. Isabella herself carried out these reforms, sometimes enforcing her mandate personally, fearless of her own safety.

The courage, intelligence and integrity of their young queen, as well as her beauty and dignity, created a great impression upon her subjects. The court circles were cleansed of the immoral and wanton atmosphere of the previous reign. Although Isabella raised court life to a high standard of virtue and dignity, it lacked nothing in splendour. Its fêtes and tournaments were magnificent and attended by all the trappings of chivalry. To it were invited artists, poets, musicians and men of letters which gave the Spanish court a true intellectual atmosphere.

Isabella's independence of Rome, her restriction of the secular power and influence of the Church in Spain, and the setting up of her own Inquisition independent of the Papacy are among the distinguishing features of this strong Catholic monarchy.

Not all of her enactments were constructive or enlightened. Medieval Spain differed from other European countries by the large numbers of Moors and Jews within its borders, among whom there was undoubtedly a lot of the kind of heresy which the Inquisition had been created to deal with. The Jews were the historical enemies of Christianity and had been persecuted for centuries. In 1478 Isabella set up the Spanish Inquisition to deal particularly with the Jews.

Why the virtuous, upright and intelligent Isabella allowed the establishment of this cruel and shameful institution of religious barbarity in her fair and smiling realm of Castile is not so surprising as has been made out. Isabella—for all her admirable qualities—was a woman of her age. It was a superstitious, bigoted and cruel age. Criminals were dealt with harshly. Torture and cruel death were not considered incompatible with the workings of justice. Isabella's pious upbringing had brought her very much under the influence of priests and monks, some of whom nourished ambitions of power when they knew their young charge was destined to become queen. None was more ambitious than a certain Dominican monk, Thomas de Torquemada, who became her confessor and who extorted from her a promise that when she came to the throne she would devote herself to the extirpation of heresy. The time arrived when Torquemada demanded that she should keep this ominous promise.

She was reluctant, perhaps for obvious reasons of humanity. Under tremendous priestly pressure, she decided finally to demand of the Pope a bull authorizing an Inquisition which would be answerable to her, not to the Papacy. Her desire to have control over this terrible instrument of religious persuasion was doubtless prompted by the best possible motives. Sixtus VI did not like the idea at all, but was unable to resist the powerful monarchy which was bringing order and prosperity to the Spanish peninsula.

Thus the Spanish Inquisition was established and it became a powerful and sinister institution, which in the hands of the Spanish crown was used to further the power of Spain rather than that of the Church. Isabella and Ferdinand were in fact determined to control the Church in the same way as they had controlled their nobles, their cities and their economy.

The Spanish Inquisition was established in Castile in 1480 and Torquemada became Inquisitor General in 1483. Soon the Inquisition was operating over all the dominions of Ferdinand and Isabella. Their first victims were the converted Jews and Mohammedans. In twenty-five years nearly 350,000 suspected heretics were dealt with, of which 28,000 were condemned to death, and 12,000 actually burnt at the stake. Most of these victims of the Holy Office were tortured unspeakably, and those not condemned to die were fatally injured or maimed for life.

So great was the terror which fell upon the Jews, who were the principal sufferers, that many fled to France, Germany and Italy, where the accounts of their treatment added to the accumulating scandal on the condition of the Mother Church. The scandal was so great that Sixtus himself was moved to rebuke the intemperate zeal of the Spanish Inquisitors, though the Holy Father soon digested his conscience; for in 1483 he was encouraging Isabella—who seemed to have a twinge of conscience herself at the time—to further efforts in seeking out heresy.

In 1494 the Pope conferred upon Ferdinand and Isabella the title of "the Catholic Monarchs", on account of their virtues, their zeal for the faith, the subjugation of Granada, and "the purification of their dominions from the Jewish heresy".

The conquest of Granada—the last remaining bastion of Mohammedanism in the Spanish peninsula—was successfully undertaken between the years 1481 and 1492. The brilliant Moorish civilization had flourished in Spain while the rest of Europe was sunk in barbarism. Although its great days were long over, it had contributed much to Spain. The Moors' beautiful and desolate ruins even now haunt the landscape of the fair country they made their own for seven centuries.

The conquest of this last Moorish stronghold by the Catholic monarchs was prosecuted with fanatical zeal and with all the barbaric usages of the time. Though not to be compared with the horrors of modern warfare, it was rich in both atrocity and chivalry, and was concluded with an ungenerous peace which leaves yet another stain upon the memory of Ferdinand and Isabella.

In 1492 Ferdinand and Isabella issued a decree expelling all Jews from Spain. The odium for this action is not entirely theirs. The high priests of the Inquisition had been long urging it. Torquemada in particular had great power over Isabella's mind. She felt bound to surrender her own judgement in matters of conscience to her religious guardians. But Isabella cannot be held entirely blameless for this great crime against the Jews, for she, too, suffered from the deep moral depravity of the medieval Catholic Church. She did not have the spiritual courage to ask the terrible questions which were being asked in Germany at that time.

Between 160,000 and 180,000 Jews were driven out of Spain by the edict of 1492. Their departure brought great economic distress to Spain, for in turning out their most talented and industrious citizens Spain became speedily and permanently crippled economically. But even their more enlightened contemporaries did not regard it as incredible that monarchs of such political sagacity should do such an act. The expulsion of the Jews was regarded as a sublime sacrifice of temporal interests for a religious principle.

Christopher Columbus came to Spain in 1484 after having unsuccessfully tried to interest various other monarchs in his plan to sail westwards around the world to China and the Indies. Ferdinand and Isabella were in the middle of the war with Granada, and little notice was taken of Columbus. It was another of Isabella's confessors, Juan Perez, who inspired her to give Columbus her royal ear. But there was more scepticism than enthusiasm for the expedition, despite Isabella's legendary exclamation that she was ready to pawn the crown jewels of Castile if there wasn't enough money in the treasury.

Actually the expedition was very cheaply financed. It cost no more than 17,000 florins, and never did so modest a sum reap so golden a harvest. On Columbus's return in 1493 the Pope, Alexander VI, made Spain the magnificent presentation of all the lands a hundred leagues west of the Azores which had been discovered and which were to be discovered.

The exploration of Central and South America quickly followed. Conquest and conversion to Christianity soon firmly entrenched Spain in the golden lands of America, enabling her to draw rich treasure as well as to spread the true faith under the velvet terror of the Spanish Inquisition. But these fabulous riches from the El Dorado beyond the sunset did not benefit the Spanish people. It was all used to build up the glory of Spanish arms and to finance innumerable wars in Europe. Spain entered into her period of

371

colonial greatness fatally weakened economically by the anti-semitic and anti-Moorish policies of Ferdinand and Isabella.

Two of Isabella's children made marriages which had important political and dynastic effects in Europe. The Infanta Dona Catalina, known in English history as Catherine of Aragon, became the wife of Henry VIII, whom he divorced in order to marry Anne Boleyn. The Infanta Joanna was married to Archduke Philip of Habsburg. This brought the Habsburg dynasty to Spain, which was something of a disaster. Joanna's son was the great Emperor Charles V. In 1503 Joanna became insane.

Having acquired and built up an important kingdom in Europe and an empire in the new world which promised to pour into her lap all the fabled treasures of the Indies, Isabella, in the noontide of her success, was taken ill and died at the age of fifty-four, on 26 November, 1504.

Upon her death mad Joanna was declared queen, with Philip of Habsburg her consort. Ferdinand, in accordance with Isabella's will, had to give up the crown of Castile, but claimed regency in the name of his insane daughter.

The absence of Isabella's firm hand upon the helm of national affairs was immediately felt. Philip claimed the throne, and Ferdinand's authority was undermined by unrest and rebellion and he was not able to re-assert himself until Philip's early death at the age of twenty-eight in 1506.

With a mad queen on the throne, the Castilians were only too glad to have Ferdinand back as their king, if only to prevent conditions slipping back to the bad old days of Charles IV, for Ferdinand was not popular. Ferdinand shut Joanna away in a palace, where she survived for forty-seven years. Once more firmly on the throne he ruled Spain until his death in 1516, when his grandson, Charles V, inherited the throne, after whose reign the golden visions of Ferdinand and Isabella were all dissipated in the sterile religious wars which ruined and exhausted Spain during the next two centuries.

HENRY VII, KING OF ENGLAND

(1457–1509)

ON 22 AUGUST, 1485, some 20,000 men fought a battle near
Bosworth in Leicestershire, some 13,000 or so under the banner
of the King of England, Richard III, and the rest, the rebel army,
following a Welsh gentleman, Henry Tudor, Earl of Richmond,
who claimed the English throne.

Henry Tudor had landed on 9 August, at Milford Haven in
Pembrokeshire, with perhaps a couple of thousand French and Breton
mercenaries and a following of English exiles. He had gathered the
rest of his troops in warlike Wales and marched across England,
hoping for a general rising in his favour. He hoped in vain. On the
other hand, Henry was assured that his brother-in-law, Sir William
Stanley, Earl of Derby, who commanded one-third of Richard's
hastily got-together army, would not fight against him. His confidence in this treachery was not misplaced.

Like most of the battles of the Wars of the Roses, the comparatively small armies of knights and feudal retainers came quickly
to hand-to-hand combat, mostly fighting on foot. Neither side as
a rule had many archers; but both had enough to forgo the ordeal
of charging on horseback against a storm of arrows. The issue of
the battle was doubtful until Stanley's troops, who had refused to
advance against the rebels, attacked the king's army. Richard,
one of the bravest warriors of his time, dashed into the centre of
the enemy, seeking Richmond himself. He was finally killed, his
crown falling from his helmet under a bush where it was lost
until found by Stanley and placed on Henry Tudor's head. The
body of King Richard was stripped naked, tossed over a horse and,
after the face had been battered against the parapet of a bridge, was
irreverently buried in the church of Grey Friars in Leicester, a
church since destroyed. "The majesty that doth hedge a king"
had been destroyed long before this battle, and of this Henry Tudor,
Henry VII, was well aware.

Since the death of Edward III in 1377, the heirs of the great
Plantagenet had been fighting over the Crown. Richard II, the
son of the Black Prince, was deposed by Henry of Lancaster,

Earl of Hereford, known as Bolingbroke, who was a son of John of Gaunt, a brother of the Black Prince. Bolingbroke became Henry IV. Henry V had no serious challenger but fighting broke out again in 1455 during the reign of his young son Henry VI, between Lancastrians and Yorkists. By force of arms, Richard, Duke of York, son of the third son of Edward III, Edmund Langley, Duke of York, won his claim to be recognized as Henry VI's heir. He, however, was killed by the Lancastrians. His son, Edward, won the crown at Towton in 1461, to lose it again when the great Earl of Warwick changed sides, backed the Lancastrians and restored Henry VI.

Edward returned from exile, and in 1471 defeated Warwick at Barnet. He finally defeated the Lancastrians at Tewkesbury, murdering Henry VI's young son and later, in the Tower, the ineffectual Henry VI himself. As Edward IV he now reigned in peace until 1483 when he died. These major battles had been accompanied by lesser ones all over England between the nobles who supported one side or the other.

The Wars of the Roses had not affected the daily life of the people as much as might have been expected; but they had ruined the national unity created by England's earlier kings and caused a break-down in public morality and public order. But in spite of the general acceptance of murder and bloodshed, the murder by Richard, Duke of Gloucester, the brother of Edward IV, of the two Princes in the Tower, the sons of Edward IV, may well have shocked the nation and perhaps have accounted for the comparatively small army which Richard III had at Bosworth. Against this supposition must be set the fact that Richard III was extremely popular in the north of England and that, during his two years as king, he had summoned Parliament, redressed grievances and ended abuses of the previous reign and generally shown himself an enlightened monarch.

The murderer of his brother's children he probably was; but so many men's hands had been stained with blood of kin that Richard's defeat cannot, with total certainty, be put down to a moral revulsion from him. His own recklessness and contempt for Richmond may have made him fight too hastily. His character had been blackened by the great genius of Shakespeare in the play *Richard III*, which is one of Shakespeare's finest works, in spite of being propaganda for the Tudors as well.

Fortunately for England the victor of Bosworth was very different from the open-hearted, virtuous young warrior who briefly

appears in Shakespeare's *Richard III* as Richmond. Had Henry VII
been another Henry V, or a pleasure-loving Edward IV, it is very
doubtful if he would have kept his throne. Bosworth then would
merely have been another inconclusive and bloody battle of the
Wars of the Roses. Henry's claim to the throne was extremely
slender, so slender indeed as to be almost non-existent. From his
mother, Margaret Beaufort, he could claim to be a descendant of
John of Gaunt; but it was descent through an illegitimate union,
subsequently legalized by King Richard II, but with the express
stipulation that this line should have no claim to royal blood.
His father, Owen Tudor, a Welsh gentleman from Anglesey, had
married Catherine, daughter of the King of France and the widow
of Henry V.

As a result of the great slaughter of princes and nobles during
the Wars of the Roses, Henry Tudor was considered the head of the
House of Lancaster by Henry VI; but this scarcely made him an
heir of the Plantagenet throne. There were still alive those who
could claim direct descent from the last Plantagenet king through
Edmund, Duke of York. There was, first of all, the daughter of
Edward IV, Elizabeth; there was the young Earl of Warwick,
directly descended from Edward IV's brother, the Duke of
Clarence; and two sons from a sister of Edward IV, the Earl of
Lincoln and Edmund, Earl of Suffolk.

In 1483, from his exile in France, Henry Tudor, when he first
staked his claims to the throne, announced his intention of marrying
Elizabeth if he came to the throne and thus re-uniting the two
Houses of York and Lancaster. This promise he carried out, and he
married Elizabeth in January, 1486, securing the ten-year-old Earl
of Warwick in the Tower.

Before Henry married he summoned Parliament and secured
from it what is called an Act of Recognition. This act did not
in fact make him king by the will of Parliament; it merely acknowledged that he was already king, as a result of the battle of Bosworth.
Precarious claim, precarious victory. Yet from the accession of
Henry VII, the king with the least reputable title to succeed to the
throne, England was never again to be afflicted with a dynastic
struggle. There was to be a civil war during the seventeenth
century, a struggle between king and parliament, but no one
doubted that Charles Stuart was the rightful King of England. James
II, was to be driven from his throne in 1688; but it was by the will of
the overwhelming majority of the nation, and William and Mary's
claim came through Mary, who was a Stuart.

The placing of the monarchy in an unassailable position was the work of Henry Tudor and of the two great Tudor rulers who followed him—Henry VIII and Elizabeth I. When Elizabeth died without issue in 1603 her successor was James VI of Scotland, the great-grandson of Margaret, daughter of Henry VII, whom he married to James IV, King of Scotland. No Tudor monarch allowed his children to marry with their subjects as had been the custom frequently in the past. The firm establishing of his rule and that of his dynasty was the greatest of Henry's achievements. He had no easy task.

The Earl of Lincoln, with the support of his aunt, Margaret, Duchess of Burgundy, who ruled the Netherlands, raised a mercenary army in that country, and disguising his own claims under that of the Earl of Warwick, whom he alleged had escaped from the Tower, had an impersonator of Warwick, a young man called Lambert Simnel, crowned king as Edward VI in Christchurch Cathedral, Dublin. The Anglo-Irish nobility were Yorkists to a man, just as the Welsh were Lancastrians. At Stoke in 1487 the rebels were defeated, the Earl of Lincoln was killed in battle, and Lambert Simnel, after exposure to the people of London, was employed as a kitchen boy in Henry's palace. Later in life he was promoted to falconer.

The second serious rebellion, backed also by the Duchess Margaret and the Yorkists, was that of Perkin Warbeck, who impersonated the younger of the princes in the Tower, Richard, Duke of York, pretending that he had escaped when his brother was smothered in his bed by Richard III's agents. Warbeck, who also received support from Ireland and from James IV for a while, finally landed in Cornwall in 1492, but ignominiously stole away from his small army to surrender to the king on the promise that his life would be spared. He was later imprisoned in the Tower with the Earl of Warwick and, unfortunately for both, he persuaded Warwick to try a joint escape. They were easily captured. Henry's policy was to avoid executions if possible; they stank of the old order. But he nonetheless executed Perkin Warbeck and the Earl of Warwick after this. Later Henry was to execute other Yorkist claimants to the throne.

The Crown had not been merely a prize to be fought over by the nobles who claimed Plantagenet blood, but it had during the Wars of the Roses become a totally valueless bauble, pledged and indebted at home and abroad. Henry's task of breaking his rivals was accompanied by measures against the power of the great feudal families, including heavy taxes on castles and on the maintenance of retainers. When the Earl of Oxford received Henry in great state, he was flabbergasted to be fined £10,000 for unlawful display. The subjection of the nobility to Henry and the exactions of the Star Chamber which carried out the punitive measures was easier because the nobility had been weakened by the civil wars. Nevertheless, only a very bold man could have acted with the speed and rigour of Henry. By 1509, when he died, he was the richest king in Christendom. The power of the king was greater than it had ever been. The country prospered under Henry's uneventful and undramatic rule; in 1497 a Venetian diplomat thought that London had become as rich as Florence or Paris, and he noted that in the Strand which leads to the City there were more goldsmiths and silversmiths than in any city he had ever visited.

Fortunes were being made as in the reign of Edward III from wool and cloth, and Englishmen, merchant-adventurers, were beginning their travels to the New World. Schools and colleges were being founded; the new rich, so prominent in the reign of the next king, were building magnificent houses.

Henry was no constitutional innovator and in fact used Parliament less and less during the latter half of his reign, particularly when he had been able to collect the money he needed from the administration of the Crown lands and the efficient collection of established duties and taxes. When Henry made war on France in 1492, Parliament voted him money. Of fighting there was virtually none except for a token siege of Boulogne; but Henry managed to get himself bought off by the French king and so collected money from this quarter too. He ruled England as an intelligent despot, giving the country an uneventful period of efficient government.

In 1501, Henry's eldest son Arthur was betrothed to Catherine of Aragon, who brought a huge dowry. Arthur died a few months after the arrival of his fiancée in London and, in 1503, the young girl was betrothed, willy-nilly, to Henry, Prince of Wales, afterwards Henry VIII. In fact, the pair did not marry until 1509, since Henry and Ferdinand first pretended to have scruples about the legitimacy of such a match and then after-thoughts about the marriage for political reasons.

At one time it was thought that Henry VII, after he had lost his wife, intended to marry Catherine's sister, Juana of Castile, the greatest heiress of Europe, who, however, was well known to be mad. He gave up this project. After his wife's death he certainly thought of marrying the young widowed queen of Naples, and among the few human things that are known about this monarch is a report in the Memorials of Henry VII of instructions sent to certain British official visitors to the Court of Naples. The king wanted to know in great detail about the queen's appearance—the colour of her hair and eyes, the shape of her nose, her lips, and how much she owed to cosmetics and how much to high heels. The observers were to mark "whether there appeared any hair about her lips or not" and "to approach as near her mouth as they may to the intent they may feel the condition of her breath, whether it be sweet or not". Henry was, of course, primarily marrying her for her fortune and of this he already had a precise knowledge.

Yet Henry VII was not a miser. He spent largely on music and books and organized magnificent State ceremonies. He began the construction of the great Henry VII Chapel at Westminster Abbey, and he largely helped, from his own purse, the completion of King's College Chapel at Cambridge. He was rather a man who, having spent his early youth in danger and exile and who had once successfully dared fate, was determined never to be caught again in a weak position and he knew that money was power. He remained, for all his cynicism, strongly religious and respectful towards the Church. Towards the end of his life he even thought of going on a crusade against the Turks—but he added a proviso that two other monarchs should come with him.

The best-known and the best portrait of Henry VII is by an unknown French painter. It shows a stern, long-mouthed, thin-lipped face beneath black velvet cap worn at the time. The eyes are slightly hooded, the hands hold a small Tudor rose. The upper part of the dress shown in the portrait is that of a banker or merchant rather than a king, and indeed the whole face is that of a man of business, cautious, politic, unostentatious and determined. Francis Bacon called him "a wonder for wise men". Known by no nick-names, even to his contemporaries, Henry revealed little or nothing of himself to any friend or mistress or adviser. He was feared rather than loved. He has been called the cleverest king who ever sat on the throne of England. His reign was certainly one of the most beneficial to the English nation.

MONTEZUMA

(1480?–1520)

HE WAS the most bloodthirsty ruler in history. He was a cannibal and a murderer.

And yet, even those who were appalled—and frightened—by his barbarities, men of an alien, Christian, culture like the Spanish conquistador Bernal, could write, as he did years later, of Montezuma's death:

"When we least expected, they came to say he was dead. Cortes wept for him as did all of us captains and soldiers. There was not one of those of us who had known him intimately that did not lament him as if he were our father. And that was no wonder, considering how good he was."

And so, on 29 June, 1520, ended the life of one of the world's most absolute, most powerful rulers, certainly one of the richest and, in a macabre way, one of the most lovable. He was a murderer on an absolutely vast scale: he ate the limbs of those he murdered. And incredibly, he managed to instil a deep love in the breasts of those who knew him.

To understand him we must take a look at the civilization into which he was born. The Mexicans had moved slowly down the length of the North American continent, having crossed, like all the other "Indians" of the New World, from North-east Asia, via the Bering Strait to what is now Alaska. Others had preceded them, but these, when the Mexicans reached the spot they cared to settle in, were defeated and destroyed. They chose as their capital an island situated many miles inland of what we now call the Gulf of Mexico, at an altitude of seven thousand feet—an island in a vast inland lake. On this they began to build their Mexico City, in 1324. Within a few years they were the most powerful community in Central America, a tough race, and intelligent—save for one blind spot—and living in the greatest luxury, on wealth they gathered annually in taxes from nearly four hundred subject towns.

But these people, with all their fantastic stores of gold and jewellery, their beautiful cottons, their chocolate, fine rubber and tobacco, so much of it denied as yet to the people of Europe, were a frightened people, organized permanently for war. They had little need to fight their neighbours; their control was absolute, their capital impregnable: they could have sat back to enjoy their wealth. But religion, their own fantastic brand of it, taught them otherwise. They knew, with every bit as much conviction as the Christian knows his God, that they were at the mercy of all their own gods, that none was merciful, that all must be placated, constantly, unceasingly, with gifts of food.

And the only food these gods would eat was a human heart, plucked beating from a human breast and placed on the altar. It was to gather victims for this ritual sacrifice that the Mexican army was always at war with one or other of Mexico's neighbours—a war fought solely for bringing home captives, to be kept to await their fate. On the appointed day, a group of prisoners would be taken from the cages, marched to the stone altar. There, each horrified victim watched the struggles of his predecessor, watched him held down on his back by four priests, one at each limb, while a fifth forced the head back to expose the throat. The sixth, the executioner —who was often the Emperor Montezuma himself—slit it, split open the chest and reached down inside to withdraw the still-beating heart. Then the limbs were cooked and eaten.

And unless this sacrifice was carried out daily—with enormous orgies of murder on certain astrologically fixed days—the sun would fail to rise, the rain to fall, maize to grow; the enemies of Mexico, both super-natural and human, would rise and conquer.

Life, for all its daily ritual of sacrifice, its aura of fear, was pleasant enough. Mexican sculpture and engineering was of a high order, the country abounded in fine roads, aqueducts, causeways. There was a legal system, an accurate calendar and a refined picture writing. Clothes and furnishings were both luxurious and beautiful, food of all sorts abounded: fruit, vegetables, succulent turkeys, and the little hairless *chihuahua* dogs bred for the table (though cattle—and horses—were unknown). Accurate and lethal weapons were made of wood, stone and bronze.

The government was headed by an elected monarch—elected by a council from among the preceding monarch's family, rather as if, on the death of Queen Victoria, the British Cabinet had settled down to decide whether the throne should go to the Prince of Wales or to some other royal relative. Once elected, the new monarch, though he had to study the appetites of the gods, was treated as one himself, a god who ruled the twin powers of army and church, had absolute power over his subjects.

It was to this throne that Montezuma—"Courageous Lord" in the Mexican language—was elected, at the age of thirty-five, on the death of his uncle. Already a warrior and legislator, he was devout and became more so, anxiously studying the Mexican scriptures. One in particular worried him: it told of the great battle between the War God and his rival, Quetzalcoatl, which ended in the latter's exile. He had sailed away on a magic raft, sailed away to the sunrise, with a final threat: "I will return in a One-Reed Year and re-establish my rule. It will be a time of great tribulation for my people."

One-Reed Years, like our own Leap Years, were based on astronomy, though they recurred at irregular intervals. The year of Montezuma's birth, 1480, had been one—and no Quetzalcoatl had come. The next One-Reed Year was 1519. Whether the god came or not, the Mexican priesthood knew from their scriptures just what he would look like, how he would behave. He would have white skin and a black beard—unknown in that part of the world—and he would, immediately on landing from his magic vessel, announce his intention of stamping out the wholesale human sacrifice offered to his rival, the War God. Not only that, but he would demand all sacrifice be stopped, forthwith, even to himself. This had been his quarrel with the War God, all those years in the past.

What did one do? To resist him, a god, was unthinkable—yet to allow him to return would arouse the ire of the War God, for whom they would have to gather yet more human hearts. Who could tell which god would be victorious, which to support? It was a terrible dilemma: and now, few doubted that Quetzalcoatl was coming. The One-Reed Year had dawned, there had been strange portents in the sky, voices wailing in the night, the eruption of a long-dead volcano. The Sun God's temple had caught fire. Superstition and astrology pointed not only to an arrival but to an exact date: 22 April, 1519.

On that date—it was Good Friday in the Christian calendar—the pale-skinned, black-bearded Spanish soldier of fortune, Hernan Cortes, landed on the Central American coast, 350 miles east of Mexico City, Montezuma's capital.

The emperor soon learnt of the invasion—and his heart sank. He was desperately worried: it would be disastrous to allow the god to return, for he and all his subjects had been bowing down to gods which were Quetzalcoatl's sworn enemies—and yet it would be still more disastrous to resist. All he could do was send messengers to the coast with gifts, urging Quetzalcoatl not to come farther. The road was dangerous—had the great god forgotten?—and very tiring: if the great god would return to whence he had come, Montezuma would give him all the riches god or man could covet.

But Cortes, after he had built his coastal base—it became the first Spanish town in Mexico, Vera Cruz—started to move inland, on 15 August, 1519. Montezuma learnt each day of their progress, how the small, white-skinned party was defeating armies from other tribes on the way, including a huge force of the savage Tlaxcalans. He sent another message to Cortes, asking how much he would demand as annual tribute—any amount of gold, silver, precious stones, slaves—not to visit Mexico City. With the messengers he sent priceless gifts, a foretaste of what would be coming.

But on and on came Cortes, replying courteously, thanking the sender for each load of gifts as it came. Eventually, in November, his Spanish force reached the lake in which the magnificent City of Mexico stood, on its island, with causeways running, some of them miles long, to the shore. (The lake today is almost dry: the city has spread over much of the lake bed.) Guided by Montezuma's emissaries—for the emperor no longer believed it possible to stop the Spanish progress—they marched along one of the causeways, as curious Mexicans paddled about them in long canoes and bejewelled lords came down to greet them.

And then, as they passed the fortress of Xoloc on this seemingly endless causeway, mile upon mile of it, they came face to face with Montezuma.

He got down from the litter in which he had been carried from his palace, and advanced on foot towards them, under a canopy of feathers and rich embroidery. Mexican nobles held the canopy, others unrolled a carpet before him so the golden sandals would not touch common dirt.

"As we approached each other, I dismounted and was about to embrace him," wrote Cortes, "but the two lords in attendance prevented me with their hands, so that I might not touch him."

There was complete silence. Then Montezuma, standing straight and tall, his feathered headdress swaying above them, addressed the returning god. He spoke with courtesy, without servility, thanked the god for the trouble he had taken in getting back to Mexico, the hardships he had undergone, and his words were translated by the beautiful and nobly-born "Doña Marina", the Mexican girl who had been handed over to Cortes, on the coast, as a gift. "Welcome to this land. Rest now, you are tired——"

Perhaps Montezuma was hinting that his visitor, when he had taken this rest, might be content to leave, to return to that eastern land, taking gifts.

But the Conquistadores never left. With their greed, their incomprehension of the people, their beliefs and their feelings—above all, their fears—they succeeded in destroying Mexican civilization almost completely within two and a half years of Cortes's arrival in Vera Cruz. With the single, foul, exception of human sacrifice made by a frightened people, much of it was fine and worthwhile, and we are the poorer by its disappearance.

The Spaniards, made welcome by the emperor, given a sumptuous palace for their own use and all the food, drink and gifts they could—for the moment—desire, still distrusted their hosts. At last, after months of misunderstanding, culminating in a skirmish between Cortes's base party at Vera Cruz and a nearby Mexican garrison, for which Montezuma was wrongly held to blame, the emperor was removed from his own palace and taken—with the greatest courtesy—to the Spaniards' one, as prisoner.

This was Cortes's greatest, fatal, mistake. His most potent supporter in Central America was Montezuma: the emperor believed him to be Quetzalcoatl and, as many of his subjects and ministers did not, that Quetzalcoatl would defeat all other gods. Had Cortes supported Montezuma to the hilt, all might have been well—but he did nothing of the sort. By June of 1520 the emperor was doubly discredited in the eyes of his people: not only was he prisoner, but he had misled them about the intentions of the god. Time and again he had told them to be calm, that Quetzalcoatl would leave: he had revisited his kingdom, been well pleased, and was going, taking his white-skinned followers with him. He had given his word. And each time, Cortes, thirsting for yet more wealth, had broken that word.

And so, at the other end of the city, the Mexicans were electing a new emperor. Goaded to fury by the installation of a statue of the Virgin in one of their temples, urged on by another god, Smoking Mirror, who demanded Cortes's death, and, finally, enraged by the killing of some uniformed dancers in the street by one of the Spanish captains who thought they were coming to attack the garrison, they prepared to rise against the invader.

Cortes had been back at the coast, at Vera Cruz, defeating—and winning over to his side—a large Spanish force dispatched by the Governor of Cuba, Velasquez, who had learned he was being cut out of any honours or profit gained from the Mexican sortie. (It had set sail from Cuba, been largely financed by Velasquez—and Cortes was now dealing direct with the King of Spain.) On hearing rumours of a Mexican rising, Cortes rushed back, with his now greatly enlarged force, and entered a sullen, hostile city.

The Mexicans struck on 25 June. They removed bridges from the causeways, making retreat impossible, and attacked the Spaniards' palace.

The battle raged; the sun burnt down into the huge courtyard, there were shrieks and the steady thud of rocks crashing against the walls, the occasional whine of a spear. Then all would be still as attackers and attacked took stock. Finally, Cortes decided to promise, yet again, that he would leave Mexico City with his men, for ever. After all, he still had his firm base of Vera Cruz: later, if he wished, and he probably would, he could come back, retake the capital.

But to tell the besiegers this in the midst of what had become a major battle (several Spaniards had been captured already and sacrificed, hearts torn from the living body, at the top of the War God's pyramid in full view of their horrified comrades-in-arms) he would need Montezuma.

At first the emperor refused. Then, though he agreed, he said it would be useless: "I cannot get them to stop fighting against you, for they have elected another sovereign and are resolved you shall not leave the city alive." He put on his ceremonial dress, the bejewelled golden crown, with the long plume, the silken shawl, the gold sandals. About his neck was a golden chain; there were turquoise ornaments through the lobe of each ear, a piece of jade through his nostrils. His face was painted with coloured stripes— green, orange, white.

He mounted the ramparts and the Mexicans, when they saw him, lowered their weapons.

He spoke, shouted, into the sudden silence. "My people—fight no more, for it is useless and unnecessary. This time I promise you, as the great god Quetzalcoatl has promised me, that he and all his lords will go."

Some in the crowd began to weep, and the Spanish soldiers who had accompanied the emperor—the ex-emperor, for he had already been superseded, by election—lowered their shields for a moment and left him unprotected.

There was a sudden, hysterical volley from the street below and a stone struck Montezuma on the side of the head. He stood erect, hand raised, for a moment longer, then fell.

Sadly, the Spaniards carried him back through the palace to his apartments. Tenderly, they cared for him—but the will to live was gone. The Great Montezuma, as they always called him, with love and respect, grew weaker every day. On 29 June, 1520, he died.

The Conquistadores, badly cut up, many of their number sacrificed, escaped. A few months later they came back and laid siege to the city themselves. On 15 August, 1521, it fell, and was totally destroyed.

Gradually it was rebuilt, and Christian churches erected on the sites of the old temples. The Mexicans had little trouble adopting Christianity because, though they had fought him, they still believed Cortes had been their returning god Quetzalcoatl: the new religion was thus guaranteed by a survivor of the old. And to this day, in parts of Christian Mexico, there are peasants who worship, in addition to the Trinity, the twin figures of Quetzalcoatl and Montezuma.

The reign of Montezuma was a splendid and glittering one—and unbelievably cruel. Some historians have put the annual number of human sacrifices in his capital as high as 20,000.

But—perhaps—one may feel remorse that it should all, good as well as bad, have been totally destroyed by an invader—masquerading as a god.

HENRY VIII

(1491–1547)

THAT UNPRETENTIOUS and somewhat drab figure, Henry VII, had not laboured in vain to establish his succession. No king began his reign more assured of the loyalty of his subjects than did Henry's son, Henry VIII—bluff King Hal, as he was later to be called.

As a young man Henry VIII charmed not only the people and the courtiers but wise and learned men such as Sir Thomas More, Erasmus, the great Archbishop Warham of Canterbury. Just as Edward III had been the image of the chivalrous medieval king, so Henry was that of the great monarch of the Renaissance. He was hearty, dashing, affable, open-handed, a lover of sports and of music, in both of which activities he was no mean performer himself. He is the author of *Greensleeves*.

He liked popularity and he knew how to make himself popular. He was extremely handsome and fond of clothes and magnificence. An Italian diplomat wrote that he was "the handsomest potentate I have ever seen—above the usual height, with an already fine calf to his leg, his complexion very fair and light, with auburn hair and a round face so beautiful it would become a pretty woman". Then Henry was also intelligent, a great linguist, a patron of learning and the arts, and, with all that, he had an orthodox cast of mind. There was no truer son of the Catholic church than the young monarch who called himself the Defender of the Faith.

He married Catherine of Aragon in 1509; she had been kept in England for many years after her engagement to Henry's elder brother Arthur, who had died whilst her father Ferdinand and Henry VII tried to make up their minds about her future. The still-young queen, in spite of her Spanish-ness and a certain stiffness of character, was also popular and remained so during her subsequent misfortunes.

Right at the beginning of his reign Henry executed two ministers of his father, Empson and Dudley, who had been responsible for some of the more severe exactions during the late reign and who were generally, perhaps inevitably, and almost certainly unjustly, hated. They went to the scaffold on a trumped-up charge of treason.

Although this move threw a sinister light on the nature of the new king, it was widely popular, betokening an end to the rather stern period of rule from which the country had benefited but of which it was tired.

Unlike his father, Henry VIII embarked early in his reign on an ambitious foreign policy, the main aim of which was to recover English possessions in France. As the son-in-law of Ferdinand, King of Spain, and as a zealous Catholic, Henry joined Spain and the Holy Roman Empire and the Papacy in alliance against Louis XII of France. The English people seemed to welcome this new attempt to aggrandize England, and Parliament, in 1512, voted money for the war on the Continent and also for the inevitable war with Scotland likely to follow as a result of the Franco-Scottish alliance.

The king's successes on the continent were more showy and costly than real, although an English victory at the Battle of the Spurs, near Boulogne, won Henry some renown. But France was no longer the weak and divided power that she was in the fourteenth century, and England, for all the wealth that the last king had gained, was unable to keep an army on the Continent for more than a few months at a time at the most. After 1520, when Henry VIII and Francis I of France met at the Field of the Cloth of Gold at which both the French and English courtiers tried to outdo each other in splendour of appearance, Henry's policy was to hold a balance between France and the immensely powerful Emperor Charles V, whose Habsburg dominions now included Spain as well as the Netherlands. But no great success came of Henry's policy, and when, in 1521, France and the empire made peace at the Treaty of Cambrai, England's interests were not satisfied.

The only great victory won during this early part of the king's reign was against the Scots in a battle at which Henry was not present. At Flodden, in 1513, the aged Earl of Surrey won a decisive victory against James IV of Scotland, who, together with some 10,000 Scots, was killed on the field of battle. For the rest of Henry's reign English influence in Scotland remained powerful.

Whilst the king, apparently, played, England was administered by the great Cardinal Wolsey. Wolsey's career and relationship with the king had some similarity to those of Thomas à Becket with Henry II. Like Becket, Wolsey was of humble birth, the son of an Ipswich butcher. He commended himself to Henry VIII by his wit, intelligence and great efficiency and, like Becket, he loved magnificence. Wolsey took a degree at Oxford when he was fifteen, entered the Church, became Chaplain to Henry VII in 1507, a member of the King's Council when Henry VIII came to the throne; he swiftly became Bishop of Lincoln, and from 1514 Archbishop of York, and then Chancellor, and therefore the first of Henry VIII's Ministers. He obtained a Cardinal's hat and became the Papal Legate and, at one time, he even hoped to become Pope. There was no limit to his ambitions.

There seemed no limit to his power either, but for all the great offices he held, and for all his papal and ecclesiastical titles, he was never anything more than a general manager of Henry VIII's estates. Wolsey had been the main organizer of the king's military expeditions, just as it was his diplomacy which bound Henry, on the whole, to the Pope and the emperor. When Henry VIII tired of his attempts to make England a great continental power and, when he began to see the importance of the Protestant German Princes and of France, he began to criticize Wolsey and to listen to the many people who hated Wolsey for his arrogance.

Wolsey's fall came when he failed to get the Pope to annul Henry's marriage to Queen Catherine; and when it came it was sudden. Forced to resign the Chancellorship, he was allowed to attend to his duties as Archbishop of York, something he had scarcely done before, after he had given the king his magnificent palace at Hampton Court. But Henry had second thoughts. Wolsey was summoned to London on an accusation of high treason. He died on the way, at Leicester, and it is recorded that he said: "Had I but served my God with half the zeal I served my King, he would not have given me over in my grey hairs." The great Cardinal had none of Becket's spiritual power and resolution and before the king's displeasure he split like a rotten bough.

Among Wolsey's enemies had been a dark-haired maid of honour to the queen, Anne Boleyn, of whom Henry was strongly enamoured and to whom he wrote some celebrated love-letters and a beautiful poem in which he compares his love to the evergreen holly. Henry's passion for Anne Boleyn was real and he meant it when he wrote the following lines:

> Now unto my lady,
> promise to her I make,
> from all other only,
> to her I me betake.

Yet it may be that this passion perhaps only lent enchantment to Henry's decision to divorce Catherine.

It was difficult then, and it is impossible now, to assess how much infatuation and how much policy played in Henry's decision; but probably policy counted for more than passion, for though Henry was an amorous man he was even more a deeply ambitious king. Catherine had borne him seven children but none of them had survived for more than a few months, except a female child, Mary, born in 1516. The king was determined to have a son. The king's anger with Wolsey for failing to get the marriage annulled, the breach with Rome which led to the Act of Supremacy in 1534, were above all, it would seem, the consequence of the Tudor itch for a male heir and for a settled succession.

Henry had some reason to be vexed with Papal authority. His sister Margaret had obtained a divorce from her second husband, the Earl of Angus, and there had been many other cases of annulled marriages of princes. The difficulties, as Henry understood them, were simply that Catherine was the niece of the emperor, and Pope Clement VII was the emperor's prisoner. The emperor's armies had sacked Rome in 1527. Henry was determined that his marriage to Anne Boleyn should be legitimate, thinking again of an heir to the throne.

During the divorce proceedings, Sir Thomas More, Chancellor after Wolsey's fall, lost his head for refusing to accept the Act of Supremacy, as did Bishop Fisher, another former friend of Henry's. Sir Thomas More was the man whom Henry as a young king would frequently visit, putting his arm round his neck as they walked in More's beautiful garden in Chelsea. More, in those early days, had expressed surprise that the young royal theologian should so adamantly defend the power of the Pope as to say to him: "For we received from the Holy See our Crown Imperial." This was a doctrine which More, the staunchest of Catholics, had never heard advanced before.

Henry's matrimonial affairs continued, to the end of his life, to be greatly concerned with this desire for male heirs. He was unlucky in the business of begetting. Anne, after a daughter who was to become Queen Elizabeth I, had borne a still-born male child. Anne Boleyn, accused of infidelities which were probably real, went to the block for failure to help the English Crown effectively. Her marriage was annulled by Archbishop Cranmer on the grounds that marriage with a former mistress was void in the eyes of the Church. Fortunately this counterfeit argument did not make Elizabeth illegitimate.

From his third wife, Jane Seymour, Henry obtained a son, Edward VI, Henry's successor indeed, but a sickly intellectual boy

389

who was to die young of consumption. Jane Seymour herself died in childbirth. In 1540 Henry made a political marriage with Anne of Cleves, English policy then seeking a Protestant alliance against the Pope and emperor. The marriage was annulled by mutual consent and by an Act of Parliament. Anne's ugliness lost Henry's minister, Thomas Cromwell, who had planned the marriage, his head. Cromwell was hated by conservative aristocracy of whom the Duke of Norfolk was the leader.

Henry had his eye on the Duke of Norfolk's niece, Catherine Howard, and she became his fifth queen. In November, 1542, however, Parliament passed an Act of Attainder against her, and she was executed on the grounds of unchastity before her marriage and of culpable indiscretion after it. Henry's last wife, Catherine Parr, was a widow, thirty years of age, who looked after him in his last years and who survived him.

In 1529 Henry summoned a Parliament. He was now to preside over the great social and ideological revolution, the effect of which was to establish Crown and Parliament together as the bulwarks of the new England. To ensure divorce from Catherine, he had to make himself Head of the Church in England and for this he needed Parliament.

The Parliament which assembled in 1529 and which sat for seven years was the first English Parliament which represented not merely the feudal nobility but the new England of rich merchants, the new landowning classes, the rich merchants and important citizens of the towns. This Parliament expressed a new mood in the country and it was a mood which suited the king. It was bent on carrying Henry VII's administrative reforms a stage further and its principal target was the Church, which owned between one-fifth and one-third of the total land of the country. Whilst the bishops' lands formed part of the taxable wealth of the country, the extensive domains of the monasteries and convents were the property of the Pope. The dissolution of the monasteries in England was an inevitable step and no modern nation, Catholic or Protestant, could come into being when such a concentration of wealth and influence remained outside the jurisdiction of the State.

The dissolution was carried out harshly and unjustly in many places and the suppression of centres of education and of good works was bitterly resented in many parts of England. But most of the monasteries no longer performed the functions which they had done in medieval England. If the moral laxity of certain monastic houses was exaggerated by Thomas Cromwell, who was responsible for their break-up, many of the 560 houses with their great properties were occupied by some score or even less of monks or nuns, and hence were inevitably parasitic organizations.

The dissolution brought immense wealth to Henry VIII, who created from the people who bought the monastic lands from the Crown a new class of landed men. These new land-owners, unlike the remnants of the feudal aristocracy, felt themselves and their future to be intimately bound up with both the king and Parliament. The ecclesiastical legislation of Henry's reign was therefore of the first importance in carrying on and consolidating the silent social revolution begun by the first of the Tudors. When, in 1543, Henry VIII confirmed the members of the House of Commons in their freedom from arrest he said:

We be informed by our judges that we at no time stand so high in our estate royal as in the time of Parliament, when we as head and you as members are conjoined and knit together in one body politic.

It was by refusal to accept this basic idea of the inter-relation between king and Parliament that James I lost the esteem of his subjects and his son, Charles I, his head.

Henry's revolution in church affairs was not, in his mind, nor in that of the majority of his subjects, a break with the Catholic Church. It was simply an affirmation that the Church could not stand outside the law and the economic needs of England. Essentially it was the same in motivation as the various Acts of Henry II in the thirteenth and Edward III in the fourteenth century to assert Royal over Papal supremacy. Henry's revolution was anti-clerical but not anti-Catholic. The doctrine of Henry's Church was virtually unchanged after the Act of Supremacy. But, of course, a stronger movement was working in English minds at the time. The setting up of the Bible in English, which took place in Henry's reign, was of major importance for the growth of English Protestantism. But the effect of Henry's character and views was that of moderating the violence of religious reformism and, but for the Act of Supremacy, of maintaining the Church of England as part of the ancient body of European Christianity.

The end of Henry's reign saw renewed costly and also ineffective wars with France and Scotland and an extension, remarkably successfully carried out, of English administration in Wales. Henry's work for the British Navy was of great importance and it was thanks to it that towards the end of the century England could face war with Spain and defeat the Armada. Towards the end of his life Henry grew more and more tyrannical. Some years before his death an ulcerated leg gave him continued pain and prevented him taking exercise. He grew immensely fat and had to have a cage with a pulley to carry him upstairs. His face was swollen, his eyes hidden. A writer of the time describes him as having "a body and a half, very abdominous and unwieldy with fat. And it was death to him to be dieted, so great his appetite, and death not to be dieted, so great his corpulence". He died in April, 1547, holding the hand of Archbishop Cranmer, the main author of the Book of Common Prayer which remains one of the abiding glories of Henry's reign.

Over and over again Henry, to men and women, showed himself a capricious, heartless and bloodthirsty tyrant. "He spared no man in his rage and no woman in his lust," it was said of him. Hundreds of Catholics were massacred for resisting his orders, hundreds of Protestants were burnt for refusing to accept the Six Articles of the Church of England. A man was hanged for eating flesh on a Friday. His great victims to perish on the headsman's block included two queens, three ministers of the Crown, Sir Thomas More and Bishop Fisher, the Earl of Surrey, the Abbots of Fountains and Jervaulx, the Marquis of Exeter and the Countess of Salisbury—descendants of the Plantagenet kings.

Yet this toll of blood did not shake the Crown. Henry was a despot, but the satisfaction of his desires and the alleviation of his fears seemed to the majority of his subjects to be carried out in the public interest. It was for the sake of getting rid of Catherine, his first queen, that Henry embarked on the breach with Rome which led to the Act of Supremacy. But this, together with the dissolution of the monasteries, was in accordance with English thinking. The Reformation, which came, in its true form, in the next reign, divided the country. But it was because King Henry had taken the country with him in the first steps that England was spared the wars of religion which so long harassed France and devastated Germany. Henry gave England a Parliament with an importance and a representative quality which no other similar body on the Continent was to possess until after the French Revolution.

If Henry had died in 1529 his hands would not have been stained with so much blood, but he would have left the memory of a play-boy king. As it is, Henry stands out among the greatest of English kings. He showed a remarkable insight into the feelings of his subjects. Self-indulgent as he was, he was industrious and worked hard and consistently for the greatness of England. Perhaps this was why to the very last, even when he was blotched and bloated, he remained a popular monarch.

CHARLES V (Emperor)
(1500–1558)

GREAT MONARCHS nearly always have some uncommon qualities of intellect and personality. Charles V, who was certainly the greatest European monarch of his time, is a remarkable exception. An ordinary, commonplace, unprepossessing man, son of a mentally defective mother, he dominated Europe and eclipsed monarchs far more gifted than himself.

Charles was born at Ghent on 20 February, 1500, to a great heritage. He belonged to that unique European family the Habsburgs, who have married their way to power throughout the centuries.* His grandfather, Emperor Maximilian I, brought about the most gainful marriages of any Habsburg. To the Habsburg inheritance of Austria he acquired the Netherlands by marrying Mary of Burgundy. His crowning triumph of matrimonial statecraft was marrying his son Philip to Joanna, the daughter of Ferdinand and Isabella of Spain (*q.v.*). This brought a splendid inheritance to the Habsburgs which included not only Spain, but half of Italy, Sardinia and the vast and rich empire of Spain in the New World which Columbus had discovered for Isabella and Ferdinand. It was a golden windfall for the Habsburgs, but a disaster for Spain, which had just been united in nationhood by Ferdinand and Isabella and had a glorious future before it. That this future was not realized was mainly due to the intrusion into their history of the Habsburgs, none of whom—not even Charles V—had any talent for statesmanship.

Philip died and Queen Joanna went mad. Their son was Charles, who at the age of eleven inherited the kingdom of the Netherlands from Philip. His grandfather Maximilian appointed his daughter Margaret, Charles's aunt, to act as Regent for him, a job which this talented woman performed with great success.

In Spain, Ferdinand, husband of the late Queen Isabella, became king again, as his daughter Joanna, Charles's mother, was unfit to rule. Ferdinand died in 1516 and Charles inherited Spain and its great empire.

*The Habsburgs gave rise to the proverb: *Bella gerunt alii, tu, felix Austria, nube.* (While others wage war, you, happy Austria, marry.)

This youth, who was the greatest of the Habsburgs and represented them at the summit of their power, and upon whom fell a kind of illusory greatness, had a thin pale face and a projecting lower jaw which made both talking and eating difficult. He was very conscious of his impediment. He spoke little and was shy and awkward at court, where he made the worst possible impression upon foreign ambassadors who described him as a weakling, without character, and practically half-witted. At this time Henry VIII, handsome, brilliant, talented, was on the English throne, and Francis I, courtly, gallant, full of easy charm, was King of France. It was an age of young rulers, and Charles, the most powerful, looked the most unpromising.

How wrong was the contemporary assessment of this fledgling emperor is a matter of history. When it came to shaping European history, the glamorous monarchs of England and France did a great deal less than Charles who, despite his modest talent and ability, possessed a strength of will and determination which did not show in his youth. The fact that the task of ruling his vast dominions was beyond him does not detract from the fact that the tremendous and devoted effort he made was enormously to his credit and showed him to be a man of character and integrity.

He became King of Spain in January, 1516, but did not visit his Spanish dominions until the autumn of the following year, for many preparations were necessary before the royal fleet especially fitted out for Charles and his eight hundred attendants was ready to sail. Charles embarked on 8 September, dressed in a high-collared crimson satin tunic, a sleeveless cape fastened with a jewelled brooch, high leggings over scarlet stockings and a crimson cap. With the gaily attired young monarch went his sister Eleanor, and the voyage was a happy and exciting adventure for these exalted youngsters, in the springtime not only of their lives, but of this fabulous century.

Their first duty was to see their poor mad mother. Charles had not seen her for many years, so it cannot be thought that it was a particularly distressing meeting. Queen Joanna did not recognize them, as her disturbed mind could not admit to the fact that her children could have grown up.

Charles was received badly in Spain. He could rot speak a word of Spanish and he was surrounded by Flemish attendants who were distasteful to the haughty Spaniards who did not like foreigners. Spain bitterly resented the Habsburg marriage which had brought them a foreign monarch. If they were to have a Habsburg at all they would have preferred Charles's younger brother, Ferdinand, who at least had been brought up in Castile. The kingdoms of Castile and Aragon had lately been united to form Spain, which just then required wise and firm government. This the inexperienced Charles was quite unable to provide and he began his reign with some disastrous mistakes. When he took the oath before the Cortes of Castile he affronted the Castilians by appointing Flemish ministers over them. At Saragossa, the capital of Aragon, he was badly received, the Aragonese making it plain that they would rather have Ferdinand. His reception at Barcelona, Valencia and Valladolid was no better.

In 1519 he heard news of the death of his grandfather, Emperor Maximilian, and he left Spain in a hurry, appointing Bishop Adrian of Utrecht—another hated foreigner—to be regent in his place, to the grievous annoyance of his Spanish subjects who were in a state of open revolt within a few weeks of his departure. The rebels believed that Charles's mother was not really mad, but had been imprisoned in the Castle of Tordesillas so that Charles should have the throne. They could not seriously have believed this, for it was notorious that Joanna had been insane for many years. Their act of capturing the mad queen and discovering the sad truth about her condition is eloquent of their desperation to have a Spaniard on their throne. The revolt then collapsed.

The death of Maximilian, said to be the vainest of the Habsburgs, left open the question of the Imperial crown of the Holy Roman Empire, which consisted mainly of the patchwork of Germanic states. Maximilian naturally wanted to keep this in the family, but the emperors were elected by the Germanic princelings. It was not a hereditary crown. Charles, conscious, as all Habsburgs, of his destiny, thought the purple should fall to him.

But he had two rivals—Henry VIII of England and Francis I of France. Of the two Francis was more serious, and was his enemy as well as his rival. Francis and Charles were at war with each other during most of their reigns.

On his way from Spain to Germany in 1519 Charles, hearing that Francis had arranged a meeting with the King of England, forestalled him by going to see Henry first. He reckoned he had some claim on Henry who was married to his aunt, Catherine of Aragon. Cardinal Wolsey met Charles at Dover and greeted him with a long speech in Latin of which the unlettered Charles couldn't understand a word.

The following day Henry accompanied Charles to Canterbury to visit Catherine, and was impressed by his intelligent conversation and pleasant manner. The astute Henry knew he had more to gain from Charles than from Francis. When Henry attended the splendid but inconsequential Field of the Cloth of Gold given in his honour by Francis, he placed more importance on a quiet meeting he had in France with Charles who didn't have to erect pavilions of gold cloth in order to gain Henry's ear.

Francis was genuinely afraid that if Charles became emperor too much power would be concentrated in his hands, and his fears were shared by Pope Leo X, who supported Francis's candidature for the Imperial Crown. Perhaps the Pope's support of Francis was the kiss of death, for some of the electors were Protestants, or at least shared the anticlericalism which was rampant in Germany at that time. In any event they chose Charles and he was crowned emperor at Aix-la-Chapelle on 20 October, 1520.

He was twenty. He had never been to Germany before, and he could not speak the language of his imperial subjects any more than he could speak the language of his Spanish subjects.

Germany of those days consisted of a hundred or so states, each with its own method of government and taxation, its own army and foreign policy—with the emperor as its overlord. To combine these states into a united nation like France was one of Charles's ambitions. Another great problem faced him as a faithful Catholic. All over Germany voices were being raised in angry protest against the Church—its wealth, its abuses, its corruption, its immoralities. The Reformation movement led by Martin Luther was growing rapidly. Lutherans believed that obedience to the teaching of the Bible was all that was necessary to a Christian and denied the infallibility of the Pope. The Church was alarmed at this spread of heresy and demanded the destruction of Lutheranism.

Charles's election as emperor had been greeted with elation in Germany, for the reformers expected that he would be on their side. But they misjudged Charles. He believed that the Church should be reformed, but he was against any change in its doctrines. For his part he failed utterly to grasp the significance of the Reformation and could not see that the points of view of the Protestants and the Catholics were quite irreconcilable.

But Charles refused to condemn Luther unheard, despite the urging of Pope Leo, and he summoned him to the assembly at Worms, where Luther refused to recant, saying he would not act against his conscience. There was nothing more that Charles could do and Luther was outlawed. A month later the famous Edict of Worms forbade the preaching of the new doctrines.

Charles had two other big problems to deal with—the continuous war with Francis and the invasion of the infidel Turks into Hungary and against the eastern frontier of his empire.

In fact Charles was probably one of the most harried monarchs who ever lived. He spent his whole reign travelling the length and breadth of his vast dominions to meet first one enemy then another. Not only was he dedicated and conscientious in the pursuit of his impossible task. He was also brave, for he led his armies personally in the field. But he was beset with so many problems, he never had time to solve any of them. He never learned how to govern, he had so many burdens on his shoulders. All through his reign he was haunted by his early mistakes, particularly those he made in Spain. Nevertheless he did not fail. He kept his scattered empire together. He made a brave attempt to bring the Lutherans back into the fold of the Mother Church, and he held up the advance of the Turks. He did this by dogged determination and hard work.

The continual enmity of Francis involved Charles in a protracted series of wars. One of the causes of this enmity was the feeling Francis had of being hemmed in between Charles's widespread territories. Both Charles and Francis claimed Burgundy and Milan, and the fight for these and other possessions went on between France and the overgrown power of the Habsburgs long after Charles and Francis were dead.

Most of the fighting took place in northern Italy, where neither Francis nor Charles distinguished themselves on the field of battle. Charles's greatest success was at the battle of Pavia, where his army, desperate, half-starved, turned on an apparently victorious French army which was attacking Pavia, and in a spectacular reversal of fortune destroyed it. Francis was wounded and taken prisoner and had to sign the Treaty of Madrid on 13 January, 1526, in order to get his freedom.

During that year Charles married Isabella, the Infanta of Portugal. In the true Habsburg tradition, he married for her rich dowry, though he fell in love with her after marriage. He had been engaged some ten times before and had an illegitimate daughter, Margaret, but he remained true to his wife while she lived. He never had a mistress or a court favourite as was usual in that immoral age. The only women who exercised any influence over him apart from his wife were his Aunt Margaret and his sister Mary, who both took over from him the burden of government in the Netherlands. In the same way his brother Ferdinand ruled in Austria and Germany during Charles's long absences.

After Pavia Charles ran short of money, despite the golden resources of his empire in the Americas, and was unable to pay his troops, who lived by plundering. They attacked and pillaged Rome, while the Pope fled in terror to the Castle of St. Angelo. This act aroused the conscience of the world, and Charles was held responsible, for while the sacred city was being sacked and despoiled by the Spanish and German ruffians of his army he was in Spain celebrating the birth of his son Philip with tournaments and festivities.

At this time both the Pope and Henry VIII, playing the Machiavellian game, had gone over to the side of France in order to prevent Charles becoming too powerful. The Pope in particular was afraid of Charles calling a General Council of Christendom in order to settle the Lutheran controversy. This was certainly in Charles's mind, but the Papacy were firmly against it, afraid it would damage the prestige of the Church.

With both England and France now allied against him, Charles lost all his gains in Italy except Naples and Milan. He was unable to assist his armies there, for the Spanish Cortes declined to grant monies which could be used for war against the Pope. But a sudden reversal of fortune occurred when Francis caused Genoa to revolt by putting a French Governor and garrison over them. The Genoese fleet thereupon went over to Charles and the French were forced out of Genoa. With the tide turned Charles was supreme in Italy once more, and came to terms with Pope Clement, who crowned him with great pomp at Bologna in 1530. He was the last emperor to be crowned by the Pope.

In the nine years in which Charles had been absent from Germany, Lutheranism had become firmly established. In 1535 there had been a peasant revolt in which the princes had been vicious in their alarmed retaliation. Luther, horrified at the dreadful result of his teachings, changed his policy in order to re-establish the authority of the princes. In 1526 the Diet of Speyer gave the rulers the right to determine the religion of their subjects.

Charles was engaged at the far eastern boundaries of his great empire where the Turks were at the gates of Vienna. Charles, with his usual dogged energy, assembled a fine army of Spaniards, Italians, Germans and Flemings. Suleiman the Magnificent, the Turks' famous Sultan, wisely withdrew in the face of Charles's imposing host.

Charles hastened to Spain, for there was no rest for him, to face the Turks on the Mediterranean front. Leading his troops in person, he conquered Tunis and freed hundreds of Christian slaves. Acclaimed as a hero, he returned to Italy to have another war with Francis in the late 1530s which ended with yet another inconclusive truce.

For the next sixteen years Charles continued to wrestle with his three great tasks—each one of which would have taxed the energies and abilities of any ruler. From fighting the Turks in Hungary or the Mediterranean, he went to wrestle with the Lutherans' consciences, and there was always Francis harrying him in Italy and elsewhere with constant warfare. He had no hope of solving the intractable problem of the split in the Church and a bitter civil war broke out in Germany. He defeated the army of the Protestant princes' Schmalkaldic League at Mühlberg, even though he was in wretched health and suffered continuously from gout.

In 1547 Francis died, to Charles's great relief. The tired, overtaxed emperor then made great efforts to effect peace where there was no peace. By 1552 all of Germany was once more aflame with war. Surrounded by his foes, Charles left Augsburg for Innsbruck, from whence he had to make an ignominious flight in a snowstorm at midnight across the Brenner Pass, carried on a litter and with only six attendants. Weary and disillusioned, he was already considering unshouldering his enormous burden.

The bitter civil war in Germany was finally pacified by the Peace of Augsburg in 1555, which laid it down that in future any prince might be allowed to choose his own religion, and his subjects must accept his choice or go into exile.

In that same year Charles solemnly abdicated at Brussels before the assembled deputies of the Netherlands. He gave his empire and his German lands to his brother Ferdinand, and Spain, the Burgundian lands and Italy to his son Philip.

He retired to a small house attached to the monastery at Yuste in Spain. Then came the happiest time of his life, for he was by no means a recluse. He took with him his favourite books and pictures, his fine clothing and jewels, and he kept in constant touch with his friends and relations. His son Philip often came seeking his advice. He enjoyed gardening and watching Torriani at his bench making clocks and mechanical toys.

But his health was bad. He still suffered from gout and his insatiable gastronomic indulgence considerably shortened his life. He enjoyed his retirement for only two years, and a little before his death he held a rehearsal of his own funeral. The last of the great Holy Roman Emperors died on 30 September, 1558, clasping his wife's crucifix in his hands.

CATHERINE DE' MEDICI

(1519–89)

CATHERINE DE' MEDICI of France rivals Mary I of England as Europe's most vilified queen. It was fortunate for her that John Foxe's *Book of Martyrs* was published before the Massacre of St. Bartholomew, or she would have been mercilessly pilloried in that famous work of Protestant martyrology. Catherine cannot escape responsibility for that terrible event. Her name is for ever besmirched with it. But she was not the only ruthless and cynical person in Paris at that time. Religious fanaticism belonged to the people. Their rulers took political advantage of it.

The name of Medici, too, was no recommendation. As a family, they were alleged to be steeped in crime and vice and to be adept at poisoning their political rivals. Catherine de' Medici was accused of introducing this toxic form of politics into France in order to gain power. No doubt much of this was exaggerated, but in the final count Catherine does not escape blameless, even if the excuse is made for her that she was after all only a creature of her age.

Legend has it that the Medici family was founded by Perseus, and that Benvenuto Cellini's famous bronze of Perseus holding on high the head of Medusa was executed at Florence to symbolize the victory of the Medici over the republic. The Medici name is an illustrious one in the chronicles of Florence, and they were princes of the state as well as of commerce. Lorenzo the Magnificent was one of the greatest figures of the Renaissance. Two Medicis became Popes and two queens of France. They were one of the great families of Europe.

Catherine was born in 1519 at Florence, the daughter of Lorenzo II, the Duke of Urbino, and Princess Madeleine de la Tour d'Auvergne. Both her parents died when she was a child, and she was adopted by her uncle, Pope Clement VII, and educated at a convent. Clement was the Pope who refused Henry VIII his divorce from Catherine of Aragon.

Clement arranged an excellent marriage for his orphaned niece with Prince Henry of Valois, the second son of King Francis I of France. The marriage took place at Marseilles in 1533. Both bride and bridegroom were fourteen, and as was not unusual in royal marriages saw each other for the first time when they met at the altar.

Catherine went to the Court of her father-in-law and at first showed no sign of the dominant personality she later became. Straight from the convent she had much to learn, and she learnt her lesson well in the brilliant and sophisticated Court of Francis I.

When the Dauphin died in 1536, Henry unexpectedly became heir to the throne and Catherine the future Queen of France. All the same she was not liked, and malicious tongues wagged about her, saying that she had employed one of the Medici family poisoners to do away with the Dauphin.

But the greatest threat to Catherine's influence was Diane de Poitiers, a middle-aged adventuress, who completely captivated the young Prince Henry, and inflamed him with a passion which lasted until the day of his death. Diane de Poitiers was a clever and ambitious woman who successfully set out to dominate the future king. It was said that she had also been the mistress of his father, Francis I, though this story has little foundation. Francis died in 1547, and though Catherine de' Medici became Queen of France in name Diane de Poitiers was virtual queen. She set about the task of enriching herself and her family. Henry II gave her the Duchy of Valentinois as well as many of the crown jewels.

During this time Catherine de' Medici waited patiently in obscurity. For the first ten years of the marriage she bore Henry no child. Her enemies accused her of lesbianism, and there was talk of divorce even before the old king died. But Henry was fond of Catherine in a brotherly kind of way, and with his accession to the throne the necessity of having children was taken more seriously, and then Catherine bore him sons and daughters in rapid succession.

The Reformation which had been demanded in vain from the Papacy in the fifteenth century was now being brought about in the Church without the assistance of the Popes, to the accompaniment of much strife, persecution and bitterness. In France Protestantism evolved into a political party called the Huguenots, the leader of which was Gaspard Coligny, Admiral of France.

Henry II was a bigoted Catholic, and ruthlessly opposed Protestantism, using his royal authority with great severity against all opposition. His death on 10 July, 1559, following a head wound received while tilting with the Count de Montgomery at a royal tournament was no cause for universal sorrow, even though his heir was a sickly, nervous boy of fifteen, Francis II.

The first thing Catherine de' Medici did was to banish Diane de Poitiers from the Court and force her to give up the crown jewels Henry had given her, as well as many valuable lands and possessions. Diane retired to her château at Anet, where she died in 1566.

The boy king during his brief reign was completely dominated by his mother and his wife. Francis was married to Mary Queen of Scots, who, at the age of seventeen, and in the full bloom of her legendary beauty, became Queen of France. Mary was related to the powerful Guise family, who were the leaders of the Catholic faction in France. Through her, Francis Duke of Guise gained control of the army, and his brother, Cardinal of Lorraine, held a high position in the councils of State.

The youthful king suffered from a hereditary disease which made him impotent. All the same, he and his young and glamorous queen were said to be devoted to each other. Mary, at this stage in her famous career, had little interest in politics, and was content to be completely under the influence of her uncles, the two powerful Guises.

The Guises came from Lorraine and were considered by many to be no more French than the Italian Queen Mother. Their rivals were the Bourbon branch of the royal family led by the King of Navarre and the Prince of Condé, who were Protestants. In this battle for power in France Catherine de' Medici held a key position, and she now began to play a skilful game which showed that she had learned much during the years of her husband's reign when she had waited patiently in the background, living a passive but observant life. But those days were over, as France very soon discovered.

The Guises did not like her, and she was determined to break their power. She was equally determined not to throw in her lot with the Protestants. By habit and tradition a Catholic, she did not intend that the Protestants should gain the upper hand. She did not want them crushed either, as they were too valuable a counterbalance to the powerful Guises. She eventually proved a match for them all.

By the end of 1560 the sickly Francis II was in his grave and the predominance of the Guises was seriously undermined. Naturally enough they accused the Queen Mother of poisoning her son—after all she was a Medici. Catherine's second son, Charles, now came to the throne at the age of ten, as Charles IX. As was to be expected, he was completely dominated by his formidable mother, now forty-one, shrewd, vigorous, with a taste for power, and who immediately had herself made regent.

Up until that moment she had appeared to be little more than the retiring and self-sacrificing widow of Henry II. Suddenly she was supreme in France, unexpectedly imperious, and both the Bourbons and the Guises were forced to bow to her. They underrated her only at their peril, for she had a fine and subtle political sense and an Italian adroitness at intrigue. Behind her she had powerful men like Montmorency, Constable of France, Michel de l'Hôpital, who was Chancellor and her spokesman in the States General. For many years she now ruled France.

The impassioned religious battle of the Reformation, which stirred all Christendom as it had never been stirred before, left Catherine de' Medici cold. Like many people of today, she wondered what all the fuss was about. Trifles like images and vestments and whether the Mass should be said in Latin or French were certainly not worth fighting over in her opinion, and should be settled at a conference table. She shared none of the violence and intolerance of the Catholics and Calvinists, and believed that their differences could only be solved through the middle path of toleration.

She was, of course, entirely right in this, and hers was the only sane voice in France, if not Europe, at that time. But all her efforts at compromise came to nothing on account of the rage, suspicion and hatred which the division of Christianity had created in men's minds. Frenchmen found it impossible to worship God in their own particular way without fighting each other.

Her curiously modern approach to a subject which her age found quite intractable culminated in a meeting she summoned in August, 1561, of the leaders of both religious sides, at which she tried to get them to agree to some common ground. But the men of God only came to blows. Catherine then granted the Huguenots restricted rights of worship. The result was civil war.

The Wars of Religion, as they were called, began with the Massacre of Vassy on 1 March, 1562, and continued for the rest of Catherine's life. The fanaticism of both sides made the struggle more ferocious and brutal than an ordinary war. Terrible cruelties were committed, and the country was devastated. The Catholics were actively supported by Philip II of Spain, the Pope and the Italian states, while Elizabeth of England, the Lutherans and Calvinists of Germany and the Low Countries supported the Protestants.

During the first war, which lasted a year, both sides lost their leaders, including the powerful Duke of Guise, who was killed while attacking Orléans in February, 1563. The Peace of Amboise followed a month later, after which Protestants and Catholics united to drive out the English who had invaded France.

Catherine still wanted to settle the burning religious issue peacefully. She tried to persuade Philip II to form a Catholic Holy Alliance which would combat heresy without the use of force. But the time for reason and moderation was not yet, and the war broke out again. Neither side could gain a decision.

By 1570 Catherine, weary of the conflict and unable to crush the Protestant rebellion, once more tried negotiation. This time she proposed two diplomatic marriages, one between her son, Henry, and Elizabeth of England, and the other between her daughter, Margaret de Valois, and Henry of Navarre. Only the latter union was agreed, and Catherine thus became reconciled with the Protestants.

The Huguenot leader Coligny was allowed to return to Court and was admitted once more to the Council of State. It was a move Catherine quickly repented. Charles IX, now twenty, married to Elizabeth of Austria, dreamed of cutting a figure in the world. He was getting tired of being tied to the political apron-strings of his formidable mother. He received the celebrated Coligny with open arms, and the two became great friends.

Coligny, determined to emancipate the young king from the powerful influence of Catherine, put forward a proposition for ending the ruinous civil war which was tearing France apart and which threatened to break out again. He proposed a great national war against Spain. In this way the people of France would combine, regardless of their religious differences, and attack the Spanish Netherlands, with Charles at the head of the Army.

The idea appealed immensely to Charles who very much wanted to distinguish himself on the field of battle, but it greatly alarmed both the Queen Mother and the staunchly Catholic Guises. Their attempts to prevent it resulted in one of the most appalling massacres of European history.

Originally the intention was to get the dangerous Coligny out of the way by having him assassinated. This, in theory, was no difficult operation in the circumstances existing in France, and was nothing that Catherine de' Medici would have on her conscience, murder being part of the working of politics as she conceived it. The murder was arranged with Henry of Guise.

Just at this time there took place in Paris the marriage of Henry of Navarre—the heir to the French throne, should the sons of Catherine de' Medici die childless, which seemed probable—and

Margaret of Valois, Catherine's daughter. Henry of Navarre was France's man of destiny, who was to become the first of the Bourbon kings. The marriage was greatly favoured by Charles IX, though as a "mixed marriage" it scandalized the Catholics.

Three days after the marriage an attempt was made to murder Coligny as he left a Council of State meeting in the Louvre. The attempt failed and Coligny was only superficially wounded by shots.

The king was furious, and in order to prevent his discovery of her part in the attempted murder Catherine invented a story of a great Huguenot conspiracy led by Coligny. Charles took a lot of persuading, but his mother knew how to handle him and finally convinced him that what she said was true. Then the unstable Charles gave the fatal order to kill all the Huguenots in Paris.

The Huguenots had gathered in great numbers in Paris for the wedding between Protestant Henry of Navarre and the king's sister, and on the eve of St. Bartholomew's Day, 23 August, 1572, the signal was given and the massacre of the Huguenots began. Among the first to be killed was Coligny. In two days it was estimated that 10,000 Protestants had been killed. Once the slaughter had begun, it was impossible to restrain the fanatical populace, and the massacre continued in Paris until 17 September. It spread to the provinces, where it continued until 3 October. It was estimated that the number killed throughout France was 50,000.

The blame for this atrocity rests heavily upon Catherine de' Medici, who, unlike the populace, did not even have the excuse of fanaticism. She was not, however, universally blamed. Far from it. She received the congratulations of all the Catholic powers, and Pope Gregory XIII ordered that bonfires should be lighted and that this example of French loyalty to the Church should be signalized by a medal of commendation.

This shocking event did nothing to check Catherine's supremacy in France. Charles IX died two years later, haunted, fever-stricken, melancholic, and was succeeded by his brother, Henry III, another impotent weakling whom Catherine was easily able to dominate. The war and bloodshed between Protestants and Catholics continued until her death in January, 1589. Within a few months Henry III was murdered, and the religious fratricide in France was not stopped until Henry of Navarre ascended the throne as Henry IV.

He became a Catholic and under the Edict of Nantes granted toleration of worship to the Protestants. "Paris is worth a mass," he said, an attitude which Catherine of Medici would have thoroughly approved.

PHILIP II

King of Spain, Naples and Sicily

(1527–98)

THE RISE of Spain in the sixteenth century to a position of world power is one of the most dramatic events in world history. Whilst in the Middle Ages England and France, in different ways, were becoming powerful nation states, the Iberian peninsula was split up into a large number of Christian and Moorish principalities. At the end of the fourteenth century the Christian kings had conquered the Moors, all but the rich and highly civilized kingdom of Granada in the south-east. There was, however, no unity in the peninsula and it was not until the second half of the fifteenth century, when Castile and Aragon were united under Isabella and Ferdinand, that Granada fell and, with the exception of the western kingdom of Portugal, the rest of Spain acknowledged the sway of the monarchs of the two most powerful kingdoms.

Spain was born slowly and late but destined to become almost at once a world power such as had never been seen before. For a short while Spain ruled over an enormously larger part of the world than Rome had ever done. As events showed, it was an ephemeral empire constantly at war, and Spain had not the strength to sustain it nor sufficient economic foresight to use the immense wealth which she won from the New World to keep the homeland of this empire strong. But throughout the sixteenth century—from Henry VII to Queen Elizabeth—when Englishmen looked abroad they saw Spain as by far the most powerful nation of the world. Spain was a dominant power in Italy, the most civilized part of Europe, and owned the Netherlands which comprised Holland and Belgium and a large part of northern France; indeed French frontiers at that time began on the Somme. Spanish infantry were the best in Europe, and Spain's power at sea, though increasingly challenged by the English and Dutch pirates, was considered invincible until very late in the sixteenth century.

Marriage turned Spain into a European power at the same time that the Conquistadores who followed Columbus gave her a colonial empire. The daughter of Ferdinand and Isabella, Juana, married Philip, the son of the Habsburg Archduke of Austria, Maximilian I, who was also the Holy Roman Emperor, overlord, that is to say, of most of the kingdoms of Germany.

Maximilian by marriage had obtained Burgundy (which he afterwards lost to France) and the Netherlands. By another marriage he became lord of the Duchy of Milan, one of the richest parts of Italy. Now Maximilian's grandson by the marriage of Philip and Juana inherited Spain and her immense empire and also the Italian possessions of Spain—which included Sardinia, the kingdom of Naples and of Sicily. So this young Habsburg ruled over between a third and a half of Europe—excluding the large part of eastern Europe in the hands of the Ottoman Turks. This grandson, duly elected Holy Roman Emperor, was Charles V, whose aunt, Catherine of Aragon, married Henry VIII of England. The huge domains and the great ambition of Charles V led him into the wild dream, which was rather more than two hundred years old, of trying to unite Christendom. His European policy failed. Charles could, however, very fairly claim that he was a "European".

He was distinctly more an Austrian than a Spaniard in character and mind, but more than either he was a man of the Low Countries. He was most at home in Brussels, and when he came to Spain, as he did at infrequent intervals, he brought with him Flemings as advisers and friends. Towards the end of his life he grew rather more Spanish and married the daughter of the King of Portugal. After her death, he married his young son Philip to another Portuguese princess who died two years later in childbirth, bringing Philip a son, Don Carlos, who was later to cause him much misfortune.

In 1554 Charles V, still bent on his dynastic policies, married his dutiful, serious-minded son, for a second time, to a woman of thirty-six, Mary Tudor, Queen of England, the daughter of Catherine of Aragon. In 1556 the now aged Charles V summoned his son Philip from England, where he was expecting a son from his new wife, to Brussels, where he announced his abdication and his retirement to a monastery in southern Spain. But now the House of Austria limited its ambitions. The Holy Roman Empire and the lands of Austria went to Charles's brother. Philip, now Philip II of Spain, received by far the major part—Spain and its empire, the Low Countries, Milan and the old Spanish possessions in Italy.

In July, 1554, Philip landed in Southampton with the Duke of

Alba and a number of grandees and their wives and the next day he rode to Winchester, through pouring rain, where the queen was waiting for him. It poured with rain and the king was soaked to the skin. He was taken to her apartments in the bishop's palace through a number of narrow gardens between high walls and up a winding staircase to a back door into the great hall. One of Philip's biographers, Mr. William Thomas Walsh, has described the scene:

> It was Philip's first glimpse of his second wife; she was walking up and down as he entered, a short slender woman in a black velvet gown with a petticoat of frosted silver and a jewelled girdle and collar. Her complexion was red and white, her hair reddish, her face round, her nose rather low and wide, the whole expression indicating great kindness and clemency; and, adds the Venetian ambassador, to whom we are indebted for the description of Mary, were not her age on the decline, she might be called handsome rather than the contrary.

Philip on his father's instructions did everything he could to please the English, including the drinking of beer, a beverage which, according to Froude, made him shudder. He became popular with the English, though the very Protestant burghers of London distrusted him. He was a good horseman, and with his white skin, flaxen hair and beard he might have been an Englishman. The marriage was not unpopular either, and it will be remembered that Mary's mother, Catherine of Aragon, had been very much liked by the English people.

The marriage was to the advantage of England, for among its terms was that England should not be drawn into Spanish wars. Charles V, anxious about his Europe rather than his Spain, wanted to see the long-standing, close relationship between England and the Netherlands strengthened so that these countries should for ever stand as a barrier against France. When it was announced that Mary was pregnant there was much public rejoicing except among the extreme Protestant section of the population. The pregnancy turned out to be an illusion. By that time the Marian persecutions of Protestants had begun and the queen was fast losing her popularity.

Historians disagree over Philip's role in this, but most authorities consider that ever mindful of what his brief had been from his father, he advised against the persecutions and other acts liable to inflame English opinion. Philip was not against the persecution of heretics in general, but he was above all politic. He reconciled Princess Elizabeth, the daughter of Anne Boleyn, with her half-sister the queen, and after he had left England for Spain, and when it was clear that Mary would never bear him a son, he supported, by every means in his power, the accession of Elizabeth to the throne, even though she was suspect of leaning towards the Protestants. He preferred a heretic Queen of England with whom he was on good terms to the Catholic Mary Stuart who was closely bound up with France and was another pretender.

In 1559 Philip returned to Spain which he was never afterwards to leave. Not liked in the Low Countries or in Germany, he became the most Spanish of kings, and by temperament and character admirably suited to rule the Spaniards. He governed Spain as autocrat, keeping power in his own hands over everything, making his decisions slowly and after a great deal of thought. From the Escorial, the monastery-palace which he built near Madrid, the king's written orders made their way across the Atlantic and all over Europe, precise, carefully worded and no doubt by the time they reached his viceroys or commanders in Brussels or Mexico City, often infuriatingly out-of-date.

Philip believed in slowness and method. He was not an absolute monarch in the sense that Louis XIV was. Every Spanish province had its Cortes or its Junta with carefully preserved traditions and prejudices. Philip had to go before all these bodies before he received a penny in taxes or could be sure of enforcing his laws. He completed the unity of Spain, balancing the needs of sovereignty and the rights and susceptibilities of the Spanish provinces in a system of government which combined absolutism and enlightened evolution. As a recent historian has said: "Whatever else he did for the Spaniards, he knew how to govern them."

The reign of Philip II is notable for the revival of the Inquisition in Spain which had flourished in the reign of Ferdinand and Isabella. The Inquisition has incurred abroad, and particularly in Protestant countries, a hatred which it only partly deserves. In the Netherlands, where increasingly it was used not to convert heretics so much as to enforce Spanish domination, it was no doubt a detestable institution. In Spain too the burning of heretics cannot commend itself to the general conscience of mankind. But the fact is that the Inquisition was popular with the nation as a whole, and the small extremist sects of Protestants who had grown up in Barcelona or Seville were feared and disliked as allies of Spain's enemies. The people also feared, and were jealous of, the numerous converted Moors and Jews whose reliability as Christians and Spaniards was examined by the Inquisition. Heresy was strangled at birth; if the means employed were sometimes atrocious the executions and expulsions fortified the weak plant of Spanish unity and saved Spain from the religious civil wars which brought France to the brink of ruin.

From the start of his reign until its end, Philip was committed to waging wars on several fronts. The unavoidable struggle was against the Turks, a war to which he was committed as the head of the most powerful Christian kingdom of Europe, a Mediterranean power directly threatened by the Turkish fleet and the ally of Austria most threatened by the Turkish armies. In the reign of Charles V, Suleiman the Magnificent's forces defeated and killed the King of Hungary at the battle of Mohacs in 1526 and three years later nearly took Vienna. Although Charles V managed to check the Turkish advance into Europe, he suffered severe reverses on sea and in North Africa.

Philip was more successful than his father by waging war in the Mediterranean more prudently. He relieved Malta rather at the last moment. He refrained from offensive operations, concentrating on protecting Italy and the coast of Spain. In 1571, in alliance with the Pope and the Republic of Venice, the Spanish fleet commanded by John of Austria, Philip's illegitimate half-brother, inflicted a crushing defeat on the Turks at Lepanto. All the sovereigns of Europe, including Queen Elizabeth, sent messages of congratulation to Philip. Lepanto did not end the Turkish menace, but, after Lepanto, though the Turks drove Spain from parts of Tunisia, Turkish sea-power slowly declined.

In Charles V's reign Spain and France had constantly fought each other in Italy and the Low Countries, with the Pope, Venice and England now on one side, now on the other. In 1559 there supervened a period of peace between Spain and France. Philip married Henry II's daughter, Elizabeth of Valois, after Mary's death, his third diplomatic marriage. But, soon after, the wars of religion in France saw Spanish armies fighting in France on the side of the Catholic League, sometimes against the King of France. Philip considered himself the defender of the Catholic faith everywhere; but it was because a France which tolerated religious freedom would inevitably be drawn to support the revolt of the Netherlands that Philip intervened so persistently.

The Netherlands were economically of vital importance to Spain, a market for her wool and her raw materials from America and the source of her textiles, her metallurgical needs and a great deal of her munitions of war. Antwerp, Bruges, and Ghent were great banking and entrepôt centres which rendered vital services to Spain. These close economic ties made the Spanish connexion not irksome to the nobility and merchants of the Netherlands and, under Charles V, their country was part of a European empire and ruled by a prince who understood them.

Philip, however, was a Spanish king. Further, he was determined to check the rapid spread of heresy—Lutheran, Calvinist and Anabaptist—in the Netherlands, and so, little by little, the revolt against Spain became general. Spanish troops by 1557 were concentrated massively in the Low Countries under the Duke of Alba to break revolts which were gradually winning over the Flemish nobles such as Egmont and the Prince of Orange. For a time Alba and his seasoned troops succeeded in repressing revolts, and at the Battle of Gembloux in 1578 the Spanish victory decided the maintenance of the southern provinces in their Spanish allegiance. The northern provinces, which are now Holland, defied Spain on land and sea with their pirate ships.

Open war with England did not begin until 1585. Of course, England and Englishmen sympathized with the Protestants in France and with the rebels in the Netherlands. But Philip had been careful never to support, in any incriminating or decisive manner, the Catholic fifth-column in England, and Elizabeth had pursued a middle-of-the-road policy in religious matters.

The cause of the open clash between Spain and England was the activities of the English mariners who were determined to break down the Spanish ban on trade with the New World, first in the Caribbean and then in the Pacific. Piracy was a sign of England's weakness and inability to challenge Spain's empire in a serious manner. It amounted to "singeing the King of Spain's beard", in Drake's celebrated phrase. The Spanish treasure-fleets, and Spanish trade, were comparatively little affected. The exploits of Drake aroused tremendous patriotic enthusiasm in England. The feeling of insecurity which Spanish merchants and traders began to have was more important than their actual losses; nevertheless, men hesitated a little before investing in trade ventures and a great cry arose in Spain for punishing England. Philip, prudent as ever, began to see, as the exploits of British seamen grew more daring, that Elizabeth was waging an undeclared war against him at sea, and, what counted for more, in the Netherlands.

Philip's fortunes seemed to reach a new height. The Turks had been defeated; the affairs of the Catholic League in France were going well; the Pope, so often opposed to Spain, was friendly. In 1583 Philip became King of Portugal and at one stroke acquired

Portugal's vast possessions in Africa and in India. With Lisbon in his hands a vigorous emphasis on Atlantic policy was inevitable. He began to build up the Great Armada to conquer England. The defeat of this Armada in 1588 was the greatest blow Philip had ever sustained. It was a triumph for English seamanship, even if it was the winds which finally blew the huge fleet of Medina Sidonia around the inhospitable coasts of Scotland and Ireland. But the defeat of the Armada did not shatter Spain's maritime power. Yet Spain waging war now with England, Holland and France was much weaker ten years after the Armada's defeat, and the great outburst of Spanish energy which had begun a hundred years before with the conquest of Granada and the voyage of Columbus was beginning to ebb away.

Philip knew a period of great happiness from his marriage with Elizabeth of Valois, whom he sincerely loved and who bore him two daughters. To them Philip was strongly attached, and in his letters to them at various ages one gets a glimpse of the man behind the cold formal exterior. The period of domestic happiness was spoilt by the terrible affair of Don Carlos, Philip's son, with his over-large head, his stammer, recurrent fevers and violent temper. Don Carlos did not appear likely to make a suitable heir to the throne. He had absurd ambitions, among them that of being sent as Viceroy to the Netherlands. He immersed himself in intrigues which, though childish, were dangerous since he was the heir to the throne. His private behaviour grew more eccentric. He would seize women in the streets, kissing them exuberantly and, at the same time, insulting them. He was impertinent to ladies of the Court and only reverenced the queen, whom he appeared to love almost as though he would be his father's rival.

As a matter of duty, the king felt obliged to act after many provocations. In January, 1568, he kept Don Carlos in the strictest seclusion in the Alcazar Palace. Philip wrote to the Pope and to his ambassadors abroad giving his reason for this painful decision. He could not bring himself to speak of Don Carlos as insane, nor did he accuse him of sedition, but he stated that it would be dangerous for Spain and the world as a whole if Don Carlos were to be allowed to succeed him.

Then in July, 1568, Don Carlos died in prison in circumstances which are unknown. There is no evidence that he died of strangulation or beheading or poison; nor either that he died as a result of his own excesses in prison. The death of Don Carlos was followed by a bitter blow in October of the same year in the death of Elizabeth of Valois. Philip married a fourth time; his wife, Anne of Austria, gave him a son, Philip III. All who knew the King realized that his great affection for his two daughters by Elizabeth was a sign of his attachment to the only family happiness he had known.

A balance-sheet of Philip's achievements would be read somewhat as follows. Against him it can be said that he did not disengage Spain from any of the many-sided struggles against the Turks, in Italy and France, in the Low Countries and in England, which exhausted her vitality. He bears the responsibility for this because he deliberately decided everything himself. He failed to have a sufficiently practical view of economics and social affairs and he allowed the Spanish countryside to be depopulated and industries to decay, relying on the silver brought to him from the New World in his galleons. Whilst not normally a man of blood, he believed in repression and supported the Spanish Inquisition and the Roman Inquisition in the Netherlands. If his enemies accused him of frequent villainies and of the murder of Don Carlos, the latter is certainly unproven, and his general behaviour towards his enemies, or half-enemies, was no worse than that of other sixteenth-century sovereigns.

There is much to be said in his favour. He governed Spain well, completed Spanish unity and did much to favour science and the arts. Spain had conquered Mexico and Peru, and the worst excesses of the Conquistadores had taken place before he reigned. It was during his reign that Spain sent to the Americas its best bishops and monks and professors and that the great work of civilizing the colonies took place. Indian students attended the great University of Mexico, founded in his time. Latin America under Philip grew a thousand firm roots in Latin and Christian culture. By his policies, Spain preserved the Catholic faith in the southern provinces of the Netherlands and shielded her own people from religious conflict.

Finally, it must be said of Philip as a ruler that, except for the Protestant provinces of the Netherlands—those which make up Holland—he lost nothing and added Portugal to the Spanish Crown. Spain at his death was exhausted, but still for a long while preserved her hegemony in Europe. Many historians consider that Philip's father, Charles V, was a far greater man. He may have been a more attractive character in some respects. But his great dynastic designs failed, his defence of the Church was ineffective and he left the Spanish Treasury bankrupt. Philip II, on the other hand, succeeded in what he set himself to do. His device could well be that of one of Spain's enemies, the Prince of Orange: "I will maintain."

ATAHUALPA

(*d.* 1533)

OF ALL the Europeans who went to the New World in the wake of Columbus, the Spaniards made the worst colonists. While others sought trade, they sought only gold and silver, and they succeeded in turning the natives' happiness and prosperity into misery and death, and wrecking their own economy in Spain in the process. The only civilizing agency which the Spaniards took to the New World was that of their Church, which finally had to restrain the scandalous rapacity of the Castilian adventurers.

But at first there was no restraint. Cortes destroyed the Aztec civilization in Mexico in 1520 by the use of every means of guile, treachery and cruelty. Loot was the main consideration of these conquering Spaniards, and when they heard stories of the fabulous Kingdom of Gold to the south they turned their eyes to Peru where the young Inca Emperor Atahualpa had just ascended the throne in Cuzco, the ancient Andean capital.

This civilization had flourished for two and a half thousand years and had been developed by various peoples, the last of whom were the Incas, who incidentally claimed for themselves a disproportionate amount of the credit for it. While the Incas did not have the same skills as the Aztecs, they excelled at engineering, constructing great roads, tunnels and bridges, and built spectacular monuments and fortifications.

In their cities among the cloud-capped mountains dwelt extraordinary ant-like communities where every person was moulded rigidly into an unalterable caste system. It was a strict totalitarian society in which everyone had his place, had to do prescribed work, and dress in a certain manner. Commoners were allowed to wear only simple clothes. Nobles were richly attired. At the top the emperor, in the finest clothes of all, was supreme and divine. He married within his family, usually his sister, in order to keep the blood-line pure. But he enjoyed a large selection of concubines and propagated numbers of natural children. Polygamy was permitted to the nobles, but not to the commoners, who were allowed only one wife. Obedience to the law was everywhere enforced with stern severity. The Incas worshipped the sun, of which their emperor—known as the Inca—was the deification on earth. The Incas' form of state socialism involved the suppression of personality and enterprise, though it provided the people with a certain security.

Inca agriculture was probably in advance of anything in Europe at that time. They had developed spinning, weaving and pottery-making to a great art. The country was rich in gold and silver mines, which were the personal property of the emperor, as were the large flocks of llama and alpaca which provided food, wool and transport. The horse was unknown in America until the Spaniards came. Yet, despite their civilization, the Incas had not discovered the art of writing, nor how to make a wheel.

Atahualpa's father was Huayna Capac, who was one of the great Incas. Atahualpa was not his true heir, as his mother was the daughter of the King of Quito, which Huayna Capac conquered. It is not likely that this princess was Huayna's lawful wife, for according to Inca custom that could only be his sister. By his sister Huayna had a son, Huascar, who by rights should have been his heir.

But the Inca developed a great love for his son by the Quito princess, and saw in him more promising qualities than in Huascar, so he resolved to break from tradition and divide his empire between his two sons. It was not surprising therefore that after the Inca's death in 1525 the brothers fell out and went to war with each other. Atahualpa won and at his moment of triumph the Spaniards invaded.

Though a brave, ambitious and clever young man, Atahualpa did not have his father's foresight or vision. But he was bold, high-minded, and, within his lights, liberal. A talented and valorous commander, he was accused of being cruel in his wars. He was said to be handsome, though there was a fierce expression to his face, emphasized by bloodshot eyes.

Francisco Pizarro, the man whose cupidity was most aroused by the legendary wealth of the Inca empire, was a Spanish adventurer of illegitimate birth who had been with Balboa at the historic moment of the first discovery of the Pacific. Ruthless, greedy, treacherous and possessed of great courage, Pizarro had the vices, but not the virtues, of Cortes. He had got himself commissioned by Charles V to undertake an expedition of exploration and conquest down the west coast of South America, then completely unknown territory. In 1529 he was made Governor and Captain General of the Spanish colony of New Castile—as Peru was then called. His commission was to go and conquer it. He was required to take a specified number of priests with him to convert the conquered Incas.

In 1532 Pizarro arrived in the dominions of Atahualpa, then totally unaware of the fact that his ancient empire had already been annexed by a monarch he had never heard of. The Spaniards were fired by tales of the incredible wealth awaiting them in the splendid land of the Incas, where the streets of the cities were said to be paved with gold.

Pizarro cautiously penetrated into Peru. His tiny, well-equipped army consisted of a mere 180 men and 27 horses for use as cavalry. When a captured Peruvian told him that the Inca awaited him with an army of more than 50,000, Pizarro paused and decided to proceed by guile. As he approached Caxamalca, where Atahualpa had his headquarters, he sent emissaries ahead proposing a meeting.

Atahualpa sent one of his nobles to meet Pizarro. The encounter took place in a pass in the Cordilleras. The Peruvian, while extolling the military might of his master, expressed the Inca's desire to extend hospitality to the strangers. Pizarro was less diplomatic, reminding the Peruvian of the inferiority of the Inca to the great and powerful monarch who ruled over the white men, and pointing out the ease with which a few Spaniards had overrun this great continent. But he came in a friendly spirit, declared Pizarro magnanimously. He had been led to visit Peru by the fame of the Inca, and to offer him his services in his wars, and he trusted his friendly spirit would be reciprocated.

We are not told how Atahualpa received this hardly gratuitous offer of a military assistance he did not require. The Inca was not deceived by the overtures from these mysterious strangers from an unknown world who fearlessly entered his realms after a march which would have daunted the boldest spirit in Peru. Atahualpa was credited with the intention of luring them deep into his land and then destroying those he did not wish to capture.

He did not dream that Pizarro's plan was to capture him. Indeed, the audacious and inspired plan of this unprincipled Spanish adventurer must commend itself to anyone who admires desperate daring. Pizarro's dealing with the last of the Incas is reckoned to be the blackest page of Spain's shameful colonial history. But it was the only way in which he, with a mere 180 men at his command, could conquer a nation which had a large army in the field. Pizarro decided to strike right at the heart, knowing that the Incas, without their leader, would collapse.

Pizarro with his little army entered Caxamalca on 15 November, 1532, and sent an invitation to the Inca to visit him for a conference. Atahualpa agreed and came into Caxamalca the following evening. He arrived in state, carried on a magnificent litter, accompanied by unarmed attendants.

There is no doubt that Atahualpa made this visit in good faith, though he probably distrusted the Spaniards' sincerity. In accepting their hospitality, he intended to impress them with his royal state. It never occurred to him that any attempt would be made upon him—here in the middle of his own empire, where he was absolute, where his word meant life and death, and where his armies were but a few miles away. The Spaniards, despite their frightening weapons, were absurdly few in number. He plainly did not understand the sort of men he was dealing with.

The Inca was first of all approached by Vicente de Valverde, Pizarro's chaplain, a Bible in one hand, crucifix in the other. The priest, through an interpreter, stated baldly and dogmatically the tenets of the Christian faith as seen through Roman Catholic eyes. He told him that the Pope had authorized the Emperor Charles V to conquer and convert the country of the Incas. Therefore Atahualpa must abandon the errors of his own faith, become a Christian and acknowledge Charles V as his master.

Atahualpa had difficulty in grasping the chain of argument by which the priest connected Pizarro with St. Peter. But the demand that he should abdicate his monarchy in favour of another was plain. He indignantly refused to recognize Charles V. "As for the Pope of whom you speak, he must be crazy to talk of giving away countries which do not belong to him." By what authority did Valverde speak? The priest replied the Bible and handed it to Atahualpa, who looked at it and threw it contemptuously on the ground.

"Tell your comrades that they shall give me an account of their doings in my land," he exclaimed. "I will not go from here until they have made me full satisfaction for all the wrongs they have committed."

The indignant Valverde, outraged at the Inca's insult to the holy book, hastened to Pizarro and recounted what had happened. "Set on them at once," the priest said. "I absolve you." Pizarro then gave the signal and his men fell upon the unarmed Peruvians from all sides and butchered them in hundreds. The bloodthirsty Spaniards wanted to kill the Inca as well, but Pizarro rescued him with his own hands, receiving in the process a minor cut—the only wound inflicted on a Spaniard that day. The unhappy monarch, strongly secured, was removed to a building nearby under heavy guard.

Upon the news of the capture of Atahualpa, the regimented and ant-like society of the Incas was immediately paralysed. The country was so dependent upon the monarch's orders that when he was captured by the invaders Peru was helpless. Pizarro's gamble came off brilliantly.

The Spaniards kept Atahualpa prisoner for many months. He impressed them by his dignity, good humour and fortitude. He was allowed to carry on his government while in the Spanish hands, and his captors marvelled at the utter servility the Peruvians displayed to him.

The Spaniards allowed him the consolation of his wives and concubines. At the same time they were busy propagating the true faith among the heathen Incas, and they converted one of the Caxamalcan temples into a church.

Atahualpa himself was not long in discovering that amidst all this show of religious zeal the passion which burnt most fiercely in the hearts of his conquerors was the lust for gold. He therefore offered Pizarro a room full of gold and silver in exchange for his freedom. Pizarro avidly accepted, though he had no intention of keeping the bargain. Atahualpa sent his emissaries to collect the treasure and assemble it in Caxamalca.

Having ensured, as he thought, his freedom, Atahualpa became acutely conscious of the existence of his brother Huascar, whom he had dethroned and imprisoned, and who as the son of his father's sister-wife was the true heir and the true Inca. Atahualpa had everything to fear from Huascar now, so he gave secret orders for his death, which his slavish minions immediately executed. Huascar was drowned in the Andamarca River, declaring, it is said, with his dying breath that the white men would avenge his murder and his brother would not long survive him.

Pizarro was angry at the news, for Huascar was an amiable and more pliant man whom he could have bent to his will more easily than the strong-minded, independent and determined Atahualpa.

Atahualpa kept his word about the ransom and soon a vast quantity of gold and silver, worth something like three million pounds, was placed before the greedy, gloating eyes of Pizarro. The Spaniards revelled in their rich treasure and even shod their horses with silver.

Meanwhile Atahualpa's demands for the freedom he had so dearly bought fell upon deaf ears. Pizarro had heard rumours of a rising among the Peruvians and he used that as an excuse for not honouring his bargain. Atahualpa heard the rumours—which were not true—with incredulity, as he knew that not one of his subjects would dare to go to arms without his authority, in which fact lay the key to the Spaniards' success.

Things now moved rapidly towards the inevitable climax of this dismal triumph of civilization over barbarism. More Spaniards arrived from Panama. There were rumours of a large invasion from Quito, and once more Pizarro accused Atahualpa of raising the country against the Spaniards. Pizarro was now under tremendous pressure from some of his compatriots to execute the Inca. But Pizarro was answerable to his emperor in Europe, and dare not in the circumstances do this without a trial.

Atahualpa was then brought before a farcical tribunal and accused of usurping the Inca crown, assassinating his brother Huascar, misusing the public revenues of his country, idolatry, adultery, polygamy and inciting insurrection against the Spaniards. The Spaniards, of course, had no jurisdiction in any of these matters. Nevertheless, they found him guilty and sentenced him to death by being burnt alive at the stake.

This scandalous injustice was even too much for some of Pizarro's gang of bandits and criminals. Indignant voices were raised, but in vain, at this outrageous treatment of a prince who had received nothing but wrong at their hands. They had no authority to sit in judgment on a sovereign in the heart of his own dominions. This wholly reasonable, even Christian, view was not shared by Father Valverde, who gave it as his opinion that the Inca deserved death.

On 29 August, 1533, Atahualpa was led out into the great square of Caxamalca, chained hand and foot, attended by Father Valverde striving to persuade him to embrace the faith of his conquerors before he died. Valverde had made many previous attempts to convert him to Christianity, but had never been able to convince Atahualpa.

However, with the doomed Inca bound to the stake, the Spanish priest was able to give him the most convincing argument that Atahualpa had heard so far. If he became a Christian, he would be strangled quickly instead of enduring the painful death of the fire.

Upon receiving this ultimatum, the unhappy Atahualpa, looking bitterly into the face of this contemptible priest, agreed and embraced the alien God of these cruel strangers who had come to loot and ravage his country. The shameful ceremony was performed by Father Valverde, who baptized the new convert Juan de Atahualpa.

Thus the last of the Incas was garrotted at the stake like a common criminal. He was about thirty years old. With him died the Peruvian empire which swiftly fell into the hands of the Spanish invaders and became part of the far-flung territories of Charles V, Emperor of the Holy Roman Empire.

The treatment of Atahualpa was widely condemned at the time, even in Spain. Pizarro and his lieutenants all came to violent and miserable ends and did not live to enjoy the treasure they took from the Incas.

WILLIAM THE SILENT

(1533–84)

FEW MEN have won fame because of their silence, and fewer still have been passionately admired for it. William, Prince of Nassau-Orange, Stadtholder (or Governor) of the Netherlands, and chosen leader in their revolt against Spanish tyranny—a revolt whose success he did not live to witness—was indeed a wise, strong and silent man. Strength and wisdom were the salient qualities which gained him fame. His celebrated "silence" was, in a sense, a by-product of these higher qualities.

To see this more clearly we should try to view William against his turbulently varied background. In the mid-sixteenth century, the seventeen States of the Spanish Netherlands comprising what are now Holland and Belgium, owing allegiance to the Habsburg emperor Charles V in Madrid, were naturally restive; but the inevitable conflict was in itself related to *three* conflicts, which proved by no means parallel in every change of circumstance.

First, there was the national consciousness gradually rising against foreign domination; secondly, often contradicting this, was the religious conflict between Catholics and several Protestant sects, themselves by no means united, but split into Calvinists, Lutherans, Anabaptists and so on; and thirdly we find the tension, if not always actual conflict, between the northern Germanic majority (including roughly the whole of modern Holland and Flemish Belgium) and the southern Walloon minority (equivalent to the modern Belgian south). The intertwining of these three conflicts produced an incredible maze of attitudes and often apparent paradoxes; to manoeuvre a course through them to find national unity and a freedom both political and religious was the aim of every Netherlands statesman.

But few succeeded in maintaining the precarious balance, while at the same time appearing honest and selfless; and none succeeded in such a task as well as William. His "silence", epitomizing his calm temperament, cautious yet alert, stood in contrast to the more ebullient nature of more "glamorous" figures like the noble but somewhat hasty Count Egmont, a half-Walloon, who later was treacherously executed by the Spaniards. William stands for solidity as well as alert, rational action, a typical combination of Dutch qualities, which to many may seem characteristic also of the British nature in time of trial.

Hence his countrymen's enduring love for William, who was in fact the founder of the present royal house of Holland. He remains the symbol of their rise to freedom and of the prelude to the epoch when the Dutch nation shone most prominently on the European stage. It must be admitted, certainly, that William has not inspired writers or dramatists of other nations, while Egmont is the subject of Goethe's famous drama (for which Beethoven wrote incidental music), though the English historian, Motley, won international renown with his book, *The Rise of the Dutch Republic*, a passionate defence of the Netherlanders' struggle against Spain, in which William the Silent is the undoubted hero.

William was born on 25 April, 1533, the son of the Count of Nassau, at Dillenburg in Germany. In those days estates were often held in different lands, and territorial frontiers themselves tended to be loose (the so-called Holy Roman Empire still occupied large areas of many quite diverse countries); so it was not surprising when, at the age of eleven, William inherited also the title and estates of Prince of Orange.

These possessions were in the Netherlands: their centre was at Breda in Brabant, with further land in the provinces of Holland and Zealand, where later William was to become Stadtholder. His parents reserved the Countship of Nassau for his younger brother John (himself to become a stormy petrel, now helping, now hindering the more far-sighted William), while William was sent to Brussels to be educated as a Catholic at the court of the Emperor Charles V. Here he doubtless gained both personal contacts and experience of statesmanship. In 1555 it was on his young shoulders that the prematurely old Charles leant as he told the assembled States of his seventeen Netherlands provinces that he was resigning the crown to his son, Philip II, later to marry England's Queen Mary.

At this scene of abdication both Charles and his audience wept, and it is important to stress the attachment to the dynasty felt by these provinces despite many provocations. The attitude was, in fact, ambivalent; a real love of freedom lay in the Netherlandish nature, whether that of Friesland fishermen, of the burghers and merchants of the city-states, or of the landed aristocrats. Doubtless William at first shared in this; and his gradual appearance as the leader of anti-Spanish revolt shines all the more tellingly for his

prudence and lack of fanaticism. The same qualities were revealed
in his religious policy; a firm but unbigoted Catholic, he strove for
religious freedom and Protestant rights, even alienating many of
his Catholic friends.

The liberation of the Netherlands from Spain ranks as a major
event in Western European history; with Switzerland, the Netherlands produced a true democracy, in the sense of orderly freedom,
government by the people, liberty of thought and conscience, and
tolerance towards minorities and refugees. This liberation took a
hundred years and was criss-crossed by innumerable paradoxes
and complications. If one man can be said to be its architect,
William the Silent is that man. Yet he was assassinated in 1584,
at Delft, by a Catholic fanatic, eighty-one years before the final
retreat of the Spaniards. Had he lived he might or might not have
accepted a constitutional crown. His office of Stadtholder was one
held by a member of one of three great families, though in 1555,
before Charles's abdication, Philip had caused indignation by
refusing the appointment to either William or Count Egmont,
and installing a protegé of his own, the energetic Cardinal Granvelle.
His reforms—partly concerned with altering the Church authority
so as to strengthen that of the king—produced a torrent of indignation. Orange, Egmont and Hoorn, three of the main lords, withdrew
from the Council of State until Philip should recall Granvelle. This
he did angrily, and his natural sister, Margaret of Parma, was
declared Regent.

Meanwhile religious persecution under the Counter-Reformation
had reached such heights that Egmont, a fervent Catholic himself,
rushed desperately to Madrid to plead with Philip. Flattering
promises from Philip raised his hopes, soon to be dashed by the
Edict of Segovia, reinforcing persecution. This was the signal for
general unrest. William estimated a total of 50,000 victims as having
suffered by 1566, and both Protestants and humane, patriotic
Catholics felt the need for a national movement. The great nobles
resigned in protest; the coolest-headed among them, William,
bided his time. But a league of nobility was formed, including
William's Calvinist brother, Louis of Nassau, and many members
of the "lower nobility" who were less connected with the Government. The Assembly, or "Compromise", of nobles found recruits
quickly.

A petition was drawn up, demanding the end of persecution
and the Inquisition; and William—unlike Egmont—was for open
support of the league when its four hundred nobles solemnly

approached the regent in Brussels. Never had the unity of the Netherlands been so clearly expressed. All classes felt this; ballads and other revolutionary literature circulated, and the regent was frightened into caution. Her advisers prepared a scheme of "Moderation", mildly tempering the Edicts, but the people scorned it. Conceiving it to imply toleration, Protestant refugees returned, and a fierce enthusiasm prevailed, especially among the Calvinists. This led to further restrictive measures and, in turn, a mad outburst of sacrilege, image-breaking and the plundering of churches. This produced general disorder; and the Government, playing one faith against another, regained some support from the moderates. However, the people's temper made a trial of strength inevitable.

William was for armed resistance, if only Egmont and Hoorn would co-operate. Philip had threatened even more savage measures, but the co-operation did not materialize. Only the Calvinists stiffened themselves into determined resistance amid the hesitant confusion. William did all he could to assist their freedom of worship, as Stadtholder in the north and as Burgrave of Antwerp, often against the will of Catholic officials. Yet he could not openly identify himself with their cause, partly because most of his own troops came from a Catholic or Lutheran Germany.

Still in the "wondrous year" 1566 the Calvinist forces suffered sharp defeats. William, unlike Egmont, refused to take the fresh oath of allegiance demanded; but, residing at Antwerp, he also declined to admit the rebel forces marching against it. He was resolved on his own chosen "middle path"; at peril of his life he kept the city barred, while Government troops cut down the rebels outside. In this he had the backing of most of the population of Antwerp, though he was largely denounced elsewhere as a traitor. With mixed feelings he saw the revolt everywhere fade out. His position had become such that, in common with many other nobles, he left the country.

This was indeed the hush before the storm, the step backward to prepare a victorious advance. Resolved to recruit an army in Germany, he retired to his ancestral castle at Dillenburg in 1567. Well can we imagine his reflections, feelings and decisions on policy designed to further the great purpose to which he felt irresistibly called. He was to personify the united Netherlands, above all clash of race, interest and religious denomination. The ground had been well sown by the forces of that league who had presented the petition at Brussels. They joyously called themselves "the Beggars", a title that arose in humorous and accidental fashion.

As the soldiers of the league marched along, the die-hard duke, Berlaymont, scoffed at them as "that pack of beggars" in the French phrase: *"Ce n'est qu'un tas de gueux"*, French being still the Court language. The nation "Dutched" *"gueux"* into "Geus", and the cry of *"Vive le Geus!"* symbolized the national unity.

Events moved swiftly. Philip, furious at Margaret's so-called "moderation", sent the Duke of Alba, a noted commander and a bigot also, to supersede her. On his arrival the country was in exhausted, almost contrite, mood. But Alba swept aside this chance of conciliation; he cut through existing interests, made arbitrary arrests, and governed by means of his well-named Council of Blood. Egmont and Hoorn were imprisoned. And then, in Motley's words: "Upon the 16th of February, 1568, a sentence of the Holy Office condemned all the inhabitants to death as heretics." Alba's terrorism increased.

William, who had himself been summoned in January before the ominous Council of Blood, protested in the face of all Europe, and set about recruiting troops, largely from the German mercenaries whom the recent peace after the French civil war had left without a job. William's first sallies were failures, but in April Louis scored a success at Groningen. Alba was quick in revenge; amongst the heads that fell were those of Hoorn and Egmont (whose fate the Beggars' song attributed to his "inconstancy"). William's lack of funds and his unpreparedness prevented him from striking at once into Brabant, the heart of the nation. Near Trier he collected a too vast horde of rapacious mercenaries, as well as genuine patriots. He could hardly afford to pay them all. Attacks followed, often petering out owing to the indifference of the population itself; William had to retreat, his starving army running amok, while he escaped into France, still pestered for arrears of pay. This was perhaps his lowest ebb. Yet, as he sings in the Beggars' song, the "Wilhelmus", which the Dutch still treat as a national anthem: "My heart hath remained constant in adversity."

He soon was able to return to Dillenburg, but meanwhile had cemented his most valuable alliance: that with the French Huguenots. In the Netherlands, revolt had burst out at Alba's "Tax of the Tenth Penny", by which the state was to receive a tenth of the price of every article sold. Alba's folly united Netherlanders of every class and religion. But all William's scheming for support in the country itself ended in hesitation and indifference. Only gradually was real popular support to be won. A useful addition to the cause were the curious semi-piratical "Sea Beggars", centred on Emden, whose pro-Orange activities were soon regularized by the far-seeing William.

Since the peace of 1570 in France, the Huguenot leader, Coligny, wielded influence over the young king, Charles IX; from the Huguenot port of La Rochelle, Louis of Nassau came to discuss a common war against France's old enemies, the Habsburgs. In 1572 came the decisive beginning. A premature attack by the Sea Beggars captured The Brill and Flushing in William's name; soon most towns in Holland and Zealand acknowledged his authority, as did many in Friesland and the north; and the Huguenots captured Mons in the Walloon South. Yet William, who on 23 July took Roermond on the Maas, was delayed by the usual financial problem until on 27 August he crossed the river, only to learn that three days earlier the French king had betrayed the Huguenots, and ordered the Massacre of St. Bartholomew. All hopes of French help, moral, financial and military, crashed. The Spaniards struck again, and William had to retreat, disbanding his forces, and travelling to the province of Holland.

Four heroic years followed, in which (while the other provinces looked on) Holland and Zealand stood alone against the Spanish armies. After the prolonged siege of Haarlem in 1572, which fell to the Spaniards, William recruited another army of German mercenaries, annihilated near Mook in 1574. Alba had been replaced by Requesens. In 1575 William cleverly showed his hand by causing the peace negotiations at Breda (for the Spaniards were alarmed) to break down. Soon Requesens died and Philip declared himself bankrupt! The new Governor, Don John, was impatient and arrogant; and in 1577 war flared once again.

January, 1579, saw the formation of the Union of Utrecht, by which the Northern Provinces leagued together in a separate entity; with utmost reluctance, seeing its Calvinistic intolerance, William also signed. This had the natural consequence of reconciling the Walloons to the king. General confusion ensued; one group of exiles returned, a fresh one left and the towns which had supported the Beggars drove them out. But now the geographical factor, the country's configuration, especially the great strategic rivers, was to bring ultimate success to the Revolt and unity to the land.

The new Governor, the brilliant general Alexander of Parma, was more tactful than his predecessor. William invited the Duke of Anjou, brother of the French king and a Catholic, to be sovereign. His rule was unsuccessful, yet William—urged to become sovereign himself—still felt that only French help could deliver the nation. Then Anjou died on 10 June, 1584. A month later, on 10 July, a Catholic fanatic killed William himself. The enemy gloated, but the revolt showed that it had its own life. William's death proved this, as did his own refusal of absolute power; his tactful negotiations with States' assemblies and his gifts of persuasion were not to be forgotten.

Under the excellent leadership of William's son, Maurice of Nassau, and hastened by events like the collapse of the Spanish Armada, the whole territory of the Netherlands was regained from Spain by 1600, though its sovereign nationality was not recognized officially until the Treaty of Westphalia in 1648, which ended the Thirty Years' War of Central Europe. But had William the Silent never lived, the Netherlanders' fight for freedom might have ended less happily.

AKBAR

(1542–1605)

A SCREAMING mob beat down the bronze gates, burst into the great mausoleum, opened the tomb. Then, "dragging out the bones of Akbar, they threw them into the fire and burnt them. Thus does the world treat those from whom it expects no good and fears no evil. That was the end of the life and reign of King Akbar."

To the Jesuit historian who wrote those words this final act of sacrilege was the end of Akbar. But a part at least of the good and evil men do lives after them, and the name of the great Mogul emperor is unlikely to be forgotten. He was, if not the founder, at least the organizer, of that empire which at its height, during his lifetime, covered all but the bottom bit of the Indian sub-continent, and territories beyond it. He could neither read nor write —even his own name—but his knowledge and his understanding were vast. His memory enabled him to fill his mind with more facts, ideas and dreams than any dozen normal men. And though he wrote nothing, he inspired others to write about him. From these we learn, for example, that Akbar's eyes were "vibrant like the sea in sunshine"; his manners were perfect, so that he could be "great with the great and lowly with the lowly"; that he never slept for more than three hours at a stretch; that he was an epileptic.

On a less personal note we know that he brought almost the whole of India under his subjugation, and invented a new religion.

A man, in short, of many facets. Before we look at a few, let us consider the world into which he was born.

It was a changing world, even then. The age-old Hindu domination of the sub-continent had yielded to a foreign, Muslim, force, and that too had succumbed to another, also Muslim, but more powerful still, sweeping all before it. But to put these new "Mogul" invaders in perspective we must glance at those who preceded them.

It was about the year 2000 B.C. that the Indian sub-continent, that vast and fertile land to the south of the Himalaya mountains, was entered from the north-west, by light-skinned, straight-haired, invaders. These lived for some time on the southern slopes of the Himalaya before deciding to advance farther. Then, moving east and south, they pushed the aboriginal "Dravida", the dark-skinned, curly-haired people, ahead of them, and these Dravidians, as we now call them, were forced down the peninsula towards its narrow southern tip. Many were killed, many taken prisoner by the invaders.

The invaders, who brought with them a strange, "Aryan" language, an involved Hindu religion and a developed art and architecture, founded great cities, some of which, like Benares, remain to the present day. They introduced a "caste" system, dividing people into four main groups of Priests, Nobles, Men and Serfs (Brahmins, Kshatriyas, Vaisyas and Sudras), and as the last group were almost entirely from the conquered, darker-skinned folk it was reasonable that they should choose their own word for Colour to describe it.

They introduced, in fact, a Colour Bar, four thousand years ago: an unfortunate development which is neither new nor confined to the so-called "White" races.

Hindu domination became virtually complete. Other religions, like Jainism and Buddhism, sprang up, but though Buddhism spread over much of the East, neither religion succeeded in winning over a large proportion of India's inhabitants. In the fourth century before Christ, Alexander the Great burst on the scene, but his influence, by Indian time-scales, was short-lived. Hindu dynasties continued to follow each other, and at certain periods there were many of them, ruling over different parts of the peninsula. There were still invasions from the north, but those who invaded either withdrew or were absorbed, submerged in a sea of humanity, and an age-old culture and religion.

But in about the year A.D. 1000 a new type swept down from the north, invaders with a fierce proud faith they called "Islam". These "Muslims"—followers of Islam—believed in a single God and a One True Faith, and they were determined to wipe out all infidels. This Islam was not their own private religion, it was a faith shared by a large part of the world beyond India's borders, and the new invaders were pledged to be its spearhead. They would take the word of their religious leader, their caliph, to all the world, and at the same time keep in touch—forever—with that caliphate, in Baghdad: much as the settlers of Israel were to do in modern times, they would bring in others of the same fierce faith to help them settle their new territories.

From this time on India was split in two.

The Muslim invaders chose as their capital a strategic spot in the north. Here, in and around Delhi, they fought a series of major battles with the defending Hindus: by A.D. 1200 they were in complete control of a large part of India.

But a little later these Muslim rulers, the Sultanate of Delhi, were defeated by other Muslims, infinitely more warlike, more ferocious, more bigoted, than they. They swept down, from the north as before, but less with the intention of acquiring territory or riches than with a fanatical zeal to punish the earlier invaders. For these were neglecting the True Faith. In 1398 the vicious Timur swept in from Samarkand with his army of fanatics, and butchered Hindu and Muslim alike before returning whence he had come.

Timur's dubious achievement is to have destroyed the Muslim power that preceded him and to have left nothing in its place.

The stage was set for the Moguls.

They came, at the start of the sixteenth century, and though the blood of many warriors, including that of Timur, flowed through the veins of their royal house, they brought a new, gentler approach to the business of invasion. The first of them was Babur, who overthrew the Sultan of the day and had himself proclaimed, a trifle prematurely, "Emperor of All India". He was a good man, a Muslim, but open-minded, a man who loved flowers and poetry and music. He was also a fine general and soon he had indeed conquered most of India. He died, and his weak and foolish son, Humayun, an opium addict, lost a large part of that empire within a few years, as parts of it rebelled and set up autonomous states. His son Akbar was born in 1542 while Humayun was in temporary exile in Sind. Then, when Humayun had managed to fight his way back to Delhi, he slipped, fell down the long staircase of his library, and killed himself.

Akbar, aged fourteen, was Emperor of India. His reign would coincide, very nearly, with that of Queen Elizabeth in England.

At first, affairs of state were entrusted to a regent, Bahram Khan, but within a year Akbar had decided the older man was cruel and intolerant in the way he maintained order among the various sections of the Empire, which had rebelled. The young emperor took over the Government himself.

His long, eventful reign is one of the most important periods in the history of India. Like his grandfather, he was far from a fanatical Muslim, and he convinced himself that the perfect religion must be an amalgam of many. The first invaders to come by sea, the Portuguese, had settled peaceably on the coast, and Akbar now sent ambassadors to them, asking that Jesuit missionaries come to Delhi and instruct him in their faith. He would probably not adopt it, but he wished to study it. And to the adherents of Brahminism, Jainism, Buddhism, to the Parsis and others, he sent messages, asking that they come and instruct him in their thinking and their rituals.

From his detailed studies Akbar devised a new religion, and did his best, without coercion, to spread it. In this he was hardly successful: many men, anxious to win royal favour, embraced it, but few understood it, or believed. Akbar's new faith was a short-lived affair. But he has gone into history as a ruler who established and insisted on complete religious toleration. He had been, at first, a strict Muslim, but he made good friends of his Hindu subjects, in particular the warlike Rajputs, from whom he appointed many of his best generals, and who served him faithfully and well. He married several Rajput princesses who were nominally expected to embrace Islam on joining the royal household, but most of whom, as we know, did nothing of the sort. They were not punished for the omission.

With his Rajput generals Akbar introduced the modern system of an army owing allegiance to the state and being paid directly by it, not feudally by hosts of minor nobles, who might tend to appropriate the funds for other purposes and neglect its strength.

The influence of Islam, since the first Muslim invasion, had always been a strong one, dragging men's minds and hearts back to that distant caliphate, but now Akbar tried hard to emancipate minds from that influence. From now on, if his subjects refused to adopt his new religion, preferred to regard themselves as Muslims, they must have their caliph within the empire: he, Akbar, was caliph to his Muslims.

With as much zeal as earlier Muslims had enforced their faith, Akbar now set himself to enforcing toleration. He forbade the building of mosques, and pilgrimages to Mecca, refused to tolerate even the ancient Fast of Ramadan. It had always been a Muslim joy to show the superiority of the True Faith over idolatrous, cattle-worshipping Hindus, by slaughtering cattle in public. Now this, too, was forbidden. The meat of oxen could be eaten, but the slaughter would be a private, hidden, affair.

Akbar's toleration extended to all things. He built new schools all over his vast domain, and encouraged the study of literature, and art, and language, from all over the known world. He was, as we have seen, illiterate, but he had half the world's great literature off by heart, and he dictated beautiful poems of his own composition, many of which we have to this day. He urged that Muslim painters and architects should study and profit by the earlier work of Hindu craftsmen; the new art which resulted is among the world's treasures.

And—perhaps because he could not do so himself—he encouraged the writing of history. From the thousands of years of Hindu domination we have remarkably little in the way of written history, aside from a few great epic poems: most of what we know of those early days has been learnt from paintings and the ruins of their ancient cities. But the Mogul period of Indian history is well documented.

Akbar's intentions were noble: to isolate Indian Muslims from their co-religionists outside and make them more Indian, so that the empire he ruled would one day become a united whole. But in this he failed. The majority of his Muslim subjects resented this attempt to interfere with their beliefs, and though Akbar repressed a number of efforts at rebellion he was unable to put out the flame of Islam. Much as Christianity has consolidated in times of religious oppression, so a newer, more orthodox, stricter, Islam was growing in India, determined to resist any heretical influence, whether it came from outside or the emperor himself. When, in 1582, Akbar formally renounced Islam and promulgated his own new faith—without, however, forcing it upon his subjects—rebellion began to take shape.

In September, 1605, after years of stamping out that rebellion, Akbar became ill. He grew worse, with vomiting and terrible stomach pains, then appeared to get better. Court physicians diagnosed it as dysentery; then, when the symptoms suddenly recurred, agreed that it could not be.

It was almost, one of them pointed out, as if the emperor were being deliberately, carefully and slowly poisoned.

In October Akbar died.

At his death, though successors made haste to bring back orthodoxy, the Mogul Empire tottered. Bit by bit, pieces were taken or retaken, beginning with the great fortress of Kandahar, which became a province of Persia.

By the death of Akbar's descendant, Aurangzeb, a hundred years later, the Empire had almost ceased to exist.

We can remember Akbar for having been a great general and a wise and cultured man. Above all, he was a man who by devotion to the idea of toleration made his mark not only on Indian history, but on India's thinking and India's philosophy.

HENRY IV (OF FRANCE)

(1553–1610)

HENRY IV, the first of the Bourbon line who came to the throne in 1589, the year after the Spanish Armada, is the most popular of all French kings. He is also one of the most widely admired of French monarchs outside France, particularly in England, a country which was his ally. England was his friend, and Spain, England's enemy, was also his. Many British schoolboys have heard of his "white plume" which he told his soldiers to follow at the battle of Ivry, a gesture which endeared him to his people. Two of Henry's sayings are long remembered: "I want every man to have a chicken in his pot"; and "Paris is worth a mass". This latest illustrates not cynicism but Henry's tolerant mind, so exceptional in an age of violence and bigotry.

England was fortunate in that the strong Tudor monarchy saved her from the Wars of Religion, the struggle between Protestants and Catholics which was to deluge France with blood in the second half of the sixteenth century and which was to cause the terrible Thirty Years War in Germany at the beginning of the seventeenth. When the New Learning and ideas of reforming the Church became current in France at the beginning of the sixteenth century, the French king, Francis I, his sister Marguerite, Queen of Navarre, and many of the French nobility favoured them, as did Henry VIII in England. But there was no question of the French monarch becoming head of a new Church which would be acceptable to the majority of the nation. The large majority of Frenchmen were staunch Catholics; they were faced by a small but fanatical Protestant minority, strong and indeed itself a majority in certain parts of France, such as the south-west and Normandy.

The Duke of Rohan, Princes of the Blood such as Antoine de Bourbon, King of Navarre, the Prince of Condé and the great family of Châtillon were Protestants. These nobles were, however, not, for the most part, religious fanatics themselves; they were driven to extreme positions by the violence of the Catholic reaction against Protestantism. This was headed by the Duke of Guise, a soldier who had distinguished himself in the wars in Italy, and his brother the Cardinal of Lorraine. With the Guises went the City of Paris with its great University, which was, from the beginning, a dynamo of the Catholic cause. The example of Paris was followed by many other cities of the east and north. The task of the monarchy was clearly to decide a middle way not only between Catholic and Protestant intransigence but between two powerful aristocratic factions.

Unfortunately, the last Valois king capable of governing France, Henry II, died in 1559, after an accident at a tournament, a lance penetrating his eye. The three kings who were to reign from then until 1589 were all young children at their father's death: the sickly Frances II, the incapable Charles IX and the less incapable but degenerate Henry III. The House of Valois had not the art of providing the right king at the right moment. The Queen Mother, the wife of Henry II, Catherine de' Medici, attempted a vain policy of making the monarchy strong against both factions. Religious passion and blood spoke louder than reason. The first of a long series of civil wars began in 1562. Small-scale but extremely ferocious fighting took place throughout the kingdom. There were truces, arranged by the monarchy. Francis, Duke of Guise was assassinated, to be succeeded by his even more violent brother Henry, known as Scarface. Catholics were aided by Philip II of Spain, Protestants by Elizabeth of England, and both sides employed numbers of mercenary troops from Germany and Switzerland.

In 1570 the monarch, Charles IX, appeared to lean towards the more moderate Protestant leaders and to be able to enforce, with their help, a permanent truce of peace based on toleration. A marriage was arranged between the king's sister Marguerite de Valois and Henry the new King of Navarre, who had succeeded his father, Antoine de Bourbon, who had been killed in the wars. In 1572, however, the queen decided the balance of power must be restored by more drastic means. The king's consent was obtained to a massacre, on the eve of St. Bartholomew, in August, of Protestant leaders assembled in Paris for the marriage. The massacre lasted over three days and was followed by massacres in other cities. The English Court went into mourning, whilst Philip II of Spain rejoiced, saying this was one of the greatest days of his life. The massacre settled nothing, for the Protestants found new leaders and remained under arms.

By order of the king the two Protestant princes of the Blood Royal escaped the massacre in Paris. One was the Prince of Condé and the other Henry, King of Navarre. They were picked up by guards at the tennis court of the Louvre early in the morning when the massacre started and, as they were taken to the king's apartments for safety, they heard the cries of their pages and valets who were being dragged out of their rooms and slaughtered. Both chose to abjure the Protestant faith and to live. A few months later on a cold and frosty night Henry escaped from Paris and returned to his kingdom of Navarre. He was now the Head of the Protestant cause.

When the effeminate Henry III became king, and after his brother, the Duke of Anjou, died, Henry of Navarre became the legitimate successor to the throne. The House of Valois was extinguished. The Bourbons were directly descended from the sixth son of St. Louis, and though their claim was not the only one to the throne, and it was a distant one, it was far better than any other.

Henry III tried to continue the sensible policy of moderation and of refusal to be the tool of either faction. But he was opposed not only now by the Catholic nobles but by the Holy League which the anti-monarchical, almost Republican, but fervently Catholic townsmen of Paris and other cities had formed, not only for the defence of their faith but of their privileges. They were encouraged by the luxury and immorality of the Valois Court, by the hated "Italian Woman" who ruled the kingdom and brought in the English troops, forgetting that the Guises had called in the Spaniards. In 1585 Henry was forced to make peace with the League and to outlaw the Protestants.

War was not long in breaking out again. King Henry had the Duke of Guise assassinated in his palace at Blois by a group of young noblemen known as Les Mignons. Paris rose against "M. Henry de Valois". Henry III now called on the King of Navarre to support him and the two Henrys besieged Paris. On 1 August, 1589, a Dominican monk managed to worm his way into the king's presence in the camp outside Paris and stabbed him to death, the revenge for the murder of the Duke of Guise. Henry of Navarre was now King of France—but a king with a capital in arms against him and indeed with an aged Bourbon cousin proclaimed King Charles X by the League. Never came a king into his heritage under worse conditions.

In the year of his crowning, Henry IV made public the Edict of Nantes. This ensured liberty of religion to Protestants in certain parts of France, with freedom to organize a Protestant clergy. The Edict gave them 150 strongholds, mainly in the south-west, where they could organize a local militia to defend themselves.

After two victories won by Henry IV at Arques and Ivry, the League was discouraged and Paris was again besieged by the royal forces. The king had been urged by Henry III to declare himself a Catholic and so to unite the nation behind him. But Henry knew that he could not afford to discourage his Protestant supporters for the sake of Paris. He delayed his conversion for four years, determined that first of all he should be seen as the legitimate king and not owe his crown to weakness. Meanwhile he conducted the war with clemency and moderation. He allowed foodstuffs to enter Paris during the siege, saying, "I do not wish to rule over a cemetery". Nothing could have been more admirable than Henry's sense of timing and his patience. These are not often found in conjunction with the dashing military genius and panache which he also displayed.

Paris yielded at last and gradually fighting ceased throughout the kingdom. Henry was now confronted with the problem of restoring France. "Whoever would have slept these last forty years," it was said, "would have awoken to see not France but a corpse." Perhaps France was not quite as desolate as around 1450 after the Hundred Years War. But the loss of life during the Wars of Religion had been huge; sieges, skirmishes, pillaging, sackings and burnings had created ruin everywhere; there were thousands of deserted villages, millions of acres unploughed, a shortage of draught animals—men and women commonly had to hitch themselves to the plough; roads were useless, bridges destroyed, and on the sea not a ship of the king's navy. "France and I have need of a great breath," said Henry. And the king's remark that he wanted to see every man with a chicken in his pot, and the saying of Henry's great Minister Sully that "plough and pasture are the breasts of France", are the reflection of this terrible time.

France recovered with astonishing speed, as she had done before and was to do again in her history. The king was successful because in face of political or economic problems he used commonsense and persuasion rather than acting dogmatically and violently. France, he knew, had need of an all-powerful monarchy and this he successfully constructed. He was a believer in the Divine Right of Kings, as he wrote to his friend, the new King of England and Scotland, James I. But Henry was a believer in this doctrine with many a nuance and much scepticism. To his Minister Sully, a Protestant, who kept pictures of Calvin and Luther in his antechamber, he said: "When you cease to contradict me I know you will have ceased to love me." Sully laboured to reform the administration and above all to restore the real wealth of France which lay in its land.

Henry IV had his marriage with Marguerite de Valois annulled and he married in 1660 Marie de' Medici, a fat and not very intelligent queen who gave him a son. The risk of a Protestant succeeding to the throne was thus ended. Marguerite de Valois bore him no malice and indeed she herself carried the gown of the new queen at her wedding. Marguerite herself had had many lovers and Henry had had even more mistresses. This hard-working, clever and patient monarch showed another side of his character in his love affairs. So frequent were these that Henry was known as *Le vert galant*—the ever-fresh lover. His escapades at first pleased the nation, although in his latter years there was some criticism, particularly when he fell in love with a girl of fifteen, the wife of the Prince of Condé, who had to take refuge in Brussels, from which city Henry threatened to take her by force of arms. This side of his character, however, together with his other good qualities, helped to get the love of his subjects. M. Jean Duché, the author of a rather droll *History of France as told to Juliette*, writes aptly of Henry IV:

> *After the decadent depravities of the Valois, do you know what was really the marvel of marvels? It was the fundamental healthiness of the man. In Henry IV every Frenchman recognized all that was best and truest in the essence of his race.*

About to embark on a war with the Habsburgs of Austria, Henry left the Louvre Palace on 14 May, 1610, in the afternoon, to transact some business with Sully. As so often happens, his wife and his entourage had had a vague presentiment of disaster and begged him to stop at home. In the narrow Rue de la Ferronerie, a young ardent Catholic, François Ravaillac, living on charity and crippled with debts, stabbed Henry twice near the heart as he leant over the side of his carriage reading a letter. His motive was hatred of the king as the protector of Protestants—a motive which had been common to Frenchmen some twenty years before, but which later had become detestable. The ghosts of the monk who had killed Henry III, and of the Protestant de Méré who had stabbed the first Duke of Guise, lived again in this senseless act of murder. Catholics and Protestants alike mourned Henry: "You cannot be a Frenchman," said the Duke of Rohan, "without regretting the loss to her well-being which France had suffered." Of how many kings could this have been sincerely said?

QUEEN ELIZABETH I

(1558–1603)

WHEN MARY TUDOR died in November, 1558, all but devout Romanists in England heaved a sigh of relief. Her savage persecution of the Protestants had introduced an alien virulence into English religious life, and the ultimate result, the conversion of the English to Protestantism, was exactly the opposite of that intended by the fanatical queen. Her marriage to King Philip II of Spain had dragged England in the wake of Spanish ambitions, led to war with France and the loss of Calais, the last English possession on the Continent.

All this sprang from a strange mixture of religious and personal motives: to restore the Catholic Faith and Papal Supremacy, earn a heavenly blessing on her marriage and so in due course produce a male child who would also be her Catholic heir. These aims had nothing to do with the destiny of England and they were all frustrated. When Mary's half-sister Elizabeth ascended the throne at the age of twenty-five, England was torn by misgovernment, the treasury was empty, heavy foreign debts had been incurred, the people were dispirited and independence itself was threatened by France, which had one foot in Calais and the other in Scotland owing to the marriage of Mary, the Queen of Scots, to the French Dauphin, soon to be King Francis II.

As for Elizabeth, called to rule strife-torn England with its four million inhabitants, its languishing trade and its military weakness, it must have seemed unlikely to contemporaries that this tall young woman, with her auburn hair, dark eyes, sleek olive complexion and winsome manner, would do more than scratch at the surface of national problems. Her sex told heavily against her, she had never before appeared in public life, her abilities were unknown.

But Elizabeth possessed many remarkable gifts, chief among them a strong and flexible intellect. In a letter to her brother, written when she was thirteen, she was already conscious of mental powers which "nor time with her swift wings shall overtake, nor the misty clouds with their lowerings may darken, nor chance with her slippery foot may overthrow".

438

But Elizabeth's brilliant mind might have been a disadvantage to her as queen without corresponding emotional gifts, and these also she possessed: high courage in times of crisis, endurance and resilience. These qualities had been tempered by adversity in her youth, once when adolescent love for Admiral Seymour, brother of the Lord Protector under Edward VI, had seemed to involve her in a plot to oust the Protector, and again, during her sister's reign, when she was falsely accused of complicity in attempted rebellion. In peril of her life, Elizabeth had learnt the value of dissemblance and prevarication. The instinct of self-preservation had taught her to walk a tight-rope amid manifold dangers and she emerged from these years as a woman in full control of herself, a thorough realist, purposeful but cautious, beneath a blithe, often ribald, exterior as tough as steel. One quality topped all others: patriotism. Against heavy odds she herself had survived. From now on, emotionally identified with the land she governed, she would work for the welfare of England.

Elizabeth was proud of being "the most English woman of the kingdom", and not surprisingly she wanted her people's affection. To rule with their "loves" was the recurrent theme of her speeches, the aim underlying her principle never to command what voluntary co-operation would achieve. The theme, an affair of the heart between the queen and Englishmen, was struck at the start when, on the eve of her coronation, she toured the City of London, arousing impassioned loyalty by a display of dignity allied to human feeling.

But undivided loyalty came only from Protestants and only from those who were not extremists. Elizabeth faced a delicate situation. On the one hand were the Romanists, fearing a restoration of heresy in the country, established in positions of power, a pool of potential treason which might be stirred from Scotland, France or Spain. On the other, exiles from Mary's persecution were flooding back, bringing with them the teachings of Calvin and insisting on their right to organize their Church and to worship in their own way. This demand, if granted, could be extended to politics, undermining the constitution and disrupting the balance of the state. To steer a middle path and establish a Church which would attract reasonable men from both sides, so forming a nucleus round which the majority of the nation could eventually rally, was an urgent necessity and its achievement one of Elizabeth's great contributions to the peace of England.

Elizabeth herself was in no way a fanatic and her inclination was to judge religious issues from a practical point of view. The disloyal Romanist bishops were deposed and replaced by moderate Protestants. England was made Protestant by law, the queen became Supreme Governor of the Church and subjects were obliged to take an oath of spiritual allegiance. A new liturgy was introduced combining, as evidence of conciliation, Protestant doctrine with Catholic ritual and its observance was imposed by Act of Parliament. All this offered Englishmen a means of reconciling their religious convictions with their patriotic instincts and, though strife continued, Elizabeth's Church grew and prospered.

Meanwhile her throne was threatened from Scotland, where French troops were fighting to gain control of the country for Mary Stuart's mother, Mary of Guise, against the Puritan Scottish nobles. The Queen of Scots was a direct descendant of Henry VII, the nearest claimant to the English throne, and if the French prevailed her claim might be made good. For close on thirty years, indeed, she was a thorn in Elizabeth's flesh. Temporarily the danger was averted by the triumph of the Scottish Protestants, discreetly assisted from England. Then Francis II of France died, Mary Stuart returned to Scotland and became a focus for Catholic supporters on both sides of the border.

Soon the problem was complicated by Mary's marriage to the feckless Lord Darnley and the birth of a son, supplying a successor to the English throne which her Privy Council, headed by the meticulous and trustworthy William Cecil, had been vainly urging Elizabeth to provide. She had consistently refused marriage for reasons of state—to keep foreign suitors in doubt and to refuse English ones was to frustrate concerted opposition to England abroad and avert the hostility of rivals at home. But when Mary gave birth to her son James, the woman in Elizabeth lamented: "The Queen of Scots is delivered of a fair son and I am but a barren stock."

Mary's connivance in the murder of Darnley and her marriage to her fellow-conspirator, Lord Bothwell, resulted in her deposition by the infuriated Scots and flight to England, where, by no means reluctant to exchange a more powerful throne for the one she had lost, she became, abetted from Spain, a centre of Catholic intrigue against Elizabeth's life. There was no easy solution to the problem she posed. Half a prisoner, she was allowed to move from one residence to another, and Elizabeth waited on events until a Catholic rebellion in northern England obliged her to confine her rival more closely. The Pope retaliated by excommunicating the English queen; there was a danger of Catholic Europe—the forces of the Counter-Reformation—combining against her, and she strove, from now on, to weaken Catholic power in France by supporting the Huguenots and Spanish power in the Netherlands by aiding Dutch resisters against the tyranny of their Spanish overlords.

This policy was moderately successful, but at home the excommunication of Elizabeth had turned her Catholic subjects into potential if not actual traitors and the danger grew from plots centring on Mary Stuart. English priests trained in France came back to fan Catholic feeling and in later years fanatical Jesuits arrived to work for the restoration of Catholicism in England. The essential issue became a simple one: Elizabeth's removal, which was only too possible, would place the Catholic Mary on the throne. Mary's removal would safeguard Elizabeth and ensure a Protestant succession in the shape of James who had been crowned king by the Calvinists in Scotland.

A series of plots, one of them revealing plans for an attack on England by all the Catholic powers and the murder by a Spanish agent of William the Silent, leader of the Dutch Protestant revolt, convinced the Privy Council that delay might be fatal and Mary must die. But Elizabeth would not sanction extreme measures until, in 1586, there was clear evidence of Mary's complicity in a fresh plot to murder her, and after Mary's trial and conviction Elizabeth at last set her hand to the death warrant, though she attempted later to shift responsibility for the execution on to her advisers.

Meanwhile in Spain King Philip's plans matured for a crusade against heretic England and the menace of invasion loomed closer during these years. From her accession Elizabeth had pursued a tortuous foreign policy aimed at preventing a foreign combination against her, weakening the Catholic forces abroad and at the same time, if possible, remaining on good terms with France or Spain. A prime concern had been to prevent the Netherlands, the Channel ports and Brittany being used as bases for invasion. It was a policy of wait-and-see, entailing shifts, stratagems and apparent vacillation. To support it Elizabeth had only limited resources. But it was typically English in its defiance of rigid principle, feminine also in its flexibility and adherence to practical ends. As a result, France and then Spain had been cajoled into friendship, until King Philip acquired the throne, the empire, the resources of Portugal and the conquest of England seemed to him a practical possibility. The execution of Mary Stuart made war certain.

Spain had overwhelming power, but English seamen were confident. For many years they had harried Spanish possessions in South America, raided Spanish harbours, captured Spanish treasure fleets. In 1587 Francis Drake "singed the King of Spain's beard" by destroying ships and stores in Cadiz. The sailing of the Armada was postponed for a year and the queen waited calmly in London to hear of its fate as it moved up-Channel. The Spanish plan was to link up at Dunkirk with a force of veteran soldiers from the Netherlands under the Duke of Parma and transport them to the Essex coast. The Armada was pursued as far as Calais by the English, badly mauled there by fire-ships and next day failed even to sight the invasion barges it was supposed to meet. A sea-fight followed in which the Spaniards suffered further loss and then the surviving ships set off on the perilous voyage, round Britain and Ireland, towards home.

But Parma and his veterans still threatened and it was now that Elizabeth, riding a white horse, "attired like an Angel bright" with crown and breastplate, addressed her army of 20,000 men at Tilbury. She was not afraid, she said, to commit herself to them. She trusted their loyalty. "And therefore I am come amongst you, as you see, resolved in the midst and heat of the battle to live or die amongst you all, to lay down for my God and for my kingdom, and for my people, my honour and my blood, even in the dust. I know I have the body of a weak and feeble woman, but I have the heart and stomach of a king, and of a king of England too and I think foul scorn that Parma or Spain or any prince of Europe should dare to invade the borders of my realm. . . ."

But Parma did not come and in November, 1588, thanks were offered in St. Paul's for the Great Deliverance. One of the medals struck at this time bore in Latin the words: "God blew and they were scattered", and the Armada portrait of Elizabeth shows her seated in regal splendour, with one hand on the globe, while on a panel behind her the Armada founders in a providential tempest. All Englishmen now firmly believed that God watched over their destinies through his chosen instrument Elizabeth and, sensibly, she did nothing to disabuse them. The result was an upsurge of national morale.

Enterprise was already the hall-mark of the Age. Drake's voyage round the world in 1577, Martin Frobisher's attempt to find the North-west Passage, Humphrey Gilbert's acquisition of Newfoundland, the founding of Virginia, raids on Spanish possessions on both sides of the Atlantic, the expeditions of Walter Raleigh and the establishment of the East India Company reflected the national mood. In imaginative and speculative thought the Elizabethans were brilliant, too. Besides Shakespeare, Spenser, Bacon and Marlowe, many other writers in prose and in verse contributed to the greatest of all periods in English literature. Directly or indirectly the queen presided over all this creative enterprise, investing personally in the voyages of her seamen and attracting learned men to her Court.

Elizabeth never risked all on the single throw of the dice and after the defeat of the Armada she did not try to deliver a mortal blow at the Spanish Empire and the possibility of renewed invasion remained. But her diplomacy and the proven power of her navy kept England safe and troops could be spared for the last great achievement of her reign, the pacification of Ireland. After an attempt to anglicize the country had failed, inter-tribal anarchy was suppressed at heavy cost and by 1603 the reconquest of Ireland had been completed and the whole country was subjugated for the first time in its history.

Peace in England, peace, though under the sword, in Ireland, the establishment of a Protestant country over against the Catholic monarchies of the Continent, the frustration of foreign enemies— these were the gifts which Elizabeth conferred. With truth in 1591 she could say: "It is clear as daylight that God's blessing rests upon us, upon our people and realm, with all the plainest signs of prosperity, peace, obedience, riches, power and increase of our subjects."

Yet the image of Queen Elizabeth which we still cherish does not rest only on these achievements. We think of her political self: hard-working, imperious, courageous, enduring, seeking always a practical compromise in problems which admitted of no final solution, never a tyrant, yet not afraid to command, "no horse-leech for blood", as she said, at a time when torture and execution were the acknowledged accompaniments of rule. We see her in the gay and vigorous life of her Court with its bull-baiting, bear-baiting dramas, chess, cards and dancing in which she partook with uninhibited relish, familiar with the opposite sex, fishing, as it was said, for men's souls, free with pungent oaths and ribald jokes. A woman of glittering personality, accepted, then as now, as the presiding genius in an age of rampant individualism. "Queen Elizabeth of famous memory", as Oliver Cromwell called her, the "Gloriana" of Spenser's *Faery Queen*, Good Queen Bess, summing up two years before she died the theme of her reign in a speech to her Commons: "Though God hath raised me high, yet this I account the glory of my crown, that I have reigned with your loves."

GUSTAVUS ADOLPHUS

(1594–1632)

FOR DECADES seers and astrologers in the war-torn principalities of sixteenth- and seventeenth-century Germany had been prophesying the advent of the Lion of the North, a kind of militant Messiah who would bring salvation from afar. In 1621 the long-expected Lion of the North came from across the Baltic and blazed a trail of hope and victory throughout Germany where Protestantism was fighting for its life.

He was Gustavus Adolphus, King of Sweden, a brilliant and attractive figure in a none-too-attractive age, who became a myth and legend in his own time. His great enemy, Wallenstein, said of him that the German people awaited him as the Jews awaited their Messiah.

The sufferings of the German principalities resulted from the endeavours of the Roman Catholic world to check the growth of Protestantism which spread with alarming rapidity in northern Europe during the sixteenth century. The emperor Charles V (q.v.) was the first Catholic ruler to make a serious challenge to the Reformation, and his armies ranged throughout his vast empire trying to stamp out the conflagration lit by Martin Luther. He considered it his Catholic duty and he wore himself out trying to suppress the unsuppressible. The princes of northern Germany had too much to gain enriching themselves by seizing Church property and acquiring popular esteem thereby. The Papacy itself, enjoying the material fruits of the Renaissance, was in decline and was not prepared to go to very great lengths to re-establish its authority among those who had strayed from the true faith.

The Peace of Augsburg (1555), which gave to the Germanic rulers the freedom to break away from the Roman Church, was not really an act of religious toleration, as it only recognized the Lutheran type of Protestantism, and provided only for the religious consciences of the German princes, not of their subjects. The "religious conscience" of the princes was frequently guided by the material gain involved in going Protestant.

After a period of uneasy peace the Catholic powers, alarmed at

444

the continuing spread of Protestantism, particularly in Bavaria and Bohemia, once more went on to the offensive. The religious aspect of the Thirty Years War which followed (1618-48) was blurred by the political and dynastic ambitions of the contestants. Ferdinand II became the Holy Roman Emperor in 1619. A Habsburg as much as a Catholic, his enthusiasm for the Thirty Years War was more political than religious. He wanted to crush Protestantism in order to enforce the Habsburg rule over his rebellious empire.

Ferdinand enlisted the services of the notorious Albrecht Wenzel Eusebius von Wallenstein (or properly Waldstein) to lead the armies of the Catholic League against the Protestants. Wallenstein, a Catholic in name only, was as ambitious as his Habsburg master, and used the war, as Ferdinand did, to extend his personal power. His armies were drawn from the dregs of European society, were unpaid and lived off the countries in which they were fighting. As a consequence the war was savage and callous even by modern standards. The people of the German countryside suffered decades of looting, violence and rapine, for which history is hard put to find a parallel. Their suffering is impossible to describe. Many were driven to cannibalism. Whole areas became depopulated.

It was in this wretched century, when men were being told that their sufferings were divine punishment for abandoning the true Church, that they turned their eyes, not south to the ancient and decadent Papacy across the Alps, but north whence their saviour, according to the prophecy, would come.

Their great champion, who did indeed come in 1621, was the most illustrious member of the royal house of Vasa, which in the previous century made Sweden into an independent kingdom.

The Scandinavian kingdoms of Norway, Sweden and Denmark came into being at the time of Charlemagne and were established by the Germanic peoples. In 1397 the three kingdoms were united under the Union of Calmar. During the sixteenth century, at about the time of the Reformation, this Scandinavian Union was broken by Gustavus Vasa, a Swede, who led Sweden to independence and was elected king by an assembly at Strangas in 1523. In that year Protestantism came to Sweden. Vasa confiscated Church property, subdued the aristocracy and set Sweden on the way to national greatness. The Swedish kings started on an era of conquest until their kingdom extended to the eastern shores of the Baltic, which is now Finland, and into Russia, which they cut off from the sea. They cast their eyes southward to Poland and Germany, for their dream was to make the Baltic a Swedish lake.

Gustavus Adolphus was born on 9 December, 1594, eldest son of Charles IX. Charles was one of those restless warrior kings, familiar in European history, whose activities were a mixture of good and bad. A fierce and despotic champion of Protestantism and oppressor of Catholicism, he carefully nurtured Gustavus Adolphus to be a doughty defender of Protestantism. He also gave the boy an excellent education. He appointed as his tutor Johan Schroderus, a learned, widely-travelled man, who was a great linguist. By the time he was twelve young Gustavus was fluent in Swedish, German, Italian, Dutch and Latin, then an international language spoken by all educated men. Later he learned to speak Spanish, Russian and Polish as well.

His father carefully trained him in statecraft, and even gave him a share in the administration. The wise old warrior's faith in his son was not misplaced, for when Gustavus Adolphus came to the throne on Charles's death in 1611 he was a prudent, accomplished young man, brilliant alike in the arts of war and statesmanship.

He was seventeen. The first thing he did was to end the somewhat fratricidal wars his father had been waging against Denmark and Russia, and he immediately created a considerable impression by the way he handled these difficult negotiations with the Danes and the Muscovites. The young Gustavus in fact lost no time in acquiring ascendancy and authority in his own country. He had a powerful and attractive personality, and a generous spirit.

He was greatly interested in reform. In 1614 he set up the Swedish Court of Appeal, which had the effect of by-passing much clumsy medieval judicial procedure. He also instituted many industrial and agricultural reforms which had a beneficial effect upon the Swedish economy.

In 1599 Spain had adopted a copper currency. Sweden had rich copper deposits, and these were developed by Gustavus, and the greatly increased exports of copper brought prosperity and economic power. Sweden thus was able to reach a position of great strength during the reign of Gustavus Adolphus, a remarkable feat for a country whose population was less than one million.

Gustavus was formally crowned in 1617 when he was twenty-three. At this time he was engaged in re-organizing his army. In contrast to most other European armies it contained few foreign mercenaries, but was exclusively Swedish. For a country with such a comparatively small population this was a great strain and a heavy burden for the people to bear. In 1620 there were local uprisings in protest against conscription. Despite these difficulties,

Sweden raised an army of exceptional quality which accomplished great feats of arms.

Gustavus Adolphus had not forgotten his training to be the champion of Protestantism. The Thirty Years War had already broken out, and he was genuinely afflicted by the misfortunes of his Protestant brethren and anxious to assist them. But all the same he was not going to devote his energies and waste the precious treasure and the manhood of Sweden purely on a religious crusade. Gustavus was probably more altruistic than his Catholic opponents, but he had a grand political aim too—the turning of the Baltic into a Swedish lake. When he crossed into Livonia (now the Russian province of Latvia) in 1621 he was hoping to extend his domains as well as to free the Protestants from the oppression of Emperor Ferdinand II and Wallenstein's armies of the Catholic League.

Although Riga capitulated to Gustavus after a month's siege, and he obtained an important foothold on Polish soil, including the vital seaway at the entrance of the River Dvina, these successes had been obtained at the cost of enormous losses, mainly due to sickness. Gustavus was forced to negotiate a truce with the Poles, and so crippling were his initial losses that it was two years before his army was refurbished and he was in a position to continue the struggle. During this time of consolidation he reinforced his army by no fewer than 10,000 men, mainly of Swedish peasant stock. It was not until 1626 that his new army was in a position to move once more. It was without doubt the best trained and most disciplined in the field at that time. It was no rabble of itinerant mercenaries, soldiers of fortune and foot-loose criminals and cut-throats, such as comprised the forces of the Catholic League. Gustavus did his best to reduce the attendant horrors of battle which the warring soldiery have throughout history inflicted upon the hapless inhabitants of the country where the fighting takes place.

In January, 1626, he attacked once more, and annihilated the Polish army at Wallhof, the Swedish troops overwhelming the Polish cavalry which previously they had always feared. A fifth of the Polish army was killed in this battle. After this great victory, Gustavus immediately consolidated his hold on Poland and advanced westward; by the end of the year he had a large Swedish fleet with 14,000 men on board anchored in the Bay of Danzig, Konigsberg had surrendered; Pillau, the only Baltic port capable of taking naval ships, was in his hands, and Danzig was blockaded. Gustavus returned to Sweden for more reinforcements—only his own personality and peculiar brand of persuasion could persuade the Swedes to give up

their peaceful and profitable pursuits to join in the deathly struggle
on the other side of the Baltic. In May, 1627, he returned with a
further 7,000 men. After some inconclusive encounters with the
formidable Polish commander, Stanislaus Koniecpolski, Gustavus
directed his attack against Prussia, and particularly the Prussian
ports, in order to establish a powerful base for taking the war into
Germany.

Despite the ancient prophecy about the Lion of the North,
Gustavus was at first regarded with suspicion by the Protestant
princes of Germany, who feared that he came as a conqueror rather
than a deliverer. They were better off as rulers under the loose
conglomeration of the empire than they would be as part of the
kingdom of this formidable King of Sweden. Despite Gustavus's
pretension of being the divinely appointed deliverer of the Protestants, there was no doubt that his policy of expanding the territories
of Sweden was every bit as important to him. The Protestant
leaders of northern Germany therefore regarded his offers of help
with some uneasiness. They well knew that everyone was in this
war for what they could get out of it.

They were, however, engaged in a terrible and merciless struggle
with the callous armies of the Catholic League under the formidable
Wallenstein, whose arrogance and dangerous personal ambitions
made him a host of enemies on his own side. In 1630 Emperor
Ferdinand, under heavy pressure, dismissed Wallenstein from
command and appointed Johann Tzerclaes, Count Tilly, in his
place.

The minds of the Protestant princes were completely changed in
1631 by the siege and sack of Magdeburg, which was accompanied
by scenes of horror, rapine and destruction reminiscent of the days
of Genghis Khan. Twenty thousand of its inhabitants were wantonly
butchered. It was Tilly's first success, and he tried in vain to restrain
the destructive lust of the sadistic soldiers of the Catholic League.
Gustavus was at this time negotiating with the Protestant princes,
and was blamed on all sides for not going to the aid of the slaughtered
Magdeburgers.

An army such as that of Gustavus Adolphus had not been seen
in Europe since the days of the Romans. It was highly disciplined,
intensively trained, well paid, and recruited from "good yeomen
and stout soldiers of fortune". There were Scottish and German
troops among them. Led by a general of Gustavus's brilliance, it
was more than a match for Tilly's considerably larger army.

Gustavus at last reached agreement with the princes, and in

particular with the Elector of Brandenburg, who allowed him to advance across his territory. The high standard of discipline and good behaviour of the Swedish army made a remarkable impression in a country accustomed to the worst kind of behaviour from passing armies.

Gustavus met Tilly at the battle of Breitenfeld, north of Leipzig, on 7 September, 1631, and by using methods of warfare he had devised overwhelmingly defeated him. Gustavus's secret was iron discipline. His troops stood unmoved like a wall against the assaults of the enemy. The veteran armies of the League fled in disorder, leaving 6,000 dead on the field. Tilly himself, badly wounded, barely escaped with his life.

Gustavus Adolphus was now acclaimed by all Protestant Germany as the great liberator—the fabled Lion of the North. He followed Tilly south, defeated him again in Bavaria, Tilly this time being killed in the battle. The alarmed emperor hastily recalled Wallenstein, who took the League's army into Saxony, plundering and burning as he went. Gustavus met him at the battle of Lutzen on 16 November, 1632, at which Wallenstein was driven from the field after tremendous losses on both sides.

But no loss was greater than that suffered by the Swedish army. It was a wild and confused battle, fought in a thick mist. Gustavus, always in the forefront of battle, led his own cavalry in a counter-charge, and was killed. It is not known exactly how, though it is believed he was lying wounded on the ground when he was dispatched by one of Wallenstein's horsemen.

It was an overwhelming blow to Sweden. With the king's death the empire melted away, despite the efforts of the regent, Count Oxenstierna, to continue the fight in Germany. With the rigid discipline imposed by Gustavus gone, the Swedish armies soon began to behave like all other armies of the period.

The Thirty Years War dragged on until 1648 when both sides were exhausted and settled their differences in the Treaty of Westphalia. This established many political changes in Europe which were to last until the Napoleonic Wars, and marked the failure of the Austro-Spanish attempt to restore Roman Catholicism in Central Europe. It took Germany a century to recover from the destruction and atrocities of this brutal war.

Gustavus Adolphus died too young to accomplish very much of what he set out to do. He was a monarch of great promise. It was a tragedy for Sweden that his brilliant but unstable daughter, Queen Christina, did not inherit his true quality of kingship.

OLIVER CROMWELL

(1599–1658)

THERE ARE historians who would not accept it as a mark of
Cromwell's greatness that he was esteemed by the founder of
psycho-analysis. Freud wrote in his *Interpretation of Dreams* that
Cromwell had "powerfully attracted" him in his boyhood. His
juvenile hero-worship was spun out to what may have been a
psychologically interesting extent, for in due time he named his
second son Oliver, after Cromwell.

Not for the Freudians only, Cromwell's character affords a
richer vein for probing than that of any other English ruler. He was
both introvert and extrovert, temperate and ruthless, conservative
and destructive, freedom-loving and authoritarian, hag-ridden and
flexible, contemplative in thought, impatient in action. Dedicated
to the parliamentary system, he was in this degree one of its most
resounding failures. He could order the obliteration of garrisons,
and yet, by his steward's testimony, "did exceed in tenderness".
In him contradictions abounded, often to the point of paradox.

As a Puritan, that is, an extreme Protestant, he believed that his
life was being lived for him as part of the Divine Will. Yet, in the
role of God's puppet, he displayed a defiant individualism, and
occasionally an omniscience, that was at variance with the deep
humility of his religious professions. That he was the battle-ground
of desperate mental conflicts cannot be doubted. After great
agonizing, spiritual conversion came when he was twenty-eight, a
married man with five children. He suffered through the first half
of his life from a blood infection that constantly erupted in boils
and carbuncles. Cromwell on the couch would have yielded an
overflowing casebook.

Estimates of his character vary as widely as those of the sum of
his final achievements. The Royalists, unable to write him off, said
that he was "a brave, bad man", a verdict that largely dominated
discussions of his place in history for two hundred years. His
reputation hung in tatters from the gibbet of time long after his
bones had been dispersed.

The Scottish philosopher, Hume, conceded him "superior

genius", coupled with a propensity to "fraud and violence", the means by which he had "rendered himself first in the State". A later and not less remarkable Scottish thinker, Thomas Carlyle, came to see "that Cromwell was one of the greatest souls ever born of English kin".

Many supplementary views can be dismissed, if not ignored, such as that of John Forster, the biographer, who held it to be "indisputably true" that Cromwell was a traitorous hypocrite. One of the great students of seventeenth-century England, S. R. Gardiner, formed the opinion that what Shakespeare was in the world of the imagination, so Cromwell was in the world of action—"the greatest because the most typical Englishman of all time". To John Morley he was "a rare and noble type of leader".

Seen from abroad, he presented an equally striking if confusing spectacle. An Italian near-contemporary, Leti, arraigned him as a bloodthirsty ruler of men, "devoid of scruples and taste". An ambassador from Tuscany wrote of him in 1651 that "there cannot be discerned in him any ambition save for the public service". Guizot, the French statesman turned historian, showed towards him the sympathetic insight of one who himself had seen a revolution in the making, assigning Cromwell to a place in the company of "these great men, who have laid the foundations of their greatness amidst disorder and revolution". The renowned German historian, Ranke, treated him with objective respect. A later German generation, as of Italians, hailed him as a prototype of the leadership which, in the 1930s, inspired them to vociferously tragic response.

In his largely uncritical biography of Cromwell, Theodore Roosevelt, sometime President of the United States, declared him to have been the leader of "a movement that produced the English-speaking world as we know it at present". In general, American historical scholarship, infused though much of it has been by the Puritan tradition, has not countenanced admiration for Cromwell as man or leader of men. Dean Inge believed that Cromwell would have delighted in the *Battle Hymn of the Republic*.

John Buchan's biography of Cromwell endorsed Carlyle's long-pondered findings, while underlining the proposition that Cromwell left no enduring mark on the national life. In the eyes of G. M. Trevelyan, the social historian, he saved England from autocracy, Presbyterian tyranny, and final disruption. In John Drinkwater's play about him, cited here not for its historical value but for its popularity in the theatre of two continents, Cromwell was projected as one "who cared above all for the well-being of England, which for him meant the individual liberty and enlightenment of the English people". Hilaire Belloc summed him up as "Jehovah's own dragoon", valorous, chaste, and staunch, riding roughshod in the vanguard of a conspiracy designed to overthrow the Church of Rome.

What manner of man, then, was this who, after three centuries, continues to provoke, as Meredith phrased it, writing to Morley about Cromwell, "the raging of distempered advocates"? He was born at Huntingdon on 25 April, 1599, the son of a Protestant line enriched by lands acquired at the Reformation. The paternal ancestor four generations removed was a Welshman named Morgan A. Williams, who migrated to London as one of the followers of Henry VII. He settled down in Putney, then a thriving Thames-side port, as a functionary of the Crown responsible for the manor of Wimbledon. His son, likewise named Morgan, carried on the office and combined a brewery connexion with it. He married the daughter of another local brewer, Walter Cromwell, a Norfolk man who was the father of Thomas Cromwell, Henry VIII's minister charged with the dissolution of the monasteries. Richard, the son of Morgan Williams and Katherine Cromwell, moved into his uncle Thomas's household and duly assumed the Cromwell surname. He was looked on with approval by the king, became a highly favoured courtier, and a knight.

His son, Sir Henry, was Sheriff of Huntingdonshire and Bedfordshire, and the builder of the fine mansion of Hinchingbrooke, near Huntingdon, where he entertained Queen Elizabeth. The next in the succession, Sir Oliver, entering upon his inheritance in 1603, considerably depleted it by his lavish and possibly slavish hospitality to James I. He was compelled to sell Hinchingbrooke and retire to a modest property at Ramsey, near-by.

Sir Oliver's brother, Robert, lived in High Street, Huntingdon, on income from family property that brought him £300 a year, plus whatever was to be made from farming in a gentlemanly way; he owned grazing land just outside the town. He had been to Cambridge, read law, and sat in the House of Commons as the member for Huntingdon. His wife, a widow when they married, was a Norfolk woman named Steward, a corruption of Stewart. She was said to have been of the royal line. They were the parents of Oliver Cromwell, who had seven sisters and two brothers. He was educated at the Free Grammar School, Huntingdon, and at Sidney Sussex College, Cambridge.

A Debrett of his day would have shown that Oliver Cromwell

was connected, directly and by marriage, with a network of influential families holding sway in East Anglia and farther afield. At one time at least twenty of his relatives were sitting in Parliament, one of them his rich cousin John Hampden. The Cromwells were a parliamentary family whose generations had acquired almost an hereditary claim to stand for Parliament and to be elected to it.

In his turn Oliver Cromwell entered the House of Commons in 1628, when he was twenty-nine, as the member for Huntingdon. He had married Elizabeth Bourchier, the daughter of a well-to-do City knight whose main business interest was in the fur trade. His standing then was that of a squire with £500 a year, derived from the wills of two of his uncles. His wife had some money of her own. While not prosperous, they were comfortably off. Cromwell was free to give his time and energy to politics, while keeping a watchful eye on local land values. In 1631 he sold off some of his Huntingdon land and re-invested in pastures new at St. Ives. In 1640 he was returned to Parliament for Cambridge town. It was a turning-point in more than one man's life. The political despotism which the Tudors had bequeathed to the Stuarts was about to be challenged.

We have a word-sketch of him by a contemporary courtier, Sir Philip Warwick, who saw him at Westminster at about that time. "I came into the House one morning, well clad, and perceived a gentleman speaking whom I knew not, very ordinarily apparelled, for it was a plain cloth suit, which seemed to have been made by an ill country tailor. His linen was plain, and not very clean; and I remember a speck or two of blood upon his little band, which was not much larger than his collar. His hat was without a hat-band. His stature was of a good size; his sword close to his side; his countenance swoln and reddish; his voice sharp and untuneable, and his eloquence full of fervour."

Cromwell was then a back-bencher, earnest for his constituents, a dutiful observer of Parliamentary procedures, a speaker who neither emptied the House nor filled it. At home a regular church-goer, the topic that excited him to his most compelling flights as a speaker was the Church itself. Much of his parliamentary ardour was centred in religion. He was moved by a crusading urge to rid the Church of England of what he conceived to be poisonous influences and practices; genuflections, vestments, graven images, Popish symbols. To him and his fellow Puritans the Bible was the key to the spiritual life. It was to be elevated to the first place in public worship, taking precedence over the Prayer Book. Preachers were to be given more authority than priests.

In Cromwell's personal life politics and religion were fused into a force that made his will a formidable instrument of power when the opportunity came for him to use it. The Bible was always at his hand, the resources of prayer constant in his life. He was on his knees every day, often many times a day. He was capable of self-discipline to the point of mortification.

He supported a movement that endowed speakers to deliver religious "lectures" on village greens and at market crosses as a way of stressing the Church's want of fervour in preaching the Word. From it came a branch of religious nonconformity in England that is still healthy and vigorous. His antipathy to the bishops, in particular, declared itself in a speech in which he complained that Papist sympathizers within the Church were being given preferment over honest men of other opinions. The speech made him the authoritative spokesman of the Puritans of eastern England, whence had lately gone the Pilgrim Fathers on their famous quest.

Both Church and State roused in Cromwell feelings of dissidence that drove him forward along his revolutionary course. Their encroachment of power, it seemed to him, would inevitably lead to the suppression of freedom of conscience. That liberty, even when, paradoxically, he appeared to be its worst enemy, was the theme and inspiration of his life.

The Puritans were a faction, by no means the nation. As one of their stalwarts, Cromwell himself took on national stature in 1641 by his prominent advocacy of the Grand Remonstrance, demanding Church reform and the modification of the king's power. He held those provisos to be of such importance for the future of the realm that, he declared, their rejection would have obliged him to sell all that he had "and see England no more". Amid intense excitement in the House, the Grand Remonstrance was passed by 159 votes to 148. From then on Cromwell was in the grip of destiny. For him there could be no going back to the squire's life. What he and others had signed with the pen they would have to defend with the sword.

On 4 January, 1642, Charles I marched with an imposing body-guard to the House of Commons to seize for impeachment five popular members: Hampden, Pym, Holles, Haselrig, and Strode. They were tipped off in time to absent themselves from the precincts. When the king called out their names and waited imperiously, an uncomfortable silence fell on the assembled members. His demand to the Speaker for information brought that worthy to his knees with the plea that he was "but the servant of this House". Head high, eyes blazing, Charles walked out of the Chamber. As he did so there was an ominous murmuring from all sides. "Privilege! Privilege!" It was one of the great moments in English history. The bodyguard escorted the king back to Whitehall in silence. It was the five members who received the cheers.

Assuming that the king would seek to avenge his rebuff by force of arms, the Puritan party deemed it necessary that Parliament should henceforth have control of the militia. When representations to that effect were formally put to the king, he answered: "Not for an hour!" Parliament thereupon seized control, over-riding Charles's protest that no ordinance was valid without his assent and signature.

Although Cromwell was not one of the members denounced by the king, if their number had been ten, or fewer, instead of five, his name would almost certainly have been on the list for arrest. He was made a member of a committee charged with inquiring into the king's sources of advice in refusing to give up control of the militia.

By then the country was considered to be in a state of emergency. The king's obduracy had cast the shadow of civil war across the land. At Cromwell's prompting, a Committee of Safety was formed. It precipitated a cleavage that ranged the people's party on the one side, presently known as the Roundheads, and the Cavaliers, whose swords were drawn in the service of the king, on the other. The outcome was a fratricidal tragedy. Families were riven, brother set against brother. Old friendships were torn apart, loyalties wiped out. Against that sombre background, Oliver Cromwell, the cavalry captain who may never have told his men, "Trust in God, and keep your powder dry", developed the leadership that was to bear him upward to a place in the pantheon of the great rulers.

The first battle of the Civil War, fought at Edgehill, near Warwick, on 23 October, 1642, proved little except that, after an initial bloody encounter, caution was largely the mood on both sides. There was some wavering among the Parliamentary foot-troops, a situation saved by the cavalry. Four months later Cromwell was raised to the rank of colonel and given a regiment. The men in it became known as Cromwell's Ironsides. Many among them were Puritan fanatics.

From the beginning Cromwell was activated by the belief that this was a religious war, and he sought to draw into his ranks only "honest and godly men". The requirement of honesty figured in almost every letter he wrote on the subject of recruiting.

By strenuous exertions, and by taking advice from professional men of arms, he made himself the Parliamentary army's best cavalry leader. It meant, in the circumstances of the time, that he was the army's best soldier, since the cavalry was the dominant arm. His bold decision, in ordering his men suddenly to rein-in and turn on the unguarded Royalist infantry, gained the victory at Marston Moor, near York, in 1644. That success weakened the king's hold on the North, particularly in Yorkshire.

That year Cromwell became a member of a sort of inner war council, styled The Committee of Both Kingdoms. One of the first recommendations brought before it was the Self-denying Ordinance, which decreed that members of both Houses of Parliament should resign their commissions in the army in favour of professional soldiers. It also considered a plan for a new national army of 10 cavalry regiments, 12 infantry regiments, and 1 regiment of dragoons. They were to be known as the New Model Army. Sir Thomas Fairfax was appointed its commander-in-chief. Cromwell was given command of the cavalry.

Discipline in the new army was ruthlessly strict. Its officers were chosen not only for their military experience but for their ardour in the cause of defeating the king's tyranny. Remoulded, the army became a unique, single-minded, dedicated military force. Its fighting efficiency owed not a little to Cromwell's inspiration and presence; and now he was preparing to comply with the Self-denying Ordinance and hand over his command.

On 4 June, 1646, the House of Commons heard a petition from the City of London for his retention as a serving officer. A similar request came from Fairfax, who was keen to put his New Model Army to the test of battle. The House of Commons concurred and, without waiting for confirmation from the other House, Fairfax sent a message to Cromwell bidding him report to the main army headquarters at Kislingbury, near Daventry.

His arrival there, at the head of six hundred mounted men, their jingling harness brasses making fine music in his ears as he rode through the fresh green Northamptonshire lanes that June, was a personal triumph. "He was with the greatest joy received by the General and the whole army. Instantly orders were given for drums to beat, trumpets to sound to horse, and all our army to draw to rendezvous." He became the New Model Army's lieutenant-general.

As at Marston Moor, he played a decisive part in the misnamed battle of Naseby, on 14 June, 1646. The discipline of his cavalry was the best in the army. Now, once again, it proved invincible. The

battle was a shattering blow to the king, revealing to him the futility
and the folly of his cause. He surrendered to the Scots, who handed
him over to Parliament.

Under Cromwell's direction the army took the king into custody
and put him under surveillance at Hampton Court Palace. Discovering that certain members of Parliament were in secret touch
with him, the Puritan leaders sent an officer named Colonel Pride
to the House of Commons to arrest them as they entered. "Pride's
Purge" was an unconstitutional act. It meant that the New Model
Army had become a political entity.

Cromwell, with Ireton, his son-in-law, evolved a plan of pacification which they hoped would receive the approval of both sides.
It was rejected by the king. Cromwell had a number of consultations
with him, finally to the detriment of his own repute, for he was
suspected of private connivance with Charles. Already there were
muttered demands that the king's life should be forfeit. Cromwell
turned a deaf ear to them. His patience was exemplary. If there was
a way of peacefully and satisfactorily resolving the dilemma, he
wished with all his heart to find it. In his efforts to do so he frequently
retired from the public scene for long sessions of prayer.

The king broke his parole and sought refuge in the Isle of Wight.
It was a fatal mistake, a signal to the headsman to begin sharpening
his axe. Cromwell had genuinely wished for a clear and conscientious understanding with the king, subject to the latter's
readiness to acknowledge the primacy of Parliament. Charles
prevaricated, twisted, intrigued, floundered in evasions, provoking
the House of Commons to pass the resolution "that by the fundamental laws of this kingdom, it is treason for the King of England
to levy war against the Parliament and Kingdom of England".

The trial of Charles I was thus set in motion. There was no
constitutional warranty for it and Cromwell listened impatiently
to those lawyers who argued otherwise. The king refused to acknowledge the authority of the Court and to defend himself before it.
Shrinking then, as on other occasions, from frightful decision and
taking it only when it appeared to him imperatively necessary,
Cromwell tried to avoid putting his name to the document that
sent Charles to his death on the scaffold in Whitehall on 30 January,
1649. Afterwards he spoke of it as an act of justice, a word that for
him always had a higher and holier sanction than that of any human
court. Long ago he had declared himself opposed to the death
penalty except for murder and treason.

A Council of State was formed, with Cromwell as the dominant figure among its 41 members. The monarchy, the House of Peers, and their associative symbols and influences, were swept away. Virtually, it meant creating a new State, with the squire from Huntingdon at its head. Before him lay nearly a decade of supreme authority.

What he did with it vexes historical judgement today as keenly as it did nearer his time. His life and work have been the subject of a score or more biographies, numerous treatises, endlessly recurring arguments. His name is still execrated in Ireland, where he met violence with violence, on the ground that Irish Catholics had instituted massacres of English Protestants living lawfully among them. Faced with the Duke of Hamilton's southward invasion from Scotland in 1648, he reacted with equally crushing effect.

He was the honoured champion of liberty, the hated wrecker of free institutions, a defender and an oppressor: in the eyes of his critics, all those things. As the historian Gardiner has said: "All the incongruities of human nature are to be traced somewhere or other in Cromwell's career." The same authority takes care to point out that "this union of apparently contradictory forces" is characteristic of the English people, "making England what she is today".

In 1657 Parliament, recognizing in him the representative Englishman, offered Cromwell the Crown as a means of securing a return to constitutional government and the ordered society. Prayer, intense self-communion, earnest consultation, finally evoked from him the reply: "I cannot undertake this Government with that title of king; and that is my answer to this great and weighty business." Instead, he agreed to be known as the Protector, the guarantor of liberty of conscience for all. There had never been in England a ruler whose fame shone out with such brilliance as Cromwell's in the last years of his life.

He died on 3 September, 1658. Overnight, a great storm that ripped off housetops and blew down mighty oaks betokened the end, also, of Puritanism as a political power.

CHARLES I

King of England, Scotland and Ireland

(1600–49)

NO ENGLISH monarch has cast a longer shadow than Charles I. His fate still stirs prejudice and engages sympathy, though the rights and wrongs of his case have been before the world for over three hundred years. The red roses that continue to appear annually at the foot of his statue at the junction of Whitehall and Charing Cross are an emblem of more than a martyr's blood. They commemorate the crux of a great constitutional struggle, in which the execution of the king was a sombre incident rather than a shattering event. The axeman who held up the severed head to the crowd round the scaffold in 1649 was the servant of forces more imponderable than political or doctrinal discords.

Those forces had been working in society from Tudor times. Their course was run only when at last the kingly role was reformed and modified by the demolition of Divine Right. That concept, stubbornly held by Charles I, ignored shifts of social and economic emphasis that were historically more decisive than his follies or the bigotries of his Civil War enemies. A new influence had been rising in the land, that of the propertied class, the gentry, who resented subjection to the exclusive authoritarian patronage of the Court and the old nobility. It was Charles's tragedy that he was too rigidly moulded by his birth and training to be sensitive to a social change with effects as potent as those of the French Revolution or that later enacted in Russia.

He became Charles I because fate ordained that his elder brother should not come to the Throne as Henry IX. The second son of James I, Charles was made Prince of Wales when Henry died at eighteen in 1612. As a child, born in the sign of Scorpio towards the end of November, 1600, Charles was a poor human specimen, extremely weak on his legs and incapable, it seemed, of more than spasmodic speech. His chances of survival, not to say of his developing normally, were thought slender, a doubt that was resolved by the devotion of his governess, Lady Carey, who cosseted him out

459

of his protracted invalidism into an adolescence that saw him taking his place as a fearless horseman and an agile tennis player. His equestrian skill owed not a little to his small stature; he fancied that his horsemanship offset it. None the less, the physical transformation was remarkable.

Mentally, he remained a slow thinker who relied on silence to conceal the truth about himself. He was never a man of easy speech. His habit of reserve hid self-distrust and kept suitable advisers at a distance. The loneliness of his early years was accentuated by his lack of sympathy and humour. Yet by many he was thought "a creditable prince", whose personal life was in favourable contrast to that of the loose-living Court of his father. For his time and station, his code of conduct was a strict one, though dedicated more explicitly to the improvement of his physical prowess than to the refinement of his moral qualities. He had a known contempt for drunkenness, for example, and the grosser forms of debauchery evoked his disgust. The people saw virtue in him, and their cheers at his few public appearances in those years made music in the ears of one whose self-assurance was always in need of support.

His father, James I, had cherished the prospect of an alliance between England and Spain, to be clinched by the marriage of his son Henry to one of the Infantas. Five years after Henry's death, negotiations were reopened with Charles taking his brother's place in the rôle of suitor. There were frustrations and delays due to papal demands and to the king's tardiness in guaranteeing liberty of worship to Roman Catholics in England. Parliament urged a different course, petitioning the king to see to it that Charles married a Protestant princess. James told the Commons in effect to mind their business, which did not include interference with royal marriages. He caused the petition to be expunged from the official records and dissolved Parliament.

In the early spring of 1623 a small party of horsemen trotted sedately out of London towards Gravesend. Two of their number rode ahead, apparently in close companionship. They were heavily bearded and muffled in the folds of long riding cloaks. The beards of the two foremost men roused the suspicion of the mayor of Gravesend, who sent a messenger to trail the party down the Dover Road. His inquisitiveness was followed by abject silence when he learned that he was shadowing the heir to the Throne, travelling in elaborate incognito to Spain. His companion in disguise was the newly ennobled George Villiers, Marquess of Buckingham, "Steenie" to the king and Prince Charles. Buckingham, who had the king's highest favour, opened new doors on the world to Charles, initiating him into a wider experience of life, while being careful not to involve him in the private vices in which Buckingham notoriously indulged.

Arriving in Paris as John and Thomas Smith, the two young men secured admission to the Court and attended a masque at which the queen was present. She was a sister of the young Infanta whom Charles hoped to meet in Madrid. The queen's charms and graces spurred his eagerness to reach the Spanish capital; and during his five days in Paris he had no more than fleeting glances for the queen's vivacious, dark-eyed sister-in-law, Henriette Maria. It was afterwards reported that the princess had remarked that there was no need for the Prince of Wales to go so far as Madrid to look for a wife.

The news of Charles's mission to Spain was communicated to the people of England by bell ringing and bonfires lighted by royal command. Not all the citizens danced for joy. The Archbishop of Canterbury protested in the name of religion. Parliamentarians were angry because they had not been consulted in the name of the people. They gave the prince a great welcome when in the autumn of 1623 he returned to England, "not so much because he had come back", explained Gardiner, the learned historian, "as because he had not brought the Infanta with him". Archbishop Laud wrote in his diary that Charles was received with "the great expression of joy of all sorts of people that ever I saw".

The abortive match, which was politically rather than sentimentally inspired, was repugnant to Englishmen who remembered the Armada thirty-five years before. The collapse of the betrothal to a Catholic princess also gratified those who could not forget the more recent Gunpowder Plot.

The news-writers observed that the Spanish adventure had improved Charles's style as a public figure. He had become "a fine gentleman", they wrote. A new stateliness marked his deportment, perhaps in conscious or unconscious imitation of his recent hosts. He remained a singularly unimaginative young man, who was as capable of offending his friends as readily as those who were not his friends. "He has not the art to please", was a clerical comment on his often morose temperament.

Having been unmistakably apprised of the people's attitude to the marriage question, he proceeded with negotiations for his engagement to the young Henriette Maria of France. The House of Commons was upset again and exacted from him an oath, solemnly affirmed at St. John's College, Cambridge, that his marriage to a Catholic princess would mean "no advantage to the recusants at home".

The worth of the oath was limited if not nullified by an understanding secretly connived at by King James, Charles, and a Secretary of State, promising Roman Catholics in England a larger measure of liberty than they had previously enjoyed. James, in particular, was concerned to save those priests who were awaiting the utmost rigour of the law for privately administering Catholic rites to their flocks. Secret modifications of publicly enacted agreements were a common feature of the diplomacy of that age. In this instance the effects reverberated far. A dynamic mistrust developed between Charles and Parliament, leading to the English Revolution.

James I died on 27 March, 1625, making a pious and affecting end, partly brought about by excessive fruit eating, the physicians said. In the afternoon of that day Charles was proclaimed king. "Universal joy" greeted the event, according to Clarendon. The new monarch was hailed as a paragon of several virtues—sobriety, chastity, piety, dignity. He disliked flattery, was impervious to sycophancy, and his private life was without blame; he was seen to blush at immodest talk. He had a good appreciation of the arts, especially painting.

A portrait of him as a young man, painted by Daniel Mytens and believed to have been in the Royal collection, showed that, for all his lack of inches—he was a little over five feet—he was well proportioned, lithe, and of good bearing. Three days after his father's death he ratified, as king, the marriage treaty to which he had already put his name as prince.

The marriage took place on 1 May, 1625, Charles being represented by proxy at a ceremony conducted on a dais erected before the great door of Notre-Dame in Paris. A week's festivities followed before the young Queen Henriette (who in England soon became Henrietta) left for London and wifehood with Charles. He, meanwhile, had been chief mourner, garbed in a black cloak that hung to his ankles, at the funeral of his father in Westminster Abbey. There was criticism of the funeral sermon preached by the Bishop of Lincoln, who insisted that "no man ever got great power without eloquence". It was thought to be too pointed a reminder, in view of Charles's unreadiness of speech.

Having borne himself with approved gravity at those majestic obsequies, the new king rode to Canterbury to await the arrival of his French bride. She had been seen by an admiring Dover mariner disporting herself on the seashore at Boulogne. He informed the mayor and burgesses in a letter that she was a healthy and merry young thing who ventured "so near the sea it was bold to kiss her feet". History is cluttered with irrelevancies. Queen Henrietta's wet shoes have remained firmly imprinted in the sands of time.

On the evening of Trinity Sunday, 12 June, 1625, a Court messenger named Tyrwhit galloped the fifteen miles from Dover to Canterbury in thirty-six minutes to inform the king that his young queen, with her retinue of ladies-in-waiting and priestly advisers, was on English soil. By ten o'clock the next morning, Charles was at Dover to greet her. She was at breakfast in Dover Castle. When she knelt to do obeisance, "he wrapt her up in his arms with many kisses". Weeping, she disengaged from his embrace, apparently overcome by being among strangers. The contract of marriage was renewed in St. Augustine's Hall, Canterbury, without benefit of clergy. Public sensitiveness precluded the king from receiving the rites from a Roman Catholic, and the queen from an Anglican.

There being a plague in London (not to be confused with the later and more horrific visitation that is in all the history books), it was deemed wise to keep the royal couple away from the streets. Escorted by a mass of small craft filled with sightseers, they were rowed up the Thames in State barges to Whitehall. While bonfires blazed and cannon boomed, the dead-carts clattered over the cobbles with their loads for unmarked graves. Mingled with the thanksgiving in the churches were prayers for relief from the pestilence.

Charles was crowned in Westminster Abbey on 2 February, 1625, "a very bright, sun-shining day" (Archbishop Laud's diary). His young consort was not by his side. The Capuchin priests who had come over with her from France saw to that. She was proclaimed, but not crowned, queen later that year. As a Catholic, she could not accept the offices of the Church of England. In any event, as man and wife, differences were soon evident between them. A particular cause was Charles's growing regard for Buckingham, by then a duke. The little French queen detested him.

Charles had inherited a Throne with sharp thorns in the cushion: enormous debts, virtually war with Spain, and an intractable belief in the sovereign's right of personal rule. The last was a source of mounting strife between him and a House of Commons group resolved to stand fast for the privileges of Parliament and the liberties of the people. Opposition to Charles was coming also from another quarter, the Puritan party, animated by the theology of Calvin and a hatred of Rome.

Those dissidents in the House of Commons forced Charles to lay before Parliament a precise statement of his personal finances, complicated, as they were, by additional debts incurred since his father's death. They required to know the cost of maintaining the Navy, and demanded an estimate of the amount likely to be involved in a war with Spain.

Behind these requirements was deepening hostility to the king's closest adviser, Buckingham, who had too much power and was considered reckless in his use of it. One of his foremost critics in the House of Commons, Sir John Eliot, from Cornwall, later denounced him as the chief author of the nation's misfortunes, and the only begetter of the disaster that befell the naval expedition to Cadiz. As a climax of the agitation, Buckingham was impeached for having imperilled the national safety and honour.

The King reacted by sending Eliot to the Tower of London. In return, the House of Commons refused to transact any business until he was released. Charles then dissolved Parliament, an act designed as much to save his friend Buckingham as to preserve the sanctity of the "royal word". From that time on the people had to choose between the ultimate authority of king or Parliament. The prisons began to fill with men for whom the still small voice had become a loud imperative command.

By the end of the third year of his reign Charles was in dire trouble, with an empty exchequer, the prospect of having to make a humiliating peace with his enemies abroad, and his prerogative being attacked in Parliament by hitherto law-abiding gentlemen. The assassination of Buckingham by an Army lieutenant at Portsmouth in 1628 was a crowning personal disaster for Charles. It was said that he never threw off the effects of it in the twenty years that were left to him. So loyal was he to his friend's memory that the great historian Clarendon declared: "From that time almost to the time of his own death the king admitted very few into any degree of trust against whom Buckingham had ever manifested a notable prejudice."

One change in Charles's personal relationships at that time was remarked. The queen was pregnant again and his concern was such that at Court it was said that he had at last fallen in love with her. Unfortunately, their sudden access of felicity proved to be of ominous import for the nation. In his determination to avenge the death of his friend, the king showed himself too ready to surrender to the influence of his wife, who was even more rigidly attached than he to the Divine Right concept.

Thenceforward Charles relied on personal rule as the sole instrument of government. For the next eight years, until 1637, England had no Parliament. The king could count those years as the happiest and most settled of his life. They gave him an opportunity of practising his patronage of the arts, and of enjoying the company of Van Dyck and other painters. He added weightily to his collection of what an irate pamphleteer reviled as "old rotten pictures and broken-nosed marbles". The Italian sculptor, Bernini, commissioned to make a bust of the king, studied Van Dyck's portraits of him and announced that he had never seen "a countenance so unfortunate".

As always, Charles had not the wit to see the reality behind events, even when the surface was comparatively unruffled. They were being more observantly watched by an as yet hardly known Fenland squire, Oliver Cromwell, who, believing that he had attained to grace and salvation, also believed that he was called to high service in the land. Others of his kind, in protest against misguided kingship, joined in the Puritan emigration that was to lay the foundations of a great new overseas nation.

A new personality had arrived on the stage in Thomas Wentworth, to be ennobled presently as the Earl of Strafford. He was a Yorkshire baronet associated with Eliot, Hampden and others of their class who had assisted the fall of Buckingham. Endowed with a keen political sense and ambitious for a chance to exercise it in office, he identified himself with the king's party and was rewarded with titular distinctions and high authority in Ireland. That he was politically talented could not be denied; unluckily for him, he too obviously rejoiced in his gifts. "Of all his passions," Clarendon wrote, "pride was most prominent", and the historian's comment was justified by Wentworth's self-aggrandizement. Soon it was to be said of him that he was an even greater servant of the king than Buckingham had been. Yet the probability was that neither had a deep regard for the other. As for the queen, she at first disliked Wentworth as heartily as she had Buckingham, fearing his influence over her husband.

Events in Scotland, where Charles's attempt to force a new Book of Common Prayer on the Church of Scotland met fierce opposition, brought the two countries into conflict. On Wentworth's advice, the king summoned what was to be known as the Short

Parliament in the spring of 1640 and, also on his advice, dissolved it in three weeks for its refusal to grant him the means to equip and pay for an army to march against the Scots.

Another burning issue was ship money, levied on port authorities for protection from pirates who harried the coastal communities. So long as the funds thus raised were used for national purposes no one seriously objected. When the tax was extended inland the Buckinghamshire squire, John Hampden, refused to pay it. His action represented widespread resentment of the king's forced loans, of which ship money was by no means a solitary example. The smouldering fires of discontent were being blown into a fierce consuming flame. Hampden's proud resistance stirred the nation.

With shame and wrath in his heart, Charles gave way over a number of vital issues of the time, after vainly trying either to evade doing so or refusing his assent. Finally, summoning against his will what became the Long Parliament (1640), he found himself facing the people's champions, Hampden, Pym and presently Cromwell, across the dividing lines of power. By his side was the apostate Strafford (Wentworth), whose death-warrant he was soon unwillingly to sign. One of the effects of the resolute stand of those men was to halt the Puritan emigration. "The change", wrote an historian, "made all men to stay in England in expectation of a new world". It was a dream to be realized only through the blood and grief of the Civil War, with its horrible climax in Whitehall that cold afternoon of 30 January, 1649.

The inquest verdict has yet to be finally given. "If he were not the best king," Clarendon wrote in his great history, "if he were without some parts and qualities which have made some kings great and happy, no other prince was ever unhappy who was possessed of half his virtues and endowments, and so much without any kind of vice". Against the exemplariness of his private life is set the arbitrary temper he too often showed in the public domain. Some would say that Charles I was his own executioner.

CHARLES II

King of England, Scotland and Ireland

(1630–85)

YOUNG KING CHARLES II of England laughed as he smeared his face with soot in the chimney corner at Whiteladies during his flight from Cromwell's vengeful forces after the battle of Worcester, 1651. He was at risk of discovery and capture. Weariness was heavy upon him. Yet still he could laugh. His good humour, though it reflected a careless mind, was his title to the regard not only of those around him but of posterity. The simple absence of vanity from his nature perpetuated him in folk-memory, and the history books, as surely as his gallantries and the general jauntiness of his performance in the kingly role. He had no taste for tyranny, and he was too intelligent to be susceptible to the divine right theory that bedevilled his forebears on the throne.

If he was the most frivolous of England's monarchs, his wretched later upbringing could be held largely to account for it. An idyllic childhood in pleasant places, Hampton Court, Windsor, Greenwich, was all too soon shadowed by violence, tragedy, and grief. As a boy he heard the howling of the mob, and was touched by the desolation of his father's grim fate. At fifteen he was with the Royalists in the last phase of the Civil War, and saw the shambles that followed defeat in the West Country. At eighteen, he became a king with nowhere to lay his head.

Then there came the forlorn descent on England from Scotland, and, after it, shame and degradation, and the poverty of exile in France and Germany. Within a year he was eating his meals in taverns, too hard up to provide a table of his own. "I am sure the king owes for all he had had since April," wrote Edward Hyde, the Chancellor of his virtually non-existent Exchequer, in June, 1653. Beset by debt, and the indignities inseparable from it, Charles maintained an extraordinary hold over his sometimes despairing and often fractious Court by his gaiety of heart and the unquenchable good-humour that enabled him to laugh when disappointment clouded every prospect and idleness ate like gall into his soul.

He was kept going through the nine frustrating years that severed him from England by a zest for the ordinary simple satisfactions that was never subdued by his worst excesses. He loved to show off the few bits of finery that he had left; delighted in old wines and new tunes, and eagerly took lessons to improve his dancing and his knowledge of French and Italian. His buoyancy in one of the stormiest periods of English history may not have been admirable. Many must have envied it.

That he emerged from those early experiences as a sauntering cynic was unfortunate but hardly to be wondered at. He was always good company, and he could laugh at himself, which does not redeem the charge that he was a worthless character but takes some of the sting out of it. Although the adventurer in him found its commonest expression in dalliance, he had not a little of the temper of a rebel, including the courage. He was a fine horseman, who did not flinch from mounting the least trustworthy beast in the stable. He was unafraid of the sea in any of its moods. He could outwalk the sturdiest of his companions, and could hold his liquor beyond the capacity of most of them. He was a womanizer from the age of sixteen. Even Pepys blushed at his prowess in the sexual arena. Pretty or plain, well-born or quite otherwise, women contributed to Charles's life of indulgence its chiefest pleasures. His profound selfishness was not much mitigated by the courtesy and grace with which he was wont to invest his amorous escapades.

His small resources of sincerity were lavished on his sweet little sister "Minette", Princess Henrietta of England, who became Duchess of Orleans. He was her only hero. "She is truly and passionately concerned for the king, her brother," one of the courtiers wrote. She admired him above all other men. In return, he wrote loving letters to her, dutifully catching the mail each week, and telling her how impatient he was "till I have the happiness to see *ma chère Minette* again". It was his deepest and most genuine affection.

Those who cared most for his future feared that the years of exile tended to confirm him in his lack of responsibility and to weaken his moral fibre yet further. Hyde passed word to him to that effect that had come in letters from London. His advisers were even more worried because he made "no distinction of persons", but seemed content to choose his company where he found it. His privations were real enough to make their mark on his personal appearance. He was even unable to pay for the candles that lighted him to bed. Belts were tightened, cloaks closely drawn, against a winter that froze the birds' feet to the bough.

Unexpectedly, Charles's world was rocked by the news of Cromwell's death. He was in Holland, taking the country air and playing tennis when he heard it. Suddenly uplifted, and believing himself enamoured of the youngest daughter of the Dowager Princess of the Netherlands, he offered his hand in marriage. In spite of his brightened prospects, the Dowager Princess did not fancy him as a son-in-law. She soon made it known that there was no match.

By the spring of 1659 the Protectorate was consigned to the tablets of history, and the members of the new Council of State that succeeded it were making their meals off venison from the royal parks. Cromwell's monument in Westminster Abbey was tumbled down. Plots and plans were thick in the air, chief among them a projected rising of Presbyterians and Cavaliers that would descend on the capital from every shire and county, bearing Charles back to his rightful place. The secret date was 1 August, 1659. Treachery rose up to confuse the scene. It was disclosed that Charles, standing by to embark for Deal, was to be seized and done away with as soon as he landed.

Affairs in Kent went wrong; in Cheshire even more so. The great plot had misfired. Charles rode off to Rouen, where there might be a boat to take him to a West Country port. Briskly cheerful as ever, he wrote to Hyde that, though he was "not altogether so plump", he felt sanguine in his guise of "Mr. Skinner", and added the reflection that "sure people never went so cheerfully to venture their necks as we do".

Receiving no sign of success afoot in his favour in England, he set off on a jaunt to the Pyrenees, *en route* for Fuentarrabia, where the envoys of France and Spain were meeting to conclude a treaty. Charles proposed to impress them with all the charm that he could muster, hoping that they would respond with help, as much for him personally as for his cause. The journey was made enjoyable by "many happy accidents", of the nature of which we are left to guess, and by meals the like of which had been too long denied him. "God keep you", he wrote to Hyde, "and send you to eat as good mutton as we have". It was about the limit of his piety.

He was well received. Due honours were done. He was so gratified by his personal success that he offered marriage to Cardinal Mazarin's niece, Hortense Mancini. He was put off, politely, by the Cardinal, as virtual ruler of France. Unabashed, Charles bestrode his horse and, with only his valet, Toby Rustat, for company, rode back across France to see his sister Minette, awaiting him at Colombes. At first he did not recognize her, she had grown so much, and he kissed another, allegedly by mistake. He then rode on to Brussels over slushy roads after frosts. The capital was in the gloom of yet another hard winter, his loyal followers, awaiting him, utterly cast down. A new civil war threatened in England.

General Monk, commander-in-chief in Scotland, who was the first of the military caste to bow the head to the civil power, paraded his army and announced his intention to march down over the Border to assert "the freedom and rights of the three kingdoms". With snow in the sky and frost covering the ground, he set forth with seven thousand men. "I do not remember that we ever trod upon plain earth from Edinburgh to London," Monk's chaplain recorded. If the snow did not melt, resistance did. All Yorkshire came out to speed Monk's men on their way.

Ahead of them went rumour, excitement, doubts, fears. Rising from his bed on 30 January, young Sam Pepys remembered that "this was the fatal day, now ten years since, his Majesty died". Despite the melancholy memory, a song came to his lips. In his favourite wine-vaults he secretly raised his glass to the king whose crowning might now be a little nearer.

In Flanders, Edward Hyde, blowing on his cold fingers, wrote to a friend in London: "We all have some envy towards you that are in a place where you can want no fire, which we all do. When it will change, we yet know not." The hardships continued. Personal possessions, including the king's, were at the pawnbrokers. Charles was busy writing letters to England, a hundred and more on official business, and pouring out his tenderness for his sister in others. "You show me so much affection that the only quarrel we are ever likely to have will be as to which of us two loves the other best."

Monk's army passed into London on 3 February, 1660, heralded by trumpeters in scarlet and silver. When the City aldermen declined to pay taxes until a free Parliament was called, Monk marched in to demonstrate the authority of what remained of Cromwell's administration, the Rump, as it was derisively known. A week later, the general demanded writs for the return of the excluded members of Parliament, to be followed, he insisted, by a dissolution and a new and freely elected House of Commons.

When on 11 February Monk told the burgesses of the City what he had done, and was requiring to be done, long-pent emotions exploded in a great outburst of popular feeling. The expression on men's faces changed as if at the wave of an enchanter's wand. The English spirit was free again and the rejoicing was immense. Every street had its bonfires that night; in one more than thirty were counted. Butchers' knives flashed as carcases were roasted, while the people made bawdy jokes about "the Rump". Dancing, shouting, singing, "the common joy was everywhere to be seen". The same chronicler wrote that "it was past imagination, both the greatness and the suddenness of it". Within two days the entire nation knew what was afoot, and there were prayers for a fair wind from Flanders.

On the afternoon of 15 March a workman with a ladder on his shoulder and a pot of paint in his free hand arrived at that place in the City, close by the Royal Exchange, where the statue of Charles I had formerly stood. After his execution an inscription had been put on the wall above the site: *Exit Tyrannus, Regum Ultimus*—"The tyrant is gone, the last of the kings". The workman proceeded to paint out the inscription. Having done it, he threw his cap into the air and called out, as if he had an official mandate to do so: "God bless King Charles the Second!" His cry was instantly taken up by a thunderous shout within the Exchange. The next day the Long Parliament was voted at an end. General Monk saw Sir John Grenville and sent him off as an emissary to the king in Brussels.

Charles mounted his horse and left at once for Holland. At Breda, in counsel with Hyde, soon to become the first earl of Clarendon, he drafted a declaration ensuring a bloodless revolution and guaranteeing his subservience to a free Parliament. On 28 April the Speaker read the declaration aloud to the House, every member standing and bareheaded; one of the great House of Commons scenes. Acclamation followed. There was not a dissentient voice. The House voted Charles £50,000 and endorsed a prayer for his return. The sky that night was red with the glow of bonfires again. Bells rang from every steeple and tower and, it seemed, more wildly than before. Men were seen drinking the king's health on their knees in the streets. The miller of Charlton burnt down his old mill for joy. In the ports the pennants flew, the guns roared, sailors lined the yards to cheer. "Believe me, I know not whether I am in England or no, or whether I dream," and the Cavalier's wonderment was echoed by Lady Derby, who wrote that "the change is so great, I can hardly believe it. It is beyond our understanding".

Charles, who knew what it was to count the hours of his long absence, now had hardly a moment to himself. Delegations, applications, petitions, crowded in on him, so that he had to sit up till after midnight writing letters, public and private. Fourteen citizens of London, bringing with them a chest full of gold to the value of £10,000, were most warmly welcomed.

471

He went aboard the re-named flagship, the *Royal Charles*, on 22 May, 1660. To see him off there were his brothers, his sister, and his aunt, the Queen of Bohemia, she for whom *The Tempest* was written half a century before. His sister wept and clung to him, until the weighing of the anchor parted them.

He was rowed ashore at Dover in the admiral's barge on 25 May. The beach under the grey cliffs was crowded down to the waterline. Guns flamed and boomed from the escort ships and coastal forts. Stepping on to the shingle, Charles knelt as if giving devout thanks, a gesture that was pleasing to the people if not to the Almighty to whom presumably it was addressed. When he rose up it was to receive Monk's sword and the general's salutation: "God save the King!" It was echoed with a roar all along the beach and up in the town. The formalities over, Charles left by coach for London. When he was well clear of the boundaries, and the last running sightseer had been left behind, he called for his horse and, mounting it, cantered across Barham Downs to Canterbury, his first sight of England in May for what was nearly half his lifetime. "My head is so dreadfully stunned with the acclamations of the people", he wrote hurriedly to tell his sister, "and the vast amount of business, that I know not whether I am writing sense or nonsense".

It was his thirtieth birthday on 29 May; for a multitude of Englishmen, as for him, an unforgettable day. Most of them had got up with the sun, like the Lord Mayor of London, who rumbled off thus early in his coach to Blackheath, where he was to greet the king. A hundred and twenty thousand citizens assembled there, the waiting hours whiled away by observing the arrival and forming up of several regiments, and by the antics of morris dancers.

When at last the king came into view, slim and tall, with a hint of the hidalgo in his looks and style, bowing gravely to right and left and yet with no condescension in his manner, the people shouted a welcome that drowned even the church bells. At the head of "a triumph of above twenty thousand horse and foot, brandishing their swords and shouting with inexpressible joy; the ways strewn with flowers, the bells ringing, the streets hung with tapestry, fountains running with wine", Charles advanced into the capital over London Bridge and along the Strand to Whitehall, where, at last dismounted, he was "so weary as to be scarce able to speak". He was too tired to attend a service of thanksgiving in the Abbey that evening. From under his heavy-lidded eyes he smiled as he jested that he ought to have come home sooner, for everyone was telling him now that the whole nation had been longing for it.

May 29, 1660, was remarkable above many other days of great rejoicing, for it was as if overnight the past had been expunged and a new era begun. Much that was traditional, ingrained, customary, seemed suddenly deprived of force. Historical perspectives were changed. The Middle Ages, the Reformation, seemed to be set still farther back in time, their hold on the minds of men diminished. New currents moved the tide of English history, which from that time broadened out to become a great formative influence of the modern world.

Casting out the works of the Puritans, their preachments, their sobriety, their desecrations, their censorship, their oppressive godliness, the new regime rid the nation of elements of restraint and discipline that were to cost it dear in times to come, including perhaps our own. The mark of the gentleman was re-defined. He had to be adept at duelling and seduction. Excess and frivolity set the tone, amplified into licentiousness by the new race of dramatists. Privately, Charles complained of "the want of good breeding" in England. He had a preference for Paris manners.

The people at large, immunized by more than distance from the sins of Court and capital, clung to the old social order and went obediently to church again, as in former times. But a spirit of inquiry was abroad and active in distinguished minds. A new temper was manifesting itself in religion and politics. Isaac Newton had just gone up to Cambridge, in itself an event of history. Charles shared the new enthusiasms, science and philosophy, while remaining the slave of his inclinations. He became the patron of the newly founded Royal Society, signing his name with a flourish on the first page of its treasured register. He had a little laboratory of his own in the palace at Whitehall and retreated to it with unconcealed satisfaction when business became wearisome. He enjoyed distilling cordials.

The time of coronation had come. On 22 April, Charles left Whitehall at dawn by barge to make a State entry from the Tower of London to the Palace of Westminster. Once again the bells rang out while the king passed down river, smiling his pleasure in the new assurances of his popularity. He was crowned on St. George's Day. The shout that was heard at the Archbishop's bidding, "Lift up your hearts", echoed far beyond the rooftops of Whitehall. Three times Garter King-of-Arms flung the challenge to all hearers: "If anyone has cause to show why Charles Stuart should not be King of England, let him speak!" No answer came. That night a canopy of dancing light hung over London from the uncounted bonfires in the streets.

Next there was the matter of his marriage; for Charles was sure that his Commons, as he told them, would not desire him to live "to be an old bachelor". The Spanish were interested, scheming to find a way of attaching the English Crown to their purposes. They proposed several choices to him, with offers of liberal endowments, which he mistrusted. He had another prospect in view. The Queen Regent of Portugal had made it known through England's ambassador at Lisbon that if Charles would take her daughter's hand he would find that it held more than the promise of domestic felicity—keys to a chest containing half a million in gold and silver, to the gates of Tangier, and to free trade with Brazil and the East Indies. It was indeed a fabulous offer. Charles responded to it as gracefully as his more limited means permitted. When the Portuguese ambassador arrived in London Charles bestowed on him the favour of a private key to the royal garden.

It was reported in Whitehall that Catherine of Braganza was short, pretty, black-eyed, and charming. Charles wrote her letters to show that he too had charm. They were married in May, 1662, and spent their honeymoon at Hampton Court. The people were pleased with their young queen, finding her only fault to be her slightly protruding teeth.

Connubial bliss was not destined to last long. In June a son was born to Barbara Palmer, Lady Castlemaine, who christened him Charles after the king, his father. Other famous mistresses followed, the vivacious orange-seller Nell Gwynne and his beautiful French fancy Louise de Querouaille amongst them. Charles was never one to deny his own and these families were adorned with the ermine of nobility and their descendants are great names with seats in the House of Lords today.

Too indolent to be ambitious, he was often clear-seeing and could rise above the more puerile preoccupations of his temperament. Thus when the new Parliament showed an unforgiving spirit towards old antagonists, he told the members: "Let us look forward and not backward, and never think of what is past. God hath wrought a wonderful miracle in settling us as He hath done. I pray let us all do what we can to get reputation at home and abroad of being well settled." Aware of the racial discords between the two countries, he deliberately risked ill-will by sanctioning the withdrawal of English troops from beyond the Border. He was no friend of bigotry.

His moral blindness made him at times contemptible. He had a natural kindness, perhaps more accurately described as the spontaneous generosity of an essentially selfish man. He was admirably free from superstition in an age that was rampant with it. He was not utterly without religion, but he had few discernible ideals.

His attraction for the insular people whom he ruled for twenty-five years seems to have resided in his being something of a foreigner. He was the grandson of Henry of Navarre, from whom he inherited a certain courtly grace, and a good constitution, though little of the energy of that admired monarch. Politically he was also an alien, for he could understand French and Spanish motives better than those of his own country. His attachment to France was a liability that bore heavily on England.

As a king he had better talents than many who occupied the throne, and better opportunities than some of demonstrating them for his people's good. His undoubted courage lay largely dormant throughout his life, just as his cool insight into the hearts of men was rarely exercised. Only his good humour remained, and that, by the perversity of things, sufficed to give him undeserved renown.

LOUIS XIV

(1638–1715)

Louis XIV, the grandson of France's most popular king, Henry IV, was born in 1638, came to the throne in 1642 and died in 1715. If his reign is dated only from 1661, from the death of Cardinal Mazarin who had ruled France during Louis's minority, it outlasts those of Charles II, James II, William and Mary and Queen Anne. He was known in France and throughout Europe as "The Great Monarch", and certainly during his reign France dominated Europe, taking the place of Spain in the sixteenth century.

Louis did not invent the idea of Absolute Monarchy. His grandfather, Henry IV, took care to see that the king's power was unchallengeable and so, in England, did the Tudors. But Louis XIV gave a striking and dogmatic form to the Absolute Monarchy. He ruled France from his new and immense palace at Versailles, which became not only the centre of government but also of social power. Louis's system of despotism became a pattern for the small princes and dukes of Germany and Italy during the eighteenth century. Scores of palaces modelled on Versailles sprang up from Brandenburg to Calabria, and there were scores of Absolute Princes by divine right, some lords of only a few towns and some thousands of acres.

England decisively refused to accept the claims of the first two Stuart kings to Absolutism, and by 1688 the power of the English Parliament was affirmed, never to be seriously questioned. Holland and the Swiss Cantons also rejected this Absolute form of government. But no country rejected the pre-eminence of French civilization during the seventeenth century. French literature, philosophy, building, furniture, cloths and manners were copied by all Europe during Louis's long reign. "We conquered France," wrote Pope, referring to Marlborough's victories over Louis XIV at the beginning of the eighteenth century,

"But felt our captive's charms,
her arts victorious triumphed o'er our arms."

The glory of French achievements during Louis's long reign

476

became a part of his personal legend. Was Louis himself a very great man or did his pomp hide a rather narrow-minded, small man? "The greatest man ever born on the steps of a throne," the liberal historian Lord Acton wrote of him at the end of the nineteenth century; or was Louis nothing more than a glorified Postmaster-General, as a more recent French historian, Seignobos, has called him?

In 1682, twenty years after his personal reign had begun, few would have doubted about the answer; it would have been that this short, physically strong, dark-faced, full-cheeked man with his large Bourbon nose was the most successful of French kings. He had fought two victorious wars against Spain and Holland, mainly in the Low Countries. He had acquired Lille and many other towns which are parts of northern France. At the Treaty of Nimwegen, which ended the second war, French had, for the first time in history, taken the place of Latin as the language of the Treaty and of diplomacy. The French armies were the best organized in Europe, the work of a great civil servant, Louvois; a great military engineer, Vauban, constructed the most efficient fortresses to protect French conquests. Now it can be said that France's strength came in part from the exhaustion of the House of Austria and its adherents in Germany as a result of the Thirty Years War; it was the result, in fact, of the policy of the great Cardinal Richelieu, Louis XIII's minister. It could be said that the young French king had only to reap benefits won by Henry IV and Richelieu, and by Mazarin's finally successful war against Spain during Louis's minority.

But, undeniably, Louis XIV had conducted his negotiations and his wars with efficiency. England under Charles II had been, in the main, his ally and so had many of the Protestant German princes of Sweden. And there was another side of the picture which told in Louis's favour. France was inherently strong economically when Louis came to the throne, but a number of civil wars known as Les Frondes had taken place between 1649 and 1653. The nobility and the regional Parliaments, in constantly changing alliances, had fought against the regent, Anne of Austria, and against Cardinal Mazarin. As a boy Louis had been forced to submit to a deputation of rebellious Paris citizens being admitted to his bed-chamber whilst he pretended to sleep; he and his mother had had to fly secretly from the royal palace; he had seen his aunt, the daughter of the Duke of Orléans, turn the cannon of the Bastille on his royal army as it tried in vain to enter Paris. These civil wars had greatly damaged France's economy and, as during the Wars of Religion in the sixteenth century, Spanish troops had fought all over France in alliance with the rebels. Though the queen and Cardinal Mazarin had won in the end, the royal authority was shaky.

The young King Louis was popular and a gallant figure as he rode his Spanish steed at great ceremonies, his plumed hat in his hand, saluting the spectators with easy grace. Even when young he was majestic, with an air of grace and dignity—which owed much to his skill at dancing, which was very great. Before his coronation and his marriage to the Infanta of Spain, Maria Theresa, he had had many love affairs and particularly one which had been painful for him to break off with Marie Mancini, the beautiful Italian niece of Mazarin. Very few people, however, knew that this amiable incarnation of Royal Grace was also a man of much sterner qualities. The indignities the royal power had suffered affected him very strongly. He was determined he would rule as a king and not, as his father had done, as a king ruling through a great Minister. When Mazarin died, Louis, who always behaved gratefully to his friend and master, as he called him, said in private: "I do not know what I would have done if he had lived longer".

Within a year of Mazarin's death the king had imprisoned for life the man who seemed destined to step in Mazarin's shoes, Nicolas Fouquet, the all-powerful Superintendent of Finances who was much richer than the king, was allied by marriage to half the great nobility and who even had a number of private warships off the coast of Brittany. It was clear that the new reign was going to be quite different; the king was absolute master and whoever was going to rebel against the administration of France was going, henceforward, to rebel against the king himself. *L'Etat c'est Moi* (I am the State) was no idle word, although Louis never actually said this.

The king's private estate became increasingly richer once Louis had direct control of the finances of the kingdom. Louis chose as his principal agent Colbert; but he was careful to see that this great man who worked so wisely was never tempted to see himself as a powerful political personage. Louis worked eight hours a day regularly, always giving work precedence over pleasure. He was in every sense a professional king, writing: "The business of being a king is great, noble and delicious." He had, as a young man, confided to a friend that when he read in history about ineffective kings he had always felt uncomfortable. After a few years of direct rule, the king remitted a substantial part of the taxes paid by the poor. New industries were founded, old ones revived, overseas colonies, notably in Canada, were created and a large navy was built. No wonder the young king was popular—and he was victorious abroad, as we have seen.

It was in 1682 that Louis transferred his court to Versailles, a palace with innumerable fountains and avenues of tall poplars and oaks, constructed out of the barren bog where there had been neither running water nor a full-grown tree. Here, in a few months time, the court became permanently installed, housing 5,000 nobles in the palace itself with another 5,000 or so in the neighbourhood. Versailles had a political purpose; it was to make the nobles totally dependent on the king. The privileged inmates of Versailles had to leave their lands and chateaux to the management of bailiffs or younger sons. They had to pay dearly, in cash, for their lodgings at Court, and increasingly forfeited their financial independence. "He is a man I do not see at court" was a sentence which, coming from the king, doomed the greatest noble to obscurity and to no part in social life.

The descendants of the rebellious nobility of the fifteenth and sixteenth centuries now intrigued for the right to hold the king's shirt or to be included in this or that special reception. An extreme formality was the rule, for, by this, the king could give importance to the slightest favour or dispensation. The nobles as a rule were not given work in the administration—the king preferred men of humbler birth who had practical experience. They were used in war and, particularly in the latter years of the reign, many of Louis's prisoners in the gilded cage of Versailles paid for their lives of solemn frivolity with their blood.

Until towards the end of the century when the king was ageing, and when France's fortunes were turning sour, Versailles was undoubtedly a gay and stimulating place. The king had many beautiful mistresses—particularly Louise de la Vallière, who died in an odour of sanctity, and Madame de Montespan, who was accused of poisoning her rivals. Louis's numerous amours were due to his innately strong sensual nature, but also to the fact that the beauties of the day, whether married or single, offered themselves freely to the king, thinking, among other things, that gratifying his whims or passions was their duty. Yet his mistresses exerted no undue influence, nor did his love affairs prevent his treating his naïve Spanish wife, who never learnt to speak good French, with anything but respect and affection. She, too, and her children were seated on a throne of splendour above the brilliant mob of the great. Plays, books, music and painting were encouraged by this extraordinary gathering in one place of the most intelligent and rich people of the kingdom.

The king himself had good taste in the arts and both Racine and Molière owed much to his personal perception. Yet if Versailles had a valid purpose—that of making the king all-powerful and unchallengeable—it was also an exaggeration. Louis loved pomp and magnificence excessively, and so, when the gaiety seemed to go, the pomp and magnificence themselves became excessive, and finally somewhat stale. So utterly to divorce the nobility from the business of running the country created a class which became increasingly parasitic. Was there no middle way between the old disorder which had so often characterized France—and Versailles?

By the time Louis died life at Versailles was considered, even by most of the courtiers, as oppressive. The last of Louis's mistresses, Madame de Maintenon, whom, after the queen's death, he married morganatically, complained of its dullness. "Oh that I could tell you of my trials, that I could reveal to you the boredom which attends the Great and the difficulty they have in passing their time", Madame de Maintenon once wrote. She also once complained to her brother of the monotony of her life with Louis, saying she could not endure it any longer and she wished she were dead. Her brother's reply to her is reported to be: "I suppose you have been promised the Almighty as a husband."

The last twenty years of Louis's reign were clouded with misfortunes. The accountancy went wrong, faster with the death of Colbert in 1682 than it might have done. In 1681, when Europe was at peace, Louis sent French troops suddenly to occupy Strasbourg, a great free city, belonging to the Holy Roman Emperor, the Austrian Habsburg. Slowly all the powers of Europe decided that France must at all costs be checked. Holland had long been preparing for revenge. Many German princes turned against France as did the still militarily powerful Sweden. In 1688 William of Orange, the implacable enemy of Louis XIV, became king of England and Louis saw his once useful ally now firmly in the camp of his enemies.

In 1689 began the War of the League of Augsburg, which Louis started by occupying the whole of the left bank of the Rhine and devastating the Palatinate, an act which, for many years after, caused Germans to hate Frenchmen. The devastation had the purpose of creating a large area of "scorched earth" between France and her northern German enemies. During eight years of war France, on land, was victorious against all her enemies—Austria,

Spain, Holland, Savoy, England and many German princes. But
the peace of Ryswick was a peace of exhaustion. Worst of all for
Louis, the French fleet, which early in the war had transported
French soldiers to Ireland to help James II, had been destroyed by
the British at La Hougue. Louis kept Strasbourg though he had to
make territorial restitutions which angered many of his generals.
Ah, if Ryswick could have been the end of Louis's wars!

In 1701 Louis was forced, this time, into his largest, longest and
most deadly conflict, the War of the Spanish Succession. The king
of Spain, Louis's brother-in-law, died without a son, and the choice
for Spain lay between an Austrian or a French nephew. Louis tried
to find a solution by splitting up the Spanish heritage, with its
great colonial empire, in a way which would be agreeable to all
parties, without notably increasing the power of Austria. He failed.
And so, in the last resort, he had to fight for his nephew, the Duke of
Anjou, whom the Spaniards preferred as king. The war lasted until
1713 and this time it was the generals of the coalition, above all
Marlborough and Prince Eugene of Savoy, who won the great
victories.

At Blenheim, Marlborough with British, Dutch and Austrian
troops shattered a daring attempt by the French to seize Vienna.
In 1706 the Allies defeated the French at Ramillies and drove them
out of Brussels and Antwerp, occupied at the beginning of the war.
The third blow was at Oudenarde in 1708 and, the next year, 1709,
another defeat for the French at the bloody battle of Malplaquet,
near Lille. Some brilliant successes in Germany and Spain could
not compensate for defeat in this vital sector. Louis sued for peace.
The Allies came nearer and nearer to Paris. The winter of 1709 was
a ferocious one. There were food riots all over France, particularly
in Paris, and Louis and his court had to eat black bread. Much of
his gold and silver plate had to be sold for the expenses of the war.

But Louis was to avoid the humiliation of military defeat after
all. In England Queen Anne dismissed the war party and the Duke
of Marlborough; and the Tories returned to power, anxious to
consolidate their possessions overseas, including Gibraltar, which
they had taken from Spain. The Emperor of Austria had died and
his successor was the Austrian nephew, the Archduke Charles, the
claimant to the Spanish throne. It was not considered wise to
reconstitute the Spanish-Austrian Empire which had enabled
Charles V to dominate Europe in the sixteenth century. There was
a Franco-British armistice. Then the French, under Marshal Villars,
won the great victory at Denain in 1712, a reversal of fortune which

resembled the battle of the Marne in 1914. The French chased the Dutch and Austrians out of France, recovering what France had held in the Low Countries when the war began. At the Treaty of Utrecht in 1713 the Duke of Anjou was recognized as King of Spain, but no Spanish Bourbon was to be allowed to sit on the French throne. The Pyrenees were to remain the great divider. France lost Nice and Savoy, and had to destroy the fortifications of Dunkirk. She still remained the strongest power in Europe; but the victorious Absolute Monarchy had been defeated, and largely by Parliamentary and maritime England.

We poets oft begin our lives in gladness,
but thereof comes in the end poverty, despair and madness.

One can apply these lines of Wordsworth to the Great Monarch. He did not go mad. But he was overwhelmed with public and private troubles. His people had turned against him. At the beginning of his reign the French peasant was relatively prosperous and content; at the end, La Bruyère's celebrated description must be recalled:

Dotted about the countryside, one sees a number of wild animals, male and female, black livid and scorched by the sun, bent close to the ground, which they scratch and dig within implacable obstinacy. They appear to possess articulate speech, and, when they stand upright, they are seen to have human faces; and in truth, they are human beings.

Louis the man is difficult to sum up. He was not particularly well educated or particularly intelligent, but he had a great deal of common sense, so much that it amounted almost to genius. He had good taste, the sort which goes with a magnificent figure, with ability to dress with the greatest elegance and to charm women. He took his profession of a king so seriously that he lacked the spontaneity and charm of his grandfather, Henry IV. He came to welcome flattery. But much of his formality was for the sake of his job. He kept a sense of proportion and of self-control and was n.ver impolite to man or woman. John Green's summing up of Louis as a vain heartless bigot, is manifestly unfair. This judgement is the fruit of a wilful ignorance of the real man. Louis had resolution and a sense of mission. Was he heartless and something of a self-important bore? This is a question that cannot be answered. What is certain is that he was a deeply serious character.

Of his reign much can be said for and against. He established the *ancien régime* which gave an internal order and peace to France and retained its power until 1789. Was this a long or short time? 1660–1789 is a long time for internal stability to last in France. But it was a deceptive regime, not merely because it did not provide for human liberty, but because it did not go far enough in breaking down the internal barriers to commerce in France, let alone the barriers in human society. A black mark against Louis was the persecution of Protestants. In 1685 he revoked the Edict of Nantes which protected them. Hundreds of thousands of France's most industrious citizens were forced to flee abroad, to the great loss of the country. Yet this was an action which Louis XIV took against his better judgement and because the majority of his subjects wished it to be taken. They disliked the existence of a Protestant state within the state.

For many historians Louis's reign was barren of real achievements. He failed to secure France's frontiers on the Rhine; he would have been more successful perhaps if his policy had been more conciliatory, less arrogant—it is said. Voltaire said that Louis would have been the greatest of French kings if he had not built Versailles. Voltaire, an admirer of the English constitution, thought that Louis had brought clarity and order into the government of France and that this had helped to make possible the great achievements of the French spirit in what he called the Century of Louis XIV. It is a charitable judgement coming from the sarcastic critic of authority, whether royal or religious.

Voltaire may well be sounder than those who denigrate Louis XIV. With the death of Louis there began a new age, that of the eighteenth century, an intelligent, frivolous age which questioned all values. Men heaved a deep sigh of relief when Louis died. But the French seventeenth century, in the eyes of today, was a far greater age than the eighteenth century, at once more profound, more ordered, more magnificent. Louis XIV was not responsible for the genius of Pascal, of La Rochefoucauld, of Molière or Racine; but he is, in an intangible way, the necessary central political figure in a period whose achievements, particularly in literature and the arts, bear comparison with any of the very great ages in human history.

PETER I (THE GREAT)
(1672–1725)

FEW RULERS can have possessed such zest for living as Peter the Great. From his earliest days to the end of a crowded, active life he was impelled by an over-mastering urge from one activity to another, ever increasing his store of knowledge and improving his various skills in all manner of arts and crafts.

He could be described as a man ready-made for legend. Six feet eight inches in height, gaunt, tough, possessed of immense physical strength, it is said that he could snap a horseshoe in his bare hands—hands that early became calloused through the persistent vigour with which he tackled the hardest manual tasks, as an engineer, boat-builder, carpenter, waterman, cabinet maker, armourer, iron-smith, and a hundred things besides.

With his love of hard labour and skilled craftsmanship went a lively, searching mind which never ceased to quest for knowledge. He sought out the people who knew, whatever their nationality. Coming across an astrolabe, of which he could make nothing, he combed the foreign quarter of Moscow for someone who could instruct him in its uses. He introduced the first telescope to Russia; opened the first hospital; tried his deft hands on occasion as dentist and surgeon; encouraged the sciences.

This man of many parts had no liking for pomp or ceremony. He chose to dress simply; enjoyed simple food; disliked formal banquets; chose a seat near the door so that he could slip away at will, though he posted sentries to make sure that others didn't follow his example. He scorned comfort; cultivated endurance.

He disliked flattery and showed his feelings by deploring the practice among his subjects of kneeling or prostrating themselves in his presence. "I don't want people to dirty their clothes in the mud for me!" he declared.

Piety, instilled by his mother, remained with him throughout his life. He believed in God; celebrated his victories with a Te Deum; closed his letters with the phrase "God's will be done". He never spared himself. After toiling to the point of exhaustion he would take himself "to rest like Noah, and then to work again".

His capacity for working others to a standstill was matched by the gusto with which he threw himself into a night of carousal. Yet, after the wildest debauch, when his companions required two or three days in which to recover, Peter would be up and pursuing one or another of his multiple projects.

One more trait must be named. Many stories of savagery and cruelty have been told against him. He was often moved to sudden acts of violence, as when he encountered a soldier making off with a piece of copper dislodged by lightning from St. Peter's Church, Riga. Peter struck the looter so savagely that the fellow died instantly.

Without entering any plea on Peter's behalf, it must be remembered that he lived in a barbaric country in a barbaric age; and though he may have possessed one of the finest minds, it is not surprising that one so lavishly endowed with lusty appetites and great physique should be correspondingly a prey to violent passions and fits of unbridled temper.

From the foregoing summary of Peter's remarkable characteristics we may turn to consider some highlights in his momentous life. He was born in 1672, the only son of Czar Alexis. When he was acclaimed czar there was a revolt of the guards and Peter's step-sister, Sophia, had her invalid brother, Ivan, proclaimed as joint-czar, an arrangement which lasted until 1696, though Sophia was deposed in 1689 and Peter's mother was regent thereafter.

Peter spent his boyhood and early youth in the country near Moscow, evincing a great interest in military matters and forming "play regiments" with all his young friends. Records show that he made frequent demands for guns and other weapons and general equipment, for he took his military pastime very seriously indeed.

When he was only twenty-three he tasted the real thing, for he led two expeditions against the Turks and captured the fortress of Azov at the mouth of the Don, to secure access to the Black Sea.

He was already deeply interested in naval matters, and in his twenty-fourth year he set out to learn more about the outside world in general and naval construction in particular. He visited Holland and England in turn, and in both countries his principal concern was to work in the shipyards and to study navigation.

England, especially, captured his affection, and he was to say: "The English Island is the best, most beautiful, and happiest that there is in the whole world."

He crossed from Holland with a suite of sixteen aboard the *Yorke*, flagship of Vice-Admiral Sir David Mitchell. Near the mouth of the Thames he transhipped to the yacht *Mary* and, accompanied by the Admiral, sailed up-river to the Tower of London.

A modest house in Norfolk Street, Strand, was his first lodging, and he plunged straight into a great round of activity. He visited William III at Kensington Palace, and was persuaded by the king to sit for a portrait by Sir Godfrey Kneller. His days were crowded with visits to works and factories and scientific institutions. He studied watch-making closely, and wherever he went he collected drawings and models and specifications.

He soon went to study shipbuilding in the royal yards at Deptford, where, it is said, he worked with his hands as hard as anyone there. At this period he and his suite were lodged at Sayes Court, the country home of John Evelyn, the diarist. This adjoined the royal docks, to which Peter enjoyed access through a private door in Evelyn's garden. During their stay the Russians incurred a bill for damages to furniture and draperies amounting to £350 9s.— a formidable sum in those times. From itemized descriptions of the damage caused it may be guessed that plenty of revelry was indulged in by the distinguished visitors.

But with Peter, as always, such things were incidental, and he was constantly occupied with manifold interests. When not toiling in the shipyards he would be earnestly conferring with every expert he could contrive to meet. He visited Parliament, Greenwich Observatory, Woolwich Arsenal, Hampton Court, the Tower of London and the Royal Mint. The latter captivated him and he returned again and again.

He visited numerous churches, attended Quaker meetings and had discussions with William Penn and the Astronomer Royal. He watched naval manoeuvres at Portsmouth, where a 21-gun salute was fired in his honour.

When the time came for his departure he had arranged for selected experts to go to Russia. He engaged about sixty specialists in all, including ship designers, a master shipwright under whom he had worked at Deptford, an hydraulics engineer and similar key workers he knew would be needed to implement his great dream of building a modern Russian fleet. With the help of a scholar from Oxford, the first School of Mathematical Sciences and Navigation was formed in Moscow in 1701, another piece of foresight that was to pay big dividends later on.

The Baltic at that time was under Swedish domination and

Russia was locked in a struggle that was to be long and exacting. To give himself "a window on to Europe", Peter founded St. Petersburg in 1703. He entered his newly created port aboard his frigate *Standard* as part of the inauguration ceremony, accompanied by six merchant vessels. When, a little later, a Dutch vessel arrived with valuable cargo, Peter rewarded the captain and crew specially to mark this first arrival.

There were early set-backs in the struggle with Sweden, but Peter's army finally prevailed at the battle of Poltavia in 1709, and Russia gained control over Karelia, Ingermanland and Livonia.

Among the prisoners taken in this battle was Catherine Skavronskaya, the daughter of a Livonian peasant, who became Peter's mistress. Later, when he had divorced the wife who had been chosen for him by his mother when he was only seventeen, Peter was to marry Catherine and she was destined to become a great influence for good in his life. She developed into a woman of strong character, and her understanding support did much to sustain the czar in his difficult reign. It was said that Catherine alone was capable of restraining him in his more tempestuous moods; that she had only to nurse his fevered head in her lap and stroke his brow to induce in him a wonderful sense of calm and well-being.

Yet Catherine was equally tough and a vital companion to Peter in many ways. She sometimes accompanied her tireless husband on his strenuous campaigns, showing the most astonishing powers of endurance, behaving resolutely when under fire and sharing the army's hardships with the greatest fortitude.

Once a campaign ended, however, all Catherine's femininity would return and she would settle down to domestic routine. She bore Peter twelve children, and though he was suspected of occasional infidelities they were fleeting incidents and he invariably returned to Catherine, and their close bond of understanding endured. He founded the Order of St. Catherine in her honour.

By 1713 St. Petersburg had virtually replaced Moscow as capital, and Peter did all he could to encourage the use of his new port by merchants from overseas. He also started to build a Baltic Fleet. In 1715 he had the School of Mathematical Sciences and Navigation transferred to St. Petersburg and re-christened it as the Naval Academy.

In the meantime, various campaigns had gone awry. Peter's armies had suffered some reverses in Turkey, had sustained heavy defeat at Pruth, and had been forced to give back the fortress at Azov. In these desperate moments Catherine stood staunchly at the czar's side, showing the greatest courage in action, and thereby winning a regard which Peter publicly acknowledged in an official ukase that he issued in 1723.

In this document he told graphically how: "Putting aside womanly weakness, of her own will she has been present with us and has helped in every way possible, and especially in the Pruth battle with the Turks, when our troops were 22,000 in number and the Turks had 270,000 men, and it was a desperate time for us, she acted as a man, not as a woman, which is known to our whole army, and through it without doubt to the whole nation; and so for these labours of our Spouse we have decided that by virtue of the supreme power given us by God she shall be crowned which, God willing, is to take place formally in Moscow in the present winter. . . ."

Towards the close of his reign Peter had attempted to gain control of the Caspian Sea, and a struggle with Persia did, in fact, give him a foothold at Baku and elsewhere.

But throughout all his active campaigning he never once ceased to advance progressive ideas of all kinds. In his many travels, which embraced Germany, France, Denmark, Austria and Poland, he always followed his practice of cultivating the acquaintance of foreign experts. Not for him the isolation of an "Iron Curtain"; rather he clung to his own inspired conception of "a window on to Europe". He liked to know what progressive people were doing in other parts of the world, and he had the good sense to profit by such knowledge in every way he could. One typical example of such foresight was his constant engagement of foreign craftsmen and technicians. He even brought in experts for the task of seeking for minerals and other natural resources in the vast lands of Russia—things which he knew to be absolutely essential for the development of all the great industries and works that figured in his ambitious dreams for the betterment of his country.

Despite his active recruitment of the best brains and best skills he could find abroad, he must often have fretted and fumed and longed for the company and advice of people he could trust. Among his close supporters he counted Colonel Patrick Gordon, a Scot who acted as military adviser, and François Lefort, a former Swiss guard, whose special flair was the organization of official functions and ceremonies. For a time, too, in his earlier years, Peter was under the sway of a German mistress, Anna Mons, on whom he lavished many gifts until he discovered that she had played him false.

In his zest for transforming Russia into a powerful and enlightened nation Peter founded schools and colleges and saw to it that promising young Russians were given the opportunity of travelling widely and studying in other lands. Busy with the general plans for a hundred laudable projects, he yet found time to supervise the provision of various educational text-books. He also introduced a reformed alphabet and simplified form of printing, besides founding and personally editing the first Russian newspaper.

He devised extensive plans for special colleges in St. Petersburg, each designed as a watertight department concerned solely with its own particular branch of Government business. He brought in enlightened tax reforms; sponsored a variety of bold and progressive social and economic plans. Right up to the time of his death from strangury, in 1725, at the age of fifty-three, he was grappling with schemes for creating an Academy of Sciences.

Peter the Great has been justly described as "the first modern Russian". Perhaps he was too modern—too far advanced for his untutored masses whose future he strove so vigorously, and so selflessly, to fashion.

CHARLES XII

(1682–1718)

FOR THE most part Sweden has lain outside the main theatre of European history. Only now and again has this land of mountain and lake, mist and arctic cold, produced a figure who has stormed his way across the stage and driven his audience into a frenzy of admiration, of awe-struck wonder. Most impressive of these rare performers was Charles XII. The "Hero King", he has been called, and with excellent reason. But a better name for him is "the Swedish Meteor", since he flared across the sky like a meteor, and, like a meteor, disappeared into the blackness of the night from which he had so suddenly emerged.

When he succeeded his father, Charles XI, as king of Sweden in 1697 he was a youth of not quite fifteen. At that time Sweden was one of the Great Powers of Europe. The Baltic was practically a Swedish lake. The whole of Finland was Swedish, and the Swedish territories extended round the Gulf of Finland from where St. Petersburg was before long to stand, to the great port of Riga. There were also Swedish outposts in Pomerania, on the mainland immediately south of Sweden, and on the farther side of Denmark in Bremen and its neighbourhood. But Sweden was "great" not only in territory. She had an army of well-drilled veterans who had become deservedly renowned as masters of the art of war.

Young as he was, the boy-king had already shown signs of exceptional capacity, and the States-General at Stockholm lost no time in proclaiming him to be of age and investing him with full regal power. Sweden's enemies—she had plenty—were not so discerning, however; they thought the times might be propitious for an attempt at humbling the Swedish giant and restoring the balance of power in the Baltic. A good deal of plotting went on in the chancelleries of Europe, and then in 1700 Charles was called upon to meet a formidable alliance of foes. In the west, the King of Denmark and Norway sent his troops into Holstein, a duchy ruled over by a duke who had married Charles's sister, and in the east, Czar Peter—who was eventually to be styled "the Great", although there was little sign of that as yet—was set upon seizing the continental provinces of the Swedish monarchy. Nor was this all. Included in the hostile confederacy were Poland and Saxony, then united under King Augustus II.

Then it was, and so early, that Charles showed himself to be a man of commanding stature and consummate genius. Statecraft was something that he never mastered, but war—that was an art in which he had received no lessons, and needed none. Covered by an Anglo-Dutch squadron under Admiral Rooke—for by a fortunate chance Sweden and Britain were then allied—the young king led an army of five thousand Swedes across the narrow channel into the heart of Danish territory. They landed on the coast of Zealand, and Charles was among the first to leap from the transports into the water, and, sword in hand, encouraged his troops by his example. The Danes, inferior in numbers, retreated before him. Copenhagen was bombarded by the British ships, and, rather than see his capital ruined and taken by storm, the Danish king sued for terms. The war was over almost before it had begun, and Charles was left free to turn his arms against Russia and Poland.

So ended Charles's first campaign, and already he was well on the way to becoming a legend. He was still no more than eighteen, but he had proved himself a man among men. The follies of youth he left behind him, not that they had ever been much in evidence. He was not interested in women; and wine, even in moderation, was never much to his taste. Soft living did not appeal to him in the slightest. When campaigning he often disdained the use of a tent but spread his cloak on the ground and slept with his men beneath the stars. The French ambassador, used to the luxurious effeminacy of Louis XIV's court, was astounded at the plainness of the Swedish king's apparel: "no ornaments," he told his master, "and shoes with low heels!" Charles's customary dress was indeed plain, and its very plainness singled him out as we may be sure he intended.

He boasted that he had only one suit, one of blue cloth with big copper buttons, buff waistcoat, and riding breeches. On his head a coarse felt hat; round his neck a black scarf; and on his feet high boots with massive steel spurs. All external marks of rank he despised. After his first experience in the field he absolutely refused to wear a wig, and was never seen except with his hair cropped short and brushed up above his forehead. He was a soldier among soldiers, and his men adored him, even when he led them into the most impossible situations and they died in droves. He was brave to the pitch of reckless folly, he was resolute to the point of obstinacy;

he had a body that seemed to be made of iron and a mind of tempered steel. A writer of his own race has described him as "a lonely, mist-shrouded figure". Others have referred to him as a hero who might have stepped straight out of one of the ancient sagas of Scandinavia.

Leaving Sweden to be governed by his ministers—he never saw Stockholm, his capital, again—Charles crossed the sea to Livonia (Latvia) with an army of 20,000 men, and marched to meet the Russians under Czar Peter, who were besieging Narva. The Russians numbered (so it is said) 50,000 men, but they were undisciplined peasants for the most part, while Charles had with him 10,000 of the justly celebrated Swedish infantry. It was all over in a quarter of an hour. The Russian hordes fled; while as for the czar, he was already on the road back to Moscow. Such was the battle of Narva, fought on 30 November, 1700.

Now it was Poland's turn to encounter the furious Swede. Campaigning went on for three years, and ended in Charles's complete triumph. Augustus was dethroned, and a puppet prince was raised to the throne in his stead. Saxony and Poland were occupied by the Swedish armies, and Charles stood forth among European potentates as a man to be feared, and courted. Among those who visited him in his hour of triumph was the Duke of Marlborough, who, with Blenheim and Ramillies behind him, could yet manage sufficient grace to express the wish that "I could serve some campaign under so great a general as your Majesty, that I might learn what I yet do not know about the art of war".

Only Russia remained to be dealt with, and there was reason to believe that the czar would be glad to come to some arrangement. But Charles would be content with nothing less than complete victory; and as though to demonstrate his contempt for anything that Peter might do, he arrested the Russian ambassador at Dresden, a man named Patkul, and—since he had been born in Livonia and might be considered, therefore, as a renegade Swede—caused him to be put to death in the most cruel fashion. This action has left an indelible stain on Charles's memory.

Meanwhile Peter had not been idle. Twice he invaded the Swedish provinces adjoining Russia, and on each occasion had to retreat before the Swedes. But he was still a very present menace, and in 1708 Charles got together a large army and marched against the Russians. To begin with all went in his favour. At Grodno he took the czar by surprise and was within an ace of capturing him. He forced the line of the Beresina and won a battle at Smolensk. The way to Moscow seemed to lie open, the way that Napoleon was to take rather more than a century later. But now he suddenly turned southward into the Ukraine, where he apparently expected to be joined by an army of 30,000 Cossacks under their *hetman* Mazeppa (the romantic subject of Byron's famous poem), who had decided to throw over his allegiance to the czar and seek to establish an independent principality. The plot came to the ears of Peter, however, and Mazeppa brought Charles only a handful of followers. To add to Charles's worries and disappointments, a large body of Swedish reinforcements was overtaken by the czar and cut to pieces. Finally, the winter of 1708-9 was an exceptionally hard one, and Charles and his army suffered horribly from the cold and lack of supplies, deep in the heart of enemy country.

Still Charles would not abandon the idea of reaching Moscow, and although his army had now been reduced to only some 23,000 men, he insisted on continuing with the campaign. Audacious as ever, and with his customary indomitable spirit, he laid siege to the Russian stronghold of Pultowa (Pultava), north of Kiev. The defenders put up a strong resistance, long enough for the czar to bring up a large army to their assistance. The decisive battle was fought on 8 July, 1709. The Russians numbered 80,000 men, which meant that the Swedes were outnumbered by four to one. To make matters worse, Charles, who up to then had seemed to lead a charmed life, was wounded in the foot the day before, and had to be carried into battle in a litter.

At dawn the Swedish infantry were launched against the Russian field batteries, and Charles was there to give them an encouraging start. They fought as bravely as ever, but suffered horrible losses; conflicting orders were given, and they looked round in vain for their king to sort them out and give them confidence; muddle and confusion were succeeded by bewilderment and desperation, and at length the attack petered out. Most of the Swedish infantry, the pride of Charles's army, were left on the field, dead or wounded, and the rest were soon prisoners. Charles attempted to rally the remainder of his men. He had his wound dressed and ordered his bearers to take him into the thick of the struggle. The bearers were killed by a cannon-ball, and the king was mounted on a horse, his foot resting on the horse's neck. The enemy were closing in, and his capture or death seemed imminent. His horse was brought down by a Russian bullet, and he fell with it. A wounded officer proffered him his mount, which he took; and having been lifted into the saddle, he suffered himself to be led away from the scene of action. Only a couple of thousand men who had not been engaged in the battle were left to him, and further resistance was out of the question. Taking advantage of the mood of intense depression into which he had been cast, his staff urged him to lose no time in taking the only way of escape left open to him. Accompanied by a handful of troops, he crossed the frontier into Turkey, where he was hospitably received at Bender, on the Dniester.

For the next three years Charles was an honoured guest rather than a prisoner of state. During that time all his expenses, and those of his numerous household, were paid by the Turkish Government, and gifts and honours were heaped upon him with oriental profusion. But from the day of his arrival at Bender his one thought was to involve Turkey and Russia in war. In this he was at length successful, and in an action on the banks of the Pruth, Peter was surrounded by Turkish soldiers and escaped barely with his life. An armistice was arranged, on terms which Charles must have thought were far too lenient. He continued his intrigues, and to render himself more secure established himself in a fortified house a short distance from Bender, surrounded by a strong guard of devoted Poles and Swedes. The Porte—the Turkish Government— which up to now had treated him with a most singular generosity, took alarm, suspecting that whatever the king had in mind was likely to do them no good. Charles was asked to explain his actions, and when his answers proved unsatisfactory it was resolved to bring him to heel. A force of several thousand Janissaries (foot-guards) surprised his little camp and took his two hundred guards prisoners. They then attacked the house, which Charles and forty of his suite defended desperately. Charles fought like a madman, killing many of his assailants. Only when the roof was burning over his head and his very eyebrows were singed and his clothes burnt did he at length give the signal for surrender.

For a while he was kept in captivity—still an honourable one; until in November, 1714, he found the way of escape open. Sending a respectful message of farewell to the Porte at Constantinople, he set off on horseback across the continent, and the Turks must have been highly relieved to see him go.

With only two attendants, travelling by day and night, he reached Stralsund—almost the only Swedish possession left on the mainland —late at night on 21 November, 1714, after a journey of sixteen days. The Governor was in bed, but on hearing that an officer had arrived from Bender with important dispatches he gave orders that he should be admitted, and at once recognized him by his voice. The town was illuminated when the king's arrival became known, but in fact the people had small cause to rejoice. Charles's enemies at once took the field against him, and after a siege of about a year Stralsund was compelled to surrender and Charles sailed away to Sweden.

Still he was filled with those irrepressible hankerings after military glory and conquest. Everything that he had accomplished in Europe in his earlier years had been reversed, and his loss had proved Czar Peter's gain. Now, however, in an evil hour he listened to the promptings of his chief adviser, Baron von Görtz, a German officer who had been with him in Bender. Let him make peace with the czar, and then—what might he not achieve? After all, he was not much in the thirties! Fantastic dreams passed through Charles's brain; he would invade and conquer Norway, and then he would lead an army across the sea into Scotland and put the Jacobite Pretender on the throne of his fathers!

Early in 1716 he attacked Norway, having come to terms with the czar by agreeing to cede all his Baltic provinces, and for a time things went well with him. Towards the end of 1718 he was besieging the Norwegian fortified town of Frederikshald. On the afternoon of 11 December he was visiting the trenches with several members of his staff and some French officers, to see how things were going. It got dusk, but still he stayed there, leaning against the parapet, and staring across at the enemy walls. His companions urged him not to expose himself in so foolhardy a fashion, but he turned their protests aside with contempt. Suddenly his head sank down on to the folds of his cloak, his left arm dropped . . . "The king is shot!" was the cry. Death in fact must have been instantaneous.

So sudden was his end that there were some who whispered that he had been the victim of assassination. The rumours persisted, so that in 1746 his tomb in the Riddarholm church in Stockholm was opened and his corpse was given a very unscientific examination. The result was inconclusive, but a further examination in 1859 put the matter to rest. It was proved then that a musket-ball had gone through his head, and that it had been fired from above and in front.

And what was the end of it all? What was there to show for the years of warfare, the marchings, the campaignings, the days of victory and the longer days of defeat? A country brought to the edge of ruin, an empire dissipated, tens of thousands of the bravest of his race left to rot on foreign fields. Something remained, however—his legend, and as long as men hold bravery, however misdirected and fruitless, in high honour, Charles XII's name will live on. "Were Socrates and Charles the Twelfth of Sweden both present in any company," Boswell reports Dr. Johnson as asserting, "and Socrates were to say, 'Follow me and hear a lecture on philosophy'; and Charles, laying his hand on his sword, to say, 'Follow me, and dethrone the Czar'; a man would be ashamed to follow Socrates". That would have been the Doctor's own reaction, we may be pretty sure, for years before Johnson had put Charles into his poem *The Vanity of Human Wishes* as the supreme illustration of the mutability of military glory. The poem is a worthy one, the best thing in verse that Johnson ever wrote; and the concluding passage is as well known—deservedly so—as almost anything in the books of quotations:

> *His fall was destin'd to a barren strand,*
> *A petty fortress, and a dubious hand.*
> *He left the name, at which the world grew pale,*
> *To point a moral, or adorn a tale.*

FREDERICK II (THE GREAT)

(1712–86)

THE EXECUTION was fixed for 7 a.m. Only two hours before, when the massive fortress of Küstrin in East Prussia was still shrouded in November darkness, the eighteen-year-old Crown Prince Frederick was informed that his fellow-prisoner and best friend, Lieutenant von Katte, would be beheaded by the sword below the windows of his cell and that his father's orders were that he should be a witness. Their offence? Frederick had tried to escape King Frederick William's tyranny by fleeing abroad and his friend had helped him. The attempt had failed. Mad with rage and thirsting for blood, the king had clapped both young men in jail, had condemned von Katte to death, waiving preliminary torture only because he was a noble, and was now bent on teaching his son an object lesson before deciding his fate. He was brooding on the thought of death for him, too.

In those two hours Frederick was delirious with remorse and terror. He pleaded for his friend's life, offered to die in his stead, or be imprisoned for life, or renounce the throne. In vain. When the time was up he was led to the window of his cell. Katte passed below and they exchanged a last affectionate farewell. The sword severed the head at the first stroke and Frederick collapsed unconscious in the arms of his jailers.

This was Frederick William's culminating act of savagery towards his son. It had been preceded by ten years of sadistic ill-treatment which had driven the highly intelligent, sensitive and imaginative boy to despair. He had been humiliated in public, dragged by the hair, thrashed, insulted and threatened—all because his brutal father failed to see in him the makings of a soldier, thought him effeminate because he played the flute and was enraged by his refusal to surrender will and personality in return for approval. After his friend's execution Frederick's life was spared, but the shock closed his heart to love for ever and in its place grew acrid cynicism, ruthlessness and a burning urge, born of parental derision, to prove that he was not a milksop, but capable of leading the fine army which Frederick William created but never used to deeds of heroism which would win for him the respect of mankind.

So, in 1740, when his father died, two Fredericks ascended the throne of Prussia: a cultivated young man, devoted to music, literature, versifying, a tranquil life among congenial friends; and a snarling, rejected son, full of rage and thirsting for action. The rulers of Europe knew nothing of this second Frederick and expected him to leave the government to his ministers while he devoted himself to the arts. There would be no fireworks, they felt sure, from Frederick. But they were soon disillusioned.

Prussia at that time consisted of two widely separated territories, the March of Brandenburg and the former Polish fief of East Prussia, and otherwise of small, scattered areas in the west of Germany in which the ruler of Prussia was not even entitled to call himself king. The population totalled 2,200,000, ranking about thirteenth in size among the states of Europe, and partly because he did not wish to risk his splendid army (including giant grenadiers whom he collected all over the Continent), Frederick William had pursued a pacific policy which, in an age of rapacious monarchs, had not enhanced his country's prestige. His son inherited a semi-feudal social structure, a sound administration, a submissive people—and the magnificently trained army, as large as Austria's, of 80,000 men, half mercenaries, half Prussians. At once young Frederick's eye lighted on this formidable machine and within four months of his accession he launched his troops on their first war-like operation: object, to bully an aged bishop into paying a huge indemnity in return for the undisputed ownership of a small village in Western Germany. Though a minor incident, it had been cynically provoked and aroused widespread condemnation. Europe was now much concerned with the personality of this new king. From Berlin diplomats reported that he was soft-spoken, but his courtesy could not conceal a mocking, contemptuous trait. He spoke a great deal without listening to others, gesturing forcefully with white hands overloaded with rings. When provoked he could flare into uncontrollable rage . . .

Before the year was out Frederick delivered his second blow, the invasion of Silesia, one of Austria's richest provinces, at a moment when the disputed accession of the 24-year-old Maria Theresa promised weak opposition. The king, as he wrote to a friend, was frankly an opportunist, athirst for glory and bored with a sedentary life. A large army, a well-filled treasury and a lively temperament did the rest. So, with a flimsy legal claim to only part of the territory, he marched, purloined the whole of the province and then awaited reactions. The Austrians promptly took up arms, were defeated in Silesia and four years of sporadic warfare followed from which Frederick emerged as a great military commander and diplomatist, unscrupulous even by the standards of that age. Three times he had allied himself with France and then backed out of hostilities when the French seemed to become too strong. Three times he made peace with Maria Theresa, only to take up arms again when Silesia was threatened or the prospect of further booty proved too alluring. Finally, after melting his palace plate to help finance the war and risking enemy occupation of his whole country, he retained Silesia, thus increasing his territories by a third. His fellow-monarchs were now heartily afraid of Frederick, his prowess in the field, his tenacity, his cunning. Because more successful than the other sharks, he was condemned as an unscrupulous knave.

But in the long interlude of peace opening in 1745 the king showed himself in a different light, as a despotic but in many ways surprisingly enlightened and humanitarian ruler. His day usually began with flute playing and ended with a concert or recitations from his own verses, but his working hours were filled with unremitting toil for his people and he demanded the same from them. In return he gave them a revised legal system providing cheap, swift and impartial justice for all. He abolished the use of torture except for high treason. He introduced complete religious toleration so that everyone could find his own path to heaven. The peasants were given adequate security against maltreatment by their overlords. Frederick set his nobles an example by declaring himself to be the first servant of the state and demanded of them a life of dedicated service, mostly in the army. Sale of office was abolished throughout Prussia and peculation kept down by repeated surprise checks on funds.

Frederick held the purse strings, he became his own minister of trade, he supervised the whole agriculture and industry of the country by regular tours of inspection each spring and every subject could have access to the king, at least in writing, to air a grievance or make a request. He was thus a benevolent despot, or almost, but like his father he never saw beyond the duties and obligations of his subjects and was not interested in their contentment except in so far as it affected their performance as efficient Prussians. "Tired of ruling over slaves," he recorded towards the end of his life, but he never did anything to set them free.

It was after a victory over the Saxons in 1745 that Voltaire called Frederick "the Great", but it was his heroism in the Seven Years' War which really earned him the title. The diplomatic manoeuvres which preceded its outbreak in August, 1756, confronted him with a coalition bent on his destruction between France, Austria and Russia—countries with populations totalling fifty times his own. That this hostile confederacy came about at all was largely his own fault. His retention of Silesia spelt the undying enmity of Maria Theresa and the certainty that if she could find allies she would make a bid to recover it. Frederick alienated the Empress Elizabeth of Russia by mocking her admittedly erratic private life and, wrongly convinced that both countries lacked the cash to make war, allowed a defensive alliance to come about between Russia and Austria. This was his first mistake. His second was even more serious. Behind the back of his ally France he signed a Convention with England with whom she was at war in the New World, and in 1756 the age-old enemies France and Austria formed a defensive alliance which soon ripened into an agreement to partition Prussia. Early in the same year Maria Theresa and the Empress Elizabeth also agreed to banish once for all the odious Frederick from the world. So, in that summer, he faced almost certain destruction unless he anticipated the onslaught and drew the sword first.

Seven long years of bitter struggle followed. Saxony was on the brink of joining the coalition. Frederick invaded, defeated the Saxon army and an Austrian force coming to its assistance. But the main fighting was yet to come and he had no illusions. His Ministers in Berlin were told that if he were taken prisoner they should pay no attention to anything he wrote from captivity, offer no ransom and prosecute the war "as though I had never existed in the world".

The new year saw another victory over the Austrians at Prague and then a bloody defeat. In an attempt to avert disaster the king himself had led his troops into the cannons' mouth and had only turned back when an adjutant called to him: "Sire, do you mean to take the battery single-handed?" He now faced armies totalling 340,000 men against his own 90,000. "Things are beginning to look vile," he wrote to one of his generals, and then sent his sister long screeds full of rhetorical indignation. East Prussia fell to the Russians. The Swedes, who had joined the fray, were walking through defenceless Pomerania, while a Croat force stormed into Berlin and exacted a heavy fine from the inhabitants before withdrawing at the approach of Prussian troops. But Frederick's resolve never

500

flagged. A brilliant victory, when outnumbered by two to one, over the French at Rossbach, made him the hero of all German patriots, and at Leuthen in Silesia he scattered a superior force of Austrians in a battle which Napoleon later declared was enough to make him immortal and place him among the world's greatest generals.

But the year 1758 was spent in inconclusive fighting, the king hurrying with dwindling troops to East Prussia, to Silesia, to Saxony in a vain effort to deal one of the allies such a blow that they would withdraw from the coalition. By Christmas he was calling himself a limping skeleton. The treasury was empty and the troops scraped together by his recruiting officers were of such poor quality that he hardly dared show them to the enemy.

But for five more years he fought on, through heavy defeats and hard-won victories, resolved in every fibre of his being to die rather than capitulate, deep at the back of his mind the lowering figure of his father to whom he had to prove himself a man. By the end of 1761 only Brandenburg and a small part of Silesia were still in his hands, and for the following year he hardly knew how he was to recruit an army, pay it and feed it. He carried a box of poison with him wherever he went. Then fortune suddenly smiled. The Empress of Russia died, to be succeeded by Peter III, an ardent admirer of Frederick, who at once concluded peace. Soon after the French were defeated by a combined English and German force and Frederick gained further successes against the Austrians. By 1763 the allies had had enough and the peace treaty left him with his country intact and still in possession of Silesia. He had shown himself a master of war, had defied the great powers of Europe and established the core of the future German nation. Yet when peace was signed he said that the happiest day of his life would be the last.

With equal energy he then turned to the reconstruction of his country, supervising everything from agriculture to the tax on coffee, and was so successful that at his death Prussia was more prosperous than at the start of the Seven Years' War, with a well-filled treasury, a growing population and a rate of taxation only slightly higher than at his accession. During his reign the territory had been increased by the seizure of Silesia and, under the partition of Poland in 1772 by the acquisition of Polish West Prussia, joining East Prussia to Pomerania.

In the closing years of his life—he died in 1786—Frederick showed himself to be a sound-hearted, brave old man. "Life", he wrote to a friend, "is a mean affair when one gets old. But there is a way of being happy and that is to rejuvenate oneself in imagination, disregard the body and to the end of the play preserve an inner cheerfulness, so strewing the last few steps of the path with flowers." More than any other man, he had provided a hero-figure round which, in the struggle with Napoleon and later, German nationalist feelings could concentrate. By establishing the power and military prowess of his country and by excluding Austria from the leadership of Germany he had made Prussia the centre of future national unity. And by his own example and that of his people he had raised hard work, discipline and tenacity to the status of Prussian if not German virtues.

But Frederick could see nothing of all this and probably did not care very much what happened to his country when he had gone. He did his duty to the end, rising at four every day, kept as close an eye as ever on the training of his army and studied meticulously the reports of his officials. At meals he talked extremely well on a wide range of subjects and was full of charm and courtesy to his guests, even if occasionally the old bitter cynicism would break through.

But he died like a Stoic, cheerful to the last though in great pain —and at once a great sigh of relief went up from his people. They were tired of being slave-driven, tired of great deeds. But outside Prussia contemporaries called him the hero of the century. Standing beside his grave in 1806, Napoleon said: "If he were still alive we would not be here", and to this day Germans revere the memory of old Fritz, the embodiment of will-power and tenacity of purpose, as brilliant and hard as a diamond, the warrior who in seven years of war showed a heroism in confronting fate unequalled since the days of Ancient Rome.

MARIA THERESA

(1717–80)

MARIA THERESA, the mother of sixteen children, the mother of her people, noble fighter against a continent in arms, wise reformer of Austrian institutions, compelling as a figure-head and enchanting as an individual, was great both as a woman and as a ruler. We see her portrayed in middle age, seated massively in a rich embroidered gown, her strong arms resting on her lap, shelving bosom tightly encased, double chin, broad smiling mouth, high forehead, beautiful complexion, fair, silken hair, and we are reminded of the Eternal Woman who, as psychologists say, dwells in the heart of every man. It was she who was the founder of the modern Austrian State, she who personified the age-old Austrian virtues of open-mindedness, spontaneity and warmth and she who brought the hitherto remote Habsburg rule close to the people's hearts.

Born in 1717, second child of the Emperor Charles VI and of his Guelph wife, Elizabeth Christine of Brunswick-Wolfenbüttel, Maria Theresa spent a happy childhood as an ordinary princess not destined to ascend the throne. Indeed, the accession of a female was barred by law. The eldest child, a boy, had died in infancy, but Charles still hoped for a male heir and meanwhile his daughter romped in the Hofburg in an atmosphere of tolerant affection. Then, as the years passed and no boy was born, Charles prepared for the future by drawing up a document called the Pragmatic Sanction. In wars against France and Turkey this foolish man had already lost Naples, Sicily, Serbia and Wallachia from his dominions. Now, in return for signatures to his piece of paper promising European support for his daughter's eventual accession, he bartered away yet further territories and rights. It was all in vain.

When in 1740 Maria Theresa came to the throne on her father's death she faced a perilous situation. An unknown quantity, un-tutored in affairs of State, married to a weak husband, the Grand Duke Francis of Lorraine, she was watched in ambiguous fashion by France, Spain, Bavaria and Saxony, late signatories to the Sanction recognizing her right and guaranteeing her territories.

Apart from Austria, the Habsburg Empire included Hungary, Bohemia and Moravia, Silesia, the Southern Netherlands, Lombardy and Tuscany, far-flung dominions, some with the weakest ties of allegiance, which invited aggression. A sign of weakness on Maria Theresa's part, a warlike move by one of her neighbours and the whole pack of alleged friends might descend on her.

Apart from this, the internal situation was forlorn. She found a bankrupt treasury, an army ill-equipped, ill-disciplined and dislocated by defeat. Three field-marshals were languishing in prison for their failure on the battlefield. Her advisers, headed by the seventy-year-old Chancellor Bartenstein, were all old men, "too prejudiced", as she later recorded, "to give useful advice, but too respectable and meritorious to be dismissed". Each thought first of how the matter under consideration would affect himself.

Within eight weeks of her accession she found herself at war. On a trumped-up pretext, athirst for glory and fame, the young Frederick of Prussia invaded Silesia, at the same time sending an envoy to Vienna to suggest the cession of the province in return for his military support of Austria. Maria Theresa indignantly refused, a force was scratched together to cut off Frederick's supplies and the two armies met at Mollwitz, where the Austrians were decisively defeated. Another month, and France, Spain, Bavaria and Saxony were agreeing to partition the Habsburg Monarchy. A French army marched through Germany to help the Elector of Bavaria seize Vienna, the Saxons moved towards Moravia, Spain started to mobilize for a campaign in Italy. Maria Theresa had no army to oppose any of these advances and in no time the Bavarian Karl Albert was within thirty miles of the capital. The government fled to Hungary and Maria Theresa followed it, to plead in an impassioned and memorable scene with the Hungarian nobility for military support. Her youth, beauty and extreme distress moved the hearts of her chivalrous subjects and as she held up her baby Prince Joseph to them they burst into shouts of joy and consecrated their lives and blood to her cause.

But the Hungarian troops were no more than a rabble and Vienna was only temporarily saved by the indecision of the Bavarians. Soon they and the French were capturing Prague, watched ineffectually by the Grand Duke Francis in command of the army fetched from Silesia, and Frederick was marching into Moravia. Austria seemed doomed and Maria Theresa's palsied advisers could only think of sacrificing territory in order to buy off the wolves. At this moment she showed her splendid courage.

To one of her ministers she wrote: "What I have I intend to hold, and all my armies, including the Hungarian, shall be destroyed before I will abdicate anything. What you cannot get voluntarily you must drag from the people by force. You will say I am cruel; I am. But I know that one day I can make good a hundredfold all the suffering I must now inflict in order to save my country."

From Italy she summoned her last remaining troops, sending their commander a stirring letter accompanied by a portrait of herself and Joseph which he showed to his men, and a few weeks later he had thrown the Franco-Bavarian army out of the country, advanced into Bavaria and occupied Munich. After a single victory at Chotusitz Frederick cautiously made peace, and the Austrians soon after forced Saxony to follow suit and recovered all the places they had lost.

Despite the dangers one must not think of Maria Theresa as obsessed by her problems. Not at all. She bore two children during this time and when she could pursued the gay life she loved, dancing, skating and riding—astride, much to the horror of elderly courtiers. She supervised the education of her growing family, watched over the morals of her ladies-in-waiting and, only too glad to be advised by men of knowledge and experience, sifted in her mind the need for internal reforms.

But major reforms had to wait, for meanwhile, in 1744, Frederick became alarmed for the safety of his purloined province of Silesia and, deciding that attack was his best course, invaded Bohemia. An Austrian army followed him and to give it the best chance of success Maria Theresa managed by dint of tears and tempers— "which made both of us quite ill"—to dissuade her husband from taking command. Her feeling about his military prowess was entirely right, but wrong about his brother's, Charles of Lorraine, whom she appointed in his stead, and the result, in the summer of 1745, was a victory for Frederick, repeated a few months later when Charles risked battle again. To Maria Theresa, Frederick by now had become a monster of supernatural proportions, but his success was bringing welcome allies for her into the field, the Russians and the Saxons.

So the future was not entirely bleak when in September she attended the coronation in Frankfurt of her benign and ineffectual husband as emperor of the "Holy Roman Empire"—in inverted commas because it was no longer a living reality. But Frederick defeated the Saxons before the Russians could move, and by the Treaty of Dresden (December, 1745) peace was patched up between

him and Maria Theresa. In the next three years, until the Peace of
Aix la Chapelle, Austria was at war with Spain in Italy and with
France in the Netherlands. As for Frederick, he knew there could be
no real agreement with Maria Theresa so long as he retained Silesia
and his motto was: "On Guard."

By the Peace the terms of the Pragmatic Sanction were confirmed
by all Powers (excepting, of course, that the Habsburg dominions
no longer included Silesia) and after 1748 there was at least a breath-
ing space when Maria Theresa could grapple with internal problems.
The diverse provinces of her domain suffered from widely differing
conditions of local rule, mostly carried out by nobles who felt a
law to themselves and were exempt from taxation.

The prime necessity was to establish the supremacy of the State,
the power to direct local government for the general good, and this
Maria Theresa sought to achieve by various means. At the same
time, justice and taxation were centralized. In the economic sphere,
the nobles' privilege was abolished, a uniform system of indirect
taxation was introduced, barriers to local trade were broken down.
Education, too, received a powerful stimulus under Maria Theresa
with the object of training useful citizens able to make their contribution to the welfare of the State.

But all these reforms were dependent on the security of the realm
and army re-organization was a necessity. The success achieved
enabled the Austrian armies to survive the Seven Years' War.

Meanwhile Maria Theresa had borne ten children and was to
produce six more between 1750 and 1756. In this task she was, as
she said, "insatiable", and it was thought extraordinary that she
could appear at the opera a few hours before the birth of a child
and be driving through the streets a few hours afterwards. But her
health and vitality were superabundant and her whole rhythm of
life, her hours of sleep, work and enjoyment reflected the fact.

She needed all her strength for the trials that lay ahead.
Immediately after Aix la Chapelle the empress's new foreign
minister Kaunitz had recommended to her a complete reversal of
the age-old hostility to France. He was sent to Paris to woo the
French, but to no effect until early in 1756 when Frederick, still
treaty-bound to them, signed a Convention with their enemy
England to exclude the entry of foreign troops into Germany.
This, seeing that Frederick had already three times deserted his
French ally, turned the scales in Kaunitz's favour and in May France
and Austria signed a "defensive" treaty. So Frederick faced two
enemies and soon there was a third, Russia, where the Empress

Elizabeth had been relying on English help against him and now turned to Austria instead.

Soon France, Russia and Austria, where Maria Theresa had never weakened in her resolve to regain Silesia, were preparing for offensive war and Saxony promised to join them later. Frederick saw clearly his mortal peril and decided to strike first by invading Saxony. So began the Seven Years' War, ending, after his triumphant defiance of countries with a total population fifty times his own, in Frederick's retention of Silesia and the acknowledgement of Prussia's and Austria's frontiers exactly as they had been in 1756.

Throughout the struggle, with its endless marches and counter-marches and battles, Maria Theresa urged on her generals, often with detailed advice, and must often have regretted not being a commander herself. They were too slow for her, too dilatory, though no doubt the implacable empress, scribbling memoranda to them in the field, did nothing to whet their initiative. But towards the end of the war she began to see that ultimate victory was impossible and tended to become apathetic.

Peace found her aged but determined as ever to give her people good government. Devoted mother though she was, if need be she would sacrifice herself and her children to the State, and at a tender age some of the girls were married in a purely dynastic interest, Marie Antoinette, for instance, to the Dauphin of France. Long screeds of advice followed them, Maria Theresa making the mistake of believing that a mature woman's paper wisdom sent half across Europe could counterbalance the effect of fresh experience on young hearts.

Her scattered family caused anxiety, but there was a greater one at home: Joseph, her problematical heir. Joseph was a Rationalist, a free-thinker, a Spartan and a firm believer that, if only the ingredients are right, happiness can be forced upon people like a pill. He was utterly sincere, but was sadly lacking in knowledge of human nature. Above all, he wished to go ahead too fast, and given the immense resistances Maria Theresa had encountered in setting up a bureaucratic State she foresaw danger here for the future. So the closing years of her life saw them working together, he as co-regent, devoted to one another but perpetually at odds, and this added greatly to her burdens.

In 1765 her husband died and she was plunged in the bitterest grief. But the trials of the ruler did not cease. Catherine of Russia had succeeded by devious means in making Poland virtually a Russian province. Then she fought a war against the Turks, won a victory and made startling claims in the Balkans. Both Frederick and Maria Theresa felt themselves threatened and the spectre of another continental war loomed, until Joseph, acting better than he knew, sent Austrian troops to occupy a small area of Poland which had formerly been German. Catherine then switched her claims and suggested the partition of Poland between Austria, Prussia and herself, and in 1772 it came about. The hearty meal banished the fear of war, but Maria Theresa had been pushed into the venture by her son and never forgave herself.

There was one more service she could render her country. In December, 1777, Joseph was able to buy Lower Bavaria from an indigent Elector in return for immediate cash, also the reversionary title to the Upper Palatinate. He thought the ageing Frederick would not react, but he did, threatening war, as Maria Theresa had foreseen. Negotiations were started, but not pursued by Joseph, with the result that in July, 1778, the King of Prussia marched into Bohemia at the head of 100,000 men. For the empress this was altogether too much and without consulting her son she wrote to the hated Frederick the first letter she had ever addressed to him in her life, asking to resume the discussions. This did not prevent war, but it shortened its length, and at the peace, with his mother's hearty concurrence, Joseph agreed to disgorge Bavaria.

And now her work was done. She could not restrain him for ever. Her health was failing and soon, for better or worse, the eager, unwise Joseph would have to tread his path alone. She had borne many children, endured long years of war, infused her easy-going people with her own sense of purpose. But she was beginning to feel a stranger in a changing world and was not sorry to see the end. It came on the evening of 29 November, 1780, after a chill caught on a long drive in a rain-storm. She was imperturbably calm, would not sleep because she wanted to see death approaching, blessed her children and then, seeing that they were overwrought, told them to leave the room. At nine o'clock the great empress died, but in the minds of Austrians she lives on as the architect of her empire's survival and as, in her own words, "the general and chief mother of my country".

CATHERINE II (THE GREAT)

(1729–96)

CATHERINE II, Empress of Russia, universally known as Catherine the Great, shares—with the English Elizabeth I and Victoria, and the Austrian Maria Theresa (Catherine's contemporary)—a fame afforded by history to but few women rulers. Catherine's almost immediate predecessor was the able, though less significant, Empress Elizabeth. Among Russian rulers since the turbulent sixteenth-seventeenth century chaos following Ivan the Terrible and Boris Godonov, only Peter the Great is Catherine's superior in importance (though not necessarily in all his policies), while among her successors in the Romanov dynasty which lasted until the Revolution of 1917 only Alexander II is comparable to her in vision, yet her inferior in personality and will-power.

The late eighteenth century was the "Age of Enlightened Despots", and to this number—stressing the noun rather than the adjective —Catherine belonged, like Frederick II of Prussia. "Enlightened" is perhaps an ambiguous term, yet in any sense of the word many of Catherine's aims and actions can be so characterized. Less obviously enlightened, though it enlightens us as to her character, was her mode of attaining the throne.

A fatal aspect of Russian monarchy—inherited perhaps from the early rivalry of princes in the Kiev period, the cradle of Russian nationhood—was the loose theory of succession. As in the later Roman Empire, havoc was wrought through uncertainty and intrigue; the eldest son by no means always succeeded to his father. Put brutally, Catherine ascended the throne through at least connivance in the murder of her husband, Czar Peter III, orphaned grandson of Peter the Great but his antithesis in character, an irresponsible "monkey" (so he was called) with almost an "arrested development".

It is ironic that both he and Catherine should have been, in different senses, outsiders: he, brought up in Sweden as a Lutheran, not speaking Russian, and even more concerned with Scandinavian and German interests; and she, not even a Russian by birth, but a princess of Anhalt-Zerbst, yet ardent for her adopted country, a student of its customs and needs, and in character not unlike previous Romanov czars. Her husband was widely unpopular, and Catherine's accession, whatever the means employed, was applauded, and her reign of thirty-four years lasted until her death.

During Catherine's reign she fostered and developed Russian institutions and reforms, conducted highly-skilled diplomatic intrigues and several wars in the "Russian interest", while conducting in a more civilized fashion Peter the Great's "opening of a door on to Europe" for a Russia still backward by general European standards. Peter imported soldiers and technicians from the West; Catherine diffused the newest French culture (hence the term "enlightened"); and it is likely that her foreign origin predisposed her to do this. She also showed a somewhat un-Russian continuity and balance in her perseverance, as distinct from the arbitrary energy of most Russian rulers, as witness the great Peter, who founded St. Petersburg (now Leningrad) on a supposedly impossible marshy site, and helped in the work literally with his own hands.

"Her brilliance was like a fountain showering down in sparks" was the way in which the French encyclopaedist Grimm described Catherine; after talking to her he would pace his own room for hours, too excited to sleep. And next day Catherine would more than likely spend some hours—she could work fifteen hours a day —in cameo-making, or engraving, or even in painting and sculpture, or in literary work, largely satirical, though none of it first-class. Still, it shows something that an autocratic sovereign should introduce satire into her country, as well as patronizing poets like Derzhavin, one of the earliest Russians still read. Catherine, as a writer, lives only in her letters; here we find her native genius for administration, especially in its diplomatic facets. Correspondence between monarchs was common in her time, but her exchanges with Joseph II, Frederick the Great and others have a unique interest. Her exchanges with Voltaire, Falconnet, Grimm, D'Alembert and other French writers and scholars helped to initiate that ascendancy of French language and culture in Russia which lasted until 1917.

Catherine admired and promoted men for their ability (and sexual charm), and showed herself generally pragmatic and opportunistic. Her diplomacy was certainly opportunist; her finesse in playing off Prussia and Austria against each other, while seemingly the friend of each, is an example. Her curiosity was both feminine and immense. History records her also as a great, frequent and changeable lover. The long roll of her partners consists roughly of two types: younger men like Mamonov or Lanskoy, treated as pets or children; and ministers and officials of exceptional quality, like Potemkin and Orlov. Potemkin was, for her, "bold mind, bold spirit, bold heart", and "cleverer than I"; and after his death, with their real intimacy long past, she felt utterly cut off. Catherine sought courageous and forceful men, and to such her letters often appear like those of one male friend to another. She liked a comradeship in which—to use her own words—"one of the two friends was a very attractive woman". Even before her rise to the throne she played seducer and seduced. She was not on the best of terms with the vigorous, sensual, and politically irresponsible Empress Elizabeth (daughter of Peter the Great). During Elizabeth's reign, when there were really two Courts—that of the empress and that of Peter (her nephew) with Catherine—a double scandal spread: while Peter was scorned as apparently both impotent and profligate, Catherine's morals caused alarm, so that Elizabeth appointed a duenna to watch over her—but Catherine responded by falling in love with the duenna's husband!

Suspicious of the cut-and-dried, Catherine yet was capable of the hardest, most concentrated work, sometimes working in great Russian bouts and sometimes in steadier German style. Employing four secretaries, she often worked a fifteen-hour day. Her nonfiction reading ran from Buffon's *Natural History* to Blackstone's *Commentaries* on law; in mastering the latter, she presaged her own studious compilation of the new humanitarian legal code, the *Instruction* (or *Nakaz*) based largely on Montesquieu, on which she worked for eighteen months.

Indeed the impression left by Catherine remains one of blended order and caprice, of idealism and opportunism. Ideas attracted her strongly; travel excited her creative thought (the Volga, she remarked, had given her ideas to last ten years). Yet in sober fact she had little right to the throne at all. "God and the choice of my subjects" was her bland reply, but some of these very subjects continued to rebel or plot against her for over thirty years. If not in league with her husband's murderers, she did reward them, without at the same time showing any disfavour towards his followers, whether through lack of malice or diplomatic guile. Even when Pugachev, leader of the greatest of the revolts, was captured, Catherine vetoed the use of torture; and she was considerate towards her servants, which was hardly a regal virtue in that Absolutist age.

Catherine was born in Germany in 1729, married the seventeen-year-old Peter III at the age of sixteen, became empress-consort with Peter as emperor in 1762—on Elizabeth's death—and seized the throne as sole ruler after six months. At her marriage she accepted the Greek Orthodox faith and was renamed Catherina Alexćivna, although like Peter she had been brought up as a Lutheran. She treated her new religion as seriously as her affinity with thinkers like Voltaire would permit, though this did not later prevent her from exiling many of the heretical "Old Believers" into the Siberian wilds, an action dictated by political diplomacy.

Her accession brought acclaim from the most important regiments, and also an open revolt of some 200,000 peasants against their squires; artillery subdued them. Her usurpation did not go unchallenged; her son Paul (who succeeded at her death) became the unwilling aim of many intrigues to place him, the legal heir, on the throne. Others favoured a youth, Ivan VI, who at the age of *one year* had reigned for a short time. Other pretenders abounded, like the adventuress called Princess Tarakanova, who claimed to be the illegitimate daughter of the late Empress Elizabeth, and who died in jail.

The Church, too, protested in the imposing figure of Arseny Matseyevich, Archbishop of Rostov, who anathematized Catherine when she confirmed Peter II's appropriation of Church estates, now called the "economic lands" of the State. Unfrocked and twice jailed, he denounced her right to the throne and died forbidden to speak to any human being. Catherine had already dubbed him "Andrew the Babbler". Other voices sang the same tune, and the merchant Smolin—for instance—wrote to the empress denouncing her "unjust government".

Still vaster hurricanes were soon in progress: notably the revolt of Pugachev in May, 1773. Catherine's first years as ruler displayed a glaring contrast between genuine progressive efforts and complacency towards appalling social conditions. Hers was indeed the age of the "gentry" (*dvoryanstvo*), a mixed class of aristocrats and servicemen, whose power over the mass of the serfs was almost unlimited. In 1771 the great plague of Moscow killed 100,000 persons, and cannon was used to suppress rioting. The Pugachev rebellion summed up a burning discontent.

A Cossack soldier and adventurer, Emilian Pugachev, after many escapes, gathered followers and even formed his own bogus court, parading as emperor and naming two of his forts Moscow and St. Petersburg! He swore he would confine Catherine in a nunnery, and slaughtered the gentry, being now in command of a vast motley force composed of Cossacks from the Don and the Dnieper, all the Tartar and Finnish groups still smarting under Russian rule, and exiles and convicts who had escaped from their guards *en route* for Siberia. Soon he had the sympathy of the people as a whole: Bibikov, sent by Catherine to stem the tide, reported: "It is not Pugachev that matters, but the general indignation." Even when Pugachev—a price of 28,000 roubles on his head—approached Moscow, Catherine (who had at first laughed at the revolt as a farce) still urged moderation. At last—aided by a famine on the Volga—the tide turned and Pugachev was executed in January, 1775, before the delighted gentry.

As a result the lot of the peasants became still more degraded. In an edict against a ruthless serf-owner, Catherine wrote: "Be so good as to call your peasants cattle." Yet her irony was wasted. In fact, serfdom increased during her—in many ways enlightened—reign. Apparently without realizing the consequences, she made enormous grants of land to her favourites, which in fact made new serfs out of the still partly-free crown peasants. Further, she extended serfdom to the vast area of the Ukraine through a "fiscal" decree, based on the equalization and centralizing of conditions throughout the country. Her son, Paul, was to extend this system. In 1773 auction-sales of serfs were allowed. The power of master over serf knew few limits: a typical punishment would be five hundred strokes of the rod for failure to attend Holy Communion.

Yet there is another side to the picture. Catherine did help in forwarding progressive ideas. Her *Instruction* (or *Nakaz*) has clauses about equality before the law; the injustice and gradual abolition of serfdom; that education is better than punishment, and that capital punishment should be limited and torture abolished; that the peasant must have food, clothing, and even peasant judges and a jury system, and be able to buy his freedom; agriculture implies property—and so forth. To debate how these principles should be implemented, Catherine, in 1766, summoned a Great Commission, elected from all classes (even the peasants) and nationalities in the empire, consisting of 564 members. It sat for a year and a half. Catherine listened, but the final upshot was disappointing.

Still, she managed to introduce certain reforms: peasants' petitions, forbidden by law, reached the sovereign; the prize essay of her Free Economic Society decided in favour of peasant proprietorship; finance, economics, justice and public health also made some advances. Local government, public welfare, roads and canals, trade with Asia, all benefited to some degree; while hospitals, schools and the St. Petersburg Public Library were founded. The

College of Medicine, founded in 1763, was followed in 1768 by Catherine's own example of inoculation against smallpox. Yet the construction of the city of Ekaterinoslav ("Glory of Catherine") stopped early through lack of funds.

It is time now to outline Catherine's foreign policy. She corresponded with foreign monarchs (180 letters to Frederick the Great alone), and induced them to visit her. How cleverly her letters cajole, and twist each point to her own advantage! In the main her interests lay in Russia's neighbours and potential foes: Sweden (then so powerful), Poland (soon to be partitioned three times), and Turkey. Early she perceived the value of a non-committal attitude towards Prussia and Austria, and it was largely through her that these states made peace in 1763. She took the most cynical advantage of the confusions of the Polish situation; bribery, invasion of the Polish Duchy of Kurland (Latvia) and then of Poland proper, enabled her and Frederick to place on the Polish throne their favourite and her former lover, Stanislaus Poniatowski, because—as she wrote—he had the least claim, and thus would always feel dependent on Russia.

She revelled in the "happy (Polish) anarchy which we can work at will". It is true that the Polish Sejm, or Diet, continued persecuting the Russian Dissidents (Greek Orthodox) in Poland. Under the famous general Suvorov, Russia seized the chance to invade; but Turkey in 1762 promised to help the Poles. Near the Turkish frontier Poles and Jews were massacred, and reprisals led to Cossacks ravaging Turkey, and the invasion of Russia by the Crimean Tartars (1768). Catherine looked forward to this war and built on it great hopes. She was greatly responsible for its success, through her naval policy which resulted in the Russian victories of Navarino and Chesme Bay. These alarmed both Austria and Prussia.

Unscrupulous intrigues then led to the first of the three partitions of Poland among the three powers. They took over a quarter of Poland's territory, with five-twelfths of her population. The war with Turkey was renewed, with Russia finally obtaining access to the Black Sea; the Crimea was declared independent, and Christians in Turkey and Moldavia (Rumania) were "protected". Shameless bargaining with Joseph II of Austria ended in a temporary stalemate, which Catherine used to annex the Crimea (1783), to which she made a triumphal visit with Joseph II, passing like a fairy queen through southern Russia with extravagant luxuries, gaiety and welcoming deputations.

There was further trouble with Turkey, but Russia was triumphant in December, 1791. Meanwhile Poland made internal and constitutional advances. Russia invaded again and a Second Partition took place, this time without Austria. The terms provoked the revolt of Kosciusko at Cracow in March, 1794, but Suvorov's forces crushed all resistance near Warsaw in November. Catherine now took the biggest share in the Third and final Polish Partition in which the whole country was swallowed up.

As the French Revolution of 1789 expanded into terror and foreign warfare Catherine was disgusted. The reactionary in her came to dominate the enlightened humanitarian: the pro-peasant writer, Radishchev, was imprisoned. In his defence he remarked that a few years earlier Catherine would have rewarded him for his sentiments.

In November, 1796, the year of Napoleon's first victories in Italy, Catherine died and her son, Paul, became czar. A magnetic and intellectual, but also capricious and somewhat unscrupulous woman, Catherine did much for Russia to ensure her place in history as Catherine the Great.

GEORGE WASHINGTON

(1732–99)

HE WAS a great ruler and a great man—and seldom in history has a great man been laden with such a dead weight of mythology, such a worthless heap of halos, crammed one on the other like a market-porter's baskets. Only—and paradoxically—in Communist China, and for much the same reason. Each state weathered a revolution, threw off the shackles of the past, buried its former idols: and new idols had to be erected in their place. Hence Comrade Mao, the god who makes the grass grow green, the rice to shoot. And hence George Washington, The-Father-of-His-Country.

"O Washington! How I do love thy name! How have I often adored and blessed thy God, for creating and forming thee the great ornament of human kind! Thy fame is of sweeter perfume than Arabian spices. Listening angels shall catch the odour, waft it to heaven, and perfume the universe!" This, in a sermon by his contemporary, Ezra Styles of Yale. And a little later, all those anecdotes, in the biography by Parson Weems, most of them, as far as we can tell, quite untrue. The cherry tree, for example. (" 'I can't tell a lie, Pa, you know I can't tell a lie. I did it with my hatchet.'—'Run to my arms, dearest boy,' cried his father in transports.")

And later still, in the *Pictorial Life of Washington*, compiled half a century after the great man's death by Horatio Weld: "The first word of infancy should be mother, the second, father, the third, WASHINGTON."

It is proof of Washington's greatness that his reputation has survived all this. And worse.

He was descended from British stock and was in many ways the epitome of an English country gentleman, fond of open-air pursuits, moderately well educated, distant with his subordinates, but scrupulously fair. The United States of America can be grateful to the bigotry and intolerance of Oliver Cromwell's adherents, in the middle of the seventeenth century, for it was they who succeeded in having the Reverend Lawrence Washington removed from his Northamptonshire living. Soon after, the vicar died in poverty, and at this two of his sons decided to sever connexion with an

516

unkind country and try their luck in an unknown one, across the sea.

They emigrated to the Colony of Virginia, and straightway made a success of it. From one of these two brothers, John, was descended George Washington, born, in Virginia, the 11th day of February, 1732. (Twenty years later the calendar was revised, adding eleven days to the date, so the correct anniversary of Washington's birth, as any American schoolboy can tell us, is 22 February). His education, by European standards, was sketchy, and not to be compared with that of some Virginian contemporaries like Thomas Jefferson: throughout his life he regretted this, and in particular his inability to speak French. When he became President, he refused to visit that country, rather than be humiliated by an interpreter. But George Washington, of a rich planting family (tobacco and wheat), was an intelligent young man who preferred the out-of-doors. He was a good shot with a rifle, a fine horseman. From childhood he was interested in a military career, an interest which had begun when his older half-brother, Lawrence, went off in the brand-new "American Regiment" to the West Indies. The expedition against the Spanish was commanded by Admiral Vernon and failed, but Lawrence so admired his commander that he re-christened his plantation Mount Vernon.

When George reached the age of sixteen he was invited to move in with this gay and gallant half-brother, and his sociable young wife, and it was with this couple that the future President of the United States got his first taste of social life, learning to dance, play cards, make conversation: though he still preferred the open air, life was gay and enjoyable. After dinner in the evenings there was animated discussion of the lands farther in, west of the Blue Ridge Mountains and the Alleghanies, and the chances of settling them. All this Washington listened to, for he was an ambitious young man. He desired not only to acquit himself well as an army officer—when opportunity arose, and he knew it would, even though impediments were put in the way of advancement for "Colonials"—but to acquire land. The most sensible way, it seemed, of getting involved in any westward settlement was to train as surveyor, and this he now did. He showed remarkable aptitude which, coupled with his family's importance, resulted in his being Surveyor of Culpeper County by the time he was eighteen. He even managed to claim, for himself, some 1,500 acres in the fertile Shenandoah Valley.

Two years later Lawrence died of TB, leaving Mount Vernon to his widow for as long as she lived; then—if none of his own children survived, and none did—to George.

And now came military opportunity. George had inherited from his half-brother not only Mount Vernon but the largely honorary job of Militia Adjutant—and for the keen young surveyor it would be as much a working job as he could make it. He persuaded Lieutenant-Governor Dinwiddie of Virginia to let him be the bearer of a written ultimatum to the French, who had started to build forts on the Ohio River.

It was not the most glorious start to a military career, but it brought him to public notice as a stubborn, fearless young man. He did the round trip to the Ohio in two and a half months, suffering great privation, being nearly killed on more than one occasion, and bringing back a polite rebuff from the French commander, in which, as Washington carefully explained to Dinwiddie, "It was their absolute design to take possession of the Ohio, and by God they would do it". He was commended on his conduct of the expedition and promoted to lieutenant-colonel.

A little later he was back in the Ohio country, successfully holding back a further French incursion and in the process capturing many prisoners. Promotion now took him to the rank of full colonel— though this was only a commission in the Colonial forces: the more important "King's Commission" was still denied him, and Washington, understandably, resented this. Commanding a mixed bag of militia and friendly Indians, he went on to encounter a vastly superior French force—at which point his Indians deserted. He was forced to retire with his remaining troops into a stockade (which he christened "Fort Necessity") and eventually to surrender. A bitter blow for a keen officer, even though the French released him immediately, with honour. They then made great propaganda from his chatty, sporting, diary which they had retained and which showed —or so they tried to point out—that the British, i.e., Washington, had been the aggressors, hounding the peace-loving French. For a while there was such a fuss that he resigned his commission.

But the call to glory was still great—doubly so after his defeat. A year later he arranged to join General Braddock's force in the same area, as unpaid A.D.C.—a gesture which could only be made by a brave, ambitious—and very rich—man.

This was total disaster, though Washington came out of it better than his general. Two horses were shot out from under him and he was noted as a very gallant soldier and an inspired commander. He was persuaded to take up his commission again, and now, at the age of twenty-three, he became not only a colonel, but Commander-in-Chief of the Virginia Army.

Soon afterwards illness struck, and he retired to Mount Vernon. His sister-in-law had moved elsewhere and was renting the property to him, and in their combined absence the plantations had suffered. He was also a poorer man, thanks largely to his quixotic military adventures, and he worked desperately hard, as soon as his health permitted, at making Mount Vernon, its slaves, its tobacco and its wheat, into a profitable investment.

By now, as a mature and much-respected Virginian of twenty-six, he was about to enter the fields of politics and matrimony. He announced his intention of severing his connexion with the militia, and it is here that we have a first indication of how valued he had been as commander and loved as a man. His officers implored him to stay. They wrote, "Our unhappy country will receive a loss, not less irreparable, than ourselves. Where will it meet a man so experienced in military affairs? One so renowned for patriotism, courage and conduct? In you we place the most implicit confidence. Your presence only will cause a steady firmness and vigour to actuate in every breast, despising the greatest dangers, and thinking light of toils and hardships, while led on by the man we know and love."

An odd bit of rhetoric—and there is no doubt of its sincerity.

But Washington said goodbye—or so he thought—to soldiering, and in January, 1759, married the prosperous young widow to whom he had long been engaged, Martha Dandridge Custis. She had two children by her first marriage (there would be no issue of this one) and George settled cheerfully down to being a good stepfather and—with the addition of Martha's considerable property —a very large landowner. He was richer than he had ever been and he and Martha began to entertain lavishly—for no better reason than that they both enjoyed doing so. Soon they had come in contact with most of the notable men from the English colonies in America.

We can picture him, sitting red-faced and smiling (despite the evidence of the lamentable, scowling, portraits that were done of him), at the head of a table gleaming in candlelight, listening with patience to a long anecdote by a distinguished guest. The guest would be working hard at his role—for it was an honour to be invited to a meal at Mount Vernon. The staid and genial host, hero of four campaigns, retired Commander-in-Chief, lacked but a fortnight to his twenty-seventh birthday.

And yet, sixteen years after this retirement, George Washington was General Washington, military leader of all thirteen American colonies. Slowly, inexorably, while he managed his estates, the tide of resentment against British control had been mounting in every colony. The process had been helped by the British defeat of the French in 1763, which drove France from North America and removed any need for British protection, but it was the result, in the main, of taxation which, though not heavy, was unexplained, and a generally heavy-handed treatment from London which made the colonists feel they were not part of Britain but some outlandish possession to be exploited.

The Stamp Act was passed, but repealed, and Washington himself was to write to England that those responsible for its repeal were "entitled to the thanks of every British subject and have mine cordially". But there was more taxation to come. All of it, in response to further outcry, was removed, save for that on tea, resulting in the famous Boston Tea Party, at which colonists dressed themselves up as Indians (nobody quite knew why) in order to throw a newly-arrived cargo of tea into the harbour, rather than pay tax on it. Tempers rose steadily, and on 15 June, 1775, the Continental Congress, meeting in Philadelphia, picked Washington to be General Commanding "all the continental forces raised for the defence of American liberty". There were many excellent reasons for the choice: he was a proved and brilliant soldier, a rich and cultivated man ("so that he may rather communicate lustre to his dignities than receive it"), and he was a Virginian. With the conflict between mother country and colonies so far confined to New England, a commander from outside New England was essential if all thirteen colonies were to be brought in.

Washington accepted, on the condition that he drew no salary, only his expenses. He was forty-three.

His first discovery was that his army was short—desperately short —of uniforms, food, blankets and ammunition, and that scoundrels all over the thirteen colonies were growing fat through holding back these supplies. His first months were spent combating graft and even treachery, making an army out of a largely rebellious (against its officers as much as against the English oppressor) rabble.

His first success came in March of the following year when he captured Boston from what were still known as "Ministerial" troops. But soon men's minds were made up: on the fourth of July the famous Declaration of Independence was signed.

Washington now suffered a series of reverses. Enemy reinforcements began to pour in from England, he was up against treachery of all sorts, from that of subordinate officers like the notorious Benedict Arnold to quarrelling factions in Congress. He handled the latter skilfully, keeping that jealous and mutually suspicious assembly briefed about his every move. He was badly defeated at the Battle of Brooklyn Heights, but went on to thrash his enemy at Trenton and again at Princeton. Two more defeats, at Brandywine and Germantown, and he took his army into winter quarters at Valley Forge, near Philadelphia. It was during this bitter winter of 1777-78, while his forces suffered horribly from exposure and a shortage of every sort of clothing and equipment, that he learnt the French were entering the war on his side.

From now on, though there was much hard fighting ahead, the outcome was clear. Yet it was not until 1781 that the British under General Cornwallis surrendered at Yorktown, their retreat cut off by the French fleet, under Admiral De Grasse.

The war over, a new republic in being, Washington resigned his post as Commander-in-Chief and went back to his plantations. He had been a superb soldier if not a perfect general. As a Virginia gentleman, a slave-owner (though a reasonably enlightened one, who made provision for them all to be freed on his wife's death), he was to most of his subordinates a stern, almost a forbidding, creature—and this has been caught in most of the surviving portraits. It is the face of a man who refuses to suffer fools gladly which glares at us from the five-cent stamp. But in 1781 Washington was a tired man, anxious to be allowed to stay on his property and try to recoup his failing fortunes. He achieved a few years of this, got his plantations working profitably once more, and then was elected, in February, 1789, first President of the United States of America. His sense of duty made him accept, and at the end of April he was inaugurated, in New York.

He did not enjoy his first four years in office. The members of his Government, though they respected him, were a quarrelsome lot, with widely differing ideas about what was best for the country and for their own individual states. He was reluctant to run for office a second time, but was persuaded to do so, was elected and this time inaugurated in Philadelphia. A few months later he laid the cornerstone of the Capitol building in the city of Washington.

He died 14 December, 1799, a fortnight before the end of the eighteenth century. Two years later his widow Martha died and the slaves were released.

No doubt there were others in the American colonies who would have made good Presidents—perhaps better. But somehow it was fitting that the tough, dignified, Virginia planter, who had proved himself in battle, should lead his country into peace.

LOUIS XVI
(1754–93)

LOUIS XVI was so overshadowed by the Revolution which destroyed him and his regime that his importance as a monarch has been perhaps overlooked. Even in the veneration accorded to royal martyrs, he is eclipsed by the tragedy of his glamorous consort, Marie Antoinette.

Louis XVI's true importance lies in the fact that the moderates, who, rather than the Jacobins, were the real makers of the French Revolution, wanted to build the new France around him. They wanted to isolate him from the courtiers of Versailles and make him into a constitutional monarch in the English style. Although the Revolution destroyed Louis, he was at first the centre of it, and he was not unsympathetic to its reasonable demands for elementary justice.

Though execrated by the Commune, Louis XVI was not in any way responsible for the conditions which led to the Revolution. The blame lies fairly and squarely with his two predecessors— Louis XIV, whose royal dictatorship undermined the ancient liberties and economic stability of his kingdom, and Louis XV, whose indolence and sloth took France to the edge of the abyss. Of the two, Louis XV—"the well-beloved"—is the most deserving of history's contempt.

Louis XVI was Louis XV's grandson. His father was the Dauphin of France and his mother was Marie Joseph of Saxony. He was born at Versailles on 23 August, 1754. When he was eleven his father died and he became heir to the throne.

Little preparation was made to fit him for his destiny. He received a sketchy education, and all knowledge of state affairs was withheld from him by his insensate grandfather. In 1770 he married Marie Antoinette, daughter of Marie Theresa, Empress of Austria.

As dauphin, Louis cut a poor figure amidst the brilliant cavaliers of his grandfather's glittering court. He was shy, reserved and harsh of voice. He lacked the excessive courtesy and exquisite manners which ever since Louis XIV the French aristocracy had cherished as something which distinguished them from the common people.

Louis XVI possessed not a shadow of the kingly dignity and regal air of his grandfather, who in consequence despised him. He was pious and lived a simple life, his one pleasure being his devotion to the chase. When he took up the blacksmith's art as a hobby, it was the cause of much hilarity at court; it greatly annoyed Marie Antoinette and was the case of many stormy scenes between them. But while a king who could use his hands at a skilled artisan's trade did not commend itself to the fastidious court of Louis XV, it did not come amiss in the spirit which was arising in France just then.

Louis XV was well aware of the storm which was brewing, but firmly believed that the existing state of affairs would last his lifetime, and that the storm was destined to burst upon the head of his successor. He therefore was safe. Indolence and ease, and the enjoyment of the passing hour alone concerned him. "*Mais après nous le déluge*", he had long been accustomed to say. In his later years he would sometimes add with a cynical smile: "I would love to know how Berry will manage to weather the coming storm."

Berry was the contemptuous name he reserved for the graceless youth who was to succeed him. Louis XV never gave him the title of dauphin.

On 10 May, 1774, Louis XV's ignoble career was terminated by a virulent attack of smallpox. Already the lick-spittle courtiers were fawning over the young king and his consort as they received the news of the end of Louis Quinze in an apartment as remote as possible from the "well-beloved's" contaminated death-room.

When the courtly sycophants saluted them as king and queen, the boy of twenty and the girl of nineteen fell upon their knees and said, "Guide us, protect us, O God. We are too young to reign." The most immoral and sophisticated court in the world knew that a very different regime had begun at Versailles.

Two hours later everyone had fled from Versailles and the infected palace was a desert. Left behind were only two or three under-servants and some priests of the "inferior clergy" whose lives were sacrificed to the fatal duty assigned them of remaining to pray by the contagious body of their late lord and master and convey it with all speed and the utmost secrecy to the Abbey of St. Denis.

The new king and his consort and the younger members of the royal family retired to La Muette and with the exception of Marie Antoinette were immediately inoculated for the smallpox by the surgeon Jouberthou. Vaccination had not then been introduced generally, though its value had been long recognized by French and German physicians.

Louis XVI during his lifetime was described by those who knew him as being the most upright man in his kingdom. His chief defect was lack of firmness. He was diffident of his own powers and conscious of his lack of proper education. He allowed himself to be influenced too much by Marie Antoinette, who was strong-minded as well as frivolous.

Louis ascended the throne at a momentous crisis in the life of the nation. There was widespread disgust at the wasted and licentious reign of Louis XV. The administration groaned beneath a mountain of debts. Trade was ruined. The nobility and clergy clung tenaciously to their age-old exemptions from taxation. The time had arrived when the abuses of the ancient regime could no longer be tolerated, and sweeping reforms were demanded.

France was aflame with new ideas. Men like Voltaire, Rousseau and Montesquieu had questioned the political institutions and created the discontent in all classes of the community which led to the Revolution.

In all this Louis XVI was out of his depth. Though he was among the first to wish to repair the damage to the nation's fabric caused by the two previous Louis, he misjudged the magnitude of the problem and the temper of his people. He had no political sagacity.

Despite his shortcomings, Louis XVI was virtuous, well-intentioned and at times liberal-minded. In other circumstances he might well have been a successful and progressive king, for all his weakness and vacillations. At all times his thoughts were for his people. This was a new departure for the Bourbons, who had always been distinguished by their selfishness and egotism.

The first thing Louis did was to summon Turgot, the economist, and one of the few honest statesmen of his day, and make him Comptroller-General. Turgot demanded the most stringent economies, particularly in the royal household, and wanted to reform the whole system of taxation.

There was no sign of economy at Louis's lavish and splendid coronation in Rheims Cathedral in June, 1775. A new crown was made costing nearly a million pounds. A luxurious new state coach was built. The impoverished treasury was recklessly plundered to provide for these and other extravagant items of expenditure.

Turgot's demands encountered the most bitter opposition from those closest to the king. Enormous sums were spent to maintain the luxuries at Versailles. The king's relatives, though they had all been well endowed by Louis XV, who had left a fortune of thirty-five million francs, were dissatisfied with their annuities and were demanding more money from the state to gratify their extravagances. Queen Marie Antoinette spent money like water.

Reforming the taxation system would have meant the privileged classes paying taxes—an unheard of thing. Turgot had no chance of putting such a revolutionary reform through against the pressures which were put upon Louis by those around him who wished to keep things as they were. Turgot's suggestions were too radical and he was dismissed in 1776.

He was succeeded by Necker, who valiantly grappled with the impossible task of keeping the leaky vessel of the old French monarchy afloat. Already France, as the ally of the United States, was involved in war against England and had sent troops to America. Not only had vast sums to be borrowed to prosecute the war, but the troops returned to France infected with the heady spirit of republicanism which was sweeping the United States. Turgot had warned Louis against this danger, in vain.

The American war helped to produce the financial crisis which was the immediate cause of the Revolution. Necker was popular at first at Versailles, for he did not discourage public expenditure. In 1781, however, he lost his popularity in that quarter when he published his famous *Compte rendu* in which he drew up a balance sheet of France, showing for the first time how much the *taille* (the heaviest tax from which the privileged classes were exempt) and the hated salt tax actually took from the people, and also how much the king spent on himself and his favourites. After that Necker was dismissed at the insistence of Marie Antoinette.

In 1789 the monarchy, and indeed the country, was bankrupt. Ministers had not enough funds to meet the regular expenses of the government. Louis then called the States-General, a national assembly of clergy, nobility and commons whose function was to advise the king, and which had not met since 1614.

Louis presided at the first meeting of this ancient body on 5 May and received a warm reception. He made a brief, formal speech. But when the assembly heard that the Third Estate, the commons, was to have no say in the conduct of the nation's affairs, its mood changed.

This marked the beginning of the Revolution. The Third Estate, finding themselves excluded from the assembly, held their own meeting in a building called the Tennis Court, and took the famous Tennis Court oath not to dissolve themselves until a new constitution had been made. Refusing to disperse, it called itself the French National Assembly. Louis, not so much alarmed as influenced by his courtiers and Marie Antoinette, brought two regiments to Versailles.

Stirred up by the Tennis Court oath and the king's counter-move, and urged on by orators and agitators, the Paris mob stormed the Bastille on 14 July, 1789. "Is this a revolt then?" asked Louis when he received the news at Versailles. "No, sire," replied the duc de Liancourt. "It is a revolution."

But Louis did not agree, and saw no cause for alarm. Other members of the privileged classes took a different view. It was then that the apprehensive aristocrats started to leave France. In the next two months twenty thousand passports were issued. They were under no illusion that the days of privilege were numbered, though none guessed the violence and intensity of the upheaval which was to come.

After the fall of the Bastille, Louis's advisers urged that the royal family should go to Metz or some other frontier fortress, escorted by a strong body of troops. Marie Antoinette was strongly in favour of this, but Louis for once would not be influenced by her. He flatly refused to leave Versailles.

Louis could not be convinced that his people would do him harm, and he was not really deluded in this. He was in fact extremely popular with the people, and he knew it. The deputies of the National Assembly, who included such statesmen as Mirabeau and Necker, wanted to build the new France around him. There was no question of a republic in the minds of responsible men in 1789.

At this moment Louis had a great opportunity to make himself a constitutional monarch, and to his credit he strove his best, within the limits of his restricted intellectual powers and the handicap of his unfortunate Bourbon background. Even without vision, but with just a little more will-power, with better advisers and a different wife, Louis XVI might have done what he desperately wanted to do —save France from bankruptcy and ruin. In order to do this he was quite prepared to become a constitutional monarch on the English style. It did not cross his mind then that the monarchy itself was in danger.

Mirabeau was pleading for a strong executive backed by a limited monarchy, and if Louis had been a man of decision this might have come about. But Louis was easy-going and good-natured. His weakness was misinterpreted as duplicity. This, combined with Mirabeau's untimely death in 1791, resulted in the destruction of the French monarchy, the Reign of Terror and the subsequent Napoleonic wars.

While the National Assembly drew up the new constitution

which abolished the *ancien régime* and issued its famous Declaration of the Rights of Man, France slipped deeper into economic distress and semi-anarchy.

Louis's hesitations and indiscretions began to try the patience of his people. He hesitated to ratify the Declaration of the Rights of Man, and the story of a dinner given by the Guardes du Corps to the Flanders Regiment at Versailles greatly angered the leaders of the National Assembly. Both Louis and Marie Antoinette were at this famous dinner, during which impassioned royalist toasts were drunk by the alcoholic grenadiers. The tricolour was trodden underfoot and the song of Blondel when seeking his captive king, Coeur de Lion, was sung. They vowed to die for Louis if he were in danger.

This highly inflammatory banquet caused great offence in Paris, though its true significance was probably exaggerated. It was rumoured that under the influence of his courtiers Louis was calling together troops loyal to him in an attempt to put an end to the Revolution.

On 5 October, 1789, the Paris mob marched to Versailles and compelled the king and the royal family to return with them to Paris. There was no antagonism shown to them. Louis was in fact at this time at the height of his popularity. The people believed that if he was in Paris away from the malign influence of the Versailles court all would be well. Louis took up residence at the Palace of the Tuileries, practically a prisoner, as it turned out.

The National Assembly, which had been holding its meetings at Versailles, followed the king to Paris, and it was the first great misfortune of the Revolution, for it placed both the king and the government at the mercy of the disorderly elements in Paris. But, although radicalism was running high in the Paris clubs, there was widespread loyalty to the king.

On 14 July, 1790, at the Festival of the Federation, Louis swore to maintain the constitution. But the high hopes and emotions of the festival did not last long. It was obvious even to Louis now that the clouds were dark in the sky. The voice of the Jacobins was being heard more insistently in the Assembly. It was in the September of 1790 that he began to think of the fate of Charles I of England, and to entertain fears that he himself might meet a similar end.

The aristocrats and nobles were fleeing in droves from France in the wake of the king's unpopular brother, the Comte d'Artois. The flight of his relatives and friends naturally reflected ill upon the king. Louis had long been urged to escape himself, but had always refused.

The flight to Varennes on 21 June, 1793, was one of his worst blunders. He may have decided to make it because the death of Mirabeau in April robbed France of the greatest statesman of the Revolution, the one man who could have reconciled the new France with the ancient monarchy. Mirabeau's death was a grievous blow to both Louis and France. The royal family's flight was too conspicuous an event to escape the notice of the countryside, and Louis ensured being recognized by continually poking the best-known head in France out of the carriage window.

Nevertheless the flight did not entirely turn the nation against him. Arrested at Varennes, he was maintained as a constitutional king after the melancholy return to Paris.

Louis's flight seems to have frightened, rather than angered, his people. Their grief at the thought of losing such an indifferent ruler clearly shows that France was still profoundly royalist. The National Assembly indeed held that he had not fled, but been carried off.

But republicanism was now a force to be reckoned with. The extremists' demand to do away with the monarchy was insistent. Many openly blamed Louis. "If this country ceases to be a monarchy," wrote Lord Gower, British Ambassador in Paris, "it will be entirely the fault of Louis XVI. Blunder upon blunder, inconsequence upon inconsequence, a total want of energy of mind, accompanied with personal cowardice, have been the destruction of his reign". Gower was hard on Louis, who was in a terrible situation after the death of Mirabeau and stood quite alone. Whatever might be said of his incompetence, he was certainly not guilty of personal cowardice, as he amply proved in 1793.

The National Assembly used the pro-Bourbon plottings in Austria as an excuse to go to war with that country in April, 1792. Louis was against the war and the unpopularity of his Austrian wife rubbed off on to him. In June a mob invaded the Tuileries and would have killed Louis if he had not consented to don the "cap of liberty", the badge of the "citizen patriots".

Louis knew now that the end was not far off. The extremists of the Commune had dominated the Assembly, which became the Convention. Its first act was to abolish the monarchy and proclaim France a republic. This was on 21 September.

The fate of the royal family was now in little doubt. A large party in the Convention held that Louis was guilty of treason in secretly encouraging foreign powers to come to his aid. They brought him to trial in January, 1793, and by a small majority condemned him to death. Already the royal family were imprisoned in the Temple in circumstances of increasing privation.

On the bitterly cold morning of 21 January, 1793, Louis went to his death on the scaffold. They drove him to the guillotine in a carriage, unlike the hated Marie Antoinette, who went in the common tumbril on 16 October of that same year. The troops were out in force—National Guards and brigades of field-pieces as well as a strong military escort for the condemned monarch's carriage.

Louis was accompanied by an Irish priest, the Abbé Edgeworth, and at the guillotine he disconcerted the executioners by his proud bearing and fearlessness. On the scaffold he cried out in a loud voice: "I die innocent of all the crimes with which I am charged. I forgive those who are guilty of my death, and I pray God that the blood which you are about to shed may never be required of France."

The knife fell and the cries of thousands of voices rent the air as the king died. People dipped their fingers into the royal blood, and one tasted it, saying, "It is vilely salty". There was no mourning in Paris that day. The theatres were full and much wine was drunk. The body was taken to the cemetery of the Madeleine and covered with quicklime.

Ten days later France declared war on England, which a century and a half before had set them the example by cutting off the head of Charles I.

NAPOLEON I

(1769–1821)

BY THE beginning of October, 1795 (*Vendémiaire* in the calendar of the French Revolution), some forty thousand armed National Guards, men of the middle classes and most of them Royalists, were confident of being able to overthrow the Convention and the weak, moderate government which, in 1794, had ended the Terror and sent the great Robespierre to the guillotine. The government was in a panic. The most resolute member of the Directorate, by name Barras, was doubtful about his generals, some of whom were unreliable, others incompetent. On the night of 4 October Barras appointed a soldier, then aged thirty-six, to take command of the forces defending the government. This was a Corsican, Napoleon Bonaparte, a brigadier thanks to some services at Toulon to the Republic, but out of employment and indeed having been obliged, recently, to sell his books and his watch to live. Generals at that time were two-a-penny.

At midnight, General Bonaparte had a large quantity of cannon dragged at the gallop into the centre of Paris. When, early in the morning of 5 October, the National Guards and a great mob marched down the Rue de Rivoli and adjoining streets in the centre of Paris, they were met with unexpected, sustained, well-directed fire from muskets and cannon. Three hundred were killed in a few minutes, numbers of dead and wounded lying sprawled on the steps of the Church of San Rocque in the Rue St. Honoré, the headquarters of the revolt. The "whiff of grape shot" had killed the Royalist reaction once and for all. It had shown that cannons speak louder than words and, in not very short a time, it had also killed the First Republic. Napoleon was made a full general, and shortly afterwards Commander-in-Chief of the army in Italy. He was set firmly on the road which was to make him Emperor in 1804, the master of Europe after Austerlitz and Jena, and finally to lead him to Waterloo in 1815 at the age of forty-six.

Napoleon's family, of Italian descent, had taken the side of France when Louis XVI had annexed Corsica in 1768, the year before Napoleon was born. Napoleon, the second son of Charles de

Bonaparte and Letizia Ramalino, a woman of exceptionally firm character, was educated at a French military school. In 1789, when the Revolution began, he was a second lieutenant in the royal army. He took the oath to the Republic in 1792, and was sent to Corsica, where he unsuccessfully tried to capture Sardinia. He remained in Corsica rather longer than he was entitled to, trying to overcome the resistance of the largest faction of the Corsicans to the Terror and the Revolution.

It is interesting that at this time Napoleon showed much greater interest in the affairs of his native island than in the battles the French Revolution was fighting throughout Europe. Rather accidentally, this young man had taken part, and a very prominent part, in the recapture of Toulon from the Royalists who were supported by English and Spanish warships. Napoleon then served in Italy where he somewhat annoyed his superiors by his self-confidence. From his exploits at Toulon he had won the esteem of Robespierre's brother, a political commissar, and of other Jacobin politicians. Consequently he was not in good odour with the now ruling moderate party.

His family had been forced to flee from Corsica which had risen against the Revolution and they were living in poverty in Marseilles, his mother and sisters obliged, at some period, to take in washing. Napoleon supported them as best he could. But in Paris, out of work himself, he could not do much. His clothes were threadbare. He looked a down-at-heels adventurer in the post-Robespierrian society which was rapidly becoming elegant. Nevertheless there was something about this short young man with his Roman profile and his burning glance and his ability to argue briefly and logically which impressed both men and women. He worked sometimes in the map department of the Ministry of War, and just before the event of *Vendémiare* he was about to take service with the Sultan of Turkey.

Shortly before he left to take his command in Italy, Napoleon married a beautiful *créole*, Josephine de Beauharnais, the widow of a general who had, since her husband's death, been forced to live on her charms. Napoleon was sincerely in love and he considered too that marriage to a woman who, even if doubtfully, belonged to the upper crust of society, advanced his fortunes.

In his Italian campaign Napoleon became the most popular of French generals and Josephine was called by the Parisiennes "Our Lady of Victories". Napoleon not only won victories, such as that of Arcole and Lodi, but he also won the hearts of most of the north-Italian population for the cause of the French Republic; he also sent a great deal of money and other spoils back to the Directory.

Realizing that, with the defeat of Austria, England was now the most serious enemy, Napoleon persuaded the Directory to mount an expedition against Egypt and the Near East to strike against England's trade and her hold on India. His fleet was destroyed at Aboukir Bay by Nelson and this expedition was largely a failure, in spite of some brilliant achievements. Napoleon abandoned his army in Palestine and returned to Paris. But this failure added to his glory, for the French imagination was excited by the spectacle of a French general reading the Bible to his officers in Nazareth, riding through the streets of Jerusalem, and standing gazing at the Pyramids of Gizeh. What did he think of the Sphinx? he was asked. "It is sad, like all greatness," Napoleon replied.

During Napoleon's absence in Egypt, the Austrians and Russians had won back northern Italy. The politicians had no hold on the imagination of the people, this young general realized, and, in November, 1799, by a *coup d'état* in which he was greatly aided by his brother Lucien, Napoleon became First Consul. The Revolution continued but under a Roman guise. Later, after a plebiscite, he became First Consul for life. He recovered Italy at the important but rather lucky victory at Marengo in 1800, whilst his generals were successful in Germany. The Austrians were completely defeated and forced to sign a humiliating treaty. Napoleon now sought peace. Britain was unbeatable on the sea, and in 1801 Nelson had destroyed the Danish fleet at Copenhagen in case it should fall into French hands. But France was everywhere victorious on land and surrounded by client republics in the Low Countries, Switzerland and Italy.

By 1804 Napoleon was determined to establish his rule on a permanent hereditary basis. On 2 December, 1804, he had himself crowned Emperor of the French, taking the Crown from the hands of Pope Pius VII who had been cajoled into coming to Paris, and placing it on his own head. He swore an oath to protect liberty, equality, the rights of property and the integrity of the Republic's territory. Beethoven, who had dedicated the Eroica Symphony to Napoleon, Hero of the French Revolution, annulled the dedication when he heard that Napoleon had been crowned.

Napoleon, after a fashion, conserved the Revolution, taking away from it some of its aspirations together with its incoherence. The French people, he said, were not interested in liberty, only in equality. He took care to dissociate himself from any suspicion of attempting a restoration of the *ancien régime*, and his abduction and murder of the Duc d'Enghien, a Royalist Pretender, was intended to show that Napoleon meant to figure in history as the heir of the Revolution.

Napoleon's fame is lasting not only because of his military genius. During the comparatively few years of the First Consulate he left his mark on France as an administrative genius. One of the first tasks he carried out was to reconcile France with the Church. Napoleon had no prejudices in favour of religion and many of his generals and closest supporters were partisans of an anti-religious State. So were many French intellectuals. When the great astronomer Laplace was explaining to Napoleon his work, the latter said: "But Monsieur, I see no place for God in your work on the cosmos"; "Sire," was the reply, "I had no need of that hypothesis." The reply pleased Napoleon. But he knew that, for the vast mass of the French peasantry, God and the Church were powerful forces.

Napoleon wanted French unity. It was during the First Consulate that was established the division of France into Departments, each of which was governed by a Prefect, the system in use today. It is essentially an authoritarian method of administration, but one which, given the instability which French political life was to experience, has undoubtedly served France well. The Council of State, Napoleon's invention, was charged with the drawing up and codifying of French Law, which codes together are known as the *Code Napoléon*. As the English historian H. A. L. Fisher has pointed out, it was the greatest of his achievements in his greatest period—before, as emperor, he became involved in perpetual war. Fisher writes:

> *The merit of the civil code is not that it is exhaustive, or that it has prevented the growth of case law, or that it is flawless in form and substance; but that in firm intelligible outline, it fixes the structure of a civilized lay society, based on social equality and religious toleration, on private property and coherent family life. The moment was opportune. A few years earlier, the Code would have glittered with revolutionary extravagances, a few years later it might have been darkened by the shades of despotism.*

It was during the Empire that Napoleon completed the great reorganization of French education, from the University to the Lycée, which has also survived until today, and founded the great post-graduate schools such as the Ecole Normale. Napoleon, mainly during the First Consulate, bequeathed to France and to the rest of the world what Professor Cobban (*A Modern History of France*, Vol. II) has described as the most effective system of bureaucratic control that the Western world has known since the Roman Empire.

> *It was not a framework for the kind of society that the idealistic liberals of 1789 had imagined themselves to be inaugurating, nor should we treat the Napoleonic system as the mere logical sequel to the* ancien régime *and*

the Revolution and Napoleon simply as the heir of Louis XIV and the Committee of Public Safety. This is to underestimate the scope of his achievement. The Great Monarch did not leave an imprint on French institutions that could be compared with the heritage of the Emperor. His immediate successors might repudiate his work, they could not undo it; and the Napoleonic State was long to outlive its author and the ends to which he had directed it.

"A throne is merely a plank covered in velvet," said Napoleon, and to his intimates he explained that he conferred titles on his supporters and held a court because one can ensure loyalty through absurdities more surely than through reason. If Napoleon was obviously not a true child of the Revolution, he was not a reactionary either. He was in truth an adventurer and his outlook belonged to the eighteenth century rather than to the nineteenth. His hero was Frederick the Great of Prussia. Unlike idealists who often neglect their families for their cause, Napoleon's triumph was that of his family in the largest sense of the word, almost, in fact, of his clan which included many of his generals. He was to make his brothers and sisters kings, queens, princes or princesses, a dynastic family in fact. They were, all of them, to cause the emperor some headaches, particularly the youngest sister Pauline with her love affairs, who was the most emotionally attached to him. He bore with them with remarkable patience. He thought his family was exceptionally gifted, all of them.

Until 1804 Napoleon can be seen to have carved his way to power by the exercise of will and his great gifts. After 1804, when war began again with England, and then with the rest of Europe, he was to win his greatest, most astounding victories, but he was also to be the victim not only of his own ambition but even more of the expansionist tendencies which had found expression in the French Revolution.

In this short essay it is impossible to do more than outline the career of Napoleon after war began in 1804. He decided to invade England, but when his admirals failed to get command of the Channel, he broke up his great camp at Boulogne. Austria had, with British subsidies and encouraged by the new Czar Alexander of Russia, begun war again. In 1805 he defeated the Austrians at Ulm, then the Austrians and Russians together at the greatest of all his victories in December at Austerlitz. He annihilated the Prussians at Jena and defeated the Russians again in 1807 at Friedland and Eylau. In 1808 Napoleon and Alexander met on a raft at Tilsit and divided up Europe. A German kingdom was made for Napoleon's brother Jerome; another brother, Louis, became King of Holland.

On the day he won the battle of Ulm, Napoleon had learnt that Nelson had destroyed the French and Spanish fleets at Trafalgar. It was to bring England to her knees that Napoleon started his continental blockade, closing the ports of Europe from the Mediterranean to Archangel to British commerce. To enforce the blockade he had to be master of all Europe, and, for this, war, constant war, was to be his lot. He made his brother Joseph King of Spain, switching him from his kingdom of Naples, where Marshal Murat, the husband of one of Napoleon's sisters, took his place.

The French never mastered Spain completely and, gradually, Sir Arthur Wellesley, later Duke of Wellington, and an English army transformed the sore place made by the Spanish guerrillas into an open wound. These ignorant Spaniards had not heard of Napoleon's great victories. Austria went to war again in 1809 and was defeated with some difficulty at Wagram in July, 1809. Marriage—Josephine was repudiated—to the Emperor of Austria's daughter did not admit Napoleon to the circle of respectable monarchs. Marie-Louise bore him an heir, the King of Rome, and this was some consolation. But now the Dutch insisted on trading with England and King Louis had to be removed and Holland made into a part of France. Finally, smouldering differences with Czar Alexander could not be settled, Russia began to open her ports to British ships. In 1812 Napoleon invaded Russia, won the battle of Borodino, took Moscow, which the Russians set fire to. The *Grande Armée* had to retreat from Moscow. After some successful fighting against the Austrians in Germany and after unwisely rejecting a chance of peace, Napoleon was defeated at Leipzig by an army three times the size of his. In 1813-14 he was fighting in France, his armies depleted in men and munitions. Yet though he defeated the Prussians and Austrians, his great skill was of no avail against the big battalions. Marie-Louise deserted him and fled to Vienna. He abdicated.

He was treated with leniency and given the Principality of Elba, a small island off the coast of Italy. Then, in March, 1815, Napoleon with a few hundred men landed in France. By 20 March he was sleeping in the Tuileries, the Bourbons having fled to Belgium. It would be untrue to say that the French nation fervently welcomed him back. But his return was welcomed by those in whom the spirit of the Revolution lived, mainly the common people, and by the army which could only respond to his call and throw away the lilies of the Monarchy for the Tricolor, the emblem of victory.

Napoleon decided, after trying to make peace with the Allies, to take the offensive against the British and Prussian armies concentrated in and around Brussels. On 18 June, 1815, was fought the battle of Waterloo. Napoleon was exiled to St. Helena in the charge of his principal foe, Britain, to whom he had deliberately surrendered. He was shabbily treated in many ways.

Until his coronation in 1804 and the beginning of the last great struggle which was to rumble in 1815, Napoleon had made no mistakes. He was that rare thing—an adventurer who remained constantly a realist. As a young man, at odds with fortune, he was never carried away by romantic or idealistic notions. He observed, studied, asked questions and then acted. All men were, as men of action, his inferiors. He observed things—the fortifications of a town, the geography of a battlefield, the defects and virtues of an administrative system—with complete concentration, mastering every detail with exceptional speed and complete accuracy. He studied men in the same way.

He was devoid neither of imagination nor of human feelings, though both were somewhat limited—the imagination a little too military, the human feelings limited too, tender sometimes, but also coarse and cynical. Of humanity in the Christian sense he had not much. But he in no way resembled many dictators in their contempt for human life, even though he did once say that he could afford to spend a hundred thousand Frenchmen a year. His career, after the empire, witnessed his most astounding victories, his masterpieces on the human stage. But, at this period, circumstances dictated to him. He was obliged to follow the path which his ambition, but not his reason, dictated and to aspire to the domination of Europe.

He is rightly called the Man of Destiny and destiny meant the retreat from Moscow and finally Waterloo. But unlike other dictators who have tried in vain to impose their wills on the world, his crimes never made him into a figure the world grew to hate. His career for all the suffering it caused was unsullied by the cruelty and by the fanaticism of other aspirants to world rule. His over-weening ambition can be seen as in large part the consequence of the explosive force of the French Revolution. So Napoleon is remembered as a man in whom were united to a superlative degree all the qualities which make up a great man of action. He is remembered as a second Alexander the Great rather than as a descendant of Attila or as an ancestor of Hitler.

ABRAHAM LINCOLN
(1809–65)

UNTIL 1937 American Presidents-elect, chosen in November, had to wait four weary, nerve-racking months for their Inauguration, for the day in March when they actually took office from their predecessors. Since 1937, when Franklin Roosevelt's inauguration for a second term was brought forward by two months, they have been more mercifully treated, take office in January.

But for Abraham Lincoln the months from November, 1860, to March of the following year were agonizing. Slowly the stage was being set for civil war: he had to stand by, impotently watching while President Buchanan's administration grew daily more futile, as the slave-owning states of the South toyed with, then decided on, a "Confederacy", prepared to secede from the Union. There was madness in the air, with the United States split into two camps moving inexorably to war; misunderstanding and pig-headed obstinacy on both sides—and no one to give an intelligent lead to public opinion.

Lincoln could have. Lincoln might have averted the most cruel war in American history. But Lincoln was a President-elect—and nothing in the American political hierarchy is lower, feebler, more ignored. Lincoln was forced to stand by while President Buchanan, pompous, desperately unsure of himself, did nothing. Right after the Presidential election, South Carolina decided to secede; within little more than a month she had been joined by Texas, Louisiana, Georgia, Alabama, Florida and Mississippi. By February of 1861, with four weeks to run before Lincoln could take office, they had formed the "Confederate States of America", named Jefferson Davis as their President.

What were the issues which brought this tragedy about?

Slavery, and its impact on men's minds. But to say that Lincoln led the North in a war to abolish slavery is a wild over-simplification. He abhorred the institution—but what mattered to Lincoln, above all else, was the preservation of the Union. That in order to preserve it he abolished slavery is from our vantage point of a hundred years' wisdom after the event, almost irrelevant. Slavery had been waning over the years; if the United States itself had not suddenly begun to double and redouble itself in size, the problem would never have reached major proportions. That wise statesman Henry Clay, the Whig on whom Lincoln in so many ways modelled himself, had forced a compromise bill through the House of Representatives in 1820 (when Lincoln was a backwoods boy of eleven) which sought to solve the problem. His bill stated that no new slave states would be allowed north of latitude 36° 30'—or north of the southern boundary of Missouri—and had the United States remained the size it had been when he tabled that bill all would have been well. There was little agitation to introduce slavery in the new states to the north and west of Missouri: those to the south and west were welcome to the institution if they preferred it. In time, Clay knew, it would die, within these confines.

But the rush westward continued, and twenty-five years after the "Missouri Compromise" there were states hundreds of miles farther west than Clay had envisaged: states like Texas clamouring to join the Union—and with slavery. And there were plenty of supporters of their cause in the existing slave states. Complicated bills, amendments, provisos, were thought out in Washington, in an effort to restrict the spread of slavery and at the same time satisfy the sentiments of the South. Tempers, over the years, rose higher. The South believed—absolutely—that slaves were better treated, better fed, housed and guarded from sin, than many of the so-called free men of the North. The North believed, with every bit as much conviction, that slavery was a sin. Voices grew louder, hatred mounted, fear spread. Men in the South began to feel they had actually been invaded, that they were already at war: those in the North convinced themselves the South was—to quote even the level-headed Emerson—"a barbarous community". Both sides expected bloodshed.

This was the scene when Lincoln was elected for his first term. Extremist politicians in the South had warned voters that a victory by his—Republican—Party would mean the plundering of their land for Yankee benefit, and the end of slavery. The South had grown angry, restless, hysterical. It was not the question of economic loss if slaves were freed—after all, not many white people owned them: it was the spectre of black savages claiming equal rights with white men, ousting them from their jobs, outvoting them. Slavery gave the poorest white a status: the black man was always below him.

In his Inaugural Address—when at last the moment came to give

538

it, in March, 1861—Lincon spoke to the South: "In your hands, my dissatisfied fellow-countrymen, is the momentous issue of civil war. The government will not assail you. You can have no conflict without being yourselves the aggressors. . . ."

But on 12 April Confederate batteries opened fire on Fort Sumter, in Charleston Harbour, and two days later its garrison surrendered. Lincoln now had no choice. He called for 75,000 volunteers—while Jefferson Davis, President of the Confederacy, demanded 100,000 to oppose them.

The war grew, went stubbornly on. A few weeks after his mobilization of the 75,000, Lincoln called up another 65,000 soldiers and 18,000 seamen and began a blockade of southern ports. His determination, now his hand had been forced, was to make the hateful war "short, sharp and decisive". As Commander-in-Chief of the Union forces he had to make many military decisions, to goad his generals to the utmost. Only one of these, Ulysses S. Grant, seemed to have any ability—and when it was objected that Grant was a heavy whisky drinker, Lincoln retorted that he wished he could give some of the same beverage to his other generals and make them fight. But there were other, perhaps more important, decisions for a President to make, and all of these Lincoln made with wisdom, understanding and, above all, compassion.

It has been shown, more than once, that the United States gets the man it deserves, at the moment he is needed, and Lincoln is the supreme example. At the same time as he was prosecuting the war he was pushing a bill through Congress offering pecuniary aid from the Government to persuade states to adopt gradual abolition of slavery. He was also overruling the edicts of commanders in the field who "abolished slavery" off their own bat, in the areas they over-ran: such hot-headed, hasty action would only prolong the war. He disapproved of slavery, he knew that in God's good time it would go, and good riddance, but, as he put it: "My paramount object is to save the Union, and not either to save or destroy slavery. If I could save the Union without freeing any slave, I would do it; if I could save it by freeing all the slaves, I would do it; and if I could do it by freeing some and leaving others alone, I would also do that." By pronouncements like this he was holding back violent and impractical reformers with one hand, gently urging forward conservatives with the other. At the same time he dealt with vexed problems of foreign policy, keeping the friendship of the Mexican people while not getting involved in hostilities against the French who "protected" that country; avoiding conflict with a Britain which, because of interdependence between Lancashire cotton mills and American plantations, tended to side with the Confederacy.

The war grew enormous. By 1863 the Union armies numbered almost a million men, a size they retained to the end—an end which came after four years of appalling bloodshed, on 9 April, 1865. The Confederate General Robert E. Lee surrendered his whole army on that date, immediately after evacuating the town of Richmond, Virginia. Lincoln, a regular visitor to his armies, had been with Sherman and entered Richmond the day after its surrender. He returned immediately to Washington and there, on 11 April, made his last public speech, urging the swift rebuilding of loyal governments in the conquered states.

It was Good Friday, 14 April, the sixth day of peace, that Lincoln, an exhausted man, conscious, as many of his cheering fellow-citizens were not, that there was much to be done before a worth-while peace was achieved, went with his wife and two young guests to the theatre. The sun had set, the clear bright evening had given way disappointingly to fog, and a chill had set in, as the Lincoln coach drew up outside Ford's Theatre, where Laura Keen was performing in *Our American Cousin*. It was half-past eight. They were late, but it had been understood they would be, there had been so much Presidential business to get through, so many people to see. The play stopped, the audience cheered, as the party entered the theatre and were led to their flag-draped box. Major Rathbone and Miss Harris, the two guests, were given front seats; Mrs. Lincoln sat a little behind them, and the President, exhausted, just able to smile, to wave at his ovation, slumped into a rocking chair at the back.

By the third act he had begun to enjoy the play: he was rested now, relaxed. He leant forward to see better.

A man entered the little corridor leading to the box, barred the door behind him, moved in behind the Presidential party.

A shot was heard, there was a scuffle in the box. The play stopped. Then a wild-eyed man, waving a huge knife (with which he had wounded Major Rathbone, who tried to stop him), leapt from the parapet of the box and crashed to the stage. People screamed. The man had damaged his ankle, he stood there for a moment rubbing it. Then he waved his fist, shouted something, and was gone.

The President had been shot, at point-blank range, through the back of the head; the bullet had penetrated the brain. There was little bleeding, and he was still alive. Tenderly, they carried him out of the theatre, across the road to the home of a small tailor, where he was laid on a bed. Doctors had been summoned, and they were soon there, giving stimulants, consulting each other, examining and adjusting the dressing on the wound—but everyone knew it was useless. Mrs. Lincoln sat in a front room, weeping, and members of the Cabinet came in, shook their heads in horror, and left.

At a few minutes after seven in the morning of 15 April, 1865, Abraham Lincoln died.

John Wilkes Booth, the half-demented actor who had selected himself to "avenge the Confederacy" in this way, a crank, starved of the success he was sure his looks, his voice, his athletic ability deserved, was run to earth and shot, twelve days later, in the barn where he was hiding.

Abraham Lincoln, whose life was snuffed out just six weeks after he had begun a second four-year term as President (elected by a huge majority: 212 electoral college votes against 21 for his Democratic opponent) and three weeks after his fifty-sixth birthday, had been born in Kentucky, of very poor parents, on 12 February, 1809. After several moves within the state they crossed the Ohio River to Indiana. The boy's father, Thomas, was shiftless and unsuccessful, working as the fancy took him, at carpentry and at farming, doing neither well, and all the family's clothes were made by Nancy Lincoln, his wife, from the skins of animals he shot—squirrels, racoons, deer, wolves. Wild turkeys abounded—as did enormous, vicious mosquitoes.

They lived for months in a "half-faced camp", a shelter of logs, enclosed on only three of its sides, with a fire constantly burning on the fourth, to keep warmth inside, animals out. For their first winter in their Indiana home the Lincoln family lived entirely on game, but they were gradually hacking out a clearing. At last Thomas laid claim, at the nearest government office, to some 100 acres, and paid the first instalment of 80 dollars, a quarter of the purchase price.

The following year disease struck both cattle and humans, and Mrs. Lincoln died. Young Abraham had loved her, but when Thomas went back to Kentucky in the winter of 1819, got himself another wife, the widow, Sarah Johnson, with three young children of her own, he and his sister fell yet more in love with her. She brought order out of the chaos and dirt of the Lincoln home, took the motherless children to her heart, saw to it that all five went to school.

The boy grew tall—to six feet four—and immensely strong. The community had grown with other settlers, and he was soon famous in it as an athlete and a clown, who could mimic preachers and the itinerant politicians of the state with a terrifying accuracy. At the same time he was a voracious reader.

When he was seventeen he got a job working a ferry across the Ohio; two years later, fascinated by the strange vessels he saw going up and down that mighty river, he left his job and contracted to take a cargo to New Orleans. It was a river journey on Ohio and Mississippi rivers of over a thousand miles. Here he made his first acquaintance with slavery, watching tired, patient, black men, loading and unloading cargoes of cotton, tobacco, sugar.

Shortly after his return the family moved again, to Illinois, where he got a job as store-keeper, then got involved in local politics. By 1832 he had decided to enter it properly, was canvassing the neighbourhood as candidate for the Illinois state legislature. He was heavily defeated. He took up law after having studied it in his spare time, but as both he and his partner were more interested in politics than the law that partnership failed. But in 1843, a year after the start of his not entirely happy marriage with the aristocratic Mary Todd, he entered into a successful legal partnership with William H. Herndon which lasted until his death.

In 1846 Mary, anxious to get out of Springfield, Illinois, drove him on to stand for election as Congressman, in Washington. He was elected—but unhappy with the chicanery and double-dealing of national politics, and when he was not re-elected he returned cheerfully to his Springfield law business. He became a familiar sight, dressed in black, wearing the high hat in which he crammed his legal documents—and famous as a brilliant speaker and an absolutely incorruptible man. He forgot about politics.

But in 1860 the new Republican Party nominated him, while he continued his law work in Springfield, as their "dark horse" candidate for the Presidency—a man not yet well-known enough, nationally, to have many enemies. He was—at last—persuaded to grow a beard and "get dignified", though he objected strongly to this bit of affectation. On 6 November, 1860, he was elected, and four months later he took over the thankless task of President.

When, a little over four years later, he was assassinated, the whole nation, North and South, mourned his death. Now that he had gone, men realized the greatness of this figure unique in American history. Without any formal education, he had made himself one of the finest orators of his time and perhaps its greatest statesman.

Ironically enough, his death healed many wounds, brought North and South nearer.

VICTORIA

(1819–1901)

ALEXANDRINA VICTORIA was born in 1819, four years after the battle of Waterloo. George III was still on the throne and Victoria's father, the Duke of Kent, was only the king's fourth son. But the children of Victoria's uncles all died and so, after the death of George IV and then of his brother, the Duke of Clarence, who succeeded him as William IV, Victoria succeeded to the throne.

Her father had died some time before and she had been brought up very strictly by her mother, a German princess of Saxe-Coburg-Gotha. Neither George IV nor his brothers were popular in England; they were either dissolute or lazy or stupid, and some were all three. They were disliked on the whole by the aristocracy and by the middle classes. The working classes, both the industrial workers and the insecure country labourers, were in a state of seething discontent. There was talk of bloody revolution. The coming to the throne of a young girl who, everyone knew, had been brought up by a mother who did not like the habits of the royal family, seemed to promise a new age. She was an attractive girl with her long fair hair, slightly protruding eyes and good figure.

The character of the new queen showed itself at once. Her first act was to remove herself from her mother's bedroom where she had always been obliged to sleep. Though a fond daughter, she saw to it that the now elderly and over-insistent Queen Mother was kept at a proper distance from the sovereign. During the Coronation Service in Westminster Abbey, a severe test of stamina for a fully-grown male monarch, the Bishop of Bath and Wells turned over two pages of the prayer book by mistake and brought the service to an end too soon. Informed of this by the sub-dean of Westminster, Victoria ordered the service to go back to where it had begun to go wrong. The procession before and after the Coronation was the finest ever staged in London. It was witnessed by thousands of foreigners as well as by the Londoners. The Turkish Ambassador was so amazed by the splendour of the display that he could scarcely walk to his place in the Abbey and kept murmuring: "All this for a woman."

Victoria, though she had a will of her own, was every inch a woman. This showed itself in the strong personal relations which, throughout her life, she was to make with some of her Ministers. From the first of these, Lord Melbourne, an intelligent rather cynical Whig, as the Liberals were then called, Victoria learned much about politics and life generally. She made her only political mistake in those early days by refusing to part with Lord Melbourne although the Tories had a majority in the House of Commons and Sir Robert Peel ought to have been Prime Minister. Not surprisingly the queen became unpopular in certain political quarters and was once hissed at Ascot and called "Mrs. Melbourne". There was not the slightest impropriety in this relationship. Lord Melbourne, who was devoted to the queen, invariably remained standing during the long sessions in which he informed his royal mistress about state affairs. Later, Queen Victoria transformed some part of her esteem and affection to Melbourne's successor, the Tory, Sir Robert Peel. Much later, her attachment to her Scottish servant John Brown, after the death of the Prince Consort, and the romantic relationship with Benjamin Disraeli, showed that throughout her life she was to remain very much a woman of feeling.

Two years after she came to the throne her betrothal to her German cousin, Prince Albert, with whom she had fallen in love almost at first sight before she was queen, was announced. At the time she first met Albert she wrote: "Albert's beauty is most striking and he is so amiable and unaffected—in short very fascinating." Whilst, with Lord Melbourne's aid and advice, she sought to ensure that her husband secured precedence in foreign countries, he was only given the title of Prince Consort in 1857. Victoria intended to reign as queen and not as the wife of a sovereign. Nor did she intend to be ordered about and, in spite of the prince's rather puritanical attitude to life, she continued to love balls which lasted after midnight and other jollities. But the prince's serious nature, his intelligent interest in politics, his practical cast of mind and organizing ability —combined with his good looks—quickly made him the real master. It was Albert who now explained state business to the queen, and though it was the queen who said yes or no, the decisions were really those of Albert.

Prince Albert worked very hard at being the power behind the throne. He concerned himself with the development of industry and with the encouragement of science and he was largely the creator of the international Great Exhibition in 1851, held in Hyde Park. His advice on political affairs, both internal and external, had to be listened to; often the prince's views had a positive affect on policy so great was the attention which he gave to the matters under discussion, so skilfully and with so much compelling and detailed argument were his memoranda drawn up. He worked himself so hard that his health suffered; he never relaxed and he grew bald rather early and constantly looked sallow and tired. In November, 1861, he caught what was wrongly diagnosed by the Royal Physician as influenza; it was in fact typhoid fever, and of this, combined with inflammation of the lungs, he died in December.

The marriage had been a great success for both, and for the queen a perfect fulfilment. Her love for Albert increased with her respect for him and then with her submission to his views and wishes. She lived with him the life she wished, homely and yet regal. They had nine children. They brought up their children to observe strictly all the middle-class virtues. They spent long holidays at Osborne, in the Isle of Wight, and at Balmoral in a medieval castle designed by Albert. The queen thrived. She grew stout, but with the plumpness of a vigorous matron full of vitality.

Albert's death was a terrible blow to her. She built the great mausoleum at Frogmore for him and, because it was so intimately connected with her life with him, she never again lived in Buckingham Palace for any length of time. Her true affection was accompanied by a sort of fetishism and, for the next forty years, Albert's clothes were laid out on a bed in what had been his suite at Windsor Castle, and each evening fresh water was poured into the wash basin. It was in deep mourning, two years later, that she witnessed the marriage of the Prince of Wales, later Edward VII, from a private pew at the St. George's Chapel at Windsor.

After Albert's death the queen, though attending as ever to state matters with regularity, withdrew from public life. "The Widow of Windsor" became unpopular and, since she spent little on public functions, the Civil List was attacked for being too large. But, gradually, her natural zest for living returned. Her friendship with Disraeli, who became Prime Minister first in 1868, was born of the latter's tributes to the Prince Consort's memory. Disraeli was a great flatterer; but he was also a genuine admirer of monarchy and also of this small vital woman with her strong emotions and strong prejudices. "Yours affly Victoria Regina et Imperatix," she signed her letters to him. Yet Disraeli treated his sovereign with the greatest deference at all times.

With Disraeli's great rival, Gladstone, Victoria did not get on so well. She used to complain that he would insist on addressing her as though she were a public meeting. She strongly disapproved of some of Gladstone's measures—in particular of the bill disestablishing the Church in Ireland—and made no secret of her opposition. But when the bill had passed through the House of Commons, the queen herself saw fit to write to the main opponent of the bill in the House of Lords, the Archbishop of Canterbury, urging him to accept it with certain concessions and not to delay its passage into law.

When in 1887 her reign of fifty years was celebrated by a Jubilee, she made many public appearances which included a review of the fleet at Spithead. She attended public performances of music and travelled abroad. In her later life she became the centre of a large international group, that of the related royal families of Europe. This, too, put her in the public eye and the public liked it. In 1897, when her Diamond Jubilee celebrated a reign of sixty years, the government of the day, of which Mr. Joseph Chamberlain was Secretary of the Colonies, made it a demonstration of the might of empire. Bonfires were lit on the hilltops throughout England, Wales and Scotland, and a huge procession, which included representatives from every territory in the empire—Dyaks from Borneo, Hausas from Nigeria, as well as Australians and Canadians—wound its way through the streets of London. The queen, whose age was seventy-eight, sat in her carriage for four hours and appeared none the worse for it.

The empire was indeed a fit theme for a great act of homage to the queen. When Queen Victoria came to the throne the empire was already far-flung; but it consisted mainly of a series of trading posts or small coastal settlements scattered throughout the world. The East India Company administered only a third of the Indian sub-continent, and Australia was still largely unexplored—was used as a place for sending convicts to. By the end of Victoria's reign she was Empress of India. New Zealand had been added to the Crown and so had South Africa and much of Central Africa, whilst Egypt and the Sudan were also coloured red on the maps. There had never been a larger empire in the history of the world. It was defended by the largest battle-fleet in the world which ensured the *Pax Britannica*, whilst British merchant ships carried by far the largest part of the world's commerce.

The changes in the United Kingdom were equally striking. England had been the workshop of the world even before Queen Victoria was born, and it was this which had enabled Britain almost alone to stand up to Napoleon. But it was still governed by the

land-owning classes who took little or no account of the workers
in the great dismal towns which were making England rich. The
average life of an industrial worker in those days was twenty-five,
whilst that of a middle-class person was fifty. The workers were
mainly voteless, and trade-unions were prohibited. By the end of
the reign the condition of the working classes still left much to be
desired, but there was a universal male franchise, a really representative Parliament, and votes for women were only some twenty years
away. A growing Labour Party existed. The public conscience about
exploitation and the direst forms of poverty had been aroused. "We
are all Liberals nowadays," said a Conservative Peer. There was
throughout the nation a feeling that the spread of education, coupled
with scientific progress, was leading to a Golden Age. A touching
illusion perhaps, but widely felt and not altogether unnatural in a
country in which science and industry had done so much and
worked so fast.

Britain was immensely wealthy. Through this long reign the
country had been involved in many wars, but they were mostly
minor ones and mainly colonial wars. There had been no major
upheaval and relatively the country had been at peace since 1815.
When Queen Victoria died in 1901, at the end of the Boer War,
the British felt that they were a race apart, the happy breed of
Englishmen.

When it is said that Queen Victoria was a "great queen" the
adjective "great" means something different from what it means
when applied to Queen Elizabeth I or to Henry II or to William
the Conqueror. As a ruler Queen Victoria had comparatively little
to do with the creation of the British Empire or with the other
main achievements of the Victorian era. She was intellectually a
very ordinary person and largely unaware of the great Victorian
achievements in literature and scholarship. Her taste in the arts was
deplorable; her personal influence was exerted in favour of what
would be considered today prudery and hypocrisy in public manners.
Yet these very limitations gave her a representative character, and
undoubtedly the Victorian public wanted the queen to embody an
ideal of perfect domestic behaviour to which they were themselves
striving. Victoria's domestic life, for example, was precisely what
the new middle-classes wanted. As Lytton Strachey has written:

*"They liked a love-match; they liked too a household which combined the
advantages of royalty and virtue, and in which they seemed to see reflected,
as in some resplendent looking-glass, the ideal image of the lives they lived
themselves. Their own existences, less exhalted, but so soothingly similar,*

acquired an added excellence, an added succulence, from the early hours, the regularity, the plain tuckers, the round games, the roast beef and yorkshire pudding of Osborne. It was indeed a model court. Not only with its central personages the patterns of propriety, but no breath of scandal, no shadow of indecorum, might approach its utmost boundaries."

It was because Queen Victoria was such a representative figure that she had and kept the admiration and respect of her subjects. She had other qualities as well. She was utterly candid, truthful and natural, and this was one of the reasons why the nation loved her. Her natural vigour and imperiousness meant that her role as queen would never be that of a do-nothing, a creature who signs documents and sighs away her hours of work. She gave advice to her ministers on most subjects in which she had some competence. She hoped this advice would be followed; but her strong common-sense always—except in the early days of Lord Melbourne—avoided a clash in which the Crown would have been opposed to Parliament.

Although it was not the work of Victoria which caused the government of England gradually to adapt itself to the new circumstances of the nineteenth century, a less perceptive monarch would have proved an obstacle to progress. Victoria never allowed her prejudices to get the better of her. The fact that the Crown rested on one head, and that that head was hers, for so long a time meant that the British monarchy which was much disliked in the early years of the century, and might well not have survived, ended up much stronger at the end of the century. It was a period when, in other countries, monarchy had disappeared or was to disappear shortly.

VICTOR EMMANUEL II

(1820–78)

IT WAS a definite, chilling, order to stop, call a halt. Garibaldi, the great guerrilla leader who had torn the island of Sicily from Bourbon grasp, liberated its inhabitants, must *not* go on from there. He would *not* cross the Straits of Messina to the mainland of South Italy.

Kings have no need to explain themselves, and King Victor Emmanuel II of Piedmont-Sardinia did not do so. But his reasons were obvious: he was nominally at peace with the Bourbon tyrants who were enslaving their "Kingdom of the Two Sicilies"—and so was France. Mighty France had been threatening the direst consequences if this insurrection went on; and these threats were too real to be ignored.

The letter which King Victor handed his trusted messenger, Count Litta Modignani, which the count now stuffed into a pocket, dealt with none of these consequences: it was an order, pure and simple.

But as the count bowed and prepared to take his leave, the king handed him another. "This," he said, "should neutralize the first".

He showed the handwritten missive to his messenger:

"To the Dictator General Garibaldi.

"Now, having written as King, Victor Emmanuel suggests to you to reply in this sense, which I know is what you feel. Reply that you are full of devotion and reverence for your King, that you would like to obey his counsels, but that your duty to Italy forbids you to promise not to help the Neapolitans, when they appeal to you to free them from a Government which true men and good Italians cannot trust: that you cannot therefore obey the wishes of the King, but must reserve full freedom of action."

Strange goings on. But Italy a hundred years ago was a strange place. Indeed, she did not exist, except as a loose geographical expression like "Polynesia", "Iberia", "South-east Asia" or "The Balkans": she was a cluster of independent states. Each state was ruled by a petty monarch who might well have no "Italian" blood in his veins, but who owed his position to the far greater rulers of lands outside the Italian peninsula, who periodically came and fought wars among themselves on Italian soil. At the end of each campaign the country was carved up, re-shuffled, and left with its little states under puppet rulers.

Yet this had not always been so. In the great days of the Roman Empire the country had been one. Then, in the fifth century A.D., everything had changed: the once-great empire began to be ruled from Byzantium, in the east; soon after, northerners like the Lombards swept down to occupy different parts of the peninsula. Soon only the cities and the island of Sicily remained part of the Eastern Empire.

Boundaries, and the balance of power, shifted; little rulers and bigger ones came, saw, conquered and vanished: Italy remained a collection of little kingdoms until the arrival of Napoleon at the end of the eighteenth century. His republican armies swept in during 1796, full of a zeal for reform, a detestation of monarchy; and by the time the majority of them had left again for home, a large part of Italy had been reluctantly united into tidier, larger, groups under awesome titles like "The Parthenopian Republic", and "The Cisalpine Republic". This latter territory was soon styled "The Italian Republic" and in 1805 Napoleon crowned himself "King of Italy" at Milan.

A decade later Napoleon had gone, exiled not only from Milan, but from all Europe. The short-lived "Kingdom of Italy" collapsed as suddenly as its king and within months the country had been distributed among the allies who had overthrown him. Petty princes were restored, former laws reinstated, reforms abolished.

For the French, during their brief ascendancy south of the Alps, had introduced a great deal in the way of social reform. Now, as the re-seated rulers of each little kingdom began to abolish these reforms, feeling rose strongly against them. The time was ripe for revolution, all the way from the toe of Italy to the Alps: revolution against petty tyrants and also against Austria which controlled so large a part of the north.

Secret societies sprang up, as they do in oppressed lands. The most powerful of these was the *Carbonari*, the Charcoal Burners. These were particularly active in the Austrian-controlled northern state of Lombardy, and in the 1820s they actually rebelled several times, but were always crushed. Somehow, though *Carbonari* membership was large, the organization had failed to enlist the sympathy of the man in the street. Better the devil one knew—even though he be an Austrian.

Under the wise guidance of Giuseppe Mazzini a new and far more effective group sprang into being. This styled itself *Giovane*

Italia, Young Italy. As the name proclaimed, it set out to enlist the zeal and patriotism of youth; the movement grew at such speed that within two years of its inception there were over fifty thousand members. One of the most vital tasks for Young Italy was the informing of all Italy of the aims of the society, and to this end literature was printed, or smuggled in from France. Mazzini himself was exiled and took over the task of sending huge quantities of revolutionary material from Marseilles.

Mazzini fanned the flame of revolution, kept it alive, and to him must go a large part of the credit for ultimately unifying and freeing Italy. But his attempts at insurrection were failures. He had one brief success when his followers rose in Rome and took over that state. He had returned from exile and for a short time was President of this new "Republic". Then the French and Austrian armies defeated the insurrection, punished the impertinence: Mazzini was forced to flee his country again.

While all this was going on a young man watched and waited his turn.

He was the new king of a small but respected state, Piedmont-Sardinia, which embraced not only Piedmont—"The Foot of the Mountain"—but the island of Sardinia. His father had been defeated in a battle against the Austrians and had abdicated, leaving his twenty-eight-year-old son as King Victor Emmanuel II.

The young king watched and listened, as risings sparked off by Mazzini burst into flame all over the peninsula and on Sicily. He admired the great patriot—but King Victor could not be expected to share Mazzini's hatred of monarchy.

Nearer at home was another great Italian patriot, a man with as deep a fervour as Mazzini's, but wiser, shrewder. Count Cavour had begun life as a soldier, gone on to take over the management of his father's great estates, then entered politics. From Minister of Agriculture in the Piedmont government he went on to become King Victor's Prime Minister, in 1852. He founded his newspaper, the *Risorgimento*, and copies of this, urging a free and united Italy, setting out methods of achieving it, were soon being handed on from man to man throughout the length and breadth of the peninsula. All Italy began to look north, to Piedmont, for leadership: leadership in first throwing out the hated Austrians, then in supplanting or at least reforming despotic rulers—who included the foreign Bourbon family at the foot of Italy and the Pope himself in the centre.

When the Crimean War broke out between Britain and France

on the one hand, Russia on the other, Cavour advised his monarch to join these two western allies. By rightly forecasting the outcome of the war and anticipating a feeling of gratitude on the part of the victorious French and British towards a tiny state which had helped them, he got Piedmont a seat at the Peace Conference which met in Paris in 1856.

Here at last Piedmont was able to present a case—a case for all Italy—to the great powers. These listened sympathetically as Cavour outlined the injustices of Austrian rule—and at the end of the Conference it was agreed that the French under Napoleon III would rush to the support of Piedmont if that small state should somehow find herself at war against Austria.

It remained only to provoke Austria into declaring war. This Cavour and his king were easily able to do.

The result, at first, was success. The Austrians were defeated by the new Franco-Piedmontese alliance at Montebello, Palestro, Magenta, Solferino. Provisional governments were set up in Modena and in Florence; revolutions broke out in the Papal states and against the Bourbons.

Then, to Italian dismay and shock, the French made peace with Austria.

It is at this point that Victor Emmanuel makes his first real entrance on the stage of history. His Prime Minister was understandably beside himself with rage at this French perfidy, and demanded that the Piedmontese go on fighting against Austria. King Victor refused, and though the argument was long and bitter and quite unlike the normal converse between king and subject he had his way. And there can be little doubt that Cavour's hot-headed patriotism on this occasion would have ended in disaster and postponed the freedom of Italy for many more years.

Victor Emmanuel understood the French point of view, even though he deplored it. Napoleon III was afraid of Prussia and at the same time unwilling to have a powerful new Italian state come into being on his frontier. If little Piedmont tried France too hard, she might well find herself at war against both France and Austria.

Garibaldi now comes into prominence. Like Mazzini—and many others—he had been exiled for his "Young Italy" work, years before. He had returned after an adventurous life in South America and begun to raise a force of "Red Shirts" in Piedmont to sail south and liberate Sicily—for a start—from Bourbon oppressors. No doubt Victor Emmanuel had mixed feelings about this fiery republican, but the king was, above all, an Italian patriot; if Garibaldi could liberate Italy from oppression, he would get King Victor's support.

The king gave his blessing to the expedition Garibaldi now raised —Garibaldi's Thousand—and the troopships sailed out of Genoa on 5 May, 1860.

A week later the Thousand landed, unmolested, in Sicily. By happy chance, two English ships had been in Marsala Harbour and, by mooring next to these, Garibaldi prevented the Bourbon fleet from opening fire. It was far too big a risk, sinking a neutral ship.

The campaign went well. Soon the whole of Sicily had been liberated.

It was at this point that Victor Emmanuel sent his two letters to the Red Shirt leader. Garibaldi studied them and gave orders for crossing the Straits of Messina.

He crossed with his force, began marching north, up the boot of Italy. His king prepared to meet him halfway.

This decision of Victor Emmanel's took considerable courage. He might easily have returned, months later, to his capital to find the Austrians or French in residence. He might easily have been molested, assassinated, by rabid republicans. He might have been disowned by the Guerrilla General himself when they met face to face, for there was little doubt that Garibaldi now had overwhelming support, not only in Italy, but outside, especially in England. Had he chosen to oppose the royal Piedmont army he could probably have defeated it, and though he had once professed loyalty to his king there was no reason to count on that loyalty remaining.

Yet King Victor set off, at the head of his force, and headed south. The stakes were high: if he stayed at home he risked having all Italy flock to the standard of a man whom he admired but could not trust, and being deposed himself; if he went south to take a part in the liberation he risked the same thing happening, with greater violence: he risked death, as well as republicanism.

He also risked excommunication by his Pope, for the citizens of the Papal states, as he passed through, demanded to be incorporated in his kingdom, and he could but agree. The excommunication was a stunning blow to a good Catholic, but King Victor took it and pressed on south.

Just north of Naples the two forces met. What would happen? Would Garibaldi, flushed with success, deny his king—or would he hand over his conquests to the royal house? There was doubt on both sides, on that early morning near the end of October, 1860, as the armies approached.

The Red Shirts heard the sound of a military band. It was playing "The Royal March". They fingered their weapons, for only Garibaldi knew what was in Garibaldi's mind. They watched him mount his horse, set out to meet the royal army.

The king came in sight, at the head of it, and men from both sides watched anxiously as the two approached each other.

Then suddenly Garibaldi, the bearded revolutionary, swept off his hat from his kerchiefed head and shouted, at the top of his lungs, "*Saluto il primo Re d'Italia!*"

The king advanced, held out his hand. "*Come state, caro Garibaldi?*"

"*Bene, Maesta, e lei?*"

"*Benone.*"

It needs little knowledge of Italian to establish that the meeting was friendly; that the Dictator acknowledged King Victor Emmanuel II as the first King of Italy.

And now, at this dramatic moment in history, almost the whole of the Italian peninsula had been annexed to the Kingdom of Piedmont. Only Rome and Venice remained outside.

On 18 February, 1861, King Victor was proclaimed King of United Italy.

There was much still to be done. He began making urgent plans for the liberation of Venice. Soon he had allied his new Italy with Prussia: by getting into war against Austria, had succeeded in adding Venice to the kingdom.

Rome still remained. And this looked like being the toughest nut of all. For the French, while prepared to help Piedmont against Austria, were not prepared to assist her in taking over the Pope's See of Rome.

But after much skilful bargaining, led by Victor Emmanuel, French troops were removed from Rome, and his own marched in. On 2 July, 1871, the Eternal City became capital of Italy.

The Pope, Pius IX, was of course unmolested, but he refused to have anything to do with the king. In fact, the two men lived in the city for the rest of their lives and never met. The Vatican became extra-territorial.

The new king, though this grieved him, had plenty of other things to worry him. He flung himself into foreign affairs, for he knew that a new and united Italy must become a voice in world affairs.

It is largely owing to her first king that she did.

But though Italy was united, and the union confirmed by plebiscite, it would be many years before she was consolidated, made into a homogeneous whole. In fact, owing to the great social differences between north and south this has not yet been fully achieved. It has been argued that some looser form of federation between north and south, with their widely divergent backgrounds, would have been preferable; that the plebiscite which married the two gave a false impression of Neapolitan eagerness to wed the north. The polling was open, and anyone who dared vote "No" risked the disapproval and worse of others.

The king worked hard to bring about a real union, though his chief interest lay in foreign affairs, in making his country great and respected in the world.

He died, his work unfinished, in 1878, at the age of fifty-eight.

He was a good man—and they called him The Honest King: *Re Galantuomo*. This honesty, this apparent simplicity (though there is nothing simple about the pair of letters to Garibaldi), has tended to make observers write him off as a political lightweight, a man who just happened to be on the spot when Italy became united. Yet nothing could be farther from the truth: he had the greatest ability as a diplomat.

To this ability we may perhaps ascribe the fact that, as Kipling might have said (but did not), he kept his throne when all around were losing theirs. Not only did he keep it, but he transformed a tiny kingdom, a sort of Mediterranean East Anglia, or Fife, or Puerto Rico, into a great and respected monarchy.

FRANCIS JOSEPH

(1830–1916)

EMPEROR FRANCIS JOSEPH began his long and remarkable reign over the Austro-Hungarian Empire in the significant year 1848. It was the year of the revolutions, and it was no coincidence that the young emperor mounted the ancient Habsburg throne just then.

The fires of freedom which the people had lit in the French Revolution were only damped down by the Napoleonic era and the restoration of the Bourbons. The popular rising in Paris of 1848 ended the efforts of the émigrés to turn back the clock, and touched off similar revolutions all over Europe where the peoples were struggling to shake off the absolutism of the old monarchies and gain the elementary freedoms of speech and franchise.

Since 1815 Europe had been dominated by Austria and Russia, or rather by the reactionary monarchies which governed those two countries, the peoples of which had no say in the conduct of their affairs. The Romanoffs and the Habsburgs were deadly enemies of the democracy and nationalism which was stirring in the patchwork of nationalities which comprised their empires. The vast Habsburg dominions of Austro-Hungary reached from the borders of Saxony to beyond Venice in the south and to the Carpathians in the east. It was a disorderly jumble of an empire with no natural cohesion, in which Czechs, Hungarians, Slavs, Italians, Austrians, Poles and Croats were ruled by a German minority at Vienna. These subject peoples, most of whom were living in a state of semi-feudalism and extreme poverty, were only kept down by forcible repression.

The Habsburgs were the deadly enemies of progress and change. They saw in the modernity which was dawning in Europe a conspiracy to overthrow everything they stood for. Their motto was: Rule and change nothing. Their blind policy of blocking all social progress and all movements towards freedom and nationalism in their ramshackle empire provoked the 1848 revolution in Vienna.

The emperor was Ferdinand I, who was weak-minded and suffered from bouts of insanity. The empire was ruled by the Chancellor, Prince Metternich, and other members of the ruling family, whose weak and witless administration fanned the flames of revolt. When the Vienna mob rose in 1848 Metternich fled. The rumours that Ferdinand intended to turn the guns of the army on Vienna provoked even more violence. Ferdinand capitulated, granted freedom of speech and promised a constitutional monarchy.

This was too much for the other members of the ruling family, who believed in giving nothing to the hated revolutionaries. The most powerful opposition to the weak Ferdinand came from Archduchess Sophia, Francis Joseph's mother, one of those remarkable Habsburg women who so often eclipsed their men in talent and determination. She dominated the Vienna court of the forties and fifties with her intelligence and strong personality. As reactionary as any despot of her age, she believed that the revolutionary movement in Europe was a thing of evil to be stamped out. When Ferdinand cringed before the revolutionaries, she planned a counter-revolution, the main object of which was to induce Ferdinand to abdicate in favour of her seventeen-year-old son, Francis Joseph, who was Ferdinand's nephew.

It was a shrewd move and it came off. She realized that the youthful emperor would appeal to the spirit of the new age. Her intention was to rule as the power behind the throne, in which ambition she was only partially successful.

Francis Joseph was a remarkably handsome youth, slim, well made, beautifully mannered and with a "faultless bearing". He had a limited intellect and cared nothing for literature and art. He was matter-of-fact, quick-witted and supremely confident of his own judgement of people, even when young. He was unsympathetic to all but the simple and natural realities of life. His military upbringing made him place exaggerated importance upon the martial virtues. His chief defect was a complete lack of imagination. He inherited his mother's ideas and was extremely hostile to any change.

Ferdinand's abdication was forced upon him by court circles led by Sophia, more on account of his alarming concessions to the revolutionaries than his weak-mindedness. Being weak of intellect, or even insane, is not usually considered a bar to sitting on a throne. Many crowns have reposed upon heads containing sluggish, ill-working brains. The Habsburgs wanted Ferdinand off the throne in order to crush the revolution, and perpetuate the rule of their house, which was more important to them than the interests of their peoples.

They accomplished this by a deliberate deception in promising that the youthful and romantically handsome emperor would become a constitutional monarch. This promise neither they nor, what was more to the point, Francis Joseph himself had any intention of keeping. He thus began his long reign with a lie on his lips.

At first he was largely under the influence of Prince Schwarzenberg, a reactionary member of the ruling clique, who encouraged and developed the young man's inherent despotism. The early years of the reign were marked by the suppression of liberty in Germany, Italy and Hungary, where the Magyars were ruthlessly crushed with the help of Russian forces.

In 1851 Francis Joseph revoked the constitution he had promised to the Austrian people, and at Schwarzenberg's death in 1852 he refused to appoint a successor and ruled in person. He did not believe in constitutional methods of government. He was divinely ordained to rule and for his authority to be challenged by his people was to him something like blasphemy. To maintain this out-of-date conception of kingship, his authority had to be reinforced with an oppressive system of political espionage and secret police.

Francis Joseph was no idle or feckless monarch. He worked inexhaustibly at the business of kingship and was diligent and conscientious in everything he did. He once said that the term "irresponsible sovereignty" had no meaning for him. In the early part of his reign his rule was purely personal, and for all the ruthless repression of liberty he did enact some not unwise reforms. An absolute monarch at the age of twenty-two, he displayed a remarkable self-confidence.

Bismarck, who met him at that time, wrote of him: "The youthful ruler of this country makes a very agreeable impression on me—the fire of the twenties, coupled with the dignity and foresight of riper years, a fine eye, especially when animated, and a winning openness of expression, especially when he laughs. The Hungarians are enthusiastic about his national pronunciation of their language and the elegance of his riding."

The young emperor's foreign policy at this time can hardly be judged a success. Just before the Crimean War he was on terms of close personal friendship with the Czar, but he antagonized the Russian autocrat by vacillating between one side and then the other, and he succeeded in pleasing neither. He caused severe internal economic difficulties by piling up huge armaments for use in a possible war.

The fifties were a decade of reverses for Francis Joseph. He not only lost the friendship of Russia, and gained the resentment of England and France, but the Italian part of his empire began to slip from his grasp, and by 1859 he had lost Lombardy.

In Austria he was very unpopular. His love of uniforms and military display alienated him particularly from the Viennese who had no love for the army which had so ruthlessly put down the 1848 rising. The emperor was not forgiven for going back on his solemn promise to become a constitutional monarch. The Austrians treated him with scorn and indifference, and the more he tried to become a just but severe ruler, the more his undevoted people turned against him, for they could not forgive his bad faith. They had a passionate desire for the constitutionalism he denied them.

Francis Joseph's obstinate refusal to come into the nineteenth century caused large numbers of his subjects to emigrate to the New World, among them the leaders of the 1848 revolution, and this caused the revolutionary spirit to die down into a kind of sullen apathy. Not even the attempt on Francis Joseph's life by a Hungarian named Janos Libényi reconciled him to his people, though the deed aroused much natural sympathy for him, for he sustained a deep wound and showed great courage.

Francis Joseph's marriage to Elizabeth of Wittlesbach, daughter of Duke Max of Bavaria, whose wife was the Archduchess Sophia's sister, was one of those rare royal unions which was a true love match. Elizabeth was sixteen, the most beautiful princess in Europe and indeed one of the most beautiful women of her century. Clever, brave, a little eccentric, a dreamer, a lover of literature and art, this legendary creature, who so exquisitely ornamented the imperial throne, was everything that the Habsburgs were not. The young emperor was fascinated, for she was a great enchantress. The deep differences between their two natures, which were to develop so tragically later, were not obvious to either at first.

Sophia was against the marriage. She wanted her son to marry Elizabeth's elder sister, but Francis Joseph, though greatly under the influence of his mother, would not be dictated to in affairs of the heart.

A general amnesty following the wedding on 12 April, 1854, brought great popularity to the fairy-tale princess, and some of this popularity rubbed off on to Francis Joseph, for the prisoners who were released were mainly political offenders, victims of his grim secret police.

But the happiness of the marriage was short-lived. Elizabeth could not endure the dreary rigours of Habsburg court life, or the interference of the emperor's tiresome and domineering mother. Elizabeth had been brought up in a cultured background of complete freedom, living the simple life of outdoor pursuits, and she was a fish out of water among the half-educated Habsburgs and their court of aristocratic illiterates. She constantly fled from the stifling atmosphere and spent long months abroad. Francis Joseph frequently followed her to snatch a few days out of his busy life in her treasured company. The truth was that being an empress bored her.

She was a magnificent rider who would storm bareback across the hills and follow the most strenuous hunts. She went to great lengths to preserve her famous slender figure, and would run for hours in the mountains, with her luckless lady-in-waiting panting beside her, followed by a footman whose duty it was to pick up various articles of attire the empress discarded as she quickened her furious pace.

In order to show her wonderful figure at its best on horseback, she always had her riding habit sewn on to her by her tailor before mounting. She was intensely proud of her long and beautiful hair which reached well below her waist, and the washing of which was almost an affair of state, for which twenty bottles of the best French brandy and the yolks of a dozen eggs were used.

The only son of Francis Joseph and Elizabeth, Crown Prince Rudolph, was an unusually talented young man, who inherited the artistic qualities of his mother rather than the more dynastic urges of the Habsburgs. He was everything his father was not—a liberal, an intellectual, a free-thinker.

His death at his hunting lodge of Mayerling near Vienna on the night of 30 January, 1889, is one of the many tragedies which befell Francis Joseph's family, and still remains something of a mystery. Rudolph and his mistress, Baroness Marie Vetsera, were both found dead and it was officially announced that they had both perished by Rudolph's hand. This tragedy gave rise to the wildest rumours. Everyone connected with the affair was sworn to secrecy, and the official dossier was not found when the state archives were open to inspection after the revolution which finally terminated the Habsburg rule.

There were stories that the Crown Prince's skull was smashed in and pieces of bottle glass found embedded in it, and that Marie Vetsera's body had been found nude and riddled with bullets; that the killing had been done by her jealous husband, or by Jesuitical intriguers in order to prevent a liberal emperor coming to the throne, or by Hungarian nobles with whom Rudolph had become compromised. Nevertheless, the official explanation of a suicide pact is generally accepted by historians.

The loss of their son was a terrible blow to the emperor and empress. Elizabeth never fully recovered from it. Her health had already failed and she fled from spa to spa in her attempts to escape from the Habsburgs and reality.

But there was no escape for the conscientious, plodding Francis Joseph, whose unenlightened spirit grappled manfully with the imponderable problems of the advancing century, which brought with it an ever-insistent demand for a more liberal administration. Reluctantly, and step by step, he was forced into the path of consti-tutionalism, though he was still a long way from permitting the people to govern. Austria lost her great influence in Europe by being defeated by Prussia in the war of 1866.

His life was clouded with personal tragedies. His brother Maxi-milian, who had become Emperor of Mexico at the foolish whim of Empress Eugénie, consort of Napoleon III, was shot by a firing squad of Mexico's leader, Benito Juarez. His heir, Francis Ferdinand, was assassinated at Sarajevo in 1914. His sister-in-law, the Duchess of Alençon, had been burnt alive, and then there was the Mayerling tragedy.

But the greatest blow he had to endure was the murder of the Empress Elizabeth by an Italian anarchist on 10 September, 1898, when she was boarding a steamer at Geneva. He stabbed her to the heart with an iron file, and this remarkable woman, no longer young but still beautiful, rather than lose her royal dignity, managed by a superhuman effort of will to walk nearly a hundred yards with a firm step before she collapsed and died.

"The world does not know how much we loved each other," Francis Joseph said in a voice choked with sobs when he heard the news. And this was the plain truth. The years of tragedy, misunder-standing and olympian loneliness had forged a deep bond between these two.

Francis Joseph had eighteen years yet to rule the great Habsburg empire he still held together. He became mellowed and his foreign policy increasingly pacific. His subjects now revered him. Very few of them could remember a time when the grizzled old emperor was not on the throne.

During the latter part of his life he had a close and long friendship with Katharina Schratt, a Viennese actress, a relationship which had been encouraged by the empress herself. It was almost certainly platonic.

By 1914 he had allowed the conduct of affairs to slip from his hands owing to advancing age, and he would probably have avoided declaring war on Serbia, which led to the First World War.

In his old age he was a kindly, likeable old man, adored by his modest court and his servants, who wept unrestrained at his death on 21 November, 1916, at the age of eighty-six.

Francis Joseph's importance lies not only in the fact that his long reign spanned two entirely different worlds. He was a supreme ruler in Central Europe at a time when its peoples were struggling to gain the elementary freedoms which we in Britain have long taken for granted.

His death signalled the final end of the Habsburg monarchy. His grand-nephew, Charles, entered upon an imperial destiny as brief as Francis Joseph's had been long. In 1918 the Austro-Hungarian Empire disintegrated, Austria was declared a republic and the Habsburgs were told that their presence was no longer welcome in the country. Their wealth and property were confiscated and used for the benefit of the victims of the Great War.

CETEWAYO

(c. 1836–84)

CETEWAYO, WHO ruled over 250,000 Zulus, was a nephew of the redoubtable Chaka. Incredible family strife marked Cetewayo's rise to power. He was the son of Mpande (or Panda) who, with his brother, Dingaan, had conspired in Chaka's assassination. Then the assassins had turned on each other and Mpande defeated Dingaan in battle, as, in a repetition of history in 1856, Cetewayo was to defeat his own brother, Umbulazi.

It was at his father's Mlambongwenya kraal, near Eshowe, that Cetewayo was born in 1826. Like all Zulu boys he was sent out to herd sheep and goats. In 1833 Mpande moved his kraal to Mangweni, on the Amatikulu River, in the shelter of the Ngoye Hills. During his struggles with his brother Dingaan, many of the latter's warriors came over to his side, and when Mpande ultimately proved victorious the Boers declared him to be King of the Zulus.

When Dingaan was later killed in battle with the Swazis, hereditary enemies of the Zulus, Cetewayo was about fifteen years old. But he was accorded no favours as crown prince. He had to undergo the same harsh military training prescribed for all young Zulus. He was required to prove himself and was sent to the Tulwana Regiment. He grew into a first-class warrior, but he was also carefully schooled in all tribal laws and customs.

In 1843, when the Boers were aggressively grabbing land from the Zulu people, they staged a commando raid, made off with a lot of cattle, and took seventeen boys and girls with them into virtual slavery. Sir George Napier, Governor of Cape Colony at the time, sent a small infantry force and, in a subsequent clash, the Boers offered little resistance. The British annexed Natal in 1844, and their Zulu neighbours to the north-east occupied an area of some 10,000 square miles.

In 1853-54 Cetewayo had full opportunity for proving himself as a warrior in an attack upon the Swazis. He joined battle with a party of the enemy, slew many in single combat and put the rest to flight. Thus his reputation grew. He displayed some of his uncle Chaka's characteristics as a leader.

Soon Cetewayo set up his own kraal at Ondini, on the south side of the Umhlatuzi River. He gathered more and more followers, especially when more trouble simmered up with the Boers and Mpande betrayed indifference. Cetewayo's younger brother, Mbuyazi, jealous of being out of things, appealed, without success, for British aid. A clash was pending between the brothers, and a young hunter-adventurer named John Dunn offered his services as mediator. He could not prevent the clash, however, and in the ensuing battle of Ndondakusuka, the army of Mbuyazi was routed and he himself was slain. So fearful was the carnage that the site became known thereafter as Mtambo—the Stream of Bones*. Among the 23,000 slain were many helpless women and children.

This holocaust moved Sir Theophilus Shepstone, then Secretary of Native Affairs in Natal, to report: "I fear that Cetewayo's successes will make him a troublesome neighbour."

The fear was to become mutual, for one result was the construction of a chain of British forts on the Natal side of the Tugela River.

In the hope of enlisting a useful ally Cetewayo invited John Dunn, who had escaped the carnage, to settle in Zululand as his personal adviser. Dunn merely made hay for himself by bartering out-of-date arms—receiving ten head of fine cattle for a musket worth about 10s. 6d. He cashed in further by setting himself up as a kind of chief over various natives he gathered into a new tribe.

Cetewayo was, to all intents, already ruler of Zululand. His nomination as Mpande's successor was clinched when Shepstone paid a visit to the royal kraal, calmly facing some angry warriors, unarmed, thereby winning their respect and that of Cetewayo himself. Mpande died in 1872, and when, in the following year, Cetewayo's coronation was officially staged, he invited Shepstone to participate in the ceremonies.

The Governor of Natal, Sir Benjamin Pine, sent a Volunteer escort consisting of 110 officers and men, with two field guns. This expedition, with a major in command, and including about 300 natives, duly reached Zululand, but Shepstone was a little put out on finding that Cetewayo had "jumped the gun" and that part of the coronation ceremony had already been completed. However, the British visitors did their best to make the final function as impressive as possible and to give it political significance as well.

A great many presents were put on display in a big marquee, specially erected for the occasion, and Shepstone's party also provided a ceremonial "crown", devised by one of the military tailors

* *The Last Zulu King*, C. T. Binns.

and modelled on a Zulu chief's head-dress. On the appointed day a glittering cavalcade marched to the royal kraal, providing a spectacle which doubtless impressed the 10,000 Zulu warriors who flocked round for the ceremony.

The occasion was seized upon by the British to proclaim new laws. Henceforth, the indiscriminate shedding of blood was to cease; no Zulu was to be condemned without open trial, and there was to be right of appeal to the king; no Zulu's life should be taken without previous knowledge and consent of the king; there should be no death penalty for minor crimes.

The coronation ceremony concluded with a seventeen-gun salute.

Before leaving Zululand Shepstone met Cetewayo with members of the King's Great Council and discussed such vexed problems as the antagonism with the Boers and difficulties with Christian missionaries over the Zulu practice of polygamy. To Cetewayo is attributed the assertion that a Christian Zulu was a Zulu spoiled. Against this it was argued that often the riff-raff among the Zulus attached themselves to the missions for easy pickings. Bishop Schroeder, anyway, made no bones about describing Cetewayo as "an able man, but for cold, selfish pride, cruelty and untruthfulness worse than any of his predecessors".

Be that as it may, it was certainly not long before trouble became manifest. The king had his fine, highly-trained Impis chafing at prolonged inaction, and though, to his credit, he organized large-scale hunting sorties to provide his full-blooded warriors with some kind of safety-valve for release of their pent-up energies, it was quite evident that he could not hope to restrain them indefinitely. Besides, from what they had already seen of land-grabbing propensities of white strangers the king and his people were naturally apprehensive.

British authorities were no less on edge, and it is not surprising that even minor frontier incidents magnified the tension. There was a case where some outraged Zulu husbands crossed into Natal to bring back a party of runaway wives; and a second incident occurred when two British surveyors were hustled by Zulu scouts who feared that the intruders were planning sites for possible gun-emplacements on sandbanks in the Tugela River.

Tension was at its height when Sir Henry Bartle Frere was appointed Governor-General of Cape Colony and High Commissioner of Natal in 1877. Sir Theophilus Shepstone, who had understood Cetewayo so well, had been succeeded as Secretary for Native Affairs by his brother, J. W. Shepstone. Sir Bartle Frere never, in fact, met Cetewayo, and had to rely on second-hand reports of frontier troubles and complaints of Zulu savagery from missionaries of different nationalities.

He was genuinely alarmed by the presence across the border of the powerful Zulu impis, and one of his first acts was to call for reinforcements. But the Government wanted to avoid a major clash and the request was refused.

Frere sent an ultimatum to Cetewayo which included, among other things, an impossible demand that the Zulu army be disbanded. Cetewayo asked for time; Frere thought this "arrogance". Troops under Lord Chelmsford were moved to the border.

Cetewayo mobilized, but gave implicit orders that his impis must not cross the frontier. He remained in his kraal. At fifty-two, fat and lazy, he had no mind for a major clash either. But he refused to be intimidated. His plea for time was rejected. In January, 1879, British forces advanced into Zululand in three main columns. Sir Henry Bartle Frere stated that the intention was merely to enforce compliance with undertakings made at Cetewayo's coronation, and added that the British Government had no quarrel with the Zulu people.

Cetewayo addressed his 25,000 warriors personally. "You are to go against the column at Rorke's Drift," he told them, "and drive it back into Natal. You will attack by daylight as there are enough of you to eat it up, and you will march slowly so as not to tire yourselves"*.

The first clash came in the battle of Isandhlwana, when the Umcityu impi, four-thousand strong, followed by others, hurled themselves upon the British column. Undeterred by heavy fire and severe losses the Zulus closed in for desperate hand-to-hand fighting in which assagais and short stabbing spears were pitted against sword and bayonet. The Zulus had been sighted at 8 a.m. By 2 p.m. the impis were victorious and in hot pursuit of survivors seeking to escape.

Then came the battle of Rorke's Drift, where a Swedish mission station had been turned by British forces into a base hospital and store depot. On the day of the Zulu assault the post was under the command of a young subaltern with 100 men and 28 patients. The story of the epic stand of this small garrison against the full fury of a Zulu impi has been told many times, and here it must suffice to record that, outnumbered by 20 to 1, the defenders repulsed repeated attacks; that 11 Victoria Crosses were won that day, and that the stubborn stand probably saved Natal from invasion.

* *Natal Witness*, 20 February, 1879.

But the disaster at Isandhlwana had driven the central British column back into Natal. Cetewayo did not send his troops after the invaders.

Pressure from London led to the removal of Sir Bartle Frere, while General Sir Garnet Wolseley replaced him as High Commissioner for Natal and the Transvaal and also superseded Lord Chelmsford as Special Commissioner and Commander-in-Chief.

For a time the Zulus inflicted humiliating defeats on the invaders until a clash at Kambula, where Zulu losses amounted to 2,000 against British casualties of under 100. This, again, was due largely to neglect to heed the king's advice about avoiding attacks on entrenched positions.

By this stage British forces were being reinforced and three columns were slowly approaching Ulundi. Messengers from the king asked that hostilities should end. Certain provisos were suggested, but ignored. The advance continued to within a day's march of the royal kraal.

At 5.30 a.m. on the morning of 4 July the distance was narrowed to 700 yards. The British forces, about 4,000 strong, with 1,000 native supporters, then waited for the Zulus to attack. This they did in force, showing their usual valour in the face of devastating fire from field guns and Gatling guns. As advancing waves were mown down, others came on, the Umcityu impi breaking through to within yards of the British ranks, only to be met by a surprise cavalry charge. By 9.30 a.m. the Zulus were in flight, having lost 1,500 men against the British losses of 12 killed and 88 wounded.

Cetewayo, watching from a ridge, also took flight.

Cavalry patrols scoured the country for him, and though a price was placed on his head, no one betrayed him. For a time he sought sanctuary in the kraal of his chief induna, Umnyamana, from whence he issued orders that peace should be made with the conquerors. Later he fled to his brother's kraal, forty miles from Ulundi; and then into the depths of the great Ngome Forest, finally reaching a kraal at Kwa Dwasa. Then, on 27 August, cornered by a detachment of dragoons, he was escorted back to Cape Town. For a time he was held a prisoner, but in the following year he was conducted to England, where his future and that of his country were candidly discussed. Terms for his restoration were finally hammered out, Cetewayo conducting himself with the greatest dignity. Queen Victoria granted him a fifteen-minute audience at Osborne, and later ordered a court artist, Carl Sohn, to paint his portrait*.

* Now in Durban.

On his restoration, in 1883, Cetewayo soon found himself in conflict with rival factions; and, in the following year, he died suddenly in circumstances which suggested that he had been poisoned. The precise truth of his sudden end could not be discovered, for his followers flatly refused to permit the king's person to be subjected to the indignity of a post-mortem. He lies buried in a remote part of Zululand—the last of the Zulu kings.

It is impossible to read the story of Cetewayo without feeling more than a little sympathy for this resolute monarch who, when forces of destiny seemed to be closing in so relentlessly upon him, was moved to protest that he had not attacked the British in Natal; they had attacked him in his own country. He had tried to defend it and had failed.

Though Cetewayo grew up in a savage country where the law was kill or be killed; and though he proved himself as a fearless warrior in youth, he developed great depth of character. In all tribulations he carried himself with dignity and restraint, and it is impossible to escape the reflection that had he been handled with more understanding a different solution to the Zulu problem might have been found, and the needless sacrifice of brave men on both sides could have been avoided.

It is ironical indeed that those who confirmed his accession and even went to the trouble of concocting a "crown" for his ceremonial coronation should so soon afterwards have destroyed him. And there is double irony in the fact that the field-pieces that fired the seventeen-gun salute in his honour may conceivably have been used to blast his valiant warriors into eternity.

Let Sir Theophilus Shepstone, who saw the Zulu monarch's rise and fall, add yet one more touch of irony and speak his epitaph:

He was a man of considerable ability, much force of character, and dignified. In all my conversations with him he was remarkably frank and straightforward, and he ranks in every respect far above any Native Chief I have ever had to do with.

EDWARD VII

(1841–1910)

EDWARD VII, portly, bearded, beautifully dressed, with his big cigar and hat tilted at a rakish angle, gazes at us with royal dignity from contemporary photographs as though from another planet. Edwardianism, in the spacious, care-free sense which the king epitomized, has gone for ever and lies on the far side of that great divide when the lights went out over Europe and were never rekindled.

They were times when seven thousand people owned four-fifths of the land in England, income tax was trifling and death-duties were non-existent. There were extremes of wealth and poverty, and though an ancient, hierarchical society was still respected and preserved it was being undermined by the new popular press, the development of working-class political activity and the spread of startling, iconoclastic ideas by writers like Bernard Shaw. But meanwhile, wealthy, industrialized England was still the hub of the greatest empire the world had ever seen and every Englishman had his place in one of the social strata, watching with more pride than envy the glittering cavalcade of high society headed by the king who as time passed became increasingly the living symbol of English manliness, sportsmanship, good nature and optimism.

The king was an ardent race-goer, liked travel and excitement, ate rich food with a Gargantuan appetite, gambled at baccarat and was a connoisseur of beautiful women. To most of his subjects these tastes were their own, writ large. They brought him down to popular level. They made him human, and it is as a human being, the first king to popularize the monarchy, that he comes down to us, with all his zest, charm, weaknesses and courage.

King Edward supplied the answer to a problem which beset his parents: how to maintain the prestige of the monarchy in an age when the sovereign reigned, but no longer ruled. What was Queen Victoria's function in a constitutional democracy where she could neither prescribe the policies of governments, nor dismiss them, nor appoint ones of her own choosing? The prince consort's answer was to make himself more expert than the experts in many departments of state and, through the queen's right to be consulted, to become a kind of permanent, unofficial cabinet minister. This solution worked well as long as he lived, but it derived from the personal talents of himself and the queen and could not be repeated. King Edward, who was not an intellectual, enjoyed the full glare of publicity on the race course, at the opera and theatre, on tours of inspection in provincial cities and as the centre-piece of the London season. From paper-work and private consultation he drew out the monarchy into public life, and gave it a democratic flavour which it has never since lost. "Good old Teddy!" shouted touts, louts and even policemen when he won the Derby for the third time—and in that cry lies an echo of his achievement.

The feat was doubly notable in that, true to their own idea of royal functions, his parents paid no attention whatever to his true personality, but tried to turn the boy Edward into a paragon of learning, industry and virtue—with the result that his performance finally proved less than average in all three. He was born on 9 November, 1841, and in December, two days before he was created Prince of Wales, his mother wrote to King Leopold of the Belgians: "I hope and pray he may be like his dearest Papa. . . . You will understand how fervent are my prayers to see him resemble his father in every respect, both in body and mind."

These prayers coincided with Albert's wish, and in consultation with his own former tutor, Baron Stockmar, he devised a stringent educational plan typical of an age which believed that education was a process of moulding, not of developing. Edward was to be treated as an empty vessel waiting to be filled and then labelled: "Fit for kingship." Taught English, French and German before he was seven-and-a-half, he was then segregated from other children, placed under a band of conscientious tutors and put to work for long hours on six days of the week, imbibing a dozen or more subjects ranging from religion to chemistry. Holidays were short and few, the pressure was intense, the luckless boy felt himself to be the constant focus of critical attention. At times, from sheer exhaustion, he sulked or burst into uncontrollable rage.

A visit to Paris, which dazzled and delighted him, showed, too, that he resented his parents' severity. "I would like to be your son," he is said to have told the Emperor Napoleon III, and he begged the Empress Eugénie to let him stay on for a few days when his parents went home.

But gradually, with great caution, the monastic seclusion was relaxed and Edward, aged fifteen and actually allowed to choose his own neckties, was sent with an adult escort on a walking tour of Dorset, to the Lake District and, for the purposes of study, to Königswinter on the Rhine. There for the first time he kissed a pretty girl, was suitably admonished and provoked the long-range ire of Mr. Gladstone, who, on hearing of the incident, called it "this squalid little debauch" and expressed the fear that the prince was being educated to wantonness.

Queen Victoria, too, was fearful for his future. He was "idle" and "weak" and his only safety, as she wrote to her daughter in Germany, lay "in his implicit reliance in everything on dearest Papa". In a few years he would come of age. Meanwhile, before freedom ruined him for ever, Papa's image must be pumped into his soul and persuaded somehow to stay there. A heavy dose of Walter Scott and French classics were considered helpful and, bored to distraction, the prince asked in vain for a military career.

All this time his true self was largely obscured for want of outlet. But his father had already noted his "remarkable social talent", and this burst into the open on a visit to Berlin when he charmed his brother-in-law, the future Emperor Frederick III, and convinced his sister Victoria that he was far from being a "very dull companion", as their mother described him. He discovered an enormous zest, sharpened by deprivation, for the colourful side of life, and that this zest had survived intact despite early training was a tribute to the vigour of his personality.

Studies at Oxford, where he did moderately well, were punctuated by visits to Canada and the United States, where his social flair was first put seriously to the test. In the States particularly he achieved a personal triumph with his tact, good humour and youthful charm, and when the queen heard of this her heart was softened. She had often rebuked him. Now she felt that he deserved the highest praise.

In September, 1861, the Prince of Wales met for the first time the beautiful young lady whom his parents had selected for him as a possible bride, Princess Alexandra, daughter of the heir to the Danish throne. Soon after, a terrible rumour reached the Prince Consort. When training at the Curragh military camp near Dublin in the summer, his son, it appeared, had had an affair with an actress. The rumour was true. Edward confessed, adding that the liaison was now over. But his father was greatly distressed and within a few weeks was dead. The cause of death was typhoid, but in the abyss of grief Queen Victoria ascribed it to her son and he was shortly dispatched on a tour of the Near East because she could hardly bear to set eyes on him.

Marriage to Alexandra, whom the queen likened to an angel from heaven, helped to reconcile mother and son, though they drew further apart in their lives, Victoria immured in black at Windsor and Osborne, while the prince, with a vast and colourful wardrobe, slipped with effortless ease into the role of social sovereign which was to last for nearly fifty years. The queen professed to see great danger to the country's stability in the frivolous existence led by the Upper Ten Thousand and deplored that her son caroused with such people. But in fact they were only part of his acquaintance, he was far too gregarious to confine his friendships to the idle rich, and as time went on he cultivated successful men in all walks of life, so widening the appeal of the monarchy at a time when the whole social fabric was undergoing a kaleidoscopic change.

Would he turn into another George IV? The queen feared that he might—and *that* the country never would stand. But she overlooked his innate moderation and good sense and also forgot that the pursuit of pleasure was almost the only activity she had left open to him. She would not allow him to represent her in public; for ten years after his father's death he was not initiated into the affairs of state and a quarter of a century passed before he was allowed a key to the red boxes containing Cabinet papers. Meanwhile the social round, the opera, the theatre, gambling, yachting, racing, shooting, country house-parties, visits to foreign relatives and trips to Paris *en garçon* filled in his time. His popularity, normally high, was temporarily damaged when he was involved in a divorce case and a gaming scandal, but it rose again when he nearly died of typhoid and soared to dizzy heights when he won the Derby for the first time in 1896.

Though condemned to the fringes of state business, he was still able as Prince of Wales to be of use in the field of semi-official diplomacy, and here his personal qualities made him supreme. A visit to India shortly before the queen became empress was a tremendous success. In Paris, friendship with men in public life allayed suspicions of England, and in Russia he won the affectionate confidence of the weak young czar, Nicholas II. Only in Berlin, where from 1888 ruled the flashy, erratic and conceited William II, was he eyed with mistrust, and relations between uncle and nephew never rose above the level of guarded hostility. To the warped view of a German observer, Edward talking to William reminded him of "a fat, malicious tom-cat playing with a shrewmouse".

Edward was sixty when he became king in January, 1901. His conciliatory temper, his patience, modesty and shrewd judgement of men had been partially obscured in the long years of idleness and there were some fears whether he was fitted to occupy the throne. But from the start of his reign, when he revealed a remarkable gift for impromptu speech-making, his personality, the innovations he made and the routine he set himself were seen as welcome contrasts to the Widow of Windsor and her semi-anonymous rule. He enhanced the ceremonial aspect of monarchy, his court became the most colourful since Charles II's, he dined out at the homes of his subjects and for at least half the year—four months of the remainder being spent abroad—he was on show to his subjects in London or the provinces.

But he was not merely a figure-head. He took an active part in speeding up final victory in the Boer War. His interest in the Navy prompted him to give unswerving support to Admiral Sir John Fisher, who put through, against the strongest service opposition, a series of much needed naval reforms, and he followed closely, with alternate encouragement and criticism, the creation of a new model army and the reorganization of the War Office carried through by Lord Haldane.

His most notable achievement was the creation in France of a more friendly attitude to England. His interest in foreign affairs was always intense and in 1901 he had done all he could to foster negotiations for an Anglo-German alliance. The project had foundered on the rock of mutual distrust and the British Government then began to consider a *rapprochement* with France. Progress was made in settling spheres of interest in Central Africa and a wider agreement was desired on both sides. But the stumbling-block was public opinion. France was suspicious of British good faith: Britons had no confidence in French strength or stability. It was at this point that King Edward was invited, on his way home from a European tour, to lunch privately with President Loubet at the Elysée. On his initiative the visit was turned into a state occasion and contrary to widespread fears proved a triumphant success.

The crowds were undemonstrative as he drove along the Champs-Elysées to the British Embassy and when he went with his host to the theatre that night his reception was icy. But his unruffled good humour, his acknowledged love for Paris and France, quickly made critics feel churlish and thawed public opinion. Within two days Paris performed a *volte-face* and milling, enthusiastic crowds were yelling at him in the street: "*Vive Edouard! Notre bon Edouard!*" The same scenes were repeated when he left. There had been cheers for the Boers on his arrival; now there were cheers for what street-hawkers called "the Czar of all the Englands". The British Ambassador reported home on a "success more complete than the most sanguine optimist could have foreseen", and before long similar enthusiasm greeted the French President in England. A year later, a far-reaching Anglo-French Agreement was signed which would certainly have been impossible but for the cordial feeling between the two countries aroused, in the first instance, by King Edward.

The king was not much interested in the colonies and was bored by home affairs, where his efforts were confined to political conciliation and protecting the royal prerogatives. From his youth he inherited a dislike of desk work, a dread of being alone and a need for constant stimulus, variety and entertainment. While the skies slowly darkened towards Armageddon he was happy, as the living symbol of British goodwill and solidity, to speed across Europe, to Paris, Berlin, Rome, St. Petersburg, in the cause of friendship and peace—equally happy to take the waters at Marienbad, cruise in the *Victoria and Albert*, or attend the Doncaster Races, and happier still perhaps in the company of his son George, heir to the throne since the death of his elder brother, to whom he was devoted. His taste for pomp and pageantry suited the mood of his people, and most of his qualities, which combined to put the monarchy in the shop window for the first time in history, helped to enhance its popularity in an age of transition. Edward was the first truly democratic monarch and the last of the play-boy kings. His optimism and broad enjoyment of life reflected times, now gone for ever, when men still believed that reason could solve all human problems and Britannia was eternally destined to rule the waves.

On the day before he died, in May, 1910, the king, with bronchitis and failing heart, gave formal audiences all day. Next morning he put on a frock-coat (he was always punctilious about dress) and lit a large cigar. In the afternoon he collapsed, and a series of heart attacks followed. But he would not go to bed and sat hunched in a chair, receiving friends who came to say goodbye. Later, he was told that one of his horses had won at Kempton Park. "I am glad," he said, then lapsed into a coma. His last words were: "I will go on. . . . I will go on. . . ."

Shane Leslie said of him: "He lived like an Epicurean and died like a Stoic", and a year later Lord Fisher wrote his epitaph in a letter to a friend: "How *human* he was! He could sin, 'as it were with a cart-rope', and yet could be loved the more for it! What a splendour he was in the world!"

MEIJI MUTSUHITO

(1852–1912)

IN JULY, 1912, a funeral took place in Tokyo—at night, under the glare of lamps. The huge procession which followed the coffin on its ox-drawn cart included a detachment of British Royal Marines.

At the very instant the cortege started from the Imperial Palace, General Nogi and his wife, sitting in the spacious front room of their house, committed *hara-kiri*.

A little later, when the body was interred, the effigies of four warriors in full armour were buried with it.

These two happenings, so dissimilar, were in fact very closely linked—for it was by the ancient custom of *junshi* that the nobles closest to a Japanese emperor killed themselves on his death and were buried with him, in order that they might accompany him to the next world. The custom had happily fallen into disuse—partly because there had been few noteworthy emperors for hundreds of years—and now only earthenware effigies of warriors were buried. But General Nogi, in a sudden, horrifying, and probably unpremeditated gesture, showed the world that the custom was not dead. Though he had left it too late to be buried in the royal grave, he would go to the next world with his emperor.

The being who had occasioned this gesture was the one-hundred-and-twenty-second Emperor of Japan, Mutsuhito. He had succeeded to the throne while still in his teens, some forty-five years previous, and like all emperors before, or since, he was descendant of the first one, Jimmu Tenno. Jimmu, according to Japanese history, founded the empire in 660 B.C. (The date rests on no historical fact, but it is an important one, and on the 2,600th anniversary in 1940 there were great celebrations.) But Mutsuhito was the first *real* emperor to rule Japan for nearly seven hundred years.

The chain of events which brought about this virtual "restoration" of a line of emperors came about independently of young Mutsuhito —but, fortunately for Japan, he was to grow into a great and wise ruler, the most highly esteemed emperor in Japanese history. The day in July, 1912, when he was buried is known, in Japan, as The End of the Grand Era.

575

To put Mutsuhito—or the Emperor Meiji, to give him his official title of "Enlightened Government"—into perspective we must go back in years. Not quite to that dubious date of 660 B.C., but to the twelfth century A.D. Up to this time the emperor, though his power had dwindled, was still ruler of Japan, even though the great families were taking over much of the business of government. The Fujiwara family had been in a position of great importance for years, by the simple expedient of marrying off its young heiresses to young emperors, then persuading the emperor to abdicate the moment a male child was born and allow a Fujiwara elder to be regent. Why bother with the cares of government?—this had been the Fujiwara advice—when you can live in pomp and luxury as the husband of an heiress. The family wielded great power during the hundred years up to the time of the battle of Hastings, when a deep internal struggle in the house of Fujiwara weakened and destroyed it. (There is, of course, no connexion between the two events: the Fujiwara had never heard of England, far less Hastings: the Conqueror can hardly have heard of Japan.)

And now, with violent struggle among the Fujiwara, power fell into the hands of yet another family, the Taira. This family took over much of the remaining power of the Imperial Court, until it, too, was overthrown in a bloody campaign ending in the great sea battle of 1185. The victors were the Minamoto family, and with their coming the last vestiges of royal power vanished. Even the capital was moved—in order to get away from the "enfeebling atmosphere" of a royal court—from Kyoto to the town of Kamakura.

And yet, despite this, the emperor was still sacrosanct. Even if he did wrong—though he was getting less and less chance to do anything —he was not to blame.

From now—until the accession of Meiji—Japanese life became strongly militaristic: the *samurai*, those armoured knights, made their appearance; so did the disembowelling process of *hara-kiri*. Government was taken from the feeble hands of the court and put under a *bakufu*, or "camp office". The head of such a government was given the highest *samurai* rank of *shogun* ("Grand General for Conquering the Tribes"), and from this first, Minamoto, *shogun*, until Meiji's accession in 1876, Japanese emperors were completely impotent, constitutional monarchs.

What, then, brought about the change?

Contact with a thrusting, greedy, outside world. At first this contact, with the arrival of Portuguese Christian missionaries, was friendly, so that Francis Xavier writing home to Portugal was able to say, "It seems to me we shall never find among heathens another race to equal the Japanese". But soon, with the arrival of Spaniards, Dutch and English, who quarrelled disgracefully among themselves and denied each other's religions, Japanese enthusiasm died. The government decided to banish the lot—this would be the simplest, indeed the only, method of getting rid of these fanatical foreign creeds. So during the seventeenth century almost every foreigner was banished and Japan retired into her shell: if this was the outside world, she wanted no part of it.

But two hundred years later, in 1853, the United States, resentful at this policy of isolation and at the callous way shipwrecked American sailors had been treated, sent Commodore Perry with four warships. All four were far vaster, better armed, than anything the Japanese had seen, and, wonder of wonders, two of them were driven by steam. Perry patiently, but firmly, set out his government's demands: the opening of at least one port to American trade, the provision of coaling stations in Japan, better treatment for shipwrecked sailors. He then showed them a model railway and a model telegraph, before sailing away. He would be back in a month or so, when they had thought it out.

The Japanese, shocked by what they had learnt of the west, furious with their own rulers for having kept them so utterly in the dark about western progress, set themselves frantically to building up an army and a navy and copying, as best they could, western ocean-going vessels.

Soon after Perry's departure a Russian vessel arrived, on the same errand. The Japanese knew they stood no chance against a combination of such forces, and agreed hastily to all of Perry's demands.

But the decision was by no means unanimous: many thought the hated foreigners should be repulsed by force. The shogun, who had "so meekly acquiesced", became overnight a hated figure.

In fact this particular shogun was a wise man and he was right in his summing up of the foreign opposition. For the time being Japan *must* agree to all demands.

Opposition to the shogun and his advisers mounted at terrifying speed, so much so that even the emperor, Meiji's predecessor, over-ruled his instructions and gave his own order for foreign ships to be bombarded. This was done, and resulted in a terrifying return bombardment of the port of Shimonoseki, in 1864, by the fleets of Britain, France, Holland and the U.S.A. Unrest in the country rose toward civil war, and with it the influence of the shogunate declined: all criticism of the way things were being handled, had always been handled, was now directed against the shogun. In particular there was a powerful rising of clans in the west of the country, clans like the Hizen and Tosa, bent on getting rid of the shogunate.

At this point a far-seeing Englishman, Sir Harry Parkes, came on the scene. He was an experienced man, had been captured and tortured by the Chinese, and he now decided, in his capacity of British Minister, that he would back these western clans, and let it be known that the British Government favoured their claims against *bakufu*, "camp office" rule, which had gone on for too long. The emperor, Parkes announced, should come back. Being a wise and statesmanlike man, he was able to convince the western clans that this must be the end-product of their policy.

At the height of this unrest the young shogun died and was reluctantly succeeded by an elderly guardian. A year later the Emperor Komei died and was succeeded by his fifteen-year-old son, Mutsuhito—and soon after that the shogunate handed over all powers to the imperial throne. Confused fighting was to follow, but in 1869 peace came and the young emperor was able to get on with the unfamiliar job of ruling his country.

He set about it with a will, and with the ardent support of his countrymen, even those who, on the face of it, seemed most likely to suffer with the abolition of feudalism. The four western lords who had been instrumental in returning the emperor to real power now addressed a remarkable document to him: "There is no soil within the empire that does not belong to the emperor, and no inhabitant who is not a subject of the emperor, though in the Middle Ages the Imperial power declined and the military classes rose, taking possession of the land and dividing it among themselves as the prize of their bow and spear. But now that the Imperial power is restored, how can we retain possession of land that belongs to the emperor and govern people who are his subjects? We therefore reverently offer up all our feudal possessions so that a uniform rule may prevail throughout the empire."

And the statement went on: "Thus the country will be able to rank equally with other nations of the world."

The young emperor rose to the challenge of this last sentence. Soon, great numbers of Japanese, delegations from every craft, every city in the land, were touring London, Paris, New York and other world centres, behaving with the impeccable good manners so little in evidence in foreigners who had visited Japan. One delegation went with the single intention of getting revision of the treaties imposed by Commodore Perry and other western exploiters, who had given themselves extra-territorial jurisdiction and the advantage of low tariffs. The delegation failed, and on receipt of the news the emperor redoubled efforts to modernize and strengthen the country: in future Japan would stand on her own feet, resist all encroachment.

Railways began to slide their tentacles from town to town; elaborate dockyards sprang up to service a new deep-water fleet; printing presses, telegraph offices, banks—everything the visiting Japanese had seen or read of—were introduced into Japan, with the emperor urging, encouraging, all the way. Party politics was introduced. A newly-restored emperor might well have felt this a usurpation of his new power, but Meiji was convinced that this western-style method of government was best for his country. He introduced a cabinet system under a prime minister in 1885, and presented that prime minister, in 1889, with a written Constitution. But Meiji had no intention of backing off the stage: the Constitution made it abundantly clear that he, the emperor, had graciously presented it to his people and had not been forced to do so. It stated that the country would be "reigned over and governed by a line of emperors unbroken for ages eternal", and this was gladly accepted by the people. In fact, Meiji's power was great—far greater than that of any other constitutional monarch—and he was able to initiate legislation by himself. This legislation was to be laid before the Imperial Diet at its "next session", and the Diet could—which was unlikely in the extreme—invalidate it.

And now the Japanese industrial revolution began to speed, during this second half of the Emperor Meiji's long reign. Factories sprang up like mushrooms, and the ships which had so shocked and impressed the Japanese in 1853 and which they subsequently ordered, one by one, from the western world, began to be made, even faster, in Japanese yards. The foreign monopoly of the crowded and important steamship trade between Japan and China was broken by a thrusting, new, government-sponsored "Japan Mail Line". A western-style army and navy began to grow.

But despite this tremendous material achievement (or perhaps because of it) the people themselves felt ever more strongly about the extra-territorial rights of foreigners, for these suggested Japan was not regarded as a civilized fellow-nation. The foreigners showed no sign of being prepared to relinquish their concessions—until a sudden war between Japan and China over Korea. Then, with Japan winning a rapid and rather surprising victory, opinion changed. An agreement was signed in 1894 between Japan and Britain, and this was followed by agreements with other countries, giving up extra-territorial status.

But the aftermath of the China war brought sudden bitterness against the West. In the hateful "Triple Intervention", France, Russia and Germany refused to allow Japan to occupy the mainland territory she had acquired as a result of the treaty (though she could retain her new acquisition of Formosa). There were angry threats in the Japanese Diet and in the press: Japan had conquered China, she must go on, conquer the world, for her rights.

It was the Emperor Meiji who calmed this agitation. He knew, from his close study of western affairs, that Japan, if she were foolish enough to engage any western power now, would lose all she had so painstakingly built up.

He was, of course, right. And nine years later, in 1904, when Russian encroachment had grown too much to bear, the far stronger Japanese nation attacked Russia and won a decisive and startling victory. As at Pearl Harbour many years later, she struck before war was declared, though negotiations had obviously broken down. But there was little indignation in 1904. As the London *Times* put it: "The Japanese Navy has opened the war with an act of daring which is destined to take a place of honour in naval annals."

Japan was at last established as the equal of any nation—but there was no resting on laurels. The visits of beaming, polite, little men all over Europe and the United States, absorbing silently and with absolute accuracy everything they saw and heard, went on, encouraged as before by the emperor. Meiji journeyed widely himself, setting a novel precedent and coming back regularly to his domains with plans for still more improvement, expansion in education, science, industry.

This, to many, was the Grand Era, the Golden Age of Japan. And when, in 1912, the Emperor Meiji died, though it caused no check in the accelerating process of advancement which he had begun, the grief all over Japan was great. The divinity who had passed on into a new and finer world had taken over his country as a squabbling oriental state: he had left it, forty-five years later, one of the world's most respected nations.

CHULALONGKORN

Rama V of Siam

(1853–1910)

"'I HAVE sixty-seven children,' said His Majesty. 'You shall educate them and as many of my wives, likewise, as may wish to learn English. And I have much correspondence in which you must assist me. And moreover, I have much difficulty for reading and translating French letters: for French are fond of using gloomily deceiving terms. You must undertake and you shall make all their murky sentences and gloomy deceiving propositions clear to me. And furthermore I have by every mail foreign letters whose writing is not easily read by me. You shall copy on round hand, for my readily perusal thereof'."

Anna Leonowens, as play- and film-goers will know, went to Siam in the middle of the nineteenth century. The king of that country had sent for an English lady to undertake the education of his children and Major Leonowens's young widow (he had just died of heat-stroke in Malaya) accepted the post.

The account of what befell her in that kingdom provides a basis for the smash-hit musical production, *The King and I*. But for a less fanciful version of what really happened we must turn to Anna's own story, *The English Governess at the Siamese Court*, first published in 1870. The passage above gives us some idea of the Asian monarch who employed her. His name was Maha Mongkut, but he figures, in Siamese history, as Rama IV.

His son Chulalongkorn, who was to gather knowledge, ideas and a radical point of view from Mrs. Leonowens—a point of view which would greatly affect his country during a long and illustrious reign—became King Rama V. We remember him better as Chulalongkorn.

Siam, or Thailand, is a proud and independent kingdom of the Indo-Chinese peninsula. Our knowledge of the area before the fourteenth century A.D. is fairly limited. We do know that Siam, in ancient times, was inhabited by primitive aboriginal people and that gradually more sophisticated colonists moved in from neighbouring Cambodia, bringing customs and religion from India. Immigration and movement continued and a Thai race evolved.

From the fourteenth century history is clearer. There is a history compiled between the fourteenth and eighteenth centuries, *The Annals of Ayuthia*, which provides a great deal of information, and from the seventeenth century there were European missionaries who reported at length on what they found. The people were proud, handsome and with a sense of humour, possessed of an astonishingly beautiful and fertile land, and ruled by absolute monarchs of ancient lineage. Though Siamese kings today are only constitutional rulers, the basic facts are unchanged: the people are gay and kind and beautiful and almost everything grows for them, in a pleasing and varied climate. Their chief crop, for home consumption as for export, is rice, but Siamese teak is as fine as any in the world, and she produces more of it than any other country. The majority of the people are Thais, but successive migrations have settled Laos, Chinese, Malays, Cambodians and Burmese within her boundaries.

And Siam owes much to the wisdom and humanity of some of her rulers, and in particular to Chulalongkorn—King Rama V.

His father, who employed Anna Leonowens, was a devoted ruler. He did much to improve the condition of his country, planning canals, making roads, building ships and introducing the art of printing. He was the first Siamese ruler to turn his back on warfare and devote himself to the arts of peace: in Rama V's reign campaigns were no longer launched against Burma or Cambodia. His Majesty, in fact, looked far beyond these lands, to the stars, for his favourite science of astronomy became an obsession, and finally killed him: he caught a chill during an expedition in 1868 to observe an eclipse. A little later he was dead, and Chulalongkorn, aged fifteen, was King Rama V.

So deeply was the tradition of education implanted in the royal house that the country remained under a regency for five years, while the young king completed the course of study begun for him by Anna by going to observe, at first hand, the forms of government in India and the Dutch East Indies. He was the first Siamese ruler to travel outside his own domains.

But thanks to Anna Leonowens we know a good deal about his youthful upbringing. As this is not only important to our assessment of the man, but delightful in itself, we can spend a moment considering it.

He was born in 1853, eldest son of the Queen Consort, and was thus the heir-apparent when Anna came to take charge of him. He was nine, and, we are told, "a handsome lad of stature neither noticeably tall nor short; figure symmetrical and compact; with dark complexion. He was, moreover, modest and affectionate, eager to learn and easy to influence". He was familiar with slavery—and later, as a man, was to abolish it—but slavery of a kind far less degrading and unpleasant than has been usual in history. A best friend was a slave, playing games with him in the royal palace, treated as a member of the family. He studied hard, mastering the fluent idiomatic English which had eluded his father, familiarizing himself with the literature, the thought and the history of the English people. As he grew towards manhood, he began to have doubts. He would rather be poor and have to earn his living, he told his governess, than be a king. "'Tis true, a poor man must work hard for his daily bread, but then he is free. And his food is all he has to lose or win. He can possess all things in possessing Him who pervades all things—earth, and sky, and stars, and flowers and children. I can understand that I am great in that I am a part of the Infinite, and in that alone; and that all I see is mine, and I am in it and of it. How much of content and happiness should I not gain if I could but be a poor boy!"

He was ten years old.

But there was little question of Chulalongkorn being a poor boy. Only, and for a few months, when he was admitted in sackcloth to the royal monastery, "chanting", as Anna noted, "those weird hymns".

He remained there, as Siamese princes do, for half a year. When he emerged he was deemed too old to study with his brothers and sisters. He was a man now, with his own private residence, "Rose-planting House", and here he took his lessons, alone with Anna. During the last months of book-study he remained a lovable, thoughtful young man, and she was to note, years later, that "even from this distant time and place, I look back with comfort to those hours".

And as she looked, the young king was completing the education she had begun, by touring, pencil and paper in hand, the capitals of Asia.

In 1873, at the age of twenty, he took up the reins of government.

Immediately—and he must have considered it again and again as he grew up—he introduced a startling series of reforms. He abolished slavery, set up efficient and incorruptible courts of law, made important changes in the methods of gathering revenue, built huge numbers of schools. Where his father had toyed with canals, young Chulalongkorn went and laid out railways.

But, of course, his path, like those of all good men, was beset with obstruction. The rich, who had grown richer through official corruption, not unnaturally resented attempts to abolish it. At the same time, the French, empire-building in that peninsula, caused him much worry, and took up valuable time which could have been devoted to improving the lot of his people. He bitterly begrudged this. The tension mounted to bloodshed and with typical nineteenth-century diplomacy the French put in gunboats and exacted a humiliating and unfair treaty, under which they were to occupy a part of South-east Siam for many years. It was not until 1896 that Britain intervened, suddenly fearful of French designs on her own empire. A treaty was signed between Britain and France, guaranteeing the autonomy of Siam.

And now, with external affairs in order, he was able to embark on an unprecedented seven-months' tour of that outside world with which he had been forced to quarrel. He visited much of Europe and was warmly welcomed in Paris. During the tour he soaked up, like a sponge, the innovations which might help his country, while carefully considering and rejecting those that would not.

On his return he built better schools, better hospitals. But he was in little doubt of his country's real position in the world, and with particular reference to the French who had greeted him so fervently in Paris, and in Asia were eyeing him quite differently. He built up, at speed, a modern army and navy.

And by this proof of a determination to resist any further encroachment, coupled with astute diplomacy, he made of his erstwhile enemy a good and loyal friend.

He replaced a complicated system of coinage, varying from district to district, by a standard one. Then he furthered the work of unification by introducing a modern apparatus of Posts and Telegraphs and personally seeing that it worked.

And, modestly aware that he owed much of the thinking behind his reforms to western civilization, he sent several of his sons to be educated in England.

The list of reforms and improvements made by Chulalongkorn during his long reign as King Rama V of Siam is almost endless. Sadly, it makes very dull reading. Sanitation and sewage farms fail to seize the imagination: even the spread of electric lighting scarcely speeds the pulse. But all these things were needed and urgently. With Chulalongkorn, Siam got them.

He died in 1910, deeply mourned, and not only in Siam. It was the same year as brought the death of Britain's Edward VII, but

Chulalongkorn's was after a far longer reign, of forty-two years. He was only fifty-seven when he died, and it was generally agreed that his unceasing work for his people had hastened the end.

He was succeeded by his son Vajiravudh, who became, in the same tradition, King Rama VI, and reigned for fifteen years before being succeeded, on his own death, by his brother Prajadhipok. A bloodless *coup d'état* in June of 1932 turned the benevolent but absolute monarchy of the country into a constitutional one, much like England's.

A long friendship between Siam and Britain, fostered by Chulalongkorn, was broken during the Second World War. There had been a non-aggression pact between the two countries, ratified in July, 1940, but when Japan invaded Malaya at the close of the following year, Siam, surrounded by Japanese forces, was compelled to declare war on Britain and the United States, which she did on 25 January, 1942, thereby leaving the way clear for Japan to invade Burma.

During the war Bangkok, the capital, was bombed by allied air forces. But with the coming of peace, Britain and India supported Siam's entry into the United Nations.

The present king, who was born in 1928, succeeded as a minor, and shortly afterwards, the council of regency was overthrown by Siam's "strong man", Pibul Songgram, who became prime minister. Yet another *coup*, in 1951, served only to strengthen Songgram's position, leaving the king as an honoured but virtually powerless constitutional monarch.

From time immemorial Thailand has leant towards the West, and this tendency was much strengthened by Chulalongkorn at the close of the nineteenth century and the beginning of our own. The West has good reason to be thankful for this inclination—though the West has not always deserved it.

We can be grateful to Chulalongkorn, and, like his own people, grateful for the statesmanship and genius of a man who brought his country from slavery and ignorance and gave it a degree of political, social and scientific advance unique in South-east Asia.

WILLIAM II

German Emperor and King of Prussia

(1859–1941)

WHEN IN 1888 the twenty-nine-year-old William II ascended the imperial throne of Germany the country had been united for only seventeen years, since, after the defeat of France, Bismarck had made William's grandfather, the King of Prussia, the first modern German Emperor. The old man had been much revered, but he was out of keeping with the spirit of a youthful nation, and his son Frederick, William's father, had succeeded him as an invalid with cancer of the throat and had died after a reign of only ninety days. Now, at last, Germans believed they had been given the figurehead they needed, and their gushing vitality, their sense of movement towards a mighty future, seemed to be matched by the young and enterprising monarch.

William certainly had intelligence and a love of display which well suited his people's mood. How were they to foresee that his reign would coincide with a period of mounting tension in world affairs, calling for infinitely more caution and sagacity than he could muster, or that it would end in world war, defeat for Germany and his ignominious abdication and flight to Holland? "Hail, Kaiser, to thee!" they shouted as, with his bristling moustache, with his own monogram planted on his face, he processed in scarlet cloak from his palace in Berlin to open the Reichstag in person, the first German Emperor ever to do so.

Inwardly William himself was far from feeling so confident. By nature he was subject to alternate moods of elation and gloom. An accident at birth had left him with a withered left arm six inches shorter than the right. This had undermined his self-assurance, and a harsh childhood discipline, designed to overcome the disability, had fanned aggressive instincts. They had been further aggravated by a supine father and an autocratic, strong-willed mother, Victoria, Queen Victoria's eldest child. William had grown into an arrogant, vain and touchy youth, at loggerheads with his mother and eager to imbibe from outsiders the flattery he never found at home. The Kaiser's inner weaknesses were obscured, however, by his frenzied activity during the first years of his reign. On the affairs of the

Fatherland or for pleasure he was perpetually on the move, until his breathless people called him the *Reisekaiser*, the travelling emperor.

With youthful idealism William conceived, soon after his accession, an ambitious programme of social legislation. This brought him into conflict with Bismarck who, as the undisputed master of Germany for fourteen years, resented the young monarch's interference and also considered that sops to the workers were dangerous at a time of industrial unrest. So, in 1890, Bismarck resigned, never to return to office, and William was left with mingled feelings of triumph and fear, mouthing phrases about "full steam ahead" for the Ship of State and wondering where he could find a new Chancellor. On one thing, however, he was determined: from now on he would have a major voice in foreign affairs.

Almost at once, under Bismarck's successor Caprivi, an error was committed by the abandonment of a Reinsurance Treaty with Russia which Bismarck had engineered. As a result, France and Russia drew closer together and Germany was confronted with a set of pincers whose jaws were forever ready to close. Other factors made caution necessary. The Turkish Empire seemed on the point of collapse, thus threatening a power-vacuum in the Balkans which would attract the conflicting ambitions of Austria-Hungary and Russia. Austria herself, Germany's only firm ally, was weakened by hostile nationalities within her own borders, while in Africa and the Far East the scramble for colonies and spheres of influence promised to keep international rivalry at fever-pitch. But, convinced that he enjoyed God's special protection and eager as ever to shine, the Kaiser threw caution to the winds and embarked on an aggressive policy, a "world policy" for the first time in German history.

Soon the world awoke to the fact that Germany was demanding her "place in the sun". After the Sino-Japanese war Kiau-Chau was leased from the defeated Chinese and further acquisitions in the Far East followed. When the Jameson Raid was defeated by the Boers, William at first thought of demanding a German protectorate over the Traansvaal, but was persuaded to send a congratulatory telegram to President Kruger instead—the only result being to infuriate Britain and compromise in advance the possibility of a firm Anglo-German understanding. Right up to the outbreak of the world war this was made yet more difficult by William's obsession with his dream-child, a large German battle-fleet, which came into being under the direction of Admiral Tirpitz. For these and other reasons an understanding with Britain was never reached and this calamity was in a large part directly due to the Kaiser.

William's megalomania, his vanity, his provocative speeches, his unreliability, his moodiness, his verbal aggression, his lack of realism and inability to learn from experience—these characteristics fairly burst the seams of contemporary memoirs and it was a tragedy that in perilous times he should have wielded such power. World suspicion of Germany grew as the Kaiser's opportunistic strokes became known: an attempt, for instance, to frighten Russia into the German orbit by pretending that an alliance was imminent with Britain, a visit to Turkey involving noisy efforts to spread German influence in the Near East. . . . Worst of all, dismissing an understanding between Britain, France and Russia as an impossibility, he failed to grasp Britain's proffered hand of friendship. So, while Germany sat on the fence, these nations came closer together and the "encirclement" of Germany came about, creating the climate for her reckless encouragement of Austria-Hungary in 1914, without which world war might at least have been postponed.

Meanwhile the zig-zag course of German foreign policy in the early 1900s was largely due to the Kaiser, the pursuit of small colonial advantages at disproportionate risk and a game of see-saw between the European powers in the erroneous belief that they would all have to pay court to Germany in the end. And when his instinct at last warned him of danger, as in the Morocco crisis of 1905, he proved unable to influence events. By that time Britain, France, Russia and Italy were all drawing together and the ring seemed to be closing round Germany. A German attempt to break it, even at the risk of war, by humiliating France on the question of French influence in Morocco, ended in disastrous failure entailing Anglo-French military conversations, and the Kaiser was left plaintively protesting to his advisers: "I told you so."

Fundamentally William was both bellicose and timorous. He possessed an aggressive spirit, but lacked a warrior's soul. He allied himself with the tradition of Frederick the Great, even of Napoleon, but never in his life seriously wanted war, at least world war. He contributed no doubt to its coming, but blindly, as one unable to conceive policy as a whole or visualize the probable results of his actions, and as the clouds gathered over Europe he watched helplessly the approaching storm, the victim of past mistakes, the victim of his excitable and erratic temperament, the victim, like all other rulers, of a chain of cause and effect which no one man could break.

As early as 1908 the European situation gave cause for alarm. The nations were aligned in two camps: Austria and Germany faced the recently formed Triple Entente comprising Britain, France and

Russia. In the Balkans, Slav nationalism was a deadly menace to Austria, on the other hand Russia hoped to profit from it when the Turkish Empire collapsed. There was a prospect, therefore, of conflict between Austria and Russia and so between the two groups of powers into which Europe was divided, and this danger was increased by Austrian intentions of crushing Serbia, the focal point of Slav agitation, when the time was ripe.

But if the local conflict led to world war, Austria would be heavily dependent on her German ally. This meant that Germany might prevent drastic Austrian action against Serbia by refusing support or threatening to refuse it. The key to the whole situation therefore lay in Berlin: if the Kaiser had made it clear to Austria that he, as the senior partner in the alliance, must call the tune, world war might have been postponed, if not averted altogether. But this, it seems, was never realized until too late and the reason was simple: to restrain Austria would have required clear-sightedness and courage. Neither William nor his Chancellors—Bülow followed by Bethmann-Hollweg—possessed these qualities, and so in 1908, in a situation closely resembling that of 1914, Austria was supported to the hilt in a rash annexation of Bosnia and Herzegovina, the Kaiser stood by his ally "in shining armour" and Russia began to prepare for a war which she now held to be one day inevitable.

From now on Germany's actions, dictated by William and his squabbling advisers, tended to increase rather than ease international tension. The illusion persisted that Germany could afford a tough policy regardless of her neighbours' feelings. Unrealistic political demands were made in return for a naval agreement which Britain requested. A renewed attempt was made to humiliate France over Morocco; as the price of her goodwill Germany demanded an exchange of colonial territories and, humiliated indeed, France drew yet closer to Britain. From this the Kaiser falsely concluded that a yet stronger fleet was necessary in order to force Britain into the German camp. This view was put to the test in 1912 when the British again tried to reach an agreement on outstanding points of contention, political, colonial and naval. It foundered on William's perverse refusal to sacrifice a single gunboat from his building programme in return for a friendship which he believed he could ultimately obtain at the pistol-point.

But truculence, always uppermost in his dealings with Britain, was succeeded by fear when in 1912 the Balkan countries drove out their Turkish overlords. Once again Germany supported Austria, this time in protests against an increase in Serbian territory. Once again Russia was incensed, to the point of mobilization. But once again world war was avoided. With horrid clarity the Kaiser saw that Germany had become a satellite of Austria and he longed to disentangle his country from complications involving the danger of war. But this mood did not last. Fear swung to the opposite pole and he began to feel that the survival of his ally depended on her dealing with the Serbian problem. Safety called for solidarity. Bethmann-Hollweg agreed with him, and when, in June, 1914, the Archduke Francis Ferdinand, heir to the Austrian throne, was murdered by an Austro-Hungarian citizen of Serb nationality, William was convinced that a reckoning was due and gave a blank cheque to the aged Emperor Francis Joseph to act as he chose against the Serbs.

Between the issue of the Austrian ultimatum and the invasion of Serbia William tried to draw back several times, but, unlike him, his Chancellor was ready to risk a world war and he actually frustrated last-minute attempts by William to act as mediator between Austria and Russia. Soon, in any case, it was too late for mediation. When Russia mobilized, for Germany faced with a war on two fronts the time-factor became all-important, and two days later William himself ordered mobilization. When he had signed the document he looked round at his Chancellor, at his Chief of General Staff and told them: "Gentlemen, you will live to rue the day when you made me do this. . . ." The approach of war filled him with black foreboding. At heart he was not an optimist, and when Britain ranged herself beside threatened France he was amazed, indignant and deeply disturbed. He railed against Edward VII, whom he had always detested and suspected of wishing to encircle Germany. Now he claimed that his uncle was stronger in death than he was in life. Then his thoughts turned to his adored grandmother, Queen Victoria. "If she had been alive," he told his friends, "*she* would never have allowed this!"

Throughout hostilities, though officially the War Lord, William never directed or even saw a battle, except from a safe distance. The protracted struggle exhausted and unnerved him, and though the fiction was maintained to the end that he held the reins of government in his hands, in the later stages he frequently escaped his responsibilities by retiring to the depths of the country, away from his advisers and from harassing decisions, such as the question of unrestricted U-boat warfare. In peacetime he had held the limelight, but in war he effaced himself so that, until Hindenburg became supreme commander, the Germans had no father-figure to look up to and listened in vain for encouragement from their Kaiser. William, in fact, was a broken reed, an actor who felt deeply humiliated that, in the grim reality of war, there was no place for his pageantry or his game of make-believe. Strong men in drab field-grey uniform ruled the country and he, as he complained, had nothing to do but saw wood and drink tea. His popularity survived so long as victories were being won, but rapidly waned as the prospect of final victory receded.

The final act in the imperial drama was written in October and November, 1918, when defeat faced Germany in the field and at home mutiny and red revolution were brewing. The Allies refused to negotiate with a monarchical government and wide sections of the German population were demanding William's abdication. He refused to go until finally, to avoid bloodshed in Berlin, the Chancellor, Max von Baden, announced his abdication—in fact, deposed him. Meanwhile a physical threat to the Kaiser was developing at Spa, where his own mutinous troops were approaching his headquarters, and it was to avert his capture, or worse, and the near certainty of civil war that Hindenburg advised flight to Holland. There was, indeed, no alternative. At last the Kaiser realized it. And so, at 5 a.m. on the morning of 10 November, in rain and total darkness, the last of the Hohenzollerns, who had been rulers in Brandenburg for over five hundred years, left Germany never to return.

Allied attempts to obtain his extradition from Holland for trial as a war criminal failed, and he died, still in Dutch exile, in June, 1941, an old man with white beard and moustaches who for many years had been almost happy in his seclusion and glad to avoid the limelight, the world of harsh reality which had dealt him such bitter blows. In the midst of the Second World War his passing went almost unnoticed and it is only today that historians are taking up the question again: to what extent was it fate and to what extent the Kaiser's own actions which led to the destruction of Imperial Germany?

GEORGE V

(1865–1936)

"IF THE dear child grows up good and wise, I shall not mind what his name is." Queen Victoria, benignly matriarchal, was writing to her son, the future Edward VII, about the choice of names for the latest addition to his family, the future George V. She had hoped for "some fine old name", and preferred Frederick to George, which last name, she reminded the Prince of Wales, "only came in with the Hanoverian family". She assumed that the name *Albert* (her italics) would be added: "As you know, we settled *long ago* that all dearest Papa's *male* descendants should bear *that* name, to mark *our line*, just as I wish all the girls to have Victoria after theirs." She stressed the point. "It is done in a great many families."

The "dear child" in question, born at Marlborough House, London, on 3 June, 1865, was baptized George Frederick Ernest Albert, and the verdict of posterity will no doubt be that he fulfilled his tremendous grandmother's hopes in both her stated particulars. He was good in the sense that there was no guile in him, and wise in his realization of what counts for virtue in a modern king of England. The result may well be that history will accord him a stature to which he never consciously aspired but which his character deserved.

That destiny had marked him for kingship was not apparent until he was nearing the third decade of his life. As the second son of the Prince of Wales, he was drilled from his earliest years to accept the notion that his future was with the Royal Navy, and that, subject to the demands of his place in the social order, he should look on it as his vocation. He and his elder brother Eddy (later Duke of Clarence) became cadets in H.M.S. *Britannia* at Dartmouth, where he showed up well in mathematics and still better in cutter sailing. The life contrasted sharply, at times painfully so, with what he had known before. "It never did me any good to be a Prince, I can tell you," he recalled, speaking to a member of the Household in later years, "and many a time I wish I hadn't been. It was a pretty tough place . . . the other boys made a point of taking it out of us on the grounds that they'd never be able to do it later on". When he got into a fight and came out of it with a bloody nose, he saw after-wards that it was "the best thing that could have happened—the doctor forbade me fighting any more". He passed out of *Britannia* when he was fourteen, having done "quite well" in the examinations.

His next three years were spent in H.M.S. *Bacchante*, a training vessel, in which he made three separate cruises, the last being the longest in that it took all but two years and made him acquainted with South America, South Africa, Australia, Japan, China, Singa-pore, and Egypt. He returned home as a midshipman in 1882, taller, heavier, and dismayed because he was quite unable to master the seasickness to which he was prone. When the *Bacchante* suffered damage in a fearful storm, he acquitted himself as well as any. Though in later years the public liked to picture him as the typical naval officer, his knock-knees and wine-bottle shoulders tended to discount that popular image.

For "Georgie", as his family called him, his naval years provided training in more than seamanship. The pattern of his future develop-ment as a man, if not as a king, was firmly drawn in those fifteen years at sea. The habits of thought, the outlook, the tastes and prejudices, the loyalties, that he formed then remained a constant of his life. He was not exposed to the doubts and re-assessments of more subtly endowed men. He had no intellectual pretensions. His values were simple, his opinions frank, his purposes honest.

Attained to man's estate, and being given command of a torpedo-boat as a lieutenant, R.N., he took part in his first State occasion by accompanying his father on an official visit to Berlin. Young Prince George was invested by the Kaiser with the Order of the Black Eagle and given honorary rank in a Prussian regiment. His mother, the Danish-born Princess of Wales, disliked the Germans, including their young emperor, Wilhelm. "So Georgie boy," she wrote to that young son of hers, "has become a real live filthy blue-coated Picklehaube German soldier ! ! ! Well, I never thought to have lived to see *that*! Better that, though," she added with more exclama-tion marks, "than Papa being made a German admiral—that I could not have survived".

The bias implanted by his mother obviously influenced his senti-ments when there arose the question of a bride being found for his elder brother, the heir but one to the throne. Prince George had read an article about it in *Vanity Fair*, which urged that the Duke of Clarence should marry an English girl. "It struck me as so sensible," George wrote to his mother. "I am afraid that both Grandmamma and dear Papa wish him to marry a German." Although the family's

variegated connexions encouraged the cosmopolitanism which
Edward VII practised so thoroughly, it had no attraction at all for
the future George V. His ideal was the life of the squire, not the
boulevardier.

The question of his elder brother's marriage was satisfactorily
settled when in December, 1891, an engagement was announced
between H.R.H. the Duke of Clarence and Princess Mary of Teck,
maternally descended from George III. Six weeks later the bride-
groom-to-be died at Sandringham, a victim of the great influenza
plague of that year. The brothers had been closer in sympathies than
they knew, and the younger was overwhelmed by a grief from
which he took many months to recover. "Alas! it is only now that
I have found out how deeply I did love him." To his distress of
mind was added the apprehension of immense unsought responsibilities piling up before him like cumulus clouds over a suddenly
shadowed landscape.

He was created Duke of York to give him a seat in the House of
Lords. "I am glad you like the title. I am afraid I do not," his
grandmother wrote to say. The name for her had "not very agreeable associations", a reference to her Hanoverian connexions. His
mother wrote cheerfully: "Fancy, my Georgie boy now being a
grand old Duke of York!" for once restrained in her use of exclama-
tion marks. He was given a wing of St. James's Palace that was
subsequently named York House, and provided with his own
personal staff. From there he attended House of Commons debates,
by way of acquainting himself with the personalities and opinions
of the leading political figures, and of learning something of the
intricacies of parliamentary procedure. Gladstone, at eighty-three,
impressed him greatly. "He made a beautiful speech and spoke for
two and a quarter hours," introducing his second Home Rule Bill.
Making a speech himself on receiving the freedom of the Merchant
Taylors Company, "I was horribly nervous, but got through fairly
well".

His grandmother, the ageing queen, was "in a terrible fuss" about
his marrying, so his father informed him. Her "most cherished
desire" was that he should become engaged to his late brother's
fiancée, Princess Mary of Teck, known in the family as May. To
what extent his affections were committed, whether or not he
married for love, or whether he saw his betrothal as a duty, what
his inclinations really were is not a matter of history. What unmistakably did emerge from such doubts as there may have been
was a successful union, one of the most felicitous in the annals of

the monarchy. The marriage took place in the Chapel Royal, St. James's, on 6 July, 1893. The honeymoon was at Sandringham, "the place I love better than anywhere in the world," he would write in after years, when he had seen more of the habitable globe than most men.

Through the now legendary 'nineties, George Duke of York was comparatively little in the public eye. Mostly he lived the life of a prematurely retired naval officer who is fond of country things. He was frequently at Sandringham, relaxed and happy in his freedom from the distractions of court life in London. His few official tasks included a visit to Ireland, from which he returned with a permanent liking for that country and the belief that the political animosities of its people were not directed against the Crown. So strong was his conviction that he begged his grandmother to consider setting up a royal establishment in or near Dublin. The cabinet approved, the queen did not.

At her behest the young duke was privately tutored during and after 1894 in constitutional history by a Cambridge don, J. R. Tanner, of St. John's College. Indispensable to his study of the subject was Walter Bagehot's *English Constitution*. The school exercise book in which he summarized his reading of that work is preserved in the Royal Library at Windsor. He noted, for example, that "where a monarchy of the English type already exists, it offers . . . a splendid career to an able monarch; he is independent of parties and therefore impartial, his position ensures that his advice would be received with respect and he is the only statesman in the country whose political experience is continuous". Inferentially, it was an important precept. It governed and perhaps inspired his conduct in the regnant years that were to come.

The South African War gave him an alarming glimpse of the risks to which persons of his station in life were exposed when human passions outran reason. His parents were fired at by an anti-British fanatic while they were waiting in their train at the Gare du Nord, Brussels. Soon afterwards he was invited to Berlin by the Kaiser for the crown prince's coming-of-age celebrations.

"It is certainly very disagreeable to me," George wrote to his mother, "having to go to Berlin just now and in fact anywhere abroad as they apparently all hate us like poison". His entourage was booed by pro-Boer sympathizers in Berlin. That was all; but life for him could never be quite the same again. "Goodbye Nineteenth Century," he wrote, not necessarily with relief, in his diary for the last day of 1900.

Three weeks later Queen Victoria died, and he was being prayed for in the churches as George, Duke of Cornwall and York. Before the year was out his father, the new king, conferred on him the title of Prince of Wales. The delay much annoyed his private secretary, Sir Arthur Bigge (later Lord Stamfordham). He was the direct heir to the throne for the next nine years, an apprenticeship in which Bigge was one of his wisest and principal mentors. Speaking of that faithful servitor in the fullness of time, he declared: "He taught me how to be a king."

George V's accession, in consequence of the sudden fatal illness of Edward VII in the first week of May, 1910, was to make him not only head of the oldest dynasty in Europe but monarch of all that he surveyed in the very real sense that he was the first head of the British Empire who had personal knowledge of the dominions and colonial possessions comprising it. He could look back not only on his circumnavigations as a naval officer, but on the still more comprehensive voyage that he made with his wife in 1901, when they journeyed 33,000 miles in the *Ophir* and a further 12,000 miles overland, visiting Australia, New Zealand, South Africa, and Canada, and when, between them, they shook hands with 24,855 persons. (The statistics of the eight months' travelling were formidable, recorded in a no less intimidating volume of 488 pages.) George's sense of responsibility was immeasurably deepened by his overseas experiences. Yet it was his insularity that finally commended him to the hearts of his people.

Between his accession in 1910 and the outbreak of the First World War in 1914 he witnessed the diplomatic embroilments, the political struggles, the industrial strife, the social upheavals, of an age that was heading for convulsion as by a natural law. As part of those troubled times, the new king had to deal with a matter that impinged unpleasantly on his personal life. For many years there had been whispered rumours of his alleged association with an admiral's daughter whom he was supposed to have secretly married in Malta during his navy time. In 1911 new currency was given to them in print. A paper called *The Liberator*, published in Paris, purported to give factual information about the affair. A charge of criminal libel was laid against the journalist concerned. The case came before the Lord Chief Justice and a special jury. The evidence conclusively disproved the story, which the king characterized in his diary as "a damnable lie that has been in existence now for twenty years". His hope was that "this will settle it once and for all".

Against advice, he had insisted on the case going forward, a decision that aroused greater interest than the cause of it. The king himself could not be called into court. After sentence had been passed the Attorney-General read out, "by his Majesty's command", a firm denial of the rumours. That he showed moral courage, rather than mere obtuseness, was generally agreed. It was a matter of conscience to him that he should stand before his people as one who was to be trusted as fully in his private life as in his public role. His mother, Queen Alexandra, was prompt with her sympathy. "To *us* all it was a ridiculous story yr having been married before ... ! ! Too silly for words. My poor Georgie—really it was too bad and must have worried you. It only shows how unfair the world is & how the wicked love to slander the upright and good & try to drag them down on their own level."

The coronation and a wonderful summer made 1911 a brilliantly memorable year, its climax for the king and queen the great Delhi durbar held in November. That event, the first of its kind to be recorded by news-reel cameras, was given its touch of anxiety when the Gaekwar of Baroda, making his obeisance, appeared to disdain the necessity of doing so. The newspapers gave the incident the prominence of an event. Official comment brushed it aside as having "lent itself to misrepresentation". For George V it cannot but have been an awkward episode, one more reminder of the unease of the imperial burden.

Foreign affairs engaged his attention more imperatively in those years before the storm. His personal relations with his cousin, the Kaiser, blended amicability with protocol. That monarch, and the policies of his government, increasingly exercised the king's thinking on current problems. He was in constant touch with Sir Edward Grey, the Foreign Secretary, and through him encouraged the British ambassadors in Europe to communicate direct with the private secretary, Lord Stamfordham, amplifying or explaining their official reports. He was seeing at the same time the foreign ambassadors in London, inviting them for week-ends at Windsor or Balmoral. The overriding theme of the conversations was the growing menace of Germany, particularly in terms of naval supremacy. As a sailor, King George often tested the patience of Paul Cambon, of France, and Count Benckendorff, of Russia, by dwelling on that topic to the exclusion of others of equal interest. Both were impressed by his grasp of affairs, by his great store of knowledge of what was going on in the world, by his close identity with the attitudes prevailing in Downing Street, and by his robust temper.

While he was making his mark in the private councils and

colloquies, the king was by no means unreservedly esteemed by the masses. To them he was still a remote personage who, dutifully doing what was required of him, engaged their homage but rarely their sympathies. That perspective was only momentarily fore-shortened by the wave of emotion that passed through the crowd clamouring for his appearance on the balcony of Buckingham Palace when war broke out. As soon as the glass doors closed behind him he receded again in the public mind to his symbolic sceptre-bearing status as head of the Commonwealth and Empire.

Then, in October, 1915, he had a riding accident while inspecting men of the Royal Flying Corps at the Front. His mount, lent to him by General Sir Douglas Haig, took fright at a burst of cheering and fell backwards, the king still in the saddle. He was more seriously hurt than was at first disclosed; in fact, "he was never quite the same man again", by the testimony of his biographer, Sir Harold Nicolson. The news evoked a spontaneous concern that was felt rather than expressed, though the bulletins were given front-page priority. Identified thus dramatically with the casualty lists, the king was seen to be a partaker of the common human lot, no more immune from misfortune than the next man. From then on he could count on affection as well as respect. The extraordinary extent to which science would enlarge and consolidate his popularity was not then within the realm of feasible conjecture.

That he came out of the ordeal of the war with enhanced personal prestige was not questioned. His exemplary behaviour over the drink question, when it was postulated by the Prime Minister, Lloyd George, as a menace to production in the war factories, was noted in responsible sections of the community, while his contempt for reprisals against prisoners of war, of whatever side, also showed his wisdom. His part in smoothing out the frictions between political and military leaders was frequently effective, though unacknow-ledged at the time.

His conciliatory services were sought again when in the first post-war decade Labour thrust its way to power for the first time. He established cordial relations in particular with the railwaymen's leader, J. H. Thomas, M.P., who in due course became Colonial Secretary. During the General Strike in 1926 the king's moderating counsel was successfully proffered on more than one outstanding issue. He warned the government of the danger of introducing pro-vocative orders and bills, and expressed his keen dislike of an intention to prohibit banks from paying out funds to the strikers' unions. When Winston Churchill made it known through the government's emergency newspaper, the *British Gazette*, which he edited, that the armed forces of the crown would receive full support in any action they might deem necessary for the security of essential services, the king communicated his displeasure to the War Office. "His Majesty cannot help thinking," wrote the private secretary, "that this is an unfortunate announcement."

The grave illness that struck the king down in the last weeks of 1929 moved the nation to depths of feeling unmatched by any similar crisis that was remembered. At a meeting of the Privy Council called to prepare a warrant for the appointment of a Council of State, his hand had to be guided by his physician, Lord Dawson of Penn, in signing the requisite document. Churches were open day and night for prayers of intercession. He was an invalid for more than three months, as a sequel to a severe lung draining operation. Shortly after the service of thanksgiving at St. Paul's for his recovery he sent for J. H. Thomas, the trade-unionist with whom he was on the friendliest terms. One of Thomas's anecdotes set him laughing so much that he had a relapse, and had to submit to a second operation, in which a rib was removed. Those around him believed that the illness had permanently weakened his constitution. It made him look older than his sixty-four years.

The world economic crisis, with its dramatic repercussions in England in 1931, was for the king a source of additional strain, not easily borne. While those closest to him saw and in some instances suffered the effects of it in his increasing querulousness and sharpness of temper, to the millions who heard his first Christmas broadcast, in 1932, he was the benign father of his people who personified the virtues of sincerity, honesty, and love of home and family. It was all there in his voice, which proclaimed him to be free of affectation and cant, a patriarchal voice rich with the overtones of experience, wisdom, and authority. It made as deep an impression in the wider world as at home. "Oh, if only he were our king too!" a German woman wrote to a London newspaper from out of the mounting anguish of life under her country's dynamically vengeful new leadership.

Jubilee year, 1935, is still remembered for the extraordinary fervour at the heart of the celebrations. "A never-to-be-forgotten day" it was, too, for the king himself, as he wrote in his diary for 6 May, after returning from the service in St. Paul's. There were flood-lit balcony appearances before vast crowds outside Buckingham Palace every night that week. When the pageantry was over, he and the queen drove through the meaner streets of the metropolis; first,

Battersea, Kennington, and Lambeth; then Whitechapel, Shoreditch, and dockland; and finally the teeming northern suburbs of King's Cross and Camden Town. His nurse, Sister Catherine Black, of London Hospital, recalled his pleasure in the welcome he had everywhere been given. "I'd no idea," he said, "they felt like that about me. I'm beginning to think they must really like me for myself." It was the naïve satisfaction of an unconceited man, who always liked appreciation and to have letters of gratitude even from obscure persons who received honours or other favours at his hands.

Broadcasting at the end of Jubilee day, he asked his myriad listeners at home and throughout the Commonwealth: "How can I express what is in my heart? I dedicate myself anew to your service for all the years that may still be given to me." The plural was poignantly redundant. His health declined after his autumn stay at Balmoral. The death of his favourite sister, Princess Victoria, was a shock. "No one ever had a sister like her," he wrote in the diary that he had kept faithfully every day for more than fifty years. His enfeeblement grew so marked that in January, 1936, a Council of State had to be convened again to act in his place. And once again Dawson of Penn was obliged to guide his hand, kneeling by the bedside. The king objected to merely making his mark, as was suggested, and struggled hard to write his usual signature. "Gentlemen," he said to the Privy Councillors as he lay back wearily on his pillow, "I am sorry to keep you all waiting like this—I am unable to concentrate."

The last diary entry was made by Queen Mary, his tower of strength throughout his reign. "My dearest husband, King George V, was much distressed at the bad writing above & begged me to write his diary for him next day. He passed away on January 20th at 5 minutes before midnight."

His great achievement was to prove to the world, through some of its most testing decades, that a constitutional monarchy is one of its soundest institutions provided that the monarch is equal to its demands and sensible always of his duties and obligations. "A king of England who is willing to be a man of his people," a Belgian diplomat had written long before, "is the greatest king in the world. But if he wishes to be more, by heaven, then he is nothing at all". George V was in all respects the man of his people, reflecting their qualities and ideals, private and public, with a sureness of touch that was akin to genius. So it is that he stands before history as one of the most respected kings of modern times.

SUN YAT-SEN

(1866–1925)

CHINA IN the second half of the twentieth century is one of the world's most powerful nations, with the enormous potential of a vast and energetic population. But this was not always the case: half a century ago it seemed unlikely that China would ever awake from what, to outsiders, seemed a complacent slumber. It was true —there had been a time, centuries before, when she was reckoned great, but now China was no more than a limping anachronism, gleefully bested by any nation which cared to come and impose "trade" upon her, a trade which was simply exploitation. The gulf between China and the world seemed to widen every day.

The man destined to lead China across that gulf was born in November, 1866. Whatever changes have taken place since his day, may yet take place, nothing will ever equal the dramatic change that came over Chinese thinking, Chinese behaviour, during the comparatively brief working life of Sun Yat-sen.

He was born in a village in the south of the country, not far from the Portuguese island settlement of Macao. He started his education in the village school and, like nearly everyone in that village and in tens of thousands of other villages throughout China, he and his family were poor. They were kept that way by high rents they were forced to pay for their land and by the depredations made upon them and their crops by imperial soldiers. For this was the day of the Manchu dynasty, the last emperors (did they but know it) of a China which had been an absolute monarchy for thousands of years. The Manchus in fact were pigtail-wearing foreigners and comparative newcomers, who had swept down over the Great Wall as recently as the seventeenth century and seized this huge and fertile country. They had forced the population to adopt this pigtail, the long, plaited queue of hair. This is often associated with ancient China—but it was a hated and compulsory innovation. During Sun Yat-sen's time one of the least important, but most emotionally-charged, manifestations of the fight for freedom was the cutting off of this hated symbol of Manchu oppression.

But this was all in the future. Young Sun, in his village, thought himself fortunate in being able to leave China at the age of fourteen and go to work for one of his two elder brothers, an enterprising fellow who had settled in Honolulu and ran a successful shop. He liked Honolulu, for the work was pleasant and left him with time to attend a Christian school. It was here that he became finally converted to that Christian faith which he had viewed with interest but without conviction from his village.

But so rapidly did Sun assimilate not only Christianity but the English language and western ways, with all manner of strange ideas about "democracy", that his alarmed older brother packed him off home to China.

And now it seemed as if the young man's link with family and village had been severed for ever. In no time he had managed to enrage the elders of the village by speaking disparagingly of idols in the local shrine: he was promptly banished from the village and sent, at the age of eighteen, to Hong Kong.

He settled well into this strange, cosmopolitan, town, for he was thirsty for new ideas, thirsty for a new philosophy which would make not only his own life more worthwhile, but that of all China. He found friends who thought as he did, and they sat up late, night after night, when studies were over, discussing the future of the world and the impact on parts of it of the exciting new, western, "Socialism". He was summoned back to his village, to be married, as was the custom, to a girl he had never met, and he went obediently. He married the girl, then left her at home with his mother while he went back to Hong Kong to finish his studies. He had just finished with one school, was going on to another; he had become firm friends with an American missionary who welcomed his help with the Chinese language and was about to baptize him in the Christian faith: a young, un-asked-for, wife had no part to play in this new awakening. He would send for her, of course, but in the meantime Sun Yat-sen was too busy for matrimony. China and her future obsessed him. Not only was he actively considering becoming either a missionary or a revolutionary—perhaps both— but he was about to embark on a medical career. One concrete, useful thing he could do for his people was to become a doctor and minister to their ills.

So, at the age of twenty-one, he entered the new Alice Memorial Hospital in Hong Kong, just started by Dr. James Cantlie. He was immediately drawn to Cantlie, they became close friends and remained so for many years.

Sun was a good student, and he graduated with honours five

years later, one of the first graduates of the hospital. But though the obvious move on graduation was to find a post as doctor, young Sun's mind was teeming with ideas of revolution. He had joined a group sworn to overthrow the Manchu dynasty, replace it with a form of Socialism, and he had been busy writing for them—writing brilliant, provocative, tracts. Now, in China where these tracts were circulating, urging overthrow of the Manchus, it was hardly surprising that a price was on his head. If he wished to look after the sick of his own people he would have to practise medicine, either in Hong Kong, which was British territory, or Macao, which was Portuguese.

How little factors—luck, the spin of a coin—affect our lives! He chose Macao, and suddenly a ban on all doctors in the territory without Portuguese qualifications ended his professional career. From now on, Dr. Sun Yat-sen would devote his energies to bringing about a new era for the Chinese people.

First, with no money and a price on his head, he would have to travel in other lands, preach the urgency of revolution in China, and beg for funds.

He went back to Honolulu, was successful in his mission and then unexpectedly met his good friend Dr. Cantlie. If Dr. Sun wanted to interest people in his exciting new ideas for a different China he should go to England.

Sun sailed, via the United States, for London.

The visit, as Cantlie had prophesied, was a success: he raised both money and moral support. But it was in the greyness of London, thousands of miles from his beloved China, that Sun Yat-sen realized the determination of the Manchu government to get rid of him and his ideas. He was lured into the Chinese Legation, overpowered and taken prisoner. He would almost certainly have been smuggled back to China and a painful death if he had not managed to get a message out to his friend Cantlie—who, like some personal deity, had returned to England, and was able to help him a third time. Cantlie was now Sir James, and a man of considerable importance in Britain. When he objected loudly about the incarceration of his friend in the Chinese Legation, no less a figure than the Foreign Secretary, Lord Salisbury, was forced to intervene. Reluctantly, angrily, the Legation handed over its prisoner.

And, a little later, revolution began in China. It was not revolution as Sun had envisaged it, and it urgently needed guidance, but it indicated at least that there were people in China dissatisfied with things as they were. The so-called "Boxers" (so styled by a European journalist who had heard they regarded themselves as "Heavenly Fists", destined to destroy all foreigners) had taken the law into their own hands, behaving much like a greatly less inhibited Ku Klux Klan, and were butchering foreigners and Chinese converts to Christianity. The Manchus, under the wily, brilliant and vicious old dowager empress, T'zu Hsi, were busily encouraging them while publicly holding up hands in horror at this "outbreak of lawlessness".

Whichever way things turned out, China was no longer asleep. Sun disapproved strongly of the action being taken against Christians, and he did what he could to arrest it, but his main work must be the consolidation of a strong revolutionary party, sworn to take over when the suitable moment arrived. He had formed his "Chinese Revolutionary League" with branches in Europe and Japan, and he had raised a great deal of money. This was being employed, for the time being, in disseminating literature which Sun wrote and which was published by a rich Chinese supporter, the American-educated Charlie Soong. Soong's firm masqueraded as a publisher of religious tracts, but in reality it devoted most of its time to printing far more explosive ones written by Sun.

(Years later Sun was to divorce the wife he had wed unseen and marry Chingling, one of Charlie Soong's three beautiful and highly educated daughters, who would be a source of strength and inspiration to him during what was left of his life. The other two Soong girls would also make interesting matches: one would become the wife of the wealthy banker, H. H. Kung—the other, Madame Chiang Kai-shek.)

The death of the dowager empress in 1908, a day after the young emperor whom she had kept virtual prisoner for many years, accelerated the process of revolution. Sun's teachings were now known all over that vast country: even his physical presence was known by many, for although much of his life had been spent outside China he was completely without fear and paid a number of visits deep into the country, despite the price on his head.

In 1911 the revolution came at last, with a rising in Hankow and the revolt of its royal garrison. Sun at the time was in America raising funds, but the revolt was acknowledged as his brainchild and he was immediately nominated first President of the new "Republic of China". He read the fact in a newspaper, halfway across the United States, and prepared to make his way back.

In January of the following year he was sworn in to the new office. He had, over the years, planned down to the last detail a

Republican government, his "Kuomintang", or "National Republican Party", and though he had little hankering for power himself he had hopes that stable government would follow the coup.

He was to be disappointed—so much so that the only way he was able to ensure stable government was by handing over, almost immediately, to the sort of President he thought the new Republic needed: a strong and ruthless man, not a behind-the-scenes idealist and reformer who had spent most of his time abroad. He urged, and it was agreed, that General Yuan Shih-kai be appointed—a doughty, if not altogether trustworthy, fighter who had wielded great influence in the Manchu court and had actually persuaded the regent, who followed T'zu Hsi, to abdicate.

But Yuan, to Sun's great disillusionment and distress, soon showed that he wanted to be dictator of this new China and had no interest at all in democracy or socialism or any of the other ideals for which Sun had been fighting. He declared himself "Emperor of China" and managed to keep himself in this anachronistic position, despite Sun's every attempt to make him see reason, right until his death, which fortunately perhaps came within a year.

A little later there came a landmark in Chinese history: the Fourth of May Incident. It was May of 1919 that the Chinese, still struggling to put their new house in order, learnt that the Treaty of Versailles, ending the First World War, had ignored them. The extra-territorial rights by which foreigners held sizeable parts of Chinese territory would be retained. The military encroachment already made by Japan would be legalized.

Angry, incredulous—for had there not been noisy praise throughout the western world for China's step into the twentieth century? Peking students marched on the foreign legation quarter to protest.

They were not allowed in. Legation quarters were extra-territorial.

And now the disillusioned Sun and his followers turned to the Soviet Union. If the West refused to help China, perhaps the U.S.S.R. would.

The U.S.S.R. did, with gifts of arms and money. And from that emotion-filled fourth of May in 1919 sprang the infant Chinese Communist party, born of gratitude to Russia. Sun, though never becoming a Communist himself, took steps to reorganize his Kuomintang party more efficiently, into Soviet shape. The Communists, for the time being, remained a small group, broadly sympathetic to Sun's aims.

Others were not. China was still divided, north from south, with the Kuomintang nominally in charge in the south and a pack of mutually antagonistic war-lords in the north. Even in the south, Sun found it again necessary, for the good of his people, to resign. He remained behind the scenes until 1921, when he was called in. A year later he was driven out by the disaffected General Chen Chiung-Ming and made a dramatic escape to Shanghai.

His loyal supporter General Chiang Kai-shek now rallied to him and General Chen was defeated. Sun Yat-sen ruled, nominally at least, over southern China.

He never succeeded, in his lifetime, in uniting the country: the war-lords were in effective control of the north when he died on 12 March, 1925. The mantle of Kuomintang leader fell on Chiang Kai-shek, who now, to raise himself above the herd of squabbling generals, styled himself "Generalissimo".

From Sun's death the Kuomintang under Chiang's conservative leadership (he believed firmly in a landlord-and-peasant economy) drew further away from the ideals of the new Communist party. Unco-ordinated civil war gave way to a clear-cut struggle between Chiang and the Communist leader Mao Tse-tung, culminating in 1949 with Communist victory and the exile of the Kuomintang to Formosa.

Had Sun Yat-sen lived longer—he was only fifty-nine when he died—it is possible this split need never have happened. But in any case, present-day Communist China, with its flexing muscles, owes its biggest debt to one man—the little Christian doctor whose energy and strange ability to make men follow in search of an ideal brought China out of the middle ages and made it a nation.

PILSUDSKI

(1867–1935)

Marshal Joseph Pilsudski of Poland was one of the great war figures of his time. All his life he fought for the regeneration of his unhappy country. Between 1905 and 1914 he built the disorganized Polish army into an efficient force which he commanded during the First World War; but his greatest achievements came after the Armistice. In 1920 he saved Poland from Bolshevik invasion, thereby earning the gratitude of the whole of Europe. In 1926 he emerged from retirement and ruthlessly reconstituted the entire system of Polish government, afterwards introducing a firm foreign policy which brought a sense of security to a people who, because of their geographical position, had been subjected to constant interference by their more powerful neighbours for over two hundred years.

Pilsudski was born at Zulova, a big estate forty miles north-east of Wilno (Vilna) in Lithuania, on 5 December, 1867, and was the fourth child of well-born parents whose ancestors had rendered signal services to the state. His father was a restless man full of strange enthusiasms, one of these being the yeast factory he ran at Zulova; his mother, a frail woman who burned with a patriotic ardour which she passed on to her twelve children.

Little Joseph (or Ziuk, the Polish equivalent of Joe) was a bright, alert child who loved exploring the countryside with his elder brother Bronislas. From his father he inherited a venturesome spirit; from his mother, whom he adored, he learned how Poland had been a great kingdom before her greedy neighbours the Swedes, Austrians, Germans and Russians had snatched parts of her territory. Catherine the Great had been the arch-enemy, since she had annexed the rich black lands of the Ukraine, the Grand Duchy of Lithuania and the province of Courland, thus turning a shrunken Poland into the Vistula provinces of Russia. The Congress of Vienna had promised amends, but nothing had been done until, in January, 1861, the Poles themselves had staged a hasty and ill-organized rebellion which was quickly squashed by the Czar's troops.

Joseph was seven when the family moved to a large flat in Wilno following a fire which destroyed their home and factory at Zulova, and young as he was he soon found ample proof of his mother's teachings. The Pilsudskis were devout Catholics, yet the children had to receive religious instruction from Orthodox priests, while in their schools lessons were given in Russian and use of the Polish language forbidden. Joseph and Bronislas became adept in dodging the frequent Russian ceremonies and stayed mute when told to chant "One Czar, one faith, one language!" They offended so often that though they were good scholars they were continually in trouble.

At that time Lithuania was dominated by Governor Muraviev, known as "The Hangman", a sadistic man who delighted in humiliating the Poles, Jews and Letts who formed the bulk of the population. His methods so angered Joseph that at the age of twelve he wrote and circulated among his friends a paper called *The Zulova Pigeon*, which called on all young Poles to rescue their motherland from durance vile. This was so popular that Joseph and Bronislas formed a secret "League", members of which read and discussed forbidden books and papers on Socialism that had been smuggled into the country. Their mother was delighted by their enterprise but was already suffering from an incurable disease. When Joseph was sixteen she died, leaving a void in his life which was never filled. While still dedicated to her romantic ideal, he felt he should explore the socialistic societies being formed by young Russians and went to the Ukrainian University of Kharkov to study medicine. There he found many other Polish students, but their apathetic attitude towards their own country and the triumph of czardom over the Russian movement known as the "People's Will" so angered him that after a year he returned to Wilno, where he and Bronislas revived and expanded their secret "League".

Wilno was not very far from St. Petersburg where the students, infuriated by the constant surveillance of the police, were forming terrorist bands, one of which began to devise an elaborate plan to assassinate Czar Alexander III. Bombs were to be thrown at him when he attended a memorial service for his murdered father early in 1887, and in order to ensure success they proposed to add poison to the explosives. They appealed to the Wilno League for chemicals, revolvers and funds and these were smuggled to the capital. The plot was discovered and some conspirators, including Lenin's brother, were executed, Bronislas was sent to Siberia for eight years, and Joseph, whose part had been small, for three.

With a score of others Joseph began the interminable journey to Irkutsk, where they were thrown into gaol until the Lena river froze and they could travel down it by sled. Conditions were so appalling that they revolted and were beaten unconscious by the guards. When they came to their senses they found three of their number missing, so they staged a hunger strike which proved effective but led to six months' imprisonment for Joseph and other ringleaders when they finally reached Kirensk, seven hundred miles down-river. He was put to work as a clerk in the hospital, a job which gave him an opportunity of getting to know the Russian patients and, more important, the bureaucracy which oppressed them. Memories of his ill-treatment by the Irkutsk guards smouldered within him and his determination to free Poland from the Russian yoke deepened. Through his friendship with an aged Polish exile who had been a mighty rebel in his day, he learnt many subtleties of technique and he also studied books on military strategy.

A boy had gone to Siberia: a man of single purpose returned to Wilno. Polish Socialists had now split into two groups, the P.P.S. (Polish Socialist Party) and the National Socialists. Pilsudski joined the P.P.S. but found to his dismay that they talked too much and did too little. Their leaders, working secretly from London, felt that this fiery young man with his cry of "Romantic plans, practical execution!" was too extreme altogether, but the rank and file loved him and before long he dominated the movement. His task was complex to a degree. In the Vistula provinces the Poles feared the Russians, in Galicia the Austrians, in the western districts the Germans. They had been browbeaten by foreign masters so long that they had lost all desire for a free Poland. Undaunted, Pilsudski set about rekindling the flame of patriotism in their breasts.

He scorned the safety of exile and worked inside Poland. He married a doctor's widow, also an ardent revolutionary, and they lived in the industrial town of Lodz, where Pilsudski and his friend Wojciekowski wrote and printed a paper called the *Workman*, which they smuggled to different centres in suitcases. Over the years the circulation reached over 100,000 copies and many socialist publications from outside were also distributed, and in addition to his printing and journalistic activities Pilsudski was constantly on the move, striving to bring Poles in various parts of their disrupted country into one united party. Inevitably there were periods when he had to go into voluntary exile for a time, and in 1900 the Russian police seized his printing press and imprisoned him in the Tenth Pavilion in Warsaw Citadel, from which escape was impossible. Here he feigned madness so convincingly that he was transferred to the St. Nicholas asylum in St. Petersburg, from whence a Polish doctor helped him escape.

Pilsudski and his wife then fled to London, but privation had given him arthritis and produced a tendency to tuberculosis, so they returned secretly to the mountains south of Cracow where he slowly regained strength. The outbreak of the Russo-Japanese war gave him fresh hope, and though discovery meant a life sentence Pilsudski boldly entered Russian territory to rally his supporters, while later he journeyed to Tokyo in an abortive attempt to induce the Japanese to finance a Polish rising. Finally, since the P.P.S. was desperately short of funds, he relaxed his rule of non-violence and organized several raids, the most notable of which was the Bezdany train robbery in September, 1908, which brought the Party some £33,000.

Since he was convinced that the Russians would soon rise against czardom, Pilsudski turned his energies to the training of a brigade of Polish riflemen. The weapons and ammunition were begged from sympathizers all over Europe, others were borrowed and not a few were stolen. The Poles were good fighters and there was no shortage of recruits. They had to train hard, submit to rigid discipline and live under spartan conditions, but by superhuman effort Pilsudski managed to turn them into a small but remarkably efficient force before the outbreak of war in 1914.

More than ever now was Poland the nut in the nut-cracker with the Russians massing in the east, the Germans in the west and the Austro-Hungarians in the south. Pilsudski, having made some successful forays against the Russians, boldly approached the Austrian High Command and offered the services of his new-styled Polish Legion (whose standard bore a white eagle) if they and the Germans would recognize Poland as an independent state. The answer was a grudging affirmative, for if Poland were given true freedom then the Hungarians would also demand it, while Italy's position might be swayed by any decisive announcement. Until 1916 Polish status remained undefined, though the Poles continued to fight gallantly for the Axis powers. In the December President Wilson declared that a free Poland was essential, and in the spring of 1917, when the tide was turning against them, the Germans and Austrians agreed to the creation of a free Polish state. Various pointers showed Pilsudski that this freedom was purely nominal, and in June, when every Polish soldier had to swear to obey the orders of Kaiser William II's High Command, he tendered his resignation to von Beseler, the German Governor in Warsaw. In their final interview at the Belvedere Palace von Beseler assured him that his army would be given the latest equipment, while he would receive fame and many honours. "Does your Excellency believe," replied Pilsudski, "that the hand which throttles Poland will throttle her the less if it has on every finger a ring which bears an eagle?"

The Polish Legion was disbanded, and on 22 July, Pilsudski and his Chief-of Staff, Sosnkowski, were arrested and driven to Germany. Over the next fifteen months Pilsudski experienced solitary confinement in four different fortresses, Posen, Danzig, Spandau and Magdeburg. News was kept from him, but he accepted everything philosophically, busying himself with writing accounts of the Legion's battles and long expositions on the state of his unhappy country. Suddenly, at the beginning of November, 1918, revolutionary groups surged through Magdeburg streets and Pilsudski was hurriedly conveyed to Berlin. On 9 November the Kaiser abdicated, and as he was being driven to the station Pilsudski saw the Imperial car, smothered in red flags, being paraded down the Unter den Linden. The following morning—the day before the Armistice— he arrived in Warsaw and as he feasted his eyes on that proud city rising from the Vistula he knew that all he had fought for was at last about to come true.

The task before him made all previous ones pale into insignificance. The so-called Regency Council was riven by political schisms, the garrison was German manned, the Polish Legionaries were scattered to the four winds, the country had no economy, the Polish National Socialist Committee based in Paris had names, like Paderewski, far more illustrious than his own. It is a measure of Pilsudski's greatness that, under his dictatorship, order took the place of chaos within a year and that the signatories to the Treaty of Versailles, well aware of Poland's strategic position between Bolshevik Russia and defeated Germany, restored her territories and gave her full and legal independence.

Then came Pilsudski's major error. The War of Intervention made him determined to win back the rich Ukraine and his troops advanced to Kiev, from which they were driven back with heavy losses by Marshal Budenny's Red cavalry. They were still licking their wounds when news came that Red forces under Tukhachevsky, a brilliant ex-czarist officer, had reached the Vistula and were about to storm Warsaw. A grim Pilsudski rallied his men and succeeded not only in saving the capital but in pushing Tukhachevsky's army back to Brest-Litovsk. He then began the laborious task of re-stabilizing the Polish Government and in 1924 he retired to live quietly near Warsaw with his second wife and two tiny daughters.

In 1926 some of his old enemies in the Polish Senate and Seym

(House of Commons) spread about the most scurrilous rumours asserting that Pilsudski had worked solely for personal gain and had even appropriated the Polish crown jewels from the Belvedere. Poland was still full of warring factions, many of whom believed the scandalous tales, and to quell the rumours once and for all Pilsudski marched on Warsaw at the head of three loyal regiments. Needless to say he routed his enemies and, although he refused to resume the Presidency, appointing his trusted friend Ignatius Moscicki in his stead, he continued to be virtual ruler of Poland until the end of his life.

By 1934 his public appearances had become few and those who met him reported he was mortally sick. In truth he was suffering from cancer and on Sunday, 12 May, 1935, he died. Political rancour was forgotten as all Poland mourned the country's greatest son. His bones were encased in a solid silver sarcophagus, but, at his special request, his heart was placed at his mother's feet in her grave at Wilno.

LENIN

(1870–1924)

THE RUSSIAN REVOLUTION of 7 November, 1917 (25 October in the Julian Calendar), was the greatest upheaval of its kind the world had ever known and it was engineered and led with complete efficacy and ruthlessness by one man, V. I. Lenin. Who was he, this man who changed the whole concept of life for some 170,000,000 inhabitants of one-sixth of the earth's land surface and profoundly influenced the minds of men and women in many different countries?

Lenin's real name was Vladimir Ilich Ulyanov and he was born in 1870 at Simbirsk, a Volga town later renamed Ulyanovsk in his honour. His father was of Tartar stock, a man of substance who was Inspector of Schools for the region: his mother was a German doctor's daughter and a devout Lutheran. Vladimir and his elder brother Alexei attended a good school where, strangely enough, one of their teachers was the father of Alexei Kerensky, leader of the 1917 Provisional Government. Both brothers were good scholars, wore neat dark suits with Eton collars, were devoted to the dogs, cats and birds they kept as pets and shared a favourite book, *Tom Sawyer*. Alexei was the more venturesome and made many school friends: Vladimir was a reserved child who liked nothing better than to creep into his father's study each evening and listen to intellectual discussions between Ulyanov and his friends.

From these debates the boy learnt much, and he supplemented this knowledge by voracious reading. Among Russian writers Turgenev especially appealed to him, and through the sufferings of the tragic Bazarov in *Fathers and Sons* he grew intensely interested in nihilism, reading everything he could find on the subject. Next he studied the doctrines of Engels and Hegel, and finally he discovered Karl Marx, the man who became his god; and *Das Kapital*, the book which became his bible. (The Russian authorities had allowed a translation to be issued because they thought it too incomprehensible, too dull, "to do anybody harm!") The adolescent Vladimir read and re-read the book until his head seethed with revolutionary ideas and, naturally, he confided these to Alexei, who received them enthusiastically. Night after night the brothers talked into the small hours about the plight of Russia and how she could be freed from the crushing tyranny of the czar, the civil service and the secret police. The impetuous Alexei was all for instant action and, despite his more cautious brother's repeated warnings, set off to begin his studies at St. Petersburg University confident that there he would find many young men who shared his views.

Shortly afterwards Vladimir entered the University of Kazan to study law. Shy and aloof, with a high domed forehead, a jutting chin and the oblique-set eyes of his Tartar forebears, he won the approval of his mentors by his diligence, though his contemporaries thought him over-serious. A few months later came the dire news that Alexei had been involved in a terrorist plot to assassinate Czar Alexander III. The plot had failed, but though his part in it had been a very minor one he was arrested and thrown into the fortress of Peter and Paul on Neva river. Madame Ulyanov was beside herself with anxiety, so Vladimir escorted her to the capital where she made hysterical pleas for her son's release. Her efforts proved useless: Alexei was executed and the broken-hearted mother returned to Simbirsk.

His brother's death had a profound influence on Vladimir. It crystallized all his ideas, transforming them into a burning desire to follow the long dangerous road that led to national revolution. Hard-headed, without illusions, he looked coldly upon the various nihilist groups which had sprung up all over the country, and even more coldly upon the followers of Plekhanov, Herzen and Bakunin, the leading Russian exponents of Marxism, for none of them had any constructive policy; they talked too much and did too little. He knew that it was impossible to overthrow the existing regime in a matter of months or even years: it had to be undermined slowly, stealthily, and a complete governmental system must be ready to put in its place when the final collapse came. Vladimir established the first Bolshevik "cell" in Russia, a move which resulted in his expulsion from Kazan University. Undaunted, he continued his studies in St. Petersburg and, after graduating, returned to practise law in the Volga town of Samara (now Kuibyshev).

His outward image was that of a rising young barrister, but underneath this façade he burrowed like a mole to make the tunnels linking an ever-growing number of cells. He had become, and was to remain, a fanatical visionary inspired by the belief that he was destined to "liquidate" the czarist regime and establish a dictatorship of the proletariat, and he possessed qualities of leadership which drew followers like a magnet. He had ferocious energy, a brilliant penetrating mind, a gift for succinct speech rare in a Russian and an unparalleled capacity for humiliating any disciple who had the temerity to argue with him.

In the early 1890s the Secret Police began to watch Vladimir's every movement. There was something suspect about this young man of good family whose brother had been executed and who had himself been expelled from Kazan. Quick to sense their surveillance, he moved back to St. Petersburg where he was less likely to attract attention, and pursued his underground work with such thoroughness that by 1895 he had a veritable honeycomb of cells under his control. He had a certain amount of money which he used to further his schemes, living frugally in cheap lodgings, frowning upon the creature comforts with which some of his followers surrounded themselves. He refused to have an easy chair in his room or a soft pillow on his bed, detested cut flowers and—a peculiar fetish— always insisted on his watch being fifteen minutes slow. According to Maxim Gorki he read a newspaper as if his eyes "were burning holes in it" and possessed a mind which had "the cold glitter of steel shavings". This last quality exerted such a magnetic influence that in one interview he could secure a man's life-long allegiance. As a rule he shunned feminine society, saying jestingly that no woman was capable of understanding chess, a railway time-table, or dialectical materialism, but he made an exception in the case of Nadezhda K. Krupskaya, a young woman of noble birth who shared his worship of Marx and was later to become his wife.

Vladimir imposed rigid rules of secrecy on his followers, but it was inevitable that some young hothead should extol his leader in public, and in 1897 such an event led to his arrest. He was sentenced to three years of exile in eastern Siberia and took the long nightmare journey to a place near Yakutsk on the Lena river. As a political prisoner he was not forced to labour in the Yakut goldmines and he quite enjoyed his Siberian sojourn since it gave him time to write the first few of the fifty-five books which expound his theories. Nor did he neglect the Social Democratic Labour Party of which he was founder and leader. Despite transport difficulties a steady stream of instructions reached the network of cells all over vast Russia. In these, for the first time, he signed himself "V. I. Lenin", though nobody seems sure if he took this name from the River Lena or just invented it. Ever cautious, he never used the terms Communism or Bolshevism in his communiqués—the time for that was not ripe, a fact he impressed on Nadezhda Krupskaya, whom he had married during his exile.

The Lenin who returned to St. Petersburg in 1900 was a far more mature, more powerful figure than the Vladimir Ulyanov who had gone to Yakut; so powerful that the authorities were about to exile him permanently when, of his own volition, he left Russia for Switzerland, leaving behind him a band of dedicated men to carry out the orders he sent. From shabby lodgings in Geneva Lenin published the Party newspaper *Iskra* (the spark), a smudgy ill-printed sheet which achieved an ever-growing circulation and, by its incandescent fervour, gained fresh adherents with every issue. One of these was Yosif Stalin, the shambling Georgian on whom Lenin relied more and more as his early co-adjutors Trotsky, Zinoviev and Kamenev suffered recurrent terms of imprisonment or exile. Stalin shared Lenin's quality of ruthlessness, carried out a big bank robbery to gain funds for the Party and possessed a Houdini-like gift for escaping from czarist gaols.

In 1902 Lenin and Krupskaya moved to London, where they remained for several years. Occasional meetings of the Party executive were held in London, Tammerfors and Poznan, while Lenin made two or three brief secret visits to Russia; but for the most part he remained in obscurity, pulling a multiplicity of strings with superb accuracy. Always he dreamed of the day when every Russian family should have a home of its own and electric light, but his humanitarianism was on so vast a scale that it ignored individual suffering. He welcomed Russia's frequent famines because hunger enraged the peasants against the czar, and wars because conflict between capitalist nations was bound to lead to the more terrible civil war between classes through which alone Communist peace could be established. Communism for Russia first and for the rest of the world afterwards was his programme, and not all the wild agitators among his followers could budge him. His obstinacy on this point, coupled with his denunciation of the 1905 Revolution as a rash error deserving of failure, led to a Party split which resulted in Lenin's assuming control of the Bolsheviks, while the few who urged an instant attempt at World Revolution called themselves Mensheviks and formed an opposition Party.

On the outbreak of the First World War Lenin was living in Galicia, but the Austrians kept an uneasy eye on their unwanted guest and finally deported him as an undesirable alien. He went back to Switzerland and was still there on 8 March, 1917, when rioting broke out in St. Petersburg. The army refused to quell the rioters, the Duma ignored an Imperial decree for its dissolution; on 15 March Czar Nicholas II was forced to abdicate and Kerensky formed his Provisional Government. This Revolution was not Bolshevik inspired; it was a revolt of the people against the gross incompetence of the Russian High Command and the utter collapse of the domestic economy. For the Germans the war was going badly and in Lenin they saw the instrument which would remove the Russian forces from the field, so they sent him and his companions by sealed train to St. Petersburg, where they received a tumultuous welcome on 16 April.

The Kerensky Government immediately set a huge price on Lenin's head, but he eluded capture by disappearing as suddenly as he had arrived and went to ground in Vyborg, then in southern Finland, where he spent a fruitful summer planning every least move in the coming struggle while watching the Provisional Government limping to disaster. Despite his manifold responsibilities he also found time to write *The State and Revolution*, one of his best-known books.

By the autumn the time was ripe. On 7 November Lenin's Bolsheviks struck and with a total loss of only a few hundred lives the greatest revolution in history was accomplished.

Lenin had triumphed, but power did not go to his head. Behind the slogans of "Peace! Land! Bread!" and "All Power to the Soviets" boomed the solemn warnings "He who does not work, neither shall he eat", and "From each according to his abilities, to each according to his needs". With remarkable speed he withdrew the Russian troops from the First World War, nationalized banks, industries and land, appointed the sadistic Felix Dzerzhinsky as head of the Cheka (Secret Police) and Trotsky as Commander of the Red Army. He also ensured that no leader, himself included, drew more than a living wage.

The mass of the peasants were behind him to a man; he had saved them from a war which had sapped their strength and rescued them from centuries of oppression. The Cossacks, however, who had long received gifts of land as reward for guarding Russia's frontiers, rose in revolt and civil war broke out. Foreign powers—Britain, France, Poland, Czechoslovakia and Japan—started the War of Intervention to help the White Russians to defeat the Red rabble. The Royal Navy blockaded the Gulf of Finland, Admiral Kolchak forged ahead in Siberia and in the south General Denikin fought grimly to hold the lower Volga while the Poles marched into Kiev. With hindsight we can see how intervention proved a help, not a hindrance, to the Bolsheviks. All Russians have a passionate love for Mother Russia, and the mere sight of foreigners fighting over her soil roused them to fury, and many czarist officers joined the Red Army. Trotsky chased the Poles out of Kiev and defeated Kolchak in Siberia, while Voroshilov and Stalin held Tsaritsin (Stalingrad) on the Volga, thus preventing Denikin from seizing the grain barges. The naval blockade caused terrible hardship in the northern provinces, and all over Russia incalculable damage was done, but in the end the Red Army proved victorious.

Meanwhile, in August, 1918, Lenin was shot and seriously wounded by a wild young anarchist named Fanny Kaplan, but on recovery drove himself as relentlessly as before, pressing ahead with urgent plans for universal education since 90 per cent of the population were illiterate. In 1921, however, two things forced him to beat a "strategic retreat": famine struck the Volga regions and the sailors mutinied at Kronstadt naval base. Communism was proving too heady a draught, so Lenin instituted the New Economic Policy, under which banking and agricultural systems were modified and some private trading allowed. This form of state capitalism worked (though it would have horrified Marx) and things were at last going well when, in 1922, Lenin suffered the first in a series of severe strokes. His brain was as alert as ever but he lost the power of speech and he had to sit immobile at Politburo meetings watching the bitter quarrels between Stalin and Trotsky, who hated each other. He agreed to Stalin becoming General Secretary, then appalled by his error scrawled on a pad: "He is too rough . . . this cook will make too peppery a stew. . . . I propose the Comrades find a way to remove . . ." The effort was too much. He had yet another stroke and died on 21 January, 1924.

Three-quarters of a million Russians queued up in the Arctic cold of 30 below zero to pass through the hall where he lay in state. They worshipped him. He was the man who had miraculously led them out of their medieval darkness into the light of the twentieth century. Since his death more than eight thousand large editions of his works have been published, and even today, forty-seven years later, the long queues wait patiently each day in the Red Square to enter the mausoleum where the embalmed body of their dead leader lies in its glass case, its left hand clenched in the Communist salute. To the Russians Lenin is more than a man: he is a religion.

ALBERT I
King of the Belgians
(1875–1934)

THE COUNT OF FLANDERS, brother of Leopold II, King of the Belgians, had two sons, Baudouin, born in 1869, and Albert, born in 1875. When Leopold lost his only son, a child of ten, Baudouin became the heir-presumptive.

As was only natural, the Count and Countess of Flanders, an irreproachable couple highly esteemed by the Belgians, devoted most of their time to Baudouin, and while Albert was neither unloved nor neglected he was more or less given over to the care of his two tutors. Unfortunately for him, both were mediocrities from whom he learnt almost nothing.

Shortly before his sixteenth birthday Albert was sent to the Military Academy. Suddenly flung, after the semi-seclusion of his home life, into the midst of a crowd of boisterous cadets, he felt like the proverbial fish out of water. Shyness made him awkward, and he rarely brought himself to join in the conversation of his class-mates. The sense of his own inadequacy manifested itself in sudden bursts of nervous laughter and equally sudden fits of reasonless rage which caused his fellow-cadets to think that he must have a screw loose. "My parents should never have sent me there," Albert told his biographer, Charles D'Ydewalle, "I had had no preparation for that kind of life. The study, the atmosphere, and the talk were entirely strange to me."

Luckily for Albert, he found a release for his pent-up feelings in outdoor sport. Too short-sighted to play a good game of tennis or golf, he loved riding, swimming, skating, climbing, particularly climbing.

Albert had been less than a year at the academy when Baudouin went down with pneumonia while in camp with his regiment—within three weeks he was dead.

The realization that he would one day be king must have seemed like a nightmare to Albert. It was fortunate indeed that two men of outstanding ability, Major Jungbluth and Major de Grunne, were appointed to act as his advisers. Thanks to them he gradually became filled with a new spirit of confidence.

Albert completed the course at the academy and was gazetted a second lieutenant in the Grenadier Guards. During the next few years he went on a series of travels abroad accompanied by Major Jungbluth.

Leopold duly drew up a list of eligible brides for his nephew, a list that did not include the girl of Albert's choice, Elisabeth, daughter of Duke Charles-Theodore of Bavaria. "Uncle Leo", however, could not raise any objection to the match, for the Duke had illustrious relations, none less than the great Wittelsbachs. Elisabeth, who had fallen as deeply in love with Albert as he with her, was gay and intelligent, and as fond of outdoor sports as he was—she was to be a lasting source of happiness to him, his good angel. They made a fairy-tale couple at their wedding in 1900—she so slight and tiny, he towering protectively above her.

Albert and Elisabeth settled down in Brussels in a house in the Rue de la Science, and here their three children, Leopold, Marie-José and Charles, were born.

During these peaceful years Albert set himself to fill in the great gaps in his education. He borrowed text-books and notes from his secretaries who had taken university courses in economics and politics, and pored over them as if he had been some needy student. Reading he loved and his literary tastes ranged from Paul Valéry's poems to Darwin's essays.

In 1909, Albert as king-to-be went on a state visit to the Congo, Belgium's recently acquired colony.* Nothing could have pleased him more for he had always longed to see Africa. From Johannesburg, accompanied only by an aide and a colonial official, he made an epic journey to the heart of the dark continent, covering the five thousand miles on horseback, on foot, by bicycle. In the colony he asked innumerable questions about the administration, the economy, and made notes of all the answers. This was the time when angry voices in Britain were denouncing the Belgian atrocities; naturally Albert saw nothing of this ugly side of the picture, but he was to outline a wide programme of social reform for the Congo in his first speech from the throne. This speech was not long delayed; four months after his return to Brussels, Leopold II died.

The Belgians shed no tears for the old king who had disgusted and shocked them by his behaviour to his family. Albert was the antithesis of his uncle, a devoted husband and father, and they gave the new royal family a warm welcome.

* The Belgian Congo began as an independent state, the Congo Free State, ruled by Leopold II who had financed Stanley's expeditions in this region. In 1908 he reluctantly handed it over to his country.

Albert soon showed that, unlike Leopold II, he was deeply interested in the welfare of his people. He became a familiar figure in the poorer quarters, and his humble subjects took him to their hearts. The members of the aristocracy were somewhat disenchanted, probably because they were seldom invited to the Palace of Laeken. (The truth was that Albert and Elisabeth found them a dull lot, and preferred to surround themselves with men and women who had something to contribute to the world: writers, artists, musicians, scientists, and so forth.) The conventional Belgians deplored Albert's ill-fitting suits, his hair worn carelessly long (Albert hated wasting time with his tailor and barber), and while they said patronizingly: "He's quite a good sort", they invariably added: "But what a bourgeois!" Albert, because of his shyness, was apt to be awkward at official functions, and this caused fools to remark: "What a mediocrity—he'll never hit the head-lines. . . ."

In 1913 Albert went to Germany to review the Luneberg Dragoons, of which regiment he was honorary colonel. During his short visit to Potsdam the Emperor William II burst into a violent anti-French tirade, and reminded him with a wink of complicity that he, William, had promised Leopold II to enlarge the frontiers of Belgium provided that, in the event of a war against France, he would allow the German armies free passage. He wound up by pointing to Von Kluck and remarking loudly: "That's the general who'll lead the offensive on Paris." Used as he was to the Kaiser's rantings, Albert was seriously alarmed, so alarmed in fact that he took the unprecedented step of warning the French ambassador, Jules Cambon. On his return to Brussels he confided his fears to his premier, who became equally apprehensive. The strength of the standing army was raised, and its complete reorganization begun. It was a race against time, a race that was lost: on 26 June, 1914, the Archduke Francis Ferdinand was assassinated at Sarajevo.

The events that followed need no re-chronicling. Let us move straight on to that fateful first week in August when the German ultimatum was delivered to Belgium. Either Belgium would allow free passage to her armies or she would take the consequences. . . .

White-faced, filled with icy rage, Albert strode up and down, up and down in the Palace grounds. On 3 August he mounted his horse and rode to Parliament.

The atmosphere in the crowded Chamber was tense with anxiety as the king entered in military dress, his sword at his side, and quietly took his place in the centre. It was a new Albert the spectators saw, or rather the true Albert—the born soldier, the born leader, the born king. There was no trace of awkwardness now, he was completely sure of himself. Slowly, simply, he began to speak, and when he reached the words: "I ask you, gentlemen, have you irrevocably decided to preserve inviolate the sacred land of our forebears?" all present sprang to their feet, cheering wildly. When silence fell at last he said what little more he had to say, and ended with the moving credo: "I have faith in our destiny. God will be with us in our righteous cause. Our country will not perish."

On 4 August the first enemy shell exploded on Belgian territory, killing a Belgian trooper.

From Staff headquarters at Louvain the king immediately gave the order to Liège and Namur to resist to the last. Two of the army's six divisions were sent to these fortified cities, the remaining four were dispatched to the Gette. Liège and Namur held out for far longer than the forty-eight hours that Ludendorff had predicted, but inevitably they fell. All might yet have been saved if Joffre, through a gross miscalculation of the enemy forces, had not left the divisions on the Gette to bear the entire weight of the massive German attack. It was impossible for them to contain the grey hordes who continued to advance wave after wave. In this grave hour Albert did not flinch; he possessed that almost supernatural courage which enables a man to look disaster squarely in the face and never so much as dream of the word surrender.

Antwerp had become the "national refuge". Elisabeth had taken her sons to England (Marie-José was safe in Italy) and had returned to her husband. The first stories of German atrocities began to trickle through, and new lines of care furrowed Albert's stern face. He had known that the war would be long and bloody, but never had he envisaged a campaign of terror directed against harmless civilians. Only Elisabeth gauged the depths of his anguish for his martyred people. Thanks to the king, the population of Brussels were spared the horrors that the inhabitants of the towns and villages engulfed by the war had suffered; after frantic efforts, he managed to get through to the capital and ordered the authorities to declare it an open city.

The news worsened day by day. Albert alone sustained his people's courage. As a French officer, General Agan, wrote: "The Star-spangled Banner is the national flag of the United States, but Belgium has a more vital, a more glorious standard: the king . . ."

In the first week of October the ring round Antwerp was pierced. The Government went to Le Havre; the evacuation of the city began, and Albert and Elisabeth shared in the confusion and misery of the retreat along roads jammed with refugees and ambulances carrying the wounded.

The Belgian Army, or, rather, what was left of it, had at last linked up with the British and French forces who had established a line on the Yser. Albert went to Nieuport, and stopped at the Villa Crombez to draw up the order of the day. "Oh God, what will become of us?" burst out the daughter of the house. Exhausted as he was, he managed to smile at her and say reassuringly: "All will be well—your king is with you."

From the Villa Crombez the king went to the trenches to hearten and encourage his army. Here is part of his proclamation:

Soldiers: Up till now you have been alone in this immense conflict. You are now fighting side by side with the gallant French and British armies. It behoves you with that courage of which you have given so many proofs, to uphold the reputation of our army. Our national reputation is at stake . . . face the future undaunted, fight on bravely. In the position in which I have placed you, may you look straight ahead, and call him a traitor who thinks of yielding. . . .

The Belgian Army lived up to these high words; during the battle of the Yser which began four days later, it displayed the utmost gallantry. From his nearby headquarters the king, unmoved by the rain of shells, watched the course of the battle. On 25 October the Germans concentrated the full force of their attack on the sector of the line held by the Belgians, and in spite of their heroic resistance it became plain that they could not contain the enemy. On 27 October, to save the threatened French flank, the king was forced to give the order for his army to fall back to the railway embankment and for the sluices to be opened. The Germans were flooded out, their ammunition was washed away and the pressure on the French was thus relieved, but the king looked at the swirling waters with a heavy heart: every Belgian soldier had been thrown into the battle-line, he had no more reserves—for him the Battle of the Yser was the end of his active participation in the war.

Albert joined Elisabeth at La Panne, and now began the strange half-life that was to endure for months. Through the secret network radiating from Brussels he was kept informed of what was happening in Occupied Belgium—it was by means of this network that he learnt of the execution of Edith Cavell. Driven almost to breaking-point by his enforced inactivity, Albert would mount his horse and gallop madly across the dunes. Visitors came and went, amongst them the Prince of Wales; Albert, had he wished, might have gone with Elisabeth to England, but he would not leave La Panne, sustained by the knowledge that, even though there was nothing he could do, his people, so long as he remained on Belgian soil, would not give up hope. The only highlights in those grey, monotonous days were the sea-going expeditions in search of enemy submarines that he made aboard the destroyer commanded by Sir Roger Keyes.

At last, in 1918, the tide of war turned. By autumn the Germans were on the run in Belgium and the bells began to ring out. They rang for the Joyous Entry of Albert and Elisabeth into Ghent; for their Joyous Entry into Bruges; and they rang out a delirium of welcome when, a few days after the Armistice had been signed, the king and queen made the Joyous Entry into Brussels, their capital.

Now wherever he went Albert was greeted with a storm of acclaim. He had become a living legend: the Warrior King. There were to be few monarchs left in post-war Europe; at Versailles, Clemenceau was busy sweeping them away. Albert rightly foresaw that in going too far and too fast Clemenceau was endangering the peace, and told the Tiger so outright. The Tiger replied with a left-handed compliment. "Oh, kings!" he said. "Hardly two of them in a century are worth a thought. . . ."

The closing years of Albert's reign were the happiest, and towards the end there was only one cloud on the horizon: his fear of old age. To decline in strength, to be ill, infirm—this was what he dreaded most of all. It was not to be. . . .

Albert was fifty-nine. On Saturday, 17 February, 1934, he had got through the usual routine by midday. He was to preside that evening at a cycling rally, and he felt a great need to relax in the open air. He would go climbing near Namur, he decided, and, radiating health and fitness, kissed Elisabeth goodbye—for the last time.

At 2 a.m. in the morning, the party of searchers summoned by Van Dyck, his faithful valet, when his royal master had failed to return at the hour he had appointed, found the body of the king on the rocky ledge where he had fallen to his death.

In the war the king had been the standard of his people. Did any of them think as the funeral cortège wound its slow way through the streets they silently lined that the flag which symbolized Belgium's story also symbolized that of their greatest king? Black, red, yellow: these were the colours that epitomized his life: Out of Darkness, Through Fire, Into Light.

KEMAL ATATURK

(1881–1938)

As THE nineteenth century progressed the Turks became increasingly a problem to themselves and to the rest of the world. They held large Christian possessions in Europe, and owing to its geographical position the Ottoman Empire blocked Slav ambitions in the Balkans or, if it collapsed, would provide a power-vacuum making all too probable a clash between Austria-Hungary backed by Germany and the Slavs supported by Russia.

So the European powers eyed Turkey with intense misgiving, made more acute by the volcano of nationalism in South-east Europe. In 1875 revolt against Turkish misrule had broken out in Bosnia and Herzegovina. Its savage suppression brought Russia into the field against Turkey. The triumph of the Russians lopped large territories from the Ottoman Empire at the ensuing Congress of Berlin: the provinces were put under Austrian administration, an independent Bulgaria and Eastern Rumelia were created, Cyprus was ceded to Britain. The Turk, the "Sick Man of Europe" as he was called, had long since lost Greece. The seizure of Algeria by France was to follow, the occupation of Egypt by Britain and the capture of Crete by the Greeks. One by one the Turkish tree was losing its branches—and the roots were rotten.

Alone among the great powers Turkey had not advanced for centuries. With Muslim fatalism the people groaned under a corrupt government headed by the cruel and despotic Sultan Abdul Hamid. The country was bankrupt, taxation oppressive, justice an inextricable tangle of religious prescript. The Turk was by nature brave, but he had long since stagnated in a land ruled by outworn custom, lethargy and brutality. The people were almost all illiterate. Britain pressed for reforms, but they were impossible so long as the Sultan, "the doom of his race" as Lord Salisbury called him, retained his prerogatives and exercised arbitrary power. So before the First World War Turkey faced a triple menace: internal decay, control from outside, or dismemberment of the remaining empire by some of the Christian powers who waited eager as jackals for it to die. A crisis was at hand—but so was the man who would master it.

In 1881 in the Turkish quarter of Salonica a son had been born to a minor government clerk named Ali Riza and his illiterate peasant wife Zubeida. On the early death of his father the penniless family moved to an uncle's farm where the boy, Mustafa, helped to clean the stables, feed the cattle and tend the sheep. A short period of schooling followed, but Mustafa ran away after a teacher had thrashed him and a place was found for him in the State-subsidized military cadet school in Salonica. He was an apt pupil, and soon the blue-eyed, sandy-haired youth found himself under the special protection of a Captain Mustafa who, to distinguish him from himself, gave him the second name of Kemal, "Perfect".

At seventeen he passed out well from the cadet school and was sent to the Senior Military School at Monastir, which was still part of the Ottoman Empire. Greece had just seized Crete and the normally dull provincial town was seething with seditious talk. Mustafa had rebellion in his blood, but to him freedom meant root-and-branch reform, not independence from Turkish rule. He studied Voltaire, Rousseau, Hobbes, John Stuart Mill, learnt French, harangued his fellow-cadets and was promoted at the age of twenty to the General Staff College in Constantinople with the report: "a brilliant, difficult youth with whom it is impossible to be intimate."

True, he never sought real human intimacy. But the danger of conspiracy was a powerful lure. At the college he joined a revolutionary society, the Vatan, dedicated to the total reform of Turkish life, and after passing a General Staff course and promotion to captain became its leader. One night, alerted by spies, the police raided a meeting and arrested all the conspirators. After weeks of solitary confinement Mustafa was released because of his military prospects and sent to Syria where his regiment was skirmishing with the Druses.

In Damascus he organized another branch of the Vatan, but a revolt starting from Syria was impossible, and hearing that the Balkans were still seething with discontent he got friends to smuggle him to Salonica. Chased by the Sultan's spies he soon had to return to Syria and then took refuge in Gaza until, there being no positive evidence against him, he was able in 1907 to persuade the War Office to post him back to Salonica, to the staff of the Third Army.

He tried to expand the Vatan, but learnt that there was another and more powerful organization, "Union and Progress", with links with the Young Turk Movement and Italian Free Masonry. Mustafa joined the committee and found its members a polyglot crowd with international ambitions far from his taste. Its leader, Enver, was a young man of humble origins, cloaking strong ambition behind dazzling charm and social grace. Mustafa, the angular misfit, hated him from the start. Dimly in his mind was dawning a vision of a modernized Turkey, but Enver and his friends thought merely of grafting new on old: the retention of the Sultanate, but the enforcement of a Constitution drafted in 1876 and never put into effect. Mustafa poured scorn on them; they excluded him from their councils, and when revolution suddenly broke out in July, 1908, supported by most of the army, it was Enver who took a leading part and reaped the applause.

At the pistol-point Abdul Hamid accepted the Constitution and a progressive government took office. Then, fanned by reactionaries, counter-revolution broke out in Constantinople and the Committee sent forces from Macedonia with Mustafa Kemal as Chief-of-Staff to a division. The insurrection was crushed, the Sultan was deposed and replaced by his feeble cousin Mehmet V. Mustafa went back to soldiering in Salonica, dissatisfied, but biding his time.

Enver and his friends were now the rulers, and Mustafa, climbing the ladder from Commandant of the Officers' School in Salonica to the General Staff, eyed them with critical disgust. To all who would listen he preached efficiency, modernization and Turkey for the Turks, until his voice reached Constantinople and in a panic Enver had him transferred to the War Office, where he could be watched.

The Italian invasion of Tripoli in 1911 sent him back to real soldiering with intense relief. But at the scene of action he was again overshadowed by Enver till Mustafa was beside himself with rage and jealousy.

A year later a mortal threat developed. All the Christian Balkan States combined to attack Turkey. Peace was quickly made with Italy. Mustafa hurried back to Constantinople and was ordered to defend the neck of the Gallipoli Peninsula against the Bulgarians, a key position guarding the Dardanelles. Meanwhile Enver made a clean sweep of his doddering colleagues in the government. But the Christians were triumphant. Macedonia had to be surrendered and it was only in the following year that Adrianople and eastern Thrace could be recovered and the threat to the homeland averted.

Enver now called on the Germans to help reorganize the army. Mustafa protested vociferously against this "national insult" and was sent, for his pains, to cool off as Military Attaché in Sofia. He was still there in October, 1914, when to his horror Turkey entered the world war on Germany's side.

Months later, while Enver was away ineffectually fighting the Russians, he was appointed to command an infantry division as yet only existing on paper to defend the Gallipoli peninsula. An English attack was known to be impending and when it came in the following April Mustafa was ready with his men fully trained. His superior, the German General von Sanders, expected the onslaught at the neck of the peninsula, but it fell on the area held by his division. The chance to act independently, without waiting for orders, brought out all that was best in him. For weeks with great courage and resolution he fought back the Australians from the key heights of Chonuk Bair, which dominated the whole of the peninsula, and by July there was stalemate. Then came the surprise landing at Suvla Bay and Mustafa Kemal was given command of scratch troops collected to meet the new threat. Again there were battles for the heights, the Turks were nearly outflanked and would have panicked but for his example. At last he sent the British reeling down the slope and with tireless energy kept the invaders at bay for three more months. When the British withdrew in December the nation looked on him as the saviour of Turkey.

But in the capital he aggravated Enver by clamouring against the Germans and, posted to command an army in Syria in the spring of 1917, he soon quarrelled with General Falkenhayn and his plans to stem the advancing British. With a lesser reputation he would have been court-martialled, but Enver allowed him to resign his command and return to Constantinople, dispatching him shortly with the Crown Prince Vaheddin on a State visit to Germany.

On his return he fell seriously ill with kidney disease, and in 1918 he was barely fit for active service when in August he was sent back to Syria to command the 7th Army, or what was left of it. The British attacked and smashed the Turkish line. With the few survivors he could collect he retreated to Damascus and, already outflanked again, from there to Aleppo—and with new vigour was fighting off his pursuers when in October an armistice was signed.

Vaheddin was now Sultan. Enver and his friends had bolted abroad and been replaced by a weak government amenable to the victors. The Ottoman Empire had been smashed. Turkey was in the grip of her enemies, and when Mustafa Kemal, the only successful general in Turkey, got back to Constantinople, Allied officers were supervising the police, the port, the dismantling of forts and the demobilization of the army.

Without success Mustafa schemed for the fall of the government and the installation of strong men. But his chance came when against strong British advice the Sultan sent him to Anatolia to quell nationalist risings and forcibly disband the last six intact divisions of the army. Kemal, it was felt, was a trustworthy soldier who would carry out his orders to the letter. He asked for and was given the widest powers—then set off, not to crush but to organize resistance under himself.

From the Black Sea coast he contacted former army commanders, the leaders of guerilla bands, local governors—all who could help to form a new army and rouse the people against the foreigners and their tool, the central government. It was agreed to call a Congress at Sivas with delegates from all over Turkey to discuss the formation of a National Assembly. On hearing of this the Sultan dismissed Mustafa from his command and he resigned his commission.

At Sivas he swept all before him. A provisional government headed by himself was formed, a "National Pact" drafted setting out the only acceptable peace terms and the delegates voted solidly for resistance to the foreigner.

This fighting spirit spread quickly throughout the country and soon the Sultan was calling on the people to fight a holy war against the Nationalists. Mustafa and his friends were outlawed and whoever killed them was promised reward in this world and the next.

For a time the hideous struggle of civil war went against the Nationalists and Mustafa was in serious danger. But he fought back relentlessly and by the autumn of 1920 popular support had turned finally in his favour. To this two events had contributed: the first session of the Grand National Assembly ending in a proud claim to be sole representative of the nation, and the Treaty of Sèvres, signed by the Sultan with the Allies, which spelt the enslavement of Turkey. Clear at last where their allegiance lay, the people closed their ranks and fell in behind Mustafa Kemal.

His troops advanced on Constantinople. The Allies were too weak to face him and in Paris the late victors, Wilson, Lloyd George and Clemenceau, looked round for help. Venizelos, the Greek Premier, had a fine army massed in Smyrna. In exchange for Turkish territory in Europe and Asia he offered to destroy the Nationalists and enforce the peace treaty—an offer gladly accepted.

For eighteen months the Greeks were irresistible. They threw a cordon to protect the quaking Sultan and his government. They drove back the Nationalists into the interior and sowed dismay among Mustafa's supporters. He rallied them with dauntless energy: "You are Turks! Will you crawl to these Greeks who yesterday were your subjects and slaves! I cannot believe it. Combine, prepare and victory is ours." He fought to maintain morale, harangued, organized, browbeat the quarrelling Nationalists and at last welded an efficient army. But the Greeks struck again in the summer of 1921. The Turks were forced to withdraw to the Sakkaria River, covering Ankara, and there for three weeks fought their hereditary enemies in a last-ditch stand. Then the Greeks fell back, burning and slaughtering as they went.

Mustafa Kemal, now called *Gazi*, the Destroyer of Christians, strengthened his army for the final reckoning. He made careful preparations and in August, 1922, launched a surprise attack, proclaiming to his troops: "Soldiers, forward! Your goal is the Mediterranean." This time nothing could stop them. The war-weary Greeks fled in utter confusion and the remnant of their army escaped by sea. Soon it was reported to be reforming in Thrace and Kemal hurried north with his tattered veterans to deliver the death-blow. Blocking his path on the eastern shore of the Bosphorus he found the small British occupation force. Taking a great risk, he marched his men through the enemy lines with arms reversed and no shot was fired. The British, their bluff called, then accepted him and his government, and a peace treaty, recognizing Turkey's full sovereignty within her own frontiers, was signed at Lausanne in the following year.

To make Turkey a strong, independent, modernized country was now the goal. Through the National Assembly he bulldozed a unanimous vote abolishing the Sultanate, and Vaheddin, with bags of jewels and the gold Imperial coffee cups, escaped to an English battleship. In his place as caliph, or spiritual ruler only, was elected his nephew, Abdul Mejid. Turkey was made into a republic and Mustafa Kemal was elected the first President. But dictatorial powers were necessary. He created a People's Party and declared it to be the only party in the State. Religion he saw as the great enemy to progress, and as long as there was a caliph he himself was not supreme and could not free the people from superstition. In March, 1924, Abdul Mejid was sent packing and the State was secularized.

There was great and growing opposition. But Kemal was utterly ruthless. Gradually he established himself as absolute dictator. With paternal rigour he then gave his people what he thought they needed. The fez, the symbol of the Ottoman past, was abolished and its wearing made a crime. Monasteries were closed, their inmates turned out to work or starve. Commercial, penal and civil codes were imported from abroad and antiquated Moslem laws were swept aside. The metric system was introduced and the Gregorian calendar. Polygamy was abolished and women were given equal rights with men. Down to the smallest detail of social life, time-honoured habits were hacked away and in the clearing made the Turk was set on his feet and told to behave like a modern man.

But only two or three per cent of the people were literate and this was partly due to the inadequacy of Arabic characters for writing Turkish. In 1928 Kemal substituted the Latin alphabet and toured the country teaching the new signs. Two years later he believed that the country was ready for a political opposition and allowed two new parties to be formed. But the experiment was a fiasco and never repeated during his lifetime. His last reform was to make compulsory the use of surnames. Hitherto men had been known by a first name followed by their trade—Ali the Ploughman, for instance. On himself the nation conferred the name Ataturk (Father Turk).

In his last years he almost withdrew from public life. Behind the father-figure was, as everyone knew, a drunken debauchee whose health had been ruined by excess. But Turks cared not a jot for his vices. The country in those years was beginning to prosper and take its place alongside the great nations of the West. The decadent past had been surmounted. There was a new spirit of enterprise. Modernization was going ahead.

All this was ascribed to Ataturk, and when he died on 10 November, 1938, the nation mourned as never before in its history. Many of his qualities were dangerous or destructive: ruthlessness, cynicism, inordinate lust for power. He was amoral and irreligious. But when he came on the scene Turkey needed a strong man and there was a corner of his heart aflame with patriotism and in love with civilization. Independence, strength, civilization were the watchwords which he left to his country. During the Second World War they guided Turkish policy and today they are as valid as ever.

FRANKLIN D. ROOSEVELT

(1882–1945)

IT WAS 1910: the Democratic Party in the State of New York had found themselves in an embarrassing difficulty. State elections were being held, for the State Senate in Albany, and for the first time in history no candidate was forthcoming. The reason can hardly have been far to seek—no Democrat had won this particular seat for twenty-eight years—but it was still a blow to Party officials that no one was prepared to contest it: however lost the cause, the candidature had always appealed to someone. Surely there was such a man still available—young and sufficiently resilient not to mind losing?

Someone suggested Franklin Roosevelt, the junior partner in a firm of lawyers, a young man from a rich and respected family. After a hurried consultation, he was approached.

Roosevelt asked for twenty-four hours to think it over. At the end of that time he had decided that, though he would certainly lose, a campaign like this would be valuable experience for a fledgling lawyer. He agreed to stand—or, to use the more vital American phraseology, to "run".

As with everything he had done, all his life, he put heart and soul into it. On 8 November, 1910, a very surprised Franklin Roosevelt was elected to the New York State Senate. He embarked on his political career, not knowing whether it would be a life's work or a few years' experience, with a light heart.

Twenty-two years later, when he was elected President of the United States, he faced a different situation with a heavier heart—but with courage and quiet optimism. The four months that elapsed between election and inauguration made the situation more ominous. By Inauguration Day—in March, 1933—a crisis of terrifying magnitude had built up. All over the country a rising flood of panic-stricken men and women was stampeding to the bank counters, demanding to withdraw savings, put them back under the mattress, in the jam-jar, up the chimney, anything rather than have them lost in a strange "depression", which had become a whirlpool.

As he stood there, at the front of the platform outside the Capitol, hand on bible to take the oath of office, there were a hundred thousand men and women in front, who had swarmed into Washington to see him do so, millions more listening at home to his words. Could this new President, returned by the biggest majority ever, justify his country's faith in him? There was silence as he ended the oath, "—so help me God," then turned from the Chief Justice, Charles Evans Hughes, to give his Inaugural Message.

It was a moving speech, interrupted many times by wild cheering, the cheering of men and women who, rightly or wrongly, felt their salvation was at hand, and the words that lingered in each mind when it had ended were: "The only thing we have to fear is fear itself——"

There was hysterical cheering when he had finished. But among men and women listening to radios all over the United States there were those who doubted his ability to deal with a superhuman problem: millions of unemployed, farms and businesses bankrupt, queues of starving people in the streets. Surely, they must have asked themselves, is *this* a time to cheer?

It was. Almost as soon as the ceremony was over, Roosevelt went into action. Bankers from all over the country had been summoned to Washington, and with them Governors of the forty-eight States. He had believed, and now he proved, that there was an old law, the "Trading-With-the-Enemy Act" of 1917, which could be used to give him emergency powers over the country's money. He rushed it into effect and soon his decisions were announced to a waiting world: from 6 March all banks would suspend operations, with the exception of making change and allowing depositors access to safe-deposit boxes, thereby getting hoarded money back into circulation; there would be, instantly, a five-hundred-million dollar cut in Federal expenditure.

Retrenchment was followed, within weeks, by the imaginative Industrial Recovery Act providing for a three-thousand-three-hundred-million dollar public-works programme, giving employment to no less than *seven million* workers. Action—drastic, controversial action—was taken over railways, house mortgages, disarmament, agriculture, the currency, reforestation, prohibition. And when the special session he had called of the 73rd Congress was over, only one of the many major bills passed had originated outside of the White House.

Never, in time of peace, had an American president, democratically elected, so dictated to his people—or had them so firmly behind him in each decision he took. (Though, when the crisis eased, panic was over, there was criticism, some of it vociferous, and the Supreme Court adjudged some of his legislation unconstitutional and therefore invalid. But by this time its work had been done.)

This crisis of March, 1933, was the second in Franklin Roosevelt's life, the second of three that tested him and which he overcame. The first was poliomyelitis: it crippled him from the waist down at the age of thirty-nine and seemed to everyone but himself, his wife and his devoted helper Louis McHenry Howe to put a complete and final stop to a political career.

The third was the Second World War, which he helped so greatly to win, and whose victory he never lived to see. He died on 12 April, 1945, a few weeks before the end of war in Europe, at the age of sixty-three.

He had been born, 30 January, 1882, at Hyde Park, the family estate on the Hudson River outside New York, with the proverbial silver spoon in his mouth, and Dutch, French and English blood in his veins. His ancestor, Claes van Roosenvelt, had come to "New Amsterdam" from Zeeland in 1644, at much the same time as his maternal ancestor, Philippe de la Noye, later Delano, arrived in Massachusetts from Leyden. Twenty years later New Amsterdam fell to the English, became New York. The Roosevelt family made one small concession to this forcible anglicization and changed —but not immediately—the name to Roosevelt. From this pioneer family were descended both Franklin and his fifth cousin Theodore, President before him, from 1901 to 1908, and whose niece Eleanor became his wife.

Despite the boy's great passion for the navy, for ships of all sizes and sorts, he was sent to Groton School and to Harvard, not to the Naval College at Annapolis. Reluctant at first, he decided to become a lawyer, went on to do post-graduate work at the Columbia Law School in New York. By this time a dormant interest in politics had been awakened by the assassination of President McKinley at the Pan-American Exposition in Buffalo. This had brought Theodore Roosevelt, as Vice-President, to the supreme office on 6 September, 1901. He was a Republican, a member of the Party to which so many Roosevelts, originally Democrats to a man, had switched at the time of the Civil War, when the South was Democrat. Franklin Roosevelt's branch had remained true to the original party, but though he and his now illustrious cousin differed in political belief, the mere fact of having him in the White House aroused in the younger man a curiosity in the affairs of government—if only to question the more conservative views of the President.

He was married in 1905 to the shy cousin who had been his constant feminine companion. The date, 17 March, was chosen by the fact that Theodore would be coming to New York to inspect the annual St. Patrick's Day parade and wanted to give the bride away. After a wedding reception (where the young couple were completely overshadowed by their distinguished guest) they set up house and Franklin went back to his law studies. Two years later he was admitted to the bar and joined a New York law firm.

It was three years after this that the Democratic Party called on him to run for State Senator—and as we have seen, he confounded the experts by winning.

By the Presidential election of 1912 he knew a great deal more about politics, and had developed a deep respect for the quiet, idealistic Governor of New Jersey, Woodrow Wilson. Wilson had been persuaded to run for nomination as Democratic candidate for the Presidency, and Roosevelt was among those who went to the Party convention in Baltimore to support him. Here he had a first experience of the rough and tumble of American politics—and found he could be as tough as the next man. He learnt that the supporters of one of Wilson's opponents, "Champ" Clark, were proposing to storm the convention and sway the vote with a hundred men wearing Clark badges and shouting, "We want Clark!" To do this they had bribed the doormen to let in anyone with a Clark badge. Roosevelt quickly rounded up two hundred supporters of Wilson, gave them each a Clark badge, told them to show it to the doormen and be let inside.

To the astonishment of the assembled delegates, the sound of men wearing Clark badges and shouting "Clark, Clark—we want Clark!" was completely drowned by twice that number of men—also wearing the Clark badge—roaring "We want Wilson".

Whether or not this influenced the nomination we cannot say—but Wilson became the Democratic candidate and, a few months later, President of the United States. By the hallowed "spoils" system of American electioneering, Franklin Roosevelt, who had worked so hard to achieve this result, was offered a post in the new government. He refused—but then Josephus Daniels, Secretary of the Navy, asked if he would care to be his Assistant.

This was too much for a small boy who had been forbidden to join the navy. Now, aged thirty-one, he accepted with excitement and gratitude and moved his wife and family to Washington.

Here, much as his contemporary, Winston Churchill, was doing across the Atlantic, he threw himself into the business of making a modern navy out of a neglected one. He scrapped old ships, built new ones, converted the age-old "navy yards" to major industrial plants, each specializing in the manufacture of certain equipment.

And one of the first things the new Assistant Secretary did was teach his navy to swim. A large proportion of it came from the interior of the United States, miles from the sea, and a considerable number of land-reared sailors was being drowned each year. Roosevelt issued an order that each recruit be able to swim before being posted to a ship, then donated a cup to be awarded annually to the ship with the best swimmers.

War ended—a war in which his new, modernized navy played a large part—and he was nominated, in 1920, to stand as Vice-Presidential candidate with the Democratic Presidential nominee, Governor Cox of Ohio. But so unpopular had the unfortunate Wilson become, with his misunderstood, unwanted, League of Nations, his "involvement" with Europe and the world, that the Democrats were soundly beaten. The Republican Harding became President, with Coolidge, not Roosevelt, as Vice-. Having resigned his Assistant Secretaryship in order to campaign, Roosevelt found himself, for the first time in ten years, entirely out of politics. He had few regrets.

And now—disaster struck. Or, what at first seemed certain, final disaster, but what many believe spurred him on to greatness. In August, 1921, on holiday with Eleanor and the five children on his favourite island of Campobello, off the coast of Maine, he was struck down with poliomyelitis.

And it was now that he was helped enormously by a little man whose effect on American—indeed, world—affairs has yet to be determined. Louis Howe was a newspaperman from Albany, in up-state New York, older, more experienced in both politics and public relations than the "F.D.R." he met and admired. Here, Howe felt, was a wise, gifted and incorruptible man, with every additional advantage from extreme good looks to the doubtful one of wealth. At the outset, Howe decided: if Roosevelt would have him, he would become his adviser. He did so.

With the 1920 elections over, and F.D.R. back at his chosen career as lawyer, Howe headed for Campobello to say farewell. He had his own newspaper work—and a New York lawyer had no need for a chain-smoking little journalist hardened by the ways of politicians. But by the time Howe reached Roosevelt the blow had fallen. Once again the little man set aside his own work, resolved to get his protégé back into action. . . . But Roosevelt had already made up his mind to do just that, and his wife was backing him to the hilt. He went back to the office on crutches. A little later, when his old friend "Al" Smith, Governor of New York State, asked him to be Campaign Manager when he stood for Democratic Presidential nomination, Roosevelt agreed. Despite a brilliant, wildly applauded nomination speech from a Campaign Manager on crutches, Smith just failed to get the nomination—but by now it was obvious to all that physical handicap would not keep Franklin Roosevelt out of politics.

Soon after this, he learnt from another good friend (can any man have had more friends than F.D.R.?) of a small place in Georgia called Warm Springs. The waters were believed to help paralyzed people. He took a few days off from work, went there, and found to his delight that swimming in them, using his powerful arms to keep himself afloat, made his legs stronger. His visit was soon over, but he came back, again and again—to the last day of his life—to get that little added strength. In 1927, in order to share the secret with others, he started his "Warm Springs Foundation" for the relief of polio, endowed it with his own money. Only when he was absolutely convinced of the value of Warm Springs as a treatment did he enlist the aid of the general public. Money poured in—a million dollars and more—and the future of the Foundation was assured.

By 1928 he was as well as he ever would be, able to drive his own car, no longer using crutches, only a pair of canes. In that year he was elected Governor of New York State, and his four years in the office covered the 1929 stock-market crash and its immediate aftermath. His handling of the crisis within the state, his championing of the "forgotten man at the bottom of the economic pyramid", resulted in his being nominated in 1932 as Democratic candidate for the Presidency, and later in the year being elected as President by a landslide.

Within his first hundred days of office he had got a despairing country moving as it had never moved before. He made enemies, seemed even to enjoy making them, and was never afraid of making mistakes—or of putting them right. In 1936 he was returned for a second term by another huge majority. By this time he was trying, steadily and with some success, to drag the U.S. from its policy of isolation. "If war comes," he declared in 1937, "let no one imagine the United States will escape."

In September, 1939, it came. In November, against great opposition, Roosevelt recast the Neutrality Act so that Britain and France could buy arms on a "cash and carry" basis. This was followed by a series of moves to help a suddenly-isolated Britain (moves without which Britain could not possibly have survived) and which brought down storms of abuse on his head from large isolationist and pro-German forces in his country. Despite this, he was elected for a third term—the first President ever to embark on a ninth year in the White House. He pushed through the Lend-Lease Act, and the trickle of food and munitions across the Atlantic became a flood.

By the second half of 1941 Britain and the United States were allies in all but name: it took the Japanese attack on Pearl Harbour in December of that year to rationalize the situation. Now he took the sweeping and not unquestioned decision to finish off Germany first, before turning his country's might on the Japanese.

The tide of war turned slowly in the Allies' favour: in June, 1944, they invaded France from north and west. He agreed to stand for yet a fourth term, and was elected in November.

His brief Inaugural Message—his fourth—on 20 January, 1945, was the first wartime one since Abraham Lincoln's, eighty years before. He was a sick man now, with the strain of thirteen crisis-packed years in office showing only too obviously when he went for a final war-time conference to Yalta on the Black Sea, with Churchill and Stalin. A month after that the Rhine was crossed and the end was near. He never lived to see it. He had gone to his beloved Warm Springs for a few days desperately needed rest and there, on 12 April, 1945, he died of a cerebral haemorrhage.

As with Lincoln, who died in the moment of victory (but had six days in which to see it), his task was complete. He had taken charge of his country in its darkest hour, had pulled it to prosperity, self-respect, and—ultimately—military victory.

A grateful Britain passed the Roosevelt Memorial Act, empowering the Government to erect and maintain in perpetuity a statue of Franklin Roosevelt in London. He stands there still, leaning on the two thin canes he taught himself to use, amid the bustle of Grosvenor Square.

CHARLES DE GAULLE
(1890–)

EXCEPT FOR four years during the Second World War, when the Vichy Government, which called itself the *Etat Français*, was in existence, France has been a Republic since 1876. If General de Gaulle is the only French president to be discussed in this book, it is not because he is considered the most remarkable or the greatest of French presidents—though many people would consider he is—but because he is the first president to govern France, to influence all government policy to a great extent and particularly to determine foreign policy.

The French presidents of the past, very soon after the republican constitution was in being, were men who performed only representative functions. Some of them had a great influence on politics, but they exerted this indirectly and as a result of their aptitudes rather than their constitutional function. The Deputies of the National Assembly were extremely jealous in case a French President should tend to abuse the prestige his function as Head of State gave him. It often seemed that the Deputies and the Senators who, with the Mayors and other notabilities of national and local government, elected the president, preferred not to see a powerful or a popular individual as Head of the State. They feared that he might subvert republican institutions.

After the 1914 war a nonenity was chosen in place of Clemenceau, who had been so largely responsible for final victory. After the Second World War, France had, for the first seven years, a very influential and popular President in M. Vincent Auriol. But he was not as popular in parliamentary circles at the end of his term of office as at the beginning. It was felt he had done rather too much. General de Gaulle, who succeeded M. René Coty, who was M. Auriol's successor, has been in every sense of the term a ruler. Indeed he has been responsible for French policy in much the same way as an American president, constitutionally the supreme executive, governs the United States.

How were the French led to accept the immense power wielded by General de Gaulle? The answer lies in two things: the first, the immense prestige of de Gaulle, won by his actions during the Second World War; and the second the failure of the French political system after the war and the consequent discredit of the political parties and politicians. One should note *en passant* that de Gaulle has never been a dictator. He has governed according to the constitution of the Fifth Republic, accepted by 80 per cent of the nation. He may have stretched his powers somewhat, but when he was elected for a second term in 1965 and there had been two polls, he remarked aptly: "People say I am a dictator—but whoever heard of a dictator who had to go for a second ballot?"

Born in 1890 of an upper-middle-class family with a strong Catholic, intellectual and military background, Charles André Joseph-Marie de Gaulle chose the army as a career, served in the 1914 war with gallantry, being mentioned three times in Army Orders. With the help of Marshal Pétain, the commander of the first regiment in which he had served, Charles de Gaulle had a successful career, becoming in 1932 Secretary to the National Defence Council which advised governments on military policy. In the thirties he annoyed some of his superior officers by advocating a French armoured force to meet the challenge of the Panzer divisions which Hitler was preparing. With Paul Reynaud, a very able conservative politician later to be Prime Minister, as a partner he engaged in public controversy, a thing the army authorities did not like. Nevertheless, he had no thoughts of being anything but a soldier, and it was not until the Battle of France, after he had led the only two French offensives during the battle, that, at the age of fifty, in 1940, he as it were left the ranks and stepped on to the stage of history. "Gaullist" became part of the international vocabulary— at the same time as "Quisling".

The originality of his achievement during the war was that, from the very beginning, in June and July, 1940, de Gaulle insisted that his, at first, small movement, Free France, which had more reverses than successes, was the legitimate custodian of France's rights, which the Vichy Government could never be since it had betrayed France's honour. He had many quarrels with Churchill—bitter quarrels of temperament and circumstance; with Roosevelt there was a fundamental dislike. Roosevelt refused to accept de Gaulle and considered him a narrow-minded French bigot. Churchill, during the many quarrels between the Anglo-Americans and the French National Committee, tended to side with Roosevelt, though, in the last resort, he refused to abandon de Gaulle. In a well-known passage in his Memoirs he wrote of de Gaulle at that time:

I had continuous difficulties and many sharp antagonisms with him. There was, however, a dominant element in our relationship . . . I always recognized in him the spirit and conception which across the pages of history the word France would ever proclaim. I understood and admired while I resented his arrogant demeanour. Always even when he was behaving worst, he seemed to express the personality of France, a great nation with all its pride, authority and ambition.

General de Gaulle and the French National Committee emerged triumphant in the end and, from 1944 until January, 1946, de Gaulle conducted French government with vigour and restored confidence that France was not down and out. When he failed to convince other French political leaders to give greater authority to the President of the French Republic and to the government, as opposed to the legislature, in the new constitution of the Fourth Republic which was being drawn up, he abruptly left power. This was in January, 1946. An unsuccessful attempt to make a strong national party which could reform the constitution did not alter his prestige. He remained in exile at Colombey les deux Eglises and, from 1952, only making speeches on great occasions. He became a hope both for men of the Left and of the Right: the former saw him an enlightened soldier who might have to be called on to save the republic; the latter, a man who believed in a strong State and in French greatness.

The great writer François Mauriac, who was not at that time a Gaullist, when he interviewed General de Gaulle, for a French newspaper in 1954 at a time when the Laniel government was in power and French prestige at its lowest, saw him as follows:

His words are like a cold wind, coming from very far and very high, from the past when France was a great nation. He persuaded us of this at the darkest and most shameful moment of our history and there are still millions of Frenchmen who have not forgotten it. I did not ask him: "Do you agree with the Laniel government?", because, by his very presence, General de Gaulle makes the dictatorship of Lilliput invisible to the naked eye.

At this period de Gaulle may have believed that his career was over and he said to Mauriac:

I sometimes wondered—perhaps it is my mission to represent in the history of our country its last upsurge towards the lofty heights. Perhaps it is my lot to have written the last pages in the book of our greatness.

France was on the verge of civil war in May, 1958, and, indeed, had been so for some six months before, when President Coty summoned "the most illustrious Frenchmen" to form a government.

The basic reason was that in the Assembly there was no majority for any consistent policy towards the Algerian nationalist revolt which had begun in November, 1954. A majority of the Deputies knew that France could not hold Algeria down and that a purely military policy would be useless. France had already given Morocco and Tunisia their freedom. A majority of the active part of public opinion was of the same view. But there were in Parliament, and in the nation generally, and above all among the French in Algeria, a strong contrary feeling that Algeria must be kept French at all costs. And the French army in Algeria, a large part of which had fought for years after the war in Indo-China, had also become determined not to give Algeria to the Algerian rebels.

Now, since the general election of 1956 there had been a majority in the Assembly in 1956 for a policy of negotiations after a cease-fire with the F.L.N., the principal organ of the rebellion. But in fact the hold of this majority on Parliament was so unsure, and the majority itself so divided, that M. Guy Mollet, the Socialist Prime Minister from January, 1956, to July, 1957, had been obliged to do almost the opposite of what he had been elected for the purpose of doing. In *100 Great Events that Changed the World* the author has described in some detail how the clash between the army and a weak government led to the return of General de Gaulle to power. What should be noted in this essay, which is concerned with de Gaulle as a ruler, is that the breakdown of the French system of government caused by Algeria followed a long series of failures by Parliament during the Fourth Republic to decide firmly and at the right time on vital policies. A similar weakness had affected the Third Republic and many Frenchmen had felt acutely the harm which the constant instability of governments had done to the country in the thirties when there were fourteen governments in less than seven years.

When Hitler went into the Rhineland in 1936, only a caretaker government was in being. France's defeat in 1940 had, in large part, sprung from the failure of the government of the time to summon the energies of the nation to fight. The French, in fact, had begun to realize that an all-powerful National Assembly, which was itself composed of a large number of undisciplined parties and groups, might be, in theory, a perfect form of democracy but that it did not work in time of stress. Governments were not really responsive to public opinion as they were in Britain or Scandinavia or in the United States and they consequently lacked vitality. The need for a stronger State and also for a stronger executive had been one of the principal aims not only of General de Gaulle and his Free France but also of the much more Left-wing Resistance movement inside occupied and unoccupied France during the Second World War. Now at the moment of truth in May, 1958, the politicians and public opinion in France turned towards General de Gaulle.

The socialist leader, M. Mollet, and the conservative, M. Pinay, and the President of the Republic, M. Coty, turned to de Gaulle, in fact, because he was the only man whom the army in Algeria would obey and who could save the Republic from a military dictatorship or civil war. Many politicians thought that General de Gaulle could end the Algerian civil war. Having done this, they counted on his impatience with politics and with what they quite wrongly thought his incapacity to deal with everyday affairs to make him resign. He was already in 1958 only two years off seventy. Politicians guessed too that he was unlikely to try to become a dictator however great his popularity might be. He could have ruled France against the political parties in 1946, and indeed he had said this when, dramatically, one Sunday morning in January of that year, he had announced that he was abandoning his office of Prime Minister:

The exclusive régime of parties has re-appeared. I disapprove of it. But apart from establishing by force a dictatorship which I do not desire and which would inevitably end badly, I have no means of preventing this experiment. I must therefore withdraw.

The drama which had marked de Gaulle's career did not end with his apotheosis as President of the Republic. It took him nearly four years to end the Algerian war and he had to overcome the implacable determination of many of the generals and colonels and junior officers of the French Army, as well as the fighting despair of the French-Algerians, before the Evian Agreements of 1962 were signed with the Algerian nationalists. There was a serious wavering of discipline in the army in 1960 and the General put on his uniform and on several occasions faced crowds of Europeans and Muslims in Algeria alone and unguarded. In 1961 a fresh revolt of the army in Algeria led by four generals was only overcome by de Gaulle's calm hold on the people. Four attempts were made to assassinate him.

After 1962 the drama of his career was associated rather with his policies, which aroused great controversy, than with his personal acts. In 1963 he virtually vetoed Britain's attempt to enter the Common Market whilst negotiations were going on in Brussels between Britain and the Six—an act which angered not only the

British but France's partners in the European Economic Community. He recognized Red China. He took France out of N.A.T.O. in 1966 and in that same year he paid a twelve-day State visit to Russia in which, an unparalleled concession on the part of the Soviet rulers, he was allowed to address huge crowds in the principal cities. Like his State visit to Britain in 1960 and that to West Germany in 1962 this old man aroused a reaction rarely given to other contemporary statesmen.

Late in 1966 he went to Ethiopia, Cambodia and the Pacific, his presence invariably arousing a sort of political excitement and anticipation not usual with State visits. He once said to Mr. Duff Cooper in Algiers in 1943: "Every day I spend five minutes thinking how what I am going to do today will appear in history." Certainly wherever he went, stopped and made speeches, often very repetitive ones, whether it was in Latin America or in the less-populated departments of France which no previous French president had ever visited, he managed to convey the feeling that an historic event was taking place.

One of his more judicious French critics has called de Gaulle "A man of Yesterday and a man of Tomorrow"; it is in the light of that phrase that one can perhaps make some judgement, a very tentative judgement, of his policies. He has constantly shown himself a man of tomorrow—that is to say, a man gifted with foresight. Early in his life there was the question of the need for armoured divisions, and in 1940 he correctly judged that Britain was "down" after the Battle of France but not "out". He correctly saw that the multi-party system combined with an Assembly which was all-powerful and in which governments were weak could not adequately govern France in times of stress. He realized with clarity that the age of holding colonial peoples in subjection was over. A long time before he returned to power in 1958 he saw correctly that Europe must have a greater degree of independence of American policy and that, to achieve this, there must be economic and political co-operation between the countries of Europe. Now over the question of tanks, and over his judgement of the world situation in 1940, he can claim to have been one of the very few Frenchmen to judge correctly. In his other judgements, and this adds to rather than detracts from their importance, he was rather the vehicle by which a widespread view became effective. De Gaulle triumphed in Algeria and freed French Africa south of the Sahara at the stroke of a pen as it were, because the majority of the French nation agreed with him even if they had found no way of expressing their opinion before.

In striving constantly to increase France's independence, General de Gaulle got rid of the humiliations and frustrations which the French had experienced after the defeat of France in 1940, a defeat followed by a series of weak governments which were alternatively cajoled and bullied by the Americans and the British. The French as a whole were glad to see that France is once again listened to by the non-aligned nations of the world, in Latin America and the Far East. De Gaulle's visit to the Soviet Union was widely approved of since it was a sign that France was capable of steering her own way in international politics. Many Frenchmen thought that by leaving N.A.T.O., the military part of the Atlantic Alliance, France had diminished the risk of world war or, if it should begin, of France's involvement.

One of the achievements of the Fourth Republic had been, first, the reconciliation with Germany begun soon after the war by Robert Schuman and Dr. Adenauer, and then the creation of common economic institutions among the Six of Europe. By 1957 the Treaty of Rome brought into being the European Economic Community with its main organism the Common Market. There was no question in General de Gaulle's mind in 1958 of France backing out of the E.E.C. He made this clear, and among the first measures which his government took was the stabilization of the franc to make it possible to accept the challenge of the Common Market. Nor did he reverse the process of Franco-German reconciliation; on the contrary, through his personal friendship with Dr. Adenauer, he brought the two countries closer than ever together. The Franco-German Treaty of 1963 provided for routine consultations between French and German ministers and, at regular intervals, between the Heads of State. Though the Germans have not in fact followed French policy towards the Atlantic Alliance, and clearly have reservations about Franco-German political co-operation, the Treaty remains a considerable achievement.

So in policies of continuing and strengthening France's membership to the Common Market and of asserting France's independence, General de Gaulle has been expressing a common purpose of the French. This accounted for the difficulty of political opposition in France; many agreed that personal rule was deplorable, but only the convinced "Europeans" who believed in the European super-State were prepared to go in for out-and-out criticism of Gaullist foreign policy, while, on economic matters, the conservative and centre parties did not agree with the Socialists and Communists.

The "Man of Yesterday" can be seen probably in de Gaulle's

excessive attachment to the idea of the Nation-State and in his suspicion of international co-operation. He may have been right that men will only die for their country and not for ideals or ideologies. But he did not point the way to a world free from national rivalries; on the contrary, he poured scorn on those who believe even in a United States of Europe.

Whether the man of yesterday predominates over his counterpart or not, it is certainly the conjunction of the two which make up de Gaulle, and one cannot help thinking that the old-fashioned nationalist, through whom speak many generations, supplies the tenacity and force of will which has enabled the man of tomorrow to act inflexibly and boldly in the present. De Gaulle is a rare combination of military man and thinker, an imaginative, cunning operator trained to command and so to know when to strike, yet also a man of far-reaching views, without either class or racial prejudices. Shortly after the First World War, de Gaulle married, in 1921, Yvonne Vendroux, the daughter of a family of industrialists in northern France. Madame de Gaulle, who with her children came to England in 1940, has fully accepted the many challenges of her husband's career. De Gaulle is a writer of great ability and, if he had remained a simple soldier, his talent as an author would probably have given him some renown. As it is, his life has been dominated by one of the highest forms of ambition, the desire to serve his country. No one has better expressed his feelings for that supernatural being *La France*, in whose existence all Frenchmen, whether of Right or Left, tend to believe, than has de Gaulle in the opening pages of his war memoirs.

All my life I have kept alive in myself a certain idea of France. Feeling has inspired it as well as reason, and I early came to believe that France, like the princess in a fairy tale or the Madonna of the frescoes, had an eminent and exceptional destiny. Instinctively, I imagined that Providence had created her for outstanding successes, or misfortunes which are to be a warning to the world. When it happens that mediocrity marks her acts or her attitude, I have a feeling of an absurd anomaly, imputable to the defects of the French but not to the genius of the nation. And the positive side of my mind convinces me that France is only really herself when she is in the front rank; that only great enterprises can compensate for the disrupting ferment which her people carry in themselves; that our country as she is, among the others, such as they are, must, under pain of mortal danger, aim high and stand upright. In brief France in my view cannot be France without greatness.

MAO TSE-TUNG

(1893–)

AN ARMY of children, marching past the reviewing stand like wooden puppets on a million strings. There are thousand upon thousand of them, stretching down the long and dusty street; thousands of feet padding along in unison, thousands of voices raised in a hoarse yet high-pitched yell. It might be a cheer, or a cry of defiance.

Thousands of left hands raised: it is this which gives the appearance of a puppet army, apart from the fact that so many of the soldiers are very small and very young. And in each hand a small red book, like a passport, a driving licence. A prayer-book.

And each book, every single one of the thousands brandished in the air, has the picture of a round-faced person who might—if one did not know the face so well—be either man or woman. A pleasant, effeminate, hairless face, under a squashed brown cap. Ageless, too: the face might be thirty, sixty, ninety years old.

What better face for a god? For Mao Tse-tung is God Incarnate to millions more people than worship or even acknowledge a Christian deity. A god is a remote being, and though we each may have a private picture in our minds, some image of our god, it would be a presumptuous soul who gave his god an age, or even a sex.

And though these "Red Guards" marching down the Peking street are mostly very young and shrieking for the obliteration of a past they have never known, there are millions of grown men and women who sincerely do believe in the divinity of Chairman Mao Tse-tung, ruler of all China.

Before we consider how this very human, very fallible Chinese schoolmaster has been elevated to a position over the hearts and minds of men never achieved in the whole of history, let us see who he is and what he has done.

He was born in Hunan Province, in the southern half of the great land mass which is China—on Boxing Day, the day after Christmas, in 1893. Not that Christmas is likely to have had an effect on him, for he was a grown man before he had even heard of it. We are told that his parents were poor, but not as poor as many, for they farmed several acres near the village of Shao Shan. The Province of Hunan has soil as fertile as any in China, and the tough, resourceful men and women who farm it deserve their reputation, in the old, old saying: "China will be conquered when the last man in Hunan is dead."

For three hundred years China had been ruled by a cruel and largely corrupt dynasty, the Manchus. Mao as a young man was inspired with determination to join with others in attempting its overthrow. A very great Chinese, to whom present-day China owes a debt even greater than that owed to Mao, had published some remarkable writings on the subject. Dr. Sun Yat-sen, a southerner who had lived years in Hawaii and gone on to practise medicine in Hong Kong, was giving up his practice to devote himself to saving his country from the Manchus. All over China men were meeting in secret to discuss Dr. Sun's writings, consider how they could be put into effect.

Opportunity knocked—with the explosion of a bomb in Hankow. The Manchu dynasty took the opportunity of arresting some supporters of Sun Yat-sen for their alleged part in the "plot" and executing them out of hand. The army revolted, and Mao Tse-tung and others rushed to join it. Within a few days the Manchu governors had been driven from a number of Chinese cities and the revolution seemed well on the way to success. Mao, who had never considered a military career, became almost overnight a superb soldier with a grasp of guerrilla tactics which half the world now acknowledges, for he soon put his views on tactics into writing. He wrote other things, too: reports on conditions in Hunan, on the chances of final success for the revolution in that province; and wall-newspapers, a peculiarly Chinese institution, with headlines like "Out with the Manchus" and "Set China Free", which he stuck on the walls of buildings.

And the revolution *did* progress, at a startling rate. Within a few months Nanking had fallen to Sun Yat-sen's forces: a little later an infant "Chinese Republic" was declared. Sun Yat-sen, who had been driven from the country with threats on his life—indeed a sentence of death—now came back as its first, provisional, president.

Mao, the brilliant guerrilla fighter, resigned from the army: he had no intention of remaining a soldier; he would be, as he had always intended, a schoolmaster. In this role he could mould the minds of young men and women, make them acknowledge the rightness of Sun Yat-sen.

He spent the years 1912 to 1918—aged nineteen to twenty-five—at the Changsha Normal School in Hunan, studying to be a teacher. It was not until he went there that he saw, for the first time, a map of the world—and he was astonished. No wonder China, which had once been so certain it was the centre of the world, was not viewed in that light outside its own borders. China not only didn't occupy most of the world's surface: it was not even the largest nation.

But it would—and this fact, central to all Mao's thinking ever since, impressed itself on him at that moment—it would always have the largest population.

The supporters of Dr. Sun Yat-sen now formed themselves into a party, the National People's Party, or Kuomintang. Sun had made the old Imperial General Yuan the first president of the new Chinese republic when he himself stepped down from the "provisional" presidency. Yuan was not a man to be trusted, but he commanded some allegiance in the country and at first this seemed a wise and diplomatic move, now that he had foresworn allegiance to the Manchu emperor.

To Sun Yat-sen's dismay the old man plotted a Manchu revival, with himself as emperor. He even succeeded in outlawing the Kuomintang and producing, if not a new Manchu dynasty, at least utter chaos.

Mercifully, General Yuan died less than three months later. By this time hundreds of petty "war lords", self-styled generals, were fighting among themselves to grab as much of the territory of China as they could before order was restored. Once again Sun Yat-sen found himself in danger of his life, and he escaped, in the nick of time, to Japan.

From here he appealed, fervently, for Western help. Without outside assistance China would dissolve in total anarchy. Was it not worth while for the rest of the world, having a strong, friendly, China?

Apparently it was not: no help was offered.

Then, as world war ground to a bloody close in late 1918, hopes rose. The American president, Woodrow Wilson—and he, like Mao, was a teacher—had produced his Fourteen Points which, if implemented, would do much to help China. For a start the hateful "extra-territorial rights" which Western powers had enjoyed in Chinese cities would end.

But in May of 1919 came terrible news: the powers meeting at Versailles had no intention of supporting a new regime in China;

even less of abandoning their own extra-territorial rights within her.

The youth of China, outraged, prepared to storm foreign legations. On 4 May five thousand of them marched on the legation quarter in Peking to demand that American and European diplomats intercede with their own governments. Rioting broke out.

Much of Communist history is dotted with dates and slogans, and this "May the Fourth Incident", which sparked off riots all over China, is the most seminal of all. Probably it did, as claimed, set off the second stage in the Chinese Revolution; for the Chinese turned to Russia for help.

Quite possibly the whole course of world history was altered in May, 1919. If that be so, the Western powers are entirely to blame.

The Russians responded lavishly and fast: money, arms, advisers, all poured in—and with them, a half-understood creed called Communism.

Young Mao Tse-tung, not yet twenty-six, was an eager convert. He joined the new Communist party, sworn to dispossess big landlords, as in Russia, and make the fruits of man's endeavour equally available to all. The party grew rapidly, was acknowledged and accepted by the only slightly more senior Kuomintang: friendship reigned between the two.

And now, tragically for China—in the opinion of many observers —Sun Yat-sen died. His place as ruler of the infant republic was taken by the greatest of the war lords, Chiang Kai-shek. To raise himself above the proliferation of petty "generals" in the country, he now styled himself, as he does today, "Generalissimo".

The new, self-appointed, Generalissimo viewed Communist aims with straightforward hostility. For Chiang Kai-shek the age-old system of big landlord, little peasant, was the only feasible one for China.

Chiang's final resolve to wipe out the new Communist Party came as a result of a report, one of the many treatises which young Mao Tse-tung had produced. It called itself "Report on an investigation into the Peasant Movement in Hunan", and it was no less than a blunt suggestion for overthrowing landlords and dividing their land among peasants.

In this Mao was ahead of his party, which preferred to wait for such a development. But Chiang, who had seen Mao's Report, decided not to wait a moment longer: the infant Communist movement must be strangled, and strangled now.

There were sudden, bloody massacres by Kuomintang troops. Many people totally unconnected with the Communist movement

—plus of course thousands who were deeply involved—were killed. By 1927 the Party had gone underground. In August of that year, another history-book slogan—"The Autumn Crop Uprising"— took place and failed to achieve anything. Its instigator, Mao Tse-tung, was arrested and sentenced to death.

Dramatically, just before he was about to be beheaded, Mao escaped. Within weeks he was hidden away in the hills between Hunan and Kiangsi—and a fanatical army with him.

Chiang Kai-shek sent Kuomintang troops against them: these were wiped out, all their arms being captured for use against the next Kuomintang attack. This duly came, was similarly repulsed, and the Communist armoury swelled to an impressive size. School-teacher Mao Tse-tung set up a First Red Army, with himself in command.

And now, from all over China, recruits flooded in. Mao's friend Chuh Teh arrived with a complete army of his own, and joined the force. Between 1930 and 1931 this Communist force repelled four major assaults by the armies of Generalissimo Chiang Kai-shek—and then came the fifth and biggest of all.

Chiang had imported, at considerable cost, arms and advisers from Germany. He had mobilized a million men.

The Kuomintang force headed into the Kiangsi mountains. There followed some of the bloodiest fighting ever to take place in Asia. At one point it seemed as if the Generalissimo had been repulsed for a fifth time: the next day it seemed Communism in China had been wiped out.

The stage was set for the greatest historical landmark in Chinese Communist history. Mao's forces had been badly cut up and forced to split in little groups. If these were ever to coalesce, they would have to make a way, licking their wounds, to another part of China, free of Kuomintang armies. Mao decided to lead them on an almost incredible march, to the north-west provinces of Kansu and Shensi. From here, backs literally against the Great Wall of China, they would be able to resist any Kuomintang attack. For there was another threat now, which to Mao was as serious as that of the Kuomintang: the Japanese had invaded, were slowly occupying more and more of China. The Communist armies, regrouped and reorganized, would deal with that threat, a threat which was being overlooked by the Kuomintang.

Mao Tse-tung's march—and it is, above all, his—was one of six thousand miles. Six thousand miles on foot against every enemy, human and otherwise, that imagination could dream up.

It began in October, 1934, and lasted a year, during which time the Communist forces were attacked by bitter cold, burning heat, the countless armies of private war lords—and the Kuomintang itself. This "Long March" is and will remain the greatest incident in Chinese history—at least for so long as a Communist government is in power.

The march was not only an exodus: it was a hugely successful recruiting campaign and propaganda stunt. Mao organized the various parties into self-sufficient groups containing among other things a theatrical company. At every stop, however hard the day's march, the company would give a performance. During the performance orators would explain to the audience the need for a Communist China.

The march passed through eleven provinces, with a total population of two hundred million people. These were shown that "only the road of the Red Army leads to liberation". Ideas would be seeded among these two hundred million that would "sprout, grow leaves, blossom into flowers, bear fruit and yield a harvest in the future".

They did, and the power of the party grew. From its new H.Q. in the north-west it continued recruiting and by the end of 1937 Mao was the absolute ruler of ten million people. He began to worry about the fact that he had never travelled outside China, and made plans to rectify this: he never had the time.

A few months before this his forces had dramatically captured Chiang Kai-shek and the Generalissimo's life had been spared by Mao himself. A promise was extracted that Kuomintang forces would stop harrying Communists and help get rid of the Japanese.

The war against Japan was won—thanks to that country's disastrous miscalculation over Pearl Harbour—and by 1945 the Chinese Civil War was raging again. By 1949 it had been won by the Communists, and Chiang Kai-shek's discredited forces had retired to Formosa as "Republic of China" in exile.

Meanwhile Mao rushed ahead with the building of party power in the country he had just inherited. With his advisers he set to work to set himself up as a god and ensure that he remained one. The image of godliness must be constantly kept up to date: only in this way could he ensure the unswerving loyalty of the Chinese people.

We cannot even guess. But, whatever happens, history must record that without Mao China would be still a feeble, helpless giant —not one of the greatest nations in the world.

GEORGE VI

(1895–1952)

IN HIS selfless devotion to duty, his unaffected warm friendliness to all his people of every rank and class, his frank honesty of spirit and the ability with which he carried out the responsibilities of his charge, King George VI stands pre-eminent among the constitutional monarchs of Britain. It was his lot to guide the nation and Commonwealth through the dark years of the deadliest war in her history and into a new era of peace and social justice. They learned to know him not alone as their king, but as a man whom they loved.

He had neither expected nor desired the Crown. He was unprepared for its tasks and handicapped by uncertain health and a stammering speech. But when the monarchy had been shaken to its foundations by the events leading to his brother's abdication, he took up with quiet heroism the burden thrust upon him, and ascended the tottering throne.

Prince Albert Edward Arthur George, the second son of the Duke of York (later King George V), was born on 14 December, 1895, at Sandringham. His childhood had its grim aspects, for his navy-trained father was a rigid disciplinarian with fixed conventional notions. He thought left-handedness a shameful deformity; and Albert proved to be left-handed. His father's efforts to rectify this caused Albert to develop a stammer which plagued him all his life.

Like his elder brother, Edward, he was educated at home by tutors, thus losing the early training of human contacts, competitive games and studies, which a preparatory school could have given him. At the age of thirteen he was entered at Osborne Royal Naval College where, shy, nervous and hampered by his stammer in answering questions, he lingered near the bottom of his form. Two years later, in January, 1911, he moved on to Dartmouth. Here his qualities began to show themselves. He was an unyielding long-distance runner, a capable left-handed tennis player, a good horseman, good shot, gay and mischievous, warm-hearted, quietly helpful and friendly. On 18 April, 1912, he was confirmed and, in his preparation for this, experienced a spiritual awakening which persisted all through his life.

His father designed him for a naval career, and on 17 January, 1913, Prince Albert joined the cruiser *Cumberland* as a cadet for a cruise to the Caribbean and Canada. In September he was made a midshipman, and appointed to the battleship *Collingwood*. In those days life as a "snotty" was tough, but he neither received nor asked for any privileges.

He was at sea when on 4 August, 1914, the First World War broke out. But his career in the Navy was doomed to be gravely interrupted and ultimately broken off by his poor health. A month after the declaration of war he was hurriedly brought ashore for an operation for appendicitis. Still suffering internal trouble, he struggled back to his ship in February, 1915, and served in *Collingwood* in May, 1916, at the Battle of Jutland, getting a mention in dispatches for his cool courage. But his health repeatedly failed. In November, 1917, a duodenal ulcer was diagnosed and he underwent an operation. Medical opinion forbade his return to the Navy, so he transferred to the Royal Naval Air Service, and in January, 1918, was appointed to their station at Cranwell. Three months later the Service and the Royal Flying Corps were amalgamated as the Royal Air Force, and on 1 August Prince Albert joined an R.A.F. Cadet Force at St. Leonards-on-Sea, where he soon took charge of a squadron. In July, 1919, he gained his wings as a pilot. In October he went with his brother Edward to spend two terms at Trinity, Cambridge, reading history, civics and economics. On 3 June, 1920, the king created him Duke of York.

His experiences with the Royal Navy and the Air Service contributed to the development of his character, and brought to the fore those qualities which were in future years to shape his career. In the Navy he learned the great lesson of complete and unselfish devotion to duty and unremitting attention to the details of a task. He also began that keen interest in machinery which later made him a very knowledgeable visitor of works and factories.

His time among the young recruits to the flying services did a great deal to bring out Albert's gifts as a leader. He drilled them, counselled them, lived among them as their friend, and reached a sympathetic understanding of them. This inspired his scheme for setting up the Duke of York's Summer Camps, which he started in 1921. Two hundred youths from industrial establishments and two hundred senior boys from public schools met for a week's camp at the seaside, and mixed, joined in games and athletic sports and came to know and like one another. The duke himself came down for one day each year, mixing with the campers as one of them, joining in their games and entertainments and in singing the Camp Song, "Under the spreading Chestnut Tree". These camps did much to dissolve class barriers and prejudices, and to develop among the young fellows a warm friendliness for the duke and the monarchy. They continued until 1939.

At a small dance in 1920 Prince Albert met Lady Elizabeth Bowes-Lyon, youngest daughter of the Earl of Strathmore, and in the autumn he visited her home of Glamis Castle with his sister Mary. The Countess was unwell, and Elizabeth entertained her guests. Albert was greatly attracted by his young hostess, and in the next two years set about doggedly pressing his suit. Elizabeth was reluctant to exchange the happy freedom of her home for the official duties and tiresome protocol hedging the royal circle, but Albert's persistence triumphed, and on 13 January, 1923, he wired his success to Queen Mary. They were married in Westminster Abbey on 26 April.

The importance of their union for Albert's career and his life's happiness was beyond all estimation. The nation at once took to its heart this handsome and devoted couple, and for the rest of Albert's life his wife was his indispensable support and comfort, encouraging him to overcome his shyness and diffidence and to face with quiet confidence the duties thrust upon him. Their happy home life and complete mutual loyalty gave him a solid foundation on which to rest.

During the next dozen years Albert was busily engaged in those many public functions at which the presence of royalty is traditionally expected: receiving as the king's deputy various distinguished visitors to this country, and touring distant parts of the Commonwealth. In 1924-25 he went with "The Little Duchess", as Elizabeth was affectionately called, to visit Kenya, Uganda and the Sudan. In 1927 they made an extensive tour of New Zealand and Australia. Here he officially opened the new Parliament House at Canberra. At home, the duke presided in 1925 over the Wembley Exhibition; and in 1929 acted as Lord High Commissioner at the Act of Union of the Church of Scotland and the United Free Church.

He carried out such tasks with charm, efficiency and full success. The king, his father, came more and more to rely on him as his representative. Though the Duke of York lacked the gay magic of his elder brother, the Prince of Wales, he was sympathetic, responsive, cheerful and brotherly. But few realized what an ordeal these functions were for him, or how fine a courage he drew on to face them. The stammer which from childhood had afflicted him, making him tongue-tied, shy and retiring, was a heavy handicap when he was called on to make speech after public speech. Fortunately in 1926 he came upon a speech specialist from Australia, Mr. Logue, who helped him to master this defect, and ultimately he achieved a workable fluency. The matter in his addresses was always first-class.

His private life with his family was unalloyed gold. He and Elizabeth maintained an ideally happy home. In 1926 their first daughter, Princess Elizabeth—now Queen Elizabeth II—was born, and in 1930 their second, Princess Margaret. In September, 1931, they settled into the Royal Lodge in Windsor Great Park, where the duke became a great authority on shrubs, especially rhododendrons. He was an excellent shot, a keen horseman and tennis player. With sharp regret he sold his racing stud in the financial crisis of 1931 to help the nation's finances. So far as official engagements permitted, he enjoyed wholeheartedly the life of an English country gentleman.

In 1936 this peace was rudely shattered. On 20 January King George V died, to be succeeded by the Prince of Wales as King Edward VIII. He had unhappily been for some time in love with an American woman who, after divorcing her first husband, had married an Englishman, Mr. Simpson. King Edward spent much time in her company, and when, in October, 1936, her second marriage to her husband was dissolved, he made known his intention of marrying her. That this would make his abdication inevitable was borne in on him by the leaders of Church and State, and the Duke of York strove passionately to dissuade him: but in vain.

For the duke, the prospect thus opened was appalling. He was next in succession, but had never imagined he might have to ascend the throne. He had received no training in the tasks and duties of the British monarchy, and considered himself, with his faltering tongue and rather uncertain health, by no means competent for that uniquely responsible role. For a time he held out against the urging of the Prime Minister and the Primate. But his life-long dedication to the call of duty prevailed. The Throne, the central pivot of the nation and Commonwealth, was in peril, and with a supreme act of quiet courage he consented to take up the post his brother was vacating. The relief and joy of the nation and Commonwealth were unbounded.

He could not foresee how grim and heavy his new task was during the next ten years to prove. But though without any advance training in its complexities—he had never previously been shown a State Paper—he was equipped with the discipline of a naval training, with a human sympathy, a store of common sense, and a humble trust in the guidance of Almighty God. The wisdom of the simple-hearted can often yield wiser solutions than the ingenious schemings of the would-be clever.

Shadows were already beginning to gather over the world scene. Hitler had begun his aggressive moves in Europe with his re-militarization of the Rhineland, and Mussolini had snatched Abyssinia in defiance of the League of Nations, while Japan had overrun Manchuria. The system of collective security was a vanished dream. The one bright gleam came from the increasing friendship of Britain and the U.S.A., which was immensely strengthened by a State Visit which King George and Queen Elizabeth in May and June, 1939, paid to Canada and the United States. It was the first time in history that a reigning British sovereign had entered the U.S.A., where the people were amazed and delighted to find them not stiff figures but friendly, informal and charming. They won the hearts of all, especially of President Roosevelt, and the resulting good-will was to prove a priceless asset in the years of world war which loomed so closely ahead.

On 1 September, 1939, Hitler invaded Poland, and even the reluctant Chamberlain was compelled two days later to declare war. King George VI found himself at the head of a nation drawn into the most devastating conflict in modern history, against the most powerful, unscrupulous and dangerous foes that had ever combined for world-wide aggression.

The British people will ever remember with pride how nobly their king and queen bore themselves through the horrors of that struggle, where the battlefields were not only on land and sea but in the air all over the island. They refused to withdraw to some remote safety, but usually stayed on in the heart of London at Buckingham Palace, which was repeatedly bombed before their eyes. Whenever any town or city was badly blitzed the royal couple might be found next morning inspecting the damage and cheering and consoling the sufferers. They visited aircraft factories, munition works, coal mines, encouraging the war workers in their tasks. With his engineering experience, King George was no mere distinguished visitor, but an understanding and sympathetic friend of the men and women on the shop floor.

Repeatedly the king travelled to the battle-fronts to move about among the troops. In October, 1939, he spent two days with the Fleet at Invergordon, and in December visited the British Expeditionary Force in France. In June, 1943, he spent some days with the British forces in North Africa, and paid a surprise visit to Malta, where he was greeted by the beleagured islanders with wild enthusiasm. Ten days after D-day he crossed to the Normandy beaches to witness the progress of the Allied troops.

While as a constitutional monarch he left the final decisions on the multitudinous political and military issues to his Ministers, King George's advice and suggestions about them were of crucial value, and provided the best answers to a number of difficult problems. By untiring application and shrewd good sense he had made himself a master of statecraft.

The national welfare benefited richly from this when, at the end of the war, a Labour government for the first time took office with a sweeping parliamentary majority, and initiated a far-reaching programme of changes in domestic and imperial affairs. The king's conduct in face of the critical issues that arose was constitutionally faultless, and his brotherly goodwill and sound sense led the Labour leaders to a new high esteem for the value of the British monarchy.

In 1947 the king took his family with him on a visit to South Africa, where for the time the racial and political discords with Britain were submerged beneath an outburst of loyal affection. Soon after their return he gave his consent to the betrothal of Princess Elizabeth to Lieutenant Philip Mountbatten, formerly a prince of the Greek Royal House. It was an ideal love match, and the nation welcomed it enthusiastically. The day before their wedding on 20 November, the king created Philip a Royal Highness and Duke of Edinburgh. Britain has deep cause for thankfulness that its future queen gained so splendid a Consort—manly, valiant, clear-thinking, energetic, high-principled. But for King George joy was tinged with sadness at parting from his beloved daughter.

On 26 April, 1948, King George and Queen Elizabeth celebrated their Silver Wedding, and faced a great and spontaneous demonstration of their people's love and loyalty. Through those past twenty-five years they had knit Crown and Nation together by their unsparing public service and warm-hearted leadership and example. They had become a symbol of unfaltering fidelity to duty, warm devotion to their people's welfare, and the kindly relations of family life.

But by November the king's health began to fail. He had to undergo an operation on his legs in the following March. Then in 1951 cancer of the lung was diagnosed, and a major operation became necessary. Medical opinion recognized that the end could not be far away. Yet he had a cheerful Christmas with his family at Sandringham, and at the end of January, 1952, he saw Princess Elizabeth and her husband off at the airport for a visit to East Africa. Returning to a pleasant gathering of friends at Sandringham, he had a good day's shooting there on 5 February. Peacefully he retired at night to rest. His waking was to a dawn that does not fade.

History will record him as a monarch universally and deservedly beloved, who reached the highest pinnacle of honour, not by brilliance of his gifts, but by courage, kindliness, humility and utter loyalty to the call of duty.

JOHN F. KENNEDY

(1917-1963)

THREATS TO one's life are not taken very seriously if one is president of the United States: John Kennedy had received no less than eight hundred and sixty during his first year in the White House. There were renewed threats when, after thirty-four months as President, he decided to visit Dallas, Texas—but by now the total of threatening letters and telephone calls had become uncountable. Kennedy had been pressing hard for a Civil Rights Bill which would guarantee equal status with whites for the American negro, and in the process had alienated much of the south, which from time immemorial had always voted for his Party, the Democrats, but now showed some sign of changing its affiliation.

Courage was never lacking in Kennedy's make-up, and it required political courage to push a bill which many regarded as political suicide: it also needed physical and moral courage to set out on a tour of the hostile south at this moment. But in November, 1963, John Kennedy and his young wife did so.

There were awkward incidents, but on the whole the tour had been a success, when on the 22nd they flew into Dallas airport. Here, as in other centres, were the cheering crowds and a band—even if the crowd were not as big as others that had greeted them. A quick review of a detachment of soldiers at the edge of the tarmac and the president and his wife got into an open car with Governor and Mrs. Connally to drive into the Dallas city centre.

There were twelve cars in the procession, with theirs in the lead, all of them keeping to a strict twenty-five miles an hour, as they came into town. Here the crowd was denser.

Suddenly there was a shot. Then two more in rapid succession. A woman screamed, the scream was taken up, and the first car in the "motorcade", the presidential car, accelerated in an instant to forty, fifty, seventy miles an hour and tore off alone.

It was minutes before anyone knew what had happened; to this day there is doubt. But somehow John Kennedy had been shot and was dying, his head cradled in his wife's lap, as the big car roared through the centre of Dallas to hospital.

It was too late: the president was dead when they reached it. An hour later Lyndon B. Johnson, the vice-president, and a Texan himself, who had been travelling two cars behind in the procession, was sworn in as 36th president of the United States. John Kennedy, the youngest elected president in American history, was dead. (Theodore Roosevelt had been younger on taking office—but he, like Johnson, took over at a moment of tragedy, with the assassination of McKinley.) Where, asked the world, do we go from here?

He had been born in Brookline, Massachusetts, a suburb of Boston, on 29 May, 1917. His grandfather was an immigrant who had left Ireland in the grip of potato famine and made a fortune in his new country, which he passed on to John Kennedy's father, Joseph, and which was enormously increased by that shrewd businessman's handling of it. Joseph arranged a trust fund for each of his nine children, to give each of them one million dollars at the age of twenty-one. At the same time he set out to organize his children's future in other ways: he had dealt with the little matter of finance, none of them was likely to feel the need of money or what it could buy; all that remained was to see that each boy and girl used what talents the Good Lord had given and grew up a credit to God and to old Joe.

For a start, young Joe—Joseph P. Kennedy, Jr.—would be President of the United States.

This has always been the American dream, but few parents can have taken it as seriously as Joe Kennedy—or had more right to do so. For as one of the richest men in the United States, a lavish contributor to Democratic Party funds who would become, in the late nineteen-thirties, American Ambassador to the Court of St. James, on first-name terms with the great of both countries, Kennedy Senior had every reason to believe his intelligent—and dutiful—eldest son capable of getting to the White House. He asked him to take up politics: the boy agreed.

But fate played tricks and Joe Junior was killed fighting for his country in a war Joe Senior had made every effort to keep away from, even to the extent of letting Britain, its Court of St. James and the rest of it, sink quietly into the sea. Fortunately for Britain and the world, this ambassadorial advice was rejected by President Roosevelt.

With the death of young Joseph Kennedy the plan had to be thought out again, and it became the turn of his younger brother John to become a politician—a prospect which appealed very little. He had distinguished himself in the navy, being wounded yet getting the crew of his sunk torpedo-boat to safety, towing another wounded man through many miles of shark-filled Pacific by a lifebelt strap gripped between his teeth, and after a long spell in hospital he took up journalism. While his father was ambassador he had studied under the famous Professor Laski at the London School of Economics, and had written, during the first months of the war, a thesis about Britain's unpreparedness. It was a remarkable, well-argued document and it was later published as a book, under the title *Why England Slept* (of which Joe Senior gave copies to both Winston Churchill and King George VI).

But before long parental pressure and his own fascination by the game decided him on a political career. He was elected Congressman for Massachusetts in 1946, at the age of twenty-nine. With his father's enthusiastic support, financial as well as moral, he went on to become a United States Senator, from Massachusetts, at the age of thirty-five. But we must not fall into the trap of believing great wealth responsible for his successes. In many ways his inherited wealth, his father's well-known ambitions, and in particular the family's Catholic faith, were a great disadvantage: John Kennedy, with a clear, incisive mind of his own, made his own way.

In 1956 he ran for the vice-presidency of the United States, and though he failed to achieve it, he had made a name for himself in national politics. The Democratic Party began to consider him as an outside possibility for the Presidential election of 1960. The possibility grew when he was returned to the Senate in 1958 with a record-breaking majority: when 1960 came round he was nominated Democratic Presidential candidate, with the Texan, Lyndon B. Johnson, as candidate for Vice-President—a junior role which the older man at first refused.

The campaign and the election, between Kennedy and Richard Nixon, President Eisenhower's Vice-President, was hard-fought and bitter. For the first time there were televised debates between the two candidates, seen and studied all over the United States, from Kennedy's east coast state to Nixon's California. The Junior Senator from Massachusetts did well in these debates, showed a calm mastery of his facts and of his temper which impressed viewers— while at the same time his very presence on ten million television screens served to make this almost unknown young man as familiar a public figure as the Vice-President of the United States.

But Kennedy was a Roman Catholic, and this political disability, which had effectively blocked the much-loved "Al" Smith's progress to the White House a generation before, did much to hinder him.

On 8 November he was elected—by a very small margin indeed. Later, research showed that his faith cost him a million-and-a-half votes, so we can take it that his majority was a very adequate one, on the real issues involved.

Much like his great democratic predecessor, Franklin Roosevelt, Kennedy made major government appointments largely from the ranks of "intellectuals", men who had distinguished themselves academically, or in the highest echelons of industry. These included Adlai Stevenson as Ambassador to the United Nations, and Dean Rusk as Secretary of State. He chose his younger brother Robert as United States Attorney-General, an appointment which—naturally —brought forth cries of "nepotism" and "a royal family", but which to the surprise even of some of John Kennedy's greatest supporters and believers was a considerable success.

He had married, when he was a junior member of the Senate, and she a junior reporter detailed to interview him, the dark-eyed, attractive Jacqueline Bouvier, and she now made an instant hit as "First Lady". Like her husband she had definite ideas on most things, including interior decoration. Her extensive changes to the inside of the White House made her hit on the happy idea of doing a televised "tour" of the building, followed from room to room by a camera, while she described to the people of the United States the interior of a great home most of them would never see. Even in a more cynical Britain the programme was a marked success.

The two Kennedy children, too, in a world which has its doubts about American children, caught the imagination of millions.

But all this is incidental: why was John Kennedy great? Pretty wives, well-behaved children, wartime bravery, great wealth, vast charm—none of these, together or separately, is a passport to Valhalla.

Let us cast our minds back to October, 1962. For some of us, in Britain as in other parts of the world, this may be acutely embarrassing. For when Kennedy was taking the decision which was, if not to save western civilization and life itself, at least to postpone its destruction, almost all the British press—and much of it among America's other allies—was vociferously shouting him down. Only one major British paper came out whole-heartedly in his support; the editor of one of the greatest even telephoned New York and suggested to radio commentator Alistair Cooke that Kennedy's action was based on a monstrous American fraud: that the pictures Adlai Stevenson was showing to the United Nations of Russian missile bases in Cuba were ingenious snapshots of papier-mâché.

But despite this—and one wonders whether some of the same thoughts passed through John Kennedy's mind in 1962 as had passed through his father's, in 1940—the President of the United States held firm. The world, which for the first time in history had stood on the actual brink of nuclear war, came back from the edge.

The crisis had been brewing for months. As early as July, American intelligence knew that the Soviet Union was increasing its aid to Cuba. When pressed, the Russians had assured the U.S. that this build-up, so close to American shores, was all part of Cuba's defence.

But near the end of October a reconnaissance aircraft brought back a picture which told a different story. Missile bases of a type which could only be offensive were now facing deep into the North American continent; more were being finished. Experts studied the prints far into the night, but there was no question about it.

Kennedy took the firm decision not to allow the bases. A mere promise by the Russians not to use them, to stop sending any more weapons to Cuba, would be quite insufficient—though this was the absolute maximum most of the world wanted him to demand. The island of Cuba would be blockaded by the United States Navy, ceaselessly observed from the air, until bases and weapons were removed.

The world—aghast—held its breath. Would the Russians back down, or would one or other of the antagonists fire the first and fatal shot?

The blockade was imposed, despite Russian threats of instant, devastating, retaliation. Then Mr. Krushchev backed down, agreed to remove his bases, and Kennedy wisely resisted any temptation to gloat. He imposed no time limit for the removal of the weapons, demanded only assurances that they were, in fact, going to be removed, assurances which he would then verify by aerial reconnaissance.

In four weeks they had been dismantled, the Soviet troops and technicians were on their way home. For the first time, a part of the western world had stood up to the Soviet Union and, paradoxically, Soviet-United States relations were better immediately after this crisis than at any time since the end of the war.

A year later John Kennedy was dead. He had made his mark in the world and at home and no doubt he would have offered himself for re-election in 1964 and served a total of eight years, for his record was outstanding in many fields. Apart from his battle of nerves with Mr. Krushchev in 1962, he had been forced to handle, within three months of his inauguration in the previous year, the fiasco of a disastrous "rising" in Cuba—a deplorably planned insurrection which was to be aided by an invasion of Cuban exiles. Kennedy, who inherited the plan from his predecessor and had no chance to alter it, was abused from all sides, for its inception and its failure, but he took the abuse calmly—though it stung—and went on with plans for a meeting with the Russians, for the huge increase in space research which he instigated and, above all, for his Civil Rights Bill —which was passed, with hardly a word of dissent, after his death. Like Lincoln, whose death from an assassin's bullet did much to smooth the way to peace at the close of the Civil War, Kennedy's did a great deal to ensure the passage of one of the most important and controversial pieces of legislation in American history.

He was dead, the world mourned, and its great flew to Washington to walk behind his coffin. As for his assassin, Lee Harvey Oswald— who recently bought a rifle similar to the one found in the Dallas building from which the shots had come, and who had been seen leaving it—was arrested and almost immediately shot dead by another man who announced, to shocked and astonished bystanders, "I did it for Jackie Kennedy".

A Commission was set up to investigate the assassination: its report, "The Warren Report", stated that Oswald was without doubt the assassin. Many people, particularly outside the United States, found, as they sifted through the pages of printed evidence for themselves, that they could not agree. In the hearts and minds of many, the case, the tragedy, is still unsolved.

But in those same hearts and minds, as in millions of others, the name Kennedy will remain: reminder of a great man who fought for his country and his principles—and died for them.

INDEX

671